BOOKS BY RALPH AND TERRY KOVEL

American Country Furniture, 1780–1875

A Directory of American Silver, Pewter, and Silver Plate

Kovels' Advertising Collectibles Price List

Kovels' American Art Pottery: The Collector's Guide to Makers, Marks, and Factory Histories

Kovels' American Silver Marks, 1650 to the Present

Kovels' Antiques & Collectibles Fix-it Source Book

Kovels' Antiques & Collectibles Price List

Kovels' Bid, Buy, and Sell Online

Kovels' Book of Antique Labels

Kovels' Bottles Price List

Kovels' Collector's Guide to American Art Pottery

Kovels' Collectors' Source Book

Kovels' Depression Glass & Dinnerware Price List

Kovels' Dictionary of Marks—Pottery & Porcelain

Kovels' Guide to Selling, Buying and Fixing Your Antiques and Collectibles

Kovels' Guide to Selling Your Antiques & Collectibles

Kovels' Illustrated Price Guide to Royal Doulton

Kovels' Know Your Antiques

Kovels' Know Your Collectibles

Kovels' New Dictionary of Marks—Pottery & Porcelain

Kovels' Organizer for Collectors

Kovels' Price Guide for Collector Plates, Figurines, Paperweights, and Other Limited Editions

Kovels' Quick Tips—799 Helpful Hints on How to Care for Your Collectibles

The Label Made Me Buy It: From Aunt Jemima to Zonkers—The Best-Dressed Boxes, Bottles and Cans from the Past

A Collector's
Directory
of Names,
Addresses,
Telephone and
Fax Numbers,
E-mail and
Internet Addresses—
to Make Selling,
Fixing, and
Pricing Your
Antiques and
Collectibles Easy

RALPH AND TERRY KOVEL

RANDOM HOUSE REFERENCE
NEW YORK TORONTO LONDON SYDNEY AUCKLAND

KOVELS'
YELLOW
PAGES

SECOND EDITION

Published by Random House Reference, an imprint of the Random House Information Group, 1745 Broadway, New York, New York 10019. Distributed by the Random House Information Group, a division of Random House Inc., New York, and simultaneously in Canada by Random House of Canada Limited, Toronto.

Random House is a registered trademark of Random House, Inc.
www.randomhouse.com

Printed in the United States of America

DESIGN BY ELINA D. NUDELMAN

ISBN 0-609-80624-6

10 9 8 7 6 5 4 3 2 1

SECOND EDITION

Contents

READ THIS FIRST   *xi*

PART I
HOW TO SELL YOUR ANTIQUES AND COLLECTIBLES

HOW TO SELL
The Contents of a House   3
How to Set Prices   5
Where to Sell Your Antiques
    and Collectibles   12

PART II
THE COLLECTIBLES

THE COLLECTIBLES A-Z
Advertising Collectibles   27
Architectural Antiques   39
Autographs   48
Barber Collectibles   51
Black Collectibles   53
Books & Bookplates   54
Bottles & Go-Withs   63
Breweriana   73
Carousels   75
Celebrity Memorabilia   80
Clocks & Watches   84
Coin-Operated Machines   93
Comic Art   99
Dollhouses   106
Dolls   108

Fashion	120
Fireplace Equipment	126
Folk Art	127
Frames & Mirrors	131
Furniture	136
Glass	160
Hardware	184
Holiday Collectibles	192
Ivory	195
Jewelry	199
Kitchen Paraphernalia	212
Lighting Devices	218
Magazines	230
Marble	234
Metals	236
Military Memorabilia	248
Movie Memorabilia	253
Musical Instruments	255
Numismatic Collectibles	262
Paintings	270
Paper Collectibles	279
Paperweights	289
Phonographs	293
Photography	300
Plastic	309
Political Memorabilia	311
Postcards	314
Pottery & Porcelain	319
Prints	355
Radio & TV	360
Rugs	364
Scientific Collectibles	366
Silver & Silver Plate	370
Smoking Collectibles	379
Sports Collectibles	383
Stamps	392
Stocks & Bonds	397
Stoves	399
Telephone Collectibles	401
Textiles	404
Tools	414

Toys   417
Transportation   440
Trunks   450
Western Artifacts   453
Wicker, Rattan & Basketry   457
Writing Utensils   460
All the Rest   462

PART III

GENERAL INFORMATION & SOURCE LISTS

GENERAL INFORMATION FOR COLLECTORS

Reference Books   475
Price Books   476
Buyer Books   478
Clubs & Their Publications   478
Other Publications   478
Archives & Museums   483
Useful Sites   483
Appraisal Groups   483
Selling Through Auction Houses   485
Conservation Supplies   514
Conservators & Restorers   520
Displaying Collectibles   531
Shipping, Insurance & Recovery of
   Lost Items   533
Matching Services   537
Useful Internet Addresses   552

INDEX   554

Acknowledgments

EVERYONE KNOWS THAT BOOKS ARE NOT MADE BY AUTHORS ALONE. This book is no exception. For the first time, we are part of the Random House Information Group headed by Bonnie Ammer, president and publisher, and Sheryl Stebbins, vice president and publisher, who adjusted to our idiosyncrasies and helped with our most serious challenges. Nora Rosansky and Elina Nudelman designed the book and gave it the new slick look. Beth Levy, Pat Ehresmann, and Merri Ann Morell handled every detail from manuscript to bound book. Dorothy Harris, our editor, kept things going, as always, with encouragement and deeds. We also had the help and expertise of many at our office, especially Marcia Goldberg and Karen Kneisley. Linda Coulter, Grace DeFrancisco, Katie Karrick, Liz Lillis, Heidi Makela, Tina McBean, Nancy Saada, Julie Seaman, June Smith, and Cherrie Smrekar also helped. But the most credit for this book should go to Gay Hunter, who has written thousands of letters to check on sources, has continually updated everyone and everything on her computer, has done last checks on proofreading, has kept us all at our tasks, and has managed to get the book out on time. To all we say thank you. We couldn't have done it without you.

Read This First

EVERYONE HAS SOMETHING TO SELL OR FIX. Maybe the table your mother gave you twenty years ago that she said was "very old and valuable," or the broken chair that rattles, or the baseball card collection from your childhood that is taking up needed space and could be worth thousands of dollars. Newspapers are always reporting stories of unsuspected treasures that have been sold at auction. A dealer listed a gold 1950s space gun PEZ dispenser on an online auction site. By the end of the first day the item had reached $1,500. He didn't know how rare the dispenser was in that color. It is one of the only two known and ended up selling for $6,262. A reader wrote to us that she had purchased a pair of glass vases embossed with a blueberry pattern for $10. She then found out they were made by the Consolidated Glass and Lamp Company and sold the pair for $195.

This book will tell you where you can get the information about what, when, where, and how to sell or fix your collectibles. It is based on years of knowledge and information we have gathered for reporting prices and writing about the antiques and collectibles market. *Kovels' Antiques & Collectibles Price List* is a best-seller found in almost every library and bookstore. More than three million copies have been sold. Our newspaper column, "Kovels: Antiques and Collecting," appears in hundreds of newspapers. We read thousands of letters each month, many of them filled with questions about what to sell, how to sell, and how to determine value. There have been so many questions that twenty-nine years ago we started a monthly newsletter, *Kovels on Antiques and Collectibles,* a subscription publication for those who collect or actively buy and sell antiques. We write about the sales and trends in the world of collecting each month. To fill the need for information about other collectibles, we have authored special price books about bottles, advertising collectibles, Depression glass, dinnerware, Royal Doulton, collector plates, and more. We have written books about art pottery, country furniture, pottery and porcelain marks, silver marks, package labels, and even how to buy and sell on the Internet. And we have written several books filled with information for beginning collectors. Our TV shows about collecting have been seen on The Discovery Channel and public television, and our newest series, *Flea Market Finds with the Kovels,* is on Home & Garden Television (HGTV) each week.

Have you ever thought about the value of your Barbie or Shirley Temple doll, your glass dishes from the 1930s, your silver candlesticks, your Eames chairs, or Great-grandmother's dishes? If you wanted to, could you sell them for the best possible price? Barbie doll dresses have sold for as much as $800 each, but her boyfriend's clothes are priced even higher. Wouldn't you like to get $1,000 for Ken's tuxedo? One sold for that price in 1989. Would you ever dream of asking thousands of dollars for a pink Mayfair Federal–pattern Depression glass shaker when other shakers sell for under $50? If you ask the right questions and sell in the right places, you can get top dollar for your items.

"What is my antique worth?" "Where can I sell it?" "How do I know if I am being cheated?" "Should I sell my things to a collector or a dealer?" All these questions arise when you decide to try to sell an antique or collectible that is no longer of interest to you. Dealers know the answers to these questions because they make a living buying and selling antiques. You should know the answers before you lose money by selling foolishly. This book has been written to help you dispose of a few items or a houseful of treasures accumulated over the years. It will warn you about legal and ethical pitfalls. (For example, it is illegal to sell any form of firearm, even a World War I souvenir, without a special license. It is bad form to sell an American flag; it should be given away.)

Usually an antique should be sold "as is," with no restoration or repairs. But sometimes, a repair will help you to get the most money for the antique. This book lists antiques and collectibles by type and suggests how to price them and who might buy them. Be sure to use the Index to find the special instructions for selling the type of collectible you own. Part III (General Information & Source Lists) at the end of the book lists recent price books, general research sources, auction houses, appraisal associations, matching services, and other important information on where to sell, how to price, and how to care for a collection. There are many price guides in print; this book lists most of those published from 1999 to 2002. We have also included some older price books that are still useful because of the pictures and research information. We write an entire book each year giving 50,000 up-to-date prices, *Kovels' Antiques & Collectibles Price List*, so we have not listed many actual prices here. We also have a website, www.kovels.com, that gives free pricing information. Our price book helps identify and price collectibles, but there are many other sources, too. These are included in Part III.

Some of the books listed here are privately printed or out of print, and it may take extra effort to find them. Ask at your local bookstore or library or order from an Internet "bookstore." A bookstore can order books if they are still in print, and we have included all the necessary information about publisher and source in our lists, even for privately printed books. If the book is out-of-print, you may find it from a book dealer at an antiquarian bookstore or on the Internet.

If your library does not have the book, it can find out where it is available for loan. Ask the librarian to locate the book through an interlibrary loan. The smallest library can make interlibrary loan arrangements. Don't ignore the libraries in museums, universities, historical societies, or those listed on the Internet. But remember if using the Internet not all sites are written by experts and there is some unintentional misinformation on some sites. Also try to visit places like the National Bottle Museum, The National Museum of Civil War Medicine, or the National Yo-Yo Museum. These and many more museums and websites are useful. The government also has useful information like patent dates, information about fake newspapers printed on wallpaper, and many other unexpected subjects.

We contacted every source listed to verify the address and other information. Those that did not respond are not listed. We felt if they did not respond to our letters and calls, they would not answer you. The list is accurate as possible. Check the Kovels' Online Yellow Pages on our website (www.kovels.com) for updated information. If you have additions or corrections, write to us at PO Box 22192, Beachwood, OH 44122.

When writing to the companies listed in this book, be sure to send a long SASE (self-addressed, stamped envelope) for the literature. When calling, remember the time zones and call at the appropriate time. Noon in New York is nine o'clock in the morning in California. It may be useful to consult *The Official Museum Directory*, published by R. R. Bowker/National Register Publishing Company,

121 Chalon Road, New Providence, NJ 07974. A copy should be in your library. There are also many virtual museums on the Internet. The register lists many types of museums that may be able to help you identify pieces. When trying to repair or replace collectibles, don't forget that many manufacturers have old parts available, will sometimes restore their older machines, and sometimes remake old pieces that can be useful to you.

—*Ralph and Terry Kovel*

PART I

HOW TO SELL YOUR ANTIQUES AND COLLECTIBLES

How to Sell

THE CONTENTS OF A HOUSE

If you plan to empty an entire house or apartment, be methodical. Keep the house locked and do not allow anyone inside without an escort. This includes relatives, friends, the landlord, and lawyers who may be handling the estate.

Don't throw away or dispose of anything before you check on its value. Everything can be sold, from old magazines to half-filled bottles or broken toys. The biggest mistake you can make is to throw away items before you offer them for sale. We once helped settle the estate of a recluse. The family cleaned the house before we were called. We noticed a shelf of stamp-collecting books and asked to see the collection. "The only stamps we saw were on some old letters and postcards. We threw them away." They also burned fifty years of old magazines (probably worth over $2 an issue) because the basement was too crowded. Another, wiser family had a well-advertised house sale after they found their elderly aunt had saved clothes—some with the original price tags. They found over 2,000 dresses (which were sold for $10 to $25 each), 500 hats ($10 each), 25 plastic purses ($30 each), and hundreds of scarves, bolts of fabric, belts, gloves, etc. The clothing stored in the closets and attic brought more money than the furniture, china, and silver.

Preparing the house for a sale is hard physical work. Get some helpers you can trust. Teenage children are useful. You must first sort the merchandise. Empty every cupboard, trunk, drawer, and closet. Try to sort everything into the separate categories used in this book; put the pottery and porcelain in one place and the linens in another. You may have to borrow or rent tables. Then your job is to decide the best place to sell the items and an approximate value for each item. If there are records of purchase prices through the years, or insurance covering major items, use these lists. But remember, inflation has raised all of the values.

After you have sorted through the objects for sale, assemble your tools: a ruler, magnet, magnifying glass, marking crayon (one that can be used on porcelains), paper tags (that can be pinned on clothing), small sheets of paper for notes to be placed with items, several different color dot stickers, pencil, pen, flashlight, loose-leaf notebook with lined paper, a price book (we suggest the latest edition of *Kovels' Antiques & Collectibles Price List*), and perhaps a laptop computer to help with prices and lists.

Examine all the items, and make notes about any of the marks, labels, breaks, or family history. Measure all large pieces of furniture you want to sell. Check to see whether the metal pieces are bronze, brass, or iron (a magnet will stick to iron), and see if the clocks, toys, and musical items work. If you decide you do not want to sell an object, try to move it to another area. Put your notes on the small pieces of paper, and put the paper in or on the object.

If you have friends who are collectors or even flea market and house sale buffs, you might ask for advice. This can be complicated because they may be your best customers later. Explain that you are in the investigative stages and will not sell anything yet. Put a colored dot on anything you might later want to give or sell to your

KEEP PROPER RECORDS

If you are still buying antiques and plan to sell them someday, start keeping proper records now. Buy a notebook, a card file, a computer inventory program, or an inventory book, and record each item with a description, including size, color, marks, condition, price paid, where purchased, any history, and the date. You will need this for proof of loss in case of fire or theft, tax responsibilities when the piece is sold, and to help you set a selling price in later years. Keep all labels, stickers, auction catalogs, and original boxes. They all add to the selling price of the antique. A toy car from the 1940s with a box is worth at least 25 percent more than the toy without the box. If the antique belonged to a famous person, try to get a letter from the seller with any of the history. It will also add to the resale value. If you reframe, restore, or repair your antique, be sure to list all costs in your inventory. Proper restoration can often add to the value. Improper restoration will lower the value.

advisers. Otherwise you might forget it, and you could possibly lose a friend.

When you have enough knowledge and information, use a price book to look up the retail prices of your antiques. Include these in your notes. There will be many pieces that you will not be able to identify or price at this time. Do not be discouraged. Remember, the more you know about antiques and collectibles, the higher the price you can ask. We have a friend with a very rare prisoner-of-war ship model made in about 1820. We tried to determine the price for months. Prices for these models range from $1,000 to $25,000. We learned an ivory model is more valuable than a wooden one, and the original glass case and straw mat almost double the value. The question was, should our friend ask $5,000 from a dealer and see what happens, or should he sell it at auction where it could fetch as little as $1,000, or possibly more than $5,000? We asked many dealers at shows about this model and one day a collector called from another city. He had been told about the model and offered $2,500 for it. This seemed fair, so the model was sold.

HOW TO SET PRICES

One of the most difficult aspects of selling an antique is determining the price. If you have a salable item, everyone wants it. Dealers will offer to buy, but they will almost always insist that you set the price. Friends and relatives may want the antique, but will either expect it as a gift or will tend to offer less than the top price you might get from a stranger.

Your old Christmas ornaments are worth more to a collector of ornaments than to anyone else. And you would probably think an ornament shaped like an angel is worth more than one that looks like a potato. It isn't. (An old potato ornament is very rare and is currently worth over $100.) The problem is that you must know what categories of collectibles are in demand and who wants them, and you must learn the requirements of the serious collector. For example, a recent out-of-production Madame Alexander doll in used condition is worth about 20 percent of its original price. That Madame Alexander doll in mint condition is worth about 80 percent of its original price. The same doll in mint condition with the original box in mint condition is worth at least 30 percent more than the original price. This is true of most collectibles; the original finish, box, labels,

EXAMPLES OF HOW PRICES ARE SET

EXAMPLE 1

An antiques dealer buys a rare French paperweight for $1. It is offered for sale in the shop for $1,000, which might be the appropriate price for such a rarity. That markup would be based on expert knowledge of the actual value of the item, rather than on its cost.

EXAMPLE 2

A dealer buys a spindle-back oak chair at a flea market for $40. He does minor refinishing and prices it at $79, which is roughly a 100 percent markup. It would not be priced at $80, because the psychology of pricing for antiques is much like that at a grocery store. A $79 item sells much faster than an $80 one. He puts the chair in his shop. At another sale he sees an identical chair for $60. He purchases it at a 20 percent dealer's discount and returns to his shop, where he prices the pair of chairs at $225. (A pair is usually worth more than two singles.) His cost for the two chairs is $88, and now his markup for the two is about 155 percent. If another dealer comes to the shop to buy the chairs, the selling price might have to be $180 (that 20 percent "dealer's discount" has to be considered). This means the chairs cost only $88 and were sold for $180, a profit of $92 with a markup of about 105 percent. Usually the dealer who is buying is getting a large number of items or is a good customer, so a discount is a form of promotion for the shop.

EXAMPLE 3

A dealer has a customer for a large oak dining-room table. While bidding at an auction, the dealer sees a table that is just what the customer wants and bids $350. She moves it to the shop at a cost of $25, calls the customer, and offers the table for $500, which was the top price the customer seemed prepared to pay. The markup from a cost of $375 to a sale price of $500 is only 33 percent. A quick sale with a low profit margin is sometimes a good idea when you are not sure when a better deal might come along.

EXAMPLE 4

A "picker" buys a tin toy for $5 at a church rummage sale and sells it for $10 to a flea market dealer, who then sells it to a toy dealer for $18. The toy dealer goes to a toy show in Ohio and sells the toy to another dealer for $35. It is sold again to another dealer from California for $70. A customer in California walks into the shop and eagerly buys the toy for $175. (It sometimes happens this way.) We always joke that if the dealers ever stopped buying from each other, there would be no antiques business. An item is often bought and sold four or five times before it reaches the ultimate collector. Each time there is an increase in price. This is not too different from the food industry. A farmer sells peas to a processor who sells to a distributor who sells to a grocery store who sells to the consumer. Each time the price rises.

and directions add to the value. Poor condition, flaked paint, chips, dents, or missing parts may make a collectible almost worthless. Repairs may add or detract. A good repair to an old, usable nineteenth-century country chair will add to the price you can ask, but a new coat of paint on an old tin toy will lower the price by 80 percent. The toy would be worth more with the old, flaking paint.

Watch for these price-increasing features:

- Original box.

- Mint condition.

- Provenance. Absolute proof that the item belonged to someone of historical importance—from rock stars to authors to Civil War generals. Proof must be a letter or photograph linking the person to the item. Family gossip doesn't count.

- Maker's label.

- Direction book that might have come with the item.

- Miniature version of a normally full-sized item.

- Event-related objects, such as souvenirs of World's Fairs, coronations, or political campaigns.

- Brands or makers that are especially popular, such as Hummel, Coca-Cola, R.S. Prussia, or Lalique.

- Anything that pictures a railroad, streetcar, train, airplane, the Wild West, or sports.

- Complete sets. A pair is worth more than two items sold as singles; a full set is worth more than the sum of the parts.

- Occupation-related objects like medical instruments.

- Documents or objects related to local or national history.

- Objects related to the women's movement, black history, or the American Indian lifestyle and history.

- The "naughty factor." We first heard this term from an auctioneer with a prestigious New York City gallery. He said the rule was, "The more erotic the piece, the higher the price." Collectors seem to pay higher prices for anything connected to tobacco, alcohol, gambling, drugs, or sex.

There is not always one correct price. You must decide whether you want to set a low price in order to sell the item quickly. In general, the more work you do studying the antique or collectible and who might want to buy it, the higher the price you will get. This takes time, but it can also be fun, especially if you sell high. Your sale price to a dealer will be a third to a half of the advertised price. If you decide to try selling through the mail yourself, you should ask for the full price.

These are the only six places to learn the correct price for an antique or collectible. Please note that there are advantages and disadvantages to each source.

1. A knowledgeable collector friend. Your friend's advice is free, but as the old saying goes, "You get what you pay for," and it could be wrong.

2. A price book. Price books come in all qualities. Bad ones are inaccurate and may misinform you. Good ones tell prices, but often you must know a lot about the subject to be able to locate the exact item and its price in these guides, and this takes time. There is a list of recent general price books in Part III at the back of this book. Specialized price books are listed with each category. Almost all are available at your library.

3. Some antiques publications (see Part III) have a few "for sale" ads with descriptions and sometimes pictures. Most of them report on sales. You can try to confirm your prices by reading these ads and articles. You may have more success with specialized or club publications devoted to specific collectibles. We list pertinent clubs and publications in each chapter.

4. The Internet has replaced the classified sections of many antiques publications. Thousands of pictures and prices are to be seen on the Internet each day in the shops, malls, newsletters, chat rooms, club sites, and auctions. Most of these pieces are small, easy to mail, and less than fifty years old. The descriptions may be incomplete or, like a price book, may require some special knowledge of antiques.

5. Visits to shops, shows, auctions, flea markets, and house sales. Your observations, although free-of-charge, can be time-consuming, but they may help you to understand why one chair is worth more than another. Don't be insistent or demanding because you may want a favor. Talk to the dealer. If the dealer isn't busy, you can get an abundance of information.

It is possible to send a picture and description (include size, condition, history, and marks) of a seemingly valuable item to an out-of-town auction gallery and ask what it would bring at auction. Some galleries will write an answer to this type of inquiry. They are under no obligation to answer your inquiries, and you are under no obligation to sell your antique through the gallery, although you may later decide it is the best way to sell it. You should include a self-addressed, stamped envelope to encourage an answer and the return of your pictures.

All dealers and matching services buy as well as sell. A matching service buys old pieces of silver, glass, or china and resells them to customers who are trying to complete old sets. This solves the constant problem of what to do when you chip the twelfth cup or grind up Grandma's silver teaspoon in the garbage disposal. If you are trying to sell a standard item like Depression glass, silver flatware, or Haviland china, you can check the retail prices of these items at shows or through mail-order listings or Internet sites. You should be able to sell your pieces to these or other dealers for about a third to half of the quoted prices. Some of the larger matching services will quote buy or sell prices over the phone. (See list in Part III.)

6. A formal appraisal. An appraisal is usually expensive. Appraisers are like doctors. They sell their expertise and training, and their time is valuable. The average big-city appraisal costs about $150 an hour or more. Never get an appraisal for a few inexpensive items; however, jewelry, sterling silver, or large collections of coins, stamps, or other specialties probably should be appraised if you do not plan to sell at auction. There is no reason to have an appraisal if you sell at auction. The estimate placed on the item by the auction house is the appraised value. You may want to put a reserve on the piece at auction to ensure that, through bad weather or other factors, you do not risk your item being sold well below value.

There are auction galleries in some cities that give free appraisals. They need merchandise to sell, and this is one of their forms of advertising. Check in the Yellow Pages of the phone book for auction houses. Watch the antiques section of want ads in your newspaper for special announcements of free appraisal days by out-of-town galleries.

There are other points to remember about appraisals. Never hire an appraiser who sets charges based on a percentage of the value of the items. Never expect the person who appraises your antiques to buy them. If your appraiser offers to buy at the appraised value, beware! Do not expect a dealer to be a free appraiser. The dealer is trying to buy at the lowest possible price and will not want to tell you what your antiques are worth unless you are paying for that information. A dealer will often ask to be permitted to buy (at the price you set) rather than take the job of appraising for a fee.

All of this "dancing around" by dealers is frustrating to those who know very little and wish to sell some antiques or collectibles, but that is how the market works. Dealers are selling antiques to make a living and not to make you happy. The better they buy, the more they make. The more they buy, the more they have for sale.

There is a list of national appraisal associations in Part III of this book. Other appraisers can usually be found in the Yellow Pages of your telephone book under "Appraisers." Most auction galleries will appraise. Many antiques dealers and household liquidators can appraise average items. Ads for antiques shops in the Yellow Pages of the telephone book often include information about appraisers. Information about specialized appraisers is listed in the appropriate categories in Part II of this book. Many of the auction houses, repair services, and matching services listed in this book will also appraise.

MORE PRICING HELP

Some types of antiques and collectibles are purchased because they are inexpensive, attractive substitutes for new department-store furniture and tableware. If you are trying to sell dishes, silver flatware, furniture, or even linens, you should always check on the price of comparable new ones at your local gift or department store. Your old furniture and dishes will sell quickly at a third to a half the price of the new, so that should be the lowest price you should ask. But remember they could be worth more than the new. Old, used linens usually sell for 20 to 30 percent less than new ones, unless they have hand embroidery or lace, or a design that's characteristic of an era, like free-form-design 1950s tablecloths, or unless they are in very unusual, hard-to-find sizes, like a five-yard tablecloth.

HOW PRICES WORK IN THE ANTIQUES MARKET

Once you have learned the correct retail price for an antique, you must still be concerned about how to price your item. No matter which method of selling you use, you are not selling from a retail store. An antiques dealer must at least double or even triple the cost of an item when selling it. This is considered a fair business practice because the dealer must pay rent, advance money to buy stock, pay expenses to move the item, and store it until it is sold. In addition, an item might have to be restored. The dealer must meet a payroll, pay taxes and insurance, advertise, and cover the other expenses of a small business. If you have your own garage or flea market sale, you will learn that dealers and many other customers usually expect you to give at least a 20 percent discount for buying more than one item. Collectors are often given this 20 percent "dealer discount" at shops, sales, and shows if they ask for it. There is also a quantity discount. Dealers and collectors expect a "lump sum" price for ten items to be less than the sum of the ten prices.

How does all of this affect the price of the collectible you are selling to a dealer? You should be warned that prices in the antiques business are based on supply and demand. The closer you can get to selling it to the ultimate collector, the higher the price you can ask. The general rule is that a dealer's gross profit margin should be 100 percent of the antique's cost. A dealer usually charges double what he pays you. This means that when you look in *Kovels' Antiques & Collectibles Price List* and see a doll worth $100, you should plan on selling yours to a dealer for half, or about $50. You must also remember that most of the prices listed in price books are those found in retail shops, not from small flea market dealers or yard sales. We often hear people complaining that they sold an antique to a dealer and later saw it in the shop at a much higher price. Of course! The dealer must make a profit! No one complains that a dress shop buys new clothes for $10 and often sells them for $30, tripling their money. Many other shops sell this way. There are few that sell for less than a 100 percent markup, which is the typical pricing formula for the antiques dealer.

PRICES AND THE AUCTION GALLERY

Auction galleries sell for a commission that usually ranges from 10 to 25 percent of the sale price, so you receive less than the announced sale price. If your dresser sells at auction for $150, you will get from $135 to $112.50, depending on the commission you contracted for. If the dresser sells for $300, you get from $270 to $225, depending on the commission rate. If you have given the auction gallery instructions not to sell the dresser for less than $150 and no one bids high enough, you will still owe the auctioneer a fee for trying to sell it, probably 5 percent, or $7.50.

GIVE TO A CHARITY AND SAVE

Sometimes it is far more profitable to donate your items to a charity than it is to sell them. The tax deduction for charitable contributions can be valuable if you are in a high tax bracket. There may be a fee to pay for an appraisal if the item is worth more than $5,000 (part of the tax laws). Some things are very valuable to a museum but very hard to sell elsewhere because of limited interest.

We once appraised a donation of annotated sheet music that was used in a landmark-status burlesque house. For historic reasons, the music was of great value to the music section of a large public library. Architects' drawings, old photographs of local scenes, historical documents, and old maps are often worth much more as a donation. The tax laws seem to change each year, so if you are considering a large gift, consult your accountant or the local Internal Revenue Service office.

WHERE TO SELL YOUR ANTIQUES AND COLLECTIBLES

There are ten ways to sell your antiques and collectibles. Each of these methods requires some work. The more you work, the more money you will probably be able to keep after the sale. You get your cash immediately by some methods, while others can take months. Each of these methods is successful only if you learn the rules and secrets of others who sell antiques and collectibles. Remember that the usual rules of credit apply. Get cash or assure yourself that the check offered will be good. You don't know the customer, and once in a while there are problems with checks or credit. Don't let anything leave your possession until you have cash, a check, or a written agreement about the sale.

1. SELL TO AN ANTIQUES DEALER, FRIEND, OR ACQUAINTANCE

The easiest way to sell an antique or collectible is to call a dealer and sell anything you can for whatever price is offered. This might be a good method if you are from out of town, have inherited a few large pieces, and must move them as soon as possible. The dealer will probably not set the price, so if your asking price isn't low enough, your item won't sell. The dealer's travel time counts, so try the closest dealers for best and quickest results. Find a list in the Yellow Pages of the phone book or in the antiques publications listed in Part III in the back of this book.

Never let anyone in the house when you are not there. If possible, make sure at least two people are in the house when a potential buyer arrives. The antiques business is never run on credit: Be sure you get the money when the collectibles are taken. If a dealer sold you or your relative the antique you are trying to sell, try to sell it back to the same dealer. The dealer knows the piece, liked it before, and knows how it will sell, so usually the original dealer will often offer the highest price.

Sometimes friends and relatives want to buy from you. Offer the antique to them first, at the price you plan to ask from the dealer. Tell them that if the dealer refuses at that price, you will offer it to them again at a lower price. Would you give your friend a $100 bill? Then don't give away your antiques for lower-than-wholesale prices. If you want to give an antique to a friend as a gift, don't charge anything. Sometimes it is best to avoid even offering to sell to friends and relatives. It can become a source of friction that can last for years.

If you have just a few antiques and a lot of time, you can look up your items, determine the best price a dealer can offer, and take the items or a picture of the items to nearby dealers.

2. SELL AT A YARD, GARAGE, ESTATE, OR HOUSE SALE

If you have a house full of goods, you can call one of the local house sale (in some areas better known as a tag sale or estate sale) firms or auctioneers. Look in the Yellow Pages of the phone book under "Liquidators" or in your newspaper's weekly listing of sales. The entire sale (advertising, pricing, security, permits, staff, and special problems) can be handled by these people. You pay them a percentage on all items sold. Be very sure that you check references for the people you hire. They will be handling your money, and the money you receive is based on their records. Before anything is started, you must have a written contract, which should list your responsibilities and the seller's responsibilities and fees. Be sure the seller is insured in case of serious damage or loss. Be sure the insurance covers damage to the house and that either you or the seller have insurance to cover accidents involving customers or workers at the sale.

Many of us are emotionally involved with some of our collectibles. They bring memories. If you are, do not attend the sale. You may be upset and may even interfere with the sale and discourage a potential customer. If you are fond of some pieces, set a price and tell the staff not to sell below that price without your approval. It is always best to cut prices on the last day so that you can sell whatever is left. Arrange in advance (put it in the contract) that it is the responsibility of the seller to be sure the unsold pieces are sent to your favorite charity and the house is left "broom clean." If you have only a few items to sell, the dealer might be able to place them in someone else's sale. This is illegal in some cities, but silver, jewelry, and furs are often sold in this way.

You can join a group of friends and arrange a big garage or house sale. Choose the most prestigious address. It helps if it is near parking and a main road. Go over the methods of bookkeeping and payment very carefully beforehand. There is often confusion about who owned the items sold. Price your own items, and be sure everyone knows all the rules about cutting prices. This works best if at least one member of the group has had experience with this type of sale. The advantage to a joint sale is that expenses are shared and so is some of the work. Color code the price tags so you can settle accounts properly. A large sale usually does better business because customers like to see tables filled with merchandise.

Anyone can run a garage or house sale. There are books about how to do it in most libraries. Before making any arrangements, check with the local police to learn about permits for sales, parking, signs, sales tax, and other problems. Some apartment buildings and complexes and towns do not allow sales. It is important to check with the police about other local sales laws: In some states it is illegal to sell guns, alcoholic beverages, endangered-animal parts, used mattresses, bedding, some Indian relics, gambling devices, and other objects. Be sure electrical appliances can be plugged in to show that they work.

Try going to some local sales, and take note of their setup for the sale, their security precautions, their tagging and pricing, and even their price reduction policy, if possible. Your local newspaper may offer a free garage sale kit, including directions and signs. Advertising is always important. Place your ad in the weekly or daily paper for your neighborhood on the day that all the garage and house sale ads appear. Study the ads: There is a more or less standard form. Include the address for the sale with directions if it is on a side street, the date and hours of the sale, a phone number that can give information, a list of the best large items to spark interest, and as much else as possible. When you place the ad, the newspaper will probably make other suggestions.

A successful sale takes work and preparation. Look through the entire house. Almost anything can be sold, including lawnmowers, out-of-date clothes, old tools, baskets, half-filled bottles, and gardening supplies. Some things like buckets and baskets are useful for display of small items, but be sure to put a price on the basket too. If you sell clothes, have a mirror so customers can see how things look. The sale should usually run for three days. The first day, the regular shoppers arrive. The second day, more casual buyers will browse and the third day, prices should be cut to get rid of the remaining pieces. If you decide to have a one-day sale outdoors, be sure your ad includes a rain date. There is much debate about letting a special group of dealers into a sale early. We avoid house sales run by professionals who let dealers and special customers in first. Most of the good stuff is gone when the sale opens to others. If you are settling an estate or cleaning a house and having a one-time-only sale, you may be surprised to see dealers trying to get in well before the announced time. Decide ahead of time what you will do—but do not open the doors before you have security in place.

You must price everything. Either use tags, stickers, or grease pencil marks. Be sure the prices cannot be switched. The day before the sale, get small bills and change from the bank. Keep the money in a safe place during the sale, probably at the headquarters table. Never leave the sale or the cash unattended, not even to go to the bathroom. Have a calculator, paper, pencils, bags, boxes, and newspapers for wrapping.

Theft is the biggest problem for a novice running a house sale. Watch out for large open bags, pocketbooks, unbuttoned raincoats, or any sort of box or bag that is brought into your sale. If possible, have shoppers check all large items and coats at the door. If you are having a garage sale, never let anyone in your house—not even to use the bathroom or get a glass of water. If you are having a house sale, always have one salesperson in each open room, so they can watch and discuss prices. Be sure each sales slip is written by your salesperson in the room with that particular item. For example, have one sales helper in charge of all linens and clothes, and put all of these items in one room. Keep small, valuable items like jewelry in a special closed case near the cashier. All money should be paid in one place, preferably on a table that faces the exit door, and the money box should be watched at all times. If it is a very large sale, it might be advisable to hire an off-duty policeman. Be sure all other exit doors are locked, and tape shut any doors to cabinets that do not contain merchandise for sale. Before leaving at night, check all window and door locks. Burglars have been known to visit a sale, open a window, and return later that night for "free" antiques, knowing the house is unoccupied. Thieves might even take sinks, radiators, and copper plumbing. It is sensible to inform your local police of the sale, so they can put an extra watch on the house at night. After all, you did place an ad in the paper telling everyone that there is an unoccupied house filled with merchandise. Expect to have some losses. We have heard stories from professional house-sale staffs that are hard to believe. Price tags are often switched. Boxes are filled with unpaid-for items. A two-foot-high vase disappeared from a room that was guarded by a policeman. One saleslady even lost her lunch because she brought it in a fancy department-store bag.

3. TAKE YOUR ITEMS TO A CONSIGNMENT SHOP

Most cities have consignment shops. These stores sell other people's merchandise and charge a commission. Some antiques shops will take merchandise on consignment for sale with their own antiques. Look in the Yellow Pages of the phone book for "Consignment Shops." Visit the stores to see if your collectibles will fit in with the other items for sale. Ask antiques dealers if consignment is possible in their shops or at shows. Be sure to get a signed copy of the consignment agreement, which should include all charges, how long your money is held, and how the items are insured while in the shop. You, in turn, will probably have to sign an agreement with the shop, and you should retain a copy. On the consignment agreement, write a full description of the objects, including the words "dented" or "flaked paint" or any other indication of wear. If your item doesn't sell and you take it back, you want to be sure that it has not been damaged in the store. The shop or dealer is probably best able to set the price. Visit the shop after a few weeks to see if your item has sold. If it has not, you should discuss reducing the price.

4. SELL THROUGH AN AUCTION GALLERY

Most major collections, important paintings, sculptures, and large antique furniture pieces are sold through auction galleries. These pieces require a special buyer who is either a professional antiques dealer or a knowledgeable collector. The gallery should mail announcements of the sale to these people, advertise in national antiques publications and local papers, and handle all the problems of the sale. Everything is negotiable at an auction gallery if you have enough items or very high-priced items to consign. The printed rates usually say the consignor must pay 10 to 25 percent commission. Most auction galleries charge the buyer 10 to 15 percent of the purchase price—a "buyer's premium"—as well as the 10 to 25 percent commission charged to the seller.

Always try to get the best rate. With negotiation, many of the extras, such as charges for shipping, pictures in the catalog, etc., could be free. You can ask for extra advertising, a catalog, even a pre-view party. No demand is unreasonable if your items are important enough to be a major sale for the gallery. Of course, a major sale in New York City is very different from a major sale in a small town.

If you permit the auctioneer to use your name in the advertising, it may mean higher prices at the sale. Collectors like to buy "fresh" antiques; these are pieces that have not been sold and resold in shops recently. Be sure to get a written contract from the auctioneer stating the terms, the approximate date the pieces will be sold, the time of payment to you, extra charges, and details regarding the advertising that is to be placed. Make sure the gallery has fire and theft insurance. If you are unfamiliar with the auction house, ask for references, and find out whether the money for your items is kept in a separate escrow account. This helps protect you from loss if the gallery has financial problems.

Check the credit rating of the auctioneer. Should the auctioneer go bankrupt, you have very little chance of getting your money for items that were sold. You may even have trouble proving that you own the unsold but consigned pieces. Discuss the "reserve." Some-times you decide you do not wish to sell below a certain price. This is the reserve price. If no bid is made above this reserve, you must usually pay a fee of approximately 5 percent of the agreed reserve price to the auctioneer. Do not place a high reserve on a piece. If you want too much, it will not sell, and you should not be auctioning it at all. Some major auction houses and many small auctioneers pre-fer only sales without reserves. If your antique does not sell above the reserve price, you can decide if you want to take your item back or have the auction gallery "sell it out the back door." In other words, if your antique fails to sell, the auctioneer can often sell it privately after the auction for a lower price. The usual commission rates apply for this kind of sale.

If you go to the auction, remember that it is not only in poor taste, but also illegal in some states, to bid on your items. If you bid the item up, you are a "shill." If you end up with the high bid, you would still owe the gallery the buyer's premium plus your charges.

5. SELL AT A COUNTRY AUCTION

At a country auction, which is very different from an auction gallery, the auctioneer usually goes to the house or farm and sells the items on the site. There is very limited advertising, no catalog, and often no chairs for the buyers. There are rarely reserves, the seller's commission may be lower, and there is almost never a buyer's premium. This is a very successful method of emptying a small-town or rural house filled with the accumulation of a lifetime. If there are valuable pieces of antique furniture, the major dealers somehow seem to find out and pay good prices. If there are no major items, just typical seventy-five-year-old things, you will be pleased at the prices you can get for some items that an auction gallery would sell in box lots or not at all. The half sets of dishes, basement tools, old lawn mower, and even torn magazines and rolls of chicken wire will sell to someone.

6. SELL AT AN INTERNET AUCTION OR THROUGH YOUR OWN WEBSITE

The Internet has become another place to buy and sell antiques. Antiques are bought and sold through general Internet sites and specialized ones. There are websites with classified advertisements and those that offer online auctions.

To find antiques and collectibles on the Web, you can use a search engine. (See Part III for a list.) You can also go to a site like Collect.com (www.collect.com), which features classified ads. There are also "Internet malls," like The Internet Antique Shop (www.tias.com), that host dealer-operated pages. This is worthwhile if you have many items to sell. Most Internet malls have self-serve programs that guide you through the process of setting up your pages.

Selling antiques and collectibles through online auctions is very similar to using classified advertising. For example, the largest auction site, eBay (www.ebay.com), lets sellers list their own items. The items are posted for a set time period, like a week. The seller can choose the minimum asking price. Most auction sites offer detailed directions with step-by-step instructions for buying and selling. Many Web sites require users to register before they can browse or search. They want a name, an e-mail address, and maybe some other information about you. After you fill in the information, you will be assigned a password to use when you return to the site. If you decide to buy or sell an item, you will be asked for more information, including a credit card number.

Remember, advertising your collection online isn't that different from advertising in a newspaper or magazine. In fact, many antiques publications, like the *Maine Antique Digest,* will run your ad in their newspaper and on the Internet for a small added charge. All of the rules of security for mail order apply to sales over the Internet. Like any sale by mail, the buyer pays for shipping and handling. If there are problems, you can report it the same way as mail fraud.

7. GO TO A FLEA MARKET OR SHOW AND OFFER YOUR ITEMS TO A DEALER

A slightly sneaky way to sell antiques and collectibles is to sell to dealers or even customers at shows and flea markets, although this is discouraged at most big shows. Take clear photographs of anything you want to sell. Record the size, marks, and any other interesting history on the back of the picture. You might also include a price, but write it in code so only you can read it. (The easiest code uses letters. Pick a special word or words of ten different letters. Try "my antiques." In that code, m = 1, y = 2, etc. The letters "AQM" are the code for $371.) Check in the local newspapers for dates and go to a major antiques show. Put the small antiques in the trunk of your car and take the photographs with you. Find a dealer at the show who sells items similar to yours, and wait until the booth is empty. Never start a selling discussion when a dealer has a customer. Ask the dealer if he is interested in buying, then show your pictures. Dealers are usually interested because it is harder to buy than to sell. Most dealers will ask you to set the price. Add 20 percent to the lowest price you will accept and negotiate from there. If you ask too much, the dealer will just say no. Remember, the dealer should be able to sell the piece for at least twice what you ask. Sometimes a dealer will not want your items but can suggest a customer, possibly another dealer or a collector who is attending the show. Be discreet. Don't bring big objects into the show. The dealer has paid for the exhibit space. If you are selling in competition with the dealers, you might be asked to leave. Don't expect a free appraisal. You must know the value of your antique to be able to sell it.

8. SET UP YOUR OWN BOOTH AT A FLEA MARKET OR MALL

If you have time, enjoy crowds, and don't mind packing and unpacking, you can set up your own booth at a flea market or mall. Look in the local newspaper or an antiques paper in your area (see Part III). Flea markets will be listed. Visit a few, talk to the dealers, and get information about how to rent space. Sometimes a table for the day is under $10. Notice how the tables are arranged and what to do in case of rain. It is also important to know whether to bring lunch, or if there is a lunch stand on the premises. Always ask how early you can set up. Dress for all types of weather: Bring umbrellas or sunshades, sweaters or heavy boots. Bring a chair. Bring a closed box to hold money, and newspapers and bags for wrapping. Try to take an assistant. You may want to eat, go to the restroom, or visit other booths, and you should never leave your booth unattended. You must stay for the full day, even if it rains. You must price the items, keep records, and give receipts. It is almost the same as having your own garage sale. Learn the state sales tax regulations. You may need a resale license. Flea markets are often checked by state inspectors. Remember that in some states it is illegal to sell items like guns, slot machines, liquor, endangered species' pelts or parts, and a few other things. Watch out for theft, too.

You may be able to rent temporary space in an antiques mall. Ask for the rules, charges, and responsibilities. The mall cases are good for small items, but you probably can't get temporary space for big items. You may be able to work out a selling agreement with a permanent mall dealer.

9. PLACE AN AD AND SELL BY MAIL

Specialized collections of small items, like political campaign material, lady head planters, or souvenir spoons, can be sold by mail. Don't ignore selling at an Internet site. (See method 6, Sell at an Internet Auction or Through Your Own Website.) The best pieces to sell this way are well-known, easy-to-describe pieces like Royal Doulton figurines, carnival glass, beer cans, or Depression glass. Large items are difficult. Furniture is almost impossible unless it will be picked up by the buyer. Check the ads in the antiques papers. Anyone selling antiques may be buying antiques, so anyone offering to sell an item like yours is a prospective customer. There are also "antiques wanted" ads that can give you leads.

When you place an ad for your antiques, be sure to request a self-addressed, stamped envelope (SASE) from anyone asking for more information. Otherwise you may find you have to pay for first-class postage on each letter to answer queries, and that can add up. A United States resident should ask for a check payable in U.S. funds on a U.S. bank, because a foreign bank check will cost you a fee to deposit. International sales are easiest by credit card. If you are selling between the United States and Canada, be sure to specify the currency expected and the exchange rate.

You may offer to send out a numbered list of the objects, with a full description of each, including size, marks, and condition. Include every defect, and set a price. If possible, take pictures or make copies and add these to the list. Make copies of the complete list and send it with a letter of explanation. Include your name and address, zip code, and phone number, including the area code. Include a fax number if you have one. Enclose a self-addressed, stamped envelope (SASE) for the return of your list and pictures. Don't try to sell damaged items by mail.

You will have to pack and ship the items. Breakage is your problem, so wrap carefully and always insure all packages. Ask for payment before you ship the antique and be sure the check or credit card is good. Offer the pieces with geography in mind. Some items sell for higher prices in the West than in the East. Get a return receipt to show that the package arrived. It should be understood that there are full return privileges and that the antique may be returned to you for a refund. The buyer pays the return postage or shipping.

If you place an ad in the local paper or the antiques papers to sell your items, study the format of other ads for ideas in composing your own. Include a full description and either a phone number or address, and ask for an SASE for inquiries. Security may be a problem, so don't use your home address if you live alone. Consider renting a post-office box. Make appointments to show the antiques, but always have someone else with you for security. In the antiques papers it is best to include the price. In your local paper it is not necessary. A local ad is best for large items like a dining-room set.

10. FIND A CUSTOMER BY WRITING OR CALLING

A few special pieces might be sold to a particular customer who is nationally known. You may own an early piece made by a company or have some historical pictures that relate to a firm. Write to that customer or the appropriate museum, enclosing a picture, description, price, your phone number, and an SASE. Museum collections are listed in *The Official Museum Directory* by the American Association of Museums (National Register Publishing Co., Wilmette, IL 60091). The annual directory can be found in your local library or perhaps at your local historical society or art museum.

A few magazines, books, and Internet sites list names and addresses of collectors and dealers who want to buy antiques and memorabilia—everything from firecracker labels to rare art pottery or things made in Hawaii. See the list of "buyer books" on page 478.

Many general publications also have a section of "want ads" that will help you locate a buyer. (See page 478.) These publications make it clear that they are not responsible for any misunderstandings between buyer and seller. You can also find Internet sites that list want ads by using a search engine. The rules of caution are the same as for Internet sales, phone sales, or mail-order sales: You don't know the seller; you will not see the merchandise you are buying. If you are selling, you have no guarantee of getting the money. Check references carefully. Send money or objects by mail so if there is a problem it can be turned over to the postal authorities. Do not deal with anyone who avoids the postal system.

Part II

THE COLLECTIBLES

The Collectibles A-Z

IT'S BEAUTIFUL. It's valuable. But it's broken. If you want to preserve the value of your antiques by keeping them in top condition or if you want to restore them properly, read on. But remember, it is not usually a good idea to repair an item to sell it. Fix it if you want to keep it. Listed are hard-to-find repair shops and sources for replacement parts located in all parts of the country.

More than sixty different types of collections are discussed here. A short paragraph tells what flaws should be repaired, how repairs affect value, and other tips. Craftsmen, supply sources, informative books, and other material related to restoring antiques are listed. If you are missing the wheel on a toy truck, need a glass liner for your silver mustard pot, or want a restorer for your Tiffany lamp, a source is listed.

At the end of the book (in Part III) are lists of those who repair and refinish many different types of antiques, sources of supply for conservation materials, and ways to display collections. This is where you will find places to buy acid-free paper, special waxes, and products for wood graining, gold leafing, and the like. We also list auction houses, appraisal groups, clubs, publications, and matching services.

We have tried to make this book easy to use, but we realize that many subjects overlap. If you are restoring or selling a piece of furniture, start with the Furniture section, but also look under Wicker, Rattan & Basketry, Hardware, Metals, Textiles, and other headings. You will find helpful comments like "See also Metals" in the Fireplace Equipment section. Also use the index at the end of the book.

Many useful books and leaflets are included. We have also listed available reprints of original instruction books. Although most of the books are in print and can be found at a bookstore or library, a few are harder to locate. These can be ordered at your library through an interlibrary loan. Ask the librarian to help you.

To assemble the names in this book, we wrote to the thousands of suppliers, restorers, and repair services we had heard about. Only those who replied are included. We felt that if we could not get an answer to an offer to give a free listing, you would have trouble getting mail-order repair information or service. There are many other reliable repair services and conservators we have not yet heard about and we welcome any suggestions for additions or corrections in future editions. We have not used the services of everyone listed in this book, and inclusion here should not be considered an endorsement of any kind. You will find local restorers' names in the Yellow Pages of your phone book.

Each listing in this book includes the address, phone number, fax number, e-mail, and website addresses if available. If you write, send an SASE (self-addressed, stamped envelope) or an LSASE (long, self-addressed, stamped envelope). If you telephone, don't forget the time listed is the time in the area where the restorer lives. If the number is wrong, check for a new area code. Many have changed recently. The listings are alphabetized by computer so that all names of companies and individuals appear in alphabetical order by first word.

Always contact the company by phone or letter before sending anything. The firm will tell you the best way to ship: postal service, delivery service company like UPS or Federal Express, or motor freight. Insure your piece when sending it. If using the post office, send it registered, with a return receipt requested. Other delivery services can track the package from your receipt number.

When we list a company as doing repairs by "mail order," that does not necessarily mean that it is only by mail. If you live nearby, you may be able to take the piece into the shop. Many places that do a primarily walk-in business will send you a part by mail if you

A NOTE ABOUT ABBREVIATIONS

THE ABBREVIATIONS USED IN THIS BOOK ARE:
MAG for magazine, NP for newspaper, and NL for newsletter. All listings are alphabetical by name or title.

Clubs are listed first along with the names of their publications, followed by listings of publications not connected to a club.

pay in advance. We have found that a good craftsman will try to fix out-of-the-ordinary items if the challenge and pay are appropriate. It doesn't hurt to inquire about difficult repairs.

The last corrections were made to the lists in this book March 2003. Some firms may have had a change of location or phone number since then.

ADVERTISING COLLECTIBLES

The country store and its contents have delighted collectors for years. Around 1955 the first serious collectors of advertising materials began searching for signs, containers, bottles, store bins, and other objects found in an old country store. It became the vogue to decorate restaurants, homes, and shops with nostalgic collectibles from old stores, and prices rose as supplies dwindled. A Cy Young cigar can is worth $6,700. A Welch's Grape Soda sign from 1910 sells for $5,500.

There are collectors clubs for people who specialize in everything from produce seals to tin containers. The nostalgia craze in restaurant decorating and the "country look" for homes have made unusual items with interesting graphics and company names into prize pieces. There are clubs for collectors interested in brands like Planters Peanuts or Coca-Cola, for collectors of tobacco tins and signs, sugar packets, bottles, and fast-food restaurant memorabilia. Publications for many of the clubs accept advertisements, and these are the best places to offer your items for sale. You can also write to dealers to advise them you are selling items, or you can place an ad. Ads in general-interest publications also sell items. A visit to dealers at mall shows, flea markets, or antiques shows where advertising pieces are sold will help you locate a possible buyer. Highest prices are paid at special advertising shows. These shows are announced in the general publications for collectors. There are several auction houses that frequently schedule special sales of advertising collectibles. They are always interested in good pieces (see auction list at the end of this chapter).

The Internet is quickly becoming a good source for many collectibles. Advertising memorabilia is bought and sold through auction and dealer websites. To find an item, use a search engine (see Part III for a list). Type a specific name, like **PLANTERS PEANUTS**, or category, like **JIM BEAM BOTTLES**. You can also go directly to an

Internet antique mall or auction website. Use its search function to help you browse through the collectibles.

Tin containers with lithographed designs, signs, bottles, boxes, giveaways, can or box labels, cutout magazine ads, or any advertisement can be sold. Neon signs, cash registers, calendars, old tobacco tins, lunch boxes with brand names or attractive graphics, gas-pump globes, or any other auto-related, brand-marked items sell quickly. If your advertising collectible pictures a train, automobile, airplane, flag, bottle, black person, American Indian, or partially clad female, it is worth a premium, up to 50 percent more. If it includes the name **COCA-COLA**, **CRACKER JACK**, **HEINZ**, **HIRES ROOT BEER**, **JELL-O**, **MCDONALD'S**, **PEPSI-COLA**, or **PLANTERS PEANUTS**, it is worth two to ten times as much as a similar item for a less popular brand. If it is an ad for whiskey, beer, cigarettes, or a drug-related product, it will sell quickly. A tin sign is worth ten times as much as the same sign on paper. If you have a set of old roly-poly tins or a Coca-Cola sign dating before 1900, it could be worth thousands of dollars. Beer can collectors have their own clubs, publications, and shows. They usually trade cans rather than buy them. Only the very unusual or the old cone-top cans sell well. For more information, see the Breweriana section.

Large items like a saloon bar, counter, floor-standing coffee grinder, and popcorn wagon are expensive, but there are dealers who specialize in them. Look for ads in special publications, or talk to dealers at the shows. These items often sell through an ad in a local newspaper or at a large auction.

You may think you own a piece of advertising art, but an auction gallery may consider it folk art. Folk art brings higher prices. If you have a handmade wooden piece, a very large figure like a cigar store Indian, or an unusual clock, it might bring the highest money at an auction gallery that usually would not sell advertising collectibles. Advertising clocks sell to both advertising collectors and clock collectors, so check publications and shows for both groups.

LABELS

All types of labels can be sold: cigar box labels, fruit crate labels, food can labels, labels for luggage, beer or wine bottles, tobacco packages, perfume, and brooms. Most labels you find offered by dealers were found in old print shops or canneries. Thousands of a single design were found, then resold in small groups to dealers, often for less than 5 cents each. They were eventually sold as single labels to collectors. All sales and resales included markups, so if you are buying common labels, you pay far more than twice the amount you will get if you are selling common labels. If you are fortunate enough to find an attic filled with the remains of your grandfather's label company, you have a treasure that should be sold to dealers at the wholesale level. If you have a few orange crate labels that were framed and hung in your kitchen, you should sell them to a collector friend or at a flea market. Cigar box and fruit crate labels are the best known, the largest, and the most decorative, and so sell the highest. Other labels, from broom handle to beer bottle, are often traded or sold for less than a dollar.

There have been a lot of ads selling "stone-lithographed cigar box labels" as rare and valuable art. Some labels are rare, but most were found in bundles of a thousand and are not rare. Framed, matted examples found in gift shops are priced as decorative pictures and do not have the resale value you would hope for in the antiques market. There are special publications, dealers, and sales dedicated to cigar box labels. Some very rare examples sell for hundreds of dollars each. An inner Daniel DeFoe cigar box label sells for $450.

REPRODUCTIONS

Beware of reproductions. Many lithographed tin and paper items originally made for the gift shop trade are now found at flea markets. New belt buckles and watch fobs with brand names have been made in old styles. One dealer boasts that he has sold over a half million new printed tin signs—some copies of old ones, some "concoctions" made with the help of art from old magazine ads. Reproduction wall mirrors are also common.

REPAIR

Many companies publish books on their histories that will serve as visual guides to help with restoration of old materials. These are available from the companies, many listed in this book. Reproductions of decals and other details of trademarked pieces are available. It is also possible to buy old parts through ads in collectors' publications.

When restoring old advertising, less is best. Don't repaint tin or paper unless the defect is glaring. Frame all paper items with appropriate nonacid mounts.

Old brass cash registers are now wanted by both collector and shopkeeper. Many are in use in stores that feature nostalgia. The machines made by National Cash Register or other companies can often be restored by a local company that repairs registers. A call to the local sales representative is a quick way to find out. Parts are available for some models. Remember, inflation has had a great impact; early machines register only to $10 or perhaps $100, not the high numbers seen today.

•→ SEE ALSO CLOCKS & WATCHES, COIN-OPERATED MACHINES, DOLLS, GLASS, METALS, PAPER COLLECTIBLES, POTTERY & PORCELAIN

REFERENCE BOOKS

The Art of the Cigar Label, Joe Davidson (Wellfleet Press, Secaucus, NJ, 1989).

British Biscuit Tins, 1868–1939: An Aspect of Decorative Packaging, M.J. Franklin (distributed by Schiffer, Atglen, PA, 1979).

The Label Made Me Buy It: From Aunt Jemima to Zonkers—The Best-Dressed Boxes, Bottles, and Cans from the Past, Ralph and Terry Kovel (Crown, New York, 1998).

Over the Counter and on the Shelf: Country Storekeeping in America, 1620–1920, Laurence A. Johnson (Charles E. Tuttle, Rutland, VT, 1961).

Smoker's Art, Joe and Sue Davidson (Wellfleet Press, New York, 1997).

PRICE BOOKS

Advertising Cutlery, Richard D. White (Schiffer, Atglen, PA, 1999).

Advertising Paperweights: Figural, Glass, Metal, Richard Holiner and Stuart Kammerman (Collector Books, Paducah, KY, 2002).

Advertising Thermometers, Curtis Merritt (Collector Books, Paducah, KY, 2001).

American Tobacco Cards: Price Guide & Checklist, Robert Forbes and Terence Mitchell (Tuff Stuff Publications, Richmond, VA, 1999).

Antique Advertising Encyclopedia, 3rd edition, Ray Klug (Schiffer, Atglen, PA, 1999).

Antique Advertising: Country Store Signs and Products, Rich Bertoia (Schiffer, Atglen, PA, 2001).

Antique and Contemporary Advertising Memorabilia, B.J. Summers (Collector Books, Paducah, KY, 2002).

Antique Pocket Mirrors: Pictorial & Advertising Miniatures, Cynthia Maris Dantzic (Schiffer, Atglen, PA, 2002).

Antique Tins, Book III, Fred Dodge (Collector Books, Paducah, KY, 1999).

Antique Trader Advertising Price Guide, Kyle Husfloen, editor (Krause, Iola, WI, 2001).

B.J. Summers' Guide to Coca-Cola, 3rd edition, B.J. Summers (Collector Books, Paducah, KY, 2001).

Bears & Dolls in Advertising: Guide to Collectible Characters and Critters, Robert Reed (Antique Trader Books, Dubuque, IA, 1998).

Beer Advertising, Donald A. Bull (Schiffer, Atglen, PA, 2000).

Campbell's Soup Collectibles, David and Micki Young (Krause, Iola, WI, 1998).

A Century of Crayola Collectibles, Bonnie B. Rushlow (Hobby House Press, Grantsville, MD, 2002).

Cereal Box Bonanza: The 1950s, Scott Bruce (Collector Books, Paducah, KY, 1996).

Children's Paper Premiums in American Advertising, 1890-1990s, Loretta Metzger Rieger and Lagretta Metzger Rajorek (Schiffer, Atglen, PA, 2000).

Cigar-Label Art, 1998 Price Guide, 4th edition, Wayne H. Dunn (PO Box 3902, Mission Viejo, CA 92691, 1998).

Classic Coca-Cola Serving Trays, Allan Petretti and Chris Beyer (Antique Trader Books, Dubuque, IA, 1998).

Coca-Cola Trays, 2nd edition, William McClintock (Schiffer, Atglen, PA, 1999).

Collecting Paint Advertising and Memorabilia, Irene Davis (Schiffer, Atglen, PA, 2000).

Collecting Toy Premiums: Bread, Cereal, Radio, James L. Dundas (Schiffer, Atglen, PA, 2001).

A Collector's Guide to the Gerber Baby, Joan Stryker Grubaugh (Joan Stryker Grubaugh, 2342 Hoaglin Rd., Van Wert, OH 45891, 1997).

The Collector's World of M&M's: An Unauthorized Handbook and Price Guide, Patsy Clevenger (Schiffer, Atglen, PA, 1998).

Commemorative Coca-Cola Bottles: An Unauthorized Guide, Joyce Spontak (Schiffer, Atglen, PA, 1998).

Country Store Advertising: Medicines and More, Rich Bertoia (Schiffer, Atglen, PA, 2001).

Cracker Jack: The Unauthorized Guide to Advertising Collectibles, Larry White (Schiffer, Atglen, PA, 1999).

Door-to-Door Collectibles: Salves, Lotions, Pills & Potions from W.T. Rawleigh, C.L. Miller (Schiffer, Atglen, PA, 1998).

Encyclopedia of Advertising Tins: Smalls & Samples, Volume II, David Zimmerman (Collector Books, Paducah, KY, 1999).

The Encyclopedia of Fast Food Toys: Arby's to IHOP and *The Encyclopedia of Fast Food Toys: Jack in the Box to White Castle,* 2 volumes, Joyce and Terry Losonsky (Schiffer, Atglen, PA, 1999).

The Encyclopedia of Pepsi-Cola Collectibles, Bob Staddard (Krause, Iola, WI, 2002).

Encyclopedia of Porcelain Enamel Advertising with Price Guide, 2nd edition, Michael Bruner (Schiffer, Atglen, PA, 1999).

The Esso Collectibles Handbook: Memorabilia from Standard Oil of New Jersey, J. Sam McIntyre (Schiffer, Atglen, PA, 1998).

Fast Food Figures, Elizabeth Beech (Schiffer, Atglen, PA, 1998).

Fast Food Toys, 3rd edition, Gail Pope and Keith Hammond (Schiffer, Atglen, PA, 1999).

Gas Globes: Amoco to Mobil and Affiliates, Scott Benjamin and Wayne Henderson (Schiffer, Atglen, PA, 1999).

Got a Drop of Oil? An Introduction & Price Guide to Small Oilers, David J. Moncrief (L-W Book Sales, Gas City, IN, 1998).

Guide to Vintage Trade Stimulators & Counter Games, Richard M. Bueschel (Schiffer, Atglen, PA, 1997).

Gulf Oil Collectibles, Charles Whitworth (Schiffer, Atglen, PA, 1998).

Huxford's Collectible Advertising, 4th edition, Sharon and Bob Huxford (Collector Books, Paducah, KY, 1999).

An Illustrated Guide to Gas Pumps, Jack Sim, (Krause, Iola, WI, 2002).

Kiddie Meal Collectibles, Robert J. Sodaro (Krause, Iola, WI, 2001).

Linda Mullins' Teddy Bears & Friends, Linda Mullins (Hobby House Press, Grantsville, MD, 2000).

McDonald's Happy Meal Toys around the World: 1995–Present, Joyce and Terry Losonsky (Schiffer, Atglen, PA, 1999).

McDonald's Happy Meal Toys from the Nineties, Joyce and Terry Losonsky (Schiffer, Atglen, PA, 1998).

McDonald's Pre-Happy Meal Toys from the Fifties, Sixties and Seventies, Joyce and Terry Losonsky (Schiffer, Atglen, PA, 1998).

Modern Collectible Tins, Linda McPherson (Collector Books, Paducah, KY, 1998).

Mom and Pop Saloons: A Compendium of Statuary Tools for Display and Value Guide, Michael A. Pollack and Richard A. Penn (Pennyfield's Publishing, PO Box 1355, Waterloo, IA 50704-1355, 2002).

More Gulf Oil Collectibles, Charles Whitworth (Schiffer, Atglen, PA, 1999).

More PEZ for Collectors, 2nd edition, Richard Geary (Schiffer, Atglen, PA, 1998).

More Root Beer Advertising & Collectibles, Tom Morrison (Schiffer, Atglen, PA, 2000).

Official Coca-Cola Collectors Series, 4 volumes, *Cars and Trucks,* Kyle Foreman; *Santas,* Karleen Buchholz, et al.; *Bean Bags and Plush,* Linda Lee Harry; and *Polar Bears,* Linda Lee Harry and Jean Gibbs-Simpson (Beckett Publications, Dallas, TX, 2000).

Overstreet Toy Ring Price Guide, 3rd edition, Robert M. Overstreet (Collector Books, Paducah, KY, 1997).

Paper Advertising Collectibles: Treasures from Almanacs to Window Signs, Robert Reed (Antique Trader Books, Dubuque, IA, 1998).

Pepsi Memorabilia . . . Then and Now, Phil Dillman and Larry Woestman (Schiffer, Atglen, PA, 2000).

Petretti's Coca-Cola Collectibles Price Guide, 11th edition, Allan Petretti (Krause, Iola, WI, 2001).

Petretti's Soda Pop Collectibles Price Guide, 2nd edition, Allan Petretti (Antique Trader Books, Dubuque, IA, 1999).

Planters Peanut Collectibles Since 1961, Jan Lindenberger (Schiffer, Atglen, PA, 1995).

Planters Peanut Collectibles: 1906–1961, 2nd edition, Jan Lindenberger (Schiffer, Atglen, PA, 1999).

Price Guide to Vintage Coca-Cola Collectibles, 1896–1965, Deborah Goldstein Hill (Krause, Iola, WI, 1999).

Radio & TV Premiums: A Guide to the History and Value of Radio and TV Premiums, Jim Harmon (Krause, Iola, WI, 1998).

Sinclair Collectibles, Wayne Henderson and Scott Benjamin (Schiffer, Atglen, PA, 1997, values 2000).

Soapine Did It: An Illustrated History of Kendall's 19th Century Soap Advertising Campaign, Dave Cheadle and W.H. "Bill" Lee (TCCA Books, 3706 S. Acoma St., Englewood, CO 80110, 2000).

Soda Advertising Openers, Donald A. Bull and John R. Stanley (Schiffer, Atglen, PA, 2000).

Texaco Collectors 1998 Price Guide (R&B Collectibles & Marketing, PO Box 406, Frenchtown, NJ 08825, 1998).

Tobacco Containers from Canada, United States, and the World, Norman Carlson (New Antique Ventures, Medicine Hat, Alberta, Canada, 2002).

Ultimate Price Guide to Fast Food Collectibles, Elizabeth A. Stephan, editor (Krause, Iola, WI, 1999).

An Unauthorized Guide to Mobil Collectibles: Chasing the Red Horse, Rob Bender and Tammy Cannoy-Bender (Schiffer, Atglen, PA, 1999).

Victorian Trade Cards: Historical Reference & Value Guide, Dave Cheadle (Collector Books, Paducah, KY, 1996).

Vintage Anheuser-Busch, Donna S. Baker (Schiffer, Atglen, PA, 1999).

Warman's Advertising, Don and Elizabeth Johnson (Krause, Iola, WI, 2000).

Westcott Price Guide to Advertising Water Jugs and Associated Collectables, Volume 2, David Westcott (Westcott Publications, PO Box 245, Deniliquin, NSW 2710, Australia, 1999).

Wilsons' Coca-Cola Price Guide, Helen and Al Wilson (Schiffer, Atglen, PA, 2000).

Winchester Rarities, Tom Webster (Krause, Iola, WI, 2000).

CLUBS & THEIR PUBLICATIONS

Antique Advertising Association of America, *Past Times* (NL), PO Box 5851, Elgin, IL 60123, e-mail: AAAA1121@aol.com.

British Beermat Collectors' Society, *British Beermat Collectors' Society Newsletter* (NL), 69 Dunnington Ave., Kidderminster DY10 2YT, UK, e-mail: cosmic@tmmathews.freeserve.co.uk, website: www.british beermats.org.uk.

Cash Register Collectors Club of America, *The Brass Idol* (NL), PO Box 20534, Dayton, OH 45420-0534, e-mail: mhenne2002@aol.com.

Citrus Label Society, *Citrus Peal* (NL), 131 Miramonte Dr., Fullerton, CA 92835, e-mail: trspellman@prodigy.net, website: www.citruslabel society.com.

Coca-Cola Collectors Club International, *Coca-Cola Collectors News* (NL), 4780 Ashford Dunwoody Rd., Suite A, PMB 609, Atlanta, GA 30338, website: www.cocacolaclub.org.

Cracker Jack Collectors Association, *Prize Insider* (NL), 5469 S. Dorchester Ave., Chicago, IL 60615, e-mail: waddyTMR@aol.com, website: www.collectoronline.com/cjca.

Dr Pepper 10-2-4 Collectors Club, *Lion's Roar* (NL), 3100 Monticello, Suite 890, Dallas, TX 75205.

Farm Machinery Advertising Collectors, *Farm Machinery Advertising Collectors* (NL), 10108 Tamarack Dr., Vienna, VA 22182-1843, e-mail: schnakenbergdd@erols.com, website: farmmachineryadvertise.com.

Florida Citrus Labels Collectors Association, 2135 Regent's Blvd., West Palm Beach, FL 33409, e-mail: BBurne1003@aol.com, website: members.aol.com/burnassoc.

International Swizzle Stick Collectors Association, *Swizzle Stick News* (NL), PO Box 1117, Bellingham, WA 98227-1117, e-mail: veray.issca@shaw.ca, website: www.swizzlesticks-issca.com.

Jell-O Collectors' Club, *Jell-O News Bulletin* (NL), PO Box 56, St. James, MO 65559-0056.

M&M Collectors Club, c/o Ken Clee, Acting Treasurer, PO Box 11412, Philadelphia, PA 19111, e-mail: danwolfe@mail.microserve.net, website: mnmclub.com.

McDonald's International Pin Club, *McDonald's International Pin Club* (NL), PO Box 328, Coopersburg, PA 18036-0328, e-mail: mike@mipc.com, website: www.mipc.com.

National Association of Paper and Advertising Collectors, *P.A.C., The Paper & Advertising Collector* (NP), PO Box 500, Mount Joy, PA 17552, e-mail: pac@engleonline.com, website: www.engleonline.com.

National Pop Can Collectors, *Can-O-Gram* (NL), PO Box 163, Macon, MO 63552-0163, website: www.one-mans-junk.com/NPCC.

New England Moxie Congress, *Nerve Food News* (NL), 445 Wyoming Ave., Milburn, NJ 07041, e-mail: njmoxie1@worldnet.att.net, website: www.moxieland.com.

Peanut Pals, *Peanut Papers* (NL), 804 Hickory Grade Rd., Bridgeville, PA 15017, e-mail: peanuts999@aol.com.

Pepsi-Cola Collectors Club, *Pepsi-Cola Collectors Club Newsletter* (NL), PO Box 817, Claremont, CA 91711, e-mail: spdrago@wavetech.net, website: www.dataflo.net/~jpepsi.

Watkins Collectors Club, *Watkins Collectors Club Newsletter* (NL), W24024 SR 54-93, Galesville, WI 54630-8249, e-mail: beanpot@triwest.net.

Whisky Pitcher Collectors Association of America, *Black & White* (NL), 19341 W. Tahoe Dr., Mundelein, IL 60060-4061, e-mail: thdpubjug1@aol.com, website: pubjug.com.

OTHER PUBLICATIONS

Card Times (MAG), 70 Winifred Ln., Aughton, Ormskirk, Lancashire L39 5DL, UK, e-mail: david@cardtimes.co.uk, website: www.cardtimes.co.uk (cigarette cards, trading cards, sports and nonsports cards, phone cards, printed ephemera).

Chili Label Reviews (NL), 10802 Greencreek Dr., #203, Houston, TX 77070-5365.

The Crunch (NL), 9 Weald Rise, Tilehurst, Reading, Berkshire RG30 6XB, UK (food-related packaging, toys, and ephemera).

Please Stop Snickering (NL), 4113 Paint Rock Dr., Austin, TX 78731, e-mail: khfoster@texas.net, website: khfoster.home.texas.net (produce labels).

The Premium Watch Watch (NL), 24 San Rafael Dr., Rochester, NY 14618-3702, e-mail: watcher1@rochester.rr.com (promotional, advertising and premium watches).

ARCHIVES & MUSEUMS

American Advertising Museum, 211 NW Fifth Ave., Portland, OR 97209, 503-226-0000, fax: 503-226-2635, website: www.admuseum.org.

American Sign Museum, 407 Gilbert Ave., Cincinnati, OH 45202, 513-421-2050 or 800-925-1110, fax: 513-421-5144, website: www.signmuseum.org.

Barker Character, Comic & Cartoon Museum, 1188 Highland Ave., Cheshire, CT 06410-1624, 800-224-CELS, e-mail: fun@barkeranimation.com, website: www.barkeranimation.com. Click on museum link.

Coca-Cola Co. Archives, Industry & Consumer Affairs, PO Box 1734, Atlanta, GA 30301, 800-438-2653, website: coca-cola.com. Click on contact link for e-mail question form.

Creatabilitoys! Museum of Advertising Icons, 1550 Madruga Ave., Suite 504, Coral Gables, FL 33146, 305-663-7374, fax: 305-669-0092, website: www.toymuseum.com.

Dr Pepper Museum, 300 S. 5th St., Waco, TX 76701, 254-757-1025, website: drpeppermuseum.com.

Historical Society of Western Pennsylvania, 1212 Smallman St., Pittsburgh, PA 15222, 412-454-6000, fax: 412-454-6031, website: www.pghhistory.org.

Hook's American Drugstore Museum, 1180 E. 38th St., Indianapolis, IN 46205, 317-924-5886, fax: 317-924-5825, e-mail: hookamerx@aol.com.

McDonald's Archives, Kroc Dr., Oak Brook, IL 60523-1900, 800-244-6227, website: mcdonalds.com.

The Museum of American Financial History, 28 Broadway, New York, NY 10004, 212-908-4519, 800-98-FINANCE, fax: 212-908-4601, website: www.financialhistory.com. Company histories and artifacts.

Nabisco Food Group, Public Relations Plaza, Floor 3, Parsippany, NJ 07054, attn.: David R. Stivers, Archivist, 800-NABISCO, website: www.nabisco.com.

NCR Archive, The Montgomery County Historical Society, 7 N. Main St., Dayton, OH 54502, 937-228-6271, website: www.daytonhistory.org/ nat_treasure.htm.

Pepsi-Cola Co. Archives, One Pepsi Way, Purchase, NY 10577, 914-253-2000, website: www.pepsi.com.

USEFUL SITES

Ad*Access (Duke University Library), scriptorium.lib.duke.edu/adaccess.
The Trade Card Place, www.tradecards.com.

APPRAISERS

Many of the auctions and repair services listed in this section will also do appraisals. *See also* the general list of "Appraisal Groups" on page 483.

AUCTIONS

➥ **SEE ALSO "SELLING THROUGH AUCTION HOUSES," PAGE 485.**

Autopia Advertising Auctions, 19937 NE 154th St. #C2, Woodinville, WA 98072-5629, 425-883-7653, fax: 425-867-5568, e-mail: win@Autopia Auctions.com, website: www.AutopiaAuctions.com. Mail and phone bids accepted. Buyer's premium 10%. Prices realized mailed after auction. Restoration and conservation available. Appraisals.

Buffalo Bay Auction Co., 5244 Quam Cir., St. Michael, MN 55376, 763-428-8480, e-mail: buffalobayauction@hotmail.com, website: www.buffalobayauction.com. Internet auctions of advertising and country store collectibles. Mail, phone, e-mail, and Internet bids accepted. Buyer's premium 10%. Prices realized available on website after auction.

Cigar Label Art, PO Box 3902, Mission Viejo, CA 92691-6036, 949-582-7686, fax: 949-582-7947, e-mail: wayne@cigarlabelart.com, website: www.cigarlabelart.com. Absentee auctions of cigar labels. Mail, phone, fax, and e-mail bids accepted. High bid prices updated on website daily. No buyer's premium.

Dave Beck Auctions, PO Box 435, Mediapolis, IA 52637, 319-394-3943, fax: 319-394-3943, e-mail: adman@mepotelco.net. Specializing in auctions of advertising watch fobs. Mail, phone, fax, and e-mail bids accepted. No buyer's premium. Prices realized mailed after auction. Free catalogs. Yearly subscription $15.

Frank's Antiques, PO Box 516, 2405 N. Kings Rd., Hilliard, FL 32046, 904-845-2870, e-mail: franksauct@aol.com. Mail, phone, and fax bids accepted. Buyer's premium 10%. Annual advertising and country store auction.

Gary Metz's Muddy River Trading Co., PO Box 18185, Roanoke, VA 24014, 540-344-7333, fax: 540-344-3014, e-mail: metz@rbnet.com, website: www.muddyrivertrading.com. Antique advertising auctions. Mail, phone, and Internet bids accepted. Buyer's premium 12.5%. Prices realized mailed after auction and available on website.

Hake's Americana & Collectibles, PO Box 1444, York, PA 17405-1444, 717-848-1333, Mon.–Fri. 10 A.M.–5 P.M., fax: 717-852-0344, e-mail: hake@hakes.com, website: www.hakes.com. Twentieth-century nostalgia collectibles including comic characters. Mail, phone, and Internet bids accepted. No buyer's premium. Catalog $7; yearly subscription $30. Sample catalog free. Appraisals.

Howard B. Parzow, PO Box 3464, Gaithersburg, MD 20885-3464, 301-977-6741, fax: 301-208-8947, e-mail: hparzow@aol.com, website: www.hbparzowauctioneer.com. Americana, advertising and country store, drug and apothecary, coin-operated machines, toys. Mail and phone bids accepted. Buyer's premium 10%. Appraisals.

Just Kids Nostalgia, 310 New York Ave., Huntington, NY 11743, 516-423-8449, fax: 631-423-4326, e-mail: info@justkidsnostalgia.com, website: www.justkidsnostalgia.com. Auctions of advertising and other pop culture memorabilia. Mail, phone, fax, and e-mail bids accepted. Prices realized mailed after auction and available on website.

McMurray Antiques & Auctions, PO Box 393, Kirkwood, NY 13795, 607-775-5972, fax: 607-775-2321. Specializing in drugstore, apothecary, patent medicines, and advertising. Three auctions per year. Mail and phone bids accepted. Buyer's premium 10%. Catalog $15. Prices realized mailed after auction. Appraisals.

Nostalgia Publications, Inc., Allan Petretti, PO Box 4175, River Edge, NJ 07661, 201-488-4536, fax: 201-883-0938, e-mail: nostpub@webtv.net. Soda-pop mail, phone, and fax auctions. No buyer's premium. Catalog $10; subscription $25 for three auctions. Two auctions per year. Prices realized printed in the next catalog. Appraisals.

Past Tyme Pleasures, 2491 San Ramon Valley Blvd., PMB 204, San Ramon, CA 94583, 925-484-6442, fax: 925-484-2551, e-mail: pasttyme1@attbi.com, website: www.pasttyme1.com., Antique advertising, general store, tobacco, soda, and breweriana. Mail, phone, fax, and e-mail bids accepted. Buyer's premium 10%. Prices realized mailed after auction and available on website. Appraisals.

Randy Inman Auctions, PO Box 726, Waterville, ME 04903-0726, 207-872-6900, fax: 207-872-6966, e-mail: inman@inmanauctions.com, website: www.inmanauctions.com. Specializing in antique advertising, coin-operated machines, toy, and related items. Mail and phone bids accepted. Buyer's premium 10%. Prices realized available after auction. Appraisals.

Richard Opfer Auctioneering Inc., 1919 Greenspring Dr., Timonium, MD 21093, 410-252-5035, fax: 410-252-5863, e-mail: info@opfer auction.com, website: www.opferauction.com. Advertising, antiques, and collectibles. Buyer's premium 10%. Mail and phone bids accepted. Prices realized mailed and available on website after some auctions. Catalog prices vary from $3 to $35, depending on sale. Referrals given for restoration and conservation. Appraisals.

Victorian Images, Box 284, Marlton, NJ 08053, 856-354-2154, fax: 856-354-9699, e-mail: rmascieri@aol.com, website: tradecards.com/vi. Absentee auctions of trade cards, ephemera, nineteenth-century advertising. Mail, phone, and Internet bids accepted. Buyer's premium 10%. Prices realized mailed after auction and available on website. Catalog $18; yearly subscription $90. Appraisals.

William Morford Auctions, RR #2, Cazenovia, NY 13035, 315-662-7625, fax: 315-662-3570, e-mail: morf2bid@aol.com, website: morfauction.com. Absentee auctions of antique advertising. Mail, phone, and Internet bids accepted. Buyer's premium 10%. Prices realized mailed after auction and available on website. Catalog $12; yearly subscription $20. Restoration and conservation. Appraisals.

REPAIRS, PARTS & SUPPLIES

➤➤ SEE ALSO "CONSERVATORS & RESTORERS," PAGE 520.

Andy Karaffa, 1875 S. Pearl St., Denver, CO 80210, 303-744-1615, fax: 303-744-7920, e-mail: akaraffa@aol.com. Antique brass cash registers serviced and restored; parts.

Chuck Kovacic, 9337 Sophia Ave., North Hills, CA 91343-2820, 818-891-4069, e-mail: cfkovacic@aol.com. Restoration of antique advertising: paper, cardboard, metal, porcelain, tins, and trays.

Daniel's Den, 720 Mission St., South Pasadena, CA 91030, 323-682-3557, fax: 626-799-3671, e-mail: danielsden@social.rr.com. Repair and restoration of Baranger motion window displays using original parts and art. Send SASE for free brochure.

Fine Gold Sign Co., 1644 Wilmington Blvd., Wilmington, CA 90744, 310-549-6622, fax: 310-549-0180, e-mail: rick@esotericsignsupply.com, website: www.esotericsignsupply.com. Restoration and conservation of pre-pro reverse glass signs.

Graphic Conservation Co., 329 W. 18th St., Suite 701, Chicago, IL 60616, 312-738-2657, fax: 312-738-3125, e-mail: info@graphicconservation.com, website: www.graphicconservation.com. Preservation of works of art on paper, including billboard advertising and paper memorabilia. Dry cleaning, stain reduction, flattening, deacidification, inpainting, tear repairs and fills. Archival matting. Free brochure.

Heimbolds, 2950 SW Persimmon Ln., Dunnellon, FL 34431, 352-465-0756. Art conservation restorers. Restoration of signs. Free estimates. Free brochure.

Hickory Bend Antiques and Collectibles, 2995 Drake Hill Rd., Jasper, NY 14855, 607-792-3343, fax: 607-792-3309, e-mail: hickorybend @infoblvd.net, website: www.hbacgroup.com. Antique cash register restoration, repair, and parts.

L.A. Allen, 5201 Wakonda Dr., Norwalk, IA 50211, 515-285-5347, 8:00 A.M.– 9:00 P.M. e-mail: allenslabels@aol.com. Supplies for spool cabinets: labels for front, sides, and back; hardware pulls for drawers; curved glass for Merrick's cabinets. Free brochure.

Precision Arcade Repair, 1315 Sandpiper Ln., Lilburn, GA 30047-2027, 770-985-4697, e-mail: gyrogames@aol.com, website: www.tristan mulrooney.com. Neon sign repair and servicing, also custom neons made to order.

Tony Orlando, 6661 Norborne, Dearborn Heights, MI 48127-2076, 313- 561-5072. Conservation and restoration of cigar store figures.

Weber's Nostalgia Supermarket, 6611 Anglin Dr., Fort Worth, TX 76119, 817- 534-6611, fax: 817-534-3316, e-mail: info@weberspump.com, website: www.weberspump.com. Gas pump restoration supplies and game- room/restaurant decor, including globes, decals, signs, parts, nostal- gic photos, books, and novelties. Catalog $4, refundable with order. Mon.–Fri. 8:30 A.M.–5:00 P.M.

➤ **ALUMINUM, SEE METALS**
➤ **AMUSEMENT PARK COLLECTIBLES, SEE CAROUSELS**

ARCHITECTURAL ANTIQUES

The tops of stone pillars, pieces of carved wooden fretwork, doors, windows, stair railings, iron fences, fountains, urns, statues, exterior tiles, wooden flooring, paneling, even old bricks and other pieces of buildings are now bought and sold in the antiques market. Many of these items are large, heavy, and difficult to move, but there are spe- cialists who deal in architectural antiques. Sometimes they are sal- vage dealers who demolish buildings and remove any salable parts. If you have rights to a large building or an old house that is about to be destroyed, examine it carefully for valuable collectibles that can be saved. Not only the wood or stone carvings, but many other parts of a building can be sold. Any sort of ornamental ironwork is in demand, including elevator doors, radiators and radiator covers, ventilator grills, locks, handles, or hinges. Light fixtures, church pews, marble benches, marble slabs, wooden doors, and anything decorative is desirable. Any unusual stone or tile piece could be used as a garden ornament. Even special wall coverings or carpeting can be sold.

Usually, the best way to sell architectural items is to place an ad in the paper and have the buyers come and take their pieces out of the building. (Don't be surprised or upset if they knock down the walls or floor to remove something.) If you own doors, phone booths, or wrought-iron fencing, you can sell them through an ad or by contacting an auctioneer or a dealer who sells this type of collectible. There are a few auction houses that specialize in architectural pieces, room paneling, large fireplaces, statues, fences, etc. One that advertises heavily is Red Baron (see the auctions section at the end of this chapter). Most dealers are not interested because architectural pieces sell slowly.

Unlike smaller antiques and collectibles, architectural and garden ornaments are not readily available on the Internet. This makes good sense—would you want to buy a new door for your restored Craftsman house sight-unseen? Delivery is also a problem.

There is added value if a building or house was designed by a well-known architect. To price architectural pieces, think of them in terms of use. A plain, used door should sell for less than a new door. A door with a carving sells for its decorative value.

REPAIR

Most cities now have dealers or specialists who have architectural pieces and can help you restore any pieces you might find. Marble yards and tombstone makers can help. Wrought-iron fence makers can often make the parts you need to reuse a radiator grille as a door or a gate as a wall ornament. Some cities are so concerned with saving the best of the past they have established government-run shops to recycle the architectural pieces found through urban renewal.

➼ SEE ALSO HARDWARE, LIGHTING

➼ WINDOW AND DOOR PARTS, SEE GLASS

REFERENCE BOOKS

Old-House Journal Restoration Directory, annual (2 Main St., Gloucester, MA 01930).

CLUBS & THEIR PUBLICATIONS

Association of Restorers, *Restorers Update* (NL), 8 Medford Pl., New Harford, NY 13413, e-mail: aorcca@alelphia.net, website: www.assoc-restorers.com.

International Brick Collectors Association, *Journal of the International Brick Collectors Association* (MAG), 1743 Lindenhall Dr., Loveland, OH 45140, e-mail: frenchie@one.net, website: www.msinter.net/tweety.

National Trust for Historic Preservation, *Preservation* (MAG), 1785 Massachusetts Ave. NW, Washington, DC 20036, e-mail: members @nthp.org, website: nthp.org.

OTHER PUBLICATIONS

American Bungalow (MAG), PO Box 756, Sierra Madre, CA 91025-0756, e-mail: Ambungalow@aol.com, website: ambungalow.com.

Architectural Digest (MAG), PO Box 59061, Boulder, CO 80328-9061, e-mail: subscriptions@archdigest.com, website: www.archdigest.com.

Old-House Interiors (MAG), 108 E. Main St., Gloucester, MA 01930, website: oldhouseinteriors.com.

Old-House Journal (MAG), P.O. Box 420235, Palm Coast, FL 32142-0235, e-mail: OHJ@palmcoastd.com, website: www.oldhousejournal.com.

Victorian Homes (MAG), PO Box 68040, Anaheim, CA 92817-9800, e-mail: editorial@victorianhomesmag.com, website: www.victorianhomesmag.com.

ARCHIVES & MUSEUMS

Cooper-Hewitt National Design Museum, 2 E. 91st St., New York, NY 10128, 212-849-8400, website: www./ndm.si.edu.

The National Building Museum, 401 F St., NW, Washington, DC 20001, 202-272-7706, fax: 202-272-2564, e-mail: mail@nbm.org, website: www.nbm.org.

APPRAISERS

Some of the auctions and repair services listed in this section also do appraisals. *See also* the general list of "Appraisal Groups" on page 483.

AUCTIONS

➜ SEE ALSO "SELLING THROUGH AUCTION HOUSES," PAGE 485.

Great Gatsby's, 5070 Peachtree Industrial Blvd., Atlanta, GA 30341, 800-428-7297 or 770-457-1903, fax: 770-457-7250, e-mail: internet @greatgatsbys.com, website: www.greatgatsbys.com. Live auctions in Atlanta in February, May, and October. Catalogs $10 for one-year subscription. Mail and phone bids accepted. Buyer's premium. Online auctions continuously on their website. Appraisals.

Red Baron Auctions, 6450 Roswell Rd., Atlanta, GA 30328, 404-252-3770, fax: 404-252-0268, e-mail: rbaron1@bellsouth.net, website: www.red-baronsantiques.com. Auctions of architectural elements, furniture, garden items, and fine art. Phone bids accepted. Buyer's premium. Catalogs. Prices realized available after auction.

REPAIRS, PARTS & SUPPLIES

➳ SEE ALSO "CONSERVATORS & RESTORERS," PAGE 520.

A.F. Schwerd Manufacturing Co., 3215 McClure Ave., Pittsburgh, PA 15212, 412-766-6322, 8:30 A.M.–5:00 P.M., fax: 412-766-2262. Reproduction wood columns, standard styles or custom. Aluminum bases for exterior. Call or write for free brochure.

Andrea Pitsch Paper Conservation, 212-594-9676, Mon.–Fri. 9:00 A.M.–5:00 P.M, fax: 212-268-4046, e-mail: apnyc@interport.net. Conservation and restoration of paper-based objects, including architectural drawings and blueprints. Consultation on condition of paper collections, prospective purchases, storage, and handling. Brochure $1 and SASE. By appointment only.

Antique Hardware & Home Store, 19 Buckingham Plantation Dr., Bluffton, SC 29910, 800-422-9982, 8:30 A.M.–6:00 P.M., e-mail: treasure @hargray.com, website: www.antiquehardware.com. Claw-foot tub supplies, high tank toilets, plumbing fittings; floor grills, tin ceilings.

Antique Hardware and Mirror Resilvering, 763 West Bippley Rd., Lake Odessa, MI 48849, 616-374-7750, fax: 616-374-7752, e-mail: antiquehardware@robinsonsantiques.com, website: www.robinsons antiques.com. Original antique restoration hardware, door hardware, doorknobs, doorbells, hinges, locks, latches, registers, and more. Original parts from 1650-1925. Free search. Free matching service.

Architectural Antiques Exchange, 709–15 N. Second St., Philadelphia, PA 19123, 215-922-3669, fax: 215-922-3680, e-mail: aaexchange@aol.com, website: www.architecturalantiques.com. Architectural salvage. Antique and reproduction wood and marble mantels, doors, stained glass, lighting, and more. Appraisals.

Architectural Detail, 512 S. Fair Oaks, Pasadena, CA 91105, 626-844-6604, fax: 626-844-6651. Home restoration resources. Used building materials from 1880–1960, including doors, doorknobs, hinges, mail slots, windows, molding, plumbing, hardware, tiles, lighting, etc. Specializing in materials from Pasadena and Greater Los Angeles. No mail order.

Architectural Emporium, 207 Adams Ave., Canonsburg, PA 15317, 724-746-4301, e-mail: sales@architectural-emporium.com, website: architectural-emporium.com. Architectural antiques, including vintage plumbing, mantels, hardware, stained glass, lighting, garden statuary, and all architectural items.

Artisans of the Valley, 103 Corrine Dr., Pennington, NJ 08534, 609-637-0450, fax: 609-637-0452, e-mail: woodworkers@artisansofthe valley.com, website: www.artisansofthevalley.com. Conservation and restoration services; hand-crafted custom woodworking. Old finishes restored, missing carvings and moldings made, leather restored.

Etched and stained glass work. Consultation services to architects, contractors, and curators. Free catalog.

Bathroom Machineries, 495 Main St., PO Box 1020, Murphys, CA 95247, 209-728-2031 or 800-255-4426, fax: 209-728-2320, e-mail: tom@deabath.com, website: deabath.com. Antique plumbing fixtures. Original and reproduction claw-foot tubs, high tank toilets, pedestal sinks, hard-to-find plumbing parts; faucets, mirrors, medicine cabinets, old keys. Free catalog.

Bedlam Brass Restoration, 520 River Dr., Garfield, NJ 07026, 800-BEDLAM-1, fax: 800-BEDLAM-2, e-mail: sales@bedlam.biz, website: bedlam.biz. Custom architectural metal fabricated. Carpet hardware.

Bradbury & Bradbury, PO Box 155, Benicia, CA 94510, 707-746-1900, fax: 707-745-9417, e-mail: info@bradbury.com, website: www.bradbury.com. Hand-printed Neoclassical, Victorian, Edwardian, and Arts and Crafts wallpapers, borders, and ceiling papers. In-house design service. Catalog $12.

Brass Foundry Castings, Brasted Forge, Brasted, Kent TN16 1JL, England, 011-44-1959-563863, fax: 011-44-1959-561262, e-mail: bfc@antique-restorations.org.uk, website: www.antique-restorations.org.uk. Hand-crafted reproduction antique brass architectural and interior design fittings, castings, escutcheons, finials, etc., dating back to the 17th century. Handmade, including wear and blemishes, and produced by the lost wax casting process. Detailed mail order catalog of over 900 fittings, £19.50 + £9 p&p. (Can order online at www.antique-restorations.org.uk)

The Brass Knob, Architectural Antiques, 2311 18th St. NW, Washington, DC 20009, 202-332-3370, e-mail: bk@thebrassknob.com, website: www.thebrassknob.com. Architectural antiques and salvage, including lighting and many other old house parts. Second location, The Back Doors Warehouse, is located at 2329 Champlain St. NW, Washington, DC 20009.

BRING Recycling, PO Box 885, Eugene, OR 97440-0885, 541-746-3023, 9:00 A.M.–5:00 P.M, e-mail: bring@efn.org, website: www.efn.org/~bring. Resale yard of used building materials for refurbishing older homes. Doors of all kinds, double-hung sash windows, bathtubs, plumbing supplies, hardware, light fixtures, mirrors, screens, gutters, etc. Free catalog.

Brooks Art Glass, Inc., 821 1/2 E. Miller, Springfield, IL 62704, 217-789-9523, fax: 217-789-6423, e-mail: brooksartglass@hotmail.com, website: www.brooksartglass. Repair and restoration of stained glass, including removal, complete rebuilding, and installation. Custom stained glass from design to installation. Decorative sandblasted designs.

Chelsea Decorative Metal Co., 8212 Braewick Dr., Houston, TX 77074, 713-721-9200, fax: 713-776-8661, website: thetinman.com. Pressed-tin for ceilings and cornices, Art Deco to Victorian. Can be used for back splashes or behind wood stoves. Send $1 for brochure.

Classic Ceilings, 902 E. Commonwealth Ave., Fullerton, CA 92831, 800-992-8700, fax: 714-870-5972, e-mail: ceilings@classicceilings.com, website: www.classicceilings.com. Tin ceiling panels. No-obligation lay-out service. Ceiling moldings and medallions. Free brochure.

Cohen and Cohen, 1963 Merivale Road, Ottawa, ON K2G 1G1, Canada, 866-937-3873, e-mail: kenbill@cohenandcohen.com, website: www.cohen andcohen.com. Repair and restoration of architectural antiques.

Conner's Architectural Antiques, 701 P St., Lincoln, NE 68508, 402-435-3338, fax: 402-435-3339, e-mail: connersaa@aol.com, website: www.ConnersArchitecturalAntiques.com. Architectural elements from old structures, including columns, doors, fireplace mantels, hardware, light fixtures, stairways, and windows. Stained, etched, and beveled glass windows. Parts for lighting fixtures; old and new hardware.

Cumberland Woodcraft Co., Inc., 10 Stover Dr., PO Box 609, Carlisle, PA 17013-0609, 800-367-1884 or 717-243-0063, fax: 717-243-6502, e-mail: saks@cumberlandwoodcraft.com, website: www.cumberlandwood-craft.com. Period architectural millwork, fireplace mantels, wooden screen doors, wood carvings, appliques and onlays, turnings and spindles, moldings and ornaments, period wallcoverings, and much more. Catalog $5, refundable with order.

David Wixon & Associates, Inc., 189 Kenilworth Ave., Glen Ellyn, IL 60137, 630-858-7618, fax: 630-858-7623, e-mail: wixonglass@aol.com, website: www.wixonartglass.com. Restoration and construction of stained and beveled glass for both residential and church clients. Historic architectural glass a specialty. Free brochure.

Delphi Creativity Group, 3380 E. Jolly Rd., Lansing, MI 48910, 800-248-2048 or 517-394-4631, fax: 800-748-0374 or 517-394-5364, e-mail: sales@delphiglass.com, website: www.delphiglass.com. Hand-blown glass for window repairs. Color matching service for repairs of antique stained-glass windows. Glass etching and engraving supplies, stencils; stained-glass kits and supplies; beveled glass; books and tools. Free catalog.

Ephraim Forge, Inc., 8300 W. North Ave., Frankfort, IL 60423, 815-464-5656, e-mail: roger@ephraimforge.com, website: www.ephraim forge.com. Restoration and replication of old ironwork. Custom black-smithing. Architectural ironwork, interior and exterior.

Ernest Porcelli/Art Glass, 543 Union St., 3A, Brooklyn, NY 11215, 718-596-4353, fax: 718-596-4353, e-mail: eporcelliart@c.s.com, website: ernestartglass.com. Restoration of stained glass windows. Custom work. Duplication of old windows to contemporary designs.

Harvard Art, 49 Littleton County Rd., Harvard, MA 01451, 978-456-9050, fax: 978-456-9050, e-mail: sjackson@harvardart.com, website: harvardart.com. Gilding conservation and restoration of architectural elements. Securing of loose elements, structural repair, missing pieces replaced, gesso fills, ingilding, and toning to match.

Hyland Studio at Manufacturers Glass Ltd., 650 Reed St., Santa Clara, CA 95050, 408-748-1806, e-mail: jim@manufacturersglass.com, website: www.manufacturersglass.com. Decorative glass and doors; traditional lead work. Historic restoration and duplication of traditional leaded glass windows. Custom beveled glass windows, historic and custom designs. Etched and carved glass; glue chipping.

International Fine Art Conservation Studios, Inc., PO Box 81509, Atlanta, GA 30366, 404-794-6142, fax: 404-794-6229, e-mail: Geoffrey.Steward @ifacs-inc.com, website: www.ifacs-inc.com. Conservation and restoration of murals, frescoes, ornamental plasterwork, interior and exterior decorative painting, etc. Surveys and scientific analysis.

John Scott, New York Conservation Center, 519 W. 26 St., New York, NY 10001, 212-714-0620, fax: 212-714-0149, e-mail: NYConsnCtr@aol.com, website: www.nycf.org. Consulting and hands-on conservation of art and architecture, including outdoor sculpture. Analysis, cleaning, and preservation of painted, unpainted, or patinated surfaces; inpainting, revarnishing, repatination; structural and surface repairs. Condition examinations, surveys, and reports.

Linoleum City, Inc., 5657 Santa Monica Blvd., Hollywood, CA 90038, 323-469-0063, fax: 323-465-5866. Natural linoleum sheet and tiles, cork, sisal, sea grass. Specialty floors, including hexagonal and pebblestone (tile). All major manufacturers. Some samples available. Catalogs available, prices vary.

Old and Elegant Distributing, 10203 Main St. Ln., Bellevue, WA 98004, 425-455-4660, fax: 425-455-0203. Custom metal refinishing and restoration. Cabinet and door hardware replication. Custom faucet and bath fixture design. Architectural wood and iron.

Old World Restorations, Inc., 5729 Dragon Way, Cincinnati, OH 45227, 513-271-5459, fax: 513-271-5418, e-mail: info@oldworldrestorations.com, website: www.oldworldrestorations.com. On-site architectural restorations of murals, frescoes, and gold leaf. Restoration and conservation of sculpture, stone, metals, and more. Fire and water damage restoration. Specialized packing and shipping. Nationwide service. Send or e-mail photos for preliminary estimates. Free brochure.

Outwater Plastics Industries, Inc., 4 Passaic St., PO Box 403, Wood Ridge, NJ 07075, 800-631-8375 or 973-340-1040, fax: 800-888-3315 or 973-916-1640, e-mail: outwater@outwater.com, website: www.outwater.com. An international supplier of more than 40,000 component products, including architectural moldings and millwork, columns and capitals, plaster architectural elements, fireplace surrounds, wrought iron components, lighting, brass tubing and fittings, fasteners, hardware, and much more. Free catalog.

Phyllis Kennedy, 10655 Andrade Dr., Zionsville, IN 46077, 317- 873-1316, fax: 317-873-8662, e-mail: philken@kennedyhardware.com, website: www.kennedyhardware.com. Architectural hardware, pressed fiberboard, and more. Wholesale catalog $3.

Pinch of the Past, 109 W. Broughton St., Savannah, GA 31401, 912-232-5563, e-mail: pinchopast@aol.com, website: pinchofthepast.com. Architectural items, hardware, and lighting, antique or reproduction. Custom castings in metals or plaster. Repair and restoration of architectural antiques, lighting, and metals. Brass and metal cleaning and polishing. Lighting restoration. Gold leafing, faux finishing. Custom casting and pattern making, welding and sandblasting. Restoration consultation. Appraisals. Free brochure.

Renovation Source, Inc., 3512 N. Southport, Chicago, IL 60657, 773-327-1250 phone/fax. Salvaged architectural details, including doors, moldings, hardware, lighting fixtures, fireplace mantels and tile, staircase components, stained and beveled glass, terra-cotta, and iron; columns, fretwork, exterior porch posts and spandrels. Light fixture restoration, hardware polishing and coating, wood refinishing. Open Tues.-Sat. 10:00 A.M.–6:00 P.M.

Renovator's Supply, Renovator's Old Mill, Millers Falls, MA 01349, 800-659-0203, 7:00 A.M.–midnight, fax: 413-659-3796 orders, website: www.rensup.com. Lighting and plumbing fixtures; firebacks, ceiling medallions, hardware, and more. Free catalog.

Restoration by Design, 1644 NW 34th Terr., Ft. Lauderdale, FL 33311, 954-791-6305, fax: 954-791-6330. Traditional (water and oil) and contemporary gilders: carat and composition gold, silver, and copper leaf. Conservation and restoration of period gilded picture and mirror frames. Reproductions made to order. Architectural element gilding, interior only.

Restoration Studio, PO Box 3440, Glens Falls, NY 12801, 518-743-9416, e-mail: anna98@nycap.rr.com. Restoration and conservation of interior decorative plaster work, frescoes, and ceramic objects of art. Restoration lessons given at the studio. Free estimates. Free brochure.

Salvage One, 1840 W. Hubbard St., Chicago, IL 60622, 312-733-0098, e-mail: staff@salvageone.com, website: www.salvageone.com. Architectural artifacts for home and garden, including mantels and fireplace accessories, lighting, iron, and terra-cotta, etc.

Sue Connell, The Clayton Store, Canaan-Southfield Rd., Southfield, MA 01259, 413-229-2621, fax: 413-229-2621. Restoration and reproduction of walls, floors, woodwork, and furniture. Color matching a specialty. Cleaning and grooming of painted and decorated surfaces. Dry scraping of later layers to original surface.

Sunflower Showerhead Co., PO Box 4218, Seattle, WA 98104, 206-722-1232, fax: 206-722-1321, e-mail: deweyusa@deweyusa.com, website: deweyusa.com/deweyusa. Antique reproduction solid brass showerheads and arm brackets. Deluge-type showerheads available in 8-inch, 10-inch, and 12-inch diameter; stone and brass unit; two-headed needle shower system; custom and hard-to-find mountings, arms, and fittings. Free brochure.

Tile Restoration Center, Inc., 3511 Interlake N., Seattle, WA 98103, 206-633-4866, fax: 206-633-3489, e-mail: trc@tilerestorationcenter.com, website: www.tilerestorationcenter.com. On-site restoration of tile installations. Reproductions of Arts and Crafts period tiles. Specializing in reproductions of Batchelder and Claycraft tiles. Custom design, custom color matching. Catalog $10.

United House Wrecking, 535 Hope St., Stamford, CT 06906, 203-348-5371, fax: 203-961-9472, e-mail: unitedhouse.wrecking@snet.net, website: www.unitedhousewrecking.com. Architectural elements, including doors, mantels, and woodwork; lighting; sinks and tubs; stained glass; garden benches, fountains, statuary; lighting; and more. Open seven days a week, Mon.–Sat. 9:30 A.M.–5:00 P.M., Sunday noon–5:00 P.M. Free brochure.

Van Dyke's Restorers, PO Box 278, Woonsocket, SD 57385, 605-796-4425, 800-558-1234 orders, fax: 605-796-4085, e-mail: restoration @cabelas.com, website: www.vandykes.com. Kitchen and bathroom plumbing supplies. Mail order worldwide. Catalog.

Vintage Hardware, PO Box 9486, San Jose, CA 95129, 408-246-9918, e-mail: vhprs@earthlink.net, website: www.vintagehardware.com. Reproduction hardware for the restoration and rehab of Victorian homes and buildings. Distributor of Heritage Lighting, reproduction antique lighting including neo-rococo gas lighting from 1840. "Pottery plaster" ceiling medallions. Color catalog, 80 pages, $4.

Vintage Plumbing Bathroom Antiques, 9645 Sylvia Ave. Northridge, CA 91324, 818-772-1721, e-mail: info@vintageplumbing.com, website: vintageplumbing.com. Antique bath and kitchen fixtures. Claw-foot bathtubs, pedestal sinks, showers, toilets, Victorian bathroom fixtures, nickel-plated brass accessories, and architectural salvage.

Vintage Wood Works, PO Box 39, MSC 3944, Quinlan, TX 75474-0039, 903-356-2158, e-mail: mail@vintagewoodworks.com, website: www.vintagewoodworks.com. Handcrafted reproductions of Victorian architectural details, including balusters, brackets, corbels, fittings, gables, posts, screen doors, stair parts. Porch, gable, and eave decorations. Mail order. Master catalog $3.

The Wood Factory, 111 Railroad St., Navasota, TX 77868, 936-825-7233. Authentic Victorian millworks. Custom turnings, gingerbread, screen doors. Specializing in custom-matching existing porch parts original to older homes. Send $2 for catalog.

AUTOGRAPHS

Nineteenth-century autograph collectors wanted just the signatures of famous people. They cut names from the bottoms of letters or other documents, destroying much of their value. Today's collector prefers the entire letter or document. Never cut out a signature! If you find old books, letters, deeds, or even scribbled notes signed by an author or famous person, keep them intact. Never cut, erase, or repair anything. Torn pages are preferred to taped pages. Glue from the tape can eventually destroy the paper.

All correspondence can have a value. This includes letters from distant relatives describing a war, an old Western town, the food eaten for dinner, or many other everyday events. Content, condition, date, place written, signature, postmarks, and other factors all affect the value. Very high prices are paid for letters or diaries about American life, especially if they describe disasters, the Gold Rush, Indians, whaling, the Revolutionary or Civil wars, or pioneer life. Hand-drawn maps, sketches by artists, and inscribed or annotated books are all of value.

Very high prices are paid for letters and documents of presidents, signers of the Declaration of Independence, important political and military figures, composers, authors, actors, or scientists. But many government documents were signed by secretaries or even by machines that reproduced a president's signature, and these are worth very little. Land grants, army discharges, and many other legal papers were signed with the president's name and not always hand-signed by the president. There are many of these, and their value is very low. Slave-related documents have become more valuable because of their historic value, and they sell best at black collectibles shows or historical document auctions.

There is little interest in documents written in foreign languages, so you may find a letter written by a famous French statesman will sell for a high price in France but not in an English-speaking country. Some autograph dealers have international outlets and get good prices for foreign material.

Supply and demand is the key to pricing an autograph. Button Gwinnett and Thomas Lynch Jr. signed the Declaration of Independence and died soon after. Because there is such great demand for a complete set of signatures of the Declaration's signers, these two autographs have a very, very high value. Other, more important men signed the Declaration, but there is an ample supply of their writings. This same pricing rule holds for more recent signatures, like those of James Dean or Marilyn Monroe.

Autographs and letters that are forgeries, copies, or reproductions have almost no resale value. You must own an original. Most libraries have excellent books about autograph collecting that offer many hints about what is valuable. Autographs can be sold to local antiques dealers, antiquarian book dealers, or sports memorabilia dealers who also handle autographed materials. If no local dealers are to be found, you may be able to sell important material through an out-of-town auction gallery. There are galleries that specialize in autographs and historic material.

Out-of-town dealers who buy autographed materials will not buy based on a description or photocopy. Carefully pack the material between pieces of cardboard, place it in a strong envelope, and seal with tape. Always get references before you send anything. Send the material first class, insured if it is worth under $300, or registered mail, tracked UPS, or FedEx if it is worth more. Keep a photocopy for yourself as well as a list of what you sent. The dealer will usually send you a check. This is one of the very few areas of collecting where you are not expected to set the price.

REPAIR

It is better to keep a complete damaged autographed piece than to trim any of it for a better appearance. If the damage is unsightly, frame the paper with acid-free mounts so only the perfect parts show.

➔ SEE PAPER COLLECTIBLES FOR REPAIR AND CONSERVATION INFORMATION
➔ SEE ALSO BOOKS & BOOKPLATES

PRICE BOOKS

The Official Autograph Collector Price Guide, 3rd edition, Kevin Martin (Odyssey Publications, Corona, CA, 2002).
Signatures of the Stars: An Insider's Guide to Celebrity Autographs, Kevin Martin (Antique Trader Books, Dubuque, IA, 1998).
The Standard Guide to Collecting Autographs, Mark Allen Baker (Krause, Iola, WI, 1999).

CLUBS & THEIR PUBLICATIONS

International Autograph Collectors Club, *Eyes, Ears and Voice of the Hobby* (MAG), PO Box 848486, Hollywood, FL 33084, e-mail: skoschal@aol.com, website: www.iaccda.com.

Manuscript Society, *Manuscripts* (MAG), *Manuscript Society News* (NL), 1960 E. Fairmount, Tempe, AZ 85282-2844, e-mail: manuscript @aol.com, website: www.manuscript.org.

Universal Autograph Collectors Club, *Pen and Quill* (MAG), PO Box 6181, Washington, DC 20044-6181, website: www.uacc.org.

OTHER PUBLICATIONS

Autograph Collector (MAG), 510-A S. Corona Mall, Corona, CA 91719-1420, e-mail: dbtogi@aol.com, website: www.autographs.com.

Autograph News (MAG), PO Box 580466, Modesto, CA 95358-0466, e-mail: Editor@autographnews.com, website: www.autographnews.com.

Autograph Review (NL), 305 Carlton Rd., Syracuse, NY 13207, e-mail: jmorey@twcny.rr.com, (autographs of sports figures, entertainers and military).

Autograph Times (MAG), PO Box 5790, Peoria, AZ 85305, e-mail: info@autographtimes.net, website: www.autographtimes.net.

APPRAISERS

Many of the auctions listed in this section also do appraisals. *See also* the general list of "Appraisal Groups" on page 483.

AUCTIONS

➨ **SEE ALSO "SELLING THROUGH AUCTION HOUSES," PAGE 485.**

Alexander Autographs, Inc., 100 Melrose Ave., Suite 100, Greenwich, CT 06830, 203-622-8444, fax: 203-622-8765, e-mail: info@alexauto graphs.com, website: alexautographs.com. Auctions of historic letters and manuscripts. Mail, phone, fax, and e-mail bids accepted. Buyer's premium 15%. Catalog $20. Prices realized on website. Appraisals.

Baltimore Book Co., 2114 N. Charles St., Baltimore, MD 21218, 410-659-0550. Auctions of autographs, photographs, and books. Mail bids accepted. Buyer's premium 15%. Catalog $5, $25 for eight issues. Prices realized mailed after auction. Appraisals.

Early American History Auctions, PO Box 3341, La Jolla, CA 92038, 858-459-4159, fax: 858-459-4373, e-mail: history@earlyamerican.com, website: www.earlyamerican.com. Absentee auctions of autographs and Americana. Mail, fax, phone, and e-mail bids accepted. Buyer's premium 15%.

Gallery of History Auctions, 601 W. Sahara Ave., Promenade Suite, Las Vegas, NE 89102-5822, 800-GALLERY (800-425-5379) or 702-364-1000 for international calls, fax: 702-364-1285, e-mail: galleryofhistory @galleryofhistory, website: www.galleryofhistory.com. "History for Sale" absentee auctions six times a year. Mail, phone, fax, and Internet bids accepted. Buyer's premium 15%. Catalogs by mail or on website. Prices realized published in next auction catalog and on website.

Paul Riseman Auctions, 2205 S. Park Ave., Springfield, IL 62704-4335, 217-787-2634, fax: 217-787-0062, e-mail: riseman@riseman.com, website: www.riseman.com. Absentee auctions of collectible popular sheet music, entertainment-related memorabilia, ephemera, and autographs. Mail, phone, fax, and e-mail bids accepted. No buyer's premium. Prices realized mailed after auction. Free catalogs. Appraisals.

R & R Enterprises, 3 Chestnut Dr., Bedford, NH 03110, 603-471-0808, fax: 603-471-2844, e-mail: bid@rrauction.com, website: www.rrauction.com. Auctions of vintage and contemporary autographs. Mail, phone, fax, and e-mail auctions. Buyer's premium 17%. Catalog $20; yearly subscription $199.

R.M. Smythe & Co., 26 Broadway, Suite 973, New York, NY 10004-1703, 800-622-1880 or 212-943-1880, fax: 212-908-4670, e-mail: info@smytheonline.com, website: www.smytheonline.com. Auctions of autographs, photographs, historic Americana, and stocks and bonds. Mail, phone, fax, and Internet bids accepted. Buyer's premium varies with amount of sale, 10%, 12%, and 15%. Prices realized mailed after auction. Catalog $25, subscription $87.50 in U.S. Appraisals.

Swann Galleries, Inc., 104 E. 25th St., New York, NY 10010, 212-254-4710, fax: 215-979-1017, e-mail: swann@swanngalleries.com, website: www.swanngalleries.com. Autograph auctions. Buyer's premium varies. Mail, phone, and fax bids accepted. Catalogs.

Waverly Auctions, Inc., 4931 Cordell Ave., Bethesda, MD 20814, 301-951-8883, fax: 301-718-8375, e-mail: waverly1660@earthlink.net, website: waverlyauctions.com. Auctions of autographs. Mail, phone, and Internet bids accepted. Buyer's premium 15%. Prices realized mailed after auction and available on website. Catalog $7; yearly subscription $38. Appraisals.

REPAIR SOURCE

Museum Shop, Ltd., 20 N. Market St., Frederick, MD 21701, 301-695-0424. Restoration of documents, autographs, etc. Free brochure.

BARBER COLLECTIBLES

The barber pole is said to have been made to represent blood-soaked bandages wrapped around the pole in earlier days. The red-and-white-striped pole has been a symbol of the pharmacist or barber since the eighteenth century. Old wooden barber poles are now considered folk art. Information about selling and repair can be found in the folk-art section.

Other barber collectibles such as bottles, shaving mugs, or even old chairs have a value to special collectors. About once a year there seems to be a special auction for barber and medical collections. Barber chairs have a very special market and sell best through an ad in the local paper or an antiques paper. Because they are heavy, few dealers will offer to buy. You must find a collector.

➥ **SEE ALSO BOTTLES & GO-WITHS, POTTERY & PORCELAIN**

REFERENCE BOOKS
The Encyclopedia of Ephemera by Maurice Rickards (Routledge, 29 West 35th St., New York, NY 10001, 2000).

PRICE BOOKS
Barbershop: History and Antiques, Christian R. Jones (Schiffer, Atglen, PA, 1998).

CLUBS & THEIR PUBLICATIONS
National Shaving Mug Collectors Association, *Barbershop Collectibles* (NL), c/o Anise Alkin, 544 Line Road, Hazlett, NJ 07730, e-mail: papgn62@aol.com, website: www.nsmca.org, (shaving mugs, barber bottles, razors, barber poles, spittoons, advertising and other barber and shaving memorabilia).

ARCHIVES & MUSEUMS
Ed Jeffers Barber Museum, 2½ S. High St., Canal Winchester, OH 43110-1213, 614-833-9931, website: www.edjeffersbarbermuseum.com.

APPRAISERS
The auction and repair services listed in this section may also do appraisals. *See also* the general list of "Appraisal Groups" on page 483.

AUCTIONS
➥ **SEE ALSO "SELLING THROUGH AUCTION HOUSES," PAGE 485.**

Glass-Works Auctions, Box 180, East Greenville, PA 18041, 215-679-5849, fax: 215-679-3068, e-mail: glswrk@enter.net, website: www.glswrk-auction.com. Absentee auctions of glass barber-shop memorabilia and antique bottles. Mail, phone, and fax bids accepted. Buyer's premium 12%. Prices realized mailed after auction.

REPAIRS, PARTS & SUPPLIES
➥ **SEE ALSO "CONSERVATORS & RESTORERS," PAGE 520.**

William Marvy Co., 1540 St. Clair Ave., St. Paul, MN 55105, 800-874-2651 or 651-698-0726, fax: 651-698-4048, e-mail: marvys@aol.com, website: www.wmmarvyco.com. Restoration of barber poles. Parts for almost every barber pole that has been made. Catalog/brochures are available at no charge.

BLACK COLLECTIBLES

Anything that pictures a black person or is related to black culture is considered a "black collectible." This includes everything from early slave documents and photographs of life in earlier times to advertisements, figurines, and other stereotypical depictions. In a price book listing of black collectibles you will find items related to **AUNT JEMIMA, RASTUS THE CREAM OF WHEAT MAN, AMOS 'N' ANDY**, a fast-food chain known as **COON CHICKEN INNS**, and many nameless black people. There are books about black items and several special shows every year. Many black-related items are sold at historic document auctions.

Black collectibles are also bought and sold at advertising or general antiques show. Black rag dolls are classed as both folk art and collectible dolls and are sold by dealers in both of these specialties. Some of the black material is derogatory, and you may be concerned about the propriety of offering it for sale. Remember that the majority of the dealers who specialize in black items and the majority of the collectors of black items are themselves black. They want the pieces as part of their heritage, and are eager to buy. Of great interest are any slave-related documents, pictures, or memorabilia.

Any item picturing a black person will sell at a good price. Amos 'n' Andy toys are worth 50% more than comparable toys showing white cartoon figures. Even small, dime-store "joke" figurines of past years are selling for over $75 each. Visit an antiques show and check prices on black collectibles before you try to sell yours. Many sell for far more than the amateur would believe.

PRICE BOOKS
Black Postcard Price Guide, 2nd edition, J.L. Mashburn (Colonial House, Enka, NC, 1999).
The Encyclopedia of Black Collectibles, Dawn E. Reno (Wallace-Homestead, Radnor, PA, 1996).
Images in Black: 150 Years of Black Collectibles, 2nd edition, Douglas Congdon-Martin (Schiffer, Atglen, PA, 1999).
More Black Memorabilia, Jan Lindenberger (Schiffer, Atglen, PA, 1999).

OTHER PUBLICATIONS
Blackin' (NL), 559 22nd Ave., Rock Island, IL 61201.

ARCHIVES & MUSEUMS

Black Archives Research Center and Museum, Florida A&M University, Tallahassee, FL 32307, 850-599-3020, website: www.famu.edu/acad/archives.

Jim Crow Museum of Racist Memorabilia, Ferris State University, Big Rapids, MI 49307, 231-591-2760, website: www.ferris.edu/news/jimcrow/index.htm.

APPRAISERS

The auction listed in this section will also do appraisals. *See also* the general list of "Appraisal Groups" on page 483.

AUCTIONS

➻ SEE ALSO "SELLING THROUGH AUCTION HOUSES," PAGE 485.

Collection Liquidators, 341 Lafayette St., Suite 2007, New York, NY 10012, 212-505-2455, fax: 212-505-2455, e-mail: coliq@erols.com, website: www.collectionliquidators.com. Absentee auctions of black Americana and Ku Klux Klan memorabilia. Mail, phone, fax, and e-mail bids accepted. Buyer's premium 10%. Prices realized mailed after auction and available on website. Catalogs $10; yearly subscription $26. Restoration and conservation. Appraisals.

BOOKS & BOOKPLATES

Selling books presents different problems from selling other types of collectibles. Age is one of the factors that determine price, but it is not as important as people believe. Some books written during the past twenty-five years are worth more than books that are 200 years old. The value of a book is determined by rarity, condition, edition, and age. It is also influenced by whether it has the original wrapping intact, who owned it, if there is a bookplate or a signature, who printed it, who did the illustrations, and the subject.

Books can be sold at house sales, auctions, and on the Internet.

QUARANTINE YOUR SICK BOOKS

If the leather binding on your book is deteriorating into red crumbles, there is little that can be done. Don't leave it near other leather-covered books—it is a contagious condition.

They also can be sold to stores that carry used books and to anti-quarian book dealers. It is necessary to think about a possible customer for your unusual books. For example, old local history books might be needed by a historical society library. You can also sell to private buyers if you are persistent and find the right customer.

If you have hundreds of books that were purchased over a period of time by an average book buyer, not a serious collector, you can sell the group at a house sale. Some cities have cut-rate bookstores that buy any type of used books. You can call in a book dealer or friend to buy, but try to sell the entire collection. Otherwise you may find that the best books have been sold and the ones remaining have little value. Don't discard any books. Give them to a charity book sale and get a tax deduction.

If you have a number of rare books, contact an antiquarian bookseller. They are listed in the Yellow Pages of the phone book or can be found selling books at one of the many antiquarian book fairs. *Buy Books Where—Sell Books Where* by Ruth Robinson and Daryush Farudi is an annual publication listing sellers of out-of-print books. Most book collectors specialize by type or subject, and Robinson's book may give you some ideas about what is valuable.

There are many Internet sites devoted to out-of-print and rare books. Book dealers we have talked to say they sell more books through their websites than in their stores. Because the customer usually is knowledgeable about books, short descriptions of title, author, edition, and condition are all that is needed. Try a search engine to look for specific titles, book dealers, and Internet sites, such as www.amazon.com or www.bookmallventura.com.

VALUE GUIDE

First editions of important books are often valuable. To determine if a book is a first edition, look at the copyright page to see if it says "First Edition." For books printed before about 1975, look on the title page to see whether the date agrees with the copyright date. Most books published since then have a row of about ten numbers (usually running from 10 to 1) on the copyright page. These tell if the book is a first edition. The lowest number in the row indicates which printing it is. If the number "1" is included in the row, then it is the first printing. First editions by the best 1930s and 1940s mystery writers are popular, but the books must have original dust jackets for highest value. Books printed by certain small private presses and special artistic printings of books are very valuable. Book-of-the-

Month Club editions, special collector editions made in quantity, or reissues of old books have little value.

Bibles, encyclopedias, dictionaries, and textbooks have very low value. McGuffey readers, disaster books (describing a flood or earthquake), and books later made into important movies are of little value unless they are first editions. The first McGuffey, the first edition of an important movie book, or a rare disaster book does sell well. Old cookbooks, decorating books, catalogs, horticulture and flower arranging books, sports books, history books, and early books on science and medicine have value. Very early children's books and illustrated books in good condition are wanted.

Books with unusual photographs, engraved illustrations, hand-tinted engravings, or other attractive pictures are worth money. Unfortunately, the pictures are sometimes worth more out of the

READ THE BOOK ADS

b & w, b.w.—black and white illustrations
colophon—inscription at end of book giving facts about its production
dj—dust jacket
eng., engr.—engraved
endp., e.p.—endpaper
folio—large sheet of paper folded once so that it forms two leaves, or four pages
Foxing—brown or yellow stains
hb—hardboard
ld., ltd.—limited (edition)
octavo—page size of book made of sheets folded into eight leaves, each leaf (page) being 5 x 8 inches to 6 x 9½ inches. Abbreviated 8 vo.
o.p.—out of print
p., pp., pg.—pages
pb—paperback
P.P.—privately printed
quarto—page size of a book made of sheets folded into four leaves, or eight pages, each leaf (page) being approximately 9 x 12 inches. Abbreviated 4 to.
r., recto—right-hand page (front side of a leaf)
sig.—signature
unb(b)—unbound
v., verso—left-hand page (back side of a leaf)
vell.—vellum

book than the entire book is worth. That is why many nineteenth-century books of flower prints have been taken apart.

"Association" books are collected. Any book with a signature by an important owner or author or with an inscription to an important person has the added value of its association with that person. Sometimes the autograph is more valuable than the book. Some bookplates are also very valuable; a Charles Dickens or Paul Revere plate is worth hundreds of dollars.

Covers are important; leather bindings, elaborate gold-decorated bindings, and paper dust covers of special interest add value. Fore-edge painting (pictures on the front edge of the page) and pop-up illustrations also add value.

Paperback books that are first editions in good condition sell well. You can tell age by the price printed on the book and sometimes by low numbers used by publishers for identification. If there is a bar code, it is not an early paperback. The book was published after 1973. Some collectors specialize, buying only books with lurid covers or with art by well-known illustrators. Worn paperbacks sell only to buyers who want a low-priced book to read.

Condition is important for all types of books. Would you want a chipped cup? A torn book is the chipped cup of the book business. If you mail a book to a buyer, wrap it in a padded book bag, and send it book rate, insured. Postage for books, magazines, and other printed materials is a bargain. Ask your post office.

REPAIR

Rebinding antique books reduces their value and should be avoided unless it is absolutely necessary. However, if you must, there are bookbinders in many cities. They are listed in the Yellow Pages under "Bookbinders" or you can learn about them from some of the better bookstores or decorating studios. Do not try to repair torn pages or covers unless you know how to use archival materials. Transparent-tape repairs lower value.

Bookplate collecting was a major hobby fifty years ago and many fine old books were mutilated by eager collectors who only wanted the bookplates. That is not recommended today. Unless the book is in very bad repair, it is worth more with the bookplate than a mutilated book and a cut-out bookplate. Little can be done to restore a bookplate outside of simple cleaning and pressing with an iron. Nothing can be done if old glue has stained the plate.

Keep bookplates, books, and all paper items in a controlled environment where they will not become too wet or dry or be attacked by insects, bookworms, or rodents. Attics and basements are usually too hot or damp. If you collect paper items, it would be wise to buy the necessary humidifier or dehumidifier for your home.

REFERENCE BOOKS

Binding and Repairing Books by Hand, David Muir (Arco Publishing Co., New York, 1987).

Care of Fine Books, Jane Greenfield (Lyons & Burford Publishers, New York, 1988).

Cleaning and Caring for Books, Robert L. Shep (Sheppard Press, London, 1983).

Cleaning and Preserving Bindings and Related Materials, Carolyn Horton (American Library Association, 1975).

PRICE BOOKS

Collecting Little Golden Books, 4th edition, Steve Santi (Krause, Iola, WI, 2000).

The Insider's Guide to Old Books, Magazines, Newspapers and Trade Catalogs, Ron Barlow and Ray Reynolds (Windmill Publishing Co., 2147 Windmill View Rd., Dept. AT2, Cajon, CA 92020, 1995).

The Official Price Guide to Collecting Books, 4th edition, Marie Tedford and Pat Goudey (House of Collectibles, New York, 2002).

Old Magazines Price Guide (L-W Book Sales, Gas City, IN, 1994, 4th printing 2000).

The Secret of Collecting Girls' Series Books, John Axe (Hobby House Press, Grantsville, MD, 2000).

Vintage Cookbooks and Advertising Leaflets, Sandra J. Norman and Karrie K. Andes (Schiffer, Atglen, PA, 1998).

CLUBS & THEIR PUBLICATIONS

American Society of Bookplate Collectors & Designers, *Ex Libris Chronicle: The International Collector* (MAG), *Year Book* (annual), PO Box 380340, Cambridge, MA 02238-0340, e-mail: exlibris@att.net, website: www.bookplate.org.

Big Little Book Club of America, *Big Little Times* (NL), PO Box 1242, Danville, CA 94526, e-mail: llarry@sirius.com, website: www.biglittlebooks.com.

Cook Book Collectors Club of America, *Cook Book Gossip over the Back Fence* (NL), PO Box 56, St. James, MO 65559-0056.

Cook Book Collector's Club of California, *Cook Book News* (NL), 4756 Terrace Dr., San Diego, CA 92116, e-mail: cookwithbabs@cox.net, website: communitylink.sdinsider.com/groups/cookbook.

Horatio Alger Society, *Newsboy* (NL), PO Box 70361, Richmond, VA 23255, e-mail: rkasper@hotmail.com, website: www.ihot.com/~has.

International Society of Bible Collectors, *Bible Editions and Versions* (MAG), PO Box 20695, Houston, TX 77225-0695, e-mail: skodouay@msn.com.

International Wizard of Oz Club, *Baum Bugle* (NL), 1407A St., Suite D, Antioch, CA 94509, e-mail: postmanofoz@aol.com, website: ozclub.org.

The Movable Book Society, *Movable Stationery* (NL), PO Box 11654, New Brunswick, NJ 08906, e-mail: montanar@rci.rutgers.edu, website: www.rci.rutgers.edu/~montanar/mbs.html.

Philip Boileau Collectors' Society, *Philip Boileau Collectors' Society Newsletter* (NL), 1025 Redwood Blvd., Redding, CA 96003-1905, e-mail: pboileaucc@aol.com, website: hometown.aol.com/PBoileauCC/index.html.

Society of Phantom Friends, *Whispered Watchword* (NL), PO Box 1437, N. Highlands, CA 95660, e-mail: dolladopt@aol.com (girls' series books).

Tasha Tudor Fan Club, *The Letter* (NL), 1234 Larke Ave., Rogers City, MI 49779.

Thornton W. Burgess Society, *Burgess Book Collectors' Bulletin* (NL), 6 Discovery Hill Rd., East Sandwich, MA 02537, e-mail: tburgess @capecod.net, website: www.thorntonburgess.org.

Zane Grey's West Society, *Zane Grey Review* (MAG), 708 Warwick Ave., Fort Wayne, IN 46825, e-mail: tbolin3194@aol.com, website: www.zanegreysws.org.

OTHER PUBLICATIONS

Book Source Monthly (MAG), PO Box 567, Cazenovia, NY 13035-0567, e-mail: books@dreamscape.com, website: www.booksource monthly.com.

Bookmark Collector (NL), 1002 W. 25th St., Erie, PA 16502-2427.

Cookbook Collectors' Exchange (NL), PO Box 89, Magalia, CA 95954, e-mail: editor@ccexonline.com, website: www.ccexonline.com.

Dime Novel Round-Up (NL), PO Box 226, Dundas, MN 55019-0226, e-mail: cox@stolaf.edu or cox@rconnect.com.

Fern Bisel Peat (NL), 20 S. Linden Rd., Apt. 112, Mansfield, OH 44906, e-mail: marwelmer@aol.com, website: www.fernbiselpeat.com.

Firsts: The Book Collector's Magazine (MAG), PO Box 65166, Tucson, AZ 85728-5166, e-mail: firstsmag@aol.com, website: www.firsts.com.

The Letter (NL), Elaine's Upper Story, 1234 Larke Ave., Rogers City, MI 49779 (Tasha Tudor collectibles).

Martha's KidLit Newsletter (NL), PO Box 1488 K, Ames, IA 50014, e-mail: marti@isunet.net (out-of-print and antiquarian children's books).

Modern Library & Viking Portable Collector (NL), 340 Warren Ave., Cincinnati, OH 45220-1135.

Paperback Parade (MAG), PO Box 209, Brooklyn, NY 11228-0209, website: www.gryphonbooks.com.

Yellowback Library (MAG), PO Box 36172, Des Moines, IA 50315 (novels and related juvenile series literature).

MUSEUMS

The Museum of Printing, 800 Massachusetts Ave., North Andover, MA 01845, 978-686-0450, website: www.museumofprinting.org.

The Museum of Printing History, 1324 W. Clay St., Houston, TX 77019, 713-522-4652, fax: 713-522-5694, website: www.printingmuseum.org.

APPRAISERS

Many of the auctions and repair services listed in this section will also do appraisals. *See also* the general list of "Appraisal Groups" on page 483.

AUCTIONS

➤ SEE ALSO "SELLING THROUGH AUCTION HOUSES," PAGE 485.

Baltimore Book Co., 2114 N. Charles St., Baltimore, MD 21218, 410-659-0550. Auctions of books. Mail bids accepted. Buyer's premium 15%. Catalog $5, $25 for eight issues. Prices realized mailed after auction. Appraisals.

New Hampshire Book Auctions, PO Box 678, Wolfeboro, NH 03894-0678, 603-569-0000, e-mail: dragonflies@metrocast.net. Mail bids accepted. Phone bids taken until 5:00 P.M. the night before the auction, not during the auction. Buyer's premium 10%. Prices realized available by request. Appraisals.

PBA Galleries, 133 Kearny St., 4th Floor, San Francisco, CA 94108, 415-989-2665 or 866-999-7224, fax: 415-989-1664, e-mail: pba@pbagalleries.com, website: www.pbagalleries.com. Auctioneers and appraisers of rare and antiquarian books and works on paper. Buyer's premium 15%. Mail, phone, and Internet bids accepted. Prices realized mailed after auction and available on website. Catalog $15, yearly subscription $175.

Swann Galleries, Inc., 104 E. 25th St., New York, NY 10010, 212-254-4710, fax: 215-979-1017, e-mail: swann@swanngalleries.com, website: www.swanngalleries.com. Over 20 rare book auctions per year. Buyer's premium varies. Mail, phone, and fax bids accepted. Catalogs.

Waverly Auctions, Inc., 4931 Cordell Ave., Bethesda, MD 20814, 301-951-8883, fax: 301-718-8375, e-mail: waverly1660@earthlink.net, website: waverlyauctions.com. Auctions of used and rare books. Mail, phone, and Internet bids accepted. Buyer's premium 15%. Prices realized mailed after auction and available on website. Catalog $7; yearly subscription $38. Appraisals.

REPAIRS, PARTS & SUPPLIES

➻ SEE ALSO "CONSERVATORS & RESTORERS," PAGE 520.

Archival Conservation Center, Inc., 8225 Daly Rd., Cincinnati, OH 45231, 513-521-9858, fax: 513-521-9859. Repair and restoration of works of art on paper, including books and family Bibles. Smoke odor removal. Freeze drying of water-damaged materials. Free brochure available upon request.

Cellar Stories Books, 111 Mathewson St., Providence, RI 02903, 401-521-2665, fax: 401-454-7143, e-mail: cellarstor@ids.net, website: cellarstories.com. Referral for bookbinding and repair. Appraisals.

Colophon Book Arts Supply, 3611 Ryan St. SE, Lacey, WA 98503, 360-459-2940, fax: 360-459-2945, e-mail: colophon@earthlink.com, website: home.earthlink.net/~colophon. Supplies for hand bookbinding, marbling, and Suminagashi (the ancient art of Japanese marbling). Workshops available. Mail order worldwide. Catalog $2.

Harcourt Bindery, 51 Melcher St., Boston, MA 02210, 617-542-5858, 8:30 A.M.–4:00 P.M, fax: 617-542-9058, e-mail: sam@harcourtbindery.com, website: www.harcourtbindery.com. Hand bookbinding, repair, and restoration in leather and cloth. Protective boxes. Free brochure.

Hollinger Corporation, PO Box 8360, Fredericksburg, VA 22404, 800-634-0491, 8:30 A.M.–5:00 P.M., e-mail: hollingercorp@erols.com, website: www.hollingercorp.com. Archival boxes and other products to store books and more. Free catalog.

James Macdonald Co., Inc., 25 Van Zant St., East Norwalk, CT 06855, 203-853-6076, 7:30 A.M.–4:30 P.M. Restoration of old and rare books. Full-cloth and quarter-leather slipcases. Cloth, quarter, or full leather binding.

Linda A. Blaser, 9200 Hawkins Creamery Rd., Gaithersburg, MD 20882, e-mail: blaser@erols.com. Conservation of books and flat paper items. Collection condition surveys. Speaker services.

Metal Edge, Inc., 6340 Bandini Blvd., Commerce, CA 90040, 800-862-2228 or 213-721-7800, fax: 888-822-6937, e-mail: info@metaledgeinc.com, website: www.metaledgeinc.com. Storage, conservation, and identification supplies. Book storage boxes, book and document repair supplies. Free catalog.

Muir's Book Repair, 1617 Willis St., Redding, CA 96001, 530-241-1948. Books repaired and restored. Old and new books, rare books, paperbacks, comic books, magazines, and newspapers repaired. Moisture or water damage, fire damage, lost covers, loose or torn pages repaired. Mail order worldwide. Send SASE for more information.

Northeast Document Conservation Center, 100 Brickstone Sq., Andover, MA 01810-1494, 978-470-1010, fax: 978-475-6021, e-mail: nedcc@nedcc.org, website: www.nedcc.org. Nonprofit regional conservation center specializing in treatment of art and artifacts on paper, including books. Preservation microfilming, duplication of historical photographs, preservation planning surveys, disaster assistance, technical leaflets. Free brochure. Open 8:30 A.M.–4:30 P.M. Monday through Friday.

Peregrine Arts Bookbindery, PO Box 1691, Santa Fe, NM 87504, 505-466-0490, 9:00 A.M.–5:00 P.M. Hand-bookbinding and book restoration services designed to restore, preserve, and protect books and related items. Single books or limited edition binding in cloth or leather, encapsulation, portfolios, slipcases, clamshell boxes. Gold stamping on cloth, paper, or leather. Hand-marbled papers by Katherine Loeffler.

Philadelphia Print Shop, Ltd., 8441 Germantown Ave., Philadelphia, PA 19118, 215-242-4750, fax: 215-242-6977, e-mail: philaprint@phila printshop.com, website: www.philaprintshop.com. Conservation services for art on paper. Handcrafted binding and refurbishing of rare and special books. Appraisals and research.

Poor Richard's Restoration & Preservation Studio Workshop, 101 Walnut St., Montclair, NJ 07042, 973-783-5333, fax: 973-744-1939, e-mail: jrickford@webtv.com, website: www.rickford.com. Restoration, conservation, archival, and preservation services for Bibles and other books. Restoration of family memorabilia and keepsakes. By appointment, Tues.–Fri. noon–5:00 P.M., Sat. noon–3:00 P.M.

Richard C. Baker Conservation, 1712 (rear) S. Big Bend Blvd., St. Louis, MO 63117, 314-781-3035, e-mail: baker@RichardCBaker.com, website: www.RichardCBaker.com. Offers a full range of conservation services for books and printed works on paper and parchment. Treatments include binding restoration, facsimile binding, box making, adhesive tape removal, stain reduction, washing, aqueous and non-aqueous deacidification, lining, mending, and in-painting.

Scott K. Kellar/Bookbinding & Conservation, 2650 Montrose Ave., Chicago, IL 60618-1507, 773-478-2825, fax: 801-760-6843, e-mail: skkellar@earth link.net. Conservation of rare books and printed material. Deacidification and archival encapsulation of documents, maps, and posters.

Talas, Division of Technical Library Service, Inc., 568 Broadway, Suite 107, New York, NY 10012, 212-219-0770, Mon.–Fri. 9:00 A.M.–5:30 P.M., fax: 212-219-0735, e-mail: info@talasonline.com, website: www.talas online.com. Supplies for all areas of conservation, restoration, and storage. Archival storage, tissues, papers, boards, cleaners, bookbinding supplies, tools, and more. Catalog online and in print.

Talin Bookbindery, 947 Rt. 6A, Cranberry Ct., Yarmouthport, MA 02675, 508-362-8144, e-mail: talinbookbindery@yahoo.com. Hand bookbinding. Restoration. Marble papers.

BOTTLES & GO-WITHS

Bottles can be divided into two separate selling markets. Modern figural bottles like Jim Beam, Ezra Brooks, and Avon have been collected since the 1960s. They are found at the liquor store or flea market, and there are several national collector clubs for them. Their market has gone up and down, and today some people have large collections that are worth less than their original cost. Old and antique bottles are favored by a very different group of people. They are serious collectors who dig for bottles, trade bottles, belong to antique bottle clubs, go to shows, and think of bottles as a part of the fun in their lives.

It is easy to price modern bottles, but it is hard to sell them. The recent figural bottles, including Avon and liquor decanters, are listed with detailed descriptions and retail prices in price guides such as *Kovels' Bottles Price List*. You will be fortunate to get 50 percent of that price if you have a new bottle in mint condition with original labels. Be sure to check local laws. It is illegal to sell filled liquor bottles in some states. There are many national clubs for modern bottle collectors. An ad in the publications for these clubs is often the best place to sell. Some states have active collectors and clubs that sponsor modern bottle shows, but in other areas there is little interest.

You'll find many bottles for sale on the Internet because many are mass-produced and easily described. There are websites devoted entirely to bottle dealers. Auction sites, even general ones like eBay, are great places to find bargains because many bottles are sold with no minimum bid.

Machine-made bottles with no redeeming features sell best at flea markets or house sales. Any type of perfume bottle and attractive figural bottles sell at antique shows and bottle shows.

Make a list of your bottles. Only those in perfect condition sell. Damaged bottles are worth pennies at a garage sale. Determine the prices and offer to sell either to dealers, on the Internet, or by mail to collectors who read the ads in bottle and general publications. Bottles that picture trains, cars, or sporting events, like many Beam bottles, are going up in price a little because they sell well to sports memorabilia collectors or to train and car collectors. (See Sports Collectibles, Toys)

Old bottles, especially rare ones, sell best at bottle shows and bottle auctions. Highest prices are paid by serious dealers and collectors. Many of these bottles are listed in *Kovels' Bottles Price List*. The listed price is very close to the price you should ask from a collector. Dealers buy at 30 to 50 percent less. Many types of old bottles are collected, including milk bottles, fruit jars, inks, inkwells, medicines, bitters, sodas, poisons, whiskeys, figurals, and most desirable of all, historical flasks. In the past few years, applied color labels or ACL bottles have gained in value. These are bottles with labels printed on the glass, not on paper. Most popular are soda and milk bottles.

Old bottles worth thousands of dollars have rare colors and markings. Common bottles can sell for a few dollars. Aqua-colored glass with bubbles is common. In the last few years, the color of some bottles has been enhanced by radiation. These colored bottles are not valuable. Desirable original colors are cobalt blue, dark purple, honey amber, clear green, yellow, and sometimes white milk glass.

A rough scar on the bottom of a bottle is called a pontil. This is usually an indication of a hand-blown bottle. Seam marks on the neck of the bottle usually indicate a newer, machine-made bottle. Old is usually more valuable than new.

Beginning collectors make several mistakes. Bottles are collected for their beauty and history. Years ago it was common to soak the

DECODING ADVERTISING COPY

- ABM—automatic bottle machine
- ACL—applied color label
- BIMAL—blown in mold, applied lip
- Dug—literally dug from the ground
- FB—free-blown
- IP—iron pontil (a black spot on the bottom of the bottle)
- ISP—inserted slug plate. Special names were sometimes embossed on a bottle, especially a milk bottle, with a special plate inserted in the mold.
- OP—open pontil (a rough spot on the bottom of the bottle)
- Pyro—pyroglaze or enamel lettering often found on milk bottles and soda bottles. It is an ACL (applied color label).
- SC—sun-colored, glass that has changed color because of exposure to the sun
- SCA—sun-colored amethyst, the light purple colored glass that has changed to that color from long exposure to the sun
- irradiated—glass that has been exposed to radiation and has turned deep purple, green, or brown

labels off, but it is not being done today. Do not remove or destroy any paper labels, tax stamps, or other paper glued to a bottle. Save the original box, if available. The box and labels add to the value. Today advertising collectors and some specialty bottle collectors pay a premium for bottles with original paper labels, even if the labels are damaged. When regluing a label, be sure to use an adhesive that will not stain the paper.

Uninformed collectors sometimes misunderstand the marks embossed on bottles. Don't think that the date 1858 in raised numerals in the glass of your fruit jar means that it is either old or rare. The date is the year the screw-top jar with a shoulder seal was patented, and the number was used for many years after 1858.

GO-WITHS

Anything that pictures or advertises a bottle or was used with a bottle is of interest to bottle collectors. This includes bottle openers, jar openers, milk bottle caps, canning jar rubber rings and tops, corkscrews, fancy bottle corks, ads, and pamphlets. These items can all be sold. The corkscrew and bottle-opener collectors have very specific wants, and the best place to sell good examples of these is through the collector clubs and ads.

Don't underestimate the value of old openers. The current record price for a corkscrew is over $30,000. Figural bottle openers often sell for over $50.

REPAIR

An old privy or dump may not seem like the perfect vacation spot. To a collector of old bottles, it is heaven. Some of the best bottles are dug from old dumps or construction sites, or are pulled from river bottoms. Many are in need of repairs. Local bottle clubs always welcome members; bottle shows are filled with collectors who delight in talking about their hobby, the bottles they have found, and experts who have restoration services.

Some manufacturers now have their own publications and books, which are usually available at bottle shows. Many collectors of specialties like inks or sodas possess historical information about the correct appearance of the bottles, which could help with repairs.

Beware of "sick" bottles. The cloudy effect inside the bottle is etched in the glass. If the bottle is for display, you can swish some clear mineral oil in the bottle, then seal the bottle. This temporarily covers the cloudy look. It is possible to polish the inside of a bottle, but it is very expensive, requires talent, and is a risky repair. Usually, only the most expensive historic flasks or early bottles are restored in this manner.

Bottles can be repaired with modern plastics. Some of the repairs are invisible except under black light, but there is an even more expensive plastic that cannot be seen by black light.

◆→ SEE ALSO GLASS

REFERENCE BOOKS

American Bottles & Flasks and Their Ancestry, Helen McKearin and Kenneth M. Wilson (Crown, New York, 1979).

The Art of Perfume: Discovering and Collecting Perfume Bottles, Christie Mayer Lefkowith (Thames and Hudson, New York, 1994).

Bitters Bottles, Carlyn Ring and W.C. Ham (PO Box 427, Downieville, CA 95936, 1998).

Bottle Makers and Their Marks, Julian Harrison Toulouse (Thomas Nelson, Nashville, TN, 1971).

The Compleat American Glass Candy Containers Handbook, revised edition, George Eikelberner and Serge Agadjanian (Bowden, 6252 Cedarwood Rd., Mentor, OH 44060, 1986).

Ink Bottles and Inkwells, William E. Covill (William S. Sullwold, Taunton, MA, 1971).

PRICE BOOKS

Antique Trader Bottles: Identification and Price Guide, 4th edition, Michael Polak (Krause, Iola, WI, 2002).

Antique Western Bitters Bottles, Jeff Wichmann (Pacific Glass Books, Sacramento, CA, 1999).

The Auction Price Report for Antique Bottles, William E. Brown (12247 NW 49th Dr., Coral Springs, FL 33076, 2002). (Bitters, historical flasks, medicines, whiskeys, and sodas and mineral waters are sections in the book that are available separately.)

VALUE HINTS

- Bubbles in the glass, "whittle marks," and pale aqua glass are not rare and are not indications of very expensive bottles.
- A nick or flaw is always significant even in a rare bottle, and substantially lowers its value. Condition is important and a nick, scratch, or cloudy interior can lower the value by as much as 70 percent.
- A damaged bottle that is less than fifty years old is often worthless.

Boxes Full of Corkscrews, Donald A. Bull (Schiffer, Atglen, PA, 2001).

Bud Hastin's Avon Collector's Encyclopedia, 16th edition, Bud Hastin (Bud Hastin, PO Box 11004, Ft. Lauderdale, FL 33339, 2000).

Bull's Pocket Guide to Corkscrews, Donald A. Bull (Schiffer, Atglen, PA, 1999).

Candy Containers for Collectors, Debra S. Braun (Schiffer, Atglen, PA, 2002).

Coca-Cola Commemorative Bottles, 2nd edition, Bob and Debra Henrich (Collector Books, Paducah, KY, 2001).

Collecting Applied Color Label Soda Bottles, 3rd edition, Rich Sweeney (Painted Soda Bottle Collectors Association, 9418 Hilmer Dr., La Mesa, CA 91942, 2002).

Collecting Lalique: Perfume Bottles and Glass, Robert Prescott-Walker (Francis Joseph, London, 2001).

Collector's Guide to Candy Containers, Douglas M. Dezso, Leon Poirier, and Rose D. Poirier (Collector Books, Paducah, KY, 1998).

Collector's Guide to Inkwells, Book II, Veldon Badders (Collector Books, Paducah, KY, 1998).

The Collector's Guide to Old Fruit Jars: Red Book 9, Douglas M. Leybourne Jr. (PO Box 5417, North Muskegon, MI 49445, 2001).

The Collector's World of Inkwells, Jean and Franklin Hunting (Schiffer, Atglen, PA, 2000).

Commemorative Bottle Checklist and Cross-Reference Guide: Featuring Coca-Cola Bottles, 5th edition, and *Featuring Dr Pepper, Pepsi, 7Up, NSDA and Other Soda Brands*, Richard Mix (Nerdz, Austin, TX, 1999).

Commemorative Coca-Cola Bottles: An Unauthorized Guide, Joyce Spontak (Schiffer, Atglen, PA, 1998).

Diamond I Perfume Bottles Price Guide and Other Drugstore Ware (L-W Book Sales, Gas City, IN 46933, 2000).

Digger Odell's Official Antique Bottle and Glass Collector Magazine Price Guide, 10 volumes, edited by John Odell: Barber Bottles (1), Bitters (2), Flasks (3), Inks (4), Medicines (5), Colognes, Pattern Mold, Label under Glass, Fire Extinguishers and Target Balls (6), Sodas and Mineral Waters (7), Whiskeys (8), Black Glass (9), Poisons, Drugstore & Apothecary Bottles (10); (Digger Odell, 1910 Shawhan Rd., Morrow, OH 45152, 1995–1998).

Fruit Jar Annual 2002, Volume 7, Tom Caniff, editor (Jerome J. McCann, 5003 Berwyn Ave., Chicago, IL 60630, 2002).

Jim Beam Figural Bottles, Molly Higgins (Schiffer, Atglen, PA, 2000).

Just for Openers: A Guide to Beer, Soda, and Other Openers, Donald A. Bull and John R. Stanley (Schiffer, Atglen, PA, 1999).

Kovels' Bottles Price List, 12th edition, Ralph and Terry Kovel (Three Rivers Press, NY, 2002).

Mario's Price Guide to Modern Bottles, Anthony Latello, issued semi-annually (146 Sheldon Ave., Depew, NY 14043).

Miller's Corkscrews and Wine Antiques, Phil Ellis (Octopus Publishing, London, England, 2001).

Modern Candy Containers and Novelties, Jack Brush and William Miller
(Collector Books, Paducah, KY, 2001).

Official Price Guide to Bottles, 13th edition, Jim Megura (House of
Collectibles, NY, 2000).

Ohio Bottles, the Ohio Bottle Club, Inc. (PO Box 585, Barberton, OH
44203, 1999).

Pepsi-Cola Bottles Collectors Guide, 2 volumes, James C. Ayers (RJM
Enterprises, 5186 Claudville Hwy., Claudville, VA 24076, 1995, 2001).

Wheaton's: My Favorite Collectibles, Lois Clark (Classic Wheaton Club,
PO Box 59, Downingtown, PA 19335, 1998).

*The Write Stuff: Collector's Guide to Inkwells, Fountain Pens, and Desk
Accessories,* Ray and Bevy Jaegers (Krause, Iola, WI, 2000).

CLUBS & THEIR PUBLICATIONS

American Collectors of Infant Feeders, *Keeping Abreast* (NL), 1849 Ebony
Dr., York, PA 17402-4706, e-mail: bbottlebkdj@juno.com, website:
www.acif.org.

Antique Poison Bottle Collectors Association, *Antique Poison Bottle Collectors Association* (NL), 312 Summer Ln., Huddleston, VA 24104, e-mail:
joan@poisonbottle.com, website: antique.poisonbottle.com.

Canadian Corkscrew Collectors Club, *The Quarterly Worme* (NL), One Madison St., East Rutherford, NJ 07073, e-mail: clarethous@aol.com.

Candy Container Collectors of America, *Candy Gram* (NL), 2711 De La
Rosa St., The Villages, FL 32159, e-mail: epmac27@comcast.net, website: www.candycontainer.org.

Classic Wheaton Club, *Classic Wheaton Club Newsletter* (NL), PO Box
59, Downington, PA 19335-0059, e-mail: cwc@cwcusa.com, website:
www.cwcusa.com.

Crown -Collectors Society International, *Crown Cappers' Exchange* (NL),
4300 San Juan Dr., Fairfax, VA 22030, e-mail: crownking@erols.com
(crown caps from beer and soda bottles).

Federation of Historical Bottle Collectors, *Bottles and Extras* (MAG),
June Lowry, 401 Johnston Ct., Raymore, MO 64083, e-mail: osubuck
eyes71@aol.com, website: www.fohbc.com.

WARNING!

In some states it is against the law to sell bottles with liquor inside. It is illegal
in every state to sell bottles that contain drugs such as opium or cocaine.
These drugs sometimes remain in old bottles found in drugstores from the
early 1900s, when the now-banned drugs were legal medicines.

Figural Bottle Opener Collectors, *Opener* (NL), 1774 N. 675 E., Kewanna, IN 46939, e-mail: fbocclub@att.net, website: www.fbocclub.com.

International Association of Jim Beam Bottle and Specialties Clubs, *Beam Around the World* (NL), 2015 Burlington Ave., Kewanee, IL 61443, e-mail: info@beam-wade.org, website: www.beam-wade.org.

International Chinese Snuff Bottle Society, *Journal* (MAG), 2601 N. Charles St., Baltimore, MD 21218, e-mail: icsbs@worldnet.att.net, website: www.snuffbottle.org.

International Perfume Bottle Association, *Perfume Bottle Quarterly* (NL), 295 E. Swedesford Rd., PMB 185, Wayne, PA 19087, e-mail: susan arthur@comcast.net, website: www.perfumebottles.org.

Jelly Jammers, *Jelly Jammers Journal* (NL), 6086 W. Boggstown Rd., Boggstown, IN 46110, e-mail: emshaw@in.net.

Lilliputian Bottle Club, *Gulliver's Gazette* (NL), 54 Village Cir., Manhattan Beach, CA 90266-7222.

Midwest Miniature Bottle Collectors, *Midwest Miniature Bottle Collector* (NL), 6934 Brittany Ridge Ln., Cincinnati, OH 45233, e-mail: shooter@fuse.net, website: www.miniaturebottles.com.

The Mini Bottle Club, *The Mini Bottle Club* (NL), 47 Burradon Rd., Burradon, Cramlington, Northumberland NE23 7NF, UK, e-mail: minibottle club@cs.com.

National Association of Avon Collectors, PO Box 7006, Kansas City, MO 64113, website: www.californiaperfumecompany.net/cpc_collector/naac.htm. Write for a list of Avon clubs in your area.

National Association of Milk Bottle Collectors, *The Milk Route* (NL), 18 Pond Place, Cos Cob, CT 06807, e-mail: gottmilk@msn.com, website: www.collectoronline.com/club-NAMBC-wp.html.

Ole Time Vinegar Society, *Vinegar Gazette* (NL), 745 Beth-Rural Hall Rd., Rural Hall, NC 27045, e-mail: speas@triad.rr.com, website: www.antiquebottles.com/vinegarclub.

Painted Soda Bottles Collectors Association, *Soda Net* (NL), 9418 Hilmer Dr., La Mesa, CA 91942, e-mail: aclsrus@home.com, website: www.collectoronline.com/PSBCA/PSBCA.html.

Phoenix Antiques Bottle Club, *AZ Collector* (NL), 4702 W. Lavey Rd., Glendale, AZ 85306, e-mail: Dig632@aol.com, website: phoenixantiques club.org.

Saratoga-Type Bottle Collectors Society, *Spouter* (NL), 1198 Main St., Box 685, Warren, MA 01083, e-mail: ctrtle@berkshire.net.

Society of Inkwell Collectors, *Stained Finger* (NL), 10 Meadow Dr., Spencerport, NY 14559, e-mail: soic@rochester.rr.com, website: www.soic.com.

Southeastern Antique Bottle Club, *The Whittle Mark* (NL), 143 Scatterfoot Dr., Peachtree City, GA 30269, e-mail: Fred-Taylor@worldnet.att.net, website: home.att.net/~Fred-Taylor.

Violin Bottle Collectors Association, *Fine Tuning* (NL), 24 Sylvan St., Danvers, MA 01923, e-mail: fbviobot@hotmail.com.

Watkins Collectors Club, *Watkins Collectors Club Newsletter* (NL), W24024 SR 54-93, Galesville, WI 54630-8249, e-mail: beanpot@triwest.net.

OTHER PUBLICATIONS

Antique Bottle & Glass Collector (MAG), PO Box 180, East Greenville, PA 18041, e-mail: glswrk@enter.net, website: www.glswrk-auction.com.

Avon Times (NL), PO Box 9868, Kansas City, MO 64134, e-mail: avontimes@aol.com, website: www.avontimes.com.

BBR: British Bottle Review (MAG), Elsecar Heritage Center, Barnsley, South Yorkshire S74 8HJ, UK, e-mail: sales@bbrauctions.co.uk, website: www.bbrauctions.co.uk.

Fruit Jar News (NL), FJN Publishers, Inc., 364 Gregory Ave., West Orange, NJ 07052-3743, e-mail: tomcaniff@aol.com.

Just For Openers (NL), PO Box 64, Chapel Hill, NC 27514, e-mail: jfo@mindspring.com, website: www.just-for-openers.org (bottle openers and corkscrews, with an emphasis on beer and soda advertising openers and corkscrews).

Miniature Bottle Collector (MAG), PO Box 2161, Palos Verdes Peninsula, CA 90274, e-mail: david@spaid.org, website: www.bottlecollecting.com.

ARCHIVES & MUSEUMS

Coca-Cola Co. Archives, Industry & Consumer Affairs, PO Box 1734, Atlanta, GA 30301, 800-438-2653, website: www.coca-cola.com. Click on contact link for e-mail question form.

Dr Pepper Museum, 300 S. 5th St., Waco, TX 76701, 254-757-1025, website: www.drpeppermuseum.com.

The Mount Horeb Mustard Museum, PO Box 468, 100 W. Main St., Mount Horeb, WI 53372, 800-438-6878, website: www.mustardmuseum.com.

The Museum of Beverage Containers and Advertising, 1055 Ridgecrest Dr., Millersville, TN 37072, 615-859-5236 or 800-826-4929, website: www.gono.com/vir-mus/museum.htm.

National Bottle Museum, 76 Milton Ave., Ballston Spa, NY 12020, 518-885-7589, website: family.knick.net/nbm.

Pepsi-Cola Co. Archives, One Pepsi Way, Somers, NY 10589, 914-767-6000, website: www.pepsi.com.

Seagram Museum Collection, Dana Porter Library, University of Waterloo, 200 University Ave. W., Waterloo ON N2L 3G1, 519-888-4567, ext. 2619 or ext. 3122, fax: 519-888-4322.

USEFUL SITES

Antique Bottle Collector's Haven, www.antiquebottles.com.

The Virtual Corkscrew Museum, www.bullworks.net/virtual.htm.

APPRAISERS

Many of the auctions and repair services listed in this section will also do appraisals. *See also* the general list of "Appraisal Groups," page 483.

Historic Glasshouse, Sea Cliff, NY, 516-759-6744, fax: 509-461-1572, website: www.antiquebottles-glass.com. Appraisal of 17th-, 18th-, and 19th-century antique American and European bottles. Visit the appraisal section of the website to submit your request.

AUCTIONS

➨ **SEE ALSO "SELLING THROUGH AUCTION HOUSES," PAGE 485.**

BBR Auctions, Elsecar Heritage Centre, Barnsley, S. Yorkshire S74 8HJ, UK, 011-44-1226-745156, fax: 011-44-1226-351561, e-mail: sales@bbr auctions.co.uk, website: www.bbrauctions.co.uk. Bottles, pub jugs, breweriana, and more. Mail and phone bids accepted. Buyer's premium 10%. Prices realized mailed after auction. Restoration and conservation. Appraisals.

Glass-Works Auctions, Box 180, East Greenville, PA 18041, 215-679-5849, fax: 215-679-3068, e-mail: glswrk@enter.net, website: www.glswrk-auction.com. Absentee auctions of antique bottles and glass barbershop memorabilia. Mail, phone, and fax bids accepted. Buyer's premium 12%. Prices realized mailed after auction.

John R. Pastor Antique & Bottle Glass Auction, 7288 Thorncrest Dr. SE, Ada, MI 49301, 616-285-7604. Mail and phone bids accepted. Buyer's premium 10%. Prices realized mailed after auction. Appraisals.

Monsen and Baer, PO Box 529, Vienna, VA 22183, 703-938-2129, fax: 703-242-1357, e-mail: monsenbaer@erols.com. Perfume bottle auctions. Mail and phone bids accepted. Buyer's premium 10%. Prices realized mailed after auction.

Norman C. Heckler & Co., 79 Bradford Corner Rd., Woodstock Valley, CT 06282, 860-974-1634, fax: 860-974-2003, e-mail: heckler@neca.com, website: www.hecklerauction.com. Bottles, flasks, early glass, stoneware, and related items. Both absentee and live sales. Mail, phone, and fax bids accepted. Buyer's premium 12%. Catalog $25; yearly subscription $100. Appraisals.

NSA Auctions, Newton-Smith Antiques, 88 Cedar St., Cambridge, ON N1S 1, Canada, 519-623-6302, e-mail: info@nsaauctions.com, website: www.nsaauctions.com. Early glass, bottles, pottery, and stoneware auctions. Mail, phone, and Internet bids accepted. No buyer's premium. Catalog price varies. Prices realized mailed after auction and available on website. Appraisals.

Old Barn Auction, 10040 St. Rt. 224 W., Findlay, OH 45840, 419-422-8531, fax: 419-422-5321, e-mail: auction@oldbarn.com, website:

www.oldbarn.com. Specializing in candy containers, Indian artifacts, and Civil War items. Mail and phone bids accepted. Buyer's premium 10%. Prices realized mailed after auction. Catalog $15; yearly subscription $45. Appraisals.

Pacific Glass Auctions, 1507 21st St., Suite 203, Sacramento, CA 95814, 800-806-7722, fax: 916-443-3199, e-mail: info@pacglass.com, website: pacglass.com. Mail and phone bids accepted. Buyer's premium 12%. Prices realized mailed after auction. Appraisals.

REPAIRS, PARTS, & SUPPLIES

↔ SEE ALSO "CONSERVATORS & RESTORERS," PAGE 520.

Blue Crystal (Glass), Ltd., Units 6-8, 21 Wren St., London WC1X 0HF, UK, 011-44-20-7278-0142, fax: 011-44-20-7278-0142, e-mail: bluecrystal glass@aol.com, website: www.bluecrystalglass.co.uk. Blue glass liners and other colors for silver salt and mustard pots; stoppers and bottles for silver cruet stands; claret bottles for silver mounts; hand-cut dishes for epergne stands. Antique and general glass repairs; declouding of glass decanters. Mail order worldwide. Catalog.

Chinese Snuff Bottles—Repairs, Tops and Spoons, Philadelphia area, 610-344-9357, e-mail: j.ohara@netzero.net. Repairs of hardstone and glass Chinese snuff bottles. Custom-made tops and spoons in all materials, including jade, coral, and ivory.

Clampmakers Clamps & Closures, 411 W. Windsor St., Montpelier, IN 47359, 765-728-3746, e-mail: zinclid@aol.com. Custom-made closures for fruit jars. Champion, Globe, King, Leader, Lightning, Millville, Osotight, Sun clamps, and many others. Send SASE or email for list and prices.

Fancy That, Monroe, MI 49068, 616-781-2985, fax: 616-781-7595, e-mail: fancythat@voyager.net, website: www.antiqnet.com/fancythat. Perfume atomizer parts and repair available. Appraisals.

Jar Doctor, R. Wayne Lowry, 401 Johnston Ct., Raymore, MO 64083, 816-318-0161, fax: 816-318-0162, e-mail: jardoclowry@aol.com, website: www.one-mans-junk.com/jardoc. Glass-polishing machines, tumbling canisters, and cleaning supplies for antique glass; specializing in bottles, jars, and insulators. National referral of professional custom polishing or glass repair in your area. Free brochure.

Paradise & Co. Atomizers, 2902 Neal Rd., Paradise, CA 95969, 530-872-5020, fax: 530-872-5052, e-mail: paradise@sunset.net, website: www.paradise-co.com. Repairs and replacement parts for antique perfume atomizers; sprayer tops, cord, balls, tassels. DeVilbiss catalog reproductions. Catalog free on website or send $1 and SASE.

Pop Shoppe Video Auctions, 10556 Combie Rd., #106521, Auburn, CA 95602, 530-268-6333, 6:00 P.M.–9:00 P.M. e-mail: popshoppe@aol.com. Cleaning manual for ACL (painted label) soda bottles, includes "Cleaning Secrets for ACL Soda Pop Bottles," instruction manual, and supplies. Free flyer.

BREWERIANA

Breweriana is anything related to beer and beer cans. This includes signs, labels, ads, coasters, glasses, hats, even the unpressed printed metal used to make cans. Breweriana will sell either at a beer-can collectors show or to advertising collectors.

The way collectors of beer cans and breweriana organize themselves into special-interest factions with shows, publications, and clubs can be confusing. There are collectors of early tin beer signs who attend advertising shows. There are collectors of beer bottles who are bottle collectors and go to bottle shows. Beer can collectors usually buy at beer can shows or flea markets. Books about beer often discuss cans as well as bottles, and include all of the brewery history that is broadly termed "breweriana."

There are many collectors of beer cans, but most cans are traded and not sold. The best way to get rid of a collection is to go to a show-and-swap meet for beer can collectors. The local papers and the beer can collectors publications will list them.

Cans are often sold in groups. Anyone who buys a six-pack has the start of a beer can collection at almost no cost. Best would be the cans issued for special events or with special designs used for a limited time as a promotion. Some can be traded for other cans, and there is no cost. If you sell some of the recent cans for anything, even 50 cents, you have a profit.

The best sellers are cone-top cans. They are old and not easily found. Collectors prefer cans that have been opened from the bottom. Rust, dents, and other damage destroy the value of a common can and lower the value of rare cans.

➔ SEE ALSO ADVERTISING COLLECTIBLES

REPAIR

There is one clever restoration tip for crushed beer cans that you might want to try. Fill the dented can about one-third full with dry beans, then add water and seal the can with tape. The pressure from the expanding beans will push outward and remove most of the dents.

Cone-top cans can be repaired by experts who solder new tops on the old cans. Repairing beer cans is almost the same as repairing any commercial tin container, including soft drink cans. More information about this can be found in the section on Metals.

REFERENCE BOOKS

American Breweries II, Dale P. Van Wieren (Eastern Coast Breweriana Association, PO Box 349, West Point, PA 19846, 1995).

The Register of United States Breweries: 1876–1976, 2 volumes, Manfred Friedrich and Donald Bull (Holly Press, Stamford, CT, 1976).

PRICE BOOKS

Beer Advertising, Donald A. Bull (Schiffer, Atglen, PA, 2000).

United States Beer Cans: The Standard Reference of Flat Tops and Cone Tops, Terry Scullin (Beer Can Collectors of America, 747 Merus Ct., Fenton, MO 63026-2092, 2001).

CLUBS & THEIR PUBLICATIONS

American Breweriana Association, Inc., *American Breweriana Journal* (MAG), PO Box 11157, Pueblo, CO 81001-0157, e-mail: breweriana1 @earthlink.net, website: www.americanbreweriana.org.

Anheuser-Busch Collectors Club, *First Draft* (MAG), PO Box 503058, St. Louis, MO 63150-3058, website: www.budshop.com.

Association of Bottled Beer Collectors, *What's Bottling* (NL), 127 Victoria Park Rd., Tunstall, Stoke-on-Trent ST6 6D4, UK, e-mail: JohnMann @csi.com, website: ourworld.compuserve.com/homepages/John_ Mann/abbchome.htm.

Beer Can Collectors of America, *Beer Cans & Brewery Collectibles* (MAG), 747 Merus Ct., Fenton, MO 63026-2092, e-mail: bcca@bcca.com, website: www.bcca.com.

National Association Breweriana Advertising, *Breweriana Collector* (NL), PO Box 64, Chapel Hill, NC 27514-0064, website: www.nababrew.org.

ARCHIVES & MUSEUMS

American Museum of Brewing History & Arts, I-75 and Buttermill Pike, Fort Mitchell, KY 41017, 859-341-2800.

The Beer Museum, PO Box 309, Milwaukee, WI 53201, 414-965-3281.

Seagram Museum Collection, Dana Porter Library, University of Waterloo, 200 University Ave. W., Waterloo ON N2L 3G1, 519-888-4567, ext. 2619 or ext. 3122, fax: 519-888-4322.

APPRAISERS

Many of the auctions listed in this section will also do appraisals. *See also* the general list of "appraisal groups," page 483.

AUCTIONS

◆→ SEE ALSO "SELLING THROUGH AUCTION HOUSES," PAGE 485.

BBR Auctions, Elsecar Heritage Centre, Barnsley, S. Yorkshire S74 8HJ, UK, 011-44-1226-745156, fax: 011-44-1226-351561, e-mail: sales@bbr auctions.co.uk, website: www.bbrauctions.co.uk. Bottles, pub jugs, breweriana, Doulton, Wade, Beswick, and more. Mail and phone bids accepted. Buyer's premium 10%. Prices realized mailed after auction. Restoration and conservation. Appraisals.

Fink's Off the Wall Auctions, 108 E. 7th St., Lansdale, PA 19446-2622, 215-855-9732, fax: 215-855-6325, e-mail: lansbeer@finksauctions.com, website: www.finksauctions.com. Breweriana auctions. Mail, phone, and e-mail bids accepted. Buyer's premium 10%. Catalog $15. Prices realized mailed after auction and available on website. Appraisals.

Gary Kirsner Auctions, PO Box 8807, Coral Springs, FL 33075, 944-344-9856, fax: 944-344-4421, e-mail: gkirsner@garykirsnerauctions.com, website: garykirsnerauctions.com. Specializing in auctions of beer steins. Mail, fax, and e-mail bids accepted. Buyer's premium 15%. Catalog subscription $30. Prices realized mailed after auction and available on website. Appraisals.

Glasses, Mugs & Steins, PO Box 207, Sun Prairie, WI 53590, 608-837-4818, fax: 608-825-4205, e-mail: pkroll@charter.net, website: www.gmskroll.com. Beer glasses, mugs, and steins. Mail, phone, and Internet bids accepted. Buyer's premium varies. Prices realized mailed after auction and available on website. Catalog $13 bulk mail, yearly subscription $25 for two issues.

Past Tyme Pleasures, 2491 San Ramon Valley Blvd., PMB 204, San Ramon, CA 94583, 925-484-4488, fax: 925-484-2551, e-mail: pasttyme1 @attbi.com, website: www.pasttyme1.com. Breweriana, antique advertising, and general store collectibles. Mail, phone, fax, and e-mail bids accepted. Buyer's premium 10%. Prices realized mailed after auction and available on website. Appraisals.

◆→ **BRONZE, SEE METALS**
◆→ **CALENDAR ART, SEE PRINTS**
◆→ **CANES, SEE FASHION**

CAROUSELS

The hand-carved, wooden charging horse or prancing pig that was part of the amusement park merry-go-round is now classed as "folk art" and sells for thousands of dollars. If it is possible to identify the makers of some of the animals, and if the name of the amusement park that originally owned the merry-go-round or the name of the artist can be determined, the value goes up 50 percent.

The most valuable carousel figures are the most unusual. Menagerie animals are rarer than horses and usually sell for thousands of dollars. Tigers, polar bears, pigs, ostriches, giraffes, goats, and other animals are most desirable. The quality of the carving, elaborate saddles and trappings, jeweled bridles, windblown manes, long coiled tails, imaginative figures at the saddle cantles, and glass eyes add to the value.

The figures in the outside row on a carousel were seen by the public and had the most elaborate decoration, with the "lead" horse showing off the best work. American figures bring higher prices in this country than European figures. American horses are more highly decorated on the right side because the carousel goes in a counterclockwise direction; English carousels are the reverse. Horses are called either standers (three or four feet on the ground), prancers (back feet on the ground), or jumpers (no feet on the ground, move up and down on pole). All are equally valuable.

Any part of the carousel will sell to a folk art collector: the trim above the center section, the carved carriage sides, even the signs of the maker have a value. Metal carousel horses also sell, but for much lower prices. Because carousels, carousel figures, and parts are large, they are most often sold through well-advertised auctions.

The market is nationwide. Buyers travel long distances to get a rare figure or a complete carousel, and they are not daunted by the problem of transporting a large item.

There are many other carvings and decorations from amusement parks that are now wanted by collectors: the figures from the fun house; the painted canvas backdrops from the sideshow; carts, planes, cars, and other parts of rides; and penny-arcade equipment and gifts. If you are lucky enough to own any parts of a defunct amusement park, be sure to check with local auctioneers and shops.

Most antiques are less valuable if restored. Automobiles, carousel figures, and oil paintings may be the major exceptions to this rule. Newly painted, old carousel figures sell at auction for very high prices, often much higher than for similar figures with "park paint." This is one of the few types of collectibles that go up in value if the paint is new. Stripped figures are worth 25 percent less than park paint; repainted ones are worth 25 to 50 percent more. But this is changing. Recently some collectors have been searching for park-painted figures and paying more for them.

REPAIR

The carousel has become an accepted part of American folk art. Museums and collectors are adding horses, carvings, cresting, chariots, and musical mechanisms to their collections. It is best to keep most of these wood carvings in unrestored condition. Some restorers remove the old finish and repaint the animals, or restore damaged wood and finish. Do not restore one of these figures yourself unless you are talented and trained. A poor restoration can destroy the resale value.

Be very careful if you plan to strip and paint a carousel figure. Tastes change. Original paint is becoming more popular. The new paint may lower the value. Some restorers now strip off the top layers of paint and try to restore the original first coat of paint.

CLUBS & THEIR PUBLICATIONS

American Carousel Society, *Rounding Board* (NL), 3845 Telegraph Rd., Elkton, MD 21921-2442, e-mail: carousel@dol.net, website: www.carousels.com/acs.htm.

National Amusement Park Historical Association, *NAPHA News* (MAG), *NAPHA News FLASH* (NL), PO Box 83, Mt. Prospect, IL 60056, e-mail: info@napha.org, website: www.napha.org (dedicated to the preservation and enjoyment of the amusement and theme park industry; tries to preserve historic rides and to find new homes for classic amusement rides).

National Carousel Association, *Merry-Go-Roundup* (MAG), PO Box 4333, Evansville, IN 47724-0333, e-mail: terrybnca@juno.com, website: www.nca-usa.org.

OTHER PUBLICATIONS

Carousel News & Trader (MAG), 87 Park Ave. W., Suite 206, Mansfield, OH 44902-1657, e-mail: cnsam@aol.com, website: www.carousel trader.com.

ARCHIVES & MUSEUMS

The Herschell Carrousel Factory Museum, PO Box 672, 180 Thompson St., North Tonawanda, NY 14120, 716-693-1885, website: www.carousel museum.org.

Merry-Go-Round Museum, PO Box 718, Sandusky, Ohio 44870, 419-626-6111, fax: 419-626-1297, website: www.merrygoroundmuseum.org.

The New England Carousel Museum, 95 Riverside Ave., Bristol, CT 06010, 860-585-5411, fax: 860-314-0483, website: www.thecarousel museum.com.

APPRAISERS

Many of the auctions and repair services listed in this section will also do appraisals. *See also* the general list of "Appraisal Groups," page 483.

AUCTIONS

→→ SEE ALSO "SELLING THROUGH AUCTION HOUSES," PAGE 485.

Auction under the Big Top, 7 Cooks Glen Rd., Spring City, PA 19745, 610-469-6331, e-mail: barbmgr@aol.com, website: carousel.com. Carousel auctions. Mail and phone bids accepted. Buyer's premium 10%. Free catalog. Appraisals.

Norton Auctioneers of Michigan, Inc., 50 W. Pearl, Coldwater, MI 49036-1967, 517-279-9063, fax: 517-279-9191, e-mail: nortonsold@cbpu.com, website: www.nortonauctioneers.com. Unique collections, carousels, amusement parks, museums. Buyer's premium varies. Appraisals.

REPAIRS, PARTS & SUPPLIES

→→ SEE ALSO "CONSERVATORS & RESTORERS," PAGE 520.

Alaska Carousel Parafunalia, 2905 W. 34th Ave., Anchorage, AK 99517, 907-248-5611 or 907-349-7511, 8:00 A.M.–8:00 P.M. fax: 907-248-5611, e-mail: mhv642@GCI.net. Complete restoration and painting of carousel animals. Written estimates provided.

Brass Ring Entertainment, 11001 Peoria Street, Sun Valley, CA 91352, 818-394-0028, fax: 818-394-0062, website: www.carousel.com. Carousel service. Restores, installs, moves, maintains, services, sells, appraises, and brokers new and antique carousels, carousel animals, and band organs.

Carousel Magic, 44 W. Fourth, PO Box 1466, Mansfield, OH 44901, 419-526-4009, fax: 419-526-4561, e-mail: shae@carouselmagic.com, website: www.carouselmagic.com. Carousel figure restoration and reproduction; restoration of complete carousels. Manufacturer of hand-carved carousel figures and complete carousels. Catalog $3.

Carousel Care Consultants, 10009 N. Moore, Spokane, WA 99208, 509-466-3186, e-mail: painttheponies@aol.com. Carousel restoration, appraisals, and identification. Annual workshop and consultation. Paint manual, $25 plus shipping and handling.

Custom Carving and Restoration, PO Box 771331, Wichita, KS 67277, 316-722-1872, e-mail: ccrmar@att.net, website: home.att.net/~ccrmar. Complete restoration of carousel animals, panels, and other decorative objects of art.

David Boyle, 150 Andrews Trace, New Castle, PA 16102, 724-667-8181, 8:00 A.M.–11:00 P.M. fax: 724-667-8598, e-mail: JosetteB@prodigy.net.

Restoration of carousel animals. Custom-made display stands. Send SASE for brochure.

Fabricon Carousel Co., 140 Hindsdale St., Brooklyn, NY 11207, 718-342-2440, 9:30 A.M.–5:30 P.M. e-mail: fabricon@interport.net, website: www.FabriconNY.com. Carousel restorations, individual horses and full carousels.

Great Canadian Nickelodeon Co. Ltd., RR #4, Mount Forest, ON, Canada N0G 2L0, 519-323-3582, Mon.–Sat. 9:00 A.M.–6:00 P.M., e-mail: RonaldS715@aol.com, website: members.aol.com/tgcnc. Complete restoration or repairs of all automated music machines, including monkey organs, band and fairground organs, carousel organs, etc. Custom-built parts. Brochure.

John Hughes, 7226 Rosencrans Way, San Jose, CA 95139, 408-227-4388, 9:00 A.M.–10:00 P.M. Restoration of wooden carousel figures and other wood carvings up to enamel undercoat.

Kromer Mechanical Musical Instruments, 53 Louella Ct., Wayne, PA 19087-3527, 610-687-0172. Carousel band organs, piano nickelodeons, antique reed organs, and calliopes restored. New carousel organs built; old organs rebuilt. Music rolls; CDs and cassettes of carousel and circus music. Send SASE with two first-class stamps for information.

LCM Studio, 10243 York Ln., Bloomington, MN 55431, 612-830-1152 phone/fax. Carousel horse restoration. If you have original paint under layers of "park paint," they can strip it down to the original paint, then varnish and in-paint on top to preserve as much of the original as possible.

Lise Liepman Restoration Studio, 1108 Neilson St., Albany, CA 94706, 510-525-3467, e-mail: lisegeorge@earthlink.net, website: www.liseliepman.com. Full restoration of wooden carousel figures and band organ facades. Wood repair; carving of missing parts; repainting; conservation of original paint. Crating and shipping available.

Merry-Go-Round Museum, PO Box 718, Sandusky, OH 44870, 419-626-6111, fax: 419-626-1297, e-mail: MerryGoR@aol.com, website: www.merrygoroundmuseum.org. Restoration of carousel figures and related items. The museum is dedicated to the preservation and promotion of the art and history of the carousel. Guided tours, seminars, workshops, library, and archives. Free brochure. Call for hours.

Midwest Carousel Organization, 1952 Lake Dr., Independence, MO 64055, 816-833-3573, e-mail: scarrousel@msn.com, website: www.finest1.com/hand. Carousel animal restoration. Repair, painting, and replacement of missing parts. Carving of commissioned new carousel animals.

Morris Caroussell Works, PO Box 786, Philadelphia, PA 19105, 610-383-1655, fax: 610-383-5656, e-mail: bramante@bellatlantic.net. Antique carousel figures restored and refinished. Catalog $2.

Pamela Hessey, Hawk's Eye Studio, 145 Hillside Ln., Martinez, CA

94553, 925-228-7309, e-mail: pam@hawkseyestudio.com, website: hawkseyestudio.com. Carousel animals, band organs, and carousel trim restored and painted. Conservation of original paint; historic restorations of surfaces.

Pirates Treasure Cove, 6212 E. Kracker Ave., Gibsonton, FL 33534, 813-677-1137, Mon.–Sat. 9:00 A.M.–5:00 P.M., fax: 813-671-2915, e-mail: piratestreasurecove@ij.net. Rhinestones, beading, braids, fringes, and jewels for carousel horses.

Quarterhorse Investments, Inc., 336 W. High St., Elizabethtown, PA 17022, 717-295-9188. Restoration supplies for carousel horses. Send SASE for brochure.

Quill Hair & Ferrule, Ltd., PO Box 23927, Columbia, SC 29224, 800-421-7961, 803-788-4499, Mon.–Fri. 8:00 A.M.–5:00 P.M., fax: 803-736-4731, website: www.qhfonline.com. Specialty products and supplies. Paints, brushes, and hard-to-find supplies for sign restoration, faux finishing, and gold leaf.

Rockinghorse Antiques, 111 St. Helena Ave., Dundalk, MD 21222, 410-285-0280. Restoration of carousel horses and related items. Appraisals, identification, and value. Free brochure.

Sheild Art & Hobby Shop, 4417 Danube Dr., King George, VA 22485-5707, 540-663-3711, fax: 540-663-3711 call first, e-mail: wsheild @crosslink.net. Complete carousel figure restoration with photo documentation. Wooden carved replacement pieces for damaged or missing parts; custom painting and appraisal included. Will complete carving and assist in finishing unfinished carousel figures purchased in "kit" form. Carved replacement pieces for various wooden items.

Tony Orlando, 6661 Norborne, Dearborn Heights, MI 48127-2076, 313-561-5072, 9:00 A.M.–5:00 P.M. Conservation and restoration of carousel figures. References furnished.

W.P. Wilcox, 2122 W. Midwood Ln., Anaheim, CA 92804, 714-635-0917, 9:00 A.M.–5:00 P.M. e-mail: wpwilcox@msn.com. Repair and restoration of carousel animals.

Weaver's Antiques, 7 Cooks Glen Rd., Spring City, PA 19745, 610-469-633, fax: 610-469-6845, e-mail: barbmgr@aol.com. Carousel figure restoration. Brass poles, jewels, eyes, etc. Send SASE for brochure. Appraisals $10, send several photos and SASE.

CELEBRITY MEMORABILIA

Celebrity memorabilia are bought and sold in four major categories: items related to TV, radio and recording stars; historic personality items; comic-related items; and items related to the movies. Each has a slightly different market.

TV, RADIO, AND RECORDING STARS

TV and radio materials are collected by fans and by those who are interested in old-time radio. Contact these collectors through the radio publications, at the special shops and shows, or at the large flea markets. Star Trek fans have special shows each year and buy and sell old scripts, tapes, and all sorts of memorabilia. Disneyana collectors are eager to buy Mouseketeers items. M*A*S*H, Howdy Doody, The Man from U.N.C.L.E., The Honeymooners, Hopalong Cassidy, and many others also have special collector organizations. Old TV Guides and other magazines are collected. So are newspaper and magazine ads that feature the stars. Of course, tapes, photographs, records, and song sheets are wanted.

Recording stars often appeared on TV or in movies, so there are several reasons their memorabilia would be collected. Try selling your items to dealers in records who also have "go-withs," or to the regular twentieth-century collectibles dealers. You should also contact any local fan club members if you have some rarities or a large box of material.

HISTORIC PERSONALITIES

Charles Lindbergh, any prominent political figure, the astronauts, composers, scientists, explorers, notorious criminals, and many others with a claim to fame interest collectors today. Often the best place to sell "association" items, like a chair that belonged to Teddy Roosevelt or Queen Victoria's underdrawers, is through a national or Internet auction that specializes in autographs and historic items. Less important items can be sold through these same national sales, through some mail-order auctions, or to dealers or collectors. Look for other possibilities. An astronaut's autographed picture might interest a collector of space toys. Lindbergh and his flight have fascinated airplane lovers for many years, and there are so many collectors that these items even have a special section listing the prices in Kovels' Antiques & Collectibles Price List.

If you are fortunate enough to be the descendant of an important person or have acquired a large collection of material about one person, you might offer it as a collection to the historical society that would be most interested in the hometown, state, or center of activity of the famous person. There may also be a Hall of Fame that would be interested; everything from aviation to rock 'n' roll to football has a Hall of Fame.

Be sure you contact an appraiser or auction house that will understand the value of the family heirlooms. We heard of a sad example of what can happen. George Pickett V, the great-great-grandson of the famous Civil War general, had a trunk full of the general's keepsakes. An appraiser bought the items for $87,500. Two weeks later, the appraiser sold the collection to the new National Civil War Museum for $870,000. Pickett sued. The appraiser said Pickett set the prices and that he should have contacted an outside appraiser. Pickett admits he was ignorant about his ancestor's fame and the value of his belongings, but the court agreed the appraiser misled him.

A large collection should be sold as a unit to obtain the best price. In other words, the price for the whole is greater than the price for the sum of the parts. This means you must find a dealer or auctioneer who will take all of it. If you sell one or two important pieces, you will lower the interest in the remaining collection.

➻ **COMIC-RELATED MEMORABILIA, MOVIE ITEMS, AND SPORT COLLECTIBLES ARE DISCUSSED IN THEIR OWN CHAPTERS.**

➻ **SEE ALSO PHONOGRAPHS, RADIO & TV**

PRICE BOOKS

Beatle Mania: An Unauthorized Collector's Guide, Courtney McWilliams (Schiffer, Atglen, PA, 1998).

The Beatles Memorabilia Price Guide, 3rd edition, Jeff Augsburger, Marty Eck, and Rick Rann (Antique Trader Books, Dubuque, IA, 1997).

Film & TV Animal Star Collectibles, Dana Cain (Antique Trader Books, Dubuque, IA, 1998).

Goldmine Kiss Collectibles Price Guide, Tom Shannon (Krause, Iola, WI, 2000).

The James Dean Collectors Guide, David Loehr and Joe Bills (L-W Book Sales, Gas City, IN, 1999).

Marilyn Monroe: Cover to Cover, Clark Kidder (Krause, Iola, WI, 1999).

Marilyn: Putting a Price on the Priceless Performer, Clark Kidder (Krause, Iola, WI, 2002).

The Monkees Collectibles Price Guide, Marty Eck (Antique Trader Books, Dubuque, IA, 1998).

Signatures of the Stars: An Insider's Guide to Celebrity Autographs, Kevin Martin (Antique Trader Books, Dubuque, IA, 1998).

The Ultimate Roy Rogers Collection, Ron Lenius (Krause, Iola, WI, 2001).

CLUBS & THEIR PUBLICATIONS

C.A.L./N-X-211 Collectors Society, *Spirit of St. Louis Newsletter* (NL), 727 Younkin Pkwy. S., Columbus, OH 43207-4788.

Dionne Quint Collectors, *Quint News* (NL), PO Box 2527, Woburn, MA 01888, e-mail: effanjay@webtv.net.

Doodyville Historical Society, *Howdy Doody Times* (NL), 8 Hunt Ct., Flemington, NJ 08822-3349, e-mail: jjudson@ptd.net.

Girl Groups Fan Club, *Girl Groups Gazette* (MAG), PO Box 69A04, Dept. K, West Hollywood, CA 90069, e-mail: gayboyloca@hotmail.com, website: surf.to/girlgroups (for fans of the 1960s and 1970s rock 'n' soul female groups and singers).

Hopalong Cassidy Fan Club, *Hoppy Talk* (NL), 6310 Friendship Dr., New Concord, OH 43762-9708, e-mail: lbates1205@cs.com.

International Al Jolson Society, Inc., *Jolson Journal* (MAG), 1195 Hickory Hill Dr., Green Bay, WI 54304, e-mail: JWWehrman@aol.com, website: www.jolson.org.

Marx Brothers Study Unit, *Freedonia Gazette* (MAG), 335 Fieldstone Dr., New Hope, PA 18938-1012, e-mail: tfg@cheerful.com, website: www.whyaduck.com/merchandise/gazette.htm.

Munsters & The Addams Family Fan Club, *Munsters & The Addams Family Reunion* (MAG), PO Box 69A04, Dept. K, West Hollywood, CA 90069, e-mail: gayboyloca@hotmail.com, website: www.geocities.com/tmafc.

National Association of Fan Clubs, *The Fan Club Monitor* (NL), PO Box 4340, Oceanside, CA 92052-4340, e-mail: emailnafc@aol.com, website: www.members.aol.com/lknafc/nafc/index.htm.

Roy Rogers/Dale Evans Collectors Association (RRDECA), *RRDECA Newsletter* (NL), PO Box 1166, Portsmouth, OH 45662, e-mail: LaRue@zoom.net, website: www.royrogers.com.

OTHER PUBLICATIONS

Beatlefan (MAG), PO Box 33515, Decatur, GA 30033, e-mail: goodypress @mindspring.com, website: beatlefan.com.

The Silver Bullet (NL), PO Box 1493, Longmont, CO 80502, e-mail: theloneranger@worldnet.att.net (for Lone Ranger enthusiasts and collectors).

Star Trek Communicator (MAG), PO Box 111000, Aurora, CO 80042, website: www.startrek.com.

Under Western Skies (MAG), 104 Chestnut Wood Dr., Waynesville, NC 28786-6514, e-mail: WOY76Ron@aol.com (movie, TV, and radio westerns).

ARCHIVES & MUSEUMS

The Museum of Television & Radio, 25 West 52nd St., New York, NY 10019, 212-621-6600, and 465 North Beverly Dr., Beverly Hills, CA 90210, 310-786-1000, website: www.mtr.org.

APPRAISERS

Many of the auctions and repair services listed in this section will also do appraisals. *See also* the general list of "Appraisal Groups," page 483.

AUCTIONS

•→ SEE ALSO "SELLING THROUGH AUCTION HOUSES," PAGE 485.

Leland's, 3947 Merrick Rd., Seaford, NY 11783, 516-409-9700, fax: 516-409-9797, e-mail: info@lelands.com, website: www.lelands.com. Specializing in auctions of vintage sports memorabilia, sports and non-sports cards, and specialized collections of rock 'n' roll and entertainment memorabilia. Mail and phone bids accepted. Buyer's premium 15%. Prices realized mailed after auction. Appraisals.

Paul Riseman Auctions, 2205 S. Park Ave., Springfield, IL 62704-4335, 217-787-2634, fax: 217-787-0062, e-mail: riseman@riseman.com, website: www.riseman.com. Absentee auctions of collectible popular sheet music, entertainment-related memorabilia, ephemera, and autographs. Mail, phone, fax, and e-mail bids accepted. No buyer's premium. Prices realized mailed after auction. Free catalogs. Appraisals.

Superior Galleries, 9478 W. Olympic Blvd., Beverly Hills, CA 90212, 877-782-6773 or 310-203-9761, fax: 310-203-8037, e-mail: alan@superiorstamps.com, website: www.superiorstamps.com. Stamps, sports memorabilia, Hollywood memorabilia, and other collectibles. Mail, phone, fax, and e-mail bids accepted. Buyer's premium 15%. Catalog $5. Yearly subscription $20. Prices realized available after auction on website. Appraisals.

•→ CHRISTMAS, SEE HOLIDAY COLLECTIBLES
•→ CHROME, SEE METALS

CLOCKS & WATCHES

CLOCKS

According to some collectors, a home without a ticking clock has no heart. Clocks that work always sell well. It does not seem to matter if they are old, new, Art Deco, or eighteenth-century French. One problem with pricing clocks is that two clocks that look the same to a novice may look very different to an expert. Years ago we ran a picture of a clock owned by a reader of our newspaper column. It was an 1880 wall clock with elaborate "gingerbread" trim. We gave a suggested value. The day after the column appeared, we started to receive phone calls and letters from readers. We got another, clearer picture of the clock, and when we examined the trim very carefully, we saw what our clock-expert readers had noticed. This was a rare version of the wall clock, worth thousands of dollars, not just the few hundred dollars we had suggested.

A clock must be opened to see if there is a label. Check on the type of mechanism running the clock. If it winds, the key is important.

One "Kovelism" for pricing antiques is that if it moves or makes noise, it brings a premium price. This includes animated alarm clocks, grandfather clocks with chimes, and any other clock that makes noise or has moving parts other than the hands. Figural clocks of any age sell well, but a few brands are especially valued. LUX on the label will double the price.

An old clock with replaced works is a "marriage" and is only worth 10 to 20 percent as much as an all-original clock. Grandfather or tall-case clocks are often found in an altered state. During the past 200 years, many owners will have repaired or glorified their clocks with additions or changes. If the feet or finials are new, subtract 10 percent. If the door is new, subtract 20 to 25 percent. If the base has been shortened, subtract 30 percent. If the case has been refinished badly or the carvings destroyed, deduct 25 percent or more.

A slightly restored painted dial or minor replacement of parts or case lowers the value by about 10 percent. If the dial is totally repainted, it lowers the value of the clock to the value of the case; the repainted dial is worthless. A restored, cracked, or damaged enameled dial lowers the value by up to 50 percent. If the face is old but a replacement, deduct 20 percent. A signature or label adds value. So do glass and a clean, working movement.

Antique grandfather clocks, especially American examples, should be examined by a qualified appraiser. If unaltered, they are usually worth thousands of dollars and should be sold by a professional dealer or auction house with national exposure for the best price. Also, be sure to check carefully on the value of carriage clocks, chronometers, novelty clocks, and elaborate clocks with ormolu or porcelain decorations. Many of these are worth big money.

WATCHES

To identify a pocket watch or wristwatch, you must open it and look for names, labels, and construction features. If you can't do this yourself, ask a local jeweler to help. When you check the value in a watch price book, you must know the name on the dial or movement, the number of jewels, serial number, size of case, and if it is solid gold or plate. Wristwatches that look old-fashioned are in demand and are sometimes worn as jewelry even if they do not keep time because they have not been cleaned and repaired. Dealers who specialize in old watches or jewelry will buy them. Look for these dealers at the shows or in the Yellow Pages of the phone book under "Watch Repair" or "Jewelry."

Of course, solid-gold watches are far more valuable than gold-plated or chrome-plated ones. The names **ROLEX**, **PATEK PHILIPPE**, **HAMILTON**, **VACHERON & CONSTANTIN**, **OMEGA**, **PIAGET**, **MOVADO**, **GRUEN**, **TIFFANY**, **LE COULTRE**, and **CARTIER** add value. Diamond watches must be appraised by a qualified jeweler for the diamond and gold value. The wristwatch must sell for more than the "break-down" value (see section on Jewelry).

Winding stems positioned out of sight in the back and triangular or other odd-shaped cases add value. So do calendars, stopwatches, chimes, and other special features. Look for the special buttons or levers that indicate these items on the watches. Unusual watches with psychedelic dials, moon dials, cartoon characters, moving figures, or slogans are considered novelties and can be sold, but they usually do not bring high dollars.

Pocket watches are wanted by watch collectors but not necessarily by a jewelry buyer. This is a special market, and the best prices are paid by the serious collector. A very low serial number adds to the value. Contact a watch dealer or an auction gallery if you want to sell a good, solid-gold pocket watch. Wristwatches made since the 1950s are selling well today. The Rolex "oyster" and other watches with intricate mechanisms bring thousands of dollars and sell quickly.

REPAIR

Repairing clockworks is a job for an expert. It is always best to have a specialist fix the inside of a broken clock unless you have the

IS IT SOLID GOLD?

When pricing watches, be sure to determine the difference between the markings on gold-plated and solid-gold cases. The marks can be misleading: The words "Guaranteed 5 (10, 20, 30) Years" appear on cases that are gold filled or rolled gold, and the karat mark was used with the year guarantee until 1924. After that, the government required the cases to be marked "10K gold filled" or "10K rolled gold plate." A solid-gold case will probably be marked with the karat mark and the words "Warranted U.S. Assay," or in a few instances, marked with hallmarks.

required talent. Clock face and dial repainting and reverse glass painting for clock doors require specialists, but simple refinishing of a clock case can be done at home. Clocks with pendulums need special adjustments to keep accurate time and often must be leveled on a shelf or floor. A local clock repair service will do this, or you may be able to correct the swing by following the directions available in various books. Lowering the weight makes the clock go slower.

If you acquire an electric clock that is more than twenty years old, always have the wiring checked and replaced. Old wiring is a fire hazard.

When you buy an old clock or watch, take it to an expert first to see if it needs to be cleaned. This is often the only restoration required. Old-style bands for wristwatches can be found at many jewelry stores.

➻ **SEE ALSO ADVERTISING COLLECTIBLES**

REFERENCE BOOKS

American Wristwatches: Five Decades of Style and Design, Edward Faber and Stewart Unger (Schiffer, Atglen, PA, 1988).

Book of American Clocks, Brooks Palmer (Macmillan, New York, 1950).

Britten's Old Clocks and Watches and Their Makers, G.H. Baillie et al. (Bonanza Books, New York, 1956).

Practical Watch Repairing, Donald de Carle (Antique Collectors' Club, Wappingers Falls, NY, 1969).

Repairing Old Clocks & Watches, Anthony J. Whitten (Antique Collectors' Club, Wappingers Falls, NY, 1982).

Restoring Grandfather Clocks, Eric Smith (Antique Collectors' Club, Wappingers Falls, NY, 1995).

Treasury of American Clocks, Brooks Palmer (Macmillan, New York, 1967).

Watchmakers & Clockmakers of the World, 2 volumes, G. H. Baillie, Brian Loomes (N.A.G. Press, London, 1976).

Wristwatches: History of a Century's Development, 3rd edition/1st English edition, Helmut Kahlert, Richard Mühe, and Gisbert L. Brunner (Schiffer, Atglen, PA, 1986).

PRICE BOOKS

100 Years of Vintage Watches: A Collector's Identification & Price Guide, Dean Judy (Krause, Iola, WI, 2002).

American Shelf and Wall Clocks, 2nd edition, Robert W.D. Ball (Schiffer, Atglen, PA, 1999).

Antique Clocks: Identification and Price Guide, CD-ROM and Internet Resource, Jeff Savage and Ryan Polite (eCollectica Publishing, www.ecollectica.com, 2001).

Automatic Wristwatches from Germany, England, France, Japan, Russia, & the USA, Heinz Hampel (Schiffer, Atglen, PA, 1997).

The Charlton Standard Catalogue of Canadian Clocks, 2nd edition, by J.E. Connell (Charlton Press, Toronto, 1999).

The Collector's Guide to 20th Century Modern Clocks: Desk, Shelf and Decorative, Mark V. Stein (Radiomania, 2109 Carterdale Road, Baltimore, MD 21209, 2002).

Electrifying Time: Telechron and G.E. Clocks, 1925–1955, Jim Linz (Schiffer, Atglen, PA, 2001).

Miller's Buyer's Guide: Clocks & Barometers, 2nd edition, Derek Roberts, editor (Miller's, Tenterden, Kent, England, 2001).

Wristwatches: History of a Century's Development, 4th edition, Helmut Kahlert, Richard Mühe, and Gisbert L. Brunner (Schiffer, Atglen, PA, 1999).

CLUBS & THEIR PUBLICATIONS

Antiquarian Horological Society, *Antiquarian Horology* (MAG), New House, High St., Ticehurst, East Sussex TN5 7AL, UK, e-mail: secretary@ahsoc.demon.co.uk, website: www.ahsoc.demon.co.uk.

National Association of Watch and Clock Collectors, Inc., *NAWCC Bulletin* (MAG), 514 Poplar St., Columbia, PA 17512-2130, e-mail: patti@nawcc.org, website: www.nawcc.org.

Swatch the Club, *Swatch World Journal* (NP), *Swatch News* (NL), PO Box 7400, Melville, NY 11747-7400, website: swatch.com.

OTHER PUBLICATIONS

Chronos (MAG), 2403 Champa St., Denver, CO 80205, website: www.goldenbellpress.com/goldenbellsite/Pages/aboutchronos.html.

Clocks (MAG), 1926 S. Pacific Coast Hwy., Suite 204, Redondo Beach, CA 90277, e-mail: wiseowl@sprintmail.com, website: www.wiseowl magazines.com.

InSync (MAG), 3946 Glade Valley Dr., Kingwood, TX 77339, e-mail: Webmaster@insync-watch.com, website: www.insync-watch.com.

The Premium Watch Watch (NL), 24 San Rafael Dr., Rochester, NY 14618-3702, e-mail: watcher1@rochester.rr.com (promotional, advertising, and premium watches).

ARCHIVES & MUSEUMS

American Clock and Watch Museum, Inc., 100 Maple St., Bristol, CT 06010, 860-583-6070, fax: 860-583-1862, website: www.clockmuseum.org.

Clockmakers' Library, Guildhall Library, Aldermanbury, London, England EC2P 2EJ, website: www.clockmakers.org/page3.html.

National Clock and Watch Museum, 514 Poplar St., Columbia, PA 17512-2130, 717-684-8261, fax: 717-684-0878, website: www.nawcc.org/museum/museum. htm.

APPRAISERS

Many of the auctions and repair services listed in this section will also do appraisals. *See also* the general list of "Appraisal Groups," page 483.

Timexpo Museum, 175 Union St., Waterbury, CT 06706, 203-346-5714, fax: 203-755-8531, e-mail: crosa@timexpo.com, website: www.timexpo.com. Information on Waterbury clocks, Ingersoll watches, Timex watches, Ingersoll and Timex character watches, and related memorabilia.

AUCTIONS

❖➤ SEE ALSO "SELLING THROUGH AUCTION HOUSES," PAGE 485.

Antiquorum Auctioneers, 609 Fifth Ave., Suite 503, New York, NY 10017, 212-750-1103, fax: 212-750-6127, e-mail: newyork@antiquorum.com, website: www.antiquorum.com. Auctions of important collector's watches, wristwatches, and clocks about eight times a year, of which three are held in Geneva, one in Hong Kong, and three to four sales in New York. Buyer's premium 15% up to $50,000; 10% over $50,000. Prices realized mailed on request. Appraisals.

Kenneth S. Hays & Associates, Inc., 120 S. Spring St., Louisville, KY 40206, 502-584-4297, fax: 502-585-5896, e-mail: kenhays@haysauction.com, website: www.haysauction.com. Specializing in clocks, antique dolls, and Victorian antiques. Mail and phone bids accepted. No buyer's premium. Prices realized mailed after some auctions. Appraisals.

REPAIRS, PARTS & SUPPLIES

❖➤ SEE ALSO "CONSERVATORS & RESTORERS," PAGE 520.

Another Time Restorations, PO Box 42013, Portland, OR 97242-0013, 503-656-9757. Clock repair and complete restoration.

Antique Restorations, The Old Wheelwrights', Brasted Forge, Brasted, Kent TN16 1JL, England, 011-44-1959-563863, fax: 011-44-1959-561262, e-mail: bfc@ antique-restorations.org.uk, website: www.antique-restorations.org.uk. Clock case restoration, brass castings and repair, polishing, documentation service.

Antiques Collectibles & Stuff, 12 W. Olentangy St., Powell, OH 43065, 614-846-8724, fax: 614-846-8724, e-mail: eiann41080@aol.com, website: www.antiques-collectiblestuff.com. Clock repairs and restoration.

Astrid C. Donnellan, 21 Mast Hill Rd., Hingham, MA 02043, 781-749-1441. Antique clock dials painted; reverse painting on glass. Restoration and reproduction services. Brochure.

B.D. Hutchinson, 1274 Long Pond Rd., Brewster, MA 02631, 508-896-6395 phone/fax, e-mail: timefiles@capecod.net. Antique clocks and watches repaired and restored.

Brass Foundry Castings, Brasted Forge, Brasted, Kent TN16 1JL, England, 011-44-1959-563863, fax: 011-44-1959-561262, e-mail: info@brass castings.co.uk, website: www.brasscastings.co.uk. Detailed mail order of over 900 fittings dating back to the seventeenth century, including a variety of clock mounts; a range of escutcheon pins and hand-cut nails; kidney bow keys; and many other previously unobtainable fittings, handmade and produced by the lost wax casting process.

Butterworths Clocks, Inc., 5300 59th Ave. W., Muscatine, IA 52761, 563-263-6759, fax: 888-399-8463, e-mail: bci@muscanet.com. Wholesale distributors of factory replacement clock movements for modern clocks. Representing Herle, Kieninger, Urgos, Regula, and Hubert Herr movements. Free brochure.

Chains Chains Chains, 25 N. Federal Hwy., Dania, FL 33004, 954-922-5002. Men's pocket watch chains, vest and sport chains, slide chains.

China and Crystal Clinic, 1808 N. Scottsdale Rd., Tempe, AZ 85281, 480-945-5510 or 602-478-7857 or 602-568-9008 or 800-658-9197, fax: 480-945-1079, e-mail: jbenterprises2@earthlink.net, website: chinaandcrystalclinic.com. Restoration or conservation of porcelain clocks and other objects. Appraisals.

Dial House, 3971 Buchanan Hwy., Dallas, GA 30132, 770-943-9786. Antique clock dial restoration. Second location at 3930 Brownsville Rd., Powder Springs, GA 30127.

European Watch & Casemakers, Ltd., PO Box 1314, Highland Park, NJ 08904-1314, 732-777-0111, 10:00 A.M.–6:00 P.M., e-mail: horology@web span.net. Restoration of unusual clocks and watches. Can make any part or restore any watch and can forge alloys appropriate to the period of the object. Cases made for watch movements. Consulting and appraisals. Free brochure.

Faire Harbour Ltd., 44 Captain Peirce Rd., Scituate, MA 02066, 781-545-2465, fax: 781-545-2465. Antique clock repair.

Fendley's Antique Clocks, 2535 Himes St., Irving, TX 75060, 972-986-7698, 6:30 P.M.–10:00 P.M. Specializing in wheel and pinion cutting for antique clocks. Clock parts made, spring barrels repaired or made new. Free catalog.

Ferenc Bitt, 6260–114 Glenwood Ave., Pleasant Valley Promenade, Raleigh, NC 27612, 919-789-8003. Repair of antique fine watches and clocks.

Fred Catterall, 54 Short St., New Bedford, MA 02740-2162, 508-997-8532, 9:00 A.M.–9:00 P.M., e-mail: FTicktock@aol.com. Replacement pictures for spring-driven banjo clocks in original colors and sizes. Paper dials. Brochure and color photo $1.50.

Hamilton, PO Box 815, West Newbury, MA 01985, 800-439-8774, fax: 978-363-2638, e-mail: hamfurnrestore@greennet.net, website: www.patinarestoration.com. Clock case restoration. Brass cleaning and sealing; hardware replacement. Additional services: research, consulting, inspections, condition reports, and photo documentation. Custom finishing. Lecturing. References.

Herwig Lighting, Inc., PO Box 768, Russellville, AR 72811, 800-643-9523 or 479-968-2621, fax: 479-968-6422, e-mail: Herwig@Herwig.com, website: www.herwig.com. Cast-aluminum reproduction brackets, posts, and street clocks. Free catalog.

Horton Brasses, 47-51 Nooks Hill Rd., PO Box 120, Cromwell, CT 06416, 860-754-9127, fax: 860-635-6473, e-mail: barb@horton-brasses.com, website: www.horton-brasses.com. Clock finials and hardware. Much hand-forged iron in stock. Polishes, waxes, and cleaners. Catalog $4.

Klockit, PO Box 636, Dept. KG8, Lake Geneva, WI 53147, 800-556-2548 or 262-248-7000, fax: 262-248-9899, e-mail: klockit@klockit.com, website: www.klockit.com. Clock kits and clock components, quartz and mechanical. Hands, dials, hardware, finishing supplies, and more. Free catalog. Products also available through the website.

Martines' Antiques, 516 E. Washington, Chagrin Falls, OH 44022, 440-247-6421, fax: 216-397-1048, e-mail: martines-silver@e2grow.com, website: martines-silver.e2grow.com. Clock repair.

Medford Clock & Barometer, 3 Union St., Medford, NJ 08055, 609-953-0014, fax: 609-953-0411, e-mail: medclock@aol.com, website: www.medfordclock.com. Clock repair. Antique mercury barometers repaired and restored. New mercury barometer tubes hand blown on site.

Merritt's Antiques, Inc., 1860 Weavertown Rd., PO Box 277, Douglassville, PA 19518-0277, 610-689-9541, fax: 610-689-4538, e-mail: info@merritts.com, website: www.merritts.com. Clock repair supplies, tools, books, and parts. Catalog $3.

Mike's Clock Clinic, 424 S. Pacific Coast Hwy., Rear Unit, PO Box 543, Redondo Beach, CA 90277, 310-344-1567, e-mail: atmosman@earthlink.net, website: www.atmos-man.com. Specializing in Atmos and 400-day clock repair. Most clock motors and rotors for sale. Instructions available for Atmos and 400-day clocks.

Poor Richard's Restoration & Preservation Studio Workshop, 101 Walnut St., Montclair, NJ 07042, 973-783-5333, fax: 973-744-1939, e-mail: jrickford@webtv.com, website: www.rickford.com. Restoration, conservation, archival and preservation services for clocks and other objects. Restoration of family memorabilia and keepsakes. By appointment, Tues.–Fri. noon–5:00 P.M., Sat. noon–3:00 P.M.

Rene Rondeau, PO Box 391, Corte Madera, CA 94976, 415-924-6534, e-mail: rene@hamiltonwristwatch.com, website: www.hamiltonwristwatch.com. Repair and restoration of antique Hamilton watches, specializing in electric watches of the 1950s and 1960s. Free brochure.

Reversen Time Inc., 6005 Bunchberry Ct., Raleigh, NC 27616-5454, 919-981-7323, e-mail: hamblest@mindspring.com, website: www.mind

spring.com/~hamblesl/index.html. Clock case restoration and conservation; missing elements carved; clock movements repaired.

S. LaRose, Inc., 3223 Yanceyville St., PO Box 21208, Greensboro, NC 27420-1208, 336-621-1936, fax: 336-621-0706, e-mail: info@slarose.com, website: www.slarose.com. Clock and watch parts, bands and straps, clock case parts, dials, hands, mainsprings, movements, and pendulums. Tools, supplies, books, and videos for the watchmaker, clockmaker, jeweler, or hobbyist. Catalog $2.50.

Simonson Clock Shop, 226 S. Main St., Wellington, OH 44090, 440-647-0049. Complete restoration of clocks and automata.

Swiss Time, 86 Exchange St., Portland, ME 04101, 207-773-0997. Clocks and watches restored; on-site service.

Tani Engineering, The Antique Nook, Inc., 6226 Waterloo, Box 338, Atwater, OH 44201, 330-947-2268 or 330-325-0645. Custom-made mainsprings for clocks and some watches. Repair and cut gears. Custom machine work.

Thomas R. John, Sr., PO Box 35, South Thomaston, ME 04858, 207-594-9341, 9:00 A.M.–5:00 P.M. Repair and restoration of pre-1900 wooden and brass wheel clocks.

Timewise, 5921 Moff Rd., Atwater, OH 44201, 330-947-0047, fax: 330-947-2507. Antique clock repair.

Venerable Classics, 645 Fourth St., Suite 208, Santa Rosa, CA 95404, 800-531-2891, 707-575-3626, fax: 707-575-4913 call first, website: www.venerableclassics.com. Restoration of ceramic clock cases and more. Please call with questions. Free brochure on request.

The Village Clock Shop, PO Box 773, 97 S. Main St., Waynesville, OH 45068, 513-897-0805, fax: 513-897-0805, e-mail: wood1@erinet.com. Clock repair, case restoration, clock glass and parts. Free brochure.

Village Goldsmith, 5333 Forest Ln., Dallas, TX 75244, 972-934-0449, fax: 972-934-1233, e-mail: eric.wright@att.net. Watch and clock repair.

Vod Varka Springs, 1251 U.S. Rt. 30, PO Box 170, Clinton, PA 15026-0170, 724-695-3268. Custom-made springs and wire forms. Flat-type springs for clocks. Made to order per print or sample. Can make almost anything out of wire or flat stock.

Woodcraft Supply Corp., PO Box 1686, Parkersburg, WV 26102-1686, 800-225-1153 for orders; 800-535-4482 for customer service; 800-535-4486 for technical service, e-mail: custserv@woodcraft.com, website: www.woodcraft.com. Clock repair supplies. Free catalog.

WTC Associates, Inc., 2532 Regency Rd., Lexington, KY 40503, 859-278-4171, fax: 859-277-5720. Clock repair; missing parts reproduced. Hand engraving.

Yankee Drummer House of Time, Unit 11, Londonderry Commons, Londonderry, NH 03053, 603-437-2410 or 800-457-2410, fax: 603-886-0631, e-mail: ydclockdr@aol.com. Repair and restoration of clocks and watches. Some parts available. Can fabricate parts or find a source for any part for any timepiece. European clocks a specialty. Repair and shipping services worldwide. Mon.–Fri. 10:00 A.M.–6:00 P.M., Sat. 10:00 A.M.–5:00 P.M.

➤ **SEE ALSO CONSERVATORS & RESTORERS, PAGE 520, FOR MORE CLOCK AND WATCH REPAIR SOURCES.**

➤ **CLOISONNÉ, SEE METALS**

COIN-OPERATED MACHINES

There is a corollary to the "Kovelism" that anything that moves or makes noise has a value. There is even more value to anything with a money slot. This includes most types of music-making machines, from nineteenth-century Swiss boxes to 1950s jukeboxes. Slot machines, gumball machines, and the myriad game-like machines known as "trade stimulators" or amusement park coin-ops are included in the valued "it moves and makes money" antiques.

Granny fortune-tellers, horse-race games, claw-digger steam-shovel games, love testers, and Kinetoscopes (movie machines), among many others, all sell well. Collectors are more interested in the item's "gimmick" value than in its age. A moving figure, an unusual configuration, or a very elaborate case will add value. Even perfume dispensers, match, cigarette, gumball, or sandwich machines, and all types of games of chance sell well. Be sure the machine works with U.S. coins. Some English games have been imported; their value is much lower.

"Trade stimulators" were games that encouraged the sale of cigarettes, cigars, drinks, and other products or services. A slot machine was made to pay out money from the machine, while the trade stimulator rewarded the player with products given out later by the store clerk or with free games. It was an easier machine to make but often had many of the other features of a slot machine.

Jukeboxes gained favor as collectibles during the 1970s. The general rule is that the more neon lights and Art Deco trim there is on a jukebox, the more it will be in demand and the higher the price. There are several reproductions on the market now, each selling for over $1,000.

The highest prices for slot machines and coin-operated games are paid by the dealers and auctioneers who specialize in them. Contact these people at the appropriate shows or sales listed in the antiques trading papers and in the magazines written for collectors in this area. If you are selling any type of slot machine or gambling device, be sure to check the laws in your state, since the sale of these items is illegal in some places. Even owning a slot machine is against the law in some cities.

The easiest way to sell a large game or jukebox is through pictures and descriptions. Buyers won't travel to your house if the machine doesn't seem to be a good one. You must make the effort to take pictures and write letters, place ads in publications or on the Internet, or talk to dealers, or you will get very little for the machine. A neighbor may think it would be a nice toy for the basement, but only a real collector will pay a top price.

The make, model, serial number, patent dates, address of the manufacturer, and other important information can be found on an identification plate under or behind the machine. A dealer or serious collector can identify a jukebox from a picture. (So can you, if you get the right books from the library.) Even arcade games and pinball machines can be identified from clear photographs. Take a picture of the top playing area and another of the back glass area so all details show well.

REPAIR

Any broken machine that should move or make noise is worth less than half the value it would have if it were in working condition. Although many coin-operated machines sell for thousands of dollars if perfect, some types of machines are so difficult to repair they are worth only about 20 percent if broken. But remember that many of these machines sell for thousands of dollars if perfect. Buying parts for any of the coin-operated machines requires some ingenuity. Broken machines can be found in special shops and shows, but some of the best buys are made by smart collectors who follow their local newspaper's classified section. A machine in very poor condition is still useful for parts that can be used to repair other machines. There are specialists who have the parts and know how to fix slot machines and jukeboxes.

Reprints of some of the original instruction books can also be found. There are also several books that give the history of jukeboxes and list the models and stores that sell parts or repair existing machines.

➥ SEE ALSO ADVERTISING COLLECTIBLES

REFERENCE BOOKS

An American Premium Guide to Jukeboxes and Slot Machines, 3rd edition,
    Jerry Ayliffe (Books Americana/Krause, Iola, WI, 1991).
Jukeboxes, Michael Adams, Jürgen Lukas, and Thomas Maschke (Schiffer,
    Atglen, PA, 1996).

PRICE BOOKS

The Always Jukin' Official Guide to Collectible Jukeboxes (Michael F. Baute,
    221 Yesler Way, Seattle, WA 98104, 1996).
The Complete Pinball Book, Marco Rossignoli (Schiffer, Atglen, PA, 2000).
Guide to Vintage Trade Stimulators & Counter Games, Richard M. Bueschel
    (Schiffer, Atglen, PA, 1997).
Loose Change Red Book for Trade Stimulators and Counter Games, 3rd
    edition, Daniel R. Mead, editor (Mead Publishing Co., Las Vegas, NV,
    1996, price update 1997-98).
Silent Salesmen Too: The Encyclopedia of Collectible Vending Machines, Bill
    Enes (8520 Lewis Drive, Lenexa, KS 66227-3277, 1995).

CLUBS & THEIR PUBLICATIONS

Coin-Operated Collectors Association, *C.O.C.A. Times* (MAG), 15200 Mansel
    Ave., Lawndale, CA 90260, e-mail: DJDAVIDS@earthlink.net, website:
    www.coinopclub.org.

OTHER PUBLICATIONS

Always Jukin (NP), 1952 1st Ave. S., #6, Seattle, WA 98134, e-mail:
    AlwaysJuke@aol.com, website: hometown.aol.com/AlwaysJuke.
Antique Amusements, Slot Machine & Jukebox Gazette (NP), 909 26th St.
    NW, Washington, DC 20037, e-mail: durham@GameRoom
    Antiques.com, website: www.GameRoomAntiques.com.
Gameroom Magazine (MAG), PO Box 41, Keyport, NJ 07735-0041, e-mail:
    coinop@gameroommagazine.com, website: www.gameroom
    magazine.com (arcade games, carousels, Coca-Cola collectibles,
    music boxes, neon, radios, slots, etc.).
Jukebox Collector (MAG), 2545 SE 60th Ct., #110, Des Moines, IA 50317-5099.
PinGame Journal (MAG), 31937 Olde Franklin Dr., Farmington Hills, MI
    48334-1731, e-mail: jim@pingamejournal.com, website:
    www.pingamejournal.com.

APPRAISERS

Many of the auctions and repair services listed in this section will
also do appraisals. *See also* the general list of "Appraisal Groups" on
page 483.

AUCTIONS

↦ SEE ALSO "SELLING THROUGH AUCTION HOUSES," PAGE 485.

Howard B. Parzow, PO Box 3464, Gaithersburg, MD 20885-3464, 301-977-6741, fax: 301-208-8947, e-mail: hparzow@aol.com, website: www.hbparzowauctioneer.com. Coin-operated machines, Americana, advertising, and country store. Mail and phone bids accepted. Buyer's premium 10%. Appraisals.

Randy Inman Auctions, PO Box 726, Waterville, ME 04903-0726, 207-872-6900, fax: 207-872-6966, e-mail: inman@inmanauctions.com, website: www.inmanauctions.com. Specializing in coin-operated machines, antique advertising, and related items. Mail and phone bids accepted. Buyer's premium 10%. Prices realized available after auction. Appraisals.

US Amusement Auctions, PO Box 4819, Louisville, KY 40204, 502-451-1263, fax: 502-897-7771, e-mail: webmaster@usamusement.com, website: www.usamusement.com. Auctions of video games, pinball machines, jukeboxes, darts, kiddie rides, pool tables, and redemption games held in various locations. Buyer's premium 5%.

REPAIRS, PARTS & SUPPLIES

↦ SEE ALSO "CONSERVATORS & RESTORERS," PAGE 520.

A.M.C. Publishing Co., PO Box 3007, Arlington, WA 98223, 360-653-1799, fax: 360-651-9099, e-mail: smokey1234@earthlink.net. Manuals for Bally pinball machines.

American Alloy Foundry, 112-120 S. Eden St., Baltimore, MD 21231, 410-276-1930, fax: 410-276-1947. Brass, bronze, and aluminum castings in the sand mold method. Can reproduce from originals to make exact copies. Slot machine parts, etc. Brochure $1.

American Gumball Machine Co., 13900 Tahiti Way #112, Marina del Rey, CA 90292, 800-779-2764, fax: 310-823-6932, e-mail: akra@aol.com, website: www.antiquegumball.com. Gumball machine parts and repair; reference books. Stands, candy and gum refills.

Arcade Classics, 3055 Wellbrook Dr., Loganville, GA 30052, 770-554-2379. Repairs pinball and coin-operated machines, specializing in electro-mechanical games. Will come to your home in the Atlanta area.

Bernie Berten, 9420 S. Trumbull Ave., Evergreen Park, IL 60805, 708-499-0688, fax: 708-499-5979. Springs, parts, reel strips, award cards for antique slot machine repair and restoration. Send 4 first-class stamps for 48-page catalog.

Bill & Jan Berning, 135 W. Main St., Genoa, IL 60135-1101, 815-784-3134. Coin-operated scales, parts, restorations, and repairs. Send SASE for free scale instructions, diagrams, and information.

Charles Maier, Jukebox Service, 3016 Derry Terr., Philadelphia, PA 19154-2519, 215-637-2869, fax: 215-637-2869. Repair of Rock-ola jukeboxes, amplifiers, circuit boards, and computers. Reprints of jukebox service manuals, all makes and models. Send SASE for service manual list.

Classic Slot Machines, Bob Levy, 2802 Center St., Pennsauken, NJ 08109, 609-663-2554. Repair and restoration of classic slot machines. Appraisals.

David Claxton, 2952 Lynn Ave., Billings, MT 59102-6640, 406-656-0949, e-mail: mtslots@att.net. Repair and restoration of mechanical slot machines. Appraisals of old machines.

DH Distributors, PO Box 48623, Wichita, KS 67201, 316-684-0050, Mon.–Sat., fax: 316-684-0050. Makes capacitor cans.

Donal Murphy, 22 Brighton Ln., Oakbrook, IL 60523, e-mail: donalmurphy@earthlink.net. Pinball parts: coils, caps, drop targets, flipper bushings, rollovers, doors, front moldings, backglasses, playfields, plastic shield sets, flippers, etc.

Donnie Kueller, 2671 NE 16th St., Pompano Beach, FL 33062-3232, 954-946-5883 (October 10–May 1). Summer address (May 1–Oct. 10): 51 Maulbeck Ave., Westwood, NJ 07675-3212, 732-716-9723, fax 732-716-9724. Jukeboxes from the '40s, '50s, and '60s restored and reconditioned. Parts. Rental. Catalog $2 plus two first class stamps.

Drop Coin in Slot, 13820 Country Home Rd., Bowling Green, OH 43402. Slot machines, gumball machines, trade stimulators, old arcade games, and other coin-operated machines made before 1950 repaired.

DurFee's Coin-op, 57 S. Main St., Orange, MA 01364, 978-544-3800, fax: 978-544-8250, e-mail: durfee@jukeboxparts.com, website: www.jukeboxparts.com. Jukebox parts, service manuals, and related items. Check their website for a listing of jukebox parts available.

Gameroom Warehouse, 826 W. Douglas, Wichita, KS 67203, 316-263-1848, fax: 316-263-1849, e-mail: home@gameroom.com, website: www.gameroom.com. Repair and restoration of coin-operated machines. Parts, schematics, and operating instructions for all kinds of coin-operated machines; pinball glasses; balls and cabinets for Pachinkos. Will ship worldwide.

George Bursor, 977 Kings Rd., Schenectady, NY 12303, 518-346-3713, e-mail: jukebox950@aol.com. Restoration of jukebox tube amplifiers, Seeburg '50s jukeboxes, and tube radios. Old jukebox parts available at times. Send SASE for free brochure.

Great Canadian Nickelodeon Co. Ltd., RR #4, Mount Forest, ON, Canada N0G 2L0, 519-323-3582, e-mail: RonaldS715@aol.com, website: members.aol.com/tgcnc. Complete restoration or repairs of all automated music machines: player pianos, pipe organs, monkey organs, music boxes, nickelodeons, orchestrions, jukeboxes, band and fairground organs, carousel organs, etc. Custom-built parts. Brochure.

JPBinc., Stanhope, NJ, 973-691-2585, fax: 973-691-5633, e-mail: tina@jpb inc.com, website: www.jpbinc.com. Pinball repair.

Jukebox Junction, Inc., PO Box 70, Cumming, IA 50061, 515-981-4019, fax: 515-981-4657. Reproduction jukebox parts. Restored antique jukeboxes. Catalog $2.50.

Ken Durham, GameRoomAntiques.com, 909 26th St. NW, Washington, DC 20037, website: www.GameRoomAntiques.com. Service manuals, repair guides, and books on jukeboxes, pinball machines, slot machines, and other coin-operated machines. 45 RPM records for jukeboxes. Can help you find sources for parts and repair of coin-operated machines.

Kim Gutzke, 7134 15th Ave. S., Minneapolis, MN 55423, 612-869-4963, fax: 612-798-4169, e-mail: kgutzke@mn.rr.com. Wurlitzer jukebox grille screens and Popperette Popcorn decals. Makes 45 RPM and 78 RPM records and 10-inch picture discs for jukeboxes and phonographs.

Mayfair Amusement Co., 60-41 Woodbine St., Ridgewood, NY 11385, 718-417-5050, 10:00 A.M.–5:00 P.M., fax: 718-386-9049, e-mail: themayfair @aol.com, website: www.mayfairamusement.com. Pinball parts, backglasses, and service. Circuit board repair. Vintage parts for electromechanical and solid-state pinball machines. Large selection of pinball backglasses. Schematics and manuals. Free brochure.

Mike Zuccaro—Antique Electronics Repair, 8795 Corvus St., San Diego, CA 92126-1920, 858-271-8294, e-mail: mjzuccaro@aol.com. Repair and restoration of jukeboxes from the 1920s through the 1970s.

Nabours Novelty Inc., 320 Hwy. 55 W., Box 204, Maple Lake, MN 55358, 800-657-4657, fax: 320-963-5953, e-mail: nabours@lkollink.net, website: www.pinballplace.com. Sales, service, and parts for pinball games, jukeboxes, Foosball, darts, and related amusement devices.

New England Jukebox & Amusement Co., 77 Tolland Turnpike, Manchester, CT 06040, 860-646-1533, fax: 86-646-7278, e-mail: nejukebox @aol.com, website: www.nejukebox.com. Complete jukebox services, parts, and restorations. Sales and rentals. Pinball machines, parts, and restorations. Showroom open to the public.

Paul Biechler, Home Arcade Corp., 4611 Main St., Lisle, IL 60532, 630-964-2555, fax: 630-964-9367, e-mail: arcadehom@aol.com, website: www.homearcadecorp.com. Coca-Cola machine parts. Catalog $5. Free brochure.

Penny Arcade Restorations, 28 Southfield Ave., Stamford, CT 06902, 203-357-1913, 24-hour voice mail, fax: 203-357-1913, e-mail: gtaplin @cloud9.net. Vintage coin-operated amusement machines restored. Mechanical, electromechanical, pneumatics, part fabrication, cabinetry refinishing, marbleizing, marquees, papier-mâché, glass, carving, castings, polishing, plating.

The Pinball Resource, 8 Commerce St., Poughkeepsie, NY 12603, 845-

473-7114, fax: 845-473-7116, e-mail: pbresource@idsi.net, website: pinballresource.virtualave.net. Parts, supplies, technical information (schematics, manuals, etc.) for repairing, maintenance, and restoration of pinball machines made from 1930 to the present.

Precision Arcade Repair, 1315 Sandpiper Ln., Lilburn, GA 30047-2027, 770-985-4697, e-mail: gyrogames@aol.com, website: www.tristan mulrooney.com. Neon sign repair and servicing, also custom neons made to order.

Richies TV, Radio, & Coin-Op Repairs, New Jersey, 973-694-6374 evenings, e-mail: radiorich1@yahoo.com, website: radiorich1.freeyellow.com. Repair and restoration of antique radios, TVs, and coin-operated machines. Service and parts.

Rick Frink, 2977 Eager, Howell, MI 48843. Reproduction reel strips and award cards for antique slot machines. Old slot machines and gum or peanut machines repaired. Send 8 first class U.S. stamps for brochure.

Ted Salveson, PO Box 602, Huron, SD 57350, 605-352-2165, 11:00 A.M.–6:00 P.M. Service manuals, books, and other literature on coin-operated machines. Pool cloth, pinball legs, locks, needles, all-purpose coin-machine cleaner, and other supplies. Appraisal service.

Victory Glass Inc., 3260 Ute Ave., Waukee, IA 50263, 515-987-5765 or 888-842-5853, fax: 515-987-5762, e-mail: vicglass@ix.netcom.com, website: www.victoryglass.com. Reproduction parts for Wurlitzer, Seeburg, Rock-Ola, and AMI jukeboxes of the 1930s through 1950s. Used parts. Service manuals. Free catalog.

➔ **COINS, SEE NUMISMATIC COLLECTIBLES**
➔ **CORKSCREWS, SEE BOTTLES & GO-WITHS**
➔ **CLOTHING, SEE FASHION**

COMIC ART

COMIC BOOKS

Action Comics No. 1 was the first superhero comic. In June 1938, this comic book introduced Superman. A copy recently sold for $137,000. A copy of Marvel Comics No. 1, Oct.–Nov. 1939, in mint condition, sold in 1984 for $35,000. In 1997, a collector paid $68,500 for Detective 27, the first comic book in which Batman appeared. A copy of Detective 38, the 1940 comic book in which Batman's sidekick Robin first appeared, sold for $120,750 in 2002. Most of the high-priced comics contain superheroes.

Age alone does not determine the value of a collectible comic. Comic strips started in 1896 with the introduction of the "Yellow Kid."

The first monthly comic book was the 10-cent "Famous Funnies," which appeared in July 1934. Comics were popular during the 1940s with children, young adults, and especially servicemen. After the war, there was a movement to censor comics to remove the violence and sex, and many comic books were burned. The paper drives of the war and the reformation movement after the war meant few of the old copies remain. Other copies disappeared because the newsprint used for comics was easily damaged by heat, light, and moisture.

Those comics that were not destroyed by a series of young readers were often preserved until a tidy mother decided they were no longer worth saving. It is the lucky collector who finds a box of well-preserved, old comic books in an attic where they avoided house-cleaning days. Comic books are wanted by young collectors who specialize in superheroes, Westerns, funny animals, jungle, SF (science fiction), or special issues or full years of favored comics. They are also purchased by serious older collectors who have more money and more expensive desires.

Comic collecting became an organized pastime about 1960. Several magazines and newspapers started that told the history of comics, reported on new comics, and, of course, included buy and sell ads. Today there are comic shops and comic shows in most major cities. Reprints, price books, and research materials are available. Most comic collectors are not children; they are affluent, educated adult males.

The easiest place to sell old comic books is at the special comic book stores. You may be able to find one nearby. If there is no shop listed in the Yellow Pages of the telephone book, you could try selling at a comic show, a mall show, or a store that sells used books. Check the local papers or ask your friends' children. If you find a large collection of comic books, you should go to a comics convention. Trading takes place at the convention and in the rooms of the hotel during the convention days and nights. The standard comic price guides, including the original one, *The Overstreet Comic Book Price Guide,* by Robert Overstreet, list almost every title and issue. The prices are high retail, and dealers at a comic show often start out offering to sell you a comic at half the Overstreet price. You will be paid even less for your comics, though very rare editions usually hold their value.

Condition is very important. A serious collector stores comics in special archival plastic bags to protect them from added tears, cover bends, or spine damage. When pricing comics, remember to check condition. This is one field of collecting where finding a retail price is as simple as reading a price guide available in every library and most bookstores. The comic must be in original, unrestored condition. It should not be repaired by gluing, restapling, recoloring, trimming, or bleaching. Rusty staples, bad printing, creases, even yellowed paper will lower the value. Mint copies have almost-white pages and glossy covers. A good copy has suffered slightly from average use, slight soil, possible creases, or minor tears, but has no tape or missing pages.

ORIGINAL COMIC ART

It is not only comic books that are collected, but also comic strips from newspapers, the original art from comics and cartoons, and even the original celluloid drawings used to make animated movie cartoons. Prices can be surprisingly high. The original art for a 1944 "Prince Valiant" strip sold for $20,700 in 2002. Most strips sell for hundreds: a "Lil' Abner" 1930s strip is worth around $700. Disney cels were offered for sale to tourists at Disneyland when it first opened. A framed cel was sold for about $15. Each cel was marked on the back with a short history of celluloids. Other genuine cels sold years earlier by Courvoisier Art Galleries in San Francisco (marked on the mat framing the cel and on the back) are prized by collectors. A scene from "Snow White" showing the evil queen as a hag dipping the apple into a pot of poison sold in 1986 for $30,800. A black and white cel of an early Donald Duck in "The Orphan's Benefit" brought $286,000. Other original comic art used for posters or publicity also sells for thousands of dollars. There are new cels being made today by a slightly different method. Cartoons are now made with the aid of computers and the hand-painted original cel is not needed. Special hand-painted cels are made by Disney and other studios and marketed as "cels." These are often sold for high prices because they are limited editions. Because they are so recent, the rules for selling are very different from those for old cels. They are difficult to sell and are bought by those dealing in newer cels.

The original art for comic books and comic strips was so undervalued before 1970 that it was often burned by the newspaper syndicates. The artists of the comics you read now usually own their art and either give it to special friends or sell it. A single strip is worth over $200 if it is the work of a popular artist, and under $25 if it's by a forgotten artist. The subject matter makes a difference in the price, too. Old political cartoons and sports cartoons for local papers are of minimal value. Any strip for **PRINCE VALIANT, LI'L ABNER**, or **YELLOW KID** is of value. All types of comic art sell at comic book shows.

It is easy to sell good comics by mail or Internet. Buyers look for comic books through the ads in comic collector publications and books.

REPAIR AND CARE

Collectors have become serious about original comic drawings as art. Most of these materials are now of enough historic importance to be found in universities and museums. The strips and "cels" (celluloid pictures used for movie cartoons) were not made to be permanent, and they fade and deteriorate easily. Watch out for excessive light, heat, or humidity, which quickly damages the materials. There are restorers for many of these items, but the restoration is expensive.

COMIC-RELATED MATERIALS

Little Lulu dolls, posters of Spiderman, lunch boxes printed with pictures of the Flintstones, cookie jars, and anything else that shows a cartoon character are all collected by someone. The best place to sell these items is to the comic book and comic art collectors. Dealers at flea markets, shopping mall antiques shows, and Internet malls are also looking for these items.

➥ **SEE ALSO MOVIE MEMORABILIA, PAPER COLLECTIBLES, PHOTOGRAPHY.**

REFERENCE BOOKS

Official Overstreet Comic Book Grading Guide, Robert M. Overstreet and
  Arnold T. Blumberg (House of Collectibles, NY, 2003).

PRICE BOOKS

2001 Comic Book Checklist and Price Guide, 7th edition, Peter Bickford,
  Maggie Thompson, and Brent Frankenhoff (Krause, Iola, WI, 2000).
Animation Art at Auction since 1994, Jeff Lotman (Schiffer, Atglen, PA,
  1998).
Cartoon Toys & Collectibles, David Longest (Collector Books, Paducah, KY,
  1999).
Collecting Garfield, Jan Lindenberger (Schiffer, Atglen, PA, 2000).
Collecting Original Comic Strip Art, Jeffrey M. Ellinport (Antique Trader
  Books, Norfolk, VA 1999).
Comics Buyers Guide: 2003 Comic Book Checklist and Price Guide, 9th edition,
  Brent Frankenhoff et al. (Krause, Iola, WI, 2002).
Comics Values Annual, 2001, 8th edition, Alex G. Malloy (Krause, Iola, WI,
  2001).

Looney Tunes Collectibles, Debra S. Braun (Schiffer, Atglen, PA, 1999).

More Peanuts Gang Collectibles: An Unauthorized Handbook and Price Guide, Jan Lindenberger and Cher Porges (Schiffer, Atglen, PA, 1999).

More Smurf Collectibles: An Unauthorized Handbook & Price Guide, Jan Lindenberger (Schiffer, Atglen, PA, 1998).

More Snoopy Collectibles: An Unauthorized Guide, Jan Lindenberger with Cher Porges (Schiffer, Atglen, PA, 1997).

Official Overstreet Comic Book Price Guide, annual, Robert M. Overstreet (House of Collectibles, New York).

Peanuts: The Home Collection, Freddi Karin Margolin (Antique Trader Books, Dubuque, IA, 1999).

The Unauthorized Guide to "The Simpsons" Collectibles, Robert W. Getz (Schiffer, Atglen, PA, 1998).

The Unauthorized Guide to Snoopy Collectibles, Jan Lindenberger (Schiffer, Atglen, PA, 1997).

CLUBS & THEIR PUBLICATIONS

NFFC: The Club for Disneyana Enthusiasts, *FantasyLine Express* (NL), PO Box 19212, Irvine, CA 92623-9212, e-mail: membership@nffc.org, website: www.nffc.org.

Official Betty Boop Fan Club, *Official Betty Boop Fan Club Newsletter* (NL), 10550 Western Ave., #133, Stanton, CA 90680-6909, e-mail: bboopfans@aol.com, website: www.geocities.com/drsdune/betty.

Peanuts Collector Club, Inc., *Peanuts Collector* (NL), 539 Sudden Valley, Bellingham, WA 98226, e-mail: acpodley@nas.com, website: www.peanutscollectorclub.com.

Pogo Fan Club, *Fort Mudge Most* (NL), Spring Hollow Books, 6908 Wentworth Ave. S., Richfield, MN 55423.

Toonerville Collectors Club, *Toonerville Times* (NL), c/o Asa Sparks, 6045 Camelot Ct., Montgomery, AL 36117-2555, e-mail: asasparks@mind spring.com, website: erols.com/diesel/toonerville.

OTHER PUBLICATIONS

Cartoon Times (NL), Cartoon Art Museum, 655 Mission St., San Francisco, CA 94105, website: www.cartoonart.org.

The Cel Block, PO Box 175, Geneva, OH 44041, e-mail: jenia@cel-block.com, website: www.cel-block.net (animation art auction price guide in several formats: printed, CD-ROM and online).

Comics Buyer's Guide (NP), 700 E. State St., Iola, WI 54990-0001, e-mail: info@krause.com, website: www.krause.com.

Comics Journal (MAG), 7563 Lake City Way NE, Seattle, WA 98115, e-mail: fbicomix@fantagraphics.com, website: www.tcj.com (covers the comics medium from an arts-first perspective).

Hogan's Alley (MAG), PO Box 47684, Atlanta, GA 30362, e-mail: hoganletters@aol.com, website: hoganmag.com.

Tomart's Disneyana Update (MAG), 3300 Encrete Ln., Dayton, OH 45439-1944, website: tomart.com.

ARCHIVES & MUSEUMS

Barker Character, Comic & Cartoon Museum, 1188 Highland Ave., Cheshire, CT 06410-1624, 800-224-CELS, e-mail: fun@barkeranimation.com, website: www.barkeranimation.com. Click on museum link.

Cartoon Art Museum, 655 Mission St., San Francisco, CA 94105, 415-227-8666, website: www.cartoonart.org.

International Museum of Cartoon Art, 201 Plaza Real, Boca Raton, FL 33432, 561-391-2200, fax: 561-391-2721, e-mail: administration @cartoon.org, website: www.cartoon.org.

APPRAISERS

Many of the auctions and repair services listed in this section will also do appraisals. *See also* the general list of "Appraisal Groups" on page 483.

AUCTIONS

➜ SEE ALSO "SELLING THROUGH AUCTION HOUSES," PAGE 485.

All-American Collectibles, Inc., 31-00 Broadway, 3rd Floor, Fair Lawn, NJ 07410, 800-872-8850, 201-797-2555, e-mail: all-american-collectibles @worldnet.att.net. Cartoon art, Americana, and baseball memorabilia. Mail bids accepted. Buyer's premium 10%.

Hake's Americana & Collectibles, PO Box 1444, York, PA 17405-1444, 717-848-1333, Mon.–Fri. 10:00 A.M.–5:00 P.M., fax: 717-852-0344, e-mail: hake@hakes.com, website: www.hakes.com. Twentieth-century nostalgia collectibles from comic characters to advertising and political Americana. Mail, phone, and Internet bids accepted. No buyer's premium. Catalog $7; yearly subscription $30. Sample catalog free. Appraisals.

The Mouse Man Ink, 11 Trumbull Ave., Wakefield, MA 01880, 781-246-3876, fax: 781-246-3876, e-mail: mouse_man@rcn.com, website: www.mouseman.com. Bi-monthly Internet auctions of Disneyana collectibles. Will evaluate Disney items made from the 1930s to the mid-1970s for a fee, $5 for the first item, $2 for each additional item. Does not evaluate cels or animation art.

Russ Cochran's Comic Art Auction, PO Box 469, 4 Court Sq., West Plains, MO 65775, 417-256-2224, fax: 417-256-5555, e-mail: ec@gemstone pub.com. Comic art auctions. Buyer's premium 10%. Mail, phone, and fax bids accepted.

REPAIRS, PARTS & SUPPLIES

➡➡ SEE ALSO "CONSERVATORS & RESTORERS," PAGE 520.

Bags Unlimited, 7 Canal St., Rochester, NY 14608, 800-767-BAGS or 716-436-9006, fax: 716-328-8526, e-mail: info@bagsunlimited.com, website: www.bagsunlimited.com. Products for storing, displaying, and shipping comics and other collectibles. Archival materials sold: polyethylene, polypropylene, Mylar, acid-free boards and storage boxes. High clarity, recyclable, 100% polyethylene bags. Three grades of backing boards, several sizes of storage boxes and divider cards.

Graphic Conservation Co., 329 W. 18th St., Suite 701, Chicago, IL 60616, 312-738-2657, fax: 312-738-3125, e-mail: info@graphicconservation.com, website: www.graphicconservation.com. Preservation of works of art on paper and paper memorabilia. Dry cleaning, stain reduction, flattening, deacidification, inpainting, tear repairs, and fills. Archival matting. Free brochure.

Northeast Document Conservation Center, 100 Brickstone Sq., Andover, MA 01810-1494, 978-470-1010, Mon.–Fri. 8:30 A.M.–4:30 P.M., fax: 978-475-6021, e-mail: nedcc@nedcc.org, website: www.nedcc.org. Nonprofit regional conservation center specializing in treatment of art and artifacts on paper. Treatment of cartoon cels. Preservation microfilming, duplication of historical photographs, preservation planning surveys, disaster assistance, technical leaflets. Free brochure.

S/R Laboratories Animation Art Conservation Center, 31200 Via Colinas, Suite 210, Westlake Village, CA 91362-3939, 818-991-9955, fax: 818-991-5418, e-mail: srlabs@earthlink.net, website: www.srlabs.com. Conservation services for most collectibles, including cels, artwork on paper, Disney Classic Collection figurines, and other objects. Custom frame shop. Animation art auctions twice yearly, May and October. Free information.

The2Buds.com, 462 W. Silver Lake Rd. N., Traverse City, MI 49684, 888-270-0552, Mon.–Fri. 9:00 A.M.–5:00 P.M., e-mail: postcards@the 2buds.com, website: www.the2buds.com. Archival supplies for storing and displaying vintage comics and other collectibles. Comic bags, storage boxes, and more. Internet sales only.

➡➡ COMPACTS, SEE FASHION
➡➡ COPPER, SEE METALS
➡➡ COSTUME JEWELRY, SEE JEWELRY
➡➡ COUNTRY STORE, SEE ADVERTISING COLLECTIBLES
➡➡ CREDIT CARDS, SEE NUMISMATIC COLLECTIBLES
➡➡ DECOYS, SEE FOLK ART
➡➡ DENTAL, SEE SCIENTIFIC COLLECTIBLES

DOLLHOUSES

There are many collectors of dollhouses and miniature dollhouse furniture. The older and more complete the dollhouse, the more valuable. There is also an extra interest in wooden houses with lithographed paper exteriors made by **BLISS**. The name is often included on the dollhouse. Other important names are **MCLOUGHLIN BROTHERS**, **SCHOENHUT**, and **TOOTSIETOY**.

Dollhouses were made in many sizes. By the 1870s most of them were made on a scale of one inch to one foot. Dollhouses seem to sell best at special auctions; look in the section on Toys to learn where these sales are held. Local dealers can also sell dollhouses. Houses made to scale sell well, especially those made before 1930. Price new dollhouses at a toy store, and always price yours higher than the comparable new ones. Be sure the dollhouse will fit through a normal door: The price is 50 percent less if it must be dismantled to be moved or set up in a home. Do not attempt to restore or repaint a dollhouse before selling it. Keep all loose pieces, or glue trim back in place, but do nothing major. Most buyers will want to do their own restoration. We have even seen a dollhouse sold in pieces in a plastic bag.

Dollhouse furniture was made to the same scale as the dollhouses and is always the easiest miniature to sell. However, anything in miniature is in demand and can bring surprisingly high prices. Doll-size dishes or dollhouse-size dishes, doll-size chairs or dollhouse-size chairs, and other decorative objects, from tiny needlepoint rugs to silverware and vases of flowers, sell well. A fine 4-inch chair could sell for over $100.

Many antiques dealers have a case filled with what are called "smalls" by the trade. Smalls include all the tiny, expensive, and easy-to-misplace items. Always look for a dealer with dollhouse smalls. If you own a furnished dollhouse or many pieces of furniture, try talking to dealers at a miniature show. These shows are for collectors of old and new dollhouse items and are often listed in your local newspaper. The national collector groups and collector magazines for miniature enthusiasts have complete show listings printed each month. They often list prices for new miniatures that can help you set a price for yours. Prices for any sort of old dollhouse or furnishings are listed in general price books.

There are clubs and shows for collectors of miniatures in most parts of the country. Craftsmen who make new miniatures can often repair old ones.

↪ SEE ALSO DOLLS, TOYS

PRICE BOOKS

Antique & Collectible Dollhouses and Their Furnishings, Dian Zillner and Patty Cooper (Schiffer, Atglen, PA, 1998).

Doll Furniture: 1950s–1980s, Jean Mahan (Hobby House Press, Grantsville, MD, 1997).

CLUBS & THEIR PUBLICATIONS

Miniature Piano Enthusiast Club, *Musically Yours!* (NL), 633 Pennsylvania Ave., Hagerstown, MD 21740, e-mail: MPEC2000@hotmail.com, website: www.angelfire.com/music2/miniaturepianoclub.

National Association of Miniature Enthusiasts, *Miniature Gazette* (MAG), PO Box 69, Carmel, IN 46082, e-mail: name@miniatures.org, website: www.miniatures.org.

OTHER PUBLICATIONS

Dollhouse Miniatures (MAG), 21027 Crossroads Circle, Waukesha, WI 53187, e-mail: cstjacques@dhminiatures.com, website: www.dhminiatures.com.

Dolls House World (MAG), 208 Fourth St. SW, Kasson, MN 55944, e-mail: info@dollshouseworld.com.co.uk, website: www.dollshouseworld.com.

Miniature Collector (MAG), 30595 W. Eight Mile Rd., Livonia, MI 48152-1798, website: www.miniaturecollectormag.com.

ARCHIVES & MUSEUMS

Delaware Toy & Miniature Museum, PO Box 4053, Rte. 141, Wilmington, DE 19807, 302-427-TOYS (8697), fax: 302-427-8654, e-mail: toys@thomes.net, website: www.thomes.net/toys.

Washington Dolls' House & Toy Museum, 5236 44th St., NW, Washington, DC 20015, 202-244-0024 or 202-363-6400.

AUCTIONS

↪ SEE ALSO "SELLING THROUGH AUCTION HOUSES," PAGE 485.

Theriault's, PO Box 151, Annapolis, MD 21404, 410-224-3655, fax: 410-224-2515, e-mail: info@theriaults.com, website: www.theriaults.com. Auctions of antique dolls, dollhouses, and related items. On-site and online auctions. Mail, phone, fax, and e-mail bids accepted. Buyer's premium 10%. Catalog $49; yearly subscription $189. Prices realized mailed after auction and available on website. Appraisals.

DOLLS

Dolls are easy to sell, but hard to price. Rare old French and German dolls from the nineteenth century bring thousands of dollars and should be sold to a top doll dealer or through an auction gallery. Several auction galleries have sales devoted just to dolls (see auction house list in Part III). The major collectors, with the most money and the best dolls, go to these auctions and pay high prices. Some sales even include lots of doll bodies, legs, arms, and eyes from old dolls, which are valued for repairs. We have seen a headless body sell for over $100.

Collectors categorize dolls by age. Traditionally, antique dolls are more than 100 years old, but recently collectors have changed their thinking to include seventy-five-year-old dolls. Some collectors consider dolls made before 1940 to be antique. Collectible dolls are from twenty-five to seventy-five years old, and modern dolls are those made during the past twenty-five years. Contemporary dolls are those still being made. The general rule is that it takes twenty years for a doll to start to go up in value, so the dolls whose prices are rising today are Barbie and other dolls of the 1960s, '70s, and '80s. The most valuable Barbie is the first model, from 1959, which has holes in the feet because it was made to fit on pegs on a stand.

If your dolls are not rare and over seventy-five years old, they will probably still sell well with dealers who specialize in dolls. The collectible foreign dolls of the 1930s to 1950s were difficult to sell for any price until the 1970s. Now they are found at most shops and doll sales. Stuffed cloth dolls, advertising and comic figures, composition dolls like Shirley Temple dolls, dolls that are replicas of famous people, characters from literature or movies, and, of course, the teenage dolls like Barbie sell quickly if they are priced properly. So does G.I. Joe (listed in this book in Toys). These are moderately priced dolls, although a few, like a mint original Shirley Temple or Barbie, will be worth over $1,000.

Many dolls are marked by the manufacturer. Look at the back of the neck, on the shoulders, or on the head of a hard porcelain or composition doll. Sometimes there are labels on the bottom of the feet, on the chest, in the clothes, or on extra tags. A few dolls can be accurately identified by the shape of eyes, face, feet, hands, or other parts, or by some peculiarity of construction. A doll expert can easily recognize these features.

Look for twentieth-century dolls marked **MATTEL**, **MADAME ALEXANDER**, **RAVCA**, **STEIFF**, **SCHOENHUT**, **LENCI**, **VOGUE**, and **STORY-BOOK**. Any **KEWPIE** or **RAGGEDY ANN** is worth money. Earlier dolls are often marked with initials or symbols. Look these up at your library in the two-volume *Collector's Encyclopedia of Dolls* by Dorothy S., Elizabeth A., and Evelyn J. Coleman.

Save all the boxes and hang tags that come with the doll. They add to the value. Always save all the accessories. The tiny pair of ice skates or the straw hat can add much to the value. If you should find the printed fabric that was sold to be made into a stuffed doll, don't cut and stuff it. It is worth more uncut. Paper dolls are also worth more uncut.

Don't restore any damaged doll unless that is your business. A collector prefers to see the doll before restoration. A dealer can have the restoration done at a lower price, so the economies of the market make it smarter to sell a doll "as is." Don't even wash the hair or the clothes. It lowers the value.

DOLL ACCESSORIES

Doll accessories sell well. Old clothing, doll carriages, chairs, and even old photographs of children with old dolls sell quickly. The celluloid pin found on the original Shirley Temple doll is so important that it has been reproduced. Barbie's clothes, including shoes, purse, and sunglasses, are valuable, and so are her accessories—the phonograph, her cars, airplane, or house. A purse or hat can be worth $10 to $25 alone. Complete, original Barbie clothing outfits sell for hundreds of dollars, even more if in original packaging. A "Midnight Blue" ball gown with cape, gloves, clutch purse, and shoes sold in 2001 for $2,820.

PRICES

If you have an antique doll or a collection of 1930s dolls, you have a valuable asset, but you must set the price to sell it. Dolls that are to be sold through a major doll auction need no formal appraisal. Just photograph the doll dressed and undressed if it is not mint. The pictures should show details of construction, a close-up of the face, and any marks or damage. Send the pictures and a description to a doll auction house. They will set the price if they accept the doll for sale.

If you want an appraisal so you can sell the doll to a dealer or friend, you can pay for one from a local doll dealer or doll hospital.

DECODING ADVERTISING COPY

WHEN READING THE ADS FOR DOLLS, IT MIGHT HELP TO KNOW THESE TERMS AND ABBREVIATIONS:

Alex.—Madame Alexander
A.M.—Armand Marseille
Amer. Char.—American character
b—back
bj body—ball-jointed body
bk—bent knees
bl—blue, blond, or blown
br—brown
c—circumference
cell.—celluloid
cl—cloth or closed
cl m—closed mouth
comp—composition
dh—dollhouse
dk—dark
EJ—Emile Jumeau
ex—excellent
f—front
gc—good condition
gl—glass
h—high
hd mk—head mark
hh—human hair
hp—hard plastic
IDMA—International Doll Makers Association
incl—included
jcb—jointed composition body
JDK—Johannes Daniel Kestner
jtd—jointed
K&R—Kämmer and Reinhardt
l—long, luster, leather, or lower
l.t.—lower teeth
m—mohair
mib—mint in box
mk—mark
mld hair—molded hair
mtd—mounted

NIADA—National Institute of American Doll Artists
NRFB—never removed from box
O.CL.M. or o/c—open-closed mouth (open lips parted but no opening in bisque)
ODACA—Original Doll Artists Council of America
oilcl—oilcloth
om—open mouth
orig—original
p—pierced
pm—papier-maché
pr—pair
pt—paint or part
ptd—painted
pw eyes—paperweight eyes
redr—redressed
rep—repair
repl—replacement
rt—right
S&H—Simon & Halbig
SFBJ—Société Française de Fabrication de Bébés et Jouets (a group of French dollmakers)
sh pl—shoulder plate
sl—sleeping
stat—stationary
sw. n.—swivel neck
syn.—synthetic
tc—terra-cotta
UFDC—United Federation of Doll Clubs
undr—undressed
u.t.—upper teeth
vgc—very good condition
w—wash

Some of the doll auction galleries will do appraisals by mail for a fee. Local members of the major appraisal societies (listed in Part III) may be able to tell you the value of your dolls. Doll appraisal clinics, where professional advice is available either for a small fee or free, are held in many parts of the country in conjunction with sales, and some doll shows also give verbal appraisals for a small fee.

There are many good books that give doll prices listed here; your bookstore or library will have them. Study these books carefully. You will usually find a doll similar to yours, but you will rarely find exactly the same doll. Even so, the prices provide a guide.

Condition is important. Even minor cracks and repaints lower the value of pre-1920 dolls by 50 to 75 percent. Although original clothes are preferred, replacements that are old retain much of the value. Once you have a general idea of the value of your doll, you can sell it through an auction or an Internet ad, to an antiques or doll dealer, in a shop, at a special doll show, at a house sale, or by any of the other methods discussed in the Introduction. There seems to be an emotional "something" that influences buyers of dolls and toys, so pricing is sometimes best set by determining how "lovable" your doll might be.

A word of caution! If you send your doll to a dealer on consignment or to an auction, always be sure to keep a complete pictorial record and a written description. Have the dealer sign and return your record after examining the doll. Too often there is an argument later about the doll's condition if the doll is returned because it couldn't be sold. Set dates for payment or the return of any unsold dolls.

REPAIR

Doll collectors judge their collections by beauty, rarity, age, and condition. Examine your old doll carefully. Has it been repainted? Is the body original? Are the arms and legs undamaged? Is the surface of the face uncracked?

Doll heads can be professionally mended. Many of the same restorers who mend porcelains will repair a china-headed doll.

Bodies can be restored or replaced. Old and new clothing is available, as are patterns for period doll dresses. A restored doll is worth more than a damaged doll, but much less than an all-original one.

The sound mechanisms of old dolls and stuffed animals can be repaired, but the restoration is expensive. To replace the voice in a "talking Barbie," the entire head must be removed and split, the voice mechanism's rubber parts replaced, the head reglued, and the joint repainted. It is sometimes less expensive to buy a new doll, but there are times when emotional attachment to a doll makes restoration a good idea.

There is a classic horror story told by doll collectors about the doll that went to a doll hospital to be repaired. When it was returned, it appeared to be a totally different doll, with a new head, new body, and new arms. The doll hospital insisted that it was the old doll, repaired. The collector was certain the old doll was so valuable that the dishonest repairer switched the parts. This is a legend, but there is the possibility of a misunderstanding any time you give your valuable items to another person. Repairs, new parts, and replacements sometimes seem to make flaws "appear." It is like hanging new curtains in a room. The room looked fine before, but after fresh, bright curtains are added, the woodwork and walls look nicked, smudged, and in need of paint and the carpet seems faded.

If you are taking a doll to be repaired, there are a few rules that must be followed to assure you and the doll hospital a happy transaction. Photograph the doll and the damaged parts. Take pictures of the marks, body, hair, and clothes. Get a written estimate of the cost of the repair and the work that is to be done before agreeing to the restoration. It is often easy to remember an old doll as more glamorous than it actually was, and sometimes when the restored doll is returned it appears unfamiliar. We often hear complaints that a head or body was replaced or that the repairs were more extensive than expected. The pictures and estimate will help prevent these problems.

➥ SEE ALSO ADVERTISING COLLECTIBLES, DOLLHOUSES, POTTERY & PORCELAIN, TOYS

REFERENCE BOOKS

Collector's Encyclopedia of Dolls, 2 volumes, Dorothy S., Elizabeth A., and Evelyn J. Coleman (Crown, New York, 1968, 1986).

German Doll Encyclopedia 1800–1939, Jürgen and Marianne Cieslik (Hobby House Press, Cumberland, MD, 1985).

Modern Collector's Dolls, 8th series, Patricia R. Smith (Collector Books, Paducah, KY, 1973–1996).

Toys, Dolls, Automata: Marks & Labels, Gwen White (B.T. Batsford, London, 1975).

PRICE BOOKS

15th Blue Book: Dolls and Values, Jan Foulke (Hobby House Press, Grantsville, MD, 2001).

200 Years of Dolls, 2nd edition, Dawn Herlocher (Krause, Iola, WI, 2002).

6th Doll Fashion Anthology, A. Glenn Mandeville (Hobby House Press, Grantsville, MD, 1998).

America's Early Advertising Paper Dolls, Lagretta Metzger Bajorek (Schiffer, Atglen, PA, 1999).

Baby-Boomer Dolls: Plastic Playthings of the 1950's & 1960's, Michele Karl (Portfolio Press, Cumberland, MD, 2000).

The Barbie Closet: Price Guide for Barbie & Friends Fashions and Accessories, 1959–1970, Patricia Long (Krause, Iola, WI, 1999).

The Barbie Doll Years: A Comprehensive Listing & Value Guide of Dolls & Accessories, 5th edition, Joyce L. and Patrick C. Olds (Collector Books, Paducah, KY, 2002).

Bobbing Head Dolls: 1960–2000, Tim Hunter (Krause, Iola, WI, 1999).

Buying and Selling Celebrity Dolls, Michele Karl (Portfolio Press, Cumberland, MD, 2002).

Characters of R. John Wright, Shirley Bertrand (Hobby House Press, Grantsville, MD, 2000).

Chatty Cathy and Her Talking Friends, Sean Kettelkamp (Schiffer, Atglen, PA, 1998).

Coffee with Barbie Doll, Sandra "Johnsie" Bryan (Schiffer, Atglen, PA, 1998).

Collector's Encyclopedia of American Composition Dolls: 1900–1950, Ursula R. Mertz (Collector Books, Paducah, KY, 1999).

Collector's Encyclopedia of Vogue Dolls, Judith Izen and Carol Stover (Collector Books, Paducah, KY, 1998).

Collector's Guide to Dolls of the 1960s and 1970s, Cindy Sabulis (Collector Books, Paducah, KY, 2000).

Composition & Wood Dolls and Toys: A Collector's Reference Guide, Michele Karl (Antique Trader Books, Dubuque, IA, 1998).

The Crissy Doll Family Encyclopedia, Carla Marie Cross (Hobby House Press, Grantsville, MD, 1998).

Crissy Doll and Her Friends, Beth Gunther (Antique Trader Books, Norfolk, VA, 1998).

Darci Cover Girl, Grace L. Simms (Hobby House Press, Grantsville, MD, 2000).

Doll Values: Antique to Modern, 6th edition, Patsy Moyer (Collector Books, Paducah, KY, 2002).

Dolls of the 40s & 50s, Carol J. Stover (Collector Books, Paducah, KY, 2002).

Dolls and Accessories of the 1950s, Dian Zillner (Schiffer, Atglen, PA, 1998).

Kewpies: Dolls and Art, 2nd edition, John Axe (Hobby House Press, Grantsville, MD, 2001).

Madame Alexander: Collector's Dolls Price Guide, No. 26, Linda Crowsey (Collector Books, Paducah, KY, 2001).

Madame Alexander: Store Exclusives and Limited Editions, Linda Crowsey (Collector Books, Paducah, KY, 2000).

Miniature Mannequins, Doris Mixon (Hobby House Press, Grantsville, MD, 2001).

Modern Collectible Dolls, 6 volumes, Patsy Moyer (Collector Books, Paducah, KY, 1997–2002).

More Enchanting Friends: Storybook Characters, Toys, and Keepsakes, Dee Hochenberry (Schiffer, Atglen, PA, 1998).

Nippon Dolls and Playthings, Joan F. Van Patten and Linda Lau (Collector Books, Paducah, KY, 2001).

Raggedy Ann and More: Johnny Gruelle's Dolls and Merchandise, Patricia Hall (Pelican Publishing, PO Box 3110, Gretna, LA 70054, 1999).

Terri Lee Dolls, Peggy Wiedman Casper (Hobby House Press, Grantsville, MD, 2001).

Warman's Dolls, R. Lane Herron (Krause, Iola, WI, 1998).

The World of Dolls: A Collector's Identification and Price Guide, Maryanne Dolan (Krause, Iola, WI, 1998).

CLUBS & THEIR PUBLICATIONS

Annalee Doll Society, *The Collector* (MAG), PO Box 1137, Meredith, NH 03253, website: www.annalee.com.

Cabbage Patch Kids Collectors Club, *Babyland in General* (NL), PO Box 714, Cleveland, GA 30528, website: www.cabbagepatchkids.com.

Chatty Cathy Collectors Club, *Chatty News* (NL), PO Box 4426, Seminole, FL 33775-4426, website: www.ttinet.com/chattycathy.

Doll Doctors' Association, *Doll Rx* (NL), 19720 NW 39th Ct., Coral City, FL 33055, website: www.gmdollseminar.com.

Friends of Bonniebrook, *Friends of Bonniebrook News* (NL), PO Box 902, Monmouth, IL 61462.

Ginny Doll Club, *The Ginny Journal* (MAG), PO Box 338, Oakdale, CA 95361, website: www.voguedolls.com.

International Rose O'Neill Club, *Kewpie Kourier* (NL), PO Box 61, Golden, CO 80402-0061, website: www.KewpieRoseONeillClub.com.

Madame Alexander Doll Club, *Review* (NL), PO Box 330, Mundelein, IL 60060, e-mail: info@madc.org, website: www.madc.org.

Modern Doll Club, *Modern Doll Journal* (NL), 305 W. Beacon Rd., Lakeland, FL 33803-7248.

Original Paper Doll Artists Guild (OPDAG), *OPDAG's Paper Doll Studio News* (NL), PO Box 14, Kingfield, ME 04947, website: www.opdag.com.

United Federation of Doll Clubs, *Doll News* (MAG), 10900 N. Pomona Ave., Kansas City, MO 64153, website: www.ufdc.org.

OTHER PUBLICATIONS

Antique & Collectible Dolls (MAG), 218 W. Woodin, Dallas, TX 75224.

Antique Doll Collector (MAG), 6 Woodside Ave., Suite 300, Northport, NY 11768, website: www.antiquedollcollector.com.

Barbie Bazaar (MAG), 5711 Eighth Ave., Kenosha, WI 53140, website: www.barbiebazaar.com.

Celebrity Doll Journal (MAG), 413 10th Ave. Ct. NE, Puyallup, WA 98372.

The Cloth Doll (MAG), PO Box 2167, Lake Oswego, OR 97035, website: www.TheClothDoll.com.

Collectors United (NP), 711 S. 3rd Ave., Chatsworth, GA 30705, e-mail: garyg@collectorsunited.com, website: www.collectorsunited.com.

Contemporary Doll Collector (MAG), 30595 W. Eight Mile Rd., Livonia, MI 48152-1798, website: www.scottpublications.com.

Doll (MAG), 208 Fourth St., Kasson, MN 55944, website: www.dollmagazine.com.

Doll Castle News (MAG), PO Box 247, Washington, NJ 07882, website: www.dollcastlenews.com.

Doll Costuming (MAG), N7450 Aanstad Rd., PO Box 5000, Iola, WI 54945, website: www.dollcostuming.net (for people who make and collect doll clothes).

Doll Reader (MAG), PO Box 420593, Palm Coast, FL 32142-9009, website: www.dollreader.com.

Dolls (MAG), PO Box 5000, Iola, WI 54945-5000, website: www.jonespublishing.com.

Dolls in Miniature (MAG), 30799 Pinetree Rd., Box 411, Cleveland, OH 44124-9939, www.dollsinmini.com.

Golden Opportunities: Paper Doll & Toy Quarterly (MAG), Box 252, Golden, CO 80402.

Now & Then (NL), 67-40 Yellowstone Blvd., Forest Hills, NY 11375 (paper dolls).

Paper Doll News (NL), PO Box 807, Vivian, LA 71082.

Paper Doll Pal (NL), 19109 Silcott Springs Rd., Purcellville, VA 20132, website: www.erols.com/jimfaraone.

Paperdoll Circle (NL), 28 Ferndown Gardens, Cobham, Surrey KT11 2BH, UK.

Paperdoll Review (MAG), PO Box 14, Kingfield, ME 04947-0014, website: www.paperdollreview.com.

Patsy & Friends (NL), PO Box 311, Deming, NM 88031, website: www.zianet.com/patsyandfriends.

Rags (MAG), PO Box 130, Arcola, IL 61910-0130 (Raggedy Ann and Andy collectibles).

ARCHIVES & MUSEUMS

The Fennimore Doll and Toy Museum, 1140 Lincoln Ave., Fennimore, WI 53809, 608-822-4100, 888-867-7935, website: www.fennimore.com/dolltoy.

Strong Museum, One Manhattan Square, Rochester, NY 14607, 585-263-2700, fax: 585-263-2493, website: www.strongmuseum.org.

Washington Dolls' House & Toy Museum, 5236 44th St. NW, Washington, DC 20015, 202-244-0024 or 202-363-6400.

APPRAISERS

Many of the auctions and repair services listed in this section will also do appraisals. *See also* the general list of "Appraisal Groups" on page 483.

AUCTIONS

➻ SEE ALSO "SELLING THROUGH AUCTION HOUSES," PAGE 485.

Bertoia Auctions, 2141 DeMarco Dr., Vineland, NJ 08360, 856-692-1881, fax: 856-692-8697, e-mail: bill@bertoiaauctions.com, website: www.bertoiaauctions.com. Specializing in auctions of antique toys, banks, doorstops, dolls, trains, soldiers, and folk art. Onsite auctions, live on Internet also. Mail, phone, and fax bids accepted. Buyer's premium 10%. Prices realized mailed after auction. Catalog $35.

Cobb's Doll Auctions, 1909 Harrison Rd., Johnstown, OH 43031-9539, 740-964-0444, fax: 740-927-7701, e-mail: auctions@cobbsdolls.com, website: www.cobbsdolls.com. Onsite, mail, phone, fax, and e-mail bids accepted. Buyer's premium 10%. Catalog $30; yearly subscription $100. Prices realized mailed after auction. Appraisals.

Frasher's Doll Auctions, 2323 S. Mecklin Sch. Rd., Oak Grove, MO 64075, 816-625-3786, fax: 816-625-6079. Auctions of dolls and doll-related items. Mail, phone, and fax bids accepted. Buyer's premium 5%. Catalog $39; yearly subscription $159. Prices realized available after auction. Appraisals.

Kenneth S. Hays & Associates, Inc., 120 S. Spring St., Louisville, KY 40206, 502-584-4297, fax: 502-585-5896, e-mail: kenhays@haysauction.com, website: www.haysauction.com. Specializing in antique dolls, Victorian antiques, and clocks. Mail and phone bids accepted. No buyer's premium. Prices realized mailed after some auctions. Appraisals.

McMasters Harris Auction Co., PO Box 1755, Cambridge, OH 43725, 740-432-7400, fax: 740-432-3191, e-mail: info@mcmastersharris.com, website: mcmastersharris.com. Antique dolls, vintage Barbies, and collectibles. Mail, fax, phone, and Internet bids accepted. No buyer's premium. Catalog $30; yearly subscription $99. Prices realized mailed after auction and available on website.

Meisner's Auction Service, PO Box 115, Rts. 20 & 22, New Lebanon, NY 12125, 518-766-5002, fax: 518-794-8073, e-mail: auction115@aol.com, website: www.meissnersauction.com. Antiques and dolls. Mail, phone, and e-mail bids accepted. Buyer's premium 10%. Prices realized available after auction. Appraisals.

Richard W. Withington, Inc., 590 Center Rd., Hillsboro, NH 03244, 603-464-3232, fax: 603-464-4901, e-mail: withington@conknet.com, website: www.withingtonauction.com. Antiques and antique dolls. No mail or phone bids. Buyer's premium 10%. Prices realized mailed after auction. Doll catalogs $16. Free auction brochures. Appraisals.

Theriault's, PO Box 151, Annapolis, MD 21404, 410-224-3655, fax: 410-224-2515, e-mail: info@theriaults.com, website: www.theriaults.com. Auctions of antique dolls and related items. On-site and online auctions. Mail, phone, fax, and e-mail bids accepted. Buyer's premium 10%. Catalog $49; yearly subscription $189. Prices realized mailed after auction and available on website. Appraisals.

REPAIRS, PARTS & SUPPLIES

➦ SEE ALSO "CONSERVATORS & RESTORERS," PAGE 520.

Antique & Art Restoration by Wiebold, 413 Terrace Pl., Terrace Park, OH 45174, 800-321-2541, 513-831-2541, fax: 513-831-2815, e-mail: wiebold @eos.net, website: www.wiebold.com. Fine art restoration and conservation of bisque dolls and other objects.

Antique Restorations, 1313 Mt. Holly Rd., Burlington, NJ 08016-3773, 609-387-2587, Mon.–Sat., 9:00 A.M.–6:00 P.M., fax: 609-387-2587, e-mail: ronaiello@comcast.net. Restorations of dolls' heads, china, porcelain, pottery, and art objects. Restoration supplies. Private restoration lessons. Free restoration supply catalog on request.

Artwork Restoration, 30 Hillhouse Rd., Winnipeg, MB R2V 2V9, Canada, 204-334-7090, e-mail: morry@escape.ca. Restoration of antique dolls and more.

Bits 'n' Pieces Lady, 1141 Belfair Dr., Pinole, CA 94564, 510-724-1855, fax: 510-724-4143, e-mail: PiecesLady@aol.com. Vintage Barbie doll clothing and accessories sold by the piece, not as a complete outfit. Dresses, shoes, gloves, etc. Send double-stamped LSASE for list. Lists issued every month. One-year subscriptions $15 U.S., $17 Canada, $24 overseas.

Cabbage Patch Kids, PO Box 714, Cleveland, GA 30528, 706-865-2171, fax: 706-865-5862, website: www.cabbagepatchkids.com. Cabbage Patch Kids cleaned and repaired. Research; replacement papers.

Chatty Cathy's Haven, 19528 Ventura Blvd. #495, Tarzana, CA 91356-2917, 818-881-3878, e-mail: cchaven@aol.com, website: chattycathys haven.com. Restorations to Mattel talking dolls, specializing in Chatty Cathy and her family. Restoration of Mrs. Beasley, Drowsy, Herman Munster, and all of the cloth dolls as well. Reproduction and original clothing.

China and Crystal Clinic, 1808 N. Scottsdale Rd., Tempe, AZ 85281, 800-658-9197, fax: 480-945-1079, e-mail: VictorColeman@earthlink.net. Restoration or conservation of porcelain dolls and other objects. Appraisals.

Devashan, 445 S. Canyon, Spearfish, SD 57783, 605-722-5355, e-mail: doll-maker@mato.com, website: www.devashan.com. Restoration of composition dolls. Period doll clothes made. Send SASE for brochure.

Doll & Bear's Paradise, 855½ N. Cedar, Laramie, WY 82072, 307-742-3429, e-mail: dolls2fix@fiberpipe.net. Repair and restoration of dolls and stuffed animals. Composition, plastic, bisque, porcelain, cloth, leather, and metal dolls restored, restrung, and cleaned. Wigs; hair re-rooting. Doll clothes made to order. Doll clothes hand washed. Stuffed animals cleaned and mended; fabric and features replaced.

Doll Hospital, 419 Gentry St. #102, Spring, TX 77373, 281-350-6722, e-mail: aaadolldoc@aol.com, website: www.aaadollhospital.com. Complete doll repair, including basic cleaning, stringing, reconstruction, and restoration of porcelain and composition dolls.

The Doll Lady Doll Hospital, 94 Pent Rd., Branford, CT 06405-4013, 203-488-6193, e-mail: docpatricia@webtv.net. Doll repairs. Antique doll parts, old eyes, replacement doll parts, and accessories. Doll kits, clothing, old and out-of-print books. Catalog $2.50.

The Doll Room, 9 Stuart Rd. W., Bridgewater, CT 06752, 860-354-8442, fax: 860-355-0546, e-mail: dollrm@aol.com. Antique and collectible dolls repaired and restored. Appraisals.

Dollightful Things, 1783 A Lincoln Way E., Chambersburg, PA 17201, 717-267-3488, e-mail: sdaly@innernet.net. Doll hospital specializing in repair, preservation, and restoration of all materials of antique dolls and most modern dolls. Restringing, cleaning and repair, rebuilding of body parts, cleaning of clothing.

Dollmasters, PO Box 2319, Annapolis, MD 21404, 800-966-3655, Mon.-Fri. 8:30 A.M.–5:00 P.M., fax: 410-571-9605, website: www.dollmasters.com. Authentic re-creations of antique doll clothes; doll accessories; books.

Dolly Heaven, 502 Broadway, New Haven, IN 46774, 800-660-1912, e-mail: dolly.heaven@gte.net. Doll repair and restoration, specializing in broken bisque and composition dolls. Cleaning, restringing, parts replaced. Wigs, clothes, doll accessories, and doll stands.

Hamilton Eye Warehouse, Box 1258-K, Moorpark, CA 93021, 805-529-5900, fax: 800-529-2934, e-mail: hamilton@vcnet.com, website: www.vcnet.com/hamilton. Specializing in doll eyes: glass paperweight and hollow blown glass eyes. Five styles of acrylic. Glass dollhouse doll eyes. Sizes from 2 mm to 30 mm in 14 colors. Color catalog $1.

Homestead Doll Hospital, 23482 Shephard Rd., Clatskanie, OR 97016, 503-728-3503, 9:00 A.M.–5:00 P.M., e-mail: dolldoctor@homestead collectibles.com, website: www.homesteadcollectibles.com. Restoration of all kinds of dolls: antique, composition, hard plastic, vinyl, bisque, talking, walkers, etc. Hair re-rooted; eye transplants; restringing. Doll supplies and kits.

IAO Doll Hospital, 2322 N. Charles St., Baltimore, MD 21218, 410-235-2291, e-mail: doc@iaodollhospital.com, website: www.iaodollhospital.com. Restoration and repair to all pre-1960 dolls. Specializing in bisque, china, composition, and papier-mâché. Restringing, craze repair, repainting, limb reconstruction, and more.

J & H China Repairs, 8296 St. George St., Vancouver, BC V5X 3S5, Canada, 604-321-1093, fax: 604-321-1093. Restoration of dolls, figurines, porcelain, etc.

Just Enterprises—Art & Antique Restoration, 2790 Sherwin Ave., # 10, Ventura, CA 93003, 805-644-5837, fax: 805-644-5837, e-mail: justenterprisesvc@yahoo.com, website: justenterprisesvc.com. Art and antique restoration, specializing in porcelain doll repair (heads and parts). Please remove hair and eyes and head from doll before sending.

Keller China Restoration, 4825 Windsor Dr., Rapid City, SD 57702, 605-342-6756, e-mail: KellerChina@rapidnet.com. Porcelain and bisque dolls repaired. Chips and hairline cracks repaired. Missing parts reproduced. Free brochure.

Long Island Doll Hospital, 45395 Main Rd., PO Box 1604, Southold, NY 11971, 631-765-2379, e-mail: jadav@suffolk.lib.ny.us, website: www.jandavisantiques.com. Restoration and repairs to antique and modern dolls; Steiff and other stuffed animals repaired. Restringing, resetting of eyes, hand sculpting of missing fingers and toes. Antique parts and eyes. Wigs, shampoo and sets. Appraisals. Free brochure.

Manhattan Doll Hospital, 236 3rd Ave., New York, NY 10003-2505, 212-253-9549, fax: 212-253-9549, website: www.manhattandollhouse.com. Doll repair.

Mini-Magic, 3910 Patricia Dr., Columbus, OH 43220, 614-457-3687, toll free order number 888-391-0691, fax: 614-459-2306, e-mail: minimagic@mini-magic.com, website: www.mini-magic.com. Fabrics and trim for doll clothes, sewing, and craft projects. French fashion patterns and kits. Doll stands, washing paste, acid-free boxes and tissue, muslin, buckles, buttons, hat supplies, and more.

Morgan's Collectibles, 831 SE 170th Dr., Portland, OR 97233, 503-252-3343, e-mail: joann@joannmorgan.com, website: www.joannmorgan.com. Doll restoration seminars; sewing seminars for doll clothing. Patterns and clothes for fashion and antique dolls. Mail order and Internet sales. No drop-in shoppers.

New York Doll Hospital, Inc., 787 Lexington Ave., New York, NY 10021, 212-838-7527. Repairs, restorations, and appraisals of antique dolls and animals. Doll clothes, wigs, and antique doll parts.

Poor Richard's Restoration & Preservation Studio Workshop, 101 Walnut St., Montclair, NJ 07042, 973-783-5333, fax: 973-744-1939, e-mail: jrickford@webtv.com, website: www.rickford.com. Restoration, conservation, archival, and preservation services. Restoration of dolls and other objects. By appointment, Tues.–Fri. noon–5:00 P.M., Sat. noon–3:00 P.M.

Rafail & Polina Golberg, Golberg Restoration Co., 411 Westmount Dr., Los Angeles, CA 90048, 310-652-0735, fax: 310-274-3770, e-mail: info@restorationworld.com, website: www.restorationworld.com.

Restoration and conservation of dolls, antiques, and objects of art. Custom-made parts. Free estimates via the Internet.

Restorations by Patricia, 420 Centre St., Nutley, NJ 07110, 973-235-0234. Repair and restoration of bisque, composition, and vinyl dolls. Can personalize hair, eyes, and clothing on statues and figurines, bride and groom, etc.

Simonson Clock Shop, 226 S. Main St., Wellington, OH 44090, 440-647-0049. Complete restoration of automata.

Treasured Collectibles, 1928 First St., Slidell, LA 70458, 985-646-6077, e-mail: info@treasured-collectibles.com, website: www.treasured-collectibles.com. Doll restoration and repair. Restorations of all types are possible. Any well-loved doll can be saved.

Twin Pines of Maine, Inc., PO Box 1178, Scarborough, ME 04070-1178, 800-770-DOLL (3655), fax: 207-883-1239, e-mail: nick@twince.com, website: www.twinpines.com. Supplies for cleaning dolls, doll clothes, and action figures. Doll hair care system includes shampoo, conditioner, brush, etc. Products for removal of stains and odor. Solvent-free casting resins for reproduction of original work. Free brochure.

Venerable Classics, 645 Fourth St., Suite 208, Santa Rosa, CA 95404, 800-531-2891, 707-575-3626, fax: 707-575-4913 call first, website: www.venerableclassics.com. Restoration of dolls and many other fragile decorative objects. Please call with questions. Free brochure on request.

Wilders Doll Center, 3345 Dixie Hwy., Waterford, MI 48328, 248-618-9506. Doll repair and supplies. Doll clothes, lace, fur, and suede. Patterns for clothes and doll bodies. Classes.

FASHION

There are old clothes and there are vintage clothes. Styles change so quickly that today clothes twenty years old or more can be considered vintage. Anything that is wearable, in good condition, with no permanent stains or damaged fabric, can be sold. The silly hats of the 1940s, the bowling shirts and Hawaiian prints of the 1950s, and the plastic purses of the 1960s are in demand to be worn or displayed. The white cotton petticoats and camisoles that were underwear before 1910 are now party dresses. Beaded flapper dresses or old lace wedding dresses are wanted for special occasions. Before you send old clothes to the local thrift shops, be sure they are not worth more money at a vintage clothing store.

Silk that is crumbling, fabric deteriorating under the arms, moth holes, and stains make a piece of clothing unwearable and almost unsalable. Pieces in good condition are of value. Damaged clothes (called "cutters" in ads) can be sold to be cut up and made into pillows, quilts, or other new items. Lace trim, buttons, even special embroidery, can be salvaged and sold separately.

Vintage clothing with designer names can sell for thousands of dollars. Look for **CHANEL, FORTUNY, WORTH, ADRIAN, CLAIRE MCCARDELL, BONNIE CASHIN, DIOR, GIVENCHY, PUCCI, JEANNE LANVIN, SCAASI, BILL BLASS**, and other important names. Designer dresses like these sell at special sales at the major auction houses. Off-the-rack brands, like **BOBBIE BROOKS, LEVI'S STA-PRESSED**, and **PENDLETON**, or department stores labels, like **BERGDORF GOODMAN, BONWIT TELLER, MACY'S, MARSHALL FIELD'S, PENNEY'S**, and **SEARS**, are of interest to collectors and sell at vintage clothing stores.

Very small sizes are more difficult to sell because so few people can wear them. We often think our ancestors must have been tiny because so many dresses are size 6 or smaller. Remember, their waists were cinched, so an 18-inch waist was not unusual. It's easy to make a dress smaller, but more difficult to make it larger. Many dresses were remade for use by other family members, so each time a dress was altered, it was usually done for a smaller person.

Accessories, including men's and women's hats, purses, fur pieces, scarves, and neckties, sell well. Cashmere sweaters and coats, for men and women, sell quickly. Very old Levi's and other jeans sell not only in this country but also in Japan and Europe. Ordinary men's clothes do not sell at vintage clothing stores; used shoes are also difficult to sell. Give them to a charity thrift stop and get a tax deduction.

FASHION ACCESSORIES

Combs, buckles, purses, canes, compacts, and other accessories are avidly collected. These items sell through the major antiques shows and dealers. Beaded purses have long been popular as both decorations to hang on a wall and as useful purses. Now collectors buy leather arts and crafts purses, needlepoint and petit point, plastic, hand-painted wood, and other unusual-looking pocketbooks dating from before 1980.

REPAIR

Collecting vintage clothing is a fairly recent hobby. Many cities have shops that specialize in old clothing that can be worn every day. There is usually someone at these shops who can repair old clothing or furnish the trim and material needed for repairs. A few bridal and antiques shops also sell old fabrics, lace, or dresses. Check the Yellow Pages of the telephone book under "Clothing Bought & Sold" or "Second Hand Stores" to locate the dealers who sell and repair old clothes.

Dirt and sunlight do more harm to old fabrics than cleaning. Most fabrics can be gently washed in pure soap, not detergent, or they can be carefully dry-cleaned. The rules for old fabrics are the same as those for modern ones. Some stains may be permanent, but the over-all soil should be cleaned away. Repairs to rips should be made before the pieces are cleaned. This avoids more damage. Loose beading and lace trim should be repaired as soon as damage is noticed.

Compacts, purses, combs, belts, canes and other accessories are repaired and restored by specialists who work in metal beading, leather, wood or other materials. A jeweler may be able to fix a beaded purse; a cabinetmaker may be able to restore a wooden cane handle.

◆▸ SEE ALSO METALS, TEXTILES

REFERENCE BOOKS

Antique Combs & Purses, Evelyn Haertig (Gallery Graphics Press, PO Box 5457, Carmel, CA 93921, 1983).

Cane Curiosa: From Gun to Gadget, Catherine Dike (Cane Curiosa Press, 250 Dielman Rd., Ladue, MO 63124, 1983).

Canes in the United States: Mementos of American History, 1607–1953, Catherine Dike (Cane Curiosa Press, Ladue, MO, 1994).

More Beautiful Purses, Evelyn Haertig (Gallery Graphics Press, PO Box 5457, Carmel, CA 93921, 1990).

Spectacles and Other Vision Aids: A History and Guide to Collecting, J. William Rosenthal (Norman, San Francisco, 1996).

PRICE BOOKS

3000 Shoes from 1896, Roseann Ettinger (Schiffer, Atglen, PA, 1998).

Aloha Attire: Hawaiian Dress in the Twentieth Century, Linda B. Arthur (Schiffer, Atglen, PA, 2000).

Beads on Bags, 1800s–2000, Lorita Winfield, Leslie Piña, and Constance Korosec (Schiffer, Atglen, PA, 2000).

Blueprints of Fashion: Home Sewing Patterns of the 1940s, Wade Laboissonniere (Schiffer, Atglen, PA, 1997),

Blueprints of Fashion: Home Sewing Patterns of the 1950s, Wade Laboissonniere (Schiffer, Atglen, PA, 1999).

Bowling Shirts, Joe Tonelli and Marc Luers (Schiffer, Atglen, PA, 1998).

Canes Through the Ages, Francis H. Monek (Schiffer, Atglen, PA, 1995).

Celluloid Hand Fans, Cynthia Fendel (Hand Fan Productions, 5128 Spyglass Dr., Dallas, TX 75287, 2001).

Collector's Encyclopedia of Compacts, Carryalls & Face Powder Boxes, 2 volumes, Laura Mueller (Collector Books, Paducah, KY, 1994, 1997).

Eyeglass Retrospective: Where Fashion Meets Science, Nancy N. Schiffer (Schiffer, Atglen, PA, 2000).

Fashion Plates, 1950–1970, Constance Korosec and Leslie Piña (Schiffer, Atglen, PA, 1998).

Fashionable Clothing from the Sears Catalogs, various authors (Schiffer, Atglen, PA, 1997).

Fifties Forever: Popular Fashions for Men, Women, Boys and Girls, Roseann Ettinger (Schiffer, Atglen, PA, 1998).

Handbags, 3rd edition, Roseann Ettinger (Schiffer, Atglen, PA, 1999).

Hathaway Shirts: Their History, Design and Advertising, Douglas Congdon-Martin (Schiffer, Atglen, PA, 1998).

Hot Shoes: 100 Years, Maureen Reilly (Schiffer, Atglen, PA, 1998).

Miller's Handbags, Tracy Tolkien. (Octopus Publishing, London, England, 2001).

Official Price Guide to Vintage Fashion and Fabrics, Pamela Smith (House of Collectibles, NY, 2001).

Popular & Collectible Neckties: 1955 to Present, Roseann Ettinger (Schiffer, Atglen, PA, 1998).

Popular Purses: It's in the Bag, Leslie Piña and Donald-Brian Johnson (Schiffer, Atglen, PA, 2001).

The Child in Fashion: 1750–1920, Kristina Harris (Schiffer, Atglen, PA, 1999).

The Collector's Encyclopedia of Buttons, 4th edition, Sally C. Luscomb (Schiffer, Atglen, PA, 1999).

The Evans Book: Lighters, Compacts, Perfumers, and Handbags, Larry Clayton (Schiffer, Atglen, PA, 1998).

Vintage & Contemporary Purse Accessories, Roselyn Gerson (Collector Books, Paducah, KY, 1997).

Vintage Hats & Bonnets, 1770–1970, Susan Langley (Collector Books, Paducah, KY, 1998).

Vintage Ladies' Compacts, Roselyn Gerson (Collector Books, Paducah, KY, 1996).

CLUBS & THEIR PUBLICATIONS

Antique Comb Collectors Club International, *Antique Comb Collector* (NL), 90 S. Highland Ave., #1204, Tarpon Springs, FL 34689-5351, e-mail: belva.green@verizon.net.

Antique Fan Collectors Association, *The Fan Collector* (NL), PO Box 5473, Sarasota, FL 34277-5473, e-mail: membership@fancollectors.org, website: www.fancollectors.org.

Buttonhook Society, *Boutonneur* (NL), Box 287, White Marsh, MD 21162-0287, e-mail: thebuttonhooksociety@tinyworld.co.uk, website: www.thebuttonhooksociety.com.

Compact Collectors Club, *Powder Puff* (NL), PO Box 40, Lynbrook, NY 11563, e-mail: compactldy@aol.com.

Costume Society of America, *Dress* (MAG), 55 Edgewater Dr., PO Box 73, Earleville, MD 21919, e-mail: national.office@costumesociety america.com, website: www.costumesocietyamerica.com.

Fan Association of North America, *FANA Forum* (NL), FANA Journal (MAG), 201 Palmetto Ct., St. Simons Island, GA 31522, website: www.fanassociation.org.

Fan Circle International, *Fans* (NL), Cronk-Y-Voddy, 21 Rectory Rd., Coltis-hall, Norwich NR12 7H, UK, e-mail: jdm@coltishall.freeserve.co.uk, website: ourworld.compuserve.com/homepages/helenakitt.

National Button Society, *National Button Bulletin* (NL), 2733 Juno Pl., Akron, OH 44333-4137.

OTHER PUBLICATIONS

Cane Collector's Chronicle (NL), PO Box 271668, Houston, TX 77277-1668, e-mail: pwarthur@hal-pc.org.

Vintage Gazette (NL), 194 Amity St., Amherst, MA 01002, e-mail: merrylees@aol.com.

ARCHIVES & MUSEUMS

American Textile History Museum, 491 Dutton St., Lowell, MA 01854-4221, 978-441-0400, fax: 978-441-1412.

The Bata Shoe Museum, 327 Bloor St. W, Toronto, Ontario, Canada M5S 1W7, 416-979-7799, fax: 416-979-0078, website: www.batashoemuseum.ca.

The Brockton Shoe Museum, Brockton Historical Society, 216 N. Pearl St., Brockton MA 02301, 508-583-1039, website: www.brocktonma.com/bhs/shoe.html.

Fashion Institute of Technology, 7th Ave. and 27th St., New York, NY 10001-5992, 212-217-7675, website: www.fitnyc.suny.edu/html/dynamic.html.

The Museum of Hatting, Wellington Mill, Wellington Rd. S., Stockport, Cheshire, England SK3 0EU, 011-44-161-355-7770, fax: 011-44-161-480-8735, website: www.stockportmbc.gov.uk/heritage.

Textile Museum, 2320 S St. NW, Washington, DC 20008-4008, e-mail: info@textilemuseum.org, website: www.textilemuseum.org.

USEFUL SITES

Vintage Pattern Lending Library, www.vpll.org.

APPRAISERS

The auction and some of the repair services listed in this section will also do appraisals. *See also* the general list of "Appraisal Groups" on page 483.

AUCTIONS

➝ SEE ALSO "SELLING THROUGH AUCTION HOUSES," PAGE 485.

Tradewinds Auctions, PO Box 249, Manchester, MA 01944-0249, 978-526-4085, fax: 978-526-3088, e-mail: taron@tradewindsantiques.com, website: tradewindsantiques.com. Auctions of antique canes and walking sticks only. Mail and phone bids accepted. Buyer's premium 12%. Catalog $40. Prices realized mailed after auction; partial list available on website. Appraisals.

REPAIRS, PARTS & SUPPLIES

➝ SEE ALSO "CONSERVATORS & RESTORERS," PAGE 520 AND "TEXTILES," PAGE 412.

Button Images, 1317 Lynndale Rd., Madison, WI 53711-3370, 608-271-4566, fax: 608-271-4566, e-mail: buttonldy@aol.com, website: www.button images.com. Supplies for cleaning, mounting, displaying, and storing buttons. Appraisal of antique and collectible buttons. Free catalog.

C.A. Zoes Mfg. Co., 168 N. Sangamon St., Chicago, IL 60607, 312-666-4018, fax: 312-666-4019. Leather-care products and leather finishes for use on shoes and accessories, luggage, camera cases, leather-bound books, antique leather items, antique leather trim, etc. Free catalog.

Cereus Inc., 31 Brook Ln., Cortlandt Manor, NY 10566, 914-739-0754, fax: 914-737-4333, e-mail: fanconservaotr@aol.com. Archival conservation of antique fans: pleated folding fans, brisé fans, fixed fans, European and Oriental, ivory, bone, wood, lacquer, mother-of-pearl, silver, paper, textiles, printed and painted leaves.

It's My Bagg, e-mail: Baggitt@ameritech.net. Repair and restoration of antique and vintage purses; antique bead matching for repairs of beaded purses; fringe repairs, new linings added. Custom beaded straps designed. Cleaning and conditioning of leathers, etc.

The Japanese Repository, 7705 Northwest 18th Court, Margate, FL 33063, 954-972-0287, e-mail: ivoryrepair@yahoo.com, website: www.ivory repair.com. Repair to ivory and wood carved canes and walking sticks. Repair and restoration of ivory. Repair to items of antler, bone, and horn.

The Laundry at Linens Limited, Inc., 240 N. Milwaukee St., Milwaukee, WI 53202, 800-637-6334 or 414-223-1123, fax: 414-223-1126, e-mail: linenslimited@msn.com, website: www.thelaundryat.com. European hand laundry service, specializing in cleaning fine and antique linens: bed linens, table linens, and heirloom pieces such as baptismal gowns and wedding dresses. Nationwide service. Free brochure.

Pirates Treasure Cove, 6212 E. Kracker Ave., Gibsonton, FL 33534, 813-677-1137, Mon.–Sat. 9:00 A.M.–5:00 P.M., fax: 813-671-2915, e-mail: pirates

treasurecove@ij.net. Rhinestones, beading, braids, fringes, and jewels
for theatrical costumes.

Stillwater Textile Conservation Studio LLC, 603-938-2310, fax: 603-938-2455,
e-mail: stillwaterstudio@conknet.com, website: www.stillwater
studio.org. Textile conservation. Custom dyeing of fabric and yarns.

Suzi's Purse Restoration, 15466 Los Gatos Blvd., 109-315, Los Gatos, CA
95032. Vintage beaded purses repaired and relined; small holes
repaired, beaded fringe repaired, purse reattached to frame.

➥ **FINE ART, SEE PAINTINGS, PRINTS**

FIREPLACE EQUIPMENT

An old fireplace had many pieces of equipment: a set of tools,
fireback, andirons, coal basket, fender, and aids such as bellows or
match holders. All are useful and some of the smaller pieces sell
easily. Andirons are difficult to sell because they are always heavy,
awkward to pack, and not in great demand. Fire screens from the
twentieth century were usually made to fit a specific opening to
keep sparks from flying. They are hard to sell.

Some imagination is needed to repair these items. Look in the
Yellow Pages of your local phone book for firms that make iron
fences or decorative metal pieces. Companies that replate metal
often repair it as well.

➥ **SEE ALSO METALS**

REPAIRS, PARTS & SUPPLIES

➥ **SEE ALSO "CONSERVATORS & RESTORERS," PAGE 520.**

Antique Hardware and Mirror Resilvering, 763 West Bippley Rd.,
Lake Odessa, MI 48849, 616-374-7750, fax: 616-374-7752, e-mail:
antiquehardware@robinsonsantiques.com, website: www.robinsons
antiques.com. Original antique restoration hardware. Original parts
from 1650 to 1925. Free search. Free matching service.

Country Iron Foundry, 800 Laurel Oak Dr., Suite 200, Dept. X98, Naples,
FL 34108, 800-233-9945, e-mail: sales@firebacks.com, website:
www.firebacks.com. Cast-iron firebacks, antique replica and original
designs, and stove plates. A fireback protects the back of the fireplace from heat damage while radiating more heat into the house.
Catalog $3.

Lemee's Fireplace Equipment, 815 Bedford St., Bridgewater, MA 02324,
508-697-2672, fax: 508-697-2672, website: www.lemeesfireplace.com.
Fireplace cranes, Dutch oven doors, cleanout doors, bellows, iron

hardware, firebacks, electric logs, and all kinds of fireplace equipment. Catalog $2.

McBuffers, 1420 Dille Rd., Unit F, Euclid, OH 44117, 216-486-6696, fax: 216-486-4152. Fireplace equipment. Metal finishing, repair, and replating: brass, copper, nickel, chrome, silver, and gold. Cleaning, buffing, and polishing. Brochure.

Patrick J. Gill & Sons, 9 Fowle St., Woburn, MA 01801, 781-933-3275, fax: 781-933-3751, e-mail: joe@patrickgillco.com, website: patrickgillco.com. Fireplace tools, andirons, and other metal objects replated. Metal repair, refinishing, and replating.

Retinning & Copper Repair, Inc., 560 Irvine Turner Blvd., Newark, NJ 07108, 973-848-0700, fax: 973-848-1070, website: www.retinning.com. Restoration of brass fireplace equipment and other metal items.

Sleepy Hollow Chimney Supply Co., 85 Emjay Blvd., Brentwood, NY 11717, 800-553-5322, 8:00 A.M.–6:00 P.M., fax: 631-231-2364, e-mail: fschukaz@bellfiresusa.com, website: www.bellfiresusa.com. Flue and fireplace restoration. Antique (c.1820-1860) Coalbrookdale cast iron fireplace facings. Distributor of Bellfires fireplace systems.

FOLK ART

There is an ongoing argument among experts over the definition of the term "folk art." For the purposes of this book, folk art is whatever is called folk art by some experts. It may have been made in the eighteenth, nineteenth, or twentieth century. It may be naive art by an untrained artist, or an old advertisement, or a carnival figure. This is one collecting field with few hard-and-fast rules of quality, condition, and age. Beauty is in the eye of the beholder, and what seems primitive to one may be considered superior by another. Some collectors prefer pieces with worn paint and rough wooden edges; others want pristine paint. Don't do any restoration unless the piece is so badly damaged it would be useless without restoration. If you think your folk art piece is of value, be sure to ask an expert before any work is done.

The meaning of the term "folk art" has changed. In the 1950s it referred to stiff, formal American portraits done by itinerant painters of the seventeenth and eighteenth centuries, ships' carved figureheads, cigar store figures, weather vanes, and a few other large signs and carvings. In the 1970s an important book on folk sculpture was written, and folk art took on a new meaning. Large carvings that were often exaggerated or bizarre, duck decoys, quilts, recent paintings in the Grandma Moses style, commercial factory-made weather vanes, carousel horses, and even printed advertising tins all were defined as folk art. Very primitive art done by untrained artists in the last seventy-five years is now called "outsider art."

•➤ **CAROUSEL HORSES AND PAINTINGS ARE IN THEIR OWN CHAPTERS**
•➤ **FOR QUILTS, SEE TEXTILES**
•➤ **FOR TINS, SEE ADVERTISING COLLECTIBLES**

The experts still debate the meaning of the words "folk art," but for you, the seller, folk art is what the customer wants to call folk art. Age is of little importance. Decorative value, humor, the artist's fame, and some "hype" determine the value. We watched a prestigious dealer sell an 1890s iron-bladed lawn mower for several thousand dollars at a folk art show. It had a "sculptural quality." Another dealer was selling a thirty-year-old, five-foot figure made of bottle caps for $35,000.

Look at what you want to sell. If it is primitive, colorful, attractive, or very unusual, it will be purchased. Price is arbitrary for most items. There are listed prices for decoys, carousel figures, cigar store figures, quilts, and paintings by known artists or from known schools of painting. These pieces should be researched because treasures do indeed look like trash to the uninformed in this market. There is almost no way to set a price by comparison on a hand-carved bird cage, a sideshow banner, a wooden maypole, or a cast-cement urn. It is one price at a flea market, and quite another if anointed as "art" by a prestigious dealer. (There is growing concern about tombstones, statues, and ironwork removed from cemeteries. Many have been stolen. It is illegal to own or sell them.)

Look at the folk art books in your library. Visit folk art exhibits. Talk to dealers and collectors at shows. If your object is large, colorful, and strange, price it a little higher than you might have thought possible. A collection of intricate carvings made by your grandfather or a group of nineteenth-century paintings by a distant relative should possibly be offered for sale through an auction gallery. It is the public who sets the price, and the gallery will show the pieces to more prospective buyers than you could. An appraisal of the collection will only be as good as your appraiser, and most appraisers who are not in the larger cities might not understand the market for unique folk art pieces.

An unusual piece of folk art will sell quickly. We were once offered, but didn't buy, a large cut-out tin sign of a black boy advertising a store in a small Ohio town. In two months it had been sold and resold to dealers five times until it finally appeared in an ad for a New York folk art gallery at twenty times the price we had originally seen. You will not be able to get the very top price for your folk art, but you should get a third of its retail value in the best shops. Don't ignore commercial items that might attract folk art buyers. Sideshow banners and other circus memorabilia, chalk (plaster) figures, birdhouses, garden ornaments, fraternal-order carvings and banners, even religious paintings, prints, and figures are sometimes folk art.

DECOYS

Duck decoys have attracted a special group of collectors for many years. But in the 1980s the fish decoy was "discovered." Carved wooden fish used by fishermen were eagerly bought as examples of folk art. They became so popular that new ones appeared, and today both duck decoys and fish decoys are being made for the gift shop trade to be sold as new decorations.

The record price for a duck decoy is $684,500 for a Canada goose, but many decoys sell for around $25. Most sell for prices in between these two amounts. Because decoys are collected as art, the most expensive are not necessarily the oldest. The quality of carving and decoration and the fame of the maker determine the price.

Average working decoys in poor condition sell quickly if they are reasonably priced. They should be offered through the normal antiques channels and shown to dealers, collectors, auctioneers, and friends. What is difficult is deciding if your decoys are just average or are "stars."

Once again we suggest you try doing serious research at a library. There are many books that picture decoys and tell about the important makers. Try to identify your decoys. Remember, the decoy was originally made to lure a bird, so it should be an identifiable fowl. The nondescript, rough silhouette of a bird is not a valuable decoy, although it will sell as a decorative piece of folk art.

If your decoys seem to be valuable, you should take them to an appraiser or auction gallery to get an expert opinion. If you live in an area with no decoy appraisers nearby, you should be able to get enough information by sending a clear photograph to one of the auction galleries that regularly sell decoys. The most successful decoy auctions have been on the East Coast.

Decoy collectors are a special group with their own clubs, publications, and events. It is not easy to learn about them. Talk to local collectors to learn about events in your area. Carvers and artists who make modern decoys can often restore old ones. Many decoys are included in shows and sales that interest the folk art and "country look" collectors, and a few can be found at almost every antiques mall or show.

REPAIR

Restoration of folk art should be done by a craftsman in the appropriate field. A painted figure might be restored by a carousel-figure expert or a furniture-restoration firm. Paper, glass, or metal pieces require other specialists. We once had a tin chimney replaced on a folk art house by the man putting metal heat ducts in our room addition, and painted by the house painter who worked on our walls.

CLUBS & THEIR PUBLICATIONS

Folk Art Collectors Club, *Folk Art News* (NL), Rt. 1 Box 328A, Edwards, MO 65326, e-mail: acgraph@aroundthelake.com, website: www.around thelake.com/pfaltzgraff.

Folk Art Society of America, *Folk Art Messenger* (NL), PO Box 17041, Richmond, VA 23226, e-mail: fasa@folkart.org, website: www.folkart.org.

Great Lakes Fish Decoy Collectors & Carvers Association, *Thru the Shanty Hole* (NL), 35824 W. Chicago, Livonia, MI 48150.

Midwest Decoy Collectors Association, *Midwest Decoy Collectors Association Quarterly Newsletter* (NL), 6 E. Scott St., #3, Chicago, IL 60610, website: www.midwestdecoy.org.

OTHER PUBLICATIONS

Decoy Magazine (MAG), PO Box 787, Lewes, DE 19958, e-mail: decoymag@aol.com, website: www.decoymag.com.

Folk Art (MAG), American Folk Art Museum, 555 W. 57th St., New York, NY 10019-2925, e-mail: membership@folkartmuseum.org, website: www.folkartmuseum.org.

ARCHIVES & MUSEUMS

Abby Aldrich Rockefeller Folk Art Center, PO Box 1776, Williamsburg, VA 23187-1776, 757-229-1000, website: www.history.org (part of Colonial Williamsburg).

American Folk Art Museum, 45 W. 53rd St., New York, NY 10019, 212-265-1040, e-mail: membership@folkartmuseum.org, website: www.folk artmuseum.org.

Museum of Arts and Design, 40 West 53rd St., New York, NY 10019, 212-956-3535, website: www.americancraftmuseum.org.

Shelburne Museum, Inc., PO Box 10, Shelburne, VT 05842, 802-985-3346, e-mail: questions@shelburne museum.com, website: www.shelburne museum.com.

APPRAISERS

The auctions listed in this section will also do appraisals. *See also* the general list of "Appraisal Groups" on page 483.

AUCTIONS

➼ **SEE ALSO "SELLING THROUGH AUCTION HOUSES," PAGE 485.**

Decoys Unlimited, 2320 Main St., W. Barnstable, MA 02668, 508-362-2766, e-mail: tsharmon@attbi.com, website: www.decoysunlimitedinc.com. Decoy auctions. Mail, and phone bids accepted. Buyer's premium 10%. Prices realized available after auction. Restoration and conservation services. Appraisals.

Guyette & Schmidt, Inc., PO Box 522, West Farmington, ME 04992, 207-778-6256, fax: 207-778-6501, e-mail: decoys@guyetteandschmidt.com, website: www.guyetteandschmidt.com. Decoy auctions, three per year. Specializes in antique duck decoys and shorebird decoys, fish decoys, fish carvings, waterfowl paintings and prints, duck calls, and ammunition advertising. Mail and phone bids accepted. Buyer's premium 10%. Catalog $36, subscription $108 per year. Prices realized mailed after auction. Free appraisals of antique waterfowl art and related items. Mon.–Fri. 9:00 A.M.–5:30 P.M.

FRAMES & MIRRORS

A painting or print needs a frame—old, new, or restored. Try to reframe any print or painting with a frame in the same style as the original. It is possible to buy antique frames or copies of antique frames from general antiques shops, modern frame shops, or special firms that deal only in period picture frames.

When reframing a picture, use acid-free archival mountings. The frame shop can tell you about these.

An antique mirror consists of a frame and the silvered glass. The value is higher if both parts are original. Unfortunately, old mirrors often lose some of the backing and the reflective qualities are diminished. It is possible to "resilver" the old glass or to replace the glass entirely if you do not wish to live with flawed glass.

An inexpensive way to restore some old mirrors with poor "silvering" is to remove the metallic backing from the old glass and put a new mirror behind the old glass. This saves the old glass, yet makes a mirror reflect properly. Locate local mirror installers using your local Yellow Pages.

Some of the craftsmen listed in the Furniture section also restore mirrors and picture frames.

PRICE BOOKS

Antique American Frames, 2nd edition, Eli Wilner (Avon, NY, 1999).

Collecting Picture and Photo Frames, Stuart Schneider (Schiffer, Atglen, PA, 1998).

APPRAISERS

The auctions and many of the repair services listed in this section will also do appraisals. *See also* the general list of "Appraisal Groups" on page 483.

Eli Wilner & Company, 1525 York Ave., New York, NY 10028, 212-744-6521, Mon.–Fri. 9:30 A.M.–5:30 P.M., fax: 212-628-0264, e-mail: info@eliwilner.com, website: www.eliwilner.com. Appraisals of antique frames.

AUCTIONS

➔ **SEE ALSO "SELLING THROUGH AUCTION HOUSES," PAGE 485.**

Balfour & Wessels Framefinders Inc., 454 E. 84th St., New York, NY 10028, 212-396-3896, fax: 212-396-3899, e-mail: framefinders@aol.com, website: framefinders.com. Auctions of antique frames. Mail, phone, and e-mail bids taken. Buyer's premium 15%. Catalog $10. Prices realized mailed after auction. Appraisal services; restoration and conservation.

REPAIRS, PARTS & SUPPLIES

➔ **SEE ALSO "CONSERVATORS & RESTORERS," PAGE 520.**

A Home Design, 5220 Veloz Ave., Los Angeles, CA 91356, 818-757-7766, fax: 818-708-3722, e-mail: homedesign@mail.com. Fine arts restoration, including items made from marble, wood carvings, glass, and mirrors. Operating in the southern California area.

A. Ludwig Klein & Son, Inc., PO Box 145, Harleysville, PA 19438, 215-256-9004 or 800-379-2929, fax: 215-256-9644, website: www.aludwigklein.com. Conservation and restoration of frames and more. Professional cleaning. Appraisals, insurance claims. Worldwide. By appointment. Free brochure.

Antique & Art Restoration by Wiebold, 413 Terrace Pl., Terrace Park, OH 45174, 800-321-2541, 513-831-2541, fax: 513-831-2815, e-mail: wiebold @eos.net, website: www.wiebold.com. Fine art restoration and conservation, including gold leaf frames and other objects. Missing parts replaced. Silver, gold, and brass plating.

Antique Hardware and Mirror Resilvering, 763 W. Bippley Rd., Lake Odessa, MI 48849, 616-374-7750, fax: 616-374-7752, e-mail: antiquehardware @robinsonsantiques.com, website: www.robinsonsantiques.com. Mirror resilvering.

Antique Restoration Co., 440 E. Centre Ave., Newtown, PA 18940, 215-968-2343, fax: 215-860-5465. Frames repaired. Mirror resilvering; gold leafing; glass beveling. Metal polishing, plating, and lacquering. Free brochure.

Antique Restoration Service, 521 Ashwood Dr., Flushing, MI 48433, 810-659-0505, fax: 810-659-5582. Restoration of frames and other objects. Missing parts reconstructed.

AntiqueConservation.com, Div. of Ponsford Ltd., 5441 Woodstock Rd., Acworth, GA 30102, 770-924-4848, fax: 770-529-2278, e-mail: GordonPonsford@AntiqueConservation.com, website: www.Antique Conservation.com. Conservation and restoration of fine art and antiques, frames and gilding, and more. Appraisals.

ArtsakeFraming Gallery, The French Block, Main St., PO Box 747, Damariscotta, ME 04543, 207-563-5643, e-mail: abaldwin@midcaost.com. Custom framing. Old picture frames restored and adapted for paintings. French ruled mats and conservation framing.

Artwork Restoration, 30 Hillhouse Rd., Winnipeg, MB R2V 2V9, Canada, 204-334-7090, e-mail: morry@escape.ca. Restoration of picture frames and more. Missing parts replaced.

Attic Unlimited, 22435 E. LaPalma Ave., Yorba Linda, CA 92887, 714-692-2940, fax: 714-692-2947, e-mail: atticunlimited@aol.com, website: www.atticunlimited.com. Restoration of frames and other objects of art.

B & L Antiqurie, Inc., 6217 S. Lakeshore Rd., PO Box 453, Lexington, MI 48450, 810-359-8623, fax: 810-359-7498, e-mail: information @bentglasscentral.com, website: www.bentglasscentral.com. Pattern cut and beveled mirrors, convex picture frame glass, antique seedy flat glass, beveled glass. Send SASE for more information. Mon.–Fri. 8:00 A.M.–5:00 P.M.

Basic Enterprise, 320 Krotzer Ave., Luckey, OH 43443, 419-833-5551, fax: 419-833-1251, e-mail: csarver@luckey.net. Mirror resilvering.

Chem-Clean Furniture Restoration, Bucks County Art & Antiques Co., 246 W. Ashland St., Doylestown, PA 18901, 215-345-0892, e-mail: iscsusn@att.net. Frame repair, glass bending, glass beveling, gold leafing. Appraisals. Free brochure.

Chicago Conservation Center, 730 N. Franklin, Suite 701, Chicago, IL 60610, 312-944-5401, fax: 312-944-5479, e-mail: chicagoconservation @yahoo.com, website: chicagoconservation.com. Restoration of frames and other objects of art.

Daniel Smith Artists' Materials, PO Box 84268, Seattle, WA 98124-5568, 206-224-0411, fax: 206-224-0406, e-mail: john.cogley@daniel smith.com, website: danielsmith.com. A complete line of fine art materials, including framing and matting supplies. Metal leafing supplies.

Devashan, 445 S. Canyon, Spearfish, SD 57783, 605-722-5355 Mon.–Fri.

10:00 A.M.–6:00 P.M., fax:, e-mail: dollmaker@mato.com, website: www.devashan.com. Antique frames repaired and regilded.

Edgellworks, 343 Sailors Ln., Black Rock, CT 06605, 203-335-6568, e-mail: jane@edgellworks.com. Velvet and moire easel backs made for sterling and other antique frames. References available. E-mail or phone with any question.

Eli Wilner & Company, 1525 York Ave., New York, NY 10028, 212-744-6521, Mon.–Fri. 9:30 A.M.–5:30 P.M., fax: 212-628-0264, e-mail: info@eliwilner.com, website: www.eliwilner.com. Antique frame restoration, replication, and consultation. American and European frames for sale. Appraisals.

Gold Leaf Studios, 1523 22nd St., Washington, DC 20037, 202-833-2440, fax: 202-833-2452, website: www.goldleafstudios.com. Gilded frame fabrication. Open Mon.–Fri. 9:00 A.M–5:00 P.M. and by appointment.

Harvard Art, 49 Littleton County Rd., Harvard, MA 01451, 978-456-9050, fax: 978-456-9050, e-mail: sjackson@harvardart.com, website: harvardart.com. Gilding conservation and restoration of frames, mirrors, and other objects. Securing of loose elements, structural repair, missing pieces replaced, gesso fills, ingilding, and toning to match.

Heirloom Restorations, 267 Sherry Ln., East Peoria, IL 61611-9410, 309-694-0960, e-mail: heirloom-restorations@insightbb.com. Plaster frame restoration.

Hudson Glass Co., Inc., Dept. K-8, 219 N. Division St., Peekskill, NY 10566-2700, 800-431-2964 or 914-737-2124, fax: 914-737-4447. Convex picture frame glass, tools, and supplies. No repairs. Catalog $5 ($3 refundable with order).

Inman Historic Interiors, Inc., 3367 170th St., Randolph, IA 51649-6020, 712-625-2403, fax: 712-625-2403, e-mail: jidesignasid@netscape.net, website: www.historicinteriors.com. Mirror resilvering, antique frame restoration, gilding, parts duplication, interior consulting. Hide glue and specialty waxes. Free brochure.

Intermuseum Laboratory, 83 N. Main St., Allen Art Bldg., Oberlin, OH 44074, 440-775-7331, 9:00 A.M.–5:00 P.M. fax: 440-774-3431, e-mail: sandra.williamson@oberlin.edu, website: www.oberlin.edu/~ica. A non-profit, regional art conservation center that provides preservation and conservation services and education for member and non-member museums and institutions, as well as private and corporate collectors. Conservation of frames, paintings, murals, paper based materials, and more.

Items of Value, Inc., 7419 Admiral Dr., Alexandria, VA 22307, 703-660-9380, fax: 703-660-9384. Restoration of wood, paintings, gesso, ivory, and many other types of items. Regilding, resilvering. Appraisals.

J & H China Repairs, 8296 St. George St., Vancouver, BC V5X 3S5, Canada, 604-321-1093, fax: 604-321-1093. Restoration of picture frames and other objects.

J.C. Wood Finishing Services, 918 Westwood St., Addison, IL 60101, 630-628-6161, fax: 630-628-9523, e-mail: jcwood1@worldnet.att.net. Repairs and restorations; refinishing, preventative maintenance of mirrors, glass tops, and more. Free estimates. Free brochure.

J.K. Flynn Co., 471 Sixth Ave., Park Slope, Brooklyn, NY 11215, 718-369-8934, fax: 718-369-8934, e-mail: jkflynncompany@aol.com. Period frame restoration, including oil or water gilding and full restoration of gesso, compo, or carved decorations. Fine art appraising and consulting. Free lists of services.

John Edward Cunningham, 1525 E. Berkeley, Springfield, MO 65804, 417-889-7702. Frames restored.

Ken Marshall, 2424 N. Wishon, #7, Fresno, CA 93704, 559-243-0655. Minor restoration of antique picture frames.

Leonard E. Sasso, Master Restorer, 23 Krystal Dr., RD 1, Somers, NY 10589, 914-763-2121, fax: 914-763-0851. Restoration of frames. Appraisals.

MAC Enterprises, 122 Miro Adelante, San Clemente, CA 92673, 949-361-9528, e-mail: macrestor@aol.com. Restoration of frames. Ship UPS or call for information. Send SASE for brochure.

Marylin Ash-Mower, 61 South Rd., East Kingston, NH 03827, 603-924-9499, e-mail: marylinashfa@attbi.com, website: www.MarylinAshFine Art.com. Restoration of antique picture frames. Silk and velvet easel backs renewed. Custom framing.

Museum Shop, Ltd., 20 N. Market St., Frederick, MD 21701, 301-695-0424. Restoration of oil paintings; 23K gold leafing. Restoration of paper, including documents, autographs, etchings, lithographs. Free brochure.

New England Country Silver, Inc., 25859 Wellington Rd., Crisfield, MD 21817, 410-968-3060, 9:00 A.M.–3:00 P.M. fax: 410-968-2810, e-mail: necsilver@aol.com, website: www.silverrestoring.com. Velvet backing for picture frames. Send merchandise insured mail or UPS. Free estimates. Free brochure.

New Orleans Conservation Guild, Inc., 3301 Chartres St., New Orleans, LA 70117, 504-944-7900, fax: 504-944-8750, e-mail: info@art-restora tion.com, website: www.art-restoration.com. Restoration and conservation of fine art and antiques, including frames. Appraisals and research searches. Call or write for brochure.

Oak Brothers, 5104 N. Pearl St., Tacoma, WA 98407, 253-752-4055, fax: 253-752-4055, e-mail: wmalovich@harbornet.com. Benders and sellers of curved glass for picture frames and other things. By appointment only. Call or write for more information.

Old World Restorations, Inc., 5729 Dragon Way, Cincinnati, OH 45227, 513-271-5459, fax: 513-271-5418, e-mail: info@oldworldrestorations.com, website: www.oldworldrestorations.com. Restoration and conservation of art and antiques, including frames. Free brochure.

PECO Glass Bending, PO Box 777, Smithville, TX 78957, 512-237-3600, e-mail:

glass@pecoglassbending.com, website: www.pecoglassbending.com. Convex glass for antique picture frames.

Peter J. Dugan, Fine Art Restoration, 1300 Coventry Cir., Vernon Hills, IL 60061, 847-367-0561, e-mail: pdugan6439@aol.com. Restoration of frames and other objects.

Premium Bevels, Inc., 2006 Johnson St., Lafayette, LA 70503, 800-752-3501, fax: 337-234-1646. Custom beveling of glass and mirrors. Mirror placemat sets. Reproduction of odd-shaped mirrors. Call for quote.

Restoration by Design, 1644 NW 34th Terr., Ft. Lauderdale, FL 33311, 954-791-6305, fax: 954-791-6330. Traditional (water and oil) and contemporary gilders: carat and composition gold, silver, and copper leaf. Conservation and restoration of period gilded picture and mirror frames. Reproductions made to order.

Reversen Time Inc., 6005 Bunchberry Ct., Raleigh, NC 27616-5454, 919-981-7323, e-mail: hamblest@mindspring.com, website: www.mind spring.com/~hamblesl/index.html. Small art frame repairs; gilding.

Rosine Green Associates, Inc., 89 School St., Brookline, MA 02446, 617-277-8368, fax: 617-731-3845, e-mail: rga@ix.netcom.com. Conservation and restoration of fine art, including frames and objects of art.

Thome Silversmiths, 49 W. 37th St., 4th Floor, New York, NY 10018, 212-764-5426 or 570-426-7480, fax: 212-391-8215 or 570-426-7481, e-mail: robert378@cs.com. Velvet backs for picture frames.

University Products, Inc., 517 Main St., PO Box 101, Holyoke, MA 01040, 800-336-4847, fax: 800-532-9281, e-mail: info@university products.com, website: www.universityproducts.com. Preservation framing supplies, tools, and equipment. Archival supplies for conservation, restoration, repair, storage, and display. Free catalog.

Williamstown Art Conservation Center, 225 South St., Williamstown, MA 01267, 413-458-5741, fax: 413-458-2314, e-mail: wacc@clark.williams.edu, website: www.williamstownart.org. Conservation of frames and other objects.

WTC Associates, Inc., 2532 Regency Rd., Lexington, KY 40503, 859-278-4171, fax: 859-277-5720. Mirrors resilvered; gold plating and gold leaf.

FURNITURE

The largest antiques you will have to sell are probably pieces of furniture. They are also among the most valuable, though their size creates special problems and limits your methods of sale. Antique and antique-style furniture has a market value that can be determined from price books, auctions, and shop sales. There are also many pieces of twentieth-century furniture in contemporary designs that have a value. You will hear about chairs that sell for $150,000 each, even one that brought $2.75 million, but these are the great rarities of the eighteenth century. You probably have less valuable pieces.

Any usable piece of furniture has a resale value. Higher prices are paid for pieces in fine original condition. Because new furniture is made with staples, glue, and veneers, well-constructed older pieces, even those in poor condition, can be sold. Study the price books and reference books in the library to find out about your furniture. If you have an antique-collecting friend, ask for an opinion about the pieces. A Chippendale-style chair could have been made in any year from 1760 to today.

If you own exceptionally large furniture (for example, a large bed, a grandfather clock that is over eight feet tall, or a very wide desk), be sure to determine how it can be removed from the room—maybe there is a removable finial or top cresting—and note this for the prospective buyer, since wise collectors have learned the hazards. A seven-foot-eleven-inch piece will sell for a better price than an eight-foot-one-inch piece, because most of today's homes have eight-foot ceilings. Deduct 50 percent from the value if a bookcase, desk, grandfather clock, or bed is over eight feet high or is too wide to go through an average door.

If you have any information about the furniture (old bills, where and when the pieces were bought, maker's labels, type of wood, pictures of the piece before you restored it, or written family history), present it to the prospective buyer with the furniture. A label adds to the value by 10 to 100 percent if the piece is worth less than $30,000. On the superstars of the furniture world, the pieces worth over $30,000, a label can increase the price four to five times. The fame of the maker determines how much value is added.

Elderly relatives sometimes hide money. Search all seat cushions for hidden valuables. Look for hidden compartments in desks. Look underneath drawers or inside the furniture. Carefully slit the backing on framed pictures and mirrors and look for valuable papers or money.

If you think there are some pieces of furniture over fifty years old, or if the pieces are original "fifties" style pieces, contact a local auctioneer and talk about the possible value at auction. The auction will advertise good antiques and get a higher price than you could through your own ads. If you are selling the entire contents of a house, a house sale might be best. The furniture may not bring top prices, but it will bring buyers, including antiques dealers, to the sale, and the other small items will sell for more. Do not invite a

FURNITURE STYLES YOU MIGHT FIND IN THE ATTIC

IMPORTED

Oriental (1700s–1900s; in recent books may be called *Asian*). Dark woods, often teak or rosewood, Oriental designs. Made in China, Japan, Korea, or India. Later pieces have elaborate carvings, lacquer, stone inlay. Some pieces were made in European shapes but with Oriental woods and decorations. All-wooden armchairs, screens, plant stands, large display cabinets.

Scandinavian (1700s–1900s). Brightly painted peasant designs over much of the wood. Blue and red preferred. Large cupboards, lift-top blanket chests, carved wooden chairs.

French (1770s–1900s). Louis XV style, rococo flowing lines, ornate curves, cabriole legs, asymmetrical; and Louis XVI style, dainty, neoclassical, straight legs.

Fantasy Furniture (1800–present). Carved shell chairs, Egyptian, Greek, Persian-inspired accessories, Bugatti designs.

Art Nouveau (1895–1910). Highly ornamental, asymmetrical, natural forms, plant-like motifs.

AMERICAN

Victorian Gothic Revival (1830–1850). Designs resemble gothic church arches; carvings, little upholstery. Walnut, rosewood, mahogany, maple. Straight-back chairs with carved high backs, settees, armchairs, washstands.

Victorian Rococo Revival (1845–1865). French-looking, ornamented, curved, carved fruit and flowers. Belter style. Rosewood, mahogany. Curved sofas, parlor sets, marble-topped tables, slipper chairs.

Eastlake Victorian (1870–1900). Rectangular furniture, contrasting color woods, incised lines. Walnut, burl, maple, veneer, oak. High-back beds, washstands, chairs, chests, and mirror dressers.

Colonial Revival or *Centennial* (1876–1900). Copies of the eighteenth- and early nineteenth-century William and Mary, Chippendale, Sheraton, Empire, and other designs.

Golden Oak (1880–1920). Mass-produced, heavy, dark or light oak, ash. Asymmetrical cabinets, chests of drawers, rolltop desks, claw-foot or pedestal dining tables, press-back chairs.

Cottage (1890–1920). Painted Eastlake adaptations, marbleized or solid color paint, trimmed with lines, flowers, pictorial medallions. Bedroom sets, small tables, chairs.

Mission or *Arts and Crafts* (1900–1920). Straight lines, solid wood—usually oak, no ornamentation, smooth surface. Rectangular tables, chairs, sofas, bookcases.

Office Furniture (1900–1930). Mission-inspired working pieces made for the office. Filing cabinets, large rolltop desks, lift-up glass-front stacked bookcases, captain's chairs, children's school desks.

Art Deco (1910–1930). Straight lines, geometric. Light-colored wood or black lacquer finish, mirrored surfaces. Square pedestal tables, bedroom sets.

Twig or Rustic (1890–1930). Bark-covered branches joined together to form chairs, tables, beds, plant stands, smoking stands. Animal horns, antlers, other natural materials used regionally.

Country (1700–1950). A "look," unsophisticated, worn, simple, handmade, solid wood, faded paint. Tables, large cupboards and shelf units, wooden chairs, stools. The most worn pieces are labeled "shabby chic."

Waterfall (1930s). Patterned veneer on cabinet doors, tabletops, or bed backs placed to make V-shaped design. Rounded corners, round mirrors. Base woods are poplar or ash. Bedroom and dining room sets.

French Revival (1930s). Copies of earlier brass and ormolu-trimmed furniture, especially French Louis XV and XVI. The name comes from costume jewelry, inexpensive copies of real jewelry.

Moderne (1930–1945). Sometimes called Hollywood Art Deco. The theatrical, modern-looking furniture seen in movies. Art Deco-inspired but a bit less severe and more dramatic. Coffee tables, dressing tables, glass-topped tables, rounded upholstered chairs.

Second Colonial Revival (1830s–1950s). Colonial styles, Wallace Nutting furniture.

Mid-Century Modern (1945–1970s). Sometimes called Organic. Freeform shapes, new materials and technology. Plastic, plywood, chrome, aluminum, steel. Interchangeable units and stacked chairs, coffee tables, wall-mounted shelf units. Blond "Scandinavian" sets.

Wicker (1850–1930). Victorian and Art Deco style pieces made of wicker or wickerlike twisted paper. Sometimes painted.

Brass and Iron Beds (1900–1920). Victorian to Deco styles. Solid brass or brass plated.

dealer in to pick out a few items if you are trying to sell the entire contents of the house. A smart dealer will buy the few good pieces, and you will have trouble getting anyone to come to see the remaining ones.

You need a few fast-selling items, like a rolltop desk or large dining room set, to entice dealers and collectors to a sale. Auctioneers will want the entire contents of the house only if there are some choice pieces. Price your pieces for your local market. It takes an expert to determine the age of a piece in a period style. A Chippendale chair dating from the eighteenth century is worth $1,500 to $150,000; a Chippendale-style chair from the nineteenth century is worth $1,500 to $3,000; a twentieth-century copy is worth $200 to

$500. If you have good reason to believe that your furniture is antique and may not bring a good price at a local auction, call or write to an out-of-town auction gallery about selling it. Send photographs of the front, back, and bottom construction. Oak furniture sells best in the West, elaborate Victorian in the South, and Art Deco in the East, Chicago, and southern Florida.

For period or old reproduction chairs of average quality: A pair is worth three times as much as a single; a set of four is worth six to seven times as much as a single. Six chairs are worth ten to twelve times as much as a single. A set of eight chairs is worth twelve to fifteen times the price of one chair. A set of twelve chairs including two armchairs is worth twenty times the price of one chair.

Dining-room table and chair sets should be sold as a unit. The breakfronts and buffets may be sold separately for better overall prices. A bedroom set usually brings the highest price when sold as a unit. Don't split the set so a friend can have the dresser. Offer the full set, but take bids on the individual pieces in case you can't sell the full set at a high enough price.

Sell a piano to a local piano store, or place an ad to sell it from the house. Unless they are top quality, pianos are very difficult to sell. The old square pianos do not stay in tune, sell low, and are usually purchased to be made into desks.

Serious collectors searching for pre-1875 painted furniture in original condition will pay a premium. Choice, painted furniture in good condition is worth 50 percent more than an unpainted similar piece. The paint was not as durable as polished wood; in poor condition it has to be sold at a lower price. Black ebonized Victorian furniture used to be worth 30 percent less than a similar piece with an unpainted finish, but in the early 1990s, collectors started to pay a premium for good ebonized pieces. It is very difficult to restore. If the original finish on a chair or table was painted and the piece has been stripped to natural wood, deduct 75 percent. In other words, a painted piece that is stripped is worth less than a similar piece that was originally made with a natural wood finish. Painted furniture made after 1900 is not rare and not yet in great demand.

Wicker, rustic or twig, cast-iron, and horn pieces are back in style and sell well. Furniture from the 1950s by important makers brings good prices at auction or from Art Moderne dealers. Some pieces from the 1960s and 1970s are gaining in value. Names of makers from the 1850s to 1950s such as **WOOTON, HERMAN MILLER, GUSTAV STICKLEY, L. & J.G. STICKLEY, LARKIN, HUNZINGER, POTIER AND**

STYMUS, HERTER, ROUX, NOGUCHI, NELSON, ROYCROFT, KNOLL, JUHL, PANTON, and RUSSEL WRIGHT add value.

Do not worry too much about how to move heavy antique furniture. There are always local movers listed in the Yellow Pages of your telephone book. There are also some long-distance moving companies that specialize in moving uncrated antique pieces. Ask any local antiques dealer for the name of someone in your area.

Most of the antique furniture that is bought and sold in America is English or American in design and manufacture. Other, less easily recognized types are also in demand. Pictures of all these types of furniture can be found in books at your library. Identify your piece from the pictures, then check in the price books for values.

REPAIRS

Repairs seriously change the value of an antique or collectible. The rarer the piece, the more acceptable a repair. An eighteenth-century American table can have replaced casters, a spliced foot, or even a restored edge, with no great loss in value. A twentieth-century table should be in pristine condition. The supply is greater and a perfect table probably exists, so a repaired piece loses value.

You should do easy repairs before you try to sell a piece. Dust and wipe off dirt. Rub the edges of drawers with paraffin to make them open easily. Reglue any loose parts or veneer. Tighten knobs and glue any wobbly legs by forcing the appropriate glue into the joints. Polish brasses if they need it. A light rubbing with scratch polish will often improve the look of the surface.

Sometimes an accurate restoration is impossible because there is no model to follow. We saw a Goddard block-front desk that should have been worth over $200,000. Unfortunately, all of the legs had been cut off in the 1880s, and new feet were made. There is no way to know what the original legs looked like, so the desk is worth about $20,000.

PRICING REPAIRED FURNITURE

Formulas for pricing are only a guide and not infallible. The formulas below are for pieces in attractive condition with almost invisible repairs.

Chest of drawers, good to excellent quality, pre-1850. If brasses are replacements, deduct 10 percent. If finish has been totally restored, deduct 10 percent. If one front foot has been replaced, deduct 10 percent. If two rear feet have been replaced, deduct 15 percent. If all feet have been replaced, deduct 70 percent. If important decorative carving has been replaced or if veneer is new, deduct 20 percent.

Chair, good quality, pre-1850. Look in a general price guide for a chair similar to yours. If the slip seat has been replaced, deduct nothing. If glued block braces (the structural supports under the chair) have been replaced, deduct nothing. If one or two leg brackets are restored, deduct nothing. If all leg brackets are restored, deduct 10 percent. If one leg is replaced, deduct 33 percent. If a splat or an important part of the chair back has been replaced, deduct 33 percent. If the top crest rail is replaced, deduct 10 to 15 percent.

Early nineteenth-century furniture with veneered fronts. If veneer is replaced, deduct 50 to 90 percent. Original veneer is an important part of the design of the furniture. A small, well-matched patch does not lower the value, but a totally new veneer surface cannot imitate the original appearance. Sometimes just one drawer has replaced veneer. If it is a well-matched piece of wood, deduct 50 percent. If all the veneer on the front of the piece is replaced, deduct 90 percent.

Eighteenth- or early nineteenth-century table, good quality. If top is replaced, deduct 50 percent. If one plain leg is replaced, deduct 20 percent. If all carved feet have been restored or replaced, deduct 90

BE CAREFUL WHEN YOU BUY

Some people hesitate to buy antique beds because they worry about technical problems, such as special mattress sizes and special restoration techniques. The problems can be solved in various ways:

1. Measure an antique bed carefully before buying it. Make sure the bed is not too high for your ceiling, because surgery on bedposts reduces the bed's value.
2. Rope "springs" are satisfactory, but they must be properly laced and tightened periodically. A box spring can also be used if it is supported by metal brackets. Standard brackets can be screwed into the frame, but the best solution is to have six or eight hanging supports custom-made by an ornamental ironworker. They do not harm the frame or reduce the value of the bed. If the box spring combined with a standard mattress is too high, a thinner foam-rubber mattress can be substituted.
3. Odd-sized mattresses and box springs can be custom-made in most major cities or ordered by mail.
4. Antique-style bed hangings, canopies, and rope springs are also available.

It is best to be sure your bed is one of the standard sizes in use today if you plan to use readily available sheets and bedspreads.

percent. Watch out for "marriages," a top of one table put on the legs of another. Look underneath the top for signs of this. There will be unexpected screw holes or color variations.

Desk, pre-1900. If the interior compartments or drawers are missing, deduct 30 percent. If the interior compartments or drawers are accurately replaced, deduct 20 percent. If one interior drawer or drawer front is a replacement, deduct nothing. If the desk has been created from a reworked bookshelf cabinet (drawer removed, fall front added), deduct 75 percent.

Other. If the top of a table or chest is warped but can be fixed, deduct 20 percent. If the top of a table or chest is extremely warped or split, the sides split, or inlay or marquetry badly damaged, deduct 75 percent. If the top of a table or chest has been reworked, given rounded edges, extra trim or carving, deduct 50 percent. If the marble top of a Victorian table is badly cracked or damaged, deduct 50 percent.

Watch out for repairs that affect value on later pieces of furniture. Glass doors on secretary-desks are more desirable than wooden doors because they are preferred for display. Add 50 percent to the value for original glass, but if the glass is a replacement for a solid wooden door, subtract 50 percent.

Welsh cupboards with original spoon holders are worth 50 percent more than plain cupboards, but if the spoon holders have been newly added, price the cupboard like a plain one.

REFINISHING AND RESTORING

Refinishing and restoring furniture has been discussed in dozens of books. For precise information on what to do, how to do it, and what finishes are best, we suggest that you go to your local hardware or paint store or library, and study the products, books, and methods. Local experts are listed in the Yellow Pages of your telephone book. We have listed a few of the major books and included sources for many of the materials. You may find additional sources in the hardware section of this book.

The general rule for refinishing an antique is "less is better." Never strip a piece that can be restored. Never remove a painted surface that can be saved. If you want furniture with a natural wood finish, don't buy an antique with an original painted finish. For many years, collectors used a polish made with boiled linseed oil, which has a finish that darkens with age and cannot be removed. Do not use it. Certain early paints made with buttermilk, blood, and other pigments are almost impossible to remove from wood pores. Many pieces of furniture are made of a variety of woods, so stripping and refinishing may result in a hodgepodge of colors.

Our ancestors seem to have delighted in surrounding themselves with chairs. Inventories of homes from the late eighteenth century list over a dozen chairs in a single room, even in a small bedroom. We often wonder how they found space for all of them. Whatever the reason, the chair is still one of the most popular pieces of furniture in a home. An odd chair from a different period is often placed in a room as a special accent.

Refinishing and restoring chairs can be handled by most amateurs. Recaning, upholstering, and other more complicated parts of refinishing may require a few special lessons, but many adult education centers and schools offer this type of instruction. Libraries are filled with books that furnish detailed refinishing information. Most of these services are also available through local decorating shops or services. Look in the Yellow Pages under "Caning," "Furniture Repairing & Refinishing," and "Upholsterers."

Sometimes a wooden chair needs minor "tightening." The glue has dried and the parts wobble. Special products found in hardware stores can solve this problem. Just squirt a bit of the special glue into the loose joints. If the parts are very loose, you may have to take the arm or leg off the chair, clean the pegs or posts and holes, and reglue them with modern wood glue. Brass furniture, especially a bed, requires special care. The brass can be polished and lacquered to keep it from darkening. Talk to a local metal polishing or replating shop.

◆→ SEE ALSO GLASS, HARDWARE, METALS, AND WICKER, RATTAN & BASKETRY

Buying and selling furniture on the Internet is difficult. Shipping costs and inconvenience far outweigh any advantages you might find in the enlarged audience. There are dealers who advertise furniture on their websites, but the descriptions are vague. Use the Internet to find dealers, restorers, and experts in your area and talk to them in person.

REFERENCE BOOKS

1000 Chairs, Charlotte and Peter Fiell (Taschen, New York, 1997).
American Furniture, 1620 to the Present, Jonathan L. Fairbanks and
    Elizabeth Bidwell Bates (Richard Marek, New York, 1981).
American Furniture: Queen Anne and Chippendale Periods, Joseph Downs
    (Macmillan, New York, 1952).
American Furniture: The Federal Period, Charles F. Montgomery (Viking,
    New York, 1966).

American Seating Furniture, 1630–1730: An Interpretive Catalogue, Benno M. Forman (W.W. Norton, New York, 1988).

American Windsor Chairs, Nancy Goyne Evans (Hudson Hills, New York, 1996).

Antiques Directory: Furniture, Judith and Martin Miller, editors (MJM, London, and G.K. Hall & Co., Boston, 1985).

Centuries and Styles of the American Chair, 1640–1970, Robert Bishop (E.P. Dutton, New York, 1972).

The Complete Book of Shaker Furniture, Timothy D. Rieman and Jean M. Burks (Harry N. Abrams, New York, 1993).

Decorative Art Yearbook, 5 volumes, Charlotte and Peter Fiell (Taschen, New York, 2000).

Dictionary of Furniture, 2nd edition, by Charles Boyce (Facts on File, NY, 2001).

Finnish Modern Design, Maarianne Aav et al. (Yale University Press, New Haven, CT, 1998).

Furniture of the American Arts and Crafts Movement: Stickley and Roycroft Mission Oak, David M. Cathers (New American Library, New York, 1981).

In the Arts & Crafts Style, Barbara Mayer (Chronicle Books, San Francisco, 1992).

Innovative Furniture in America, From 1800 to the Present, David A. Hanks (Horizon, New York, 1981).

The Look of the Century, Michael Tambini (DK Publishing, New York, 1996).

Modern Furniture Designs, 1950–1980s, Klaus-Jürgen Sembach, editor (Schiffer, Atglen, PA, 1997).

New England Furniture at Winterthur: Queen Anne and Chippendale Period, Nancy E. Richards and Nancy Goyne Evans (Winterthur, distributed by University Press of New England, 23 South Main St., Hanover, NH 03755-2048, 1997).

The New Fine Points of Furniture, Albert Sack (Crown, New York, 1993).

The Pegged Joint: Restoring Arts and Crafts Furniture and Finishes, Bruce Johnson (Knock on Wood Publications, P.O. Box 8773, Asheville, NC 28814, 1995).

Rustic Traditions, Ralph Kylloe (Gibbs Smith, Layton, UT, 1993).

Sourcebook of Modern Furniture, Jerryll Habegger and Joseph H. Osman (Van Nostrand Reinhold, New York, 1989).

Wicker Furniture: A Guide to Restoring & Collecting, revised edition, Richard Saunders (Crown, New York, 1990).

SOURCE FOR ADDITIONAL REFERENCES

Furniture Library, 1009 N. Main St., High Point, NC 27262, 336-883-4011, Mon.–Fri. 9:00 A.M.–5:00 P.M., fax: 336-883-6579, website: www.furniture library.com. Over 7,000 books on furniture and furniture-related subjects are available for research. Free catalog of books for sale.

PRICE BOOKS

Antique Trader Furniture Price Guide, Mark Moran, editor (Krause, Iola, WI, 2001).

The Arts & Crafts Price Guide: Furniture—Gustav Stickley, L. & J.G. Stickley, Charles Stickley, and Roycroft, A Decade of Auction Results, Treadway Gallery in association with John Toomey Gallery (Treadway, Cincinnati, OH, 1998).

The Arts & Crafts Price Guide: Furniture—Limbert, Stickley Brothers, Lifetime, Shop of the Crafters, and Frank Lloyd Wright, A Decade of Auction Results, Treadway Gallery in association with John Toomey Gallery (Treadway, Cincinnati, OH, 1998).

British Antique Furniture: Price Guide and Reasons for Values, 4th edition, John Andrews (Antique Collectors' Club, Wappingers' Falls, NY 12590, 2001).

Dunbar: Fine Furniture of the 1950s, Margaret Hockaday, editor (Schiffer, Atglen, PA, 2000).

Encyclopedia of American Oak Furniture, Robert W. and Harriett Swedberg (Krause, Iola, WI, 2000).

Fifties Furniture by Paul McCobb: Directional Designs, catalog reprint (Schiffer, Atglen, PA, 2000).

Fifties Furniture, 2nd edition, Leslie Piña (Schiffer, Atglen, PA, 2000).

French Provincial Furniture, Robin Ruddy (Schiffer, Atglen, PA, 1998).

The Herman Miller Collection: The 1955/1956 Catalog. Reprint of Herman Miller Furniture Co. catalog from 1955–56 (Schiffer, Atglen, PA, 1998).

Heywood-Wakefield Modern Furniture Identification and Value Guide, Steve Rouland and Roger Rouland (Collector Books, Paducah, KY, 1995).

Knoll Furniture, 1938–1960, Steven and Linda Rouland (Schiffer, Atglen, PA, 1999).

Late 19th Century Furniture by Berkey & Gay, Brian L. Witherell (Schiffer, Atglen, PA, 1998).

More Golden Oak, Velma Susanne Warren (Schiffer, Atglen, PA, 1998).

The 1950s/Modern Furniture Price Guide: Auction Results from the 1990's, 2 volumes (Treadway, Cincinnati, OH, 1999).

Pine Furniture: The Country Look, Nancy N. Schiffer (Schiffer, Atglen, PA, 1999).

Popular Furniture of the 1920s and 1930s: From Traditional to Early (Schiffer, Atglen, PA, 1998).

Rattan Furniture: Tropical Comfort throughout the House, Harvey Schwartz (Schiffer, Atglen, PA, 1999).

Styles of American Furniture: 1860–1960, Eileen and Richard Dubrow (Schiffer, Atglen, PA, 1997).

Warman's American Furniture, Ellen T. Schroy, editor (Krause, Iola, WI, 2001).

PUBLICATIONS

Windsor Chronicles (NL), 44 Timber Swamp Rd., Hampton, NH 03842, e-mail: info@thewinsdorinstitute.com, website: TheWinsdorInstitute.com.

ARCHIVES & MUSEUMS

The Brooklyn Museum of Art, 200 Eastern Pkwy., Brooklyn, NY 11238-6052, 718-638-5000, e-mail: information@brooklynmuseum.org, website: www.brooklynmuseum.org.

The Chicago Athenaeum: Museum of Architecture and Design, 307 N. Michigan Ave., Chicago, IL 60601, 312-372-1083, fax: 312-372-1085, website: www.chi-athenaeum.org.

Colonial Williamsburg, PO Box 1776, Williamsburg, VA 23187-1776, 757-229-1000, website: www.history.org.

Craftsman Farms, The Gustav Stickley Museum, 2352 Rt. 10-W, Box 5, Morris Plains, NJ 07950, 973-540-1165, fax: 973-540-1167, website: www.parsippany.net/craftsmanfarms.html.

Henry Francis du Pont Winterthur Museum, Rte. 52, Winterthur, DE 19735, 302-888-4600, fax: 302-888-4880, website: www.winterthur.org.

High Museum of Art, 1280 Peachtree St. N.E., Atlanta, GA 30309, 404-733-4400, website: www.high.org.

The Hitchcock Museum, PO Box 95, Riverton, CT, 06063, 203-738-4950.

The Metropolitan Museum of Art, 1000 5th Ave., New York, NY 10028-1098, 212-879-5500, website: www.metmuseum.org.

Shaker Museum and Library, 88 Shaker Museum Rd., Old Chatham, NY 12136, 518-794-9100, website: www.shakermuseumoldchat.org.

The Wolfsonian, 1001 Washington Ave., Miami Beach, FL 33139, 305-531-1001, fax: (305) 531-2133, website: www.wolfsonian.fiu.edu.

USEFUL SITES

Online Arts and Crafts Movement Resource Directory, www.ragtime.org/Ragtime_Resources.html.

APPRAISERS

The auction and repair services listed in this section will do appraisals. *See also* the general list of "Appraisal Groups" on page 483.

AUCTIONS

➻ **SEE ALSO "SELLING THROUGH AUCTION HOUSES," PAGE 485.**

Most of the major auction houses sell furniture. See the general list of auction houses in "Selling Through Auction Houses," page 485.

Willis Henry Auctions, 22 Main St., Marshfield, MA 02050, 781-834-7774, fax: 781-826-3936, e-mail: wha@willishenry.com, website: www.willis

henry.com. Shaker and decorative arts auctions. Mail and phone bids accepted. Buyer's premium 15%. Prices realized mailed after auction. Prices of catalogs vary. Advice on restoration and conservation. Appraisals.

REPAIRS, PARTS & SUPPLIES

⇥ SEE ALSO "CONSERVATORS & RESTORERS," PAGE 520.

18th Century Hardware Co., Inc., 131 E. Third St., Derry, PA 15627, 724-694-2708, fax: 724-694-9587. Duplication of missing hardware on antique furniture. Metal items cleaned and polished. Broken items repaired. Catalog $3.

3-R Artisans, 4790 Coppedge Tr., Duluth, GA 30096, 770-476-5152, fax: 770-476-4297, e-mail: pmweichild@mindspring.com. Furniture restoration, repair, refinishing, and upholstery. Custom cabinet construction and design. Free brochure.

A & H Brass & Supply, 126 W. Main St., Johnson City, TN 37604, 423-928-8220. Complete line of restoration hardware; reproduction furniture hardware, veneers, caning supplies, replacement seats, Briwax, Howard's products. Trunk supplies. Catalog $3.

A Home Design, 5220 Veloz Ave., Los Angeles, CA 91356, 818-757-7766, fax: 818-708-3722, e-mail: homedesign@mail.com. Furniture and antiques touch-ups and restoration. Fabric and leather furniture repairs, cleaning, and re-upholstering. Fine arts restoration, including items made from marble, woodcarvings, glass, and mirrors. Moving and damage claims, inspection and repair. Operating in the southern California area.

Able to Cane, 439 Main St., PO Box 429, Warren, ME 04864, 207-273-3747, fax: 207-774-6481, e-mail: boz@midcoast.com, website: abletocane.net. Restoration of antique furniture. Natural rush seating, Shaker taping, French caning, wicker repair. Caning and basketry supplies. Instruction available. Catalog upon request.

Advanced Leather Solution, 27365 Industrial Blvd., Hayward, CA 94545, 510-786-6059, fax: 510-785-9078, e-mail: kgillan@advleather.com, website: advleather.com. Restoration of leather furniture. Repairs of rips, cuts, burns, and stains. Full-color restoration and color changes, partial to full reupholstery, and custom matching. Free brochure.

Antique Hardware and Mirror Resilvering, 763 West Bippley Rd., Lake Odessa, MI 48849, 616-374-7750, fax: 616-374-7752, e-mail: antiquehardware@robinsonsantiques.com, website: www.robinsons antiques.com. Original antique restoration hardware. Furniture hardware, mirrors, locks, pulls, hinges, latches, registers, and more. Mirror resilvering. Original parts from 1650 to 1925. Free search. Free matching service.

Antique Restoration Co., 440 E. Centre Ave., Newtown, PA 18940, 215-968-2343, fax: 215-860-5465. Furniture stripping, repair, and refinishing. Cushions refilled and recovered; upholstery. Caning, rushing, and splint weave. Billiard tables restored, moved, and set up. Frames repaired. Mirror resilvering; gold leafing; glass beveling. Metal polishing, plating, and lacquering. Free brochure.

Antique Restorations, The Old Wheelwrights', Brasted Forge, Brasted, Kent TN16 1JL, U.K., 011-44-1959-563863, fax: 011-44-1959-561262, e-mail: bfc@antique-restorations.org.co.uk, website: www.antique-restorations.org.uk. Furniture restoration and conservation. Clock case restoration, brass castings and repair, polishing, upholstery, documentation service.

AntiqueConservation.com, Div. of Ponsford Ltd., 5441 Woodstock Rd., Acworth, GA 30102, 770-924-4848, fax: 770-529-2278, e-mail: GordonPonsford@AntiqueConservation.com, website: www.Antique Conservation.com. Conservation and restoration of furniture, fine art and antiques, and more. Appraisals.

Antiques on the Mend, 1428 Bellaire Dr., Colorado Springs, CO 80909, 719-630-0378, fax: 719-630-8736, e-mail: margaret@antiquesonthe mend.com, website: www.antiquesonthemend.com. Structural repairs, wobbly joints reglued, parts replaced when necessary. Veneering and veneer patching, including marquetry panels. Repairs to finishes: scratches, dents, burn marks, gouges, stains, water rings. Revive blushed, cracked, and worn finishes. Refinishing; upholstery.

Artisans of the Valley, 103 Corrine Dr., Pennington, NJ 08534, 609-637-0450, fax: 609-637-0452, e-mail: woodworkers@artisansofthe valley.com, website: www.artisansofthevalley.com. Specializes in conservation and restoration services and hand crafted custom woodworking. Old finishes restored, missing carvings and moldings made, leather restored. Consultation services to architects, contractors, and curators. Free catalog.

B & L Antiqurie, Inc., 6217 S. Lakeshore Rd., PO Box 453, Lexington, MI 48450, 810-359-8623, toll free ordering Mon.–Fri. 8:00 A.M.–5:00 P.M., fax: 810-359-7498, e-mail: information@bentglasscentral.com, website: www.bentglasscentral.com. Replacement curved glass for china cabinets and display cases, curios, etc. Pattern cut and beveled mirrors, convex picture frame glass, antique seedy flat glass, beveled glass. Send SASE for more information.

B.M.R.D., Inc. Heirloom Furniture, 9860-2 Owensmouth Ave., Chatsworth, CA 91311, 818-772-8908, fax: 818-772-8982, website: repairpro1.com. Antique furniture restoration, furniture repairs, refinishing, reupholstering. Wood turning, wood carving, veneering, gilding, pyroengraving. Will supply and fit bent glass and flat glass, both regular and "antique" glass. Pick up and delivery in local area.

Ball & Ball Antique Hardware Reproductions, 436 W. Lincoln Hwy., Exton, PA 19341, 800-257-3711, fax: 610-363-7639, website: www.balland ball.com. Reproduction furniture and cabinet hardware. Hardware and metal items repaired and refinished.

Basic Enterprise, 320 Krotzer Ave., Luckey, OH 43443, 419-833-5551, fax: 419-833-1251, e-mail: csarver@luckey.net. Furniture repair and refinishing. Chair seats and caning. Mirror resilvering.

Bedlam Brass Restoration, 520 River Dr., Garfield, NJ 07026, 800-BEDLAM-1, fax: 800-BEDLAM-2, e-mail: sales@bedlam.biz, website: bedlam.biz. Restoration and refinishing of beds, lights, etc. New brass parts.

Bob Morgan Woodworking Supplies, 1121 Bardstown Rd., Louisville, KY 40204, 502-456-2545, e-mail: info@morganwood.com, website: www.morganwood.com. Veneers for antique restoration: flexibles, 2-plys, fancy faces, burls, crotches, flitch veneers, custom-made veneer faces; inlays, chair cane. Brochure $1. Free veneering advice. Call and ask for Bob Morgan.

Bonatesta Furniture Services, 1201 Pennsylvania Ave., Natrona Heights, PA 15065-1401, 724-448-1080, e-mail: mj.bonatesta@verizon.net. Furniture refinishing; on-location repairs to wood and upholstery. Moving claims.

Brass Foundry Castings, Brasted Forge, Brasted, Kent TN16 1JL, England, 011-44-1959-563863, fax: 011-44-1959-561262, e-mail: bfc@antique-restorations.org.uk, website: www.antique-restorations.org.uk. Handcrafted reproduction antique brass furniture fittings, clock mounts, castings, escutcheons, finials, architectural and interior design fittings dating back to the 17th century. Handmade, including wear and blemishes, and produced by the lost wax casting process. Can order online on the website.

C & H Supply, 5431 Mountville Rd., Adamstown, MD 21710, 301-663-1812, Mon.–Fri. 9:00 A.M.–5:00 P.M., e-mail: CandHSupplyCo@aol.com. Reproduction brass hardware, wood and porcelain knobs, table parts, chair caning supplies, replacement chair seats, short bed rails, cannonballs for iron and brass beds, replacement trunk parts, pie-safe tins, icebox hardware, kitchen cabinet hardware, flour bins. Veneers, paint and varnish removers, stains and lacquers. Most orders shipped within 24 hours. Catalog $4.

Cane & Basket Supply Co., 1238 S. Cochran Ave., Los Angeles, CA 90019, 323-939-9644, fax: 323-939-7237, e-mail: info@caneandbasket.com, website: www.caneandbasket.com. Hand caning, French caning, blind caning, press caning, rush seating, natural and fiber. Wicker repair. Weaving. Shaker tape weaving, rawhide weaving. Supplies for the do-it-yourselfer. Free catalog.

Caning Shop, 926 Gilman St., Dept. KOV, Berkeley, CA 94710-1494, 800-544-3373, fax: 510-527-7718, e-mail: jwidess@caning.com, website: www.caning.com. Complete selection of chair caning, supplies, books, and tools. Cane, webbing spline, reed, rattan poles, sea grass, ash splints, hickory bark, rawhide, shaker tape, gourds, basketry dyes, hoops and handles, pressed fiber seats, raffia, waxed linen threads, etc. Danish furniture repair. Classes. Free brochure.

Carter Canopies, Box 808, Troutman, NC 28166, 800-538-4071, fax: 704-528-6437, e-mail: jcarter@abts.net, website: www.cartercanopies.com. Hand-tied fishnet bed canopies, window valances, and table overlays. Custom dust ruffles. Mail order nationwide. Free brochure.

Central Glass Products Inc., 405 W. Hamon Ave., Pocola, OK 74902, 888-BENTGLA(SS) 800-236-8452, fax: 888-BENTGLA(SS) 800-236-8452, e-mail: info@bentglass.com, website: www.bentglass.com. Bent-curved china cabinet replacement glass. Antique seeded glass available.

The Chair Shop, 101 South St., Chagrin Falls, OH 44022, 440-247-2126, e-mail: lnelson@oh.verio.com. Seat weaving of rush, splint, Danish cord, cane, and cane webbing. Gluing and repair. Finish cleaning and oiling.

Chairs for All Seasons, 24 Whitney Avenue, Framingham, MA, 508-872-2966, e-mail: samekm@yahoo.com. Chair caning: 7-step, fiber rush, porch weave, pressed. Also minor repairs and refinishing.

Chem-Clean Furniture Restoration, Bucks County Art & Antiques Co., 246 W. Ashland St., Doylestown, PA 18901, 215-345-0892, e-mail: iscsusn@att.net. Furniture repair and restoration; stripping, finishing, caning, re-upholstery, glass bending, glass beveling, gold leafing, marble repair, metal polishing, mirror resilvering, plastic repair, and more. Research. Appraisals. Free brochure.

Cohen and Cohen, Kris's Custom Woodworking Studio, 1963 Merivale Rd., Ottawa, ON K2G 1G1, 1-866-937-3873, e-mail: kenbill@cohenand cohen.com, website: www.cohenandcohen.com. Repair, restoration, re-furnishing (old and new), reproductions and new designs for furniture. For woodworking quotes, call or send e-mail to Kris Persaud, Ken Billings, or Gary Colautti.

Colonial Woodworks, Inc, 1709 Laurel St., Columbia, SC 29201, 803-254-7519, fax: 803-765-2643, e-mail: colonialwoodwork@aol.com. Repair and refinishing of furniture and antiques; replacement of missing parts. Chair caning and rushing, veneer repairs and replacement, pickled finishes. Upholstery and fabrics. Moving, insurance, and military claims. Serving all of South Carolina, Augusta, GA, and Charlotte, NC. Custom building and carving. In-home touch-ups.

Connecticut Cane & Reed Co., PO Box 762, Manchester, CT 06040, 860-646-6586, fax: 860-649-2221, e-mail: canereed@ntpix.net, website: www.caneandreed.com. Chair seating and basketry supplies. Free catalog.

Constantines Wood Center, 1040 E. Oakland Park Blvd., Ft. Lauderdale, FL 33334, 954-561-1716, fax: 954-565-8149, website: www.constantines.com. Woodworkers supplies, including hardwoods, veneer, tools, hardware, and cane. Free catalog. Hours: Mon.–Fri. 8:30 A.M.–5:30 P.M., Sat. 9:00 A.M.–4:00 P.M. (October 1–May 31); Mon.–Fri. 8:30 A.M.–5:30 P.M., Sat. 9:00 A.M.–1:00 P.M. (June 1–September 30).

Country Accents, 1723 Scaife Rd., Williamsport, PA 17701, 570-478-4127, fax: 570-478-2007, e-mail: caccents@msn.com, website: www.pierced tin.com. Pierced tin cupboard inserts in over 300 designs and 14 different metal finishes. Custom sizes and designs. Catalog $5. Samples: 14 pieces with catalog $22.95.

Craftsman's Passion, 105 A Pan Ridge Ct., Point Harbor, NC 27964, 252-491-5333, fax: 252-491-5334, e-mail: cpassion@pinn.net, website: www.craftsmanspassion.com. Furniture restoration and repairs, including replacement of damaged or missing parts, stripping, refinishing, veneering, turning, and carvings. Custom furniture handmade.

Dr. Michael A. Taras, 215 S. Craggmore Dr., Salem, SC 29676, 864-944-0655. Identification of domestic and foreign woods.

Excel Shop, 112 Bauer Ave., Louisville, KY 40207, 502-895-7374, fax: 502-895-7374, e-mail: excelshop@juno.com. Full service furniture restoration company. Furniture repair, stripping, refinishing, upholstery, caning, painting; distinctive fabrics and custom-built furniture. On-site touch-up, estimates, furniture hardware, fabric remnants, pick-up and delivery in local area. Free brochure.

Faneuil Furniture Hardware Co., Inc., 163 Main St., Salem, NH 03079, 603-898-7733, fax: 603-898-7839. Solid brass reproduction hardware for furniture pulls. Traditional, French, Oriental, Victorian. Knobs, ornaments, pendant pulls, escutcheons, casters, hinges, and drapery tiebacks. Catalog $5.

Final Touch, Inc., 34 Ranch Rd., Woodbridge, CT 06525, 203-389-5485, fax: 203-389-5553, e-mail: FinalTh@optonline.net. Repair and restoration of furniture, specializing in antiques. Custom color matching, faux finishing, carvings, moldings, and reproductions. Appraisals.

Florentine Antique Restoration, 86 Regan Rd., Ridgefield, CT 06877, 203-431-8726, fax: 203-431-8726. Antique furniture restoration, specializing in carving, gilding, turning, and inlay, using classical restoration techniques.

Floyd J. Rosini, 6126 Rt. 22, Millerton, NY 12546, 518-789-3582, 8:00 A.M.–4:30 P.M. fax: 518-789-6386, e-mail: RosiniAntiques@taconic.net, website: www.rosiniantiques.com. Furniture repaired, restored, and reconditioned. Furniture care products, including polish, touch-up markers, and other supplies. Workshop seminars on antique maintenance.

Frank's Cane & Rush Supply, 7244 Heil Ave., Huntington Beach, CA 92647, 714-847-0707, fax: 714-843-5645, e-mail: franks@franksupply.com, website: www.Franksupply.com. Chair caning and seat weaving supplies; wicker repair and upholstery supplies; basketry and fiber arts supplies; wood parts and wood furniture kits; raffia and hat-making supplies; bamboo and rattan poles; videos and instruction books.

Furniture Repair Works, LLC, 1426 Brevard Rd., Asheville, NC 28806,

828-670-7764, fax: 828-670-7949. Furniture repair and restoration. In-home repairs.

Gensys Inc., 104 E. Ave K-4, Suite A, Lancaster, CA 93536, 661-726-9525, fax: 661-726-9525, e-mail: id.denham@verizon.net, website: www.gensys inc.net. Gensys Inc. represents E-Z Way Restoration Products, refinishing products that eliminate methylene chloride and remove paint, varnish, and other coatings. Products for coating metal and wood. Free restoration course. Complete package for care and restoration of antiques and homeowner items. "Free Restoration Primer" on their website.

George G. Whitmore Co., Inc., 311 Farm Hill Rd., Middletown, CT 06457, 860-346-3492, e-mail: berylwthorpe@aol.com, website: www.ggwhitmore.com. Furniture repair, restoration, refinishing, and reproduction. Free brochure.

Golden's Antique Supply, 8990 Main St., Woodstock, GA 30188, 888-202-1029 or 770-924-8528, fax: 770-924-8980, e-mail: wcgolden @antiquesupply.com, website: www.antiquesupply.com. Everything for the "antiqueholic:" testing equipment, restoration supplies, archival supplies, display, hardware, books, and videos.

H.H. Perkins Co., 222 Universal Dr., North Haven, CT 06473, 800-462-6660, fax: 203-787-1161, e-mail: HPerkinsco@HHPerkins.com, website: www.HHPerkins.com. Seat weaving supplies, including cane, rush, and splint. Furniture kits, repair and restoration products, tools, stains and finishes, books, patterns, and videos. Free catalog.

Hamilton, PO Box 815, West Newbury, MA 01985, 800-439-8774, fax: 978-363-2638, e-mail: hamfurnrestore@greennet.net, website: www.patinarestoration.com. Restoration and conservation of antique and fine quality furniture. Specialized services: structural repair, carving, worm damage repair, lathe turning, French polishing, boulé and ormolu repair, clock case restoration, caning and rushing. Custom stands for trays and boxes. Brass cleaning and sealing; hardware replacement. Research, consulting, inspections, condition reports, photo documentation. Custom finishing. Lecturing. References.

Harvard Art, 49 Littleton County Rd., Harvard, MA 01451, 978-456-9050, fax: 978-456-9050, e-mail: sjackson@harvardart.com, website: harvardart.com. Gilding conservation and restoration of furniture, frames, and mirrors. Securing of loose elements, structural repair, missing pieces replaced, gesso fills, ingilding, and toning to match.

Hensler Furniture Refinishing Inc., 310 Christy Way, Saginaw, MI 48603, 989-792-1311, fax: 989-249-5291, e-mail: info@henslerfurniture restore.com, website: www.henslerfurniturerestore.com. Complete restoration of antique and contemporary furniture. Duplication of missing parts, carving, and turnings. Free brochure.

Heritage Furniture Systems, PO Box 442, Shillington, PA 19607, 800-

889-6498, fax: 800-889-0112, e-mail: hfsym@juno.com. Furniture repair and restoration, specializing in moving damage claims.

Herman Miller for the Home, 855 E. Main Ave., Zeeland, MI 49464, 800-646-4400, website: www.hermanmiller.com. Parts and service for all Eames molded-plywood products.

Horton Brasses, 47-51 Nooks Hill Rd., PO Box 120, Cromwell, CT 06416, 860-754-9127, fax: 860-635-6473, e-mail: barb@horton-brasses.com, website: www.horton-brasses.com. Reproduction brass and iron furniture and cabinet hardware. Hardware from 1650 to 1940 reproduced. Much hand-forged iron in stock. Polishes, waxes, and cleaners. Catalog $4.

Hudson Glass Co. Inc., Dept. K-8, 219 N. Division St., Peekskill, NY 10566-2700, 800-431-2964 or 914-737-2124, fax: 914-737-4447. Bent glass for china cabinets, tools, and supplies. No repairs. Catalog $5 ($3 refundable with order).

Image Restoration Services, Inc., PO Box 489, Belvidere, IL 61008-0489, 815-547-5919, fax: 815-547-6413, e-mail: kummerowdl@aol.com. Complete restoration services of furniture.

Ingrid Sanborn & Daughter, 85 Church St., West Newbury, MA 01985, 978-363-2253, fax: 978-363-2049, e-mail: sanbornanddaughters@mediaone.net, website: www.isd.pair.com. Restoration and reproduction of painted furniture. Reproduction églomisé. Restoration and reproduction of reverse paintings on glass.

Inman Historic Interiors, Inc., 3367 170th St., Randolph, IA 51649-6020, 712-625-2403, fax: 712-625-2403, e-mail: jidesignasid@netscape.net, website: www.historicinteriors.com. Furniture restoration, veneering, mirror resilvering, antique frame restoration, gilding, parts duplication, interior consulting. Hide glue and specialty waxes. Free brochure.

Items of Value, Inc., 7419 Admiral Dr., Alexandria, VA 22307, 703-660-9380, fax: 703-660-9384. Restoration work for many different types of items. Restoration of wood. Regilding. Reproduction of brass hardware. Appraisals.

J.C. Wood Finishing Services, 918 Westwood St., Addison, IL 60101, 630-628-6161, fax: 630-628-9523, e-mail: jcwood1@worldnet.att.net. Repairs and restorations; refinishing, preventive maintenance of furniture, mirrors, glass tops, pianos, kitchen cabinets. Veneering, rushing and caning, custom finishes, color matching, upholstery, leather cleaning and repair. Free estimates. Free brochure.

James Lane, 8834 N. Virginia Ave., Palm Beach Gardens, FL 33418, 561-615-0622, e-mail: antiquef@bellsouth.net, website: www.antiquerestorers.com/LEATHER.htm. Desk-top leathers. Custom colors available.

Joseph Biunno, 129 W. 29th St., 2nd Floor., New York, NY 10001, 212-629-5630, fax: 212-268-4577, e-mail: finunlim@aol.com, website:

www.antiquefurnitureusa.com. Restoration and refinishing of fine furniture and antiques.

Kistner's Full Claims Service, Inc., 520 20th St., Rock Island, IL 61201, 309-786-5868, fax: 309-794-0559, e-mail: kistners1@home.com, website: www.kistners.com. Complete furniture restoration, specializing in hand-rubbed finishes, European wax finishes, shellac finishes, and today's gallery finishes. Manufacture of new wooden parts; antique hardware replaced. Serving eastern Iowa and northwestern Illinois. Free brochure.

L.J. Cook, Fine Woodworking, 61292 C.R. 7, Elkhart, IN 46517, 219-295-1878, e-mail: larry.j.cook@gte.net. Repairs to antique furniture. Finish restorations, refinishing. Veneer repairs, inlay and inlay repairs.

Lockwood Refinishing & Restoration, 7700 N. Hwy. VV, Columbia, MO 65202, 573-442-7109, fax: 573-449-9400, e-mail: cnl46@yahoo.com, website: lockwoodrefinishing.com. Restoration, refinishing, and repair of antique and contemporary furniture. Seat caning and rushing; parts fabrication. Can help clients locate hardware. Free brochure.

McDonald's Restoration, 31 B Front St., Belfast, ME 04915, 207-338-6127, fax: 207-338-6127, e-mail: pmcd@mint.net. Restoration of period antiques.

Meeting House Furniture Restoration, 87 Waterman Hill, Quechee, VT 05059, 802-295-1309, fax: 802-296-5911. Restoration, repair, and refinishing of antique and classic furniture. Specializing in veneer and carving repair. Conservation of original finishes of woodwork and paneling. Restoration of gilded and inlaid surfaces. Brass polishing and repair. Specialists in the restoration of moving, flood, and fire-damaged furniture.

Michigan Antique Preservation Co. Inc., 2034 Eureka Rd., Wyandotte, MI 48192, 734-283-5700, fax: 734-283-4312, e-mail: mapco@wyan.org. Furniture conservation and restoration.

Mickey's Chair Caning, 233 Byrnes Dr., Waterloo, IA 50701, 319-232-5934, e-mail: mlj091554@aol.com, website: www.mickeyschaircaning.com. Specializing in the restoration of antique and modern caning and rush seating. Residential and commercial customers. Free estimates. Caning and rush material available for the do-it-youselfer: strand cane, cane webbing, spline, and rush. Call for appointment.

Mike's Antiquary, 305 S. Main, PO Box 229, Almont, MI 48003, 810-798-3599, fax: 810-798-2042 (call first), e-mail: jamm@ees.eesc.com. Refinishing, repair, and restoration. Furniture repaired: stripping, upholstery, caning, rushing, splinting. Metal polishing; silvering. Serving eastern U.S. Call for availability. Mon.–Fri. 10:00 A.M.–6:00 P.M., Sat. 10:00 A.M.–2:00 P.M.

Minuteman Upholstery Supply Co., 1905 S. Elm St., High Point, NC 27260, 800-457-0029, fax: 336-885-6890, e-mail: mkmsales@mindspringcom, website: minutemanuph.tripod.com. Products for furniture upholstering. Prewoven cane and other caning supplies, springs, jute webbing, upholstery tacks, hand tools for re-upholstering, etc. Custom feather cushions and down cushions a specialty. Free catalog.

New Orleans Conservation Guild, Inc., 3301 Chartres St., New Orleans, LA 70117, 504-944-7900, fax: 504-944-8750, e-mail: info@art-restoration.com, website: www.art-restoration.com. Restoration and conservation of furniture and fine art and antiques. Appraisals and research searches. Call or write for brochure.

Oak Brothers, 5104 N. Pearl St., Tacoma, WA 98407, 253-752-4055, fax: 253-752-4055, e-mail: wmalovich@harbornet.com. Benders and sellers of curved glass for china closets. By appointment only. Call or write for more information.

Oak Grove Restorations, Inc., 299B Broad St., Manchester, CT 06040, 860-646-1951, fax: 860-646-0770. Furniture stripping, repairing, and refinishing (wood only); antique restoration; church pew restoration.

Old World Restorations, Inc., 5729 Dragon Way, Cincinnati, OH 45227, 513-271-5459, fax: 513-271-5418, e-mail: info@oldworldrestorations.com, website: www.oldworldrestorations.com. Restoration and conservation of furniture and antiques. Fire and water damage restoration. Specialized packing and shipping. Nationwide service. Send or e-mail photos for preliminary estimates. Free brochure.

Original Mattress Factory, 4930 State Rd., Cleveland, OH 44134, 216-661-8388, website: originalmattress.com. Custom-size mattresses and box springs that will fit antique beds; Amish-built box springs, custom-sized. Innerspring models available.

Original Woodworks, 4631 Lake Ave., White Bear Lake, MN 55110, 651-429-2222, e-mail: orgwood@iaxs.net, website: originalwoodworks.com. Antique furniture and trunk conservation and restoration. Replacement cast iron Victorian bed fasteners. Reproduction Victorian easels and folding screens.

Outwater Plastics Industries, Inc., 4 Passaic St., PO Box 403, Wood-Ridge, NJ 07075, 800-631-8375 or 973-340-1040, fax: 800-888-3315 or 973-916-1640, e-mail: outwater@outwater.com, website: www.outwater.com. An international supplier of more than 40,000 component products, including furniture hardware, cabinet components, knobs and pulls, casters, fittings, fasteners, and much more. Free catalog.

Paxton Hardware Ltd., 7818 Bradshaw Rd., PO Box 256, Upper Falls, MD 21156, 800-241-9741, fax: 410-592-2224, e-mail: paxton@ix.netcom.com, website: www.paxtonhardware.com. Antique style furniture fittings and lighting. Classic pulls, handles and knobs, hinges, locks, casters, supports, catches, table and bed hardware, hooks, seat-weaving materials. Catalog.

PECO Glass Bending, PO Box 777, Smithville, TX 78957, 512-237-3600, e-mail: glass@pecoglassbending.com, website: www.pecoglassbending.com. Curved glass for china cabinets; 39 stock radiuses. Custom-made J's, S's, serpentines, and bubble glass.

Phyllis Kennedy, 10655 Andrade Dr., Zionsville, IN 46077, 317- 873-1316, fax: 317-873-8662, e-mail: philken@kennedyhardware.com, website: www.kennedyhardware.com. Hardware and parts for antique furniture, Hoosier cabinets, and trunks. Specializing in parts for Hoosier cabinets, including flour bins, bread drawers, roll doors, wire racks, and sugar jars. Pie-safe tins, ice-box hardware, bed hardware, chair seats and caning, architectural hardware, pressed fiberboard, and more. Wholesale catalog $3.

Poor Richard's Restoration & Preservation Studio Workshop, 101 Walnut St., Montclair, NJ 07042, 973-783-5333, fax: 973-744-1939, e-mail: jrickford@webtv.com, website: www.rickford.com. Restoration, conservation, archival and preservation services for furniture and other objects. By appointment, Tues.–Fri. noon–5:00 P.M., Sat. noon–3:00 P.M.

Price House Antiques, 137 Cabot St., Beverly, MA 01915, 978-927-5595. Chair caning, pressed and hand caning; porch weaving; wicker repair and restoration. Rush and most natural weaving materials.

Professional Furniture Service, 95 W. Main St., Amelia, OH 45102, 513-753-5578, fax: 513-752-3006, e-mail: kenlarbes@profurniture.com, website: www.profurniture.com. Complete refinishing and restoration of modern and antique furniture. Missing parts duplicated; touch-up and repair.

Rafail & Polina Golberg, Golberg Restoration Co., 411 Westmount Dr., Los Angeles, CA 90048, 310-652-0735, fax: 310-274-3770, e-mail: info@restorationworld.com, website: www.restorationworld.com. Restoration and conservation of antiques and objects of art, including furniture. Custom-made parts. Free estimates via the Internet.

Restoration Center–Hotline, Inc., PO Box 988, Danielsville, GA 30633, 800-332-2747, fax: 800-332-2017, e-mail: furniturehotline@msn.com, website: www.furniture-hotline.com. Nationwide referral service for furniture repairs.

Retinning & Copper Repair, Inc., 560 Irvine Turner Blvd., Newark, NJ 07108, 973-848-0700, fax: 973-848-1070, website: www.retinning.com. Restoration of brass beds and other metal items.

Richard Blaschke Cabinet Glass, 670 Lake Ave., Bristol, CT 06010, 860-584-2566, fax: 860-314-0296, e-mail: rjblaschke@snet.net, website: www.dicksantiques.com. Curved china cabinet replacement glass.

Rocky Mountain Furniture Restoration, 103 Commercial Dr., Bozeman, MT 59715, 800-230-6414, fax: 406-586-6414, e-mail: swebe16@aol.com. Complete restoration services for all types of antiques, specializing in age appropriate custom finishing.

Rosine Green Associates, Inc., 89 School St., Brookline, MA 02446, 617-277-8368, fax: 617-731-3845, e-mail: rga@ix.netcom.com. Conservation and restoration of fine art, including furniture.

Scott's Beckers' Hardware, Inc., 411 S. 3rd St., Ozark, MO 65721, 417-581-6525, fax: 417-581-4771, website: www.scotbeckhdw.com. Antique hardware, trunk parts, brass and iron bed parts, period brass knobs and pulls, kitchen cabinet parts, pierced tins, spool cabinet decals, icebox parts, wood turnings and plugs, refinishing supplies, caning supplies, and more. Catalog online and in print. Retail showroom open Mon.–Fri. 8:30 A.M.–5:00 P.M., Sat. 9:00 A.M.–3:00 P.M. Toll free order desk 888-991-0151.

Shaker Chairs, Glenn A. Carlson, 29 Shepard Rd., PO Box 278, Norfolk, CT 06058, 860-542-6881, 9:00 A.M.–5:00 P.M. Antique Shaker chair restoration. Hand-built reproduction Shaker chairs. Free brochure.

Shaker Workshops, PO Box 8001, Ashburnham, MA 01430, 800-840-9121, fax: 978-827-6554, e-mail: shaker@shakerworkshops.com, website: www.shakerworkshops.com. Replacement Shaker chair seat tape in a variety of colors, furniture kits, interior and exterior paints and stains. Free catalog.

Sheild Art & Hobby Shop, 4417 Danube Dr., King George, VA 22485-5707, 540-663-3711, fax: 540-663-3711 call first, e-mail: wsheild @crosslink.net. Furniture restoration. Carved replacement pieces for various wooden items.

Specialized Repair Co., 12101 S. 1390 W., Riverton, UT 84065, 801-254-2777, fax: 801-254-3513, e-mail: SpecRep@SoftSolutions.com. Furniture touch-up and repair. Specializing in claim service for moving companies.

Stanzione Furniture Repair Inc., 49970 Van Dyke, Utica, MI 48317, 586-739-9010, fax: 586-739-6921, e-mail: stanzione@ameritech.net. Refinishing and reconditioning of all-wood furniture, including reproduction of pieces, repair, and recoloring. Re-upholstery, custom cornice boards. Reconditioning and repair of leather furniture.

Sue Connell, The Clayton Store, Canaan-Southfield Rd., Southfield, MA 01259, 413-229-2621, fax: 413-229-2621. Restoration and reproduction of walls, floors, woodwork, and furniture. Color-matching a specialty. Cleaning and grooming of painted and decorated surfaces. Dry scraping of later layers to original surface.

Trilco Claims & Antiques Inc., 617 S. Myrtle Ave., Monrovia, CA 91016, 626-359-1010, fax: 626-357-4313, e-mail: trilco@hotmail.com. Furniture restoration and refinishing.

Van Dyke's Restorers, PO Box 278, Woonsocket, SD 57385, 605-796-4425, orders 800-558-1234, fax: 605-796-4085, e-mail: restoration @cabelas.com, website: www.vandykes.com. Furniture components, including claw feet, table pedestals, legs, bentwood chair parts, reproduction pressed chair backs, seats, supports, leather desk-top pieces, and roll-top desk components. Brass hardware of all kinds, pie-safe tins, curved-glass china-cabinet parts, isinglass for stove doors, cane, reed, veneer, upholstery supplies, tools, stains, varnishes, brushes, modeling compounds. Special parts designed to duplicate original pieces. Mail order worldwide. Catalog.

Wade Holtzman, 104 Bolton Rd., Harvard, MA 01451, 978-456-6850, e-mail: antique104@charter.net. Restoration of period and fine furniture.

West Interior Services, Inc., PO Box 540, Natrona Heights, PA 15065-0740, 724-224-2215, fax: 724-226-3233, e-mail: tomjr@westinterior services.com, website: www.westinteriorservices.com. Antique furniture and woodwork preservation. Furniture and woodwork repairs and refinishing. Free brochure.

West Woodwork, 40321 Avenida Cerro Vista, Cherry Valley, CA 92223, 909-845-8658, fax: 909-845-6598, e-mail: westwoodwork@yahoo.com. Antique furniture repair and restoration, specializing in in-home touch-up.

Wicker Fixer, 924 Prairie Ridge Rd., Ozark, MO 65721, 417-581-6148, e-mail: wckerfxr@gte.net, website: wickerfixer.com. Wicker repairs and restoration. Minor to major surgery, painting, and cleaning. Get your dog-chewed, cat-clawed, bird-pecked wicker fixed. Tip and care information on wicker available, $5.

The Wicker Fixers, 1900 Stoney Ridge Rd., Cumming, GA 30041, 770-887-8518, e-mail: dottym@mindspring.com. Chair caning, including laced (French) and pressed cane, split oak, binder cane, sea grass, Shaker tape; all types of caning. Complete wicker restoration and repair, including bamboo, rattan, and reed.

The Wicker Woman, Cathryn Peters, 1250 Hwy. 25, Angora, MN 55703, 218-666-6189, e-mail: cathryn@wickerwoman.com, website: www.wicke rwoman.com. Wicker restoration and seat weaving specialist since 1975. Restoration of all types of wicker furniture, including 1890s–1930s wicker, chair caning, paper fiber and natural rush, oak, ash, reed, and hickory splint, Danish Modern, and sea grass.

Wicker Workshop, 18744 Parthenia St., #1, Northridge, CA 91324, 818-886-4524 or 818-692-4999, fax: 818-886-0115, e-mail: shoshenosh @aol.com. Restoration and repair of wicker, cane, rattan, rush, Danish lace, split reed, cord sea grass, and herringbone. Spindles and rockers made. Wood furniture repaired. Custom finishes and paint; parts made.

William Evans Fine Handmade Furniture, PO Box 757, Waldoboro, ME 04572, 207-832-4175, e-mail: bill@www.williamevansfurniture.com, website: www.williamevansfurniture.com. Restoration of fine antique furniture. Handmade reproduction furniture. Catalog $5.

Williamstown Art Conservation Center, 225 South St., Williamstown, MA 01267, 413-458-5741, fax: 413-458-2314, e-mail: wacc@clark.williams.edu, website: www.williamstownart.org. Conservation of furniture and other objects. Analytical services.

Winter Brook Farm Antiques, 450 N. State Road, Cheshire, MA 01225, 413-743-2177, website: www.winterbrookfarm.com. Reproduction replacement hardware. Styles include Victorian, Mission, Colonial Revival, Deco, Hepplewhite, and Sheraton in brass, copper, wood, etc. Brass hardware is "aged" so it isn't bright and shiny.

Wood & Leather, 215 Ocean Forest Dr. NW, Calabash, NC 28467, 910-575-7114. Genuine leather tops made to fit your secretary, desk, etc. Gold-tooled, period designs in antique brown, green, red, or black finishes. Easy gluing directions given. Send measurements for estimate and free samples.

The Wood Works Inc., 7710 W. 63rd St., Shawnee Mission, KS 66202, 913-362-2432, fax: 913-362-0588, e-mail: tim@thewws.com, website: thewoodworksinc.com. Furniture repair and touch-up. Restoration and refinishing.

Workbench Furniture Restoration, Inc., 8631 Gravois Rd., St. Louis, MO 63123, 314-351-4224, fax: 314-353-4664, e-mail: workbenchfurniture @prodigy.com. Antique restoration and conservation of finishes. Minor touch-up and reproduction of missing or broken parts, as well as complete restoration and upholstery. Brochure.

Yesterday's Antiques & Refinishing, 203 Pacific Ave., Bremen, GA 30110, 770-537-9157, e-mail: ggpriest@aol.com, website: yesterdaysantiques andrefinishing.com. Complete furniture restoration and refinishing; parts made if necessary. Chair caning. Open Mon.-Sat.

GLASS

Glass is one of the most difficult types of antiques to identify and price. Few pieces are marked, reproductions abound, style doesn't always reflect age, and quality is not always the reason for a price. A novice will have great difficulty (some experts do, too) in identifying reproductions. It is a major task to learn the names of the many glasswares.

First, sort your glassware. Sets of goblets, plates, and cups and saucers should be put in one group. Vases, figurines, candlesticks, and other decorative items should be considered separately. We wrote *Kovels' Know Your Antiques* and *Kovels' Know Your Collectibles* for the beginner. There is a chapter on glass in each book, written to help make identifying glass a less complicated task. The colored art glass of Victorian times is described in terms of color and design. The names Pomona, Peachblow, amberina, Quezal, and others will make more sense after you study a little. Go to a large antiques show and look for glassware that resembles yours. Dealers will be glad to tell you what it is called. Then you can look up the prices in any of the books listed here. Victorian glass has been reproduced and modern versions are made today. Milk glass, purple or blue slag glass (it resembles a marble cake), pressed glass, and many types of colored glass baskets, cruets, and plates are being made for the gift-shop trade. You probably can't tell the old from the new without expert help. If you know your glass vase belonged to your great-grandmother, you should research the value carefully—don't rely on family legend. Some of the strangest-looking glass pieces are of great value.

IRIDESCENT GLASS

Gold iridescent glass is very valuable. Any piece of glass that can be identified as made by the workshops of Louis Comfort Tiffany has a high value. The Tiffany signature on a piece doubles the value. Also look for STEUBEN, DURAND, QUEZAL, KEW BLAS, and small trademarks like a fleur-de-lis or initials that identify the makers.

BLOWN GLASS

Blown glass of the eighteenth and early nineteenth centuries is older than art glass or cameo glass, but seldom brings as high a price unless it's very rare. Although English collectors eagerly buy goblets with blown and twisted stems and decanters with applied decorations, American collectors have never been as interested. Many decanters from the 1820s sell for under $350. Early blown bottles are a whole different story. Very rare mold-blown whiskey flasks can sell for tens of thousands of dollars. Even common ones sell for hundreds.

•→ SEE BOTTLES & GO-WITHS

CUT GLASS

Cut glass, especially the very elaborate pieces known as "brilliant cut," was not easy to sell until the 1970s. Suddenly, after fifty years of being out of favor, it was back in demand. The cost of making the glass is high, so the antique pieces began to rise in value. Today, old cut glass is high-priced and very much in demand, and, if in perfect condition, it sells very quickly. A water pitcher can bring $500; a 10-inch bowl is worth $350. Small or large nicks lower value by 25 to 50 percent, depending on rarity of the design. If the object is made of colored and clear glass, add 100 percent. If the glass is sick (cloudy) and does not seem to wash clean, deduct 40 percent.

If the glass is signed, add 25 percent. The signature can be difficult to find, but is usually on the smooth surface of the inside of a bowl. Because the marks are acid-etched, they are very faint and can only be seen if the bowl is turned to catch the light the right way. Ask an antiques dealer to show you a signature on a piece of cut glass and you will quickly learn how to find others. Only about one in ten pieces is signed.

There are several kinds of feet that could be put on a piece of cut glass. A round disc and short stem on a vase are common, but the same type of foot on a carafe, sugar or creamer, bowl, jug, decanter, or ice tub adds 15 percent. A tall foot on a compote is the rule, but the same tall foot on a berry bowl, spooner, cologne, sugar, or creamer adds 15 percent. If there are decorations on the feet, add 2 percent more. Peg feet on a vase, bowl, bucket, creamer, or sugar raise the value by 10 percent. Cut glass prices are listed in the general price books and in some specialized books. It is best to try to determine the name of the pattern by looking at the cut glass picture books in your library. Even without the pattern name, you can decide approximate value.

CAMEO GLASS

Cameo glass, an Art Nouveau- and Art Deco-inspired glassware, is very popular and very high priced today. Quality and signature are important. Often a small piece that will fit on a breakfront shelf is preferred to a very large vase, since serious collectors run out of space. Cameo glass is made of several layers of glass of different colors. The design is made by cutting away the top color to make patterns. French cameo glass was inspired by the Art Nouveau tradition. **GALLÉ, A. WALTER, DAUM NANCY, ARGY-ROUSSEAU, MÜLLER FRERES, DE VEZ, DELATTE**, and **LEGRAS** are names found on French cameo glass that add to the value. If cameo glass is signed by Gallé, add 100 percent. If the piece is signed by a less important maker, add 50 percent to the value of a similar unsigned piece. The record price for cameo glass is $995,400 for a Gallé vase made for a 1903 exhibition, but typical Gallé and Daum vases sell for less than $5,000. Typical pieces by other makers sell for less than $2,000. The best name of all, and rarest, is **WOODALL**. He was an English artist and his cameo glass vases are worth tens of thousands of dollars. **WEBB** is another English maker favored by collectors. The American **STEUBEN** glassworks made an acid-cut, cameolike ware that also sells well. There is increasing collector interest in Bohemian cameo glass signed **C.A. LOETZ, VELES**, or **RICHARD**. Beware of the many reproductions with fake signatures of Bohemian and French makers, as well as ones with deceptive signatures, like "Galli."

LALIQUE

LALIQUE is another marketable name. Most of the glass was made in frosted, clear, or opalescent glass. Lalique glass is still being made. The older pieces, signed "R. Lalique," were made before 1945 and are worth 100 to 500 percent more than the newer ones. (The pieces made after 1945 are signed "Lalique.") The best pieces of Lalique are the rare colored pieces. A Lalique "Roses" vase, made using the *cire perdu* (lost wax) method, sold in 1998 for $409,500.

PRESSED GLASS

Pressed glass, made in Victorian times, was a very popular collectible in the 1930s, but lost favor until the 1980s. It was inexpensive and easy to find, perhaps because the design was unfashionable or because almost-undetectable reproductions were made. Prices remained low until collectors began to realize that an 1890 pressed-glass goblet now sold for the same price as a 1930s Depression glass piece, and bargain hunters began looking for pressed glass sets again. In the late 1990s, auction houses sold the items of longtime collectors and prices climbed. A Sandwich Vine pattern goblet sold for a record $16,500 in 2000. To price your pieces, you first need to identify the pattern. Look for a good book that lists patterns, such as: *American Pressed Glass and Figure Bottles* by Albert Christian Revi (Thomas Nelson & Sons, Toronto, 1964); *Early American Pattern Glass Collector's Identification & Price Guide* by Darryl Reilly and Bill Jenks, 2nd edition (Krause Publications, Iola, WI, 2002); *Field Guide to Pattern Glass* by Mollie Helen McCain (Collector Books, Paducah, KY, 2000); *Pressed Glass in America: Encyclopedia of the First Hundred Years, 1825–1925* by John and Elizabeth Welker (Antique Acres Press, Ivyland, PA, 1985); and *Early American Pattern Glass* by Ruth Webb Lee, revised edition (Tuttle, Rutland, VT, 1984).

After you learn the name of your pattern, look in the latest edition of a price guide for a retail value. Only perfect pieces sell, because the supply is plentiful. Pressed glass sells at general antiques shows, specialized auctions, and through mail-order or Internet ads.

CARNIVAL GLASS

Carnival glass, an inexpensive iridescent glass popular in the early twentieth century, can be sold to interested collectors. The highest prices are for rare patterns and forms; punch bowls and certain pitchers and lamps sell well. Ordinary carnival glass is not high-priced, so be realistic when you set your selling price. Common pieces, like a marigold Beaded Bull's-Eye vase or a blue Persian Medallion compote, sell for $100–$200. Check the carnival glass price guides to see if you own a rare pattern or color. An aqua opalescent Peacock & Urn master ice cream bowl sold for $22,000 in 2002 because it was the only known example with butterscotch and pink iridescence. Most of the guides have sketches or photographs of each pattern. It is a bit complicated to understand how to identify the color of carnival glass. The color of the glass itself, not the color of the iridescence seen on the top, is the determining factor. The main carnival glass auctions are held in the Midwest. Several auction houses in Kansas have well-attended sales.

DEPRESSION GLASS

Depression glass began gaining favor with collectors during the 1970s. It was then that the pale pink or green lacy pattern pieces were first noticed. Sets were assembled from garage sales. A cup often cost a nickel and a plate a dime. Today there are many serious collectors of all types of Depression glass, from pastels to bright ruby, cobalt blue, or forest green. Hobnail, the Sandwich-style patterns, and even enamel-decorated pieces are wanted. The highest prices are paid at Depression glass shows. Look for show ads in your local newspaper or in general antiques publications. Many dealers now sell their wares online in Internet malls devoted to Depression glass.

Prices vary widely. A rarity, like a green Floral 24-ounce pitcher, sells for $600, while a Colonial green sherbet is worth $6. There are at least fifteen current price books on Depression glass. We like *Kovels' Depression Glass and Dinnerware Price List* the best. Reproductions of Depression glass have been made. Some are sets for everyday use; some are copies of rarities, such as the pink Cherry Blossom cookie jar that sells for hundreds of dollars if original.

ELEGANT GLASS

"Elegant glassware" is the name sometimes given to the better glass made from the 1930s to the 1970s. Included are certain patterns by **HEISEY, FENTON, FOSTORIA, CAMBRIDGE, IMPERIAL**, and **DUNCAN AND MILLER**. These and a few other American companies made fine quality, cut crystal goblets, wines, plates, and figurines for the gift-shop trade. Heisey is well known for both its decorated pieces and its heavy, modern, glass animal figures. Very high prices are paid for these figures and for the goblets with animal- or bird-shaped stems. Small is "big" with the animal figures; the small sizes sell for the most.

If your glass was inherited from parents or grandparents, you could easily have some of these pieces. They were sold in all parts of the country and were popular wedding gifts. The problem is identification. There is a Heisey glass museum in Newark, Ohio, and several clubs for the other types of glass. A clear photograph and letter to these groups may get you the information about age and pattern name that you need to determine a price using the price guides. There are books showing many of the patterns, but it is not a quick research project. A few of the pieces are signed with initials or insignia, but most are not. If you have this type of glass, go to the antiques shows and glass shows and ask questions to try to determine a price. Most small local auction galleries do very well with this type of glassware and get high prices for you. They should be able to identify it and tell you the approximate value. It is difficult to sell a partial set of drinking glasses, because the new owner may not be able to fill in the twelfth for a party. All other types of glass made after the 1930s can sell for surprisingly high prices. We have seen and purchased many pieces of unmarked Heisey for under $10 at garage sales, where they are often overlooked and underpriced by the amateur seller. Many Depression glass dealers sell "elegant" wares, too. Look for them at the same venues— online and at shows.

MID-CENTURY AND MODERN GLASS

In the 1980s, a group of buyers appeared who were willing to pay good prices for the studio and art glass made from the 1950s on. **VENINI**, **KOSTA**, **ORREFORS**, **HOLMEGAARD**, **AFORS**, **TOSO**, **BARBINI**, and **BODA** are some of the most important foreign names. There are also American makers with names like **EDRIS ECKHARDT**, **DOMINICK LABINO**, **BLENKO**, **ERICKSON**, and **HIGGINS**. In general, the more Art Moderne the appearance, the more abstract the forms, and the heavier the glass bodies, the higher the prices. Signatures are very important for these pieces. There are also collectors of modern and contemporary studio glass by makers like **DALE CHIHULY**, **HARVEY LITTLETON**, and **CHRISTOPHER RIES**. These items usually sell best at auction.

OTHER GLASSWARE

Kitchen glasswares of the 1920s to 1970s, including mixing bowls, reamers, dinner plates, mugs, and storage jars, are all collected.

Glass candlesticks of any kind are now selling very well. They seem to have come back into fashion in the 1980s. Remember, even if your glass looks like dime-store junk to you, or like a misshapen ashtray made from a glob of glass, you are selling and not buying. To the trained eye, your glass dish may be a treasure, and you must train your eye enough to recognize the high-priced items.

Selling and buying glass via the Internet is very easy. The mass-produced rule applies here, too. Most glassware, like carnival, Depression or cut glass, is mass-produced and easily described by pattern name and shape. All of the Internet antiques malls (see Part III for a list) have glass dealers and many dealers have their own individual sites. Look for glass associations on the Web, too. Many club sites feature classified ads or links to dealers.

REPAIR

Starting in the 1990s, glass of all types was being reproduced and imported, so be cautious when you buy. Publications and price guides sometimes mistakenly list the well-known reproductions. Fake glass marks are not uncommon, as it is simple to acid-stamp, etch, or sandblast a name on a less desirable piece of glass to raise the value of it for the unsuspecting buyer. To add to the confusion, many reproduced pieces can cost more than the originals.

Glass should never be kept in a sunny window. Old glass (before 1900) was made of a slightly different mixture and may turn colors. Any glass can magnify the sun and cause scorch marks on furniture or carpets, or even start a fire.

Chipped edges on glass can be ground down. A local glass-repair shop can be located through the Yellow Pages. New epoxy mixtures can be used to make repairs on glass that are almost impossible to detect without the use of a black light. This type of repair is expensive and only a few restorers offer the service. Any glass, including the insides of small-necked bottles, can be polished. There is a danger of breakage and it is a very specialized job. Stained glass can be cleaned and restored. Look for a restorer in the Yellow Pages under "Glass, Stained & Leaded." Sets of glasses can be completed with the help of a matching service. Many are listed in Part III.

➤ SEE ALSO ADVERTISING COLLECTIBLES, HOLIDAY COLLECTIBLES, PAPERWEIGHTS

REFERENCE BOOKS

20th Century Factory Glass, Lesley Jackson (Rizzoli, New York, 2000).

American Art Nouveau Glass, Albert Christian Revi (Thomas Nelson, Nashville, TN, 1968).

American Glass, 1760–1930, Kenneth M. Wilson (Toledo Museum of Art/ Hudson Hills, New York, 1994).

American Glass, George S. and Helen McKearin (Crown, New York, 1948).

Art Glass Nouveau, Ray and Lee Grover (Charles E. Tuttle, Rutland, VT, 1967).

Carved & Decorated European Art Glass, Ray and Lee Grover (Charles E. Tuttle, Rutland, VT, 1970).

Colored Glassware of the Depression Era, 2 volumes, Hazel Marie
  Weatherman (Weatherman Glassbooks, P.O. Box 280, Ozark, MO
  65721, 1970, 1974).
Contemporary Art Glass, Ray and Lee Grover (Crown, New York, 1975).
Crystal Stemware: Identification Guide, Bob Page and Dale Frederiksen
  (Replacements, Ltd., Greensboro, NC, 1997).
Field Guide to Pattern Glass, Mollie Helen McCain (Collector Books,
  Paducah, KY, 2000).
Encyclopedia of American Cut and Engraved Glass, 1880–1917, 3 volumes,
  J. Michael Pearson (402844 Ocean View Station, Miami Beach, FL
  33140, 1975–1978).
*Glass Signatures, Trademarks and Trade Names from the Seventeenth to the
  Twentieth Century,* Anne G. Pullin (Wallace-Homestead/Krause, Iola,
  WI, 1986).
Guide to Sandwich Glass, 4 volumes, Raymond E. Barlow and Joan E.
  Kaiser (PO Box 265, Windham, NH 03087, 1985).
Identifying American Brilliant Cut Glass, revised edition, Bill and Louise
  Boggess (Schiffer, Atglen, PA, 1990).
The Milk Glass Book, Frank Chiarenza and James Slater (Schiffer, Atglen,
  PA, 1998).
Nineteenth Century Glass: Its Genesis and Development, Albert Christian
  Revi (Thomas Nelson, Nashville, TN, 1967).
Reflections on American Brilliant Cut Glass, Bill and Louise Boggess
  (Schiffer, Atglen, PA, 1995).

PRICE BOOKS
'40s, '50s, & '60s Stemware by Tiffin, Ed Goshe, Ruth Menninger, and
  Leslie Piña (Schiffer, Atglen, PA, 1999).
20th Century Glass Candle Holders, Sherry Riggs and Paula Pendergrass
  (Schiffer, Atglen, PA, 1999).
Albany Glass: Model Flint Glass Company of Albany, Indiana, Ron Teal Sr.
  (Antique Publications, Marietta, OH, 1997).
American Pressed Glass and Bottles, 2nd edition, Kyle Husfloen (Antique
  Trader Books, Iola, WI, 2000).
An Unauthorized Guide to Fire-King Glasswares, Monica Lynn Clements and
  Patricia Rosser Clements (Schiffer, Atglen, PA, 1999).
Anchor Hocking Commemorative Bottles and Other Collectibles, Philip
  Hopper (Schiffer, Atglen, PA, 2000).
Anchor Hocking's Fire-King and More, 2nd edition, Gene Florence (Collector
  Books, Paducah, KY, 2000, prices 2002).
Antique Trader American and European Decorative and Art Glass Price Guide,
  Kyle Husfloen, editor (Krause, Iola, WI, 2000).
The Big Book of Fenton Glass, 1940–1970, 2nd edition, John Walk (Schiffer,
  Atglen, PA, 1999).
Bill Friedberg's Pictorial Price Guide & Informative Handbook Covering

"Official" Kentucky Derby, Preakness, Belmont, Breeders' Cup Glasses and Much More, William Friedberg (462 Hillcreek Rd., Shepherdsville, KY 40165, 1996).

Blenko Glass: 1962–1971 Catalogs, preface by Leslie Piña (Schiffer, Atglen, PA, 2000).

Blenko: Cool '50s and '60s Glass, Leslie Piña (Schiffer, Atglen, PA, 2000).

Bryce, Higbee and J.B. Higbee Glass, Lola and Wayne Higby (Antique Publications, Marietta, OH, 1998).

Carnival Glass Auction Prices, annual, Tom and Sharon Mordini (36 N. Mernitz, Freeport, IL 61032).

Carnival Glass: The Magic and the Mystery, Glen and Stephen Thistlewood (Schiffer, Atglen, PA, 1998).

Circa Fifties Glass from Europe & America, Leslie Piña (Schiffer, Atglen, PA, 1997).

Cobalt Blue Glass, Monica Lynn Clements and Patricia Rosser Clements (Schiffer, Atglen, PA, 1998).

Collectible Bohemian Glass, 2 volumes, Robert and Deborah Truitt (B&D Glass, 5120 White Flint Drive, Kinsington, MD 20895, 1995–1998).

Collectible Drinking Glasses, Mark Chase and Michael Kelly (Collector Books, Paducah, KY, 1996, prices 1999).

Collectible Glass Rose Bowls, Johanna S. Billings (Antique Trader Books, Dubuque, IA, 1999).

Collectible Glassware from the 40s, 50s, 60s . . ., 6th edition, Gene Florence (Collector Books, Paducah, KY, 2002).

Collecting Carnival Glass, 2nd edition, Marion Quintin-Baxendale (published in England; available from Krause, Iola, WI, 2002).

Collecting Crackle Glass, Judy Alford (Schiffer, Atglen, PA, 1997).

Collecting Lalique: Perfume Bottles and Glass, Robert Prescott-Walker (Francis Joseph, London, 2001).

Collector's Encyclopedia of Depression Glass, 15th edition, Gene Florence (Collector Books, Paducah, KY, 2002).

The Collector's Encyclopedia of Fry Glassware, H.C. Fry Glass Society (Collector Books, Paducah, KY, 1990, price update 1998).

Collector's Encyclopedia of Milk Glass: Identification and Value Guide, Betty and Bill Newbound (Collector Books, Paducah, KY, 1995).

Comprehensive 2000 Price Guide for "Heisey's Cut Handmade Glass," Connie Dall and Bob Ryan (Glass Press, Marietta, OH, 2000).

Coudersport Glass, 1900–1904, Tulla Majot (Glass Press, Marietta, OH, 1999).

Crackle Glass in Color, Depression to '70s, Leslie Piña (Schiffer, Atglen, PA, 2000).

Crackle Glass, Book II, Stan and Arlene Weitman (Collector Books, Paducah, KY, 1998).

Depression Era Art Deco Glass, Leslie Piña and Paula Ockner (Schiffer, Atglen, PA, 1999).

Depression Era Dime Store Glass, C.L. Miller (Schiffer, Atglen, PA, 1999).

Depression Era Glass by Duncan, Leslie Piña (Schiffer, Atglen, PA, 1999).

Depression Era Kitchen Shakers, Barbara E. Mauzy (Schiffer, Atglen, PA, 2001).

Depression Era Stems & Tableware: Tiffin, Ed Goshe, Ruth Hemminger, and Leslie Piña (Schiffer, Atglen, PA, 1998).

Depression Glass: A Collector's Guide, 3rd edition, Doris Yeske (Schiffer, Atglen, PA, 1999).

Designed & Signed: '50s & '60s Glass, Ceramics, & Enamel Wares by Georges Briard, Sascha B., Bellaire, Higgins . . . , Leslie Piña (Schiffer, Atglen, PA, 1996).

Diamond I Perfume Bottles Price Guide and Other Drugstore Ware. Original pages from Illinois Glass Co.'s wholesale catalogs, 1910–1925 (L-W Book Sales, Gas City, IN 46933, 2000).

Dugan & Diamond Carnival Glass, 1909–1931, Carl O. Burns (Collector Books, Paducah, KY, 1999).

Durand: The Man and His Glass, Edward J. Meschi (Antique Publications, Marietta, OH, 1998).

Early American Pattern Glass, 2nd edition, Darryl Reilly and Bill Jenks (Krause, Iola, WI, 2002).

Elegant Glassware of the Depression Era, 10th edition, Gene Florence (Collector Books, Paducah, KY, 2003).

The Essence of Pairpoint: Fine Glassware, 1918–1938, Marion and Sandra Frost (Schiffer, Atglen, PA, 2001).

Fenton Art Glass, 1907–1939, Margaret and Kenn Whitmyer (Collector Books, Paducah, KY, 1996).

Fenton Art Glass, 1939–1980, Margaret and Kenn Whitmyer (Collector Books, Paducah, KY, 2002 values).

A Field Guide to Carnival Glass, 2nd edition, David Doty (Glass Press, Marietta, OH, 2000).

Fifties Glass, 2nd edition, Leslie Piña (Schiffer, Atglen, PA, 2000).

Fifty Years of Collectible Glass, 1920–1970, 2 volumes, Tom and Neila Bredehoft (Antique Trader Books, Dubuque, IA, 1997).

Forest Green Glass, Philip Hopper (Schiffer, Atglen, PA, 2000).

Fostoria American Line 2056, Leslie Piña (Schiffer, Atglen, PA, 1999).

Fostoria American: A Complete Guide, 4th edition, Sidney P. Seligson (660 Preston Forest, #392, Dallas, TX 75230, 2001).

Fostoria, Useful and Ornamental: The Crystal for America, Milbra Long and Emily Seate (Collector Books, Paducah, KY, 2000).

Frederick Carder and Steuben Glass: American Classics, Thomas P. Dimitroff (Schiffer, Atglen, PA, 1998).

Great American Glass of the Roaring 20s & Depression Era, Books 1 and 2, James Measell and Berry Wiggins (Antique Publications, Marietta, OH, 1998–2000).

A Guide to Sandwich Glass: Cut Ware, A General Assortment and Bottles, Raymond E. Barlow and Joan E. Kaiser (Schiffer, Atglen, PA, 1999).

A Handbook of Morgantown Glass, Jerry Gallagher (M.C.A.-Dept. MP, 420 First Ave. NW, Plainview, MN 55964, 1995).

Heisey Glass, 1896–1957: Identification and Value Guide, Tom and Neila Bredehoft (Collector Books, Paducah, KY, 2001).

Heisey Glass: The Early Years, 1896–1924, Shirley Dunbar (Krause, Iola, WI, 2000).

Higgins: Adventures in Glass, Donald-Brian Johnson and Leslie Piña (Schiffer, Atglen, PA, 1997).

Hobbs, Brockunier & Co., Glass, Neila and Tom Bredehoft (Collector Books, Paducah, KY, 1997).

Identification Guide to Cambridge Glass, 1927–1929, Bill and Phyllis Smith (4003 Old Columbus Rd., Springfield, OH 45502, 1996).

Imperial Glass Encyclopedia, 3 volumes, James Measell, editor (Glass Press, Marietta, OH, 1995–1999).

Jadite, Joe Keller and David Ross (Schiffer, Atglen, PA, 1999).

Kemple Glass, 1945–1970, John R. Burkholder and D. Thomas O'Connor (Antique Publications, Marietta, OH, 1997).

Kovels' Depression Glass & Dinnerware Price List, 7th edition, Ralph and Terry Kovel (Three Rivers Press, New York, 2001).

Kitchen Glassware of the Depression Years, 6th edition, Gene Florence (Collector Books, Paducah, KY, 2001).

The L.G. Wright Glass Company, James Measell and W.C. "Red" Roetteis (Antique Publications, Marietta, OH, 1997).

Mauzy's Comprehensive Handbook of Depression Glass Prices, 4th edition, Barbara and Jim Mauzy (Schiffer, Atglen, PA, 2002).

The Milk Glass Book, Frank Chiarenza and James Slater (Schiffer, Atglen, PA, 1998).

Milk Glass: Imperial Glass Corporation, Myrna and Bob Garrison (Schiffer, Atglen, PA, 2001).

Miller's Glass of the '50s & '60s: A Collector's Guide, Nigel Benson (Octopus Publishing, London, 2002).

More Royal Ruby, Philip Hopper (Schiffer, Atglen, PA, 1999).

Moser Artistic Glass, 2nd edition, Gary D. Baldwin (Antique Publications, Marietta, OH, 1997).

Mt. Washington Art Glass plus Webb Burmese, Betty B. Sisk (Collector Books, Paducah, KY, 2003).

Much More Early American Pattern Glass, Alice Hulett Metz (Collector Books, Paducah, KY, 2000).

Official Price Guide to Glassware, 3rd edition, Mark Pickvet (House of Collectibles, NY, 2000).

Pattern Glass Mugs, John B. Mordock and Walter L. Adams (Antique Publications, Marietta, OH, 1995).

Peachblow Glass, Sean and Johanna S. Billings (Krause, Iola, WI, 2000).

Peanut Butter Glasses, Barbara E. Mauzy (Schiffer, Atglen, PA, 1997).

The Picture Book of Vaseline Glass, Sue C. Davis (Schiffer, Atglen, PA, 1999).

Pocket Guide to Pink Depression Era Glass, Monica Lynn Clements and Patricia Rosser Clements (Schiffer, Atglen, PA, 2000).

Popular '50s and '60s Glass: Color along the River, Leslie Piña (Schiffer, Atglen, PA, 1999).

Royal Ruby, Philip Hopper (Schiffer, Atglen, PA, 1998).

Scandinavian Ceramics and Glass, 1940s to 1980s, George Fischler and Barrett Gould (Schiffer, Atglen, PA, 2000).

Shoes of Glass, 2nd edition, Libby Yalom (Antique Publications, Marietta, OH, 1998).

Standard Encyclopedia of Carnival Glass, 8th edition, Bill Edwards and Mike Carwile (Collector Books, Paducah, KY, 2002).

Standard Encyclopedia of Millersburg Crystal, Bill Edwards and Mike Carwile (Collector Books, Paducah, KY, 2001).

Standard Encyclopedia of Opalescent Glass, 4th edition, Bill Edwards and Mike Carwile (Collector Books, Paducah, KY, 2002).

Stemware of the 20th Century: The Top 200 Patterns, Harry L. Rinker (House of Collectibles, NY, 1997).

Tiffany Favrile Art Glass, Moise S. Steeg Jr. (Schiffer, Atglen, PA, 1997).

Tiffin Glass, 1914–1940, Leslie Piña and Jerry Gallagher (Schiffer, Atglen, PA, 1996).

Tiffin Modern Mid-Century Art Glass, Ruth Hemminger, Ed Goshe, and Leslie Piña (Schiffer, Atglen, PA, 1997).

Very Rare Glassware of the Depression Years, 6th Series, Gene Florence (Collector Books, Paducah, KY, 1999).

Warman's Depression Glass, 4th edition, Ellen T. Schroy (Krause, Iola, WI, 2002).

Warman's Glass, 4th edition, Ellen T. Schroy, editor (Krause, Iola, WI, 2002).

Warman's Pattern Glass, 2nd edition, Ellen T. Schroy, editor (Krause, Iola, WI, 2001).

Westmoreland Glass, 3 volumes, Lorraine Kovar (Antique Publications, Marietta, OH, 1991–1997).

Yellow-Green Vaseline: A Guide to the Magic Glass, revised edition, Jay L. Glickman and Terry Fedosky (Antique Publications, Marietta, OH, 1998).

CLUBS & THEIR PUBLICATIONS

Akro Agate Collectors Club, *Clarksburg Crow* (NL), 10 Bailey St., Clarksburg, WV 26301-2524, e-mail: rhardy0424@aol.com, website: www.mkl.com/akro/club.

American Carnival Glass Association, *American Carnival Glass News* (NL), 5951 Fredricksburg Rd., Wooster, OH 44691.

American Cut Glass Association, *Hobstar* (NL), PO Box 482, Ramona, CA 92065-0482, e-mail acgakathy@aol.com, website: www.cutglass.org.

Candy Container Collectors of America, *Candy Gram* (NL), 2711 De La

Rosa St., The Villages, FL 32162, e-mail: epmac27@comcast.net, website: www.candycontainer.org.

Collectible Carnival Glass Association, *Collectible Carnival Glass Association* (NL), 2360 N. Old S.R. 9, Columbus, IN 47203.

Custard Glass Collectors Society, *Custard Connection* (NL), 591 SW Duxbury Ave., Port St. Lucie, FL 34983.

Early American Pattern Glass Society, *News Journal* (MAG), PO Box 266, Colesburg, IA 52035, e-mail: fredlmia@msn.com, website: www.eapgs.org.

Fenton Art Glass Collectors of America, Inc., *Butterfly Net* (NL), PO Box 384, Williamstown, WV 26187, e-mail: kkenworthy@foth.com, website: www.collectoronline.com/club-FAGCA.html.

Fostoria Glass Collectors, Inc., *Glass Works* (NL), PO Box 1625, Orange, CA 92856, e-mail: info@fostoriacollectors.org, website: www.fostoria collectors.org.

Fostoria Glass Society of America, Inc., *Facets of Fostoria* (NL), PO Box 826, Moundsville, WV 26041, website: www.fostoriaglass.org.

H.C. Fry Glass Society, *The Shards* (NL), PO Box 41, Beaver, PA 15009, website: www.rochesterpenn.com/fryglass/index.htm.

Heart of America Carnival Glass Association, *H.O.A.C.G.A. Bulletin* (NL), 7517 Evanston, Raytown, MO 64138, e-mail: bobimocg@aol.com.

Heisey Collectors of America, *Heisey News* (NL), 169 W. Church St., Newark, OH 43055, e-mail: heisey@infinet.com, website: www.heisey museum.org.

International Carnival Glass Association, *The Town Pump* (NL), Box 306, Mentone, IN 46539.

Michiana Association of Candlewick Collectors, *The Spyglass* (NL), 17370 Battles Rd., South Bend, IN 46614.

Mt. Washington Art Glass Society, *Mt. Washington Art Glass Society Newsletter* (NL), 1305 Clipper Rd., N. Myrtle Beach, SC 29582, e-mail: bankie@concentric.net.

National American Glass Club, *Glass Club Bulletin* (MAG), *Glass Shards* (NL), Box 8489, Silver Spring, MD 20907, e-mail: nagc@att.net, website: www.glassclub.org.

National Cambridge Collectors, Inc., *Cambridge Crystal Ball* (NL), PO Box 416, Cambridge, OH 43725-0416, e-mail: NCC_Crystal_Ball@yahoo.com, website: www.cambridgeglass.org.

National Depression Glass Association, *News & Views* (NL), PO Box 8264, Wichita, KS 67208-0264, website: www.glassshow.com/NDGA.

National Duncan Glass Society, *National Duncan Glass Society Journal* (NL), PO Box 965, Washington, PA 15301, e-mail: museum@nb.net, website: www.duncan-glass.com.

National Fenton Glass Society, *Fenton Flyer* (NL), PO Box 4008, Marietta, OH 45750, e-mail: nfgs@ee.net, website: www.fentonglasssociety.org.

National Greentown Glass Association, *N.G.G.A. Newsletter* (NL), PO Box 107, Greentown, IN 46936-0107, website: www.greentownglass.org.

National Imperial Glass Collectors Society, *Glasszette* (NL), PO Box 534, Bellaire, OH 43906, e-mail: info@imperialglass.org, website: www.imperialglass.org.

National Milk Glass Collectors Society, *Opaque News* (NL), 9238 Kenosha Ct., Floral City, FL 34336-2438, e-mail: membership@nmgcs.org, website: www.nmgcs.org.

National Westmoreland Glass Collectors Club, *Towne Crier* (NL), PO Box 100, Grapeville, PA 15634, website: www.glassshow.com/Clubs/NWGCC/west.html.

Old Morgantown Glass Collectors' Guild, *Topics* (NL), PO Box 894, Morgantown, WV 26507-0894, e-mail: jwiley1@adelphia.net, website: www.oldmorgantown.org.

Phoenix & Consolidated Glass Collectors Club, *Phoenix & Consolidated Glass Collectors News & Views* (NL), 41 River View Dr., Essex Junction, VT 05452, e-mail: TOPofVT@aol.com, website: pcgcc.com.

Pressed Glass Collectors Club, *Marking Times* (NL), 4 Bowshot Close, Castle Bromwich, W. Midlands B36 9UH, UK, e-mail: markingtimes @netlineuk.net, website: www.webspawner.com/users/pressedglass.

Promotional Glass Collectors Association (PGCA), *Collector Glass News* (NL), 97 Bigham Dr., Central Point, OR 97502, website: www.pgcaglass club.com.

Stained Glass Association of America, *Stained Glass* (MAG), 10009 E. 62nd St., Raytown, MO 64133, e-mail: sgaa@stainedglass.org, website: www.stainedglass.org.

Stretch Glass Society, *Stretch Glass Society Newsletter* (NL), 508 Turnberry Ln., St. Augustine, FL 32080, e-mail: stretchgl@aol.com, website: members.aol.com/stretchgl.

Swan Seekers Network, *Swan Seekers News* (NL), 9740 Campo Rd., Suite 134, Spring Valley, CA 91977, e-mail: marilyn@swanseekers.com, website: swanseekers.com (Swarovski crystal).

Tiffin Glass Collectors Club, *Tiffin Glassmasters* (NL), PO Box 554, Tiffin, OH 44883, website: www.tiffinglass.org.

Vaseline Glass Collectors, Inc., *Glowing Report* (NL), PO Box 125, Russellville, MO 65074, website: www.vaselineglass.org.

Vitrolite Glass Collectors Club, 3301 Hemlock Ave., Parkersburg, WV 26104.

Wave Crest Collectors Club, *Wave Crest Collectors Club Newsletter* (NL), PO Box 2013, Santa Barbara, CA 93120, e-mail: whntique@gte.net.

Westmoreland Glass Society, Inc., *Westmoreland Glass Society, Inc.* (NL), PO Box 2883, Iowa City, IA 52240-2883, e-mail: molockwood@webtv.net, website: www.glassshow.com/Clubs/Wgsi/wgsi.html.

OTHER PUBLICATIONS

The Acorn (MAG), *The Cullet* (NL), Sandwich Glass Museum, PO Box 103, Sandwich, MA 02563, e-mail: sgm@capecod.net, website: www.sandwichglassmuseum.org.

All About Glass (MAG), West Virginia Museum of American Glass, Ltd., PO Box 574, Weston, WV 26452, e-mail: wvmuseumof glass@aol.com, website: members.aol.com/wvmuseumofglass.

Candlewick Collector (NL), 17609 Falling Water Rd., Strongsville, OH 44136, e-mail: VRS1CW@aol.com.

Glass Art Magazine (MAG), PO Box 260377, Highlands Ranch, CO 80163-0377, e-mail: glassartm@aol.com.

Glass Messenger (NL), 700 Elizabeth St., Williamstown, WV 26187, e-mail: askfenton@fentonartglass.com, website: www.fentonartglass.com.

Goofus Glass Gazette (NP), 400 NE Martin Blvd., Kansas City, MO 64118, e-mail: goofus@mid-west.net.

Jody & Darrell's Glass Collectibles (NL), PO Box 180833, Arlington, TX 76096-0833, e-mail: scribeink@aol.com (Boyd Glass and other contemporary glass collectibles).

Network (NL), PO Box 2385, Mt. Pleasant, SC 29465, e-mail: pagewrks@awod.com, website: www.woodsland.com/thistle (carnival glass).

ARCHIVES & MUSEUMS

The Bennington Museum, W. Main St., Bennington, VT 05201, 802-447-1571, fax: 802-442-8305, e-mail: Bennington.Museum@neinfo.net, website: www.benningtonmuseum.com.

The Chrysler Museum of Art, 245 W. Olney Rd., Norfolk, VA 23510-1587, 757-664-6200, e-mail: chrysler@norfolk.infinet, website: www.chrysler.org.

Corning Museum of Glass, One Museum Way, Corning, NY 14830-2253, 607-937-5371, fax: 607-937-5352, website: www.cmog.org

Dorflinger Glass Museum, Long Ridge Rd., White Mills, PA 18473, 570-253-1185, website: www.dorflinger.org.

Greentown Glass Museum, Inc., PO Box 161, Greentown, IN 46936, 765-628-6206, website: www.eastern.k12.in.us/gpl/museum.htm.

National Cambridge Collectors Museum, PO Box 416, Cambridge, OH 43752, 740-432-4245, website: www.cambridgeglass.org.

National Heisey Glass Museum, 169 W. Church St., Newark, OH 43055, 740-345-2932, fax: 740-345-9638, website: www.heiseymuseum.org.

Oglebay Institute Mansion and Glass Museum, Oglebay Park, Wheeling, WV 26003, 304-242-7272, fax: 304-242-4203, website: www.oionline.com.

Sandwich Glass Museum, PO Box 103, Sandwich, MA 02563, 508-888-0251, website: www.sandwichglassmuseum.org.

Toledo Museum of Art, PO Box 1013, Toledo, OH 43627, 419-255-8000, fax: 419-255-5638, website: www.toledomuseum.org.

West Virginia Museum of Glass, PO Box 574, Weston, WV 26452, 304-269-5006, website: members.aol.com/wvmuseumofglass.

USEFUL SITES

Carnival Glass Tumblers of the World, www.tumblerworld.com.

Carnival Glass: Reproductions at a Glance, www.woodsland.com/carnival glass/repro.

Dictionary of Glass Marks, www.heartland-discoveries.com/dictionary.htm.

English Glass Registration Marks, 1st.glassman.com/lozengetranslator.html.

Glass Museum On Line, www.glass.co.nz.

Great Glass, www.great-glass.co.uk.

Just Glass, www.justglass.com.

Vaseline Glass: New, Reissue and Reproductions, www.maxframe.com/GLASS/Vaseline/Reproductions.

APPRAISERS

Many of the auctions and repair services listed in this section will also do appraisals. *See also* Matching Services (crystal), page 544, and the general list of "Appraisal Groups" on page 483.

AUCTIONS

➨ SEE ALSO "SELLING THROUGH AUCTION HOUSES," PAGE 485.

Collector's Sales & Services, PO Box 6, Pomfret Center, CT 06259-0006, 860-974-7008, e-mail: collectors@AntiqueChina.com, website: www.antiqueglass.com. Auctions of china and glass. Mail and phone bids accepted. Buyer's premium 10%. Appraisals.

John R. Pastor Antique & Bottle Glass Auction, 7288 Thorncrest Dr. SE, Ada, MI 49301, 616-285-7604. Mail and phone bids accepted. Buyer's premium 10%. Prices realized mailed after auction. Appraisals.

Just Glass, 405 Lafayette Ave., Cincinnati, OH 45220, 513-961-5794, fax: 513-651-0860, e-mail: justglassauctions@aol.com, website: www.justglass.com. Internet auction of glass and lighting. Appraisals.

L.H. Selman Ltd., 123 Locust St., Santa Cruz, CA 95060, 800-538-0766 or 831-427-1177, fax: 831-427-0111, e-mail: lselman@got.net, website: theglassgallery.com. Glass art and paperweight auctions. Mail, phone, fax, and e-mail bids accepted. Buyer's premium 10%. Catalog $25; annual subscription $60 for 3 catalogs. Prices realized mailed after auction and on website. Restoration and conservation services. Appraisals.

Norman C. Heckler & Co., 79 Bradford Corner Rd., Woodstock Valley, CT 06282, 860-974-1634, fax: 860-974-2003, e-mail: heckler@neca.com, website: www.hecklerauction.com. Bottles, flasks, early glass, and related items. Both absentee and live sales. Mail, phone, and fax bids accepted. Buyer's premium 12%. Catalog $25; yearly subscription $100. Appraisals.

Old Barn Auction, 10040 St. Rt. 224 W., Findlay, OH 45840, 419-422-8531, fax: 419-422-5321, e-mail: auction@oldbarn.com, website: www.oldbarn.com. General auctions; specialized auctions of candy containers. Mail and phone bids accepted. Buyer's premium 10%. Prices realized mailed after auction. Catalog $15; yearly subscription $45. Appraisals.

Pacific Glass Auctions, 1507 21st. St., Suite 203, Sacramento, CA 95814, 800-806-7722, fax: 916-443-3199, e-mail: info@pacglass.com, website: pacglass.com. Mail and phone bids accepted. Buyer's premium 12%. Prices realized mailed after auction. Appraisals.

Shot Glass Exchange, PO Box 219K, Western Springs, IL 60558, 708-246-1559, fax: 708-246-1559. Mail bids only. Two auctions per year. Buyer's premium 10% on items over $50. Prices realized mailed after auction.

Woody Auction, PO Box 618, Douglass, KS 67039, 316-747-2694, fax: 316-747-2145, e-mail: woodyauction@earthlink.net, website: www.woody auction.com. General auctions, carnival glass, and R.S. Prussia. Mail, fax, and e-mail bids accepted. No buyer's premium. Catalogs available in print and online. Prices realized mailed after auction. Free catalogs.

REPAIRS, PARTS & SUPPLIES

↝ SEE ALSO "CONSERVATORS & RESTORERS," PAGE 520.

A Home Design, 5220 Veloz Ave., Los Angeles, CA 91356, 818-757-7766, fax: 818-708-3722, e-mail: homedesign@mail.com. Fine arts restoration, including items made from glass. Operating in the southern California area.

A. Ludwig Klein & Son, Inc., PO Box 145, Harleysville, PA 19438, 215-256-9004 or 800-379-2929, fax: 215-256-9644, website: www.aludwig klein.com. Conservation and restoration of glass and more. Appraisals, insurance claims. Worldwide. By appointment. Free brochure.

Albert Post Gallery, 2291 Newbury Dr., West Palm Beach, FL 33414, 561-333-7740, fax: 561-333-7740, e-mail: apostgallery@aol.com. Restoration and conservation of art glass. Appraisals.

Allan B. Mittelmark, 366 Clinton Ave., Cedarhurst, NY 11516, 561-733-4801, fax: 561-740-1164, e-mail: amsco366@aol.com. Restoration of crystal, including Swarovski and other manufacturers.

Antique & Art Restoration by Wiebold, 413 Terrace Pl., Terrace Park, OH 45174, 800-321-2541, 513-831-2541, fax: 513-831-2815, e-mail: wiebold @eos.net, website: www.wiebold.com. Fine art restoration and conservation of glass and other objects.

Antique Restoration Co., 440 E. Centre Ave., Newtown, PA 18940, 215-968-2343, fax: 215-860-5465. Glass beveling. Free brochure.

Antique Restoration Service, 521 Ashwood Dr., Flushing, MI 48433, 810-

659-5582, 810-659-0505, e-mail: sshch@aol.com. Restoration of glass and other art objects.

AntiqueConservation.com, Div. of Ponsford Ltd., 5441 Woodstock Rd., Acworth, GA 30102, 770-924-4848, fax: 770-529-2278, e-mail: GordonPonsford@AntiqueConservation.com, website: www.Antique Conservation.com. Conservation and restoration of fine art and antiques, including stained glass. Appraisals.

Antiques Etc., 1270 Autumn Wind Way, Henderson, NV 89052, 702-270-9910, e-mail: jimchel@ix.netcom.com. Restoration and appraisals of glass.

Architectural Emporium, 207 Adams Ave., Canonsburg, PA 15317, 724-746-4301, e-mail: sales@architectural-emporium.com, website: architectural-emporium.com. Stained glass.

The Art of Fire at Chaerie Farm, 7901 Hawkins Creamery Rd., Laytonsville, MD 20882, 301-253-6642, e-mail: artofire@bellatlantic.net, website: www.artoffire.com. Glass stem and chip repair; porcelain and pottery restoration. Hand-blown glass. Classes in glass blowing. Open seven days a week. Please call ahead on weekdays.

Artisans of the Valley, 103 Corrine Dr., Pennington, NJ 08534, 609-637-0450, fax: 609-637-0452, e-mail: woodworkers@artisansofthe valley.com, website: www.artisansofthevalley.com. Etched and stained glass work. Consultation services to architects, contractors, and curators. Free catalog.

Artwork Restoration, 30 Hillhouse Rd., Winnipeg, MB R2V 2V9, Canada, 204-334-7090, e-mail: morry@escape.ca. Restoration of crystal and more.

Attic Unlimited, 22435 E. LaPalma Ave., Yorba Linda, CA 92887, 714-692-2940, fax: 714-692-2947, e-mail: atticunlimited@aol.com, website: www.atticunlimited.com. Restoration of glass religious statues and articles, antiques and collectibles, and any objects of art.

B & L Antiqurie, Inc., 6217 S. Lakeshore Rd., PO Box 453, Lexington, MI 48450, 810-359-8623, toll free ordering Mon.–Fri. 8:00 A.M.–5:00 P.M., fax: 810-359-7498, e-mail: information@bentglasscentral.com, website: www.bentglasscentral.com. Replacement curved glass for china cabinets and display cases, curios, etc. Pattern cut and beveled mirrors, convex picture frame glass, antique seedy flat glass, beveled glass. Send SASE for more information.

Bevel GlassWorks, Inc., 900 Hacienda, Belville, TX 77418, 979-865-5711. Bevel mirrors, glass shelves with plate grooves. Can copy almost anything in glass.

Beverly Standing Designs, 1026 Elizabeth St., Pasadena, CA 91104, 626-798-2306, fax: 626-798-3529, e-mail: bubbs120@aol.com. Restoration of objects of art containing glass. By appointment only.

Blue Crystal (Glass), Ltd., Units 6-8, 21 Wren St., London WC1X 0HF, UK, 011-44-20-7278-0142, fax: 011-44-20-7278-0142, e-mail: bluecrystal glass@aol.com, website: www.bluecrystalglass.co.uk. Blue glass liners and other colors for silver salt and mustard pots; stoppers and bottles for silver cruet stands; claret bottles for silver mounts; hand-cut dishes for epergne stands, etc. Antique and general glass repairs; declouding of glass decanters. Reproduction chandelier parts; glass lampshades of any size. Mail order worldwide. Catalog.

Botti Studio of Architectural Arts, Inc., 919 Grove St., Evanston, IL 60201-4315, 800-524-7211 or 847-869-5933, fax: 847-869-5996, e-mail: botti@bottistudio.com, website: www.bottistudio.com. Stained glass; beveled glass; etched, sandblasted, and bent glass; glass painting. Restoration, conservation, and consultation. Free brochure.

Brooks Art Glass, Inc., 821 1/2 E. Miller, Springfield, IL 62704, 217-789-9523, fax: 217-789-6423, e-mail: brooksartglass@hotmail.com, website: www.brooksartglass. Repair and restoration of stained glass, including removal, complete rebuilding, and installation. Custom stained glass from design to installation. Decorative sandblasted designs.

Central Glass Products Inc., 405 W. Hamon Ave., Pocola, OK 74902, 888-BENTGLA(SS) 800-236-8452, fax: 888-BENTGLA(SS) 800-236-8452, e-mail: info@bentglass.com, website: www.bentglass.com. Bent-curved china cabinet replacement glass. Antique seeded glass available.

Chem-Clean Furniture Restoration, Bucks County Art & Antiques Co., 246 W. Ashland St., Doylestown, PA 18901, 215-345-0892, e-mail: iscsusn@att.net. Glass bending, glass beveling. Appraisals. Free brochure.

China & Crystal Matchers Inc., 2379 John Glenn Dr., Suite 108-A, Chamblee, GA 30341, 800-286-1107 or 770-455-1162, fax: 770-452-8616, e-mail: chinacmi@bellsouth.net, website: www.chinaandcrystal.com. Basic chip repair on stemware.

China and Crystal Clinic, 1808 N. Scottsdale Rd., Tempe, AZ 85281, 800-658-9197, fax: 480-945-1079, e-mail: VictorColeman@earthlink.net. Restoration of glass, crystal, and many other materials. Swarovski, Lalique, etc.

The Crystal Cave, Ginny Hoppa, Repair Department, 1141 Central Ave., Wilmette, IL 60091, 847-251-1160, fax: 847-251-1172, e-mail: allcrystal1141 @aol.com, website: www.crystalcaveofchicago.com. Crystal repair, glass cutting, engraving. Retail store and workshop on the premises.

David Smith, 1142 S. Spring St., Springfield, IL 62704, 217-523-3391, fax: 217-523-0478, e-mail: davemarble@msn.com. Glass restorations. Glass marbles restored: grinding and buffing the glass. Broken or chipped pieces fixed. Brochure 50 cents. Open Mon.-Fri. 10:00 A.M.–5:00 P.M.

David Wixon & Associates, Inc., 189 Kenilworth Ave., Glen Ellyn, IL 60137, 630-858-7618, fax: 630-858-7623, e-mail: wixonglass@aol.com, website: www.wixonartglass.com. Restoration and construction of stained and beveled glass for both residential and church clients. Historic architectural glass a specialty. Free brochure.

Dean's China Restoration, 324 Guinevere Ridge, Cheshire, CT 06410, 800-669-1327 or 203-271-3659, e-mail: DSandAssociates@aol.com. Invisible restoration of all types of crystal, glass, figurines, etc. Pieces can be brought to the studio or sent from anywhere. Free estimates. Free brochure.

Delphi Creativity Group, 3380 E. Jolly Rd., Lansing, MI 48910, 800-248-2048 or 517-394-4631, fax: 800-748-0374 or 517-394-5364, e-mail: sales@delphiglass.com, website: www.delphiglass.com. Hand-blown glass for window repairs. Color matching service for repairs of antique stained-glass windows. Glass etching and engraving supplies, stencils; stained-glass kits and supplies; beveled glass; books and tools. Mosaics, hot glass, and jewelry supplies. Free catalog.

Devashan, 445 S. Canyon, Spearfish, SD 57783, 605-722-5355, e-mail: dollmaker@mato.com, website: www.devashan.com. Glass chip removal. Send SASE for brochure.

Drehobl Brothers Art Glass Co., 2847 N. Lincoln Ave., Chicago, IL 60657, 773-281-2022, fax: 773-281-2023. Restoration of leaded, stained, and beveled glass. New leaded glass custom made. Bent glass panels for shades.

Eastern Art Glass, PO Box 9, Wyckoff, NJ 07481, 800-872-3458 for customer service, 800-872-3458 for order desk, e-mail: etchgal@idt.net, website: www.etchworld.com. Glass etching and mirror decorating supplies, stencils, books and videos for the do-it-yourselfer. Glass engraving tools and craft supplies.

Ernest Porcelli/Art Glass, 543 Union St., 3A, Brooklyn, NY 11215, 718-596-4353, fax: 718-596-4353, e-mail: eporcelliart@c.s.com, website: ernestartglass.com. Full-service stained glass studio. Restoration of stained glass windows. Custom work. Duplication of old windows to contemporary designs.

Esoteric Sign Supply, 1644 Wilmington Blvd., Wilmington, CA 90744, 310-549-6622, fax: 310-549-0180, e-mail: lola@esotericsignsupply.com, website: esotericsignsupply.com. Exotic sign and gilding supplies. Gold leaf, mother-of-pearl, paints, brushes, etc. Glue chipping supplies; colored glass smalts; beach and crushed sand smalts. Catalog $3. Free price list.

Facets, 107 Boundary Rd. Leyton, London, E17 8NQ, UK, 011-44-208-520-3392, e-mail: repairs@facetsglass.co.uk, website: www.facets glass.co.uk. Glass and antique restoration company offering a wide range of services, including cleaning the inside of decanters, scent bottles, and vases; repair and restoration of egg timers and hourglasses.

Final Touch, Inc., 34 Ranch Rd., Woodbridge, CT 06525, 203-389-5485, fax: 203-389-5553, e-mail: FinalTh@optonline.net. Glass repair. Appraisals.

Fine Wares Restoration, Sharon Smith Abbott, PO Box 753, Bridgton, ME 04009, 207-647-2093, e-mail: sharonsmithabbott@yahoo.com. Glass restoration. Treatments include cleaning, bonding, gapfilling, and replacement by casting with appropriate resins. Written estimates and suggested treatment provided at no cost.

Glass Lady @ Kaleidoscope, 7501 Iron Bridge Rd., Richmond, VA 23237, 804-743-9811 or 804-743-9846, e-mail: glasslady8@aol.com. Glass repair.

Glass Restorations, 1597 York Ave., New York, NY 10028, 212-517-3287, fax: 212-517-3287, e-mail: gusjochec@webtv.net. Restoration of anything made of glass, including glassware and art glass of all kinds: Steuben, Lalique, Baccarat, Waterford, Gallé, Daum Nancy, Kosta, St. Louis, etc.

Glass Studio, 5412A Dickson, Houston, TX 77007, 713-880-1090, fax: 713-880-3544, e-mail: nfwassef@msn.com. Crystal repair.

Grashe Fine Art Restorers, 35 148th Ave. SE, #9, Bellevue WA 98007, 425-644-7500, fax: 425-644-7582, e-mail: art@grashe.com, website: www.grashe.com. Specializes in the restoration and conservation of glass and other art objects.

H.W. Kopp, Glass Grinding, 26 State St., Skaneateles, NY 13152, 315-685-5073. Repairs chips on tops of glasses; cuts broken tops of vases, bottles, etc., and polishes them; fits stoppers to bottles, drills holes. Mail order and UPS orders.

Hamlin's Restoration Studio, 14640 Manchester Rd., Ballwin, MO 63011, 636-256-8579, e-mail: hamlinsrestoration@msn.com, website: www.hamlinsrestoration.com. Repair and restoration of glass and other materials.

Heimbolds, 2950 SW Persimmon Ln., Dunnellon, FL 34431, 352-465-0756. Art conservation restorers: pottery and porcelain, glass, dolls, toys, signs, paintings, stone or organic carvings, etc. Free estimates. Free brochure.

Herbert F. Klug Conservation & Restoration, Box 28002, #16, Lakewood, CO 80228, 303-985-9261, e-mail: hgklug@qadas.com. Conservation and restoration of Lalique glass and other objects of art. By appointment only.

Hudson Glass Co. Inc., Dept. K-8, 219 N. Division St., Peekskill, NY 10566-2700, 800-431-2964 or 914-737-2124, fax: 914-737-4447. Bent glass for china cabinets, convex picture frame glass, stained glass, tools, and supplies. No repairs. Catalog $5, $3 refundable with order.

Hyland Studio at Manufacturers Glass Ltd., 650 Reed St., Santa Clara, CA 95050, 408-748-1806, e-mail: jim@manufacturersglass.com, website: www.manufacturersglass.com. Decorative glass and doors; traditional lead work. Historic restoration and duplication of traditional leaded glass windows. Custom beveled glass windows, historic and custom designs. Etched and carved glass; glue chipping.

Items of Value, Inc., 7419 Admiral Dr., Alexandria, VA 22307, 703-660-9380, fax: 703-660-9384. Restoration work for many different types of items, including glass. Appraisals.

Jar Doctor, 401 Johnston Ct., Raymore, MO 64083, 816-318-0161, fax: 816-318-0162, e-mail: jardoclowry@aol.com, website: www.one-mans-junk.com/jardoc. Glass-polishing machines, tumbling canisters, and cleaning supplies for antique glass; specializing in bottles, jars, and insulators. National referral of professional custom polishing or glass repair in your area. Free brochure.

Jonathan Mark Gershen, 1463 Pennington Rd., Ewing Township, NJ 08618, 609-882-9417. Repair and restoration of glass. Missing parts fabricated, shattered pieces restored. Historically accurate reconstruction of decorative art objects. Send for information on how to ship your items for evaluation. Worldwide service. Free brochure.

Kemxert Corp., 3195 E. Prospect Rd., York, PA 17402, 717-757-1551, fax: 717-757-1357, e-mail: info@kemxert.com, website: www.kemxert.com. U.V. materials for glass repair and lamination. Adhesives for bonding glass to glass, mirrors, and other materials. U.V. lamps. Open 9:00 A.M.–4:00 P.M.

Kim Carlisle & Associates, 28220 Lamong Rd., Dept. K, Sheridan, IN 46069, 317-758-5767, e-mail: kcarlisl@indy.net. Cloudy glass cleaned. The inside of vases, decanters, cologne bottles, salt shakers, cruets, etc., cleaned. Write for quote.

Kingsmen Antique Restoration Inc., 19 Passamore Ave., Unit 28, Scarborough, ON M1V 4T5, Canada, 416-291-8939, fax: 416-291-8939, e-mail: kingsmen@sprint.ca. Invisible mending of art objects. Restoration of glass and more. Service worldwide. Call for information on sending objects for estimates.

KLM Studios, 9525 Kenwood Rd., Suite 16-226, Cincinnati, OH 45242, 513-652-9216, e-mail: info@klmstudios.com, website: www.klmstudios.com. Restoration services for glass.

L.H. Selman Ltd., 123 Locust St., Santa Cruz, CA 95060, 800-538-0766 or 831-427-1177, fax: 831-427-0111, e-mail: lselman@got.net, website: theglassgallery.com. Glass art and paperweight restoration and conservation services. Appraisals.

Manor Art Glass, 20 Ridge Rd., Douglaston, NY 11363, 718-631-8029, fax: 718-631-0308. Repair and restoration of stained glass. Leaded, etched, and carved glass. Hand-painted glass. Custom-designed windows and doors.

Mike and Jo Baldwin, PO Box 2971, Anderson, IN 46018-2971, 765-643-7065, e-mail: gmja59@insightbb.com. Tin parts and closures for glass candy containers, as well as some lids for glass banks. Parts are die stamped. Free catalog.

Montano's Antique Glass Repair, P.O. Box 290003, Phelan CA 92329, 760-868-6598, fax: 760-868-6598, e-mail: info@montanosglassrepair.com, website: www.montanosglassrepair.com. Repairing of glass and crystal. Specializing in the repair of American Brilliant cut glass, art glass,

Lalique, Daum, Baccarat, Waterford, Steuben, Venetian, Murano, elegant glassware, and pressed glass.

New Orleans Conservation Guild, Inc., 3301 Chartres St., New Orleans, LA 70117, 504-944-7900, fax: 504-944-8750, e-mail: info@art-restoration.com, website: www.art-restoration.com. Restoration and conservation of fine art and antiques, including glass. Appraisals and research searches. Call or write for brochure.

Oak Brothers, 5104 N. Pearl St., Tacoma, WA 98407, 253-752-4055, fax: 253-752-4055, e-mail: wmalovich@harbornet.com. Benders and sellers of curved glass for china closets, picture frames, lamps, and other things. By appointment only. Call or write for more information.

Old World Restorations, Inc., 5729 Dragon Way, Cincinnati, OH 45227, 513-271-5459, fax: 513-271-5418, e-mail: info@oldworldrestorations.com, website: www.oldworldrestorations.com. Restoration and conservation of art and antiques including glass. Specialized packing and shipping. Nationwide service. Send or e-mail photos for preliminary estimates. Free brochure.

Pairpoint Crystal Co., 851 Sandwich Rd., PO Box 515, Sagamore, MA 02561, 508-888-2344, fax: 508-888-3537, e-mail: pairpoint@earthlink.net, website: www.pairpoint.com. Glass repair and reproduction. Chips and rough edges repaired. Custom work available. Can make a candlestick to match one of a broken pair. Free catalog.

Past & Present, 14851 Avenue 360, Visalia, CA 93292, 559-798-0029, fax: 559-798-1415, e-mail: P-P@ix.netcom.com, website: www.pastpresent.net. Restoration and appraisals.

PECO Glass Bending, PO Box 777, Smithville, TX 78957, 512-237-3600, e-mail: glass@pecoglassbending.com, website: www.pecoglassbending.com. Curved glass for china cabinets; 39 stock radiuses. Custommade J's, S's, serpentines, and bubble glass. Convex glass for antique picture frames. Custom-made lamp parts.

Peter Owen, 29 Murray St., Augusta, ME 04330, 207-622-3277, e-mail: lamprepair@msn.com, website: www.stained-glass-lamp-restorations.com. Replacement bent slag glass panels and other stained-glass lamp shade repairs.

Pick Up the Pieces, 711 W. 17th St., Unit C-12, Costa Mesa, CA 92627, 800-824-6967, fax: 949-645-8381, e-mail: johnnce@yahoo.com, website: www.pickupthepieces.com. Repair and restoration of glass, fine art, and collectibles.

Pleasant Valley Restoration, 1725 Reed Rd., Knoxville, MD 21758, 301-432-2721, 9:00 A.M.–7:00 P.M., e-mail: PVRfixit@aol.com. Restoration of glass and other art and antique objects.

Poor Richard's Restoration & Preservation Studio Workshop, 101 Walnut St., Montclair, NJ 07042, 973-783-5333, fax: 973-744-1939, e-mail: jrickford@webtv.com, website: www.rickford.com. Restoration, conservation, archival and preservation services for glass and other objects. By appointment, Tues.–Fri. noon–5:00 P.M., Sat. noon–3:00 P.M.

Premium Bevels, Inc., 2006 Johnson St., Lafayette, LA 70503, 800-752-3501, fax: 337-234-1646. Custom beveling of glass and mirrors. Mirror placemat sets. Stained glass assembly. Reproduction of odd-shaped mirrors. Call for quote.

Professional Restoration Studio, PO Box 435, N. 5th St., Highland, NC 28741, 828-526-4064, fax: 828-526-4064, e-mail: crystalstudio @earthlink.net. Restoration of fine crystals, including Lalique, Waterford, and more.

Rafail & Polina Golberg, Golberg Restoration Co., 411 Westmount Dr., Los Angeles, CA 90048, 310-652-0735, fax: 310-274-3770, e-mail: info @restorationworld.com, website: www.restorationworld.com. Restoration and conservation of antiques and objects of art, including crystal. Free estimates via the Internet.

Ray Errett, 101 Mohican Tr., Wilmington, NC 28409, 910-792-1807, e-mail: errettjr@aol.com. Crystal repair and restoration.

Renovation Source, Inc., 3512 N. Southport, Chicago, IL 60657, 773-327-1250, fax: 773-327-1250. Salvaged architectural details, including stained and beveled glass. Open Tues.-Sat. 10:00 A.M.–6:00 P.M.

Replacements, Ltd., PO Box 26029, 1089 Knox Rd., Greensboro, NC 27420-6029, 800-REPLACE (800-737-5223), fax: 336-697-3100, e-mail: inquire@replacements.com, website: www.replacements.com. Crystal repair.

Restoration Services, 1417 Third St., Webster City, IA 50595, 515-832-1131, e-mail: repair@netins.net, website: www.Restorationmaterials.safe shopper.com. Restoration services for glass and most other materials. Replacement parts fabricated. Supplies, videos, home study course, classes available. Glass chip filler, diamond hand pads for removing scratches, glass bonding resin, enamel glaze, stain remover, lacquers, milliput, less toxic milliput substitute, flatner, and more. Mini manual, "Glass Cleaning & Repairing."

Restorations Unlimited, 3009 W. Genesee St., Syracuse, NY 13219, 315-488-7123, fax: 315-488-7123, e-mail: d64curtin@aol.com. Glass repair.

Restorite Systems, PO Box 7096-A, West Trenton, NJ 08628, 609-530-1526. Products for restoring glass. Repair kit for restoring broken or chipped china and glass. Includes supplies necessary to mend dozens of pieces and illustrated instruction book. Mail order only. Free brochure.

Richard Blaschke Cabinet Glass, 670 Lake Ave., Bristol, CT 06010, 860-584-2566, fax: 860-314-0296, e-mail: rjblaschke@snet.net, website: www.dicksantiques.com. Curved china cabinet replacement glass.

Rosine Green Associates, Inc., 89 School St., Brookline, MA 02446, 617-277-8368, fax: 617-731-3845, e-mail: rga@ix.netcom.com. Conservation and restoration of fine art, including glass, and objects of art. Custom display cases.

Stewart's Restoration Studio, 2555 Goldenrod Dr., Bowling Green, KY 42104, 270-842-4580, fax: 270-842-4580, e-mail: stewartsrestore @aol.com. Restoration of glass antiques and collectibles.

Swan Restorations, 2627 Montrose Ave., Abbotsford, BC V2S 3TS, Canada, 604-855-6694, fax: 604-855-1720. Restoration of glass, crystal, and antiques and collectibles: Free written estimates. Open Mon.-Fri. 10:00 A.M.–5:00 P.M., or by appointment. Call before sending item to be repaired.

Tindell's Restoration, 825 Sandburg Pl., Nashville, TN 37214, 615-885-1029, fax: 615-391-0712, e-mail: info@ATindellsRestorationSchools.com, website: www.TindellsRestorationSchools.com. Restoration services, seminars, training, and products for crystal, glass, and more. Appraisals. Free brochure.

United House Wrecking, 535 Hope St., Stamford, CT 06906, 203-348-5371, fax: 203-961-9472, e-mail: unitedhouse.wrecking@snet.net, website: www.unitedhousewrecking.com. Architectural elements, including stained glass. Open seven days a week, Mon.–Sat. 9:30 A.M.–5:00 P.M., Sunday noon–5:00 P.M. Free brochure.

Venerable Classics, 645 Fourth St., Suite 208, Santa Rosa, CA 95404, 800-531-2891, 707-575-3626, fax: 707-575-4913 call first, website: www.venerableclassics.com. Restoration of crystal and many other fragile decorative objects. Restoration of Swarovski crystal collectibles. Please call with questions. Free brochure on request.

Whittemore-Durgin Glass Co., Box 2065, Hanover, MA 02339, 800-262-1790, fax: 781-871-5597, website: www.WhittemoreDurgin.com. Stained glass supplies, equipment, and instruction. Bent lampshade panels, beaded lampshade fringes, bull's-eye panes. Catalog $2.

Zorella Restoration, 1936 Mt. Royal Terr., Baltimore, MD 21217, 410-225-2141, fax: 410-462-2135, e-mail: szorella@aol.com. Restoration of glass and other antique pieces and art objects.

•→ HALLOWEEN, SEE HOLIDAY COLLECTIBLES

HARDWARE

Locks and keys have intrigued collectors since medieval times, and today collectors want everything from wrought-iron door locks to brass-tagged hotel keys. Wooden locks were used by the Egyptians about 2000 B.C. By the Middle Ages, huge metal locks were made to keep intruders out of the castle. Collectors divide locks into types and often specialize in categories such as railroad locks, trick locks, ball and chains, institutional locks, combination locks, padlocks, or locks made by special companies or for special events. A few locks have historical value because they can be traced to a maker or historic building.

Locks sell well in flea markets and antiques stores, in restored and in original condition. Missing keys are not a problem—a locksmith can replace them. The best prices are paid for locks with special features, those with unusual mechanisms or rare logos, and those in pristine condition with the original box and key.

Keys are priced by rarity, shape, and age. Old iron keys are best, but some collectors now buy brass hotel keys either tagged or with the name on the key. Look for the names **YALE**, **VAN DORN IRON WORKS**, and **WINCHESTER**.

REPAIR

Some collectors want examples of old doorknobs or iron latches to display as part of a collection, but most people want to use the old hardware. When using old doorknobs or locks, you must be sure the measurements correspond to the thickness of your door. Old doors are sometimes thicker than newer doors.

Hardware for old furniture is difficult to match but relatively easy to replace. When possible, match existing hardware—some designs are still being made. A few companies will make a copy of your hardware from the sample you submit. If the hardware is not original or can't be matched, replace it with old or new pieces. Be sure to get hardware of the correct style and period.

When replacing hardware, try buying pieces that will cover the old screw holes. Special hardware for old refrigerators, trunks, doors, and windows can be found.

⇢ SEE ALSO FURNITURE, METALS, POTTERY & PORCELAIN, TRUNKS

PRICE BOOKS
Antique Hardware Price Guide, H. Weber Wilson (Krause, Iola, WI, 1999).

CLUBS & THEIR PUBLICATIONS
American Lock Collectors Association, *Journal of Lock Collecting* (NL), 8576 Barbara Dr., Mentor, OH 44060, e-mail: dixlock@aol.com, website: alca-online.org.

Antique Doorknob Collectors of America, *Doorknob Collector* (NL), PO Box 31, Chatham, NJ 07928-0031, e-mail: KnobNews@aol.com, website: members.aol.com/knobnews.

Antique Fan Collectors Association, *The Fan Collector* (NL), PO Box 5473, Sarasota, FL 34277-5473, e-mail: membership@fancollectors.org, website: www.fancollectors.org.

West Coast Lock Collectors, *West Coast Lock Collectors Newsletter* (NL), 1427 Lincoln Blvd., Santa Monica, CA 90401, e-mail: locksmann@aol.com, website: wclca.org.

AUCTIONS

➻ **SEE ALSO "SELLING THROUGH AUCTION HOUSES," PAGE 485.**

Web Wilson's Online Auctions, PO Box 506, Portsmouth, RI 02871, 800-508-0022, fax: 401-683-1644, e-mail: hww@webwilson.com, website: www.webwilson.com. Antique hardware, tiles, and more. Phone, fax, and e-mail bids accepted. Buyer's premium 10%. Catalog posted on website or by mail. Prices realized posted on website after auction. Appraisals.

REPAIRS, PARTS & SUPPLIES

➻ **SEE ALSO "CONSERVATORS & RESTORERS," PAGE 520.**

18th Century Hardware Co., Inc., William F. Simpson, president, 131 E. Third St., Derry, PA 15627, 724-694-2708, fax: 724-694-9587. Duplication of missing hardware on antique furniture. Metal items cleaned and polished. Broken items repaired. Catalog $3.

A & H Brass & Supply, 126 W. Main St., Johnson City, TN 37604, 423-928-8220. Complete line of restoration hardware, reproduction furniture hardware, veneers, caning supplies, replacement seats, Briwax, Howard's products. Trunk supplies. Catalog $3. Separate catalog for lamp parts.

Al Bar-Wilmette Platers, 127 Green Bay Rd., Wilmette, IL 60091, 847-251-0187, fax: 847-251-0281, e-mail: info@albarwilmette.com, website: www.albarwilmette.com. Restoration of historic hardware and metal fixtures. Restoration of metal finishes; missing parts furnished, lamps and chandeliers repaired, locks refurbished, and new hardware plated to match historic finishes.

American Alloy Foundry, 112-120 S. Eden St., Baltimore, MD 21231, 410-276-1930, fax: 410-276-1947. Brass, bronze, and aluminum castings made using the sand-mold method. Can reproduce from originals to make exact copies. Replicas of antique hardware, drawer pulls, handles, bales, rosettes, and hooks. Antique car parts, boat parts, airplane parts, slot machine parts, etc. Brochure $1.

Antique Hardware & Home Store, 19 Buckingham Plantation Dr., Bluffton, SC 29910, 800-422-9982, 8:30 A.M.–6:00 P.M. e-mail: treasure @hargray.com, website: www.antiquehardware.com. Old-style hardware and accessories: door, window, cabinet, Hoosier hardware, and specialty hardware; sinks, claw-foot tub supplies, high tank toilets, plumbing fittings; specialty lamp shades, floor grills, tin ceilings. Custom hardware and plumbing fixtures. Free catalog.

Antique Hardware and Mirror Resilvering, 763 West Bippley Rd.,

Lake Odessa, MI 48849, 616-374-7750, fax: 616-374-7752, e-mail: antiquehardware@robinsonsantiques.com, website: www.robinsons antiques.com. Original antique restoration hardware, door hardware, doorknobs, furniture hardware, hinges, mirrors, locks, pulls, latches, registers, and more. Mirror resilvering. Original parts from 1650 to 1925. Free search. Free matching service.

Architectural Detail, 512 S. Fair Oaks, Pasadena, CA 91105, 626-844-6604, fax: 626-844-6651. Home restoration resources. Used building materials from 1880 to 1960, including doors, doorknobs, hinges, mail slots, windows, molding, plumbing, hardware, tiles, lighting, etc. Specializing in materials from Pasadena and Greater Los Angeles. No mail order.

Architectural Emporium, 207 Adams Ave., Canonsburg, PA 15317, 724-746-4301, e-mail: sales@architectural-emporium.com, website: architectural-emporium.com. Specializing in restored period lighting, early Victorian gas fixtures through Art Deco period. Architectural antiques, including vintage plumbing, mantels, hardware, stained glass, garden statuary, and all architectural items.

Ball & Ball Antique Hardware Reproductions, 436 W. Lincoln Hwy., Exton, PA 19341, 800-257-3711, fax: 610-363-7639, website: www.ballandball.com. Reproduction furniture and cabinet hardware. Hardware, lighting, and metal items repaired and refinished. Lighting fixtures duplicated or custom-made. Fireplace accessories.

Bathroom Machineries, 495 Main St., PO Box 1020, Murphys, CA 95247, 209-728-2031 or 800-255-4426, fax: 209-728-2320, e-mail: tom@deabath.com, website: deabath.com. Antique plumbing fixtures. Original and reproduction claw-foot tubs, high tank toilets, pedestal sinks, hard-to-find plumbing parts, faucets, mirrors, medicine cabinets, old keys. Antique replacement glass lampshades. Free catalog.

The Brass Knob, Architectural Antiques, 2311 18th St. NW, Washington, DC 20009, 202-332-3370, fax: 202-332-5594, e-mail: bk@thebrassknob.com, website: www.thebrassknob.com. Architectural antiques and salvage, including fireplace mantels, claw-foot tubs, radiators, lighting, stained glass, and many other old house parts. Second location, The Back Doors Warehouse, is located at 2329 Champlain St. NW, Washington, DC 20009.

C & H Supply, 5431 Mountville Rd., Adamstown, MD 21710, 301-663-1812, e-mail: CandHSupplyCo@aol.com. Reproduction brass hardware, wood and porcelain knobs, table parts, chair caning supplies, replacement chair seats, short bed rails, cannonballs for iron and brass beds, replacement trunk parts, pie-safe tins, icebox hardware, kitchen cabinet hardware, flour bins. Veneers, paint and varnish removers, stains and lacquers. Most orders shipped within 24 hours. Catalog $4.

Cambridge Smithy, 140 Forge Dr., Cambridge, VT 05444, 802-644-5358, fax: 802-644-5651, e-mail: pkrusch@sover.net. Repair of antique weathervanes. Custom copper weathervanes. Repair and duplication of antique forged hardware.

Classic Restoration Co., 10800 Carnegie Ave., Cleveland, OH 44106, 216-791-9050, 10:00 A.M.–6:00 P.M. Metal repairs, refining, replating of hardware and light fixtures. Missing parts reproduced.

Conant Custom Brass, 270 Pine St., PO Box 1523A, Burlington, VT 05402, 800-832-4482 or 802-658-4482, fax: 802-864-5914, e-mail: steve@conantcustombrass.com, website: www.conantcustombrass.com. Brass and copper restoration and repair. Check the website for tips on care and cleaning of brass.

Conner's Architectural Antiques, 701 P St., Lincoln, NE 68508, 402-435-3338, fax: 402-435-3339, e-mail: connersaa@aol.com, website: www.ConnersArchitecturalAntiques.com. Architectural elements from old structures, including columns, doors, fireplace mantels, hardware, light fixtures, stairways, and windows. Stained, etched, and beveled glass windows. Old and new hardware.

Constantines Wood Center, 1040 E. Oakland Park Blvd., Ft. Lauderdale, FL 33334, 954-561-1716, fax: 954-565-8149, e-mail: info@constantines.com, website: www.constantines.com. Woodworkers supplies, including hardwoods, veneer, tools, hardware, and cane. Free catalog. Hours: Mon.–Fri. 8:30 A.M.–5:30 P.M., Sat. 9:00 A.M.–4:00 P.M. (October 1–May 31); Mon.–Fri. 8:30 A.M.–5:30 P.M., Sat. 9:00 A.M.–1:00 P.M. (June 1–September 30).

Crown City Hardware Co., 1047 N. Allen Ave., Pasadena, CA 91104, 800-950-1047 or 626-794-1188, fax: 800-816-8492, e-mail: questions@restoration.com, website: www.crowncityhardware.com. Restoration hardware: cabinet hardware, doorknobs and escutcheons, hinges, window hardware, and more. Glass cabinet and door hardware. Catalog $5, refundable with purchase.

Darryl Hudson Custom Machining & Fabrication, 68 Bluegrass Dr., Aiken, SC 29803, 803-649-6641, 8:00 A.M.–10:00 P.M., e-mail: dhudson@mindspring.com, website: darryl.hudson.home.mindspring.com. Electric fan and heater parts and restoration supplies. Correct replacement parts for antique fans or heaters, including rubber grommets, rubber feet, replacement screw-in grommets, shoulder screws, brush caps, brush holders, bearings, gears, oscillator arms, etc. Glass bead blasting available. Mail order worldwide. Send $2 and SASE for current price list.

Doug Poe's Restoration Hardware, 4213W 500N, Huntington, IN 46750, 800-348-5004, 8:00 A.M.–5:00 P.M. fax: 219-356-4358, e-mail: dpoe@yahoo.com, website: www.homier.com/dougpoe. Antique restoration hardware. Stamped and cast brass pulls, die-cast brass knobs, stamped brass keyholes, keys, hooks, wood casters. Free flyer.

Eugenia's Antique Hardware, 5370 Peachtree Rd., Chamblee (Atlanta), GA 30341-2450, 800-337-1677, 770-458-1677, fax: 770-458-5966, e-mail:

eugeniashardware@mindspring.com, website: eugeniaantiquehardware.com. Antique hardware. Door and furniture hardware. Accessories: doorknockers, twist doorbells, curtain tiebacks, bin pulls, latches, and hinges. Will search for items by request. No reproduction hardware. Cleaning and restoration products.

The Fan Man, 1914 Abrams Pkwy., Dallas, TX 75214, 214-826-7700, e-mail: fanmanusa3@aol.com, website: www.fanmanusa.com. Parts, repair, restoration, rentals, and sales of antique mechanical fans. Blades, blade irons, etc. Ceiling, pedestal, and desk fans from 1895 to the present. Emerson & Hunter service/warranty centers. Catalog $3.

Faneuil Furniture Hardware Co., Inc., 163 Main St., Salem, NH 03079, 603-898-7733, fax: 603-898-7839. Solid brass reproduction hardware for furniture pulls. Traditional, French, Oriental, Victorian. Knobs, ornaments, pendant pulls, escutcheons, casters, hinges, and drapery tiebacks. Catalog $5.

Finials Unlimited, 129 W. 29th St., 2nd Floor, New York, NY 10001, 212-629-5630, fax: 212-268-4577, e-mail: finunlim@aol.com, website: www.antiquefurnitureusa.com. Manufacturers of custom drapery hardware; antique restoration and reproductions. Free brochure.

Hershberger's Hardware Ltd., 1411 Township Rd. 178, Dept. K, Baltic, OH 43804, 330-893-2464, fax: 330-698-3200. Catalog company serving the furniture manufacturing industry and the antique industry. Many hard-to-find hardware items, including pulls, latches, handles, table locks, Hoosier cabinet parts, pie-safe tins, bins, wood dowels, pegs, spindles, decals, Zap glue, and more. Wholesale catalog $4.

Horton Brasses, 47-51 Nooks Hill Rd., PO Box 120, Cromwell, CT 06416, 860-754-9127, fax: 860-635-6473, e-mail: barb@horton-brasses.com, website: www.horton-brasses.com. Reproduction brass and iron furniture and cabinet hardware. Hardware from 1650 to 1940 reproduced. Custom hand-forged iron hinges and latches for barns, doors, shutters, and other restoration projects. Much hand-forged iron in stock. Polishes, waxes, and cleaners. Catalog $4.

Jim Leonard, Antique Hardware, 509 Tangle Dr., Jamestown, NC 27282. Eighteenth- and nineteenth-century wrought-iron door hardware and fireplace equipment. Thumb latches, elbow latches, slide bolts, strap hinges, ram's-horn hinges, sawtooth trammel lighting device holders, cupboard and blanket chest hardware, etc. Send $3 for price list. Photos of hardware available.

Kayne & Son Custom Hardware, Inc., 100 Daniel Ridge Rd., Candler, NC 28715, 828-667-8868 or 828-665-1988, fax: 828-665-8303, e-mail: kaynehdwe@earthlink.net, website: customforgedhardware.com. Repair, restoration, refinishing, and reproduction of hardware, etc. Custom forged hardware and cast brass or bronze reproductions. Tools for blacksmiths, metalsmiths, and collectors: anvils, hammers, tongs, swages, etc. Catalogs available, $5.

Lee Valley Tools, Ltd., 1090 Morrison Dr., Ottawa, ON K2H 1C2, Canada, 800-871-8158, fax: 800-513-7885, e-mail: customerservice@lee valley.com, website: www.leevalley.com. Fine woodworking and finishing tools and supplies for restoration and preservation. Free introductory catalog.

Memphis Plating Works, 682 Madison Ave., Memphis, TN 38103, 901-526-3051. Repairing and refinishing of metals, including antique bronze or pot metal statues, chandeliers, and lamps. Refinishing of door and window hardware in old houses; refinishing chrome on antique and show cars.

Monroe Coldren and Son, 723 E. Virginia Ave., West Chester, PA 19380, 610-692-5651, fax: 610-918-1722. Brass, copper, and iron work. Metal work repaired and custom-crafted. Eighteenth- and nineteenth-century hardware, lighting, and fireplace accessories. Catalog available.

Muff's Antiques, 135 S. Glassell St., Orange, CA 92866, 714-997-0243, fax: 714-997-0243, e-mail: muffs@earthlink.net, website: www.muffs hardware.com. Antique restoration hardware. Hard-to-find hardware for furniture, trunks, Hoosier cabinets, iceboxes, sewing machines, oil lamps, and more. Old-fashioned locks and keys. Mail order worldwide. Catalog free online, $5 in print. Tues.–Sat. 11:00 A.M.–5:00 P.M., Sun. 1:30 P.M.–4:00 P.M.

Old and Elegant Distributing, 10203 Main St. Ln., Bellevue, WA 98004, 425-455-4660, fax: 425-455-0203. Custom metal refinishing and restoration. Cabinet and door hardware replication. Custom faucet and bath fixture design. Architectural wood and iron.

Outwater Plastics Industries, Inc., 4 Passaic St., PO Box 403, Wood Ridge, NJ 07075, 800-631-8375 or 973-340-1040, fax: 800-888-3315 or 973-916-1640, e-mail: outwater@outwater.com, website: www.outwater.com. An international supplier of more than 40,000 component products, including furniture hardware, cabinet components, knobs and pulls, casters; architectural moldings and millwork, columns and capitals, plaster architectural elements, fireplace surrounds, wrought iron components, lighting, brass tubing and fittings, fasteners, and much more. Free catalog.

Paxton Hardware Ltd., 7818 Bradshaw Rd., PO Box 256, Upper Falls, MD 21156, 800-241-9741, fax: 410-592-2224, e-mail: paxton@ix.net com.com, website: www.paxtonhardware.com. Antique-style furniture fittings and lighting. Classic pulls, handles and knobs, hinges, locks, casters, supports, catches, table and bed hardware, hooks, seat-weaving materials, lamp burners, chimneys, and shades. Catalog.

Phyllis Kennedy, 10655 Andrade Dr., Zionsville, IN 46077, 317-873-1316, fax: 317-873-8662, e-mail: philken@kennedyhardware.com, website: www.kennedyhardware.com. Hardware and parts for antique furniture, Hoosier cabinets, and trunks. Specializing in parts for Hoosier cabinets, including flour bins, bread drawers, roll doors, wire racks, and sugar jars. Pie-safe tins, icebox hardware, bed hardware, chair seats and caning, architectural hardware, pressed fiberboard, and more. Wholesale catalog $3.

R.J. Pattern Services, c/o R. J. Hoerr, 1212 W. Detroit St., New Buffalo, MI 49117, 616-469-7538, fax: 616-469-8554, e-mail: mhoerr@starband.net. Cast iron, aluminum, and brass castings. Wood and plastic (foundry) patterns and models. Antique stove and range replacement parts. Classic gas range knobs, dials, and handles.

Rejuvenation, 2550 NW Nicolai St., Portland, OR 97210, 888-401-1900 toll free or 503-231-1900, fax: 800-526-7329 toll free or 503-230-0537, e-mail: info@rejuvenation.com, website: www.rejuvenation.com. Reproduction antique hardware. For information on restoration services, call 503-238-1900 or e-mail restoration@rejuvenation.com.

Renovation Source, Inc., 3512 N. Southport, Chicago, IL 60657, 773-327-1250, fax: 773-327-1250. Salvaged architectural details, including hardware and lighting fixtures. Light fixture restoration, hardware polishing and coating, wood refinishing. Open Tues.–Sat. 10:00 A.M.–6:00 P.M.

Renovator's Supply, Renovator's Old Mill, Millers Falls, MA 01349, 800-659-0203, 7:00 A.M.–midnight, fax: 413-659-3796 orders, website: www.rensup.com. Hardware, plumbing fixtures; firebacks, ceiling medallions, and more. Free catalog.

Scott's Beckers' Hardware, Inc., 1411 S. 3rd St., Ozark, MO 65721, 417-581-6525, toll free order desk 888-991-0151, fax: 417-581-4771, website: www.scotbeckhdw.com. Antique hardware, trunk parts, brass and iron bed parts, period brass knobs and pulls, kitchen cabinet parts, pierced tins, spool cabinet decals, icebox parts, wood turnings and plugs, lamp parts, refinishing supplies, caning supplies, and more. Catalog online and in print. Retail showroom open Mon.–Fri. 8:30 A.M.–5:00 P.M., Sat. 9:00 A.M.–3:00 P.M.

Tremont Nail Co., PO Box 111, Dept. K-98, Wareham, MA 02571, 800-842-0560 or 508-295-0038, fax: 508-295-1365, e-mail: info@tremont nail.com, website: www.tremontnail.com. Manufacturer of 20 different types of cut nails. Colonial hardware.

Van Dyke's Restorers, PO Box 278, Woonsocket, SD 57385, 605-796-4425, 800-558-1234 order, fax: 605-796-4085, e-mail: restoration @cabelas.com, website: www.vandykes.com. Brass hardware of all kinds, trunk parts, pie-safe tins, clock parts, curved-glass china cabinet parts, isinglass for stove doors, cane, reed, veneer, upholstery supplies, tools, stains, varnishes, brushes, modeling compounds. Special parts designed to duplicate original pieces. Lamp parts for electric lamps and oil lamps, including Aladdin lamps. Shades and glass chimneys. Mail order worldwide. Catalog.

Vintage Hardware, PO Box 9486, San Jose, CA 95129, 408-246-9918, e-mail: vhprs@earthlink.net, website: www.vintagehardware.com. Reproduction hardware for the restoration of antique furniture and the rehab of Victorian homes and buildings. Distributor of Heritage Lighting, reproduction antique lighting including neo-rococo gas lighting from 1840. "Pottery plaster" ceiling medallions. Color catalog, 80 pages, $4.

Windy Hill Forge, 3824 Schroeder Ave., Perry Hall, MD 21128, 410-256-5890, e-mail: windy-hill-forge@juno.com. Custom and reproduction hardware for homes and furniture. Cast brass or steel furniture pulls and handles. Hand-cut keys. Colonial box locks repaired and restored.

Winter Brook Farm Antiques, 450 N. State Road, Cheshire, MA 01225, 413-743-2177, website: www.winterbrookfarm.com. Reproduction replacement hardware often found missing on antique furniture. Styles include Victorian, Mission, Colonial Revival, Deco, Hepplewhite, and Sheraton in brass, copper, wood, etc. Brass hardware is "aged" so it isn't bright and shiny.

HOLIDAY COLLECTIBLES

If your attic has been used for storage for the past thirty years or more, it probably holds some valuable holiday collectibles. Christmas ornaments, light bulbs, tree holders, cards, tinsel, Halloween papier-mâché pumpkins, skeletons, costumes, candles, candy containers, even Fourth of July banners or fireworks package labels are eagerly collected. The prices paid for old Christmas ornaments or Halloween decorations are astounding. Do your homework. Look at the books about holiday collectibles at your library or bookstore. There are six or seven books with color pictures, descriptions, and some price information. There is also price information in the annual general price lists like *Kovels' Antiques & Collectibles Price List.*

Don't just put out a box of ornaments at your garage sale; you might be giving away money. If you do not have time to do the research, take the holiday memorabilia to a local auction gallery or to a dealer who is already selling this type of merchandise. These pieces sell best the month before the holiday, so be sure to talk to the dealers several months earlier. Sell Christmas ornaments by October 1, Halloween pumpkins by August.

The savvy surfer can find holiday collectibles on the Internet by searching keywords, like **CHRISTMAS COLLECTIBLES**. There are sites devoted to single holidays or single manufacturers of new pieces. Or go straight to your favorite Internet antiques mall and start there. Halloween collectibles were among the top ten items bought and sold in one Internet mall in 1997.

In general, anything figural will sell well: Santa Claus, black cats, sleighs filled with toys, even bottles shaped like holiday symbols. Newer items are often made partially of plastic, so study anything you have that is made entirely of paper, iron, or tin. Early blown-glass ornaments are hard to date because they have been copied since the 1950s, but even relatively recent ones are worth money to the right person. Chains of bubble lights, or figural bulbs, working or not, and all sorts of old paper and tinsel ornaments can be surprisingly high-priced. The old chicken-feather Christmas trees are now classed as folk art and sell for hundreds of dollars even if they are only twelve inches high. Postcards and greeting cards sell as holiday items at regular shows and also do well at the specialty shows for paper items.

●→ SEE ALSO GLASS, PAPER COLLECTIBLES, POTTERY & PORCELAIN

REPAIR

Save the old metal caps from broken early glass ornaments. They are different from the new ones and can be used on other early glass ornaments that are missing them. It is possible to find new old-style tinsel, paper cutouts, and spun "clouds" when restoring old ornaments.

Many old glass ornaments are now being reproduced; with a little ingenuity, you could find a new glass bird for your old glass-and-tinsel bird nest, or use other combinations of old and new to save treasured pieces. Look in gift shops that sell stickers and fancy wrapping paper.

Many reprints of Victorian "scrap" figures are now available. Feather trees are being reproduced and there are a few craftsmen who can repair old trees. The old base is one of the clues to age, so don't repaint or remove it. If it is unsightly, cover it with a cloth.

Halloween or Christmas pieces made of pressed cardboard or crepe paper will fade if kept in too sunny a spot. Never light a candle in the center of a cardboard pumpkin. It may be attractive, but it is a fire hazard. Many old jack-o'–lanterns had tissue-paper inserts for eyes. You can easily make a reproduction or replacement if you can find an old one to use as a pattern.

Easter eggs and candy containers should be carefully stored where the remains of food will not attract rodents and insects. Bits of paper lace used on some Easter pieces can be replaced by using parts of paper doilies found in stores that specialize in gourmet cooking supplies.

Specialized information can be found in the Glass, Paper, and Pottery & Porcelain sections.

PRICE BOOKS

Christmas Jewelry, Mary Morrison (Schiffer, Atglen, PA, 1998).

Christmas Revisited, 2nd edition, Robert Brenner (Schiffer, Atglen, PA, 1999).

Collectible Halloween, Pamela E. Apkarian-Russell (Schiffer, Atglen, PA, 1997).

Collector's Value Guide: Hallmark Keepsake Ornaments, 3rd edition, Jeff Mahony, editor (CheckerBee, Middletown, CT, 1999).

Halloween Favorites in Plastic, Charlene Pinkerton (Schiffer, Atglen, PA, 1998).

Halloween in America, Stuart Schneider (Schiffer, Atglen, PA, 2000).

Halloween: Collectible Decorations and Games, Pamela Apkarian-Russell (Schiffer, Atglen, PA, 2000).

More Halloween Collectibles: Anthropomorphic Vegetables and Fruits of Halloween, Pamela E. Apkarian-Russell (Schiffer, Atglen, PA, 1998).

One Hundred Years of Valentines, Katherine Kreider (Schiffer, Atglen, PA, 1999).

Romantic Valentines, Dan and Pauline Campanelli (L-W Book Sales, Gas City, IN, 1996).

Santa's Price Guide to Contemporary Christmas Collectibles, Beth Dees (Books Americana/Krause, Iola, WI, 1997).

Silver Christmas Ornaments: A Collector's Guide, Clara Johnson Scroggins (Krause, Iola, WI, 1997).

The Joy of Christmas Collecting: Ornaments, Advertising, Postcards, Pails, Tins, Etc., Chris Kirk (L-W Book Sales, Gas City, IN, price revision, 1998).

Valentines for the Eclectic Collector, Katherine Kreider (Schiffer, Atglen, PA, 1999).

CLUBS & THEIR PUBLICATIONS

Golden Glow of Christmas Past, *The Glow* (NL), 6401 Windale St., Golden Valley, MN 55427-4250, e-mail: snowbaby@marymorrison.org, website: www.goldenglow.org.

National Valentine Collectors Association, *National Valentine Collectors Bulletin* (NL), PO Box 1404, Santa Ana, CA 92702, e-mail: nancyrosin@aol.com, website: www.telebody.com/valentines.

OTHER PUBLICATIONS

BooNews: The Halloween Quarterly (NL), PO Box 143, Brookfield, IL 60513-0143, e-mail: BooNews@aol.com.

Creche Herald (NL), 117 Crosshill Rd., Wynnewood, PA 19096-3511, e-mail: crecher@op.net, website: www.op.net/~bocassoc.

Trick or Treat Trader (NL), PO Box 499, Winchester, NH 03470, e-mail:

halloweenqueen@cheshire.net, website:
adam.cheshire.net/~halloweenqueen/home.html.

AUCTIONS

➨ **SEE ALSO "SELLING THROUGH AUCTION HOUSES," PAGE 485.**

Holiday Auction, 4027 Brooks Hill Rd., Brooks, KY 40109, 502-955-9238, fax: 502-957-5027, e-mail: holauction@aol.com, website: members.aol.com/holauction/index.html. Absentee auctions of holiday collectibles only. Mail, phone, fax, and e-mail bids accepted. Buyer's premium 10%. Catalog $10. Prices realized mailed after auction.

➨ **INSULATORS, SEE TELEPHONE COLLECTIBLES**

IVORY

All ivory does not come from elephant tusks. Ivory can also be from other animals, such as walruses, hippopotamuses, or whales. There is also "vegetable ivory." Some vegetable materials have a similar texture and density and look like ivory, but it is possible to see the growth rings on a large piece of an elephant's tusk. Some types of plastic look very much like ivory. Determining whether you have ivory or plastic may prove a problem. The standard test is to heat a needle red hot while holding it with pliers. Press the point of the needle into the bottom of the ivory piece. Plastic will melt, but ivory will not. Obviously this leaves a mark and should not be done where it shows. Never try this test on a piece of ivory you do not own.

The value of ivory objects is determined by the quality of the carving and its condition. If the ivory is milk white because it was washed, deduct 30 percent. If the ivory is noticeably cracked, deduct 75 percent. Oriental ivory carvings, from large elephant tusks to tiny netsuke (Japanese buttons), sell quickly to friends and dealers. New ones are being made, but premium prices are paid for the old ones. A signature adds 50 percent or more. Be careful to follow the rules about selling ivory. There are laws governing the buying and selling of new elephant ivory and the laws sometimes govern old pieces. We do not recommend dealing with ivory pieces on the Internet. You may run into legal problems.

If you suspect you have an old, top-quality ivory carving, make an appointment with the proper person at your local art museum. You should be able to learn the age and the quality, but do not ask the value. A museum cannot appraise for you. Once you know the age, it is not difficult to compare your carving with others of similar quality that you can find at good shops, shows, auctions, or for sale on the Internet. Price guides list hundreds of ivory items under such headings as Ivory, Scrimshaw, Netsuke, Orientalia, or Jewelry. Even poor-quality, modern ivory carvings can be sold, but they have a low value.

Scrimshaw is ivory or ivory-like material decorated or carved by sailors or other artists. It is a very popular, high-priced form of folk art and sells to maritime collectors and folk art enthusiasts at important shows and auctions. If you have some old scrimshaw, a carved tooth, or a small box, tool, or whimsy, it should be appraised by an expert before it is sold. Beware! Imitation scrimshaw—especially carved whale teeth—has been made of plastic for the past twenty years or more. Some reproductions are so realistic they have fooled auctioneers. Modern craftsmen make and sell "scrimshaw" made on plastic or fossilized walrus tusks.

REPAIR

Ivory requires special care and cleaning. Never make the mistake that we made many years ago when we carefully washed our first ivory carving, leaving it an undesirable white color. It has been years since we erred, and the carving has still not regained the yellow-brown tint or patina preferred by collectors. If a carving is handled, body oils and moisture will eventually help to age it, but that would take more than one lifetime. Artificial coloring is not satisfactory. Never wash old ivory. Never color old ivory. The proper steps for cleaning can be found in technical books on restoration.

Ivory can be repaired by experts. Minor breaks can be mended by using a good commercial glue. Thin slices of ivory for inlay replacement are available.

CLUBS & THEIR PUBLICATIONS

International Ivory Society, *International Ivory Society Newsletter* (NL), 11109 Nicholas Dr., Wheaton, MD 20902, e-mail: rweisblut@yahoo.com.

APPRAISERS

Many of the repair services listed in this section will also do appraisals. *See also* the general list of "Appraisal Groups" on page 483.

REPAIRS, PARTS & SUPPLIES

➻ **SEE ALSO "CONSERVATORS & RESTORERS," PAGE 520.**

A. Ludwig Klein & Son, Inc., PO Box 145, Harleysville, PA 19438, 215-256-9004 or 800-379-2929, fax: 215-256-9644, website: www.aludwig

klein.com. Conservation and restoration of ivory, jade, marble, statuary and monuments, and more. Professional cleaning. Appraisals, insurance claims. Worldwide. By appointment. Free brochure.

Antique & Art Restoration by Wiebold, 413 Terrace Pl., Terrace Park, OH 45174, 800-321-2541, 513-831-2541, fax: 513-831-2815, e-mail: wiebold @eos.net, website: www.wiebold.com. Restoration and conservation of ivory and other fine art. Missing parts replaced.

Antique Restoration Service, 521 Ashwood Dr., Flushing, MI 48433, 810-659-0505, fax: 810-659-5582. Restoration of ivory and other art objects.

Artwork Restoration, 30 Hillhouse Rd., Winnipeg, MB R2V 2V9, Canada, 204-334-7090, e-mail: morry@escape.ca. Restoration of vases, figurines, lamps, ivory carvings, Inuit soapstone carvings, and more. Missing parts replaced.

Boone Trading Co., Inc., 562 Coyote Rd., PO Box 669, Brinnon, WA 98320, 360-796-4330, fax: 360-796-4511, e-mail: sales@boonetrading.com, website: www.boonetrading.com. Legal new and fossil ivory and scrimshaw for craftspeople and collectors. Scrimshaw supplies. Ivory and bonded ivory grips. Books on ivory. Brochure $1.

Broken Art Restoration, 1841 W. Chicago Ave., Chicago, IL 60622, 312-226-8200 or 815-472-3900, fax: 815-472-3930. Restoration of ivory, stone, and other art objects. By appointment. Free brochure.

The Brushstroke, 4250 Van Cortlandt Pk. E., #1B, Bronx, NY 10470, 718-994-5989, e-mail: art_restoration@usa.com. Conservation and restoration of ivory, jade, and other objects of art. Pick-up and delivery service within 50-mile radius in tri-state NYC area. Free estimates.

Carl "Frank" Funes, 57 Maplewood Ave., Hempstead, NY 11550, 516-483-6712. Restoration of ivory and other objects.

Ceramic Restorations, Inc., 224 W. 29th St., 12th Floor, New York, NY 10001, 212-564-8669, 9:00 A.M.–6:00 P.M. fax: 212-843-3742. Restoration of ivory and other objects. Invisible or museum-style repairs, reconstruction, and replacement of missing elements. Will also restore marble, stone, and plaster.

China and Crystal Clinic, 1808 N. Scottsdale Rd., Tempe, AZ 85281, 800-658-9197, fax: 480-945-1079, e-mail: VictorColeman@earthlink.net. Restoration of ivory, jade, and many related materials.

David Warther Carving Museum, 2561 Crestview Dr. NW, Dover, OH 44622-7405, e-mail: ivorybuyer@adelphia.net, website: www.ivory buyer.com. Provides legal ivory to artisans doing restoration work in ivory. Ivory cut for guitar and violin parts, knife handles, piano keys, gun grips, and other items. Ivory insulators and finials for sterling hollowware. Free brochure.

Gepetto Restoration, 31121 Via Colinas, Suite 1003, Westlake Village, CA 91362, 818-889-0901, fax: 818-889-8922, e-mail: barrykorngiebel @mailcity.com. Specializing in the restoration of ivory, jade, etc. Appraisal of objects of art.

Grashe Fine Art Restorers, 35 148th Ave. SE, #9, Bellevue WA 98007, 425-644-7500, fax: 425-644-7582, e-mail: art@grashe.com, website: www.grashe.com. Restoration and conservation of ivory, jade, and other materials.

Hamlin's Restoration Studio, 14640 Manchester Rd., Ballwin, MO 63011, 636-256-8579 days, e-mail: hamlinsrestoration@msn.com, website: www.hamlinsrestoration.com. Repair and restoration of ivory and other fine antiques.

Herbert F. Klug Conservation & Restoration, Box 28002, #16, Lakewood, CO 80228, 303-985-9261, e-mail: hgklug@qadas.com. Conservation and restoration of ivory and other materials. By appointment only.

James Davidson, 928 Independence St., New Orleans, LA 70117-5738, 504-944-0545, fax: 504-944-0545, e-mail: cjd9440545@netscape.net. Restoration of ivory, jade, and other art objects.

The Japanese Repository, 7705 Northwest 18th Court, Margate, FL 33063, 954-972-0287, e-mail: ivoryrepair@yahoo.com, website: www.ivory repair.com. Repair and restoration of ivory and items of antler, bone, and horn. Repair to ivory and bone chess sets, ivory and wood carved canes and walking sticks, ivory and bone inlay.

John Edward Cunningham, 1525 E. Berkeley, Springfield, MO 65804, 417-889-7702. Porcelains, ivory, and jade restored. Missing parts replaced. Specializing in carving elephant ivory parts for art deco and Oriental figurines, jewelry, and inlays. Hours by appointment.

Legacy Art Restorations & Design Int'l. Inc., 4221 N. 16th St., Phoenix, AZ 85016-5318, 602-263-5178, fax: 602-263-6009, e-mail: restoration @legacyintlinc.com, website: legacyintlinc.com. Restoration of fine art and collectibles, including ivory, jade, alabaster, and stone.

Pick Up the Pieces, 711 W. 17th St., Unit C-12, Costa Mesa, CA 92627, 800-824-6967, fax: 949-645-8381, e-mail: johnnce@yahoo.com, website: www.pickupthepieces.com. Fine art and collectible repair and restoration, including ivory, jade, and bone.

Poor Richard's Restoration & Preservation Studio Workshop, 101 Walnut St., Montclair, NJ 07042, 973-783-5333, fax: 973-744-1939, e-mail: jrickford@webtv.com, website: www.rickford.com. Restoration, conservation, preservation, and archival services.

Rafail & Polina Golberg, Golberg Restoration Co., 411 Westmount Dr., Los Angeles, CA 90048, 310-652-0735, fax: 310-274-3770, e-mail: info @restorationworld.com, website: www.restorationworld.com. Restoration and conservation of antiques and objects of art, including ivory. Free estimates via the Internet.

Restoration Services, 1417 Third St., Webster City, IA 50595, 515-832-1131, e-mail: repair@netins.net, website: www.Restorationmaterials.safe shopper.com. Restoration services for ivory, jade, and most other materials. Supplies, videos, home study course, classes available.

Restoration & Design Studio, 249 E. 77th St., New York, NY 10021, 212-

517-9742, fax: 212-517-9742. Repair and restoration of ivory and other materials. Ivory insulators for tea or coffeepots.

Sano Studio, 767 Lexington Ave. at 60th St., New York, NY 10021, 212-759-6131, fax: 212-759-6131. Restoration of ivory, tortoiseshell, and other materials.

Swan Restorations, 2627 Montrose Ave., Abbotsford, BC V2S 3TS, Canada, 604-855-6694, fax: 604-855-1720. Restoration of antiques and collectibles, including ivory, jade, and soapstone. Free written estimates. Mon.–Fri. 10:00 A.M.–5:00 P.M., or by appointment. Call before sending item to be repaired.

Tindell's Restoration, 825 Sandburg Pl., Nashville, TN 37214, 615-885-1029, fax: 615-391-0712, e-mail: info@ATindellsRestorationSchools.com, website: www.TindellsRestorationSchools.com. Restoration of ivory and other objects. Restoration services, seminars, training, and products. Appraisals. Free brochure.

Venerable Classics, 645 Fourth St., Suite 208, Santa Rosa, CA 95404, 800-531-2891, 707-575-3626, fax: 707-575-4913 call first, website: www.venerableclassics.com. Restoration of ivory, jade, and many other fragile decorative objects. Please call with questions. Free brochure on request.

JEWELRY

FINE JEWELRY

Fine jewelry has a special monetary worth known in the trade as "meltdown." This is the value of the piece if it is totally destroyed and the wholesale price of the gold, silver, and gems is calculated. You must never sell for less than meltdown. It is like giving dollar bills away.

Great-grandmother left you her heirloom diamond pin, probably dating from about 1910. It is made of white metal and has many small diamonds set in the old-fashioned way. You might be able to take it to a local jeweler to learn the meltdown value. "Jewelry Buyers" are listed in the Yellow Pages of the phone book, and the ads indicate those who buy "estate" jewelry and scrap. These are the people to tell you the lowest price you should take. They will test the metal to see if it is white gold, silver, or platinum; they will check the diamonds and then tell you what they will pay. Sometimes there is a small fee for this service. Most do not take into consideration the artistic value of the piece or its significance as an antique. These dealers will buy old jewelry, broken watches, gold teeth, or anything that is made of precious stones or metals. This is the place to sell damaged silverware and jewelry.

Now that you have a base price, you can determine what a jeweler who sells antique jewelry will pay. That price would include additional dollars covering artistic value. Of course, you can also sell it to a friend, to an antiques dealer, or through an auction. Some jewelers will take the pieces on consignment. Remember, styles in modern jewelry change and influence the value of antique pieces.

The Internet sparkles with jewelry. There are websites devoted entirely to jewelry, and there are dealers in Internet antiques malls that offer jewelry among their other wares. Descriptions are clear enough to allow you to be specific when searching—look for Ciner or Art Nouveau clip. Be careful if buying from Internet dealers. Remember the rules for mail order sales (see page 20).

In recent years, large brooches have again become stylish. Bar pins, which were unsalable as wearable jewelry in the 1970s, are now in demand. Watch-slide bracelets and charm bracelets gained favor again in the 1990s. Large antique brooches have a low break-up value because the stones are usually small. So the pins are especially attractive to the insurance-conscious, mugger-wary buyer, and they sell well. If you have decided it would be nice to make a modern pin

DECODING THE MARKS

The words and symbols on jewelry can be confusing. Pure gold is 24 karat, but it is too soft to be useful for jewelry. The gold quality marks 14K (karat), 18K, 20K, and 22K indicate gold content. If it is 14 parts pure gold and 10 parts of another metal, it is 14/24 parts gold or 14 karat.

"Gold filled," "gold plated," "rolled gold," or "gold overlay" means your jewelry has limited meltdown value since it consists of only a layer of gold on another metal. Be careful, because sometimes the label is "14K gold filled," which probably means it is classed as "costume jewelry."

"Sterling," "coin," and "800" are desirable silver quality marks. Nickel silver and German silver are not silver at all, but imitations. They are white metals similar to pewter. "Quadruple plate" and "triple plate" mean the pieces have only thin layers of silver over another, less valuable metal. "Silver plate" in an English publication means solid silver, but in an American book it signifies just a thin coating of silver over another metal.

Platinum may look like silver, but it is much more valuable. If it says "PLATINUM" in tiny letters on the back of the jewelry, take it to a jeweler for a professional appraisal before you sell it.

using the old stones, be sure to check prices carefully. It might be better to sell the old piece as an antique and buy a totally new one. The old stones are often of poor quality, and the expense of a new setting for the old stones may be more than the value of the finished, reworked piece.

Jewelry can easily be sold directly to a dealer. Often shops and jewelers who sell estate jewelry will make you an offer. Some large department stores sell estate or fine antique jewelry in a special department or at special sales several times a year. The buyers for these departments might want your jewelry. If you go to an antiques show and see dealers with pieces like yours, you can probably sell your items. Because most shops and dealers specialize, it is best to look for someone with jewelry like yours. A dealer who specializes in watches and gold chains may not want a small diamond pin.

One problem with selling antiques, especially jewelry, is proof of ownership. The buyer of your jewelry must be sure that you really own the piece and have a legal right to sell it. Many pieces of stolen jewelry are offered to dealers during the year. Have good personal identification with you and offer to show it. Don't send a teenager to sell jewelry. Dealers are fearful that even if the jewelry belongs in the family, the seller is not the true owner.

DESIGNER JEWELRY

There are often marks on jewelry that add to the value. A known signature adds up to 100 percent or more. Although most marks are found on the back of a piece, be sure to check the catch on a necklace and the sides of a large piece. If it says FABERGÉ ФАБЕРЖЕ , you have a Russian piece worth thousands of dollars. If the name TIFFANY, LIBERTY, LALIQUE, FOUQUET, MARCUS, CASTELLANI, SPRATLING, or MÜRRLE, BENNETT AND CO. appears, the piece is worth hundreds to thousands of dollars. If it is a piece of silver jewelry marked GEORG JENSEN, HA (Hector Aguilar), KALO, ED WEINER, ARTHUR STONE, KEM WEBER, or LOS CASTILLO, it is probably worth hundreds of dollars. The early 1990s saw prices rise for Mexican silver pieces by famous designers. The late 1990s saw higher prices for American silver jewelry by the best studio artists. There are books available that picture jewelry from these twentieth-century silversmiths.

LOOK UP THE MARKS

The hallmarks used on silver or gold are a series of small pictures like this 🔲🔲 ⊙ Ⓓ Ⓖ that are so small you will need a magnifying glass. Check the meaning of the marks in the appropriate books. Some marks indicate the country of origin, which may be important in setting the price. English, Danish, and important Mexican silver have an added value for collectors. Some marks indicate the makers. The names that add to the value, especially the names of important designers of the Art Nouveau, Art Deco, and Arts and Crafts schools, can be found in books. The library will also have books on jewelry makers and on silver marks.

PEARLS

Irregularly shaped freshwater pearls, baroque cultured pearls, and smooth, spherical pearls are in style. The graduated pearl necklace is temporarily out of style, and the best prices today are for strings of pearls of one size. Good pearls are always strung with a knot between each bead. There is a strange rule for drop-shaped natural pearls. If they are drilled end-to-end they are worth 40 percent less than if they are drilled at the top only.

A black (ultraviolet) light will tell if your pearls are cultured or fake. When viewed by black light, cultured and real pearls look slightly fluorescent, but fake pearls glow a bright white.

PRECIOUS STONES

The glow produced by a black light will also show if stones are real or glass. If the setting is made of gold, have a jeweler check any large stones to see if they are good-quality diamonds, sapphires, or rubies, or just plain glass. Even experts are being fooled by zirconium and other new diamond substitutes. Gemstones are usually cold to the touch and very hard. A stone with worn edges is probably just colored glass.

JEWELRY FABLES TO IGNORE

Opals are unlucky unless your birthday is in October. We think they are lucky, but because of the superstition, ordinary opal jewelry sells at lower prices than similar pieces with other stones. Gem-quality opals sell at high prices.

Amber floats. Only a loose bead in salt water floats.

A fine setting will hold real stones. If no one has changed them or if they are not synthetic stones.

Pearls improve with age. They absorb skin oils and cosmetics, change color, scratch, and even rot if stored incorrectly.

ENHANCED JEWELS

Some stones, old or new, are doublets or even triplets. That means a piece of the colored stone is joined with clear stone. Almost all gem-quality opals sold today are doublets or triplets. We once bought an emerald, complete with a Colombian government guarantee of authenticity, for a bargain price. It turned out to be a clear piece of the mineral beryl, called an "emerald" when it is green. Underneath the clear part was a dark green piece of glass. The top tested as an emerald; the green glass improved the color. By making it a doublet, the color was enhanced and the finished stone looked dark green, but it had no gem value. There are some styles of very early Spanish, Hungarian, and English jewelry made with foil-backed stones. A piece of silver foil or colored foil is set behind a clear or colored stone to enhance the color. These are wanted by collectors as examples of a rare type of antique jewelry. There are also many stones that have had the color improved or changed by irradiation. Ask a jeweler if the color has been enhanced. Opals can look more "fiery" if treated with acid. Some sapphires, rubies, and other colored stones are manmade. Natural stones are of more value than enhanced stones or manufactured stones.

UNUSUAL JEWELRY

Some types of antique jewelry are not being made today. Mourning jewelry was often made of braided hair set with gold trim as a memorial to the departed. Enameled rings with images of funeral urns and special rings given as gifts at funerals are among the best-known mourning jewelry. These and other "memento mori" are wanted by collectors, although they are not considered as popular as wearable jewelry.

Berlin ironwork was made for a short time in the early nineteenth century. It was actually made of iron, instead of gold, during a time when gold was needed for the war effort against Napoleon. This is rare and valuable to serious collectors. So is gold jewelry set with feathers from China and jet (coal) or black beads made from gutta-percha or any other early composition material. These were popular as mourning jewelry in the late nineteenth century. Hatpins, elaborate combs, watch-chain slides, studs, scarf rings, posy holders, chatelaines, cuff links, watch fobs, and other similar types of jewelry are not worn much today, but are wanted by certain collectors.

Don't think that something you consider ugly, like lava stone (dirty gray) or a realistic bug pin, has no value. Gold pins and necklaces designed with snakes, beetles, and dragonflies have extra value.

CARVED GEMS

The English made a type of jewelry from carved quartz backed with a specially carved and painted picture, often of a dog or horse. The finished stone looks like glass with a piece of paper behind it. It is actually a very valuable form, usually set in cuff links for men. The Chinese made clear quartz beads like miniature crystal balls set in loops of wire; they look like glass but are very valuable.

Cameos can be made of stone, shell, lava rock, coral, or plastic. Black and white stone cameos were very popular in the nineteenth century. Agate or carnelian cameos have more value than shell cameos. Plastic cameos are used in costume jewelry. The light pink and white shell cameos are easy to identify because the curve of the shell can always be seen. Stone cameos have flat backs. The quality of the carving and the setting help determine the value. The more detail, the better. Remember, beautiful women in the nineteenth century were chubby-faced and had full noses. Today's beauty is thin and pug-nosed. This helps to date a cameo. Lava rock, a soft gray or beige stone, and coral are also used. Some cameos picture a woman wearing a necklace set with a small diamond. They were made after 1915.

SEMI-PRECIOUS MATERIALS

Don't underestimate the value of old beads of amethyst, pink quartz, garnet, jade, turquoise, amber, or colored stones. It takes an expert to recognize the quality, so be sure to show them to a qualified appraiser before you underestimate their value and put them in the junk box at your garage sale.

ARTS AND CRAFTS AND MID-TWENTIETH-CENTURY JEWELRY

Some of the important early jewelry by RENÉ LALIQUE, LIBERTY, RUSKIN, POTTER STUDIOS, ROYCROFT and other English and American Arts and Crafts designers and companies became popular in the 1990s. The hand-hammered pewter, copper, silver, or gold pieces were set with inexpensive materials like glass, base metals, cut steel, moonstones, semiprecious stones, and enamels. Asymmetrical modern pins and necklaces with unusual stones and metals are just beginning to go up in price. Pieces by well-known artists, like Ed Weiner, are already selling for thousands of dollars. The quality of workmanship can make these as valuable as gold and precious stone jewelry. Look carefully for a name.

OTHER SPECIAL JEWELRY

American Indian jewelry has a special market. If you can trace the history of an Indian necklace, pin, or ring back over fifty years, it may be very valuable. Try to sell it to a collector of Indian artifacts, or through Western dealers. Some recent silver jewelry by famous American Indian artists also sells well.

Compacts, lipstick cases, money clips, cigarette cases, and cigarette lighters are sometimes made of precious metals and stones. These should be sold like any other type of precious jewelry or to the specialist collector. Those made of imitation gold and silver also have a resale value, and they should be sold to costume jewelry dealers or to specialists who favor compacts, lighters, and other "smalls."

Arts and Crafts and mid-twentieth-century jewelry became very popular in the 1990s. The hand-hammered pewter and copper pieces with inexpensive stones or enamel by makers like Ruskin, Rebajes, and Matisse were recognized as important examples of costume jewelry.

COSTUME JEWELRY

Prices for top-quality costume jewelry are now higher than for some precious pieces. Old beads, rhinestones, marcasite, enameled Art Nouveau and Art Deco, and Bakelite pieces are all back in vogue. The major auction houses now have sales of the costume jewelry made since the 1920s. Names that add value to costume jewelry are **EISENBERG, HOBÉ, SCHIAPARELLI, HATTIE CARNEGIE, KRAMER, MIRIAM HASKELL, MATISSE, WEISS, VOGUE, HOLLYCRAFT, JOSEFF, WIESNER, REGENCY, VENDOME, FLORENZA, MONET, CORO, TRIFARI, NAPIER,** and **KENNETH LANE.** Some are still working, but pre-1960 pieces by these companies bring premium prices.

Bakelite jewelry prices have doubled and tripled in the past few years. The multicolored striped "Philadelphia" bracelet sold in 1998 for $17,600. A charm pin in a cigarette shape was $108,450 and a googly-eyed clown pin was $7,700. Unfortunately, many fakes are now being made in Asia. Watch out especially for carved or dot-decorated bracelets.

Look at the new jewelry being offered in department stores. Run-of-the-mill old pieces are worth about 60 percent of the cost of comparable new ones. Old rhinestones are probably worth more than new ones, because old rhinestones are of better quality. Two-

or three-color Bakelite plastic pins and bracelets are worth more than new jewelry. So are many of the gem-set or enameled pieces with important makers' names. Very large, impressive old pieces are worth more than similar new pieces.

Be very careful what prices you ask for costume jewelry you sell at house and garage sales. Dealers at flea markets, mall shows, vintage-clothing stores, and at the best antique stores get high prices for rhinestone and plastic costume jewelry and good Art Deco designs. The bigger and gaudier, the better.

REPAIR

Period jewelry has become very popular during the past few years, particularly Georgian, Victorian, Art Nouveau, Arts and Crafts, Art Deco, costume, Mexican silver, Fifties, and American Indian jewelry. Always be sure when buying old jewelry that you get an all-original piece. Many are changed or "married" (mismatched) or are modern copies.

Repairing old jewelry requires the greatest concern, because repairing or remodeling can destroy the antique value. Repairs should be made in the spirit of the original jewelry. Replace old stones with old stones; if you put a modern-cut diamond in a piece with old mine-cut diamonds, the new one will be too bright and look out of place. Replacing earring backs, safety catches, or pin backs or restringing beads does not affect the value of most old jewelry and will definitely help to prevent loss. Many artisans now make necklaces of old and new beads. They may also be able to restring your old beads. Many jewelers will restring pearls and other valued beads.

Many local jewelers know how to appraise and repair old jewelry, but they often consider old jewelry "scrap" and figure the value based on the meltdown of the elements. Be sure to go to someone who understands old pieces, old methods, and old stones.

Jewelry can and should be cleaned at home. Be particularly careful of pieces with pearls or opals. They can be damaged by incorrect care, oil, and temperature changes. Never store opals or pearls in an airtight bag or bank safe-deposit vault. Lack of air may dull the luster. Beads should not be soaked in water when cleaned. The string cord will eventually rot if it gets too wet. Never get hairspray on pearls or opals.

◆➤ **SEE ALSO SILVER & SILVER PLATE**

REFERENCE BOOKS

American & European Jewelry, 1830–1914, Charlotte Gere (Crown, New York, 1975).

American Jewelry Manufacturers, Dorothy T. Rainwater (Schiffer, Atglen, PA, 1988).

Messengers of Modernism: American Studio Jewelry, 1940–1960, Montreal Museum of Decorative Arts (Flammarion, New York, 1996).

Mexican Silver: 20th Century Handwrought Jewelry and Metalwork, Penny Chittim Morrill and Carole A. Berk (Schiffer, Atglen, PA, 1994).

Understanding Jewellery, David Bennett and Daniela Mascetti (Antique Collectors' Club, Wappingers Falls, NY, 1989).

PRICE BOOKS

Answers to Questions about Jewelry, 1840–1950, 5th edition, C. Jeanenne Bell (Krause, Iola, WI, 1999).

Antique Sweetheart Jewelry, Nicholas D. Snider (Schiffer, Atglen, PA, 1996).

Bakelite Bangles, Karima Parry (Schiffer, Atglen, PA, 1999).

Bakelite Jewelry: Good, Better, Best, Donna Wasserstrom and Leslie Piña (Schiffer, Atglen, PA, 1997).

The Best of Costume Jewelry, 3rd edition, Nancy Schiffer (Schiffer, Atglen, PA, 1999).

Cameos: Classical to Costume, Monica Lynn Clements and Patricia Rosser Clements (Schiffer, Atglen, PA, 1998).

Christmas Jewelry, Mary Morrison (Schiffer, Atglen, PA, 1998).

Collectible Costume Jewelry, Cherri Simonds (Collector Books, Paducah, KY, prices 2000).

Collectible Silver Jewelry, Fred Rezazadeh (Collector Books, Paducah, KY, 2001).

Collecting Rhinestone & Colored Jewelry, 4th edition, Maryanne Dolan (Krause, Iola, WI, 1998).

Lea Stein Jewelry, Judith Just (Schiffer, Atglen, PA, 2001).

Miller's Costume Jewelry, Caroline Behr (Octopus Publishing, London, England, 2001).

North American Indian Jewelry and Adornment (Harry N. Abrams, New York, 1999).

Official Price Guide to Costume Jewelry, 3rd edition, Harrice Simons Miller (House of Collectibles, New York, 2002).

Popular Jewelry of the '60s, '70s & '80s, Roseann Ettinger (Schiffer, Atglen, PA, 1997).

Sarah Coventry Jewelry: An Unauthorized Guide for Collectors, Monica Lynn Clements and Patricia Rosser Clements (Schiffer, Atglen, PA, 1999).

Signed Beauties of Costume Jewelry, Marcia "Sparkles" Brown (Collector Books, Paducah, KY, 2002).

Silver Jewelry Designs: Evaluating Quality, Good, Better, Best, Nancy N. Schiffer (Schiffer, Atglen, PA, 1996).

Vintage Jewelry: A Price and Identification Guide, 1920–1940s, Leigh Leshner (Krause, Iola, WI, 2002).

Warman's Jewelry: A Fully Illustrated Price Guide to 19th- and 20th-Century Jewelry, 3rd edition, Christie Romero (Krause, Iola, WI, 2002).

Wooden Jewelry and Novelties, Mary Jo Izard (Schiffer, Atglen, PA, 1998).

CLUBS & THEIR PUBLICATIONS

American Hatpin Society, *American Hatpin Society Newsletter* (NL), 20 Montecillo Dr., Rolling Hills Estates, CA 90274, e-mail: hatpnginia @aol.com, website: www.collectoronline.com/AHS.

American Society of Jewelry Historians, *Newsletter of the American Society of Jewelry Historians* (NL), Box 103, 1333A North Ave., New Rochelle, NY 10804-2120, e-mail: info@jewelryhistorians.com, website: jewelryhistorians.com.

Antique Comb Collectors Club International, *Antique Comb Collector* (NL), 90 S. Highland Ave., #1204, Tarpon Springs, FL 34689-5351, e-mail: belva.green@verizon.net, website: geocities.com/heartland/pointe/ 5350.

Center for Bead Research, *Margaretologist* (NL), 4 Essex St., Lake Placid, NY 12946-1236, e-mail: pfjr@northnet.org, website: www.thebead site.com.

Enamelist Society, *Glass on Metal* (MAG), PO Box 310, Newport, KY 41072, e-mail: Dviehman7en12@aol.com, website: www.enamelist society.org.

H.A.I.R. Society, *HAIRLine Newsletter* (NL), 1939 Elizabeth Blvd., Newport, MI 48166, e-mail: ruthgordon@foxberry.net, website: Hairwork Virtu.homestead.com/HairworkVirtu.html.

Hat Pin Society of Great Britain, *Hat Pin Society of Great Britain* (NL), PO Box 110, Cheadle, Cheshire SK8 1GG, UK, website: www.hatpin society.org.uk.

International Watch Fob Association Inc., *International Watch Fob Association Newsletter* (NL), 601 Patriot Pl., Holmen, WI 54636, e-mail: info@watchfob.com, website: www.watchfob.com.

National Cuff Link Society, *The Link* (NL), PO Box 5700, Vernon Hills, IL 60061, e-mail: genek@cufflinksrus.com, website: www.cufflink.com.

Victorian Hairwork Society, PO Box 806, Pleasant Grove, UT 84062, e-mail: marlys.hairwork.com, website:www.hairworkssociety.org.

Vintage Fashion & Costume Jewelry Club, *Vintage Fashion & Costume Jewelry Newsletter* (NL), PO Box 265, Glen Oaks, NY 11004, e-mail: vfcj@aol.com.

OTHER PUBLICATIONS

Adornment: The Newsletter of Jewelry & Related Arts (NL), 1333A North Ave., Box 122, New Rochelle, NY 10804, e-mail: ekarlin@usa.net, website: www.adornment.net.

Ornament (MAG), PO Box 2349, San Marcos, CA 92079-2349, e-mail: ornament@cts.com.

ARCHIVES & MUSEUMS

Cranbrook Art Museum, Cranbrook Academy of Design, 39221 Woodward Ave., Bloomfield Hills, MI 48303-0801, 248-645-3323, website: www.cranbrook.edu/art/museum.

Montreal Museum of Decorative Arts, Jean-Noël Desmarais Pavilion, 1380 Sherbrooke St. W., PO Box 3000, Station H, Montreal, QC H3G 2T9, 514-285-1600, fax: 514-844-6042, website: www.mbam.qc.ca/a-sommaire.html.

USEFUL SITES

Gemological Institute of America, World Headquarters, The Robert Mouawad Campus, 5345 Armada Dr., Carlsbad, CA 92008, 800-421-7250, ext. 4001, website: www.gia.edu.

APPRAISERS

Many of the auctions and repair services listed in this section will also do appraisals. *See also* the general list of "Appraisal Groups," page 483.

National Association of Jewelry Appraisers, PO Box 6558, Annapolis, MD 21401-0558, 410-897-0889. Appraisal services on jewelry, silver hollowware, and silver flatware. Appraisers throughout the United States.

AUCTIONS

➻ SEE ALSO "SELLING THROUGH AUCTION HOUSES," PAGE 485.

Joseph DuMouchelle International Auctioneers, 5 Kercheval Ave., Grosse Pointe Farms, MI 48236-3601, 313-884-4800 ext. 23 or 800-475-8898, fax: 313-884-7662, e-mail: joe@dumouchelleauction.com, website: www.dumouchelleauction.com. Specializing in jewelry auctions. Mail and phone bids accepted. Buyer's premium 15%. Prices realized mailed after auction. Appraisals.

Mackley & Co., 9724 Kingston Pike, Suite 1012, Knoxville, TN 37922, 865-693-3097, fax: 865-693-3097, e-mail: joseph@mackley.com, website: www.mackley.com. Online auctions of estate jewelry. The public may attend the last hour of an auction to bid and watch. Mail, phone, and Internet bids accepted. No buyer's premium. Prices realized posted on the website for one month following the auction. Online catalog only. Appraisals.

REPAIRS, PARTS & SUPPLIES

➠ SEE ALSO "CONSERVATORS & RESTORERS," PAGE 520.

AntiqueConservation.com, Div. of Ponsford Ltd., 5441 Woodstock Rd., Acworth, GA 30102, 770-924-4848, fax: 770-529-2278, e-mail: GordonPonsford@AntiqueConservation.com, website: www.Antique Conservation.com. Conservation and restoration of jewelry and other objects. Appraisals.

Beverlee Kagan Antique and Vintage Jewelry, 5831 Sunset Dr., South Miami, FL 33143, 305-663-1937, Mon.–Sat. Costume jewelry restored. Clip earrings converted to pierced earrings; earrings converted to cuff links; cuff links converted to earrings. Free brochure.

Cherished Memories, 1939 Elizabeth Blvd., Newport, MI 48166, 734-586-2027, e-mail: ruthgordon@foxberry.net, website: HairworkVirtu. homestead.com/HairworkVirtu.html. Hair jewelry repaired. Reproduction jewelry findings and fittings. Send LSASE marked "Findings" for brochure. Hair-braiding tables; bobbins for making hair jewelry. Send LSASE marked "Bobbins" for information. Seminars and classes.

Delphi Creativity Group, 3380 E. Jolly Rd., Lansing, MI 48910, 800-248-2048 or 517-394-4631, fax: 800-748-0374 or 517-394-5364, e-mail: sales@delphiglass.com, website: www.delphiglass.com. Hand-blown glass for window repairs. Color matching service for repairs of antique stained-glass windows. Glass etching and engraving supplies and stencils; stained-glass kits and supplies; beveled glass; books and tools. Mosaics, hot glass, and jewelry supplies. Free catalog.

Glass Studio, 5412A Dickson, Houston, TX 77007, 713-880-1090, fax: 713-880-3544, e-mail: nfwassef@msn.com. Some old fashion jewelry repaired.

Golden's Antique Supply, 8990 Main St., Woodstock, GA 30188, 888-202-1029 or 770-924-8528, fax: 770-924-8980, e-mail: wcgolden @antiquesupply.com, website: www.antiquesupply.com. Everything for the "antiqueholic" from testing equipment, restoration supplies, and archival supplies, to display, hardware, books, and videos.

Halcyon Studios, Koral Michael Whalton, PO Box 11525, Montgomery, AL 36111, 334-834-9560, fax: 334-270-0057, e-mail: khalscann@hot mail.com. Vintage and heirloom jewelry repairs. Specializing in costume jewelry, cameo, floating opals, Native American, bean and pearl knotting. Vintage rhinestone replacement. Tool set rhinestones (pavé replacement work). Plating in rose, yellow, and rhodium. Heirloom costume jewelry appraisals.

Heart Broken Jewelry, 1325 McKinley Ave., South Bend, IN 46617, 574-287-1615, e-mail: valerie@HeartBrokenJewelry.com. Custom jewelry made from pieces of broken china or glass. Several pieces of jewelry can be made from one broken piece of china.

Indian Jewelers Supply Co., PO Box 1774, Gallup, NM 87305, 800-545-6540 or 505-265-3701, fax: 888-722-4172, e-mail: catalogs@ijsinc.com, website: www.ijsinc.com. Jewelry-making supplies, including turquoise beads, cords, clasps, jump- and split-rings, and other bead styles. Materials, tools, and supply catalogs. Catalogs available on CD-ROM; $6 for paper version.

Matthew Ribarich, PO Box 10104, Costa Mesa, CA 92627, 949-645-9017, fax: 949-645-9020, e-mail: mrstones4u@aol.com, website: www.sparklz.com/matt. Costume jewelry stone replacement from inventory of replacement stones. Single stone or complete restoning of Eisenberg, Trifari, Coro-Duettes, and others. Stone matching service available. Free catalog of replacement stones.

Myron Toback, Inc., 25 W. 47th St., New York, NY 10036, 212-398-8300, fax: 212-869-0808, e-mail: michael@myrontoback.com, website: www.myrontoback.com. Hardware distributor for jewelry. Tools, glue, findings, chain, settings, polishing compounds. Free catalog.

Norman L. Sandfield, Netsuke, Oriental Art, 3150 N. Sheridan Rd., Chicago, IL 60657-4, 773-327-1733, fax: 773-327-1791, e-mail: norman @sanfield.org, website: www.internetsuke.com. Japanese inro cord in several colors. Ojime Miseru, silver or gold hangers that allow you to wear an ojime (Japanese slide fastener bead) on a chain or cord. Available in five standard sizes or custom made. "The Inro Knot: A Step-by-Step Illustrated Guide to Tying Different Knots for Hanging Medicine Boxes," including sample cord, $5; "The Cheat Sheet," a pocket-size reference to 102 common Japanese characters found in netsuke signatures, $2.

Patrick J. Gill & Sons, 9 Fowle St., Woburn, MA 01801, 781-933-3275, fax: 781-933-3751, e-mail: joe@patrickgillco.com, website: patrick gillco.com. Jewelry repaired and restored, silver plate or gold plate.

Poor Richard's Restoration & Preservation Studio Workshop, 101 Walnut St., Montclair, NJ 07042, 973-783-5333, fax: 973-744-1939, e-mail: jrickford@webtv.com, website: www.rickford.com. Restoration of jewelry and other objects. By appointment, Tues.–Fri. noon-5:00 P.M., Sat. noon–3:00 P.M.

S. LaRose, Inc., 3223 Yanceyville St., PO Box 21208, Greensboro, NC 27420-1208, 336-621-1936, fax: 336-621-0706, e-mail: info@slarose.com, website: www.slarose.com. Jewelry findings. Tools, supplies, books, and videos for the jeweler or hobbyist. Catalog $2.50.

Swan Restorations, 2627 Montrose Ave., Abbotsford, BC V2S 3TS, Canada, 604-855-6694, fax: 604-855-1720. Jewelry cleaning. Free written estimates. Hours Mon.–Fri. 10:00 A.M.–5:00 P.M., or by appointment.

T.B. Hagstoz & Son, Inc., 709 Sansom St., Philadelphia, PA 19106, 800-922-1006, 215-922-1627, fax: 215-922-7126. Jewelry tools and supplies.

Findings, solders, casting supplies, and many metals, including gold, sterling silver, pewter, copper, bronze, brass, and nickel silver. Catalog $5.

Trailblazer—Indian Jewelry Repair & Sales, 210 West Hill, Gallup, NM 87301, 505-722-5051, website: www.trailblaz.com. Indian jewelry repaired. Items to be repaired should be sent insured mail. Estimates given. Jewelry catalog $2.

Village Goldsmith, 5333 Forest Ln., Dallas, TX 75244, 972-934-0449, fax: 972-934-1233, e-mail: eric.wright@att.net. Restoration of antique and vintage jewelry. Repair and replacement stones for costume jewelry. Silver and gold replating.

Vogue & Vintage, 106 Middle Neck Rd., Great Neck, NY 11021, 516-773-3338, fax: 516-773-3447, e-mail: gifts@vogueandvintage, website: vogue-andvintage.com. Jewelry repaired and restored. Earrings converted from pierced to clip-on or clip-on to pierced. Specializing in repair and restoration of all antique and estate jewelry, including Hobé, Haskell, and Victorian jewelry.

WTC Associates, Inc., 2532 Regency Rd., Lexington, KY 40503, 859-278-4171, fax: 859-277-5720. Diamonds and emeralds replaced. Sterling silver repairs; gold plating; hand engraving.

KITCHEN PARAPHERNALIA

Anything that was ever used in a kitchen, from a wrought-iron kettle holder of the 1700s to a 1960s juicer or reamer or a chrome toaster, has a sale value. Most buyers want something nostalgic and decorative to put in a modern kitchen. Any unusual object will sell quickly at a house sale or flea market or to friends. Some antiques shops deal in utensils that were made before 1930 and dishes with the "country look." Very modern-looking equipment, preferably chrome, bright-colored pottery or plastic pitchers, toasters, canisters, and a few other objects with Art Deco designs are sold by a different group of dealers.

ELECTRICAL APPLIANCES

Old toasters, mixers, and waffle irons have little value unless the design is very unusual and decorative. An electric toaster with a blue willow porcelain plaque sells for over $500, a leaf-decorated 1950s glass plaque on the side will sell for over $150. The same toaster without the attractive sides is worth less than $50. A rare glass iron sells for hundreds of dollars; an electric metal iron is almost unwanted.

LARGE APPLIANCES

Don't ignore an old stove, refrigerator, vacuum cleaner, or washing machine. If decorative or very odd-looking, they will sell, sometimes to an appliance store that needs one for a window display. Stoves are often used outside for barbecue pits.

GADGETS

Think of kitchen gadgets in terms of the question, "How will it look on a wall or shelf?" Anything with red and white or green and cream wooden handles does well. These were the colors favored in the 1930s. Colored plastic handles, found on items made in the 1930s and '40s, add value to old eggbeaters and other utensils. Eggbeaters are very salable. The nineteenth-century ones are iron; by 1900, the eggbeater had an iron gear but stainless-steel beaters. The beaters and gears soon were all stainless. Many eggbeaters have dates in raised numbers on the gears. Ice-cream scoops sell for much more money than seems possible. Check the price guides carefully. Almost any scoop manufactured before 1940 is worth over $50; many are worth much more. A rare heart-shaped scoop sold with its box in 1997 for $15,400. Juicers or reamers also sell for high prices. Favored are those made of colored glass or figural shapes. All out-of-production cookie cutters, molds, nutcrackers, bottle openers, and apple peelers have value.

Mixing bowls of all kinds, pitchers, storage jars, cookie jars, and other ceramic kitchen items have a dual value. They are wanted by both kitchen and pottery collectors. (See Pottery & Porcelain.) Identify the makers from the marks, and look in both a general price guide and a kitchen price book. Even more surprising is the value of old iron pots and molds and unusual cast aluminum tea kettles and pots. Look for the name **GRISWOLD** on iron pieces. It adds value.

Your mother's and grandmother's kitchens are still filled with treasures: scrapers, cookie cutters, forks, funnels, dessert molds, ice-cream molds and pans, all either purchased new or "borrowed" from an aging parent who no longer baked. Now that microwaves, electric burners, self-cleaning ovens, and dishwashers have changed our needs, many old pots and bowls are out of favor with cooks. But don't throw anything away until you check on the value. Even molded-plastic string holders, clocks, egg timers, and menu planners can have value. All salt and pepper sets, cookie jars, and stove or refrigerator sets are collected. Cookbooks and recipe pamphlets sell well, too. (See Advertising Collectibles and Books & Bookplates.)

In general, the oldest sells for the highest price. Items that are figural, especially those picturing blacks, sell well; so do plastic, brass, copper, and colorful pottery. Anything that moves, like an apple peeler, will sell. Aluminum and chrome in very modern styles are now of interest to collectors of 1950s items. Early wooden items are wanted by "country" collectors, but sometimes not-so-old but well-worn wooden cutting boards and knives are overvalued by novice collectors. Watch for the names **DOVER** and **ENTERPRISE** on metal kitchen gadgets.

REPAIR

Collectors should remember that while old items are fine as decorations, they are sometimes not safe to use for food preparation. Some types of pottery have a lead glaze that is poisonous. Copper molds and pots should never be used unless the tin lining is flawless. Companies that re-tin pots are listed in the Metals section. Chipped graniteware could add bits of crushed glass to your food. Woodenwares should only be treated with edible oils, not linseed oil.

➼ SEE GLASS, METALS, POTTERY & PORCELAIN FOR CARE INFORMATION

REFERENCE BOOKS

The Collector's Encyclopedia of Granite Ware: Colors, Shapes and Values, 2 volumes, Helen Greguire (Collector Books, Paducah, KY, 1990, 1993).

Housewares Story: A History of the American Housewares Industry, Earl Lifshey (National Housewares Manufacturers Association, Chicago, 1973).

PRICE BOOKS

300 Years of Kitchen Collectibles, 4th edition, Linda Campbell Franklin (Books Americana/Krause, Iola, WI, 1997).

Antique Chocolate Molds, Wendy Mullen (Hobby House Press, Grantsville, MD, 2002).

Apple Parers, Don Thornton (Off Beat Books, Sunnyvale, CA, 1997).

Bakelite in the Kitchen, Barbara E. Mauzy (Schiffer, Atglen, PA, 1998).

Black Memorabilia for the Kitchen, Jan Lindenberger (Schiffer, Atglen, PA, 1998).

The Book of Griswold & Wagner, 2nd edition, David G. Smith and Chuck Wafford (Schiffer, Atglen, PA, 2000).

The Book of Wagner and Griswold, David G. Smith and Chuck Wafford (Schiffer, Atglen, PA, 2001).

Butter Molds and Stamps: A Guide to American Manufacturers, Barbara S. and Robert E. Van Vuren (Butter Press, PO Box 5782, Napa, CA 94581, 2000).

Coffee Antiques, Edward C. Kvetko and Douglas Congdon-Martin (Schiffer, Atglen, PA, 2000).

The Complete Book of Kitchen Collecting, Barbara E. Mauzy (Schiffer, Atglen, PA, 1997).

The Eggbeater Chronicles, 2nd edition, Don Thornton (Thornton House, 1345 Poplar Ave., Sunnyvale, CA 94087, 1999).

The 50s & 60s Kitchen, 2nd edition, Jan Lindenberger (Schiffer, Atglen, PA, 1999).

Griswold Cast Iron, Volume 2, (L-W Book Sales, Gas City, IN, 1998).

Griswold Muffin Pans, Jon B. Haussler (Schiffer, Atglen, PA, 1997).

Indiana Cabinets (L-W Book Sales, Gas City, IN, 1997).

Irons by Irons, More Irons by Irons, Even More Irons by Irons, Books 1–3, David Irons (223 Covered Bridge Rd., Northampton, PA 18067, 1994–2000).

Kitchenware: American and European, David T. Pikul and Ellen M. Plante (Schiffer, Atglen, PA, 2000).

Toasters, 1909–1960, E. Townsend Artman (Schiffer, Atglen, PA, 1996).

ARCHIVES & MUSEUMS

Culinary Archives & Museum, 315 Harborside Blvd., Providence, RI 02905, 401-598-2805, fax: 401-598-2807, website: www.culinary.org.

Toaster Museum Foundation, 1003 Carlton Ave., Suite B, Charlottesville, VA 22902-5974, e-mail: eric@toaster.org, website: www.toaster.org.

CLUBS & THEIR PUBLICATIONS

Association of Coffee Mill Enthusiasts, *Grinder Finder* (NL), PO Box 5761, Midland, TX 79704, e-mail: acmeman@erols.com.

Cookie Cutter Collectors Club, *Cookie Crumbs* (NL), 1167 Teal Rd. SW, Dellroy, OH 44620.

Griswold and Cast Iron Cookware Association, *The Pan Handler* (NL), PO Box 552, Saegertown, PA 16433, e-mail: dmosier@griswoldcookware.com, website: www.gcica.org.

International Society of Apple Parer Enthusiasts, *ISAPE Newsletter* (NL), 735 Cedarwood Terr., Apt. 735B, Rochester, NY 14609, website: www.collectoronline.com/clubs/ISAPE.

Maytag Collector's Club, *Maytag Collector's Club* (NL), 960 Reynolds Ave., Ripon, CA 95366, e-mail: multimotor@aol.com, website: maytagclub.com.

Mid-American Reamer Collectors, *Juicy Journal* (NL), 222 Cooper Ave., Elgin, IL 60120-2128, e-mail: antiquemax@nzantiques.com, website: www.reamers.org.

Midwest Sad Iron Collectors Club, *Pressing News* (NL), 6903 Singingwood Ln., St. Louis, MO 63129, e-mail: BruceBaumunk@gte.net, website: www.irons.com/msicc.htm.

National Graniteware Society, *National Graniteware Society Newsletter* (NL), PO Box 9248, Cedar Rapids, IA 52409-9248, e-mail: info@granite ware.org, website: www.graniteware.org.

National Reamer Collectors Association, *National Reamer Collectors Association Quarterly Review* (NL), 47 Midline Ct., Gaithersburg, MD 20878, e-mail: reamers@erols.com, website: www.reamers.org.

Old Appliance Club, *Old Road Home (MAG),* PO Box 65, Ventura, CA 93002, e-mail: jes@west.net, website: www.theoldapplicanceclub.com.

Toaster Collector Association, PO Box 485, Redding Ridge, CT 06876, e-mail: pres@ toastercollector.com, website: www.toastercollector.com.

Upper-Crust: Toaster Collectors Association, *A Toast to You* (NL), Toasters Galore, PO Box 529, Temecula, CA 92593, e-mail: rocknroles @yahoo.com.

OTHER PUBLICATIONS

Cookies (NL), 9610 Greenview Ln., Manassas, VA 20109-3320, e-mail: editor@cookiesnewsletter.com, website: www.cookies newsletter.com.

Hotwire (NL), Toaster Museum Foundation, 1003 Carlton Ave., Suite B, Charlottesville, VA 22902-5974, e-mail: eric@toaster.org, website: www.toaster.org.

Kettles 'n Cookware (NL), PO Box 247, Perrysburg, NY 14129, e-mail: panman@utec.net, website: www.panman.com.

Piebirds Unlimited (NL), PO Box 192, Acworth, GA 30101-0192, e-mail: pldonaldson@mindspring.com, website: hometown.aol.com/ acworthd/PiebirdsUnlimited.html.

REPAIRS, PARTS & SUPPLIES

➡ **SEE ALSO "CONSERVATORS & RESTORERS," PAGE 520.**

Abercrombie & Co., 9159A Brookeville Rd., Silver Spring, MD 20910, 800-585-2385 or 301-585-2385, fax: 301-587-5708, e-mail: abernco @erols.com, website: www.silverplaters.com. Metal repair, plating,

---

BEFORE YOU COOK

Iron skillets and baking pans should be seasoned. Coat an iron pot with edible cooking oil and bake it at 300 degrees for about two hours. Special dull black and rust-resistant paint is available if you want to repaint iron, but it must not be used on utensils that hold food.

and polishing. Dents smoothed or removed; handles, hinges, lids, and spouts repaired. Copper cookware tin lined. Copper, brass, and tin plated.

C & H Supply, 5431 Mountville Rd., Adamstown, MD 21710, 301-663-1812, Mon.–Fri. 9:00 A.M.–5:00 P.M., e-mail: CandHSupplyCo@aol.com. Reproduction brass hardware, wood and porcelain knobs, pie-safe tins, icebox hardware, kitchen cabinet hardware, flour bins. Veneers, paint and varnish removers, stains and lacquers. Most orders shipped within 24 hours. Catalog $4.

European Kitchen Bazaar, PO Box 4099, Waterbury, CT 06704, 888-243-8540 or 203-757-7131, fax: 203-754-6904, e-mail:. sales@european kitchenbazaar.com, website: www. europeankitchenbazaar.com. Parts for blenders, bread makers, food processors, coffee and espresso makers, and other small appliances. Free catalog.

Guardian Service Cookware, 2110 Harmony Woods Rd., Owings Mills, MD 21117, 410-560-0777, e-mail: vetelvr93@aol.com, website: members.aol.com/vettelvr93. Guardian Service cookware replacement glass covers; pressure cooker parts, racks, and handles; reproduction Guardian Service cookbooks.

Joe MacMillan, 657 Old Mountain Rd., Marietta, GA 30064, 770-427-6434, 10:00 A.M.–10:00 P.M. Color decals for double-wheel coffee mills.

Larsen's Collectibles, 757 120th St., Hampton, IA 50441-7555, 641-866-6733. Lids, handles, and spigots for stoneware crocks and jugs. Handles that will fit most rolling pins.

Lorrie Kitchen, 2258 Sylvania Ave., Toledo, OH 43613, 419-475-1759, e-mail: lorrie@kitchenantiques.com, website: kitchenantiques.com. Replacement labels for Anchor Hocking and Owens-Illinois kitchen canisters.

Muff's Antiques, 135 S. Glassell St., Orange, CA 92866, 714-997-0243, fax: 714-997-0243, e-mail: muffs@earthlink.net, website: www.muffshard ware.com. Hard-to-find hardware for Hoosier cabinets, iceboxes, and more. Old-fashioned locks and keys. Mail order worldwide. Catalog free online, $5 in print. Tues.–Sat. 11:00 A.M.–5:00 P.M., Sun. 1:30 P.M.–4:00 P.M.

Phyllis Kennedy, 10655 Andrade Dr., Zionsville, IN 46077, 317-873-1316, fax: 317-873-8662, e-mail: philken@kennedyhardware.com, website: www.kennedyhardware.com. Hardware and parts for Hoosier cabinets. Specializing in parts for Hoosier cabinets, including flour bins, bread drawers, roll doors, wire racks, and sugar jars. Pie-safe tins, icebox hardware, and more. Wholesale catalog $3.

R.J. Pattern Services, c/o R.J. Hoerr, 1212 W. Detroit St., New Buffalo, MI 49117, 616-469-7538, fax: 616-469-8554, e-mail: mhoerr@starband.net. Antique stove and range replacement parts. Classic gas range knobs, dials, and handles. Antique toy and salesman sample stove restoration.

Retinning & Copper Repair, Inc., 560 Irvine Turner Blvd., Newark, NJ 07108,

973-848-0700, fax: 973-848-1070, website: www.retinning.com. Re-tinning and repair of antique copper cookware.

Scott's Beckers' Hardware, Inc., 1411 S. 3rd St., Ozark, MO 65721, 417-581-6525, fax: 417-581-4771, website: www.scotbeckhdw.com. Kitchen cabinet parts, pierced tins, icebox parts, and more. Catalog online and in print. Retail showroom open Mon.–Fri. 8:30 A.M.–5:00 P.M., Sat. 9:00 A.M.–3:00 P.M. Toll free order desk 888-991-0151.

Uncle Tom's Hoosier Cabinets, 5680 W. McNeely St., Elletsville, IN 47429, 812-325-0833, fax: 812-935-5735, e-mail: tomandnac@aol.com. Old Hoosier cabinets, Seller's, McDougall, Wilson, etc., parts and acces-sories. Catalog $2.

➻ JUKEBOXES, SEE COIN-OPERATED MACHINES
➻ KNIVES, SEE MILITARY MEMORABILIA
➻ LAMPS, SEE LIGHTING DEVICES

LIGHTING DEVICES

All types of lamps and lighting devices, including candlesticks, rushlight holders, and railroad lanterns, can be sold. Buyers pur-chase electric lamps to give light and to be decorative. Earlier forms of lighting are purchased either as part of a historic collection or as decorative pieces. To sell rushlights, old candlesticks, or even flash-lights, you must find the proper collector. There are many who col-lect whale oil lamps, Sandwich-glass oil lamps, or some other specialty. These lighting devices are more than one hundred years old, and they sell well to dealers and at auctions. Judge the market by the device's appearance. Some belong in a "country look" home, while others are for the more sophisticated home filled with English nineteenth-century antiques, Art Deco sofas, or 1950s kitsch.

Lamp bases from the late nineteenth and early twentieth cen-turies were often made by important glass, pottery, or metalwork-ing firms. A **TIFFANY** lamp has value as a lamp and because it is by Tiffany. Consequently, it sells for many times more than a compar-able lamp without the Tiffany mark. Spectacular Tiffany lamps can sell for hundreds of thousands of dollars. Cameo glass lamps by **GALLÉ** are also priced at least 100 percent more than common cameo lamps. The signature of a less important cameo glass maker adds only 50 percent. Sell these lamps and other special types of glass-shaded lamps to glass collectors.

A pottery lamp base made by an important pottery firm sometimes sells best as a lamp; occasionally, however, a lamp base is sold as a freestanding figurine or as a vase. If a hole for wiring was drilled in the bottom of a vase and the lamp was dismantled, the freestanding vase is considered to have a flaw. Factories like Rookwood or Van Briggle often made the base with the hole—the glaze even shows it is still in original condition—but the collector still pays half as much for a vase with a hole in the bottom. Figurines can usually be removed from the base with no indication of their original use. Lamps often have decorative metal bases that hide any indication of the maker of the pottery. It is a gamble to try to see if there is a mark.

In general, table lamps, unless by known makers, do not sell well. The highest prices for ordinary lamps are obtained at house sales or flea markets. Lamp shades have suddenly become of interest to decorators, and old fringed, parchment, or oddly-shaped fiberglass shades can be sold with or without the lamp. Brass floor lamps have become popular again, because many of the new ones are not made of solid brass. They can be refinished, rewired, and resold for a good price, so some dealers will buy a good metal floor lamp in any condition. Special types of lighting, like chandeliers, wall sconces, and torchères, have limited markets. Lamps that are in eccentric modern shapes, have moving parts like dancing hula girls, or have special effects like lava lamps or "moving water" reflected on the shade sell well.

The highest-priced lamps have leaded or painted glass shades. If the maker can be identified from either design or signature, the lamp has added value. Thousands of dollars are paid for good lamps by **HANDEL**, **TIFFANY**, or **PAIRPOINT**. Lamps sell for hundreds to thousands of dollars if made by **DIRK VAN ERP**, **STEUBEN**, **BRADLEY & HUBBARD**, **DUFFNER & KIMBERLY**, **EMERALITE**, or **JEFFERSON**. If your lamp is marked by a glass or pottery company, such as **ROOKWOOD**, **ROSEVILLE**, **HEISEY**, **GALLÉ**, or **RICHARD**, look in the general price books for the maker's name. If it isn't listed, the maker was unimportant. Outstanding Art Deco or 1950s lamps sell for good prices no matter who made them; price is determined by the appeal.

REPAIR

Lamps and lighting devices are collected for many reasons, the most obvious being that they can light a room. If you are using old lamps in your home, be sure they are restored so they can be safely used. Oil and kerosene lamps have well-known hazards. Always check to be sure that all of the parts are working. Most early lamps can be converted to electricity. The original burner can be replaced with a new electric socket and cord. The unit will fit into the available space of the old lamp and can be removed or added with no damage to the antique value of the lamp. If you do electrify an old lamp, be sure to keep the old parts. The next owner may want an all-original lamp. The original brass fittings for Tiffany or Handel lamps are very important.

The light bulb was invented in 1879. That means that some electric lamps can be more than one hundred years old. If you are using any electric lamp that is more than twenty-five years old, be sure it is safe. The cord should not be frayed, and if it is an old-style silk-wrapped cord or a stiff rubber cord, it should be totally replaced. Local lamp shops can rewire any lamp. Look for them in the Yellow Pages of the telephone book under "Lamps—Mounting & Repairing." If the sockets or pull chains need repairing, ask the shop to use as many of the old pieces as possible. Old sockets were made of solid brass, but now most of them are plated. A serious collector will always want the original chain. Some pay extra to get old acorn-tipped pull chains.

Reproductions of almost all parts of old lamps are available: glass shades, lamp chimneys, sockets, hangers for chandeliers, and more. Old metal lamps can be cleaned or replated. Leaded shades can be repaired. Art glass shades are being reproduced or can be repaired.

The lamp shade and lamp finial can often make the difference between an attractive, period-look lamp and an unattractive hodge-podge. Old-looking fringed, beaded, and lace shades are again being made. Finials with old pieces of jade or porcelain are being offered by decorating services and mail-order houses.

➠ SEE ALSO GLASS, METALS

REFERENCE BOOKS

Handel Lamps: Painted Shades & Glassware, Robert De Falco et al. (H & D Press, Staten Island, NY, 1986).

The Lamps of Tiffany Studios, William Feldstein Jr. and Alastair Duncan (Harry N. Abrams, New York, 1983).

Oil Lamps: The Kerosene Era in North America, Catherine M.V. Thuro (Wallace Homestead/Krause, Iola, WI, 1976).

Oil Lamps II: Glass Kerosene Lamps, Catherine M.V. Thuro (Collector Books, Paducah, KY, 1983).

Pairpoint Lamps, Edward and Sheila Malakoff (Schiffer, Atglen, PA, 1990).

PRICE BOOKS

'50s TV Lamps, Calvin Shepherd (Schiffer, Atglen, PA, 1998).

Aladdin Collectors Manual and Price Guide No. 20: Kerosene Mantle Lamps, J.W. Courter (3935 Kelley Road, Kevil, KY 42053, 2001).

Aladdin Electric Lamps: Collector's Manual and Price Guide No. 4, J.W. Courter (3935 Kelley Rd., Kevil, KY 42053, 2002).

Antique Lamp Buyer's Guide: Identifying Late 19th and Early 20th Century American Lighting, Nadja Maril (Schiffer, Atglen, PA, 1998).

Antique Trader Lamps and Lighting Price Guide, edited by Kyle Husfloen (Krause, Iola, WI, 2002).

Better Electric Lamps of the 20s and 30s (L-W Book Sales, Gas City, IN, 1997).

Classic Lanterns, Dennis A. Pearson (Schiffer, Atglen, PA, 1998).

Collectible Dietz Lanterns, Neil S. Wood (L-W Book Sales, Gas City, IN, 1997).

Collectible Lanterns, (L-W Book Sales, Gas City, IN, 1997).

Early Twentieth Century Lighting Fixtures, Jo Ann Thomas (Collector Books, Paducah, KY, 2000).

Fairy Lamps, Bob and Pat Ruf (Schiffer, Atglen, PA, 1996).

Lamps of the 50s & 60s with Values, Jan Lindenberger (Schiffer, Atglen, PA, 1997).

Lighting Fixtures of the Depression Era, Books I and II, Jo Ann Thomas (Collector Books, Paducah, KY, 2001).

Miniature Victorian Lamps, Marjorie Hulsebus (Schiffer, Atglen, PA, 1996).

Moss Lamps: Lighting the '50s, Donald-Brian Johnson and Leslie Piña (Schiffer, Atglen, PA, 2000).

Oil Lamps III: Victorian Kerosene Lighting, 1860–1900, Catherine M.V. Thuro (Collector Books, Paducah, KY, 2001).

Price Guide for Miniature Lamps, Marjorie Hulsebus (Schiffer, Atglen, PA, 1998).

CLUBS & THEIR PUBLICATIONS

Aladdin Knights of the Mystic Light, *Mystic Light of the Aladdin Knights* (NL), 3935 Kelley Rd., Kevil, KY 42053, e-mail: brtknight@aol.com, website: www.aladdinknights.org.

Fairy Lamp Club, *Fairy Lamps: Elegance in Candle Lighting* (NL), 6422 Haystack Rd., Alexandria, VA 22310-3308, e-mail: sapp@erols.com, website: www.fairylampclub.com,

The Glow Light Collectors Club, *The Glow Light Collectors Club Newsletter* (NL), 4027 Brooks Hill Rd., Brooks, KY 40109, e-mail: holauction @aol.com, website: hometown.aol.com/holauction/index.html.

Historical Lighting Society of Canada, *HLSC Journal* (MAG), *Newsletter* (NL), PO Box 561 Station R, Toronto, ON M4G 4E1, Canada, e-mail: Goulding @idirect.com, website: www.historical-lighting.on.ca.

International Coleman Collectors, *Coleman Collector Courier* (NL), 3404 W 450 N, Rochester, IN 46975-8380.

Night Light: The Miniature Lamp Collectors Club, *Night Light* (NL), c/o Robert N. Culver, 3081 Sand Pebble Cove, Pinckney, MI 48169, website: my.voyager.net/~rculver/nightlight/nlhome.htm.

Rushlight Club, Inc., *Rushlight* (MAG), *Flickerings* (NL), 3901 Gloucester Dr., Lexington, KY 40510-9733, e-mail: info@rushlight.org, website: www.rushlight.org.

APPRAISERS

Many of the auctions and repair services listed in this section will also do appraisals. *See also* the general list of "Appraisal Groups," page 483.

REPAIRS, PARTS & SUPPLIES

➜ **SEE ALSO "CONSERVATORS & RESTORERS," PAGE 520.**

A & H Brass & Supply, 126 W. Main St., Johnson City, TN 37604, 423-928-8220. Lamp parts. Catalog.

AAMSCO Lighting, 100 Lamp Light Circle, Summerville, SC 29483, 843-278-0000 or 800-221-9092; fax: 843-278-0001, e-mail: bulbs@hudsonet.com, website: www.aamsco.com. Ferrowatt® Brand reproduction antique light bulbs. Can reproduce other manufacturers' discontinued light bulbs. Light bulbs for all worldwide voltages and hard-to-find bulbs.

Abercrombie & Co., 9159A Brookeville Rd., Silver Spring, MD 20910, 800-585-2385 or 301-585-2385, fax: 301-587-5708, e-mail: abernco@erols.com, website: www.silverplaters.com. Lamps restored and rewired. Metal repair, plating, and polishing. Dents smoothed or removed.

A-Bit-of-Antiquity, 1412 Forest Ln., Woodbridge, VA 22191, 703-491-2878, e-mail: dudleyre@erols.com, website: www.erols.com/dudleyre. Complete restoration of antique lighting, with an emphasis on oil lighting. Repair of table, piano, student, banquet, and mantle lamps. Parts replaced. Oil and gas lamps electrified; electrified lamps returned to their original state when possible.

Across-the-Board Lampworks, 167 Foster Creek Rd., Toledo, WA 98591, 888-994-LAMP, e-mail: hannah@toledotel.com, website: www.acrosstheboardwoodwork.com. Vintage fabric lampshades restored. Custom-designed lampshades of all kinds—Softbacks and Hardbacks. Lampshade frames, many hard-to-find lamp parts, new and vintage silks, satins, glass bead fringe. Catalog $5.

Al Bar-Wilmette Platers, 127 Green Bay Rd., Wilmette, IL 60091, 847-251-0187, fax: 847-251-0281, e-mail: info@albarwilmette.com, website: www.albarwilmette.com. Lamps and chandeliers repaired. Restoration of metal finishes.

American Period Lighting, Inc., 3004 Columbia Ave., Lancaster, PA

17603, 717-392-5649, fax: 717-509-3127, e-mail: conygham@yahoo.com, website: www.americanperiod.com. Traditional, period, and historical lighting, specializing in lanterns, post lights, and chandeliers for home and garden. Brochure.

Antique & Colonial Lighting, 10626 Main St., Clarence, NY 14031, 716-759-1429, e-mail: jack@thebrassman.com, website: thebrassman.com. Lighting restoration, polishing, metal spinning, and repair. Specializing in antique lighting.

Antique China Restorations by MyJolie Hutchings, 1941 Wolfsnare Rd., Virginia Beach, VA 23454-3544, 757-425-1807. Restorations of lamps.

Antique Hardware & Home Store, 19 Buckingham Plantation Dr., Bluffton, SC 29910, 800-422-9982, 8:30 A.M.–6:00 P.M., e-mail: treasure @hargray.com, website: www.antiquehardware.com. Specialty lampshades.

The Antique Lamp Co., 1213 Hertel Ave., Buffalo, NY 14216, 716-871-0508, e-mail: info@antiquelampco.com, website: www.antiquelampco.com. Lamp restoration and rewiring. Polishing, plating, missing parts replaced; electrifying. Custom shades for all types of fixtures. Old and new glass shades. Free brochure. Catalog of lampshades and parts on website. World-wide shipping. Appraisals.

Antique Restoration Service, 521 Ashwood Dr., Flushing, MI 48433, 810-659-5582, 810-659-0505, e-mail: sshch@aol.com. Restoration of lamps. Soldering and wiring if necessary.

Antique Service Center Inc., 109 E. First St., Sumner, IA 50674, 563-578-3337, fax: 563-578-8848, e-mail: asc@antiqueservicecenter.com, website: www.antiqueservicecenter.com. Replacement parts for lamps; shades; electrical work on most lamps. Polishing of most metals—brass, copper, silver, aluminum, cast iron, etc. Plating in brass, copper, and nickel.

Antiques Collectibles & Stuff, 12 W. Olentangy St., Powell, OH 43065, 614-846-8724, fax: 614-846-8724, e-mail: eiann41080@aol.com, website: www.antiques-collectiblestuff.com. Lamp repairs and lamp building. Oil and gas lamps converted to electric.

Architectural Detail, 512 S. Fair Oaks, Pasadena, CA 91105, 626-844-6604, fax: 626-844-6651. Home restoration resources. Used building materials from 1880 to 1960; lighting. Specializing in materials from Pasadena and Greater Los Angeles. No mail order.

Architectural Emporium, 207 Adams Ave., Canonsburg, PA 15317, 724-746-4301, e-mail: sales@architectural-emporium.com, website: architectural-emporium.com. Specializing in restored period lighting, early Victorian gas fixtures through Art Deco period.

B & P Lamp Supply Co., Inc., 843 Old Morrison Rd., McMinnville, TN 37110, 931-473-3016, fax: 931-473-3014, e-mail: pmbarnes@charter.net, website: bplampsupply.com. Manufacturer and wholesaler of lamp parts for the repair and manufacture of antique and early lighting. Reproduction lamps and lamp parts. Contact for a dealer in your area. Catalog $15.

Ball & Ball Antique Hardware Reproductions, 436 W. Lincoln Hwy., Exton, PA 19341, 800-257-3711, fax: 610-363-7639, website: www.balland ball.com. Lighting and metal items repaired and refinished. Lighting fixtures duplicated or custom-made.

Bathroom Machineries, 495 Main St., PO Box 1020, Murphys, CA 95247, 209-728-2031 or 800-255-4426, fax: 209-728-2320, e-mail: tom @deabath.com, website: deabath.com. Antique replacement glass lampshades. Free catalog.

Bedlam Brass Restoration, 520 River Dr., Garfield, NJ 07026, 800-BEDLAM-1, fax: 800-BEDLAM-2, e-mail: sales@bedlam.biz, website: bedlam.biz. Restoration and refinishing of lighting. New brass parts.

Blue Crystal (Glass), Ltd., Units 6-8, 21 Wren St., London WC1X 0HF, UK, 011-44-20-7278-0142, fax: 011-44-20-7278-0142, e-mail: bluecrystal glass@aol.com, website: www.bluecrystalglass.co.uk. Reproduction chandelier parts; glass lampshades of any size. Antique and general glass repairs. Mail order worldwide. Catalog.

Brass & Copper Polishing Shop, 13 S. Carroll St., Frederick, MD 21701, 301-663-4240, fax: 301-694-9190, e-mail: shineit4u@aol.com. Antique and new lamp parts and supplies. Replacement glass shades. Brass, copper, and silver polishing, repair, and lacquering. Free brochure.

Brass & Silver Workshop, 758 St. Andrew Blvd., Charleston, SC 29407, 843-571-4342, fax: 843-571-7417. Restoration to light fixtures and all metals. Services include soldering, polishing, buffing, burnishing, and dent removal.

The Brass Knob, Architectural Antiques, 2311 18th St. NW, Washington, DC 20009, 202-332-3370, e-mail: bk@thebrassknob.com, website: www.thebrassknob.com. Architectural antiques and salvage, including lighting and many other old house parts. Second location, Back Doors Warehouse, is located at 2329 Champlain St. NW, Washington, DC 20009.

Chem-Clean Furniture Restoration, Bucks County Art & Antiques Co., 246 W. Ashland St., Doylestown, PA 18901, 215-345-0892, e-mail: iscsusn@att.net. Lamp repair. Research. Appraisals. Free brochure.

Classic Restoration Co., 10800 Carnegie Ave., Cleveland, OH 44106, 216-791-9050, 10:00 A.M.–6:00 P.M. Lamps and lighting fixtures rebuilt and rewired. Metal repairs, refining, and replating. Missing parts reproduced.

Conant Custom Brass, 270 Pine St., PO Box 1523A, Burlington, VT 05402, 800-832-4482 or 802-658-4482, fax: 802-864-5914, e-mail: steve @conantcustombrass.com, website: www.conantcustombrass.com. Brass and copper restoration and repair. Custom-made lighting. Glass shades. Check the website for tips on care and cleaning of brass.

Conner's Architectural Antiques, 701 P St., Lincoln, NE 68508, 402-

435-3338, fax: 402-435-3339, e-mail: connersaa@aol.com, website: www.ConnersArchitecturalAntiques.com. Architectural elements from old structures, including light fixtures. Parts for lighting fixtures.

Delphi Creativity Group, 3380 E. Jolly Rd., Lansing, MI 48910, 800-248-2048 or 517-394-4631, fax: 800-748-0374 or 517-394-5364, e-mail: sales@delphiglass.com, website: www.delphiglass.com. Lamp bases and supplies. Free catalog.

Drehobl Brothers Art Glass Co., 2847 N. Lincoln Ave., Chicago, IL 60657, 773-281-2022, fax: 773-281-2023. Bent glass panels for shades.

Elcanco Ltd., PO Box 682, Westford, MA 01886, 800-423-3836, fax: 978-392-0870, website: www.elcanco.com. Electric wax candles, flame-like bulbs, and beeswax candlecovers; 6-volt adapters.

Faire Harbour Ltd., 44 Captain Peirce Rd., Scituate, MA 02066, 781-545-2465, fax: 781-545-2465. Antique lighting repair. Specializing in Aladdin lamps and parts, old and new.

Fleming's Lighting & Silver Restoration, 24 Elm St., Cohasset Village, MA 02025, 781-383-0684. Brass, copper, pewter, and silver repair and re-plating. Restoration of lamps, chandeliers, and sconces. Replacement fabric shades. Lamps made from vases and statues. Free brochure.

Fred Kuntz, 47 Larchwood Dr., Painesville, OH 44077, 440-352-9630, evenings and weekends, e-mail: fredkuntz@nc.web.com. Reproduction mica chimneys and some Pyrex globes for Coleman and other makes of lanterns and lamps. Labels for newer Coleman lanterns. Free information sheet on Coleman lantern chimneys.

Good Pickin', 220 N. Polk St., Jefferson, TX 75657, 866-333-5267 or 903-665-3003, e-mail: lamps@goodpick.com, website: www.goodpick.com. Parts for old Aladdin lamps: chimneys, shades, wicks, lamp oil. Burners and collars, shades for bridge lamps, Dietz lanterns and parts, gaslight shades, and more. Free brochure.

Herwig Lighting, Inc., PO Box 768, Russellville, AR 72811, 800-643-9523 or 479-968-2621, e-mail: Herwig@Herwig.com, website: www.herwig.com. Lanterns and posts. Cast-aluminum reproduction brackets, lanterns, and posts. Free catalog.

Hexagram Antiques, 426 Third St., Eureka, CA 95501, 707-725-6223, e-mail: hexagram@foggy.net. Specializing in vintage lighting; lighting restoration and rewiring.

Items of Value, Inc., 7419 Admiral Dr., Alexandria, VA 22307, 703-660-9380, fax: 703-660-9384. Restoration work for many different types of items. Appraisals.

Johnson's Lampshop, 8518 Old National Rd. (U.S. Rt. 40), South Vienna, OH 45369, 937-568-4551, fax: 937-568-9513. Antique parts and original glass for kerosene and gas lamps and fixtures. Shades. Free brochure. Hours Wed., Thurs., Fri. 10:00 A.M.–5:00 P.M.; Sat. 10:00 A.M.–4:00 P.M. Closed Sun., Mon., Tues.

Lamp Glass, 2230 Massachusetts Ave., Cambridge, MA 02140, 617-

497-0770, fax: 617-497-2074, e-mail: lamps@lampglass.nu, website: www.lampglass.nu. Replacement glass lampshades, including student shades, chimneys, hurricanes, Gone-with-the-Wind globes, torchères, banker's shades, and cased glass.

Leacock Coleman Center, 89 Old Leacock Rd., PO Box 307, Ronks, PA 17572-0307, 717-768-7174, fax: 717-768-7673 or 800-397-5234, e-mail: leacock@prodigy.net, website: www.leacockcoleman.com. Old Coleman lamp parts, lampshades, and globes. Aladdin lamp parts and shades. Lanterns repaired. Send SASE for brochure. Hours Mon.–Thurs. 7:00 A.M.–5:00 P.M., Fri. 7:00 A.M.–8:00 P.M., Sun. 7:00 A.M.–noon.

Lehman Hardware, One Lehman Circle, PO Box 41, Kidron, OH 44603-0041, 330-857-5757, fax: 330-857-5785, e-mail: info@lehmans.com, website: www.lehmans.com. Lamps and parts for Aladdin lamps, Dietz lanterns, gas lamps, and others. Old-fashioned hard-to-find items for non-electric living. Tools; books. Catalog $3.

Lemee's Fireplace Equipment, 815 Bedford St., Bridgewater, MA 02324, 508-697-2672, fax: 508-697-2672, website: www.lemeesfireplace.com. Wrought iron lighting, tin lighting, lampshades. Catalog $2.

Lights to Go, PO Box 533, Derby, KS 67037, 316-304-3051, fax: 316-788-4911, e-mail: ltg@trafficlights.com, website: www.trafficlights.com. Traffic light control sequencers for antique and collectible traffic lights. Control circuit converts your light into a stand-alone, working unit. Circuits for traffic lights, railroad crossing traffic lights, school Zone markers, Walk/Don't Walk lights, and almost any electric light display.

Lundberg Studios, 131 Old Coast Rd., PO Box C, Davenport, CA 95017, 888-423-9711 or 831-423-2532, Mon.–Fri. 8:00 A.M.–5:00 P.M. Pacific Time, fax: 831-423-0436, e-mail: lundbergstudios@earthlink.net, website: www.lundbergstudios.com. Replacement lampshades for Tiffany and Handel lamps. Special overhead and 2¼-inch fitter shades. Photos available. Free catalog.

The Magic Lamp, 200 S. Main St., Springboro, OH 45066, 937-748-8777, fax: 937-748-8419, e-mail: themagiclamp@earthlink.net, website: www.lampdoc.com. Aladdin lamps, wicks, chimneys, and parts. Replacement shades in fabric and glass for kerosene and electric lamps. Shade finials.

McBuffers, 1420 Dille Rd., Unit F, Euclid, OH 44117, 216-486-6696, fax: 216-486-4152. Complete lamp repair. Lamps and chandeliers refinished. Metal finishing, repair, and replating: brass, copper, nickel, chrome, silver, and gold. Cleaning, buffing, and polishing. Brochure.

Memphis Plating Works, 682 Madison Ave., Memphis, TN 38103, 901-526-3051. Repairing and refinishing of metals, including chandeliers and lamps.

Mike's Antiquary, 305 S. Main, PO Box 229, Almont, MI 48003, 810-798-3599, fax: 810-798-2042 call first, e-mail: jamm@ees.eesc.com.

Lamp restorations. Metal polishing. Serving eastern U.S. Call for availability. Mon.–Fri. 10:00 A.M.–6:00 P.M., Sat. 10:00 A.M.–2:00 P.M

Muff's Antiques, 135 S. Glassell St., Orange, CA 92866, 714-997-0243, fax: 714-997-0243, e-mail: muffs@earthlink.net, website: www.muffs hardware.com. Antique restoration hardware. Hard-to-find hardware for oil lamps and more. Mail order worldwide. Catalog free online, $5 in print. Tues.–Sat. 11:00 A.M.–5:00 P.M., Sun. 1:30 P.M.–4:00 P.M.

Museum Quality Restorations, PO Box 402, Palmyra, NJ 08065, 856-878-9711, fax: 856-878-0902, e-mail: jcmaue@aol.com, website: www.museumquality.net. Antique light fixture repair, parts, and accessories. Restoration services, reproduction globes, 1820–1875. Specialty metal repair and refinishing. Historic lighting consultant. Catalog and brochure.

Nadja Maril Historic Lighting, PO Box 6180, Annapolis, MD 21401, e-mail: nadjamaril@earthlink.net. Antique lighting consultation services. Antique shades and complete fixtures from the late 19th and early 20th century. Books about antique lighting; lectures on American lighting. Write or e-mail for more information.

Nowell's, Inc., 490 Gate 5 Rd., PO Box 295, Sausalito, CA 94966, 415-332-4933, fax: 415-332-4936, e-mail: sauslamp@aol.com, website: www.nowells-inc.com. Restoration and repair of old lighting fixtures. Smokeless, odorless lamp oil. Antique and reproduction lighting. Catalog $5.

Oak Brothers, 5104 N. Pearl St., Tacoma, WA 98407, 253-752-4055, fax: 253-752-4055, e-mail: wmalovich@harbornet.com. Benders and sellers of curved glass for lamps and other things. By appointment only. Call or write for more information.

Orum Silver Co., Inc., 51 S. Vine St., Meriden, CT 06450-0805, 203-237-3037, fax: 203-237-3037, e-mail: orum.silver@snet.net, website: orumsilver.com. Restoration of lighting fixtures. Gold, silver, nickel, copper, brass, and chrome plating. Free brochure.

Patrick J. Gill & Sons, 9 Fowle St., Woburn, MA 01801, 781-933-3275, fax: 781-933-3751, e-mail: joe@patrickgillco.com, website: patrickgillco.com. Metal repair, refinishing, and replating. Chandeliers, lamps, and other metal objects replated.

Paxton Hardware Ltd., 7818 Bradshaw Rd., PO Box 256, Upper Falls, MD 21156, 800-241-9741, fax: 410-592-2224, e-mail: paxton@ix.net com.com, website: www.paxtonhardware.com. Antique-style lighting. Lamp burners, chimneys, and shades. Catalog.

PECO Glass Bending, PO Box 777, Smithville, TX 78957, 512-237-3600, e-mail: glass@pecoglassbending.com, website: www.pecoglassbending.com. Custom-made lamp parts.

Peter Owen, 29 Murray St., Augusta, ME 04330, 207-622-3277, e-mail: lamprepair@msn.com, website: www.stained-glass-lamp-restora

tions.com. Replacement bent slag glass panels and other stained-glass lampshade repairs.

Phyllis' Antiques & David's Brass Works, PO Box 111, Washington, KY 41096, 606-759-7423, fax: 606-759-7423, e-mail: lamps@may-uky. campus.mci.net. Victorian lighting restoration, rewiring, refinishing, parts and supplies. Cranberry, hand-painted, and all other types of glass lampshades; silk, cloth, and parchment lampshades. Send LSASE for free brochure.

Pinch of the Past, 109 W. Broughton St., Savannah, GA 31401, 912-232-5563, e-mail: pinchopast@aol.com, website: pinchofthepast.com. Repair and restoration of lighting. Brass and metal cleaning and polishing. Restoration consultation. Antique and reproduction lighting. Appraisals. Free brochure.

Pleasant Valley Restoration, 1725 Reed Rd., Knoxville, MD 21758, 301-432-2721, 9:00 A.M.–7:00 P.M., e-mail: PVRfixit@aol.com. Lamps rewired; power cords on old electrical devices replaced.

Precision Arcade Repair, 1315 Sandpiper Ln., Lilburn, GA 30047-2027, 770-985-4697, e-mail: gyrogames@aol.com, website: www.tristan mulrooney.com. Neon sign repair and servicing, also custom neons made to order.

Rejuvenation, 2550 NW Nicolai St., Portland, OR 97210, 888-401-1900 toll free or 503-231-1900, fax: 800-526-7329 toll free or 503-230-0537, e-mail: info@rejuvenation.com, website: www.rejuvenation.com. Reproduction antique lighting. For information on restoration services, call 503-238-1900 or e-mail restoration@rejuvenation.com.

Remember When, 111 Main St., Torrington, CT 06790, 860-489-1566, fax: 860-489-1566, e-mail: karen@remwhen.com, website: remwhen.com. Antique lighting repair and restoration. Lampshades and parts. Reversible conversion of oil lamps to electric. Appraisals.

Renovator's Supply, Renovator's Old Mill, Millers Falls, MA 01349, 800-659-0203, 7:00 A.M.–midnight, fax: 413-659-3796 orders, website: www.rensup.com. Lighting, glass shades, prisms, pendalogues, and more. Free catalog.

Restoration & Design Studio, 249 E. 77th St., New York, NY 10021, 212-517-9742, fax: 212-517-9742. Repair and restoration of lighting fixtures and metals.

Retinning & Copper Repair, Inc., 560 Irvine Turner Blvd., Newark, NJ 07108, 973-848-0700, fax: 973-848-1070, website: www.retinning.com. Restoration of brass chandeliers, lighting fixtures, and other metal items.

Riverwalk Lighting, 401 S. Main St., Naperville, IL 60540, 630-357-0200, e-mail: info@enlighteninc.com, website: www.riverwalklighting.com. Repair and rewiring of all types of lighting, including halogen lighting. Broken or missing parts replaced or rebuilt, glass shades replaced or hand-painted to match the base. Replating, polishing, and lacquering metal items, including lamps and fixtures. Nickel, brass, or copper plating.

Robben Restoration, 5628 Cheviot Rd., Cincinnati, OH 45247, 877-257-0596 or 513-741-3619, e-mail: RRsilver1@aol.com. Gold, silver, and brass plate lamp restoration. Fabrication, plating, soldering, dent removal, part replacement, etc. Free brochure.

Roy Electric, Antique & Reproduction Lighting Fixtures, 22 Elm St., Westfield, NJ 07090, 908-317-4665, fax: 908-317-4629, website: www.westfieldnj.com/roy. Original Victorian gas lighting, early electric through Art Deco period. Reproduction lighting fixtures. Restoration of all types of lighting, from rewiring and adjusting to polishing, plating, and refinishing. Free catalog.

Scott's Beckers' Hardware, Inc., 1411 S. 3rd St., Ozark, MO 65721, 417-581-6525, fax: 417-581-4771, website: www.scotbeckhdw.com. Antique lamp parts, refinishing supplies, and more. Catalog online and in print. Retail showroom open Mon.–Fri. 8:30 A.M.–5:00 P.M., Sat. 9:00 A.M.–3:00 P.M. Toll free order desk 888-991-0151.

The Silk Shade, PO Box 243, Santa Monica, CA 90406, 310-395-6360. Turn-of-the-century Victorian lampshades made using vintage fabrics, vintage laces, trims, and embroidery; metallic appliques and bullion tassels. Shipped anywhere.

St. Louis Antique Lighting Co., 801 N. Skinker Blvd., St. Louis, MO 63130, 314-863-1414, 8:00 A.M.–4:30 P.M., fax: 314-863-6702, e-mail: slalco@mindspring.com. Restoration of antique lighting. Custom design and fabrication of antique lighting; exact reproduction of historic fixtures. Historic preservation consultation; appraisals. Catalog $3.

Two Brothers Antique Lighting Restorations, 36-25 164 St., Flushing, NY 11358, 718-939-9703, e-mail: twobrothers21@hotmail.com. Antique lighting restorers. Restoration of all sconces, lamps, and chandeliers. All finishes reproduced. Specializing in antique lighting only.

United House Wrecking, 535 Hope St., Stamford, CT 06906, 203-348-5371, fax: 203-961-9472, e-mail: unitedhouse.wrecking@snet.net, website: www.unitedhousewrecking.com. Lighting and architectural elements. Open seven days a week, Mon.-Sat. 9:30 A.M.–5:00 P.M., Sunday noon–5:00 P.M. Free brochure.

Van Dyke's Restorers, PO Box 278, Woonsocket, SD 57385, 605-796-4425, 800-558-1234 orders, fax: 605-796-4085, e-mail: restoration@cabelas.com, website: www.vandykes.com. Lamp parts for electric lamps and oil lamps, including Aladdin lamps. Shades and glass chimneys. Brass hardware of all kinds. Special parts designed to duplicate original pieces. Mail order worldwide. Catalog.

Victorian Lighting, Inc., 29 York St., PO Box 1067, Kennebunk, ME 04043, 207-985-6868, website: www.antiquesmap.com. Lamp repair and restoration: polishing, lacquering, repair, rewiring; shade painting and re-covering. Glass shades, new and old. Antique lighting, including chandeliers, sconces, and table lamps. Free brochure.

Vintage Hardware, PO Box 9486, San Jose, CA 95129, 408-246-9918, e-mail: vhprs@earthlink.net, website: www.vintagehardware.com. Distributor of Heritage Lighting, reproduction antique lighting including neorococo gas lighting from 1840. Color catalog, 80 pages, $4.

Whittemore-Durgin Glass Co., Box 2065, Hanover, MA 02339, 800-262-1790, fax: 781-871-5597, website: www.WhittemoreDurgin.com. Bent lampshade panels, beaded lampshade fringes, bull's-eye panes. Stained-glass supplies, equipment, and instruction. Catalog $2.

Woodman's Parts Plus, PO Box 186, East Wakefield, NH 03830-0186, 603-522-8216, 9:00 A.M.–5:00 P.M., fax: 603-522-3007. Parts for kerosene lamps. Custom-made wrought iron accessories.

Yesterday Once Again, PO Box 6773, Huntington Beach, CA 92615, 714-963-2474, telephone hours Mon.–Fri. 7:00 A.M.–9:30 A.M. and 4:30 P.M.–6:30 P.M., fax: 714-963-1558, e-mail: yesterdayonceagain@yahoo.com. Carbon filament light bulbs, replicas of Edison's 1890 bulb. Victorian-style light bulbs. Mail order worldwide. Free brochure.

Yestershades, 4327 SE Hawthorne, Portland, OR 97215, 503-235-5645. Hand-sewn Victorian fabric lampshades; custom designing on shades. Will ship anywhere. Shop hours noon–5:00 P.M. Tues. through Sat. Catalog $3.50.

→ LUGGAGE, SEE TRUNKS

MAGAZINES

You may not be able to sell a book by its cover, but that is usually the best way to sell an old magazine. It is often the cover illustration that brings the money for old but not rare magazines. A picture of Marilyn Monroe on a *Life* magazine or a Norman Rockwell illustration on the cover of the *Saturday Evening Post* means there is more value than expected for the magazine. There are other parts of magazines that sell well: advertisements, paper dolls, and stories by famous authors. There is a moral dilemma here. Should you cut up the magazine and destroy it forever, or is it better not to try to sell the parts? The whole magazine is often worth less money than the parts, but it does take time and extra research to know how to sell the individual pages. If you are selling the whole magazine, be sure that every page is still in your magazine. Missing pages lower the value dramatically. The first issue of any magazine has a value, even if the magazine is now unknown.

ILLUSTRATIONS

Collectors prize cover illustrations as well as inside story and advertising illustrations by known artists. Names to look for are JESSIE WILLCOX SMITH, ROLF ARMSTRONG, HOWARD CHANDLER CHRISTY, PALMER COX, ERTÉ, HARRISON FISHER, J. C. LEYENDECKER, F. X. LEYENDECKER, CHARLES DANA GIBSON, JAMES MONTGOMERY FLAGG, KATE GREENAWAY, WINSLOW HOMER, THOMAS NAST, ROSE O'NEILL, MAXFIELD PARRISH, COLES PHILLIPS, ARTHUR RACKHAM, FREDERIC REMINGTON, GEORGE PETTY, and NORMAN ROCKWELL.

The early hand-colored fashion illustrations from the nineteenth-century *Godey's Ladies Book* or *The Delineator* are often torn from the magazines and sold separately. The woodcuts by Winslow Homer and other important artists that appeared in *Harper's Weekly* are also cut and removed.

Photographic covers and illustrations by less well-known artists can have extra value. A *Life* magazine photograph by ALFRED STIEGLITZ or MARGARET BOURKE-WHITE, either inside or on the cover, adds value. Stories in *Life* about the Kennedys, Marilyn Monroe, sports figures, and some politicians and movie stars add value. A *Time* or *Newsweek* cover showing a baseball player, especially LOU GEHRIG, TY COBB, or BABE RUTH, a famous person from the 1920s through the 1940s, some World War II personalities such as ADOLF HITLER or GENERAL DOUGLAS MACARTHUR, or a famous movie star has added value. There is a special market for any type of Nazi and war memorabilia.

SPECIAL SUBJECTS

Paper dolls are wanted by a special group of collectors. Full-page pictures of dolls or separate paper-doll books are collected and sell best at either doll shows or with other paper ephemera. Look for the dolls called LETTIE LANE, BETTY BONNET, KEWPIE, and DOLLY DINGLE.

The buyers of other types of movie memorabilia also collect movie magazines. (See Celebrity Memorabilia.) Collectors are also trying to buy old *TV Guides* and other television-related magazines. There is interest in sports and health magazines as well.

Short stories by famous authors are collected by the same people who want old books. Often an author wrote the first version of a story for a magazine. Of special interest are science-fiction magazine stories, which sell best at a science-fiction show. (See Books & Bookplates.)

Only the early girlie magazines or men's magazines sell for good prices. Collectors want special issues that feature **BRIGITTE BARDOT**, **JANE FONDA**, **JAYNE MANSFIELD**, **MARILYN MONROE**, or **CANDY STARR**. *Playboy* generates the most interest. Because each issue includes comic strips, the comic magazine dealers often buy and sell *Playboy* issues known as "fillers." These are the issues complete except for the centerfold.

Some collectors are searching for old advertisements. Best are **CREAM OF WHEAT** ads by famous illustrators and **COCA-COLA** ads that appeared on the back cover of National Geographic magazine for many years. Small ads from magazines that were published before 1940 are often cut out and sold as individual pictures to collectors, so you might sell car ads to car collectors, food ads to advertising collectors, etc. Each ad must be matted.

"Pulps" are magazines, often printed on poor-quality paper, that published mystery and science-fiction stories. Pulps should never be cut. The value is greater for the complete magazine than for any combination of cut-up illustrations and stories. These magazines are usually wanted by book and comic dealers.

NEWS MAGAZINES

Don't be disappointed if your large stack of *Life* or *National Geographic* magazines is not worth a small fortune. It is rare for a magazine to sell at retail for over $5 unless it is mint, has an interesting cover or story, and is at least pre-1960. Many magazines have no value at all. Still, try to sell your stacks of old magazines, especially *Life, National Geographic, Playboy* and similar magazines, decorating magazines like *House Beautiful,* gardening and cooking magazines, sports, movie, TV, automobile, and special-interest magazines. If you have enough, you will find that even at less than $1 each, the value adds up. Like other bargain-priced collectibles, magazines can be sold easily on Internet auction sites.

➻ SEE ALSO MOVIE MEMORABILIA, PAPER COLLECTIBLES

PRICE BOOKS

Collectible Magazines: Identification and Price Guide, David K. Henkel (HarperResource, New York, 2000).

The Gutmann & Gutmann Artists: A Published Works Catalog, 4th edition, Victor J.W. Christie (Science Press, Ephrata, PA, 2001).

Harrison Fisher: Defining the American Beauty, Tina Skinner (Schiffer, Atglen, PA, 1999).

Old Magazines Price Guide (L-W Book Sales, Gas City, IN, 1994, 2000 prices).

CLUBS & THEIR PUBLICATIONS

The Arthur Szyk Society, *Newsletter of the Arthur Szyk Society* (NL), 1200 Edgehill Dr., Burlingame, CA 94010, e-mail: info@szyk.com, website: www.szyk.org (Szyk was an artist whose work includes illuminated manuscripts, editorial cartoons, and magazine covers).

Philip Boileau Collectors' Society, *Philip Boileau Collectors' Society Newsletter* (NL), 1025 Redwood Blvd., Redding, CA 96003-1905, e-mail: pboileaucc@aol.com or gamlin@aol.com, website: hometown.aol .com/PBoileauCC/index.html.

REPAIRS, PARTS & SUPPLIES

↦ SEE ALSO "CONSERVATORS & RESTORERS," PAGE 520.

Brodart Co., 1609 Memorial Ave., Williamstown, PA 17705, 800-233-8959, website: www.brodart.com. Acid-free products for preservation, repair, and storage of books and magazines. Free catalog.

Century Business Solutions, PO Box 2393, Brea, CA 92822, 800-767-0777, fax: 800-786-7939, website: www.centurybusinesssolutions.com. Products for organizing and storing magazines and other collectibles.

Graphic Conservation Co., 329 W. 18th St., Suite 701, Chicago, IL 60616, 312-738-2657, fax: 312-738-3125, e-mail: info@graphicconservation.com, website: www.graphicconservation.com. Preservation of works of art on paper, including magazines. Dry cleaning, stain reduction, flattening, deacidification, inpainting, tear repairs and fills. Archival matting. Free brochure.

Muir's Book Repair, 1617 Willis St., Redding, CA 96001, 530-241-1948. Magazines, comic books, newspapers, and books repaired. Moisture or water damage, fire damage, lost covers, loose or torn pages repaired. Mail order worldwide. Send SASE for more information.

The2Buds.com, 462 W. Silver Lake Rd. North, Traverse City, MI 49684, 888-270-0552, Mon.–Fri. 9:00 A.M.–5:00 P.M., e-mail: postcards@the 2buds.com, website: www.the2buds.com. Archival supplies for storing and displaying magazines and other collectibles. Sleeves, bags, storage boxes, and more. Internet sales only.

University Products, Inc., 517 Main St., PO Box 101, Holyoke, MA 01040, 800-336-4847, fax: 800-532-9281, e-mail: info@universityproducts.com, website: www.universityproducts.com. Specialized storage for comics, magazines, and other collectibles. Archival supplies for conservation, restoration, repair, storage, and display. Archival storage boxes, paper and plastic enclosures, acid-free board and papers, adhesives, and other materials. Free catalog.

MARBLE

Marble carvings sell like any other sculpture: the better the artist, the higher the price. Size is also a factor. Busts and small figures sell for hundreds of dollars. Life-sized statues, especially those suitable for a garden, sell for thousands.

The major concern regarding marble is its care and upkeep. Marble should be kept clean. Wipe up any spills as soon as possible or the marble may become etched. If the stain is stubborn, use soap and lukewarm water. Marble should be dusted with a damp cloth and washed with a little water and a mild detergent about twice a year. You can wax marble with a colorless paste wax, but white marble may appear yellow if waxed.

Minor breaks can be mended with instant epoxy glue. Most marble cutters, cemetery monument makers, tile setters, and windowsill installers have the product. Stains can be removed, but it takes time and requires some expertise. Check your library or contact a marble worker in your area.

Sometimes a white marble carving will suffer from an odd, reappearing stain. This is from dirty water that has soaked into the porous marble. It can't be cured.

Marbles are listed in the Toys section.

BROCHURE ON REPAIR

Care & Cleaning for Natural Stone Surfaces, Marble Institute of America (30 Eden Alley, Suite 301, Columbus, OH 43215, 614-228-6194).

REPAIRS, PARTS & SUPPLIES

•→ SEE ALSO "CONSERVATORS & RESTORERS," PAGE 520.

A. Ludwig Klein & Son, Inc., PO Box 145, Harleysville, PA 19438, 215-256-9004 or 800-379-2929, fax: 215-256-9644, website: www.aludwig klein.com. Conservation and restoration of marble, statuary and monuments, and more. Professional cleaning. Appraisals, insurance claims. Worldwide. By appointment. Free brochure.

Antique China Restorations by MyJolie Hutchings, 1941 Wolfsnare Rd., Virginia Beach, VA 23454-3544, 757-425-1807. Restorations of marble, ceramics, soapstone, terra-cotta, and more.

Beverly Standing Designs, 1026 Elizabeth St., Pasadena, CA 91104, 626-798-2306, fax: 626-798-3529, e-mail: bubbs120@aol.com. Restoration of objects of art containing wood, glass, or marble. By appointment only.

Ceramic Restorations, Inc., 224 W. 29th St., 12th Floor, New York, NY 10001, 212-564-8669, 9:00 A.M.–6:00 P.M., fax: 212-843-3742. Restoration of marble, stone, and other materials.

China and Crystal Clinic, 1808 N. Scottsdale Rd., Tempe, AZ 85281, 480-945-5510 or 602-478-7857 or 602-568-9008 or 800-658-9197, fax: 480- 945-1079, e-mail: jbenterprises2@earthlink.net, website: chinaandcrystalclinic.com. Restoration or conservation of marble objects, figurines, vases, and other items. Appraisals.

Grashe Fine Art Restorers, 35 148th Ave. SE, #9, Bellevue WA 98007, 425-644-7500, fax: 425-644-7582, e-mail: art@grashe.com, website: www.grashe.com. Restoration and conservation of marble, jade, and other materials.

Hadley Restorations, 4667 Third St., La Mesa, CA 91941-5529, 619-462-5290, e-mail: cphadcearthlink.net, website: www.assoc-restorers.com. Restoration of marble and other material. Free brochure.

Hamlin's Restoration Studio, 14640 Manchester Rd., Ballwin, MO 63011, 636-256-8579 days, e-mail: hamlinsrestoration@msn.com, website: www.hamlinsrestoration.com. Repair and restoration of marble, alabaster, and other fine antiques.

Herbert F. Klug Conservation & Restoration, Box 28002 #16, Lakewood, CO 80228, 303-985-9261, e-mail: hgklug@qadas.com. Conservation and restoration of marble and other material. By appointment only.

A Home Design, 5220 Veloz Ave., Los Angeles, CA 91356, 818-757-7766, fax: 818-708-3722, e-mail: homedesign@mail.com. Fine arts restoration, including items made from marble. Operating in the southern California area.

James Davidson, 928 Independence St., New Orleans, LA 70117-5738, 504-944-0545, fax: 504-944-0545, e-mail: cjd9440545@netscape.net. Restoration of marble, jade, and other art objects.

Kingsmen Antique Restoration Inc., 19 Passamore Ave., Unit 28, Scarborough, ON Canada M1V 4T5, 416-291-8939, fax: 416-291-8939, e-mail: kingsmen@sprint.ca. Restoration of marble, jade, soapstone, and more. Service worldwide. Call for information on sending objects for estimates.

Leatherman Restoration, 509 Mairo St., Austin, TX 78748, 512-282-1556, fax: 512-282-1562, e-mail: rondl@juno.com, website: leatherman services.com. Repair and restoration of stone, marble, ceramic, and wood statues, figurines, tiles, and miscellaneous items. Restoration of damaged and incomplete fossils as well as ancient artifacts.

Pick Up The Pieces, 711 W. 17th St., Unit C-12, Costa Mesa, CA 92627, 800-824-6967, fax: 949-645-8381, e-mail: johnnce@yahoo.com, website: www.pickupthepieces.com. Fine art and collectible repair and restoration.

Pleasant Valley Restoration, 1725 Reed Rd., Knoxville, MD 21758, 301-

432-2721, 9:00 A.M.–7:00 P.M., e-mail: PVRfixit@aol.com. Restoration of marble. Previous restorations detected and verified.

Rafail & Polina Golberg, Golberg Restoration Co., 411 Westmount Dr., Los Angeles, CA 90048, 310-652-0735, fax: 310-274-3770, e-mail: info @restorationworld.com, website: www.restorationworld.com. Restoration and conservation of antiques and objects of art, including marble. Free estimates via the Internet.

The Sisters, 4163 Danamar Dr., Pensacola, FL 32504, 850-484-0975 or 850-476-7513, e-mail: sjtrimble@worldnet.att.net. General restoration of marble, jade, alabaster, and more. Free brochure.

Stewart's Restoration Studio, 2555 Goldenrod Dr., Bowling Green, KY 42104, 270-842-4580, fax: 270-842-4580, e-mail: stewartsrestore @aol.com. Restoration of porcelain, pottery, ceramics, glass, and marble antiques and collectibles.

Tindell's Restoration, 825 Sandburg Pl., Nashville, TN 37214, 615-885-1029, fax: 615-391-0712, e-mail: info@ATindellsRestorationSchools.com, website: www.TindellsRestorationSchools.com. Restoration services, seminars, training, and products. Appraisals. Free brochure.

Venerable Classics, 645 Fourth St., Suite 208, Santa Rosa, CA 95404, 800-531-2891, 707-575-3626, fax: 707-575-4913 call first, website: www.venerableclassics.com. Restoration of marble, jade, and many other fragile decorative objects.

METALS

Eighteenth- and nineteenth-century iron, brass, tin, toleware, pewter, and copper utensils have long been popular collectibles and are easily sold to dealers, decorators, and collectors. The fashion for the "country look" has added to the popularity, and any old tool, trivet, or kitchen utensil that can be put on a shelf or hung on a wall is wanted. Fine Early American examples, especially those stamped with a maker's mark, sell for hundreds to thousands of dollars. These early pieces can be sold through mail-order ads, at auction, on the Internet, or to collectors or dealers. They are part of the general merchandise found in most antiques shops. (See section on Kitchen Paraphernalia for additional information.)

Twentieth-century metalwork is sometimes mistakenly sold for low prices at garage sales because the uninformed don't realize that many recent pieces have a great value in the collectors' market. A Bradley and Hubbard Whistling Jim cast-iron doorstop sold in 2000 for $11,000. An old figural doorstop with some original paint is worth $50 or more. Heavy, solid copper cooking pots are also selling well. Price these by comparing them to new ones available in gourmet cooking stores. Art Nouveau and Art Deco pewter, chrome, or copper are in demand. Hammered aluminum from the 1940s and 1950s has some value if it is in very good condition. Of special interest are chrome cocktail shakers, Art Deco pieces with Bakelite (plastic) handles, and Arts and Crafts hammered-copper bookends or vases. Look for these names: pewter, **KAYZERZINN, TUDRIC, LIBERTY**; copper, **NEKRASSOFF, DIRK VAN ERP, HEINTZ ART, ROYCROFT, STICKLEY**; aluminum, **WENDELL AUGUST FORGE, STEDE, FARBERWARE, RODNEY KENT, CHASE**.

ENAMELS

Enamel decoration on metal is created by applying a glass mixture to copper, bronze, or silver items and then firing it to create a glass-like surface. The earliest enameling process, champlevé, involved pouring molten glass into depressions in the metal. Cloisonné is made with small strips of wire, or cloisons, applied to a metal (usually brass) item. Enamel is then floated between the strips. The finished piece is smoothed until the surface shows the pattern of colored enamels and brass lines. Plique-à–jour enamels are like miniature stained-glass windows. Small sections of transparent enamel are held in metal wire. Modern enameling is more painterly. A mixture of glass powder and metal oxides is applied to the metal in layers with brushes, printed transfers, or silk-screens. Sometimes chunks of glass are added to look like jewels after the firing process.

Oriental cloisonné can sell for high prices. Age and quality determine the value. Any damage or dent lowers the value as much as 90 percent, because repairs are difficult. The new cloisonné is very similar to the old, and it takes an expert to evaluate a piece. Plique-à–jour items from Russia bring high prices, too. Good-quality old enamels should be sold to a top antiques dealer or at auction. Mid-twentieth-century enameled plates, plaques, ashtrays, and jewelry are gaining popularity with collectors. Prices are highest for signed pieces. Look for the names **ED WINTER, KENNETH BATES, KARL DRERUP, MILDRED WATKINS**, and others.

BRONZE

Bronze figures were very important decorative pieces in the 1880–1900 period, but then lost favor. A new-style Art Deco bronze, often set with ivory, became fashionable in the 1920s and 1930s and became popular again in the 1970s. The bronze figure was scorned for many years, so there may be some very valuable ones in your attic or living room. Some of the best bronzes were given to thrift shops or resale stores in the 1950s. They were purchased for a few dollars by far-thinking collectors.

Always try to check the importance of a signed marble or bronze sculpture. Even unsigned figures, if well made, sell for hundreds of dollars today. Fine marble and bronze figures have been re-created in other materials such as spelter or plaster. The most famous of these are the **JOHN ROGERS** groups, plaster composition figures made in late nineteenth-century America. They sell quickly if the original painted surface is in good condition.

A bronze can be judged by the quality of the casting, the fame of the artist, and the appeal of the subject. Age is not as important as you might think. Many modern bronzes sell better than antique examples. Western subjects, the animal figures by nineteenth-century French artists, the Art Deco designs of the 1920s, and huge masculine subjects, such as nude males wrestling or warriors on horseback, are now bringing the highest prices. To check on the artist, see *Abage Encyclopedia: Bronzes, Sculptors & Founders* by Harold Berman. Look for names like **FREDERIC REMINGTON**, **LANCERAY**, **CHIPARUS**, **PREISS**, **CLODION**, **KAUBA**, **MOREAU**, **BARYE**, **MÉNE**, **CARRIER-BELLEUSE**, or **NAM GREB**.

A group is probably worth more than a single figure by the same artist. A marble base adds value. Generally, the larger the bronze, the greater the value, although miniatures (under six inches) sell for surprisingly high prices. The artist's signature, founder's seal, number, and any other special marks increase the value.

Poor details, crossed eyes, dented noses, repaired fingers, missing parts, or cracks lower the value. If the patina has been removed or damaged, the value is lowered by 50 percent. Recast pieces have low values. If you discover a Remington or any other very famous bronze figure, take it to a qualified appraiser to find out if it is an old or new reproduction. Replicas have been made by using the original statue to make a new mold. The replicas will be slightly smaller than originals. An original Remington bust is worth over $100,000; a recast may sell for as low as a few hundred dollars.

Any auction house, antiques dealer, or art dealer can easily sell a good bronze figure, and you should have no problem selling yours.

REPAIR

Each type of metal requires particular cleaning and care. Some copper, bronze, and brass should be kept polished. Some should not be polished. Bronze should never be cleaned in any way that might affect the patina. Heintz Art copper pieces were made with a special green or brown patina that should not be cleaned. Soap, water, dusting, and even a light waxing are safe for most metal items. There are several tarnish-preventative silicon-based polishes that are safe for metals. Do not use harsh abrasives like scouring powder or steel wool on any metal. Always rinse off all polishes completely. Many polishes are made with acids that continue to "eat" the metal after it has been polished.

Do not keep bronzes in a room that is being cleaned with bleaching powders, disinfectants, or floor-washing products containing chlorine. The chlorine can harm the bronze. Never store bronzes near rubber mats. Some carpet adhesives, paints, and fabrics may contain chemicals that are corrosive.

Damaged enamels and cloisonné are very difficult to repair. Dents and chipped enamel require the attention of an expert. The cost of the repair is often more than the value of the piece. Some minor repairs might be done by a local jeweler or metalsmith. Radical changes in temperature can crack enamel, so pieces should never be kept in a sunny window or over heat ducts, or washed in very hot or cold water.

Pewter is very soft and can be damaged easily or melted. Never put a piece of pewter near a burner on a stove or in an oven. Never mechanically buff a piece of pewter; it will permanently change the color of the piece. Never use harsh scouring powder or steel wool to clean pewter. There are several commercial pewter polishes available at jewelry and grocery stores.

Tin and toleware should be kept dry and free of rust. If tin is rusty, try removing the rust with 0000 steel wool. For painted toleware, just touch up the spot, but never paint more than is necessary. A redecorated piece of toleware is of value as a new item but not as an antique. Once the tin is repainted, it has lost its value to the serious collector: but sometimes repainting is the only solution for a severely damaged piece. Serious toleware decorators often look for old pieces with worn paint to redecorate, even though it is possible to get new tinware made in the same manner as the old. Many restored-village museums have tinshops where tin is made and sold.

Dents can be removed from tin and toleware by any competent silverworker or metalsmith.

Never wrap metals in plastic or non-ventilated materials. Moisture can collect under the wrap, or the plastic may melt and cause damage.

Check in the Yellow Pages of the telephone book under "Plating" to find shops that replate, polish, and restore metal items. *See also* the section in this book on Silver & Silver Plate.

•→ SEE ALSO ADVERTISING COLLECTIBLES, FIREPLACE EQUIPMENT, HARDWARE, LIGHTING DEVICES

REFERENCE BOOKS

Abage Encyclopedia: Bronzes, Sculptors & Founders, volumes 1–4, Harold Berman (Abage Publishers, Chicago, 1974–1980).

The American Pewterer: His Techniques & His Products, Henry J. Kauffman (Thomas Nelson, Nashville, TN, 1970).

Animals in Bronze: Reference and Price Guide, Christopher Payne (Antique Collectors' Club, Wappingers Falls, NY, 1986).

Art Deco and Other Figures, Bryan Catley (Antique Collectors' Club, Wappingers Falls, NY, 1978).

The Dictionary of Western Sculptors in Bronze, James Mackay (Antique Collectors' Club, Wappingers Falls, NY, 1977).

History of American Pewter, Charles F. Montgomery (E.P. Dutton, New York, 1978).

Old Pewter: Its Makers and Marks, Howard Herschel Cotterell (Charles E. Tuttle, Rutland, VT, 1973).

Pewter in America: Its Makers and Their Marks, 3 volumes, Ledlie Irwin Laughlin (Barre Publishers, Barre, MA, 1969–1971).

Pewter Marks of the World, D. Starà (Hamlyn, London, 1977).

PRICE BOOKS

Aluminum Giftware, Frances Johnson (Schiffer, Atglen, PA, 1996).

Art Deco Aluminum: Kensington, Paula Ockner and Leslie Piña (Schiffer, Atglen, PA, 1997).

Art Deco Chrome, Jim Linz (Schiffer, Atglen, PA, 1999).

Chase Complete: Deco Specialties of the Chase Brass & Copper Co., Donald-Brian Johnson and Leslie Piña (Schiffer, Atglen, PA, 1999).

Collectible Enameled Ware: American & European, David T. Pikul and Ellen M. Plante (Schiffer, Atglen, PA, 1998).

Designed & Signed: '50s & '60s Glass, Ceramics, & Enamel Wares by Georges Briard, Sascha B., Bellaire, Higgins . . ., Leslie Piña (Schiffer, Atglen, PA, 1996).

Hubley Metal Art Goods Price Guide, Judy and Ron Rittenhouse (PO Box 1411, Lancaster, PA 17608, 1996).

Ronson's Art Metal Works, Stuart Schneider (Schiffer, Atglen, PA, 2001).

Roycroft Art Metal, 3rd edition, Kevin McConnell (Schiffer, Atglen, PA, 1999).

Tiffany Desk Treasures: A Collector's Guide, George A. Kemeny and Donald Miller (Hudson Hills Press, New York, 2002).

CLUBS & THEIR PUBLICATIONS

Cloisonne Collectors Club, *Cloison* (NL), Box 96, Rockport, MA 01966.

Enamelist Society, 6105 Bay Hill Cir., Jamesville, NY 13078, e-mail: info@enamelistsociety.info, website: www.enamelistsociety.org.

Hammered Aluminum Collectors Association (HACA), *Aluminist* (NL), PO Box 1346, Weatherford, TX 76086, e-mail: al1310@aol.com.

Pewter Collectors Club of America, Inc., *Pewter Bulletin* (NL), *PCCA Newsletter* (NL), 504 W. Lafayette St., West Chester, PA 19380-2210, e-mail: gpewter@bellatlantic.net, website: members.aol.com/pewterpcca.

Society of North American Goldsmiths (SNAG), *Metalsmith* (MAG), *SNAG News* (NL), 710 E. Ogden Ave., Suite 600, Naperville, IL 60563-8603, e-mail: info@SNAGmetalsmith.org, website: SNAGmetalsmith.org.

OTHER PUBLICATIONS

Glass on Metal (MAG), PO Box 310, Newport, KY 41072, e-mail: Dviehman7en12@aol.com, website: www.enamelistsociety.org.

ARCHIVES & MUSEUMS

National Ornamental Metal Museum, 374 Metal Museum Dr., Memphis, TN 38106, 901-774-6380 or 877-881-2326, fax: 901-774-6382, website: www.metalmuseum.org.

REPAIRS, PARTS & SUPPLIES

➤➤ **SEE ALSO "CONSERVATORS & RESTORERS," PAGE 520.**

18th Century Hardware Co., Inc., 131 E. Third St., Derry, PA 15627, 724-694-2708, fax: 724-694-9587. Duplication of missing hardware on antique furniture. Metal items cleaned and polished. Broken items repaired. Catalog $3.

A. Ludwig Klein & Son, Inc., PO Box 145, Harleysville, PA 19438, 215-256-9004 or 800-379-2929, fax: 215-256-9644, website: www.aludwig klein.com. Conservation and restoration of brass, bronze, pewter, silver, frames, statuary and monuments, and more. Professional cleaning. Appraisals, insurance claims. Worldwide. By appointment. Free brochure.

Abend Studio and Metal Repair, 22 Drumlins Terrace, Syracuse, NY 13224, 315-446-4324, fax: 315-446-4324, e-mail: aabend@twcny.rr.com. Restoration of metal antiques with the welding process. Work on brass, bronze, cast iron, steel, stainless steel, and aluminum. Repair and restoration of sculpture and antiques. Parts casting; patina restoration. Commissioned metal designs. Written repair estimates.

Abercrombie & Co., 9159A Brookeville Rd., Silver Spring, MD 20910, 800-585-2385 or 301-585-2385, fax: 301-587-5708, e-mail: abernco@erols.com, website: www.silverplaters.com. Metal repair, plating, and polishing. Dents smoothed or removed; handles, hinges, lids, and spouts repaired; garbage disposal–damaged flatware repaired; new blades, brushes, combs, and mirrors fitted. Copper cookware tin lined. Lamps restored and rewired. Silver, gold, nickel, copper, brass, and tin plated.

Al Bar-Wilmette Platers, 127 Green Bay Rd., Wilmette, IL 60091, 847-251-0187, fax: 847-251-0281, e-mail: info@albarwilmette.com, website: www.albarwilmette.com. Restoration of historic hardware and metal fixtures. Restoration of metal finishes; missing parts furnished, lamps and chandeliers repaired, locks refurbished, and new hardware plated to match historic finishes. Silver repaired and restored; silver plating.

American Alloy Foundry, 112-120 S. Eden St., Baltimore, MD 21231, 410-276-1930, fax: 410-276-1947. Brass, bronze, and aluminum castings made in the sand mold method. Can reproduce from originals to make exact copies. Replicas of antique hardware, drawer pulls, handles, bales, rosettes, and hooks. Antique car parts, boat parts, airplane parts, slot machine parts, etc. Brochure $1.

Antique & Art Restoration by Wiebold, 413 Terrace Pl., Terrace Park, OH 45174, 800-321-2541, 513-831-2541, fax: 513-831-2815, e-mail: wiebold@eos.net, website: www.wiebold.com. Restoration and conservation of silver, pewter, brass, copper. Silver, gold, and brass plating.

Antique Hardware and Mirror Resilvering, 763 W. Bippley Rd., Lake Odessa, MI 48849, 616-374-7750, fax: 616-374-7752, e-mail: antiquehardware@robinsonsantiques.com, website: www.robinsonsantiques.com. Original antique restoration hardware, door hardware, doorknobs, furniture hardware, hinges, mirrors, locks, pulls, latches, registers, and more. Original parts from 1650 to 1925. Free search. Free matching service.

Antique Restoration Co., 440 E. Centre Ave., Newtown, PA 18940, 215-968-2343, fax: 215-860-5465. Metal polishing, plating, and lacquering. Free brochure.

Antique Service Center Inc., 109 E. First St., Sumner, IA 50674, 563-578-3337, fax: 563-578-8848, e-mail: asc@antiqueservicecenter.com, website: www.antiqueservicecenter.com. Restoration of metal antiques. Polishing of most metals: brass, copper, silver, aluminum, cast iron, etc. Plating in brass, copper, and nickel. Can send items to be silver plated. Replacement parts for lamps; shades; electrical work on most lamps.

AntiqueConservation.com, Div. of Ponsford Ltd., 5441 Woodstock Rd., Acworth, GA 30102, 770-924-4848, fax: 770-529-2278, e-mail:

GordonPonsford@AntiqueConservation.com, website: www.Antique Conservation.com. Conservation and restoration of metal and other materials. Appraisals.

Ball & Ball Antique Hardware Reproductions, 436 W. Lincoln Hwy., Exton, PA 19341, 800-257-3711, fax: 610-363-7639, website: www.balland ball.com. Reproduction furniture and cabinet hardware. Hardware, lighting, and metal items repaired and refinished. Lighting fixtures duplicated or custom-made. Fireplace accessories.

Bedlam Brass Restoration, 520 River Dr., Garfield, NJ 07026, 800-BEDLAM-1, fax: 800-BEDLAM-2, e-mail: sales@bedlam.biz, website: bedlam.biz. Restoration and refinishing of beds, lights, etc. New brass parts. Can fabricate custom architectural metal. Carpet hardware.

Brass & Copper Polishing Shop, 13 S. Carroll St., Frederick, MD 21701, 301-663-4240, fax: 301-694-9190, e-mail: shineit4u@aol.com. Brass, copper, and silver polishing, repair, and lacquering. Free brochure.

Brass & Silver Workshop, 758 St. Andrew Blvd., Charleston, SC 29407, 843-571-4342, fax: 843-571-7417. Restoration and conservation of all metals. Services include soldering, polishing, buffing, burnishing, dent removal, and monogram removal. Replacement of insulators in pots; replacement knife blades; replacement of ivory and hardwood pieces; reattachment of broken finials. Restoration of weighted items. Restoration to light fixtures.

Broken Art Restoration, 1841 W. Chicago Ave., Chicago, IL 60622, 312-226-8200 or 815-472-3900, fax: 815-472-3930. Restoration of metal and other materials. By appointment. Free brochure.

Cambridge Smithy, 140 Forge Dr., Cambridge, VT 05444, 802-644-5358, fax: 802-644-5651, e-mail: pkrusch@sover.net. Repair of antique weathervanes. Custom copper weathervanes. Repair and duplication of antique forged hardware.

Carl "Frank" Funes, 57 Maplewood Ave., Hempstead, NY 11550, 516-483-6712. Restoration of arms, armor, artifacts, metalwork, and more. Rust removed from weapons. Metal objects cleaned and restored.

China and Crystal Clinic, 1808 N. Scottsdale Rd., Tempe, AZ 85281, 480-945-5510 or 602-478-7857 or 602-568-9008 or 800-658-9197, fax: 480-945-1079, e-mail: jbenterprises2@earthlink.net, website: chinaandcrystalclinic.com. Restoration or conservation of bronze or metal figures and other objects. Appraisals.

Classic Restoration Co., 10800 Carnegie Ave., Cleveland, OH 44106, 216-791-9050, 10:00 A.M.–6:00 P.M. Metal repairs, refining, replating of hardware, light fixtures, antiques, silver hollowware and flatware. Missing parts reproduced. Lamps and lighting fixtures rebuilt and rewired.

Conant Custom Brass, 270 Pine St., PO Box 1523A, Burlington, VT 05402, 800-832-4482 or 802-658-4482, fax: 802-864-5914, e-mail: store @conantcustombrass.com, website: www.conantcustombrass.com. Brass and copper restoration and repair. Custom-made hardware and lighting. Glass shades. Check their website for tips on care and cleaning of brass.

Ephraim Forge, Inc., 8300 W. North Ave., Frankfort, IL 60423, 815-464-5656, e-mail: roger@ephraimforge.com, website: www.ephraimforge.com. Restoration and replication of old ironwork. Custom blacksmithing. Architectural ironwork, interior and exterior.

Fleming's Lighting & Silver Restoration, 24 Elm St., Cohasset Village, MA 02025, 781-383-0684. Brass, copper, pewter, and silver repair and replating. Restoration of lamps, chandeliers, and sconces. Free brochure.

George Basch Co., Inc., PO Box 188, Freeport, NY 11520, 516-378-8100, 9:00 A.M.–3:00 P.M. fax: 516-378-8140, e-mail: mark@nevrdull.com, website: www.nevrdull.com. Nevr-Dull, a brand of treated cotton wadding cloth, cleans and polishes metal. Can be used on aluminum, brass, chromium, copper, gold, nickel, pewter, silver, and zinc. Cleans automotive trim, marine accessories and hardware, tools, cookware, and silverware.

Hadley Restorations, 4667 Third St., La Mesa, CA 91941-5529, 619-462-5290, e-mail: cphadcearthlink.net, website: www.assoc-restorers.com. Restoration of metal and other materials. Free brochure.

Heimbolds, 2950 SW Persimmon Ln., Dunnellon, FL 34431, 352-465-0756. Art conservation restorers. Restoration of metals and other materials. Free estimates. Free brochure.

Heirloom Restorations, 267 Sherry Ln., East Peoria, IL 61611-9410, 309-694-0960, e-mail: heirloom-restorations@insightbb.com. Brass and copper cleaning and buffing.

Hiles Plating Co., Inc., 2028 Broadway, Kansas City, MO 64108, 816-421-6450, fax: 816-421-1132, e-mail: hilespl@aol.com, website: www.hilesplating.com. Repairs on sterling silver, silver plate, coin silver, pewter, copper, and brass. Plating in silver, gold, brass, nickel, and copper. Some prices given over the phone.

Kayne & Son Custom Hardware, Inc., 100 Daniel Ridge Rd., Candler, NC 28715, 828-667-8868 or 828-665-1988, fax: 828-665-8303, e-mail: kayne-hdwe@earthlink.net, website: customforgedhardware.com. Repair, restoration, refinishing, and reproduction of hardware, etc. Custom-forged hardware and cast brass or bronze reproductions. Tools for blacksmiths, metalsmiths, and collectors: anvils, hammers, tongs, swages, etc. Catalogs available, $5.

Kingsmen Antique Restoration Inc., 19 Passamore Ave., Unit 28, Scarborough, ON Canada M1V 4T5, 416-291-8939, fax: 416-291-8939, e-mail: kingsmen@sprint.ca. Restoration of bronze, pewter, brass, white metal, cloisonné, and more. Service worldwide. Call for information on sending objects for estimates.

McBuffers, 1420 Dille Rd., Unit F, Euclid, OH 44117, 216-486-6696, fax: 216-

486-4152. Metal finishing, repair, and replating: brass, copper, nickel, chrome, silver, and gold. Cleaning, buffing, and polishing. Brass beds, fireplace equipment, lamps, chandeliers, and silverware refinished. Complete lamp repair. Brochure.

Meeting House Furniture Restoration, 87 Waterman Hill, Quechee, VT 05059, 802-295-1309, fax: 802-296-5911. Brass polishing and repair.

Memphis Plating Works, 682 Madison Ave., Memphis, TN 38103, 901-526-3051. Repairing and refinishing of metals, including antique bronze or pot metal statues, chandeliers, and lamps. Refinishing of door and window hardware in old houses; refinishing chrome on antique and show cars.

Mike's Antiquary, 305 S. Main, PO Box 229, Almont, MI 48003, 810-798-3599, Mon.–Fri. 10:00 A.M.–6:00 P.M., Sat. 10:00 A.M.–2:00 P.M., fax: 810-798-2042 call first, e-mail: jamm@ees.eesc.com. Metal polishing; silvering. Lamp restorations. Serving eastern U.S. Call for availability.

Mueller Kaiser Plating Co., Hampton Ave., St. Louis, MO 63109, 314-832-3553, e-mail: tmsk9111@yahoo.com, website: www.Mueller-Kaiser Plating.com. Restoration, repair, and plating of church metalware and religious ware: chalices, altar appointments, candelabra, sanctuary lamps, etc. Restoration, repair, and plating of tea sets, flatware, lamps, and antiques in gold, silver, brass, bronze, and copper. Custom, antique, and ecclesiastical finishes; polishing; parts made. Free brochure.

New England Country Silver, Inc., 25859 Wellington Rd., Crisfield, MD 21817, 410-968-3060, 9:00 A.M.–3:00 P.M. fax: 410-968-2810, e-mail: necsilver@aol.com, website: www.silverrestoring.com. Complete restoration service for silver plate, sterling silver, copper, brass, and pewter. Missing parts duplicated. New stainless knife blades, combs, brushes, and mirrors. Velvet backing for picture frames. Silver, gold, and copper restoring. Engraving. Send merchandise insured mail or UPS. Free estimates. Free brochure.

Newmans Ltd., 51 Farewell St., Newport, RI 02840, 401-846-4784, e-mail: newmansltd@cox.net, website: www.newmansltd.com. Conservation and restoration of fine metal objects.

Oexning Silversmiths, 320 Hwy. 197 S., Bakersville, NC 28705, 828-688-9998 or 800-332-6857, fax: 828-688-9976, e-mail: oexning@aol.com, website: www.oexningsilversmiths.com. Silver restoration, replating, and repair. Sterling, pewter, brass, and copper refinishing; copper plating, gold plating. Dent removal. Missing parts cast, including feet, handles, and ornate work. New brushes and combs; steel blades, meat forks, knife sharpeners, nail sets, letter openers. New insulators for coffee sets.

Old and Elegant Distributing, 10203 Main Street Ln., Bellevue, WA 98004, 425-455-4660, fax: 425-455-0203. Custom metal refinishing and restoration. Cabinet and door hardware replication. Custom faucet and bath fixture design. Architectural wood and iron.

Orum Silver Co., Inc., 51 S. Vine St., Meriden, CT 06450-0805, 203-237-3037, fax: 203-237-3037, e-mail: orum.silver@snet.net, website: orumsilver.com. Repairing and replating of old silver and antiques. Restoration of brass, copper, and pewter; lighting fixtures and door and cabinet hardware. Gold, silver, nickel, copper, brass, and chrome plating. Brushes, combs, and mirrors for dresser sets. Restoration of church goods, chalices, Bible stands, etc. Free brochure.

Patrick J. Gill & Sons, 9 Fowle St., Woburn, MA 01801, 781-933-3275, fax: 781-933-3751, e-mail: joe@patrickgillco.com, website: patrickgill co.com. Metal repair, refinishing, and replating. Flatware, hollowware, dresser sets, fireplace tools and andirons, door hardware, chandeliers, plumbing fixtures, and other metal objects replated. Repair of broken or damaged parts, knife blades replaced. Jewelry repaired and restored, silver plate or gold plate.

Peninsula Plating Works, 1083 Americas, San Carlos, CA 94070, 650-326-7825, fax: 650-593-2650. Repairing, polishing, and plating of silver, brass, copper, bronze, pewter, and tin items. Repair of silver flatware, hollowware, brass and copper items; tinplating of pots. Free brochure.

Poor Richard's Restoration & Preservation Studio Workshop, 101 Walnut St., Montclair, NJ 07042, 973-783-5333, fax: 973-744-1939, e-mail: jrickford@webtv.com, website: www.rickford.com. Restoration, conservation, preservation, and archival services. Fine and decorative art, brass, jewelry, silver, and other objects. Restoration of family memorabilia and keepsakes. By appointment, Tues.–Fri. noon–5:00 P.M., Sat. noon–3:00 P.M.

R.J. Pattern Services, c/o R.J. Hoerr, 1212 W. Detroit St., New Buffalo, MI 49117, 616-469-7538, fax: 616-469-8554, e-mail: mhoerr@starband.net. Cast iron, aluminum, and brass castings. Wood and plastic (foundry) patterns and models. Antique stove and range replacement parts. Classic gas range knobs, dials, and handles. Castings for antique tractor restoration. Antique toy and salesman sample stove restoration.

Remember When Restoration, 5545 Celestial Rd., Addison, TX 75254, 972-788-1411, fax: 972-385-0779, e-mail: mike@rememwhen.com, website: www.rememwhen.com. Restoration and preservation of vintage metal collectibles, specializing in iron, cast iron, steel, aluminum, galvanized, brass, copper, tin, stainless steel and corrugated, stamped, rolled, pressed and pot metal. "Repair" and "Restoration" are two different types of services. "Repair" fixes something that is broken, missing or inoperable. "Restoration" involves a complete renewal of a piece so it closely resembles its original factory appearance. As a rule, does not accept items for repair only. Call, fax, or e-mail a description of the piece to be restored.

Restoration & Design Studio, 249 E. 77th St., New York, NY 10021, 212-517-9742, fax: 212-517-9742. Repair and restoration of silver, all metals, ivory, and lighting fixtures. Ivory insulators for tea or coffee pots.

Retinning & Copper Repair, Inc., 560 Irvine Turner Blvd., Newark, NJ 07108, 973-848-0700, fax: 973-848-1070, website: www.retinning.com. Retinning and repair of antique copper cookware. Restoration of brass beds, chandeliers, lighting fixtures, fireplace equipment, and other metal items.

Richford's Restoration, 147 Michigan Ave., Daytona Beach, FL 32114, 386-239-0939, fax: 386-252-1700, e-mail: srich4d@bellsouth.net. Pot metal repair.

Riverwalk Lighting, 401 S. Main St., Naperville, IL 60540, 630-357-0200, e-mail: info@enlighteninc.com, website: www.riverwalklighting.com. Replating, polishing, and lacquering metal items, including lamps, fixtures, architectural hardware, copper boilers, and fire extinguishers. Nickel, brass, or copper plating.

Robben Restoration, 5628 Cheviot Rd., Cincinnati, OH 45247, 877-257-0596 or 513-741-3619, e-mail: RRsilver1@aol.com. Metal restoration, specializing in silver repair, but offers a complete line of restoration in all metals: gold, bronze, copper, pewter, lead, and brass. Fabrication, plating, soldering, dent removal, part replacement, etc. Wicker handle replacements, blade replacements, hand-carved ebony and ivory insulators and handles. Dresser sets restored. Gold, silver, and brass plate lamp restoration. Free brochure.

Thome Silversmiths, 49 W. 37th St., 4th Floor, New York, NY 10018, 212-764-5426 or 570-426-7480, fax: 212-391-8215 or 570-426-7481, e-mail: robert378@cs.com. Restoration of objects of art and Judaica. Silver, gold, copper, brass, and pewter repaired. Jewelry boxes relined; velvet backs for picture frames. Brass and copper polishing and lacquering. Gold and silver plating. Cleaning and polishing of flatware and hollowware; hand engraving.

Tindell's Restoration, 825 Sandburg Pl., Nashville, TN 37214, 615-885-1029, fax: 615-391-0712, e-mail: info@ATindellsRestorationSchools.com, website: www.TindellsRestorationSchools.com. Restoration services, seminars, training, and products. Metal restoration and more. Appraisals. Free brochure.

Vermont Plating, Inc., 113 S. Main St., Rutland, VT 05701, 802-775-5759, fax: 802-775-5759. Cleaning, polishing, and plating of copper, nickel, and chrome.

WTC Associates, Inc., 2532 Regency Rd., Lexington, KY 40503, 859-278-4171, fax: 859-277-5720. Sterling silver repairs, including replacement of missing parts. Silver plating; silver plate and sterling repairs; gold plating and gold leaf; mirrors resilvered; clock repair; missing parts reproduced. Diamonds and emeralds replaced. Hand engraving.

Zophy's Fine Silver Plating, 4702 Park St., Box 10, Peterboro, NY 13134, 315-
684-3062, fax: 315-684-3494. Silver plating. Copper, brass, sterling,
pewter. Mon.-Fri. 7:00 A.M.–3:00 P.M.

•→ FOR MIRRORS, SEE FRAMES

MILITARY MEMORABILIA

Collectors of military memorabilia search for everything from toy
soldiers to working guns. Many of these souvenirs are dangerous,
and any gun, hand grenade, bullets, or other military object that
might hold explosives should be checked by local police or other
experts. If you have children in a home with military memorabilia,
be sure the guns and knives are safely locked up. Old guns that are
kept for display should have the barrels filled so it is impossible to
accidentally discharge the guns. Old rifles may be unsafe to shoot,
and often even safe antique guns have a recoil that will surprise the
inexperienced.

Never attempt to sell firearms, swords, dangerous war souvenirs,
or other weapons before checking with local police about your city
and state laws. The laws concerning the sale of guns are very strict.
You could be subject to a fine or jail sentence, or even be held
responsible for any death caused by a gun you sold illegally. Don't
sell or trade firearms or weapons to friends or other collectors before
you know the law.

The safest way to dispose of a gun, rifle, or perhaps an eighteenth-
century blunderbuss is to have it auctioned or sold by a reputable
firearms dealer. They will be listed in the Yellow Pages of the phone
book under "Guns" along with antique gun appraisers. It pays to
check on the value of any large collection before offering it for sale.

War souvenirs sell well, especially medals, books, historic documents, photographs, uniform caps and insignias, foreign flags,
small firearms, and knives. Be very careful; some types of knives are
illegal and should not be sold as anything but collector's items.
Knife collecting includes everything from penknives to daggers,
regardless of their age. Don't try setting up a table at a garage sale
or flea market without knowing the law. Grenades, bullets, and
other explosive objects are dangerous, and many become unstable
with age. Never handle old explosives before you talk to the local
bomb squad. It is amazing how often an old box of souvenirs has a
dangerous grenade in it. Never let children near any of these items.

There are many serious collectors of firearms and weapons. Early swords, especially decorated Japanese ceremonial pieces, military dress uniform swords, or any good sword made before 1850, command high prices. Kentucky rifles, muskets, Civil War weapons, dueling pistols, and even World War I and II guns are in demand. Well-made military knives can also be sold to collectors of weapons.

The buyers for these items are not usually found at the average antiques show. Some flea markets have a few tables of dealers who specialize in war materials. Ask the collectors and dealers in your area who sell weapons. They can tell you about the clubs, shows, and auctions that are the best for you.

Once or twice a year some dealers travel from city to city looking for old Japanese swords and other weapons that might have been taken to the United States after World War II. They advertise and set up a buying office in a local hotel. Be sure you check on the value of your war souvenirs before you sell. Few Americans understand the great value of certain ceremonial swords. A local museum expert might be able to tell you the age or rarity of your pieces.

REPAIRS

Repairs to any sort of weapon should only be done by an expert. Many shops that sell modern firearms have staff members who can repair old guns. Other restorers can be located through the publications listed below. Because of the legal problems of shipping guns, repair work must be done locally.

Repairs on knives can be done by companies that repair or sell modern knives, or by specialists in military or hunting equipment.

PRICE BOOKS

Bowies, Big Knives, and the Best of Battle Blades, Bill Bagwell (Paladin Press, Boulder, CO, 2000).

Flayderman's Guide to Antique American Firearms, 8th edition, Norm Flayderman (Krause, Iola, WI, 1998).

Official Price Guide to Civil War Collectibles, 2nd edition, Richard Friz (House of Collectibles, New York, 1999).

Official Price Guide to Military Collectibles, 6th edition, Richard J. Austin (House of Collectibles, New York, 1998).

R.L. Wilson Price Guide to Gun Collecting, 2nd edition, R.L. Wilson (House of Collectibles, NY, 1999).

Standard Catalog of Military Firearms, 1870 to the Present: The Collector's Price & Reference Guide, Ned Schwing (Krause, Iola, WI, 2001).

CLUBS & THEIR PUBLICATIONS

Association of American Military Uniform Collectors (AAMUC), *Footlocker* (NL), PO Box 1876, Elyria, OH 44036, e-mail: AAMUCFL@aol.com, website: www.aamuc.org.

International Ammunition Association, Inc., *International Ammunition Association, Inc. Journal* (MAG), 631 Carlsbad Dr., Lincoln, NE 68510, e-mail: ammoangel@msn.com.

Japanese Sword Society of the United States, *Japanese Sword Society of the United States Newsletter* (NL), *Bulletin* (NL), PO Box 712, Breckenridge, TX 76424-0712, e-mail: tcford@texasisp.com, website: jssus.org.

Military Heraldry Society, *The Formation Sign* (NL), 77 Chiltern Gardens, Dawley, Telford, Shropshire TF4 2QH, UK.

Military Miniature Society of Illinois, *The Scabbard* (MAG), c/o Andy Hansen, 529 Burno Dr., Palatine, IL 60067, website: members.aol.com/ MMSI2K/newmmsipages/mmsimain.htm.

Military Transport Association of New Jersey, *Motor Pool Messenger* (NL), 12 Indian Head Rd., Morristown, NJ 07960, e-mail: MVehicle@aol.com, website: hometown.aol.com/MVehicle/home.htm (focused on restoring and operating historic military vehicles).

Military Vehicle Preservation Association, *Army Motors* (MAG), *Supply LIne* (NL), PO Box 520378, Independence, MO 64052-0378, website: www.mvpa.org.

Napoleonic Society of America, *Members Bulletin of the Napoleonic Society of America* (NL), 1115 Ponce de Leon Blvd., Clearwater, FL 33756, e-mail: staff@napoleonic-society.com, website: www.napoleonic-society.com.

National Knife Collectors Association, PO Box 21070, Chattanooga, TN 37424-0070, e-mail: info@nationalknife.org, website: www.national knife.org.

OTHER PUBLICATIONS

Airgun Ads (NP), Box 1795, Hamilton, MT 59840, e-mail: airgunads @bitterroot.net.

Armourer Magazine (MAG), 1st Floor Adelphi Mill, Bollington, Cheshire SK10 5JB, UK, e-mail: editor@armourer.u-net.com, website: www.armourer.u-net.com.

Blade (MAG), 700 E. State St., Iola, WI 54990-0001, e-mail: info @krause.com, website: www.krause.com.

Camp Chase Gazette (MAG), PO Box 707, Marietta, OH 45750-0707, e-mail: info@campchase.com, website: www.campchase.com (magazine for reenactors).

Civil War Courier (NP), PO Box 625, Morristown, TN 37814, e-mail: cwc1861@lcs.net, website: www.civilwarcourier.com.

Civil War Lady Magazine (MAG), PO Box 351, Clarinda, IA 51632-0351.

Civil War News (NP), 234 Monarch Hill Rd., Tunbridge, CT 05077, e-mail: mail@civilwarnews.com, website: www.civilwarnews.com.

Gun List (NP), *Gun-Knife Show Calendar* (MAG), *Military Trader* (MAG), *Military Vehicles* (MAG), 700 E. State St., Iola, WI 54990-0001, e-mail: info@krause.com, website: www.krause.com.

Gun Report (MAG), PO Box 38, Aledo, IL 61231-0038.

Knife World (NP), PO Box 3395, Knoxville, TN 37927, e-mail: knifepub @knifeworld.com, website: www.knifeworld.com.

Man at Arms (MAG), PO Box 460, Lincoln, RI 02865, e-mail: stuart @manatarmsbooks.com, website: www.manatarmsbooks.com.

Military Artifact (NL), PO Box 33071, Ottawa, ON K2C 3Y9, Canada, e-mail: sales@servicepub.com, website: www.servicepub.com (Canada and the British Empire, 1854–1953).

Military Images Magazine (MAG), PO Box 2391, Southeastern, PA 19399-2391, e-mail: milimage@yahoo.com, website: civilwar-photos.com.

North South Trader's Civil War Magazine (MAG), PO Drawer 631, Orange, VA 22960, e-mail: info@nstcivilwar.com, website: www.nstcivilwar.com.

Rimfire & Airgun (MAG), PO Box 2021, Benton, AR 72018, website: usairgun.com.

ARCHIVES & MUSEUMS

The Center of Military History, 103 3rd Ave., Fort McNair, Washington, DC 20319-5058, website: www.army.mil/cmh-pg. Online archives.

The Civil War Library and Museum, 1805 Pine St. Philadelphia, PA 19103, 215-735-8196, website: www.netreach.net/~cwlm.

The National D-Day Museum, 945 Magazine St., New Orleans, LA 70130, 504-527-6012, fax: 504-527-6088, website: www.ddaymuseum.org.

National Museum of Civil War Medicine, PO Box 470, Frederick, MD 21705, 301-695-1864, fax: 301-695-6823, website: www.civilwarmed.org.

National Museum of Naval Aviation, 1750 Radford Blvd., Suite C, N.A.S., Pensacola, FL 32508, 850-542-3604 or 850-453-2389, fax: 850-452-3296, website: www.naval-air.org.

United States Air Force Museum, 2601 E Street, Wright-Patterson AFB, OH 45433-7609, website: www.wpafb.af.mil/mua.htm. Research requests must be sent by regular mail. Phone calls are not accepted.

APPRAISERS

Many of the auctions and repair services listed in this section will also do appraisals. *See also* the general list of "Appraisal Groups," page 483.

O.C. Young, PO Box 51167, Denton, TX 76210, 940-382-1559, fax: 940-381-1075, e-mail: ocy@earthlink.net, website: www.ocyoung.com. Appraisals of antique American firearms and some European antique firearms.

AUCTIONS

➻ SEE ALSO "SELLING THROUGH AUCTION HOUSES," PAGE 485.

AAG International, 1266-B Sans Souci Pkwy., Wilkes-Barre, PA 18702, 570-822-5300, fax: 570-822-9992, e-mail: info@aagmilitaria.com, website: www.aag-militaria.com. Antique militaria, including memorabilia from World War I, World War II, and Vietnam. Mail, phone, and fax bids accepted. Buyer's premium 18%. Prices realized available after auction. Appraisals.

Greg Martin Auctions, 660 Third St., Suite 100, San Francisco, CA 94107, 415-522-5708, fax: 415-522-5706, e-mail: info@gmartin-auctions.com, website: www.gmartin-auctions.com. Auctions of fine arms and armor, historical memorabilia. Phone and Internet bids accepted. Buyer's premium 12%. Catalog $40. Prices realized mailed and available on website after auction. Appraisals.

Mohawk Arms, Inc., PO Box 157, Bouckville NY 13310, 315-893-7888 or 315-893-7889, fax: 315-893-7707, e-mail: mohawk@militaryrelics.com, website: www.militaryrelics.com. Militaria, all periods. Mail and phone bids accepted. Buyer's premium varies depending on value of item. Catalog $19.50 in U.S. and Canada; yearly subscription, 2 catalogs, $39. Prices realized mailed after auction. Appraisals.

Roger S. Steffen Historical Militaria, 14 Murnan Rd., Cold Spring, KY 41076, 859-431-4499, fax: 859-431-3113, website: steffensmilitaria.com. Militaria auctions. Mail and phone bids accepted. Buyer's premium 18%. Catalog $9; $35 for next 4 catalogs. Prices realized mailed after auction. Appraisals.

William "Pete" Harvey Gun Auctions, PO Box 280, Cataumet, MA 02534, 508-548-0660, fax: 508-457-0660, website: www.firearmsauctions.com. Firearm auctions only. Mail and phone bids accepted. Buyer's premium 10%. Prices realized mailed after auction. Catalog $35. U.S. firearms appraised.

REPAIRS, PARTS & SUPPLIES

➻ SEE ALSO "CONSERVATORS & RESTORERS," PAGE 520.

Artisans of the Valley, 103 Corrine Dr., Pennington, NJ 08534, 609-637-0450, fax: 609-637-0452, e-mail: woodworkers@artisansofthevalley.com, website: www.artisansofthevalley.com. Specializes in conservation and restoration of firearms, swords, and other military relics. Free catalog.

Carl "Frank" Funes, 57 Maplewood Ave., Hempstead, NY 11550, 516-483-6712. Restoration of arms, armor, artifacts, metalwork, and more. Rust removed from weapons. Metal objects cleaned and restored.

➻ MINIATURES, SEE DOLLHOUSES, DOLLS, TOYS
➻ MIRRORS, SEE FRAMES
➻ MONEY, SEE NUMISMATIC COLLECTIBLES

MOVIE MEMORABILIA

Movie memorabilia is a large field, ranging from movie films, soundtrack albums, comic materials, toys, and dolls representing characters in movies to ceramics commemorating movie characters and related events. It also includes movie posters, lobby cards, press kits, movie stills, costumes, and memorabilia from the stars, such as Joan Crawford's false eyelashes or Judy Garland's ruby slippers.

All this material is rightly considered movie memorabilia and can be found in any shop or show. Specialists should be familiar with the publications and shows that are devoted exclusively to movies. Special groups, like *Star Trek* enthusiasts or fan clubs of deceased stars, hold regular conventions and meetings, exchanging information and memorabilia. Anything pertaining to **GONE WITH THE WIND, MARILYN MONROE, JUDY GARLAND, ELVIS PRESLEY,** or **JAMES DEAN** has added value.

Anything related to the movie business is in high demand: old props, costumes, lobby cards, still photographs, scripts, publicity packets, promotional giveaways, signs, objects (especially clothing) owned by a star, and, of course, the movies themselves. Even scrapbooks filled with newspaper clippings or movie fan magazines are bought and sold. Although much movie memorabilia is sold through flea markets, antiques shows, and even auctions, these do not represent the major market. Several special newspapers are devoted to buying and selling movie material.

Special shows are held during the year, especially in California. There are also several mail auctions and many Internet sites selling movie material. Fan clubs want appropriate items. Try to find the movie collectors in your area. If you have a tie that belonged to John Wayne, you can find the proper fan club and contact the members. To locate the star or fan club, look in *The Address Book: How to Reach Anyone Who Is Anyone* by Michael Levine at your library or use an Internet search engine.

It is important to verify the authenticity of your movie memorabilia. Many autographs were not originally signed by the stars. Pictures were often signed by someone on the staff.

REPAIR

Because movie memorabilia is so recent and so abundant, it does not pay to repair any but the greatest rarities. Movie film is a special consideration. The old nitrate film is combustible and dangerous to store and should be copied. Contact the National Center for Film and Video Preservation to learn what to do with old nitrate film. You may phone the center at 323-856-7637, or write to: National Center for Film and Video Preservation, American Film Institute, 2021 N. Western Ave., Los Angeles, CA 90027.

➥ SEE ALSO CELEBRITY MEMORABILIA, COMIC ART, PAPER COLLECTIBLES, PHOTOGRAPHY, TOYS

REFERENCE BOOKS

The Address Book: How to Reach Anyone Who Is Anyone, 10th edition, Michael Levine (Perigee Books, East Rutherford, NJ, 2001).

Collecting Movie Posters: An Illustrated Reference Guide to Movie Art-Posters, Press Kits, and Lobby Cards, Edwin E. and Susan T. Poole (McFarland & Co., Jefferson, NC, 2001).

Illustrated History of Movies through Posters, 18 volumes, Bruce Hershenson (306 Washington Avenue, West Plains, MO 65775, 1990-2001).

PRICE BOOKS

Collecting Japanese Movie Monsters, Dana Cain (Antique Trader Books, Dubuque, IA, 1998).

Collecting Monsters of Film and TV, Dana Cain (Krause, Iola, WI, 1997).

The Galaxy's Greatest Star Wars Collectibles Price Guide, Stuart W. Wells III (Antique Trader Books, Dubuque, IA, 1998).

Miller's Movie Collectibles, Rudy & Barbara Franchi (Miller's Publications, London, 2002).

An Unauthorized Guide to Godzilla Collectibles, Sean Linkenback (Schiffer, Atglen, PA, 1998).

A Universe of Star Wars Collectibles, 2nd edition, Stuart W. Wells III. (Krause, Iola, WI, 2002).

CLUBS &THEIR PUBLICATIONS

Drive-In Theatre Fanatic Fan Club, *Drive-In Theatre Fanatic Fan Club* (NL), PO Box 18063, Baltimore, MD 21220-0163, e-mail: drivein@erols.com, website: www.drive-in.net/fanclub.htm.

The Movie Machine Society, *Sixteen Frames* (MAG), PO Box 94, Oley, PA 19547, e-mail: teclight@yahoo.com.

Three Stooges Fan Club Inc., *Three Stooges Journal* (NL), PO Box 747, Gwynedd Valley, PA 19437, e-mail: garystooge@aol.com.

Westerns & Serials Fan Club, *Westerns & Serials* (MAG), 527 S. Front St., Mankato, MN 56001, e-mail: kietzer@mctcnet.net, website: www.angelfire.com/biz2/normankietzerpubs.

OTHER PUBLICATIONS

Big Reel (NP), 700 E. State St., Iola, WI 54990, e-mail: info@krause.com, website: www.krause.com.

Classic Images (NP), *Films of the Golden Age* (NP), 301 E. 3rd St., Muscatine, IA 52761, e-mail: classicimages@classicimages.com, website: www.classicimages.com.

Cliffhanger (MAG), 104 Chestnut Wood Dr., Waynesville, NC 28786-6514 (chapter play serials).

Movie Collector's World (NP), PO Box 309, Fraser, MI 48026, e-mail: mcw@mcwonline.com, website: www.mcwonline.com.

Star Wars Insider (MAG), Wizards of the Coast, PO Box 707, Renton, WA 98057, e-mail: swfan@wizards.com, website: swfan.wizards.com.

ARCHIVES & MUSEUMS

American Film Institute, PO Box 27999, 2021 N. Western Ave., Los Angeles, CA 90027, 323-856-7600, fax: 323-467-4578, website: www.afi.com.

AUCTIONS

➻ **SEE ALSO "SELLING THROUGH AUCTION HOUSES," PAGE 485.**

Just Kids Nostalgia, 310 New York Ave., Huntington, NY 11743, 516-423-8449, fax: 631-423-4326, e-mail: info@justkidsnostalgia.com, website: www.justkidsnostalgia.com. Auctions of old toys, movie posters, TV and comic characters, advertising, sports, rock 'n' roll, and other pop culture memorabilia. Mail, phone, fax, and e-mail bids accepted. Prices realized mailed after auction and available on website.

Last Moving Picture Co., Kirtland Antique Mall, 10535 Chillicothe Rd., Kirtland, OH 44094, 440-256-3660, fax: 440-256-3431, e-mail: lastmo@aol.com, website: vintagefilmposters.com. Movie poster auctions. Mail, phone, and Internet bids accepted. Buyer's premium 15%. Catalog $10. Prices realized available on website after auction. Some appraisals.

MUSICAL INSTRUMENTS

Everyone has heard of the Stradivarius violin that sold for over $1 million. Unfortunately, very few people know that 99.99 percent of the violins labeled Stradivarius are nineteenth- or twentieth-century versions and are worth very little. Some old musical instruments have great value, but most of them should be priced as secondhand instruments to be used by young musicians. If you have an old violin or other musical instrument, the best way to start determining the value is to take it to a friend who is a competent musician. Don't forget that even the bow might be of value. Very good bows can sell for thousands of dollars. You might price a new violin and bow to get some idea of value. Anyone who plays the violin well will know if your violin is of good quality. If it seems good, take it to a local store that sells used musical instruments. They are listed in the Yellow Pages of the phone book. If it seems very good, you might try to contact a violin appraiser. This type of specialist is often listed in the phone book but is not found in every city. The only other way to sell old violins is through a local auction, through an ad in the newspaper, or even at a flea market. Few antiques dealers buy and sell average-quality musical instruments.

Collectible musical instruments are old, decorative, and often unusual in appearance. Some are no longer made or used but are often playable. These instruments might include a sarrusophone (used in marching bands from the 1860s to the 1920s) or an American harp-guitar (popular from 1800 to 1925). Banjos and mandolins with carvings and mother-of-pearl inlay appeal both to collectors who want something decorative to display and to musicians who are looking for instruments. Look at the construction of the instrument. Like fine furniture, it should be well made and have crisp detail. Inlays and carvings are often signs of quality. Collectors pay a premium for instruments in original condition and original cases, but musicians don't seem to mind restorations if it is a fine instrument that can be played.

Vintage electric guitars and keyboards are attracting attention, too. Look for the names of major manufacturers such as YAMAHA, HAMMOND, RICKENBACKER, GIBSON, SILVERTONE, FENDER, or EPIPHONE. Collectors are looking for novelty as well as performance. A metallic turquoise or flame-decaled guitar will probably sell for more than its traditional "fireglo" counterpart.

PIANOS

Because pianos are so large and difficult to move, they present special problems. Fine pianos with elaborately painted cases are very popular with decorators, especially for large apartments. The decorative value of the piano as a piece of furniture as well as the quality of the instrument are considered in determining the price. "Reproducing pianos," a special type of piano that plays automatically, bring high prices. Any top-quality piano will probably sell best at a well-advertised antiques auction. If there is no gallery nearby, it can be sold to a piano store to be resold. An average-quality piano can be sold at a house sale, through an ad in the papers, to a music store, or through an auction. The best method will depend on what is available in your area.

Square pianos, the 1880s type with rosewood case and heavy carved legs, are the most disappointing to sell. The square piano doesn't remain tuned very long. It is not a good instrument for a musician. Most of these pianos are finally sold for a few hundred dollars. The insides are removed and the case is remade into a desk.

Player pianos are wanted for entertainment. If your player piano works, it will sell quickly at a good price. The more attractive the case, the higher the price. Well-finished wood and stained-glass panels add to the price. If the piano does not play, have it checked by a piano restorer. It may not be salable because repairs are too expensive.

Small musical instruments, like harmonicas and kazoos, sell at flea markets for prices a little lower than the cost of new ones. Unusual designs, extra large or small examples, or other odd features will raise the price.

MUSIC BOXES

All music boxes, from the early cylinder types with bells and dancing figures to a ten-year-old musical powder box, are in demand. The Kovelism "If it moves or makes noise, it has value" has double meaning here. However, age, rarity, size, additional features, and the quality of the box are important in pricing it for sale. The nineteenth-century boxes that play using cylinders, teeth, and combs have values from hundreds to thousands of dollars. The REGINA boxes that play flat, round, metal disks are also high priced and easy to sell. Go to a serious music box collector (your town may have an active chapter of the Musical Box Society International) or to your library. There are many books about music boxes that will help you decide if yours is average or special. Various price books and the Internet site www.Kovels.com also price many of the boxes.

Look for anything that moves, like bells or dancers, a selection of tunes, or an elaborate case. Some boxes play paper "rolls." These are old and, if working, should sell well. Very large cylinder boxes (over three feet long) are usually of top quality. Small boxes, twelve inches long or less, were usually made for tourists and often were not as well made. Musical, animated birds are always popular with buyers. Any moving bird sells for hundreds of dollars. Twentieth-century music boxes include carved wooden figures that turn their heads and whistle tunes, musical powder boxes and jewelry cases, even carved chairs that play when you sit on them. As we said, anything that moves and makes noise or music is popular with collectors.

REPAIR

Music collectibles range from musical instruments to reproducing pianos. The value of each of these items is in the music it makes, so each piece must be in good working condition. Repairs of mechanical music-making machines are slow. Many of the restorers have two- and three-year waiting lists. If you can fix this type of antique yourself, you can usually make good buys. Be very careful if you plan to buy a machine that needs repairs that you can't do yourself.

All music boxes are delicate, intricate mechanisms that require care. Don't try to repair a music box unless you're an expert—it's a job for a professional. Restorers and parts can be found, but they are rare and expensive. You may be lucky enough to find a local music box devotee who restores or contact the Musical Box Society International for information (see club list that follows). Other restorers are listed here, but some have advised us that they are very busy and repairs may take years.

Minor repairs of instruments are possible in some cities through dealers or service shops listed in the Yellow Pages under "Musical Instruments—Repairing."

➦ SHEET MUSIC, SEE PAPER COLLECTIBLES

BOOKS ON REPAIR

The American Reed Organ and the Harmonium: A Treatise on Its History, Restoration and Tuning, Robert F. Gellerman (Vestal Press, Vestal, NY, 1997).

Piano Care & Restoration, Eric Smith (Tab Books, Blue Ridge Summit, PA 17214, 1982).

Piano Servicing, Tuning and Rebuilding, Arthur A. Reblitz (Vestal Press, Vestal, NY, 1993).

Player Piano Servicing and Rebuilding, Arthur Reblitz (Vestal Press, Vestal, NY, 1985).

Restoring and Collecting Antique Reed Organs, Horton Presley (Vestal Press, Vestal, NY, 1977).

REFERENCE BOOKS

Encyclopedia of Automatic Musical Instruments, Q. David Bowers (Vestal Press, Vestal, NY, 1972).

Treasures of Mechanical Music, Arthur A. Reblitz and Q. David Bowers (Vestal Press, Vestal, NY, 1981).

These books will help you date a guitar, piano, or organ and learn where it was made:

Gellerman's International Reed Organ Atlas, Robert R. Gellerman (Vestal Press, Vestal, NY, 1985).

Gruhn's Guide to Vintage Guitars, 2nd edition, George Gruhn and Walter Carter (Backbeat Books, San Francisco, 1999).

Pierce Piano Atlas, 10th edition, Bob Pierce (1880 Termino, Long Beach, CA 90815, 1996).

PRICE BOOKS

Antique Brass Wind Instruments, Peter H. Adams (Schiffer, Atglen, PA, 1998).

Blue Book of Electric Guitars, S.P. Fjestad, editor (Blue Book Publications, Minneapolis, 2001).

CLUBS & THEIR PUBLICATIONS

American Musical Instrument Society, *AMIS Journal* (MAG), c/o A-R Editions, Inc., 8551 Research Way, Suite 180, Middleton, WI 53562, e-mail: AMIS@AREditions.com, website: www.amis.org.

Automatic Musical Instrument Collectors Association, *AMICA Bulletin* (MAG), 919 Lantern Glow Trail, Dayton, OH 45431, e-mail: shazam@sonic.net, website: www.amica.org.

Harmonica Collectors International (HCI), *The Trumpet Call* (NL), PO Box 6081, Chesterfield, MO 63006, e-mail: hcrain@harleysharps.com, website: www.harleysharps.com.

Musical Box Society International, *Journal of Mechanical Music* (MAG), *MBSI News Bulletin* (MAG), New Member Registration, PO Box 551083, Indianapolis, IN 46205-5583, e-mail: mbsi@estreet.com, website: www.mbsi.org.

Reed Organ Society International, *ROS Quarterly* (MAG), 3575 State Hwy. 258 E, Wichita Falls, TX 76308-7037, e-mail: www.Reedsoc.org, website: sponsor.globalknowledge.nl/ros.

OTHER PUBLICATIONS

Vintage Guitar Magazine (MAG), PO Box 7301, Bismarck, ND 58501, e-mail: vguitar@vguitar.com, website: www.vintageguitar.com.

ARCHIVES & MUSEUMS

The Music House, 7377 U.S. 31 N., Box 297, Acme, MI 49610, 231-938-9300, fax: 231-938-3650, website: musichouse.org.

National Music Museum, University of South Dakota, 414 East Clark St., Vermillion, SD 57069-2390, 605-677-5306, website: www.usd.edu/smm.

APPRAISERS

Many of the repair services listed in this section will also do appraisals.

•➤ SEE ALSO THE GENERAL LIST OF "APPRAISAL GROUPS," PAGE 483.

AUCTIONS

•➤ SEE ALSO "SELLING THROUGH AUCTION HOUSES," PAGE 485.

Joel Markowitz, Box 10, Old Bethpage, NY 11804, 516-249-9405 phone/ fax, e-mail: smctr@sheetmusiccenter.com, website: www.sheetmusic center.com. Mail order auctions of sheet music. Mail, phone, and e-mail bids accepted. No buyer's premium. Catalog on website.

REPAIRS, PARTS & SUPPLIES

•➤ SEE ALSO "CONSERVATORS & RESTORERS," PAGE 520.

Another Time Restorations, PO Box 42013, Portland, OR 97242-0013, 503- 656-9757. Repair and restoration of player pianos, reed organs, orchestrions, and automatic musical instruments.

Antique Music Box Restoration, 1825 Placentia Ave., Costa Mesa, CA 92627, 949-548-1542, 8:00 A.M.–5:30 P.M., e-mail: MusicBox@Email.com. Restoration and historical research on antique music boxes. They do not repair modern, inexpensive, or toy musical pieces.

Atlanta Grand Pianos, 1182 Grimes Bridge Rd., Roswell, GA 30075, 770- 594-8000, fax: 770-587-0516, e-mail: agpianos@bellsouth.net, website: www.atlantagrandpianos.com. Custom rebuilding services.

Beehive Reed Organ Service, 11 Oak St., Suite 3, Alfred, ME 04002-0041, 207-324-0990, e-mail: beehive@cybertours.com. Reed organs, harmoniums, melodeons repair and rebuilding, including case-work refinishing.

Brady Sales and Restorations, 2725 E. 56th St., Indianapolis, IN 46220, 317- 259-4307, fax: 317-259-4340, e-mail: jlbrady@mindspring.com, website: www.bradymusicboxes.com. Restoration of antique self-playing instruments, including both disc and cylinder music boxes. Music box cases refinished.

Chet Ramsay Antiques, 2460 Strasburg Rd., Coatesville, PA 19320-4339, 610-384-0514, 10:00 A.M.–6:00 P.M. Restoration of all types and makes of antique music boxes and phonographs, 1912 and older. Shop and showroom open by appointment.

DB Musical Restorations, 75 Waters Edge Ln., Newnan, GA 30263, 770-253- 1903, fax: 770-253-7610, e-mail: cbeck93435@aol.com. Restoration of antique cylinder and disc music boxes. Comb work, cylinder repinning, gear work, governors repaired or replaced, parts fabrication. Worldwide. Call to discuss before shipping. Free brochure.

Great Canadian Nickelodeon Co. Ltd., RR #4, Mount Forest, ON N0G

2L0, Canada, 519-323-3582, Mon.–Sat. 9:00 A.M.–9:00 P.M., e-mail: RonaldS715@aol.com, website: members.aol.com/tgcnc. Complete restoration or repairs of all automated music machines: player pianos, pipe organs, monkey organs, music boxes, nickelodeons, orchestrions, jukeboxes, band and fairground organs, carousel organs, etc. Custom-built parts. Brochure.

Inzer Pianos, Inc., 2473 Canton Rd., Marietta, GA 30066, 770-422-2664, Mon.–Fri. 10:00 A.M.–5:00 P.M., Sat. 10:00 A.M.–3:00 P.M. Repair and restoration of antique pianos, player pianos, and pump organs. Parts and supplies. Free catalog.

Johnson Music, 117 Colonels Tr., PO Box 615, Mt. Airy, NC 27030, 336-320-2212. Antique pump organs rebuilt, restored, and refinished. Parts and restoration supplies, including original reeds, bellows cloth, springs, stop knobs, pedal straps, keys, and "how-to" books and tapes on pump organ restoration.

K.R. Powers Antique Music Boxes, 28 Alton Circle, Rogers, AR 72756, 479-636-2643. Cylinder and disc music box restoration.

Kromer Mechanical Musical Instruments, 53 Louella Ct., Wayne, PA 19087-3527, 610-687-0172. Carousel band organs, piano nickelodeons, antique reed organs, and calliopes restored. New carousel organs built; old organs rebuilt. Music rolls; CDs and cassettes of carousel and circus music. Send SASE with two first-class stamps for information.

The Magic Barn, Dawson's Antiques, 516 N. Ave. B, Washington, IA 52353, 319-653-5043, e-mail: radio4me@hotmail.com. Restoration of mechanical music, including reed organs, organettes, player pianos, band organs, phonographs, and antique radios.

The Musical Wonder House & The Merry Music Box, Attention: Repairs, 18 High St., PO Box 604, Wiscasset, ME 04578, 207-882-7163, fax: 207-882-6373, e-mail: musicbox@musicalwonderhouse.com, website: www.musicalwonderhouse.com. Repair and restoration of antique and contemporary music boxes, spring-wound phonographs, singing birds, and whistling figures. Musical box combs tuned and enhanced. The Musical Wonder House is a museum of mechanical musical instruments, open Memorial Day weekend through October 15. Appraisals. Mail order all year. Brochure $1.

New York Piano Center, 121 W. 19th St., New York, NY 10011, 212-229-2600, fax: 212-229-2668, e-mail: service@nypiano.com. website: www.newyorkpianocenter.com. Restoration of contemporary and antique pianos. Appraisals. Mon.–Fri. 8:30 A.M.–5:30 P.M., Sat. 10:00 A.M.–4:00 P.M., and by appointment.

Panchronia Antiquities, PO Box 400, Canastota, NY 13032-0400, 315-761-5569, e-mail: musicbox@sover.net. Restoration of antique musical boxes. Restoration supplies, including tools and specialty products. Recordings, videos, and books on all types of antique automatic musical machines. Restoration supply catalog $6; audio/book catalog $3.50.

Phoenix Reed Organ Resurrection, 593 Phoenix Way, Townshend, VT 05353, 802-365-7011, e-mail: Ned_Phoenix@PhoenixReedOrgans.com, website: PhoenixReedOrgans.com. Complete restoration of reed organs worldwide. All types, sizes, makes, and models, especially two-manual-with-pedal reed organs. Specializing in replacement reeds and tuning to A440. Case work and refinishing available during restoration. Online catalog of reed organs for sale, as well as stools, benches, pipetops, and more. Database of Estey serial numbers and dates. Reed organ books. Appraisals: ask about reed organ donor benefits. Your gift of a restored and appraised reed organ benefits you and a nonprofit of your choice.

Player Piano Co., Inc., 704 E. Douglas, Wichita, KS 67202, 316-263-3241, Mon.–Thurs. 8:00 A.M.–4:30 P.M., fax: 316-263-5480. Player piano parts and restoration supplies. Tubing, bellows cloth, and hardware for all types of roll-operated instruments or any bellows-operated instrument. White or yellowed key-tops, felts, fall-board decals, tuners' tools, and specialized parts. Orchestrion, reed organ, and melodeon parts. Manual reprints, books, and music rolls. Free catalog.

Pump and Pipe Shop, 7945 Kraft Ave., Caledonia, MI 49316, 616-891-8743. Reed pump organs restoration and information.

Randolph Herr, 111-07 77th Ave., Forest Hills, NY 11375, 718-520-1443, e-mail: aeolian@nyc.rr.com. Player pianos and other automatic music items repaired. Free brochure.

Tani Engineering, The Antique Nook, Inc., 6226 Waterloo, Box 338. Atwater, OH 44201, 330-947-2268 or 330-325-0645. Custom-made mainsprings for music boxes. Repairs and cuts gears. Custom machine work.

➨ **MUSIC BOXES, SEE MUSICAL INSTRUMENTS**

NUMISMATIC COLLECTIBLES

Do you remember going to the bank for rolls of pennies so you could search for the rare dates? Have you kept a box of foreign coins given to you by traveling relatives? Collections of this sort, even those started by Grandpa as a boy, have less value than many people imagine because of the poor condition of the coins. However, you can never be sure there is not a treasure hiding among the ordinary, so you must examine coin collections carefully.

If you have inherited a properly stored, serious collection of currency in good to mint condition, you have even more reason to be careful about selling. We remember appraising an estate that had a library full of coin books. We asked about the coins, and the almost unbelievable answer was: "Oh, there were lots of old coins. I took them to the bank and deposited them into a savings account." That is exactly the wrong thing to do.

You will find many books in the public library about coin and paper currency values and the buying and selling of them. The books use the term "numismatic," meaning anything related to currency. The prices given are the going retail prices, not what you would get for your coins from a dealer, who would probably offer half or less of the listed price. The books picture coins and indicate prices for coins in all grades or conditions. They refer to coins in proof (PRF), uncirculated (UNC or MS), extremely fine (EF or EX), very fine (VF), fine (F), very good (VG), good (G), or poor (PR) condition. Each book has a slightly different code. Beware! It takes an expert to know the condition of a coin. All you can do is learn the range of prices for your coin if it seems to be in excellent condition. That means it has the original bright, shiny finish of a new coin, no scratches, no nicks, no overall wear.

Never clean a coin! That lowers the value. The bright finish must be original. Remember, an old coin or bill is almost always worth at least the face value. Check the meltdown value of silver coins. When silver prices were high in the 1970s, coins were worth much more than face value or even coin collectors' values. Many coins in poor condition were melted and sold as silver. But few new coins have silver today.

The most obvious place to sell coins is to a coin dealer. There is a listing for "Coin Dealers" in the Yellow Pages of the telephone book, which will also list any stores that sell coins. Anyone who sells coins buys coins. Auctioneers sell good-quality coins and paper currency; local antiques auction galleries may have special sales for numismatic items or include them in regular sales; and there are also some nationally known numismatic auction houses. Some are listed later in this chapter and others can be found through the advertisements in any of the numismatic publications.

If you send your coins to be auctioned, be sure to ask who pays for insurance for the coins while at the gallery, photography of coins for the catalog, and any advertising. You must pay a fee to the auctioneer, and you should ask what percentage of the sale price that will be, get a signed contract or agreement, and send the coins by insured mail and with a full inventory list. Before you do anything, check the references of the auction house. Ask how long it will be before you are paid and be sure the payment from the buyer is kept in escrow for you by the auction house.

Information about coins and currency prices can often be obtained by telephone. A dealer can research an accurately described coin in the current edition of any of the price books, and can give you an approximate value over the phone.

If you inherit what appears to be a good collection, it might be advisable to contact a numismatic appraiser. They will be listed in the Yellow Pages of your telephone book under either "Coins" or "Appraisers." The probate court must use appraisers to determine the value of coins in an estate, and the names of these appraisers are known to the lawyers and judges in your city. A qualified appraiser should belong to some of the national numismatic organizations. The appraiser can also arrange for the sale of your collection. Be sure to ask the charge for appraisal or for disposing of the collection. We have found that an amateur does not do well trying to sell a collection of rare coins. It takes a professional auctioneer or appraiser to watch out for your interests.

Coins and paper money can often be sold to friends, to dealers at coin shows, or to jewelers who advertise for pieces for meltdown. We caution you to be sure that you do not have a very rare coin before you sell by this method. It takes an expert to understand the difference in value between a coin with a mint mark and one without it, and any of the other details that determine great rarity and value.

Coins are a hot topic on the Internet. There are sites devoted to numismatic information and history, as well as to dealers who buy and sell. This is a specialized area of collecting, so you might want to start with a website devoted to numismatics, like www.pcgs.com (Professional Coin Grading Service). Coins are also sold through these same sites.

Although many coin dealers routinely buy and sell by mail or Internet or through ads in numismatic publications, we urge caution in these dealings. Most publications try to screen the dealers, but sometimes a dishonest person may offer to buy at fair prices for months before problems surface. If you plan to sell to an unknown person, get references. Ask how long you must wait for your money and include a full list of the coins and paper currency you want to sell. If possible, have someone, perhaps a local collector, help you determine the condition of your coins. You could be wrong, and a fine-looking coin may only be extra good or an unscrupulous dealer could tell you that your coin is in worse condition than it really is. Sometimes you may find that you have to wait too long for your money from the sale of your coins. Send the coins registered mail. Postal fraud is a crime, and dishonest dealers try to avoid it.

There are many special categories for coins. You must learn what *mint set, proof set, reissue, restrike, type set,* and other words mean. If you have sets or rolls of coins, sell them as a unit; do not break them up. Paper bills are very popular, and these should be researched and sold in the same way as coins.

Solid-gold coins present a special problem. They can be sold for the gold content or for the numismatic value. In recent years many investors have started to buy gold coins. The value changes daily with the price of gold. Look for nicks in the edges that indicate bits of the gold have been removed. This lowers both values. Coins mounted in bezels as jewelry retain numismatic value if they can be removed with no damage to the coin. Of course, the coin may be scratched from wear. Coins mounted as jewelry with soldered links have lost the numismatic value even if the link is removed. The solder will damage the edge of the coin. Gold coins in good condition sell for the highest prices at coin shops and auctions.

TOKENS AND CARDS

Tokens and any other types of "money" also have value to a coin collector. Some specialize in store tokens, odd types of money that are not metal coins, misstruck coins, or error coins. Even canceled and blank checks are wanted. A relatively new collectible that can be sold is a credit card or a phone card. The AT&T phone card from the 1992 Democratic Convention in good condition has sold for $750. Store charge cards are also collected.

Almost every type of "money," from wooden nickels to casino gambling chips, has a value. If the money is an unfamiliar-looking American coin or bill, it is even more important to check the value. Medals are sold through coin dealers. Even jewelry made from coins can be sold through coin dealers.

REPAIR

The value of rare coins, perhaps more than for any other type of collectible, is determined by condition as well as rarity, beauty, and history. For this reason, coin collectors are particularly careful about handling, storing, and cleaning coins.

The perspiration from a hand will eventually damage a coin. It should always be handled with cotton gloves or by the edges. Never store coins in bags where they might rub against each other. Try storing them in an area where they will not tarnish. Keep them away from damp places, too much direct sunlight, off floors, and away from rubber bands, tape, metal, and cardboard. The sulfur in the rubber or cardboard will eventually damage the coins. There are many types of holders with spaces for specific coins, and envelopes and filing boxes that are made for coin storage.

Never clean your coins. If it must be done, consult an expert. There are dips, cleaning cloths, and other products made to clean coins, but they may cause damage if not used correctly.

Never clean a token or a medal; it lowers the value. Handle the pieces as little as possible and wear white cotton gloves.

Checks and credit cards should be stored or restored in the same way as any paper or plastic items.

REFERENCE BOOKS

American Numismatics before the Civil War, 1760–1860, Q. David Bowers (Bowers and Merena Galleris, Wolfeboro, NJ, 1998).

PRICE BOOKS

2003 North American Coins & Prices, 12th edition, David C. Harper, editor (Krause, Iola, WI, 2002).

2003 Standard Catalog of World Coins, 30th edition, Chester L. Krause and Colin R. Bruce (Krause, Iola, WI, 2002).

Coin World 2002 Guide to U.S. Coins: Prices and Value Trends, the editors of Coin World (New Signet, New York, 2002).

The Insider's Guide to U.S. Coin Values 2003, Scott A. Travers (Dell, New York, 2002).

Official 2003 Price Guide to World Coins, 6th edition, Marc Hudgeons and Hudgeons (House of Collectibles, New York, 2002).

The Official American Numismatic Association Grading Standards for United States Coins, American Numismatic Association (Krause, Iola, WI, 2002).

Standard Catalog of United States Tokens, 1700–1900, 3rd edition, Russell Rulau (Krause, Iola, WI, 1999).

Official 2003 Blackbook: Price Guide to United States Coins, 41st edition, Marc and Tom Hudgeons (House of Collectibles, NY, 2003).

Official 2003 Blackbook: Price Guide to United States Paper Money, 35th edition, Marc and Tom Hudgeons (House of Collectibles, NY, 2003).

CLUBS & THEIR PUBLICATIONS

American Credit Card Collectors Society, *Charge: The Journal of the American Credit Collectors Society* (NL), PO Box 2465, Midland, MI 48641.

American Numismatic Association, *Numismatist* (MAG), 818 N. Cascade

Ave., Colorado Springs, CO 80903-3279, e-mail: ana@money.org, website: www.money.org.

American Society of Check Collectors, *Check Collector* (MAG), PO Box 577, Garrett Park, MD 20896, e-mail: cal493@aol.com, website: members.aol.com/asccinfo.

American Vecturist Association, *Fare Box* (NL), PO Box 1204, Boston, MA 02104-1204 (transportation tokens).

Canadian Numismatic Association, *Canadian Numismatic Journal* (MAG), PO Box 226, Barrie, ON L4M 4T2, Canada, website: www.canadian-numismatic.org.

Casino Chip & Gaming Token Collectors Club, *Casino Chip & Gaming Tokens Magazine* (MAG), PO Box 35769, Las Vegas, NV 89133-5769, e-mail: hotrodrjm@ccgtcc.com, website: www.ccgtcc.com (chips, tokens, and other casino memorabilia, including ashtrays, dice, playing cards, matchbook covers, slot machines, postcards showing casinos).

Combined Organizations of Numismatic Error Collectors of America (CONECA), *Errorscope* (MAG), 35 Leavitt Ln., Glenburn, ME 04401-1013, e-mail: pfunny@telplus.net, website: conecaonline.org.

The Elongated Collectors, *TEC News* (NL), PO Box 460936, San Francisco, CA 94146-0936, e-mail: tec@liss.olm.net, website: www.money.org/clubs/tec.html (elongated coins).

International Association of Silver Art Collectors (IASAC), *The Silver Bugle* (NL), PO Box 28415, Seattle, WA 98118, e-mail: IasacNancy@cs.com (silver art bars and rounds).

International Bank Note Society, *International Bank Note Society Journal* (MAG), *Inside IBNS* (NL), PO Box 1642, Racine, WI 53401, e-mail: milana@wi.net.

International Organization of Wooden Money Collectors, *Bunyan's Chips* (NL), 5295 Beechwood Rd., Ravenna, OH 44266-9119, e-mail: RAQ56@aol.com.

Latin American Paper Money Society, *LANSA* (NL), 3304 Milford Mill Rd., Baltimore, MD 21244, e-mail: matzlansa@aol.com, website: www.crosswinds.net/%7Elansa.

Liberty Seated Collectors Club, *Gobrecht Journal* (MAG), PO Box 261, Wellington, OH 44090.

National Token Collectors Association (NATCA), *Talkin' Tokens* (MAG), PO Box 281, Ormond Beach, FL 32175, e-mail: cjcoins@att.net, website: home.pacbell.net/tokenbob/cgi-bin/natca.html.

Orders & Medals Society of America, *Journal of the Orders & Medals Society of America* (MAG), PO Box 198, San Ramon, CA 94583, website: www.omsa.org.

Society of Paper Money Collectors, *Paper Money* (MAG), PO Box 117060, Carrollton, TX 75011, e-mail: frank.clark@rediform.com, website: www.spmc.org.

Token and Medal Society, Inc., *TAMS Journal* (MAG), PO Box 832854, Miami, FL 33283, e-mail: mlighter@bellsouth.net.

World Proof Numismatic Association (W.P.N.A.), *Proof Collectors Corner* (MAG), PO Box 4094, Pittsburgh, PA 15201-0094.

OTHER PUBLICATIONS

Bank Note Reporter (NP), *Coin Prices* (MAG), *COINS Magazine* (MAG), *Numismatic News* (NP), *World Coin News* (MAG), 700 E. State St., Iola, WI 54990-0001, e-mail: info@krause.com, website: www.krause.com.

Canadian Coin News (NP), Trajan Publishing Corporation, 103 Lakeshore Rd., Suite 202, St. Catharines, ON L2N 2T6, Canada, e-mail: bret @trajan.com, website: www.canadiancoinnews.ca.

The Celator (MAG), PO Box 839, Lancaster, PA 17608, website: www.celator.com (ancient numismatics and antiquities).

Coin Connoisseur (MAG), 5855 Topango Canyon Blvd., Suite 330, Woodland Hills, CA 91367, e-mail: subscriptions@coinmag.com, website: www.coinmag.com.

Coin News (MAG), 1 Orchard House, Duchy Rd., Heathpark, Honiton, Devon EX14 8YD, UK, e-mail: info@coin-news.com, website: www.coin-news.com.

Coin World (NP), PO Box 150, Sidney, OH 45365, website: www.coin world.com.

Error Trends Coin Magazine (MAG), PO Box 158, Oceanside, NY 11572-0158, e-mail: etcmman@aol.com.

Medal News (MAG), Token Publishing Ltd., 1 Orchard House, Duchy Rd., Heathpark, Honiton, Devon EX14 8YD, UK, e-mail: info@medal-news.com, website: www.medal-news.com.

Rare Coin Review (MAG), *The Coin Collector* (NP), Bowers and Merena Galleries, Box 1224, Wolfeboro, NH 03894, e-mail: Mary@bowersand merena.com, website: www.bowersandmerena.com.

ARCHIVES & MUSEUMS

Museum of the American Numismatic Association, 818 N. Cascade Ave., Colorado Springs, CO 80903-3279, 719-632-2646, website: www.money.org.

USEFUL SITES

The United States Mint, www.usmint.gov.

APPRAISERS

Many of the auctions and repair services listed in this section will also do appraisals. *See also* the general list of "Appraisal Groups," page 483.

Professional Coin Grading Service (PCGS), PO Box 9458, Newport Beach, CA 92658, 800-447-8848 or 949-833-0600, e-mail: info@pcgs.com, website: www.pcgs.com. Coin grading and authentication. Service available to members of PCGS or through authorized dealers.

AUCTIONS

➡➡ **SEE ALSO "SELLING THROUGH AUCTION HOUSES," PAGE 485.**

Bowers and Merena, PO Box 1224, Wolfeboro, NH 03894, 800-458-4646, fax: 603-569-5319, e-mail: auction@bowersandmerena.com, website: www.bowersandmerena.com. Bowers and Merena Auctions conducts in-person auctions. Bids may also be executed by telephone, fax, e-mail, Internet, or regular mail. Its Kingswood Coin Auctions division conducts online auctions. Grading and authentication service.

C & D Gale, 2404 Berwyn Rd., Wilmington, DE 19810-3525, 302-478-0872, fax: 302-478-6866, e-mail: cdgale@dol.net, website: www.cdgale.com/catalog/exonumia.htm. Auctions of nineteenth-century U.S. tokens. Mail, phone, and Internet bids accepted. Buyer's premium 10%. Catalog free online; text-only hard copy catalog $5 for one-year subscription. Prices realized mailed after auction, $1.

Early American History Auctions, PO Box 3341, La Jolla, CA 92038, 858-459-4159, fax: 858-459-4373, e-mail: history@earlyamerican.com, website: www.earlyamerican.com. Coins, currency, and Americana. Absentee auctions. Mail, fax, phone, and e-mail bids accepted. Buyer's premium 15%.

Heritage Rare Coin Galleries, 100 Highland Park Village, Suite 200, Dallas, TX 75205-2788, 800-872-6467 or 214-528-3500, website: heritagecoin.com. Internet-only coin auctions and appraisals.

Malter Galleries Inc., 17003 Ventura Blvd., Suite 205, Encino, CA 91316, 818-784-7772, fax: 818-784-4726, e-mail: mike@maltergalleries.com, website: www.maltergalleries.com. Specializing in Greek, Roman, and Egyptian coins and artifacts. Mail, phone, and Internet bids accepted. Buyer's premium 15%. Free catalogs. Prices realized available after auctions. Restoration and conservation services. Appraisals.

R.M. Smythe & Co., 26 Broadway, Suite 973, New York, NY 10004-1703, 800-622-1880 or 212-943-1880, fax: 212-908-4670, e-mail: info@smytheonline.com, website: www.smytheonline.com. Auctions of coins, currency, stocks and bonds, and historic Americana. Mail, phone, fax, and Internet bids accepted. Buyer's premium varies with amount of sale, 10%, 12%, and 15%. Prices realized mailed after auction. Catalog $25, subscription $87.50 in U.S. Appraisals.

Stack's Coin Galleries, 123 W. 57th St., New York, NY 10019, 212-582-2580, fax: 212-582-1946, e-mail: info@stacks.com, website: www.stacks.com. Rare coins. United States, foreign, ancient, gold, and silver coins. Mail bids accepted. Buyer's premium 15%. Catalog $10. Appraisals.

Teletrade, Inc., 27 Main St., Kingston, NY 12401-3853, 800-232-1132 or 914-

339-2900, e-mail: bradj@teletrade.com or pauls@teletrade.com, website: www.teletrade.com. Absentee auctions of rare coins. Phone and Internet bids only. Buyer's premium 10%. Prices realized mailed and available on website after auction.

World Exonumia, PO Box 4143, Rockford, IL 61110, 815-226-0771, e-mail: hartzog@exonumia.com, website: www.exonumia.com. Absentee auctions of exonumia: tokens, medals, etc. Mail, phone, and Internet bids accepted. No buyer's premium. Prices realized mailed after auction. Catalog $15, deducted from purchase of $50 or more. Appraisals.

REPAIRS, PARTS & SUPPLIES

➥ SEE ALSO "CONSERVATORS & RESTORERS," PAGE 520.

Bill Cole Enterprises, Inc., PO Box 60, Dept. RK1, Randolph, MA 02368-0060, 781-986-2653, fax: 781-986-2656, e-mail: bcemylar@cw business.com, website: www.bcemylar.com. Manufacturers and distributors of archival supplies. Mylar sleeves for paper money and other paper collectibles.

Century Business Solutions, PO Box 2393, Brea, CA 92822, 800-767-0777, fax: 800-786-7939, website: www.centurybusinesssolutions.com. Products for organizing and storing coins and other collectibles.

RN Products, 39 Monmouth St., Red Bank, NJ 07701-1613, 732-741-0626, fax: 732-741-0479, e-mail: mostco@monmouth.com. Complete line of coin supplies.

University Products, Inc., 517 Main St., PO Box 101, Holyoke, MA 01040, 800-336-4847, fax: 800-532-9281, e-mail: info@university products.com, website: www.universityproducts.com. Archival supplies for conservation, restoration, repair, storage, and display. Specialized storage for coins and other collectibles. Free catalog.

PAINTINGS

Original art can be the most valuable and the most complicated antique or collectible to sell. You must be able to tell if it is an oil painting, a print, an original Remington sketch, or just a photographic copy. Find a knowledgeable friend who can tell you which pieces look authentic. It might be a local artist, craftsman, or photographer who can recognize quality. Then try to check on the artist before you offer the piece for sale.

If you live in or near a big city, ask whether the local art museum schedules a day for authenticating works of art for the general public. Many museums will tell you the age of the piece and information on the artist, but none will estimate price. Watch for an appraisal day at local auction galleries or at fund-raisers. Take the piece to the appraiser. If it is too big, take a photograph.

The work of any artist listed in *Dictionnaire des Peintres, Sculpteurs, Dessinateurs et Graveurs* by Bénézit, *Mantle Fielding's Dictionary of American Painters, Sculptors and Engravers* or *Mallett's Index of Artists* has a value. Look in the library for copies of these books. Check prices for the past ten years in the price books listed in this section and similar books found at your library, at your local art museum library, or available through some computer networks. You can also write to the National Museum of American Art, The Inventory of American Paintings, 8th & G Sts. NW, Washington, DC 20560, to learn about paintings by American artists.

Photograph the picture, write a description, copy down the artist's name, and contact a local or out-of-town auction gallery or any dealer to sell the item.

Before you decide how to sell your artwork, it would be prudent to go to some local auctions and see if paintings or expensive prints sell for good prices. Sometimes a small local gallery does not get high prices for good art because it specializes in furniture, country antiques, or other types of collectibles. National publicity in ads or online make a difference. Some local auctions hold special, well-publicized print and painting sales and get very high prices.

Valuable paintings are sometimes found in unexpected places. An American tourist in England went to a "boot sale" (flea market) and noticed a painting of two hummingbirds near a nest. He bought the picture for about $5. He vaguely remembered seeing a similar painting, so he took the oil to Christie's in London. It was identified as the work of Martin Johnson Heade, one of a group of paintings done after Heade returned from Brazil. The picture was soon sold at an auction in the United States for $96,000. Two other Heade paintings were bought at a house sale in Arizona for $88. They were auctioned in New York for $1,072,000.

When you have a piece that seems to be old and authentic, it is always wise to have an appraisal by a qualified art appraiser before you sell it. If you decide to sell it through an auction gallery, no appraisal is needed. The gallery should be able to tell you the approximate value.

It is important to know the history of family pieces. Many good pieces of art "liberated" by soldiers during World War II are now appearing in house and estates sales. Many times, the value is unrecognized by the owners. Some works were obtained illegally and might still belong to an overseas owner, so a gallery might want to investigate.

VALUE TIPS

Age does not always determine the value of fine art, but condition, quality, and the prestige of the artist do. You may think a painting is ugly, but someone else may pay a significant sum for it. The size of an average-quality painting helps to determine the price. It should fit over a fireplace or sofa. If too high and narrow, it is worth 30 percent less. If the subject matter is unappealing (dead bodies, gored matadors, or unattractive factory views), the picture will not sell as easily as landscapes, seascapes, or still lifes by the same artist. Animals, beautiful women, nudes, sweet children, Jewish subjects, Oriental views, and Paris street scenes are good sellers. Historical events, military battles, and biblical subjects are not as popular. If a landscape includes a town that can be identified, the value is at least doubled.

A good original gold-leaf frame is of added value when selling a large painting. Most buyers plan to hang the picture on a wall, and if they have to spend extra money to restore or frame a painting, it is worth less. Vintage and antique frames have become very valuable. Sometimes the frame is worth as much as the picture.

Rips and damage in the main part of the painting (on a face, for example) are considered serious problems. Small tears in the background area are not serious if the painting has value. If the pictures were in the home of an elderly relative, be sure to check under the dust cover paper on the back for hidden money or stock certificates. The labels and writing on the back may provide valuable information about the work's history.

Don't be discouraged if friends tell you what a "bad" painting you have. Beauty is in the eye of the beholder. Respectable copies of famous paintings, decorative subjects, very primitive-looking pictures, and huge pictures (especially of food) that are suitable for restaurant walls will all sell. They are bought and sold not as great art, but as decorations for boring walls or dark corners. They may even be purchased because the new owners like "kitsch," something that is so bad it has charm.

REPAIR

Oil paintings require special care. Home care should include just a light dusting of the surface once a month or less. Never wash a painting or try any at-home restoration unless you are trained.

Never entrust a good oil painting to anyone but a competent restorer or conservator. Many pictures have been completely ruined by overrestoration, too much overpainting, or an overzealous cleaning that "skinned" the picture. These procedures may cause problems that can never be rectified. A friend's mother regularly washed her oil paintings and, after many years, most of the paint was gone.

If you believe that your painting, no matter how dirty, is valuable, take it to your local museum to learn about the artist. Museums will not appraise, but they can tell you if your picture is worth restoring, and may furnish the names of local conservators. In some cities, restorers are listed in the Yellow Pages under "Art Restoration and Conservation" or "Picture Restoring."

We have listed individuals and companies that restore paintings and other forms of artwork. If you are concerned about the quality of the work or whether the firm is headed by a conservator or a restorer, you must check further. More information can be obtained through the American Institute for Conservation, 1522 K Street NW, #804, Washington, DC 20005.

➤ SEE ALSO PRINTS

REFERENCE BOOKS

Dictionary of American Sculptors, 18th Century to the Present, Glenn B. Opitz, editor (Apollo, Poughkeepsie, NY, 1984).

The Dictionary of British Artists, 1880–1940, J. Johnson and A. Greutzner (Antique Collectors' Club, Wappingers Falls, NY, 1976).

Dictionnaire des Peintres, Sculpteurs, Dessinateurs et Graveurs, 10 volumes, E. Bénézit (Librairie Gründ, Paris, 1976).

Mallett's Index of Artists: International—Biographical, Daniel Trowbridge Mallett (Peter Smith, New York, 1935, 1948).

Mantle Fielding's Dictionary of American Painters, Sculptors & Engravers, 2nd edition, Glenn B. Opitz, editor (Apollo, Poughkeepsie, NY, 1986).

The New-York Historical Society's Dictionary of Artists in America, 1564–1860, George C. Groce and David H. Wallace (Yale University Press, New Haven, CT, 1957).

Supplement to Mallett's Index of Artists: International—Biographical, Daniel Trowbridge Mallett (Peter Smith, New York, 1940, 1948).

PRICE BOOKS

Art at Auction in America, William E. Belk and Frank E. Beaty, editors (Frontier Publishing, 4933 West Craig Rd., Suite 155, Las Vegas, NV 89130, 1997).

Davenport's Art Reference & Price Guide, 2003–2004, Lisa Reinhardt, editor (Gordon's Art Reference, Phoenix, AZ, 2003).

Fine Art Identification and Price Guide, 3rd edition, Susan Theran (Avon, New York, 1996).

CLUBS & THEIR PUBLICATIONS

International Foundation for Art Research, *IFAR Journal* (MAG), 500 Fifth Ave., Suite 1234, New York, NY 10110, website: www.ifar.org.

Society to Prevent Trade in Stolen Art (STOP), *Art Intelligence* (NL), 1920 N St., Suite 620, Washington, DC 20036, e-mail: rob6960@aol.com or spiel@arttheft.com, website: www.arttheft.com.

OTHER PUBLICATIONS

American Art Journal (MAG), 730 Fifth Ave., New York, NY 10019, e-mail: AAJ@kgny.com.

The Art Newspaper (NP), PO Box 3000, Denville, NJ 07834-9776, website: www.theartnewspaper.com.

Fine Arts Trader (NL), PO Box 1273, Randolph, MA 02368, website: www.fineartstrader.com.

Wildlife Art News (MAG), 1428 E. Cliff Rd., Burnsville, MN 55337, e-mail: publisher@winternet.com, website: www.wildlifeartmag.com.

ARCHIVES & MUSEUMS

Archives of American Art, Smithsonian Insitution, PO Box 37012, Victor Building, Room 2200, MRC 937, Washington, DC 20013-7012, 202-275-1961, website: artarchives.si.edu. Online research form.

APPRAISERS

Many of the repair services listed in this section will also do appraisals. *See also* the general list of "Appraisal Groups" on page 483.

AUCTIONS

→ **SEE ALSO "SELLING THROUGH AUCTION HOUSES," PAGE 485.**

Illustration House, Inc., 96 Spring St., 7th Floor, New York, NY 10012, 212-966-9444, fax: 212-966-9426, e-mail: illushse@interport.net, website: www.illustrationhouse.com. Auctions of illustrative paintings and drawings. Two Premier (in-person) auctions and two Back Porch absentee auctions (mail and fax bids only) per year. Buyer's premium 10%. Premier catalogs $30, Back Porch catalogs $30. Prices realized available after auction.

REPAIRS, PARTS & SUPPLIES

→ **SEE ALSO "CONSERVATORS & RESTORERS," PAGE 520.**

Albert Post Gallery, 2291 Newbury Dr., West Palm Beach, FL 33414, 561-333-7740, fax: 561-333-7740, e-mail: apostgallery@aol.com. Restoration and conservation of paintings. Appraisals.

Andrea Pitsch Paper Conservation, 212-594-9676, Mon.–Fri. fax: 212-268-4046, e-mail: apnyc@interport.net. Conservation and restoration of paper-based objects, including oil and acrylic paintings on paper, watercolors and gouaches, and drawings. Brochure $1 and SASE. By appointment only.

Antique & Art Restoration by Wiebold, 413 Terrace Pl., Terrace Park, OH 45174, 800-321-2541, 513-831-2541, fax: 513-831-2815, e-mail: wiebold @eos.net, website: www.wiebold.com. Fine art restoration and conservation on oil paintings, portrait miniatures, and gold leaf frames.

Antique Restorations, The Old Wheelwrights', Brasted Forge, Brasted, Kent TN16 1JL, UK, 011-44-1959-563863, fax: 011-44-1959-561262, e-mail: bfc@antique-restorations.org.co.uk, website: www.antique-restorations.org.uk. Complete range of antique and fine art services from furniture restoration and conservation to solutions for preserving your art collections and other valuables. Documentation service.

AntiqueConservation.com, Div. of Ponsford Ltd., 5441 Woodstock Rd., Acworth, GA 30102, 770-924-4848, fax: 770-529-2278, e-mail: GordonPonsford@AntiqueConservation.com, website: www.Antique Conservation.com. Conservation and restoration of fine art and antiques, including paintings. Appraisals.

Archival Conservation Center, Inc., 8225 Daly Rd., Cincinnati, OH 45231, 513-521-9858, fax: 513-521-9859. Repair and restoration of works of art on paper, including watercolors and Oriental scrolls. Smoke odor removal. Freeze drying of water-damaged materials. Free brochure available upon request.

Attic Unlimited, 22435 E. LaPalma Ave., Yorba Linda, CA 92887, 714-692-2940, fax: 714-692-2947, e-mail: atticunlimited@aol.com, website: www.atticunlimited.com. Restoration of paintings, frames, and any objects of art.

Boston Art Conservation, 9 Station St., Brookline, MA 02146, 617-738-1126, 9:00 A.M.–5:00 P.M., e-mail: admin@bosartconserv.com, website: bosartconserv.com. Conservation of works of art on paper, Asian paintings (scrolls and screens), photographs, art/artifacts on paper, and textiles. Collection surveys. Consultations on proper storage and display. Free brochure.

The Brushstroke, 4250 Van Cortlandt Pk. E., #1B, Bronx, NY 10470, 718-994-5989, e-mail: art_restoration@usa.com. Conservation and restoration of oil paintings and other objects of art. Pickup and delivery service within 50-mile radius in tristate NYC area. Free estimates.

Carl "Frank" Funes, 57 Maplewood Ave., Hempstead, NY 11550, 516-483-6712. Restoration of paintings.

Chem-Clean Furniture Restoration, Bucks County Art & Antiques Co., |246 W. Ashland St., Doylestown, PA 18901, 215-345-0892, e-mail:

iscsusn@att.net. Art restoration. Oil paintings restored, frames repaired. Research. Appraisals. Free brochure.

Chicago Conservation Center, 730 N. Franklin, Suite 701, Chicago, IL 60610, 312-944-5401, fax: 312-944-5479, e-mail: chicagoconservation @yahoo.com, website: chicagoconservation.com. Restoration of paintings, works of art on paper, frames, murals, and more.

Conservation of Art on Paper, Inc., 2805 Mount Vernon Ave., Alexandria, VA 22301, 703-836-7757, fax: 703-836-8878, e-mail: capi@erols.com. Conservation treatments for art and historic artifacts on paper, including watercolors, drawings, pastels, and collages. Vault storage, classes and lectures, publications about caring for art on paper, collection surveys, insurance reports.

Dobson Studios, 810 N. Daniel St., Arlington, VA 22201, 703-243-7363, e-mail: ddobson@dobson-studios.com, website: www.dobson-studios.com. Conservation of watercolors, drawings, pictures, and oil paintings on various supports, including glass and silk. Most paper objects are washed and deacidified, if needed. All work and materials are reversible.

Fine Art Conservation Laboratories, PO Box 23557, Santa Barbara, CA 93121, 805-564-3438; fax: 805-568-1178, e-mail: artdoc@earthlink.net, website: www.fineartconservationlab.com. Fine art restoration and preservation. Analytical services include pigment analysis, infrared and X-radiography. Specializing in the conservation of easel paintings, art on paper, and murals in historic buildings. Free brochure.

Fine Art Restoration, 93 Knowlton Rd., Brooks, ME 04921, 207-722-3464, fax: 207-722-3475. Restoration, cleaning, and conservation of oil paintings. Send photo of your damage and size for free written estimate. If you don't have a box to ship it in, a foam-lined wooden box will be sent to you for shipping. No charge for information and photos.

Gainsborough Products Co., 281 Lafayette Cir., Lafayette, CA 94549, 8 00-227-2186, fax: 925-283-3343, e-mail: service@gainsborough products.com, website: www.gainsboroughproducts.com. Oil painting restoration products, including oil painting cleaners, varnish removers, wax-resin lining compound, putty, Damar gloss varnish, linen and canvas for lining, epoxy, and ultraviolet lights. Air purifiers. Free catalog.

Grashe Fine Art Restorers, 35 148th Ave. SE, #9, Bellevue WA 98007, 425-644-7500, fax: 425-644-7582, e-mail: art@grashe.com, website: www.grashe.com. Specializes in the restoration and conservation of paintings.

Ingrid Sanborn & Daughter, 85 Church St., West Newbury, MA 01985, 978-363-2253, fax: 978-363-2049, e-mail: sanbornanddaughters @mediaone.net, website: www.isd.pair.com. Restoration and reproduction of painted furniture. Reproduction églomisé. Restoration and reproduction of reverse paintings on glass.

Intermuseum Laboratory, 83 N. Main St., Allen Art Bldg., Oberlin, OH 44074, 440-775-7331, 9:00 A.M.–5:00 P.M. fax: 440-774-3431, e-mail: sandra.williamson@oberlin.edu, website: www.oberlin.edu/~ica. A nonprofit, regional art conservation center that provides preservation and conservation services and education. Conservation of paintings, murals, paper-based materials, frames, and more.

International Fine Art Conservation Studios, Inc., PO Box 81509, Atlanta, GA 30366, 404-794-6142, fax: 404-794-6229, e-mail: Geoffrey.Steward @ifacs-inc.com, website: www.ifacs-inc.com. Conservation and restoration of easel paintings, murals, frescoes, ornamental plasterwork, interior and exterior decorative painting, etc. Surveys and scientific analysis.

Items of Value, Inc., 7419 Admiral Dr., Alexandria, VA 22307, 703-660-9380, fax: 703-660-9384. Restoration of paintings, gesso, and many different types of items. Regilding, resilvering. Appraisals.

J.K. Flynn Co., 471 Sixth Ave., Park Slope, Brooklyn, NY 11215, 718-369-8934, fax: 718-369-8934, e-mail: jkflynncompany@aol.com. Painting restoration, including cleaning, reversible BEVA linings/relinings; restoration of tears, holes, missing paint layers; reversible inpainting (retouching); and revarnishing. Period frame restoration, including oil or water gilding and full restoration of gesso, compo, or carved decorations. Fine art appraising and consulting. Specializing in the appraisal of American and European paintings. Free lists of services.

John Edward Cunningham, 1525 E. Berkeley, Springfield, MO 65804, 417-889-7702. Oil paintings and frames restored. Hours by appointment.

Kingsmen Antique Restoration Inc., 19 Passamore Ave., Unit 28, Scarborough, ON Canada M1V 4T5, 416-291-8939, fax: 416-291-8939, e-mail: kingsmen@sprint.ca. Invisible mending of art objects and oil paintings. Service worldwide. Call for information on sending objects for estimates.

Kistner's Full Claims Service, Inc., 520 20th St., Rock Island, IL 61201, 309-786-5868, fax: 309-794-0559, e-mail: kistners1@home.com, website: www.kistners.com. Restoration of oil paintings and other objects. Serving eastern Iowa and northwestern Illinois. Free brochure.

Legacy Art Restorations & Design Int'l. Inc., 4221 N. 16th St., Phoenix, AZ 85016-5318, 602-263-5178, fax: 602-263-6009, e-mail: restoration @legacyintlinc.com, website: legacyintlinc.com. Restoration of fine art and collectibles, including oil paintings.

Leonard E. Sasso, Master Restorer, 23 Krystal Dr., RD 1, Somers, NY 10589, 914-763-2121, fax: 914-763-0851. Restoration of oil paintings, watercolors, and frames. Appraisals.

Liros Gallery, PO Box 946, 14 Parker Point Rd., Blue Hill, ME 04614, 207-374-5370, fax: 207-734-5370, e-mail: liros@lirosgallery.com, website: lirosgallery.com. Restoration of paintings; custom framing. Appraisals of paintings, prints, and icons. Free brochure.

MAC Enterprises, 122 Miro Adelante, San Clemente, CA 92673, 949-361-9528, e-mail: macrestor@aol.com. Restoration of oil paintings, frames, and collectibles. Ship UPS or call for information. Send SASE for brochure.

Museum Shop, Ltd., Richard Kornemann, conservator, 20 N. Market St., Frederick, MD 21701, 301-695-0424. Restoration of oil paintings; 23K gold leafing. Free brochure.

New Orleans Conservation Guild, Inc., 3301 Chartres St., New Orleans, LA 70117, 504-944-7900, fax: 504-944-8750, e-mail: info@art-restoration.com, website: www.art-restoration.com. Restoration and conservation of fine art and antiques, including paintings and frames. Appraisals and research searches. Call or write for brochure.

Old World Restorations, Inc., 5729 Dragon Way, Cincinnati, OH 45227, 513-271-5459, fax: 513-271-5418, e-mail: info@oldworldrestorations.com, website: www.oldworldrestorations.com. Restoration and conservation of art and antiques, including paintings and frames. On-site architectural restorations of murals, frescoes, and gold leaf. Fire and water damage restoration. Specialized packing and shipping. Nationwide service. Send or e-mail photos for preliminary estimates. Free brochure.

Peter J. Dugan, Fine Art Restoration, 1300 Coventry Cir., Vernon Hills, IL 60061, 847-367-0561, e-mail: pdugan6439@aol.com. Restoration of paintings and frames.

Peter Kostoulakos, 15 Sayles St., Lowell, MA 01851-1625, 978-453-8888, website: www.pkart.com. Cleaning and restoration of oil paintings on canvas and solid supports. Cleaning, lining, strip lining, inpainting, varnishing, custom stretchers. Résumé and sample estimate form available.

Poor Richard's Restoration & Preservation Studio Workshop, 101 Walnut St., Montclair, NJ 07042, 973-783-5333, fax: 973-744-1939, e-mail: jrickford@webtv.com, website: www.rickford.com. Restoration, conservation, and preservation of fine and decorative art. By appointment, Tues.–Fri. noon–5:00 P.M., Sat. noon–3:00 P.M.

Pratzon Art Restoration, 122 W. 26th St., Suite 1006, New York, NY 10001, 212-807-7066, e-mail: jpratzon@earthlink.net. Conservation and restoration services for paintings; cleaning, lining, tear repair, sensitive inpainting and retouching. All linings and repairs are done with archival, reversible BEVA products. Send SASE for free pamphlet.

Rafail & Polina Golberg, Golberg Restoration Co., 411 Westmount Dr., Los Angeles, CA 90048, 310-652-0735, fax: 310-274-3770, e-mail: info @restorationworld.com, website: www.restorationworld.com. Restoration and conservation of antiques and objects of art, including paintings. Free estimates via the Internet.

Renaissance Gallery, 481 S. Oak St., Ukiah, CA 95482, 707-462-3003, e-mail: jayed@email.com. Painting restoration. Two-day restoration classes offered.

Rosine Green Associates, Inc., 89 School St., Brookline, MA 02446, 617-277-8368, fax: 617-731-3845, e-mail: rga@ix.netcom.com. Conservation and restoration of fine art, including paintings and frames.

Tindell's Restoration, 825 Sandburg Pl., Nashville, TN 37214, 615-885-1029, fax: 615-391-0712, e-mail: info@ATindellsRestorationSchools.com, website: www.TindellsRestorationSchools.com. Restoration services, seminars, training, and products. Restoration of oil paintings, frames, and much more. Appraisals. Free brochure.

Tsondru Thangka Conservation, e-mail: tsondru@ns.sympatico.ca. Conservation of Tibetan thangkas, religious paintings on fabric used in meditation practices.

Williamstown Art Conservation Center, 225 South St., Williamstown, MA 01267, 413-458-5741, fax: 413-458-2314, e-mail: wacc@clark.williams.edu, website: www.williamstownart.org. Conservation of paintings, paper, 3-dimensional objects, frames, and more. Analytical services. Painting conservation now offered in Atlanta at Atlanta Art Conservation Center, 6000 Peachtree Rd., Atlanta, GA 30341, phone 404-733-4589.

Wiscasset Bay Gallery, 67 Main St., PO Box 309, Wiscasset, ME 04578, 207-882-7682, fax: 207-882-9116, e-mail: info@wiscassetbaygallery.com, website: www.wiscassetbaygallery.com. Restoration of oil paintings, specializing in fine nineteenth- and twentieth-century American and European paintings, with an emphasis on New England artists.

PAPER COLLECTIBLES

Paper collectibles were almost ignored until the 1970s, when the word *ephemera* came into common use. If you have a bookplate that belonged to Charles Dickens, a 1910 gum wrapper, a bill of sale for a slave, or an 1890 menu, it is called ephemera. They are "throwaway" bits of history.

We seem more aware today that these bits are of historic importance. Several centuries ago, paper was not common, and very little ephemera has remained. We have no accurate idea of what the Pilgrims wore on their feet because we have no photographs or personal letters. We can only make educated guesses about many of the everyday activities of the past. The history of the rich and famous remains in paintings and documents, but everyday ephemera is gone.

Menus, newspapers, maps, ration books from the wars, personal letters, letterheads, diaries, children's lesson books, paper end-labels from bolts of cloth, wallpaper, fabric sample books, and instruction books for obsolete machinery are among the items of interest to the ephemera collector. There are collectors of local-history ephemera in every part of the country. Any paper item with a city or state name can probably be sold, and it will bring the best price near the city named on it.

Old newspapers are not very valuable unless they refer to a very special historic event, like the "election" of Dewey or the death of Washington. The paper is acidic and "self-destructs" after a number of years, becoming brittle and falling apart. Many libraries are selling old newspapers and replacing them with microfilm or digital images, so the supply is larger than the demand. Most newspapers are worthless unless sold as a full-year set. A few special papers reporting interesting events are worth up to $15 to $20.

Sort through boxes of old papers and "junk" you may find in the attic. Try to imagine who would find it useful. The best way to sell many special paper items can be found in the various appropriate sections of this book. Other items can be sold through mail-order ads in general antiques publications or on the Internet. Ephemera is usually small, lightweight, and easy to mail to a buyer. There is even an international club of ephemera collectors and several newspapers devoted to the subject. Look at the want ads and try to find just the right person for your ephemera.

When all else fails, place a box filled with the papers on a table at a flea market and lightly pencil a low price on each piece. Guess the value from the subject matter. Single pieces of paper over fifty years old can be worth from ten cents to a few dollars even if they seem of no consequence to you.

SHEET MUSIC

Sheet music is collected for many reasons. Some want the music, but most want the old covers to frame as pictures. Others want covers that are celebrity- or movie-related. So there are several ways to sell the sheet music you might find in a box or a piano bench. A few pieces of sheet music may not have great value, but a pile of the music could add up to considerable money.

There is added value to covers illustrated with an old car, a train, a political event, a Gibson girl, blacks, well-known movie stars, Elvis Presley, or even a battle scene. The general rule is: the smaller the picture on the title page, the older the sheet music. Only historians want the early pieces. By the 1870s, the cover was a full picture, which was almost always lithographed. Colored lithographs sell best. Photographs were used by the early 1900s. Sheet music was printed on pages measuring 13½ by 10½ inches before 1917. Most sheet music was published on sheets measuring 12 by 9 inches after 1920. Collectors like covers made before the 1930s.

The best prices are paid for music with all the pages intact and untrimmed. After 1920, old music was often cut to fit in the piano bench. Dust the music and carefully erase pencil marks and smudges with an art-gum eraser before you sell. Transparent tape and tears always lower the value, sometimes to a few cents. Dealers in shops and flea markets sell most of the music. It doesn't sell well at auctions.

Collectors and dealers of sheet music advertise in the general antiques publications and the paper ephemera and sheet music publications. There are several dealers who sell music through the mail using monthly lists. There are also many Internet sites that trade sheet music. They could be your best customers.

REPAIR

The proper storage, display, and repair of paper collectibles is both difficult and important if you wish to preserve old maps, hand-written documents, sheet music, or other paper items.

For storage, humidity should range between 45 and 65 percent. If a room is too dry, the paper can become brittle; if it is too wet, various molds and insects can attack. Never glue or paste any paper items. Transparent mending tape can be especially damaging, as it will eventually react with the paper and make a stain. Even so-called removable tape and notes will eventually leave a mark.

Be sure to display printed paper away from strong sunlight or direct heat. The sun will fade paper and the heat will cause damage. Unfortunately, ideal conditions are almost impossible for collectors who wish to hang a Currier & Ives print or an old map as decoration.

Consider the value and the possible damage before framing any paper item. Follow these strict rules: Use acid-free matting available at art supply or framing stores. Always leave a space between the paper and the glass. Use an inner liner or spacer. Seal the back to keep it dust-free. A frame shop will be able to help you with this.

Instructions for framing and storing valuable paper collectibles can be found in most paper preservation books. If your local art supply shop or frame shop is unfamiliar with the proper materials, you can purchase them by mail through the companies listed here.

➻ SEE ALSO ADVERTISING COLLECTIBLES, BOOKS & BOOKPLATES, MAGA-ZINES, MOVIE MEMORABILIA, PHOTOGRAPHY, POSTCARDS, PRINTS

REFERENCE BOOKS
Encyclopedia of Ephemera, Maurice Rickards (Routledge, New York, 2000).

PRICE BOOKS
A Bit of Brundage: The Illustration Art of Frances Brundage, Sarah Steier and Donna Braun (Schiffer, Atglen, PA, 1999).

Collectible Sheet Music: The Gold in Your Piano Bench, Marion Short (Schiffer Publishing, Atglen, PA, 1997).

Covers of Gold: Collectible Sheet Music, Marion Short (Schiffer, Atglen, PA, 1998).

From Footlights to "The Flickers": Collectible Sheet Music—Broadway Shows and Silent Movies, Marion Short (Schiffer, Atglen, PA, 1998).

Hollywood Movie Songs: Collectible Sheet Music, Marion Short (Schiffer, Atglen, PA, 1999).

Leonard's Posters & Photographs, Susan Theran, editor (Auction Index, 30 Valentine Park, Newton, MA 02165, 1995).

More Gold in Your Piano Bench: Collectible Sheet Music, Inventions, Wars and Disasters, Marion Short (Schiffer, Atglen, PA, 1997).

CLUBS & THEIR PUBLICATIONS
American Business Card Club, *Card Talk* (NL), PO Box 460297-K, Aurora, CO 80046-0297, e-mail: suzykat@hiwaay.net, website: www.expage.com/abcc.

The Daguerreian Society, *The Daguerreian Society Newsletter* (NL), 3045 West Liberty St., Suite 9, Pittsburgh, PA 15216-2460, e-mail: dasocpgh@aol.com, website: www.daguerre.org.

Ephemera Society of America, Inc., *Ephemera News* (NL), PO Box 95, Cazenovia, NY 13035-0095, e-mail: info@ephemerasociety.org, website: www.ephemerasociety.org.

Hermon Dunlap Smith Center for the History of Cartography, *Mapline* (NL), Newberry Library, 60 West Walton St., Chicago, IL 60610-3380, e-mail: smithctr@newberry.org, website: www.newberry.org.

International Map Collectors Society, *IMCOS Journal* (MAG), 7 E. Park St., Chatteris PE16 6LA, UK, e-mail: samantha@pearce1.demon.co.uk, website: www.imcos-mapcollecting.org.

National Association of Paper and Advertising Collectors, *P.A.C. The Paper & Advertising Collector* (NP), PO Box 500, Mount Joy, PA 17552, e-mail: pac@engleonline.com, website: www.engleonline.com.

National Sheet Music Society, *Song Sheet* (NL), 1597 Fair Park Ave., Los Angeles, CA 90041-2255.

Transport Ticket Society, *Journal of the Transport Ticket Society* (MAG), 4 Gladridge Close, Earley, Reading RG6 7DL, UK, e-mail: courtney@gladridgecl.demon.co.uk, website: www.btinternet.com/~transport.ticket.

OTHER PUBLICATIONS

Calendar Art Collectors' Newsletter (NL), 4 Henchman St., Suite #8, Boston, MA 02113-1445, e-mail: JollyJoan@aol.com.

Card Times (MAG), 70 Winifred Ln., Aughton, Ormskirk, Lancashire L39 5DL, UK, e-mail: david@cardtimes.co.uk, website: www.cardtimes.co.uk (cigarette cards, trading cards, sports and nonsports cards, phone cards, printed ephemera).

Collect! (MAG), 700 E. State St., Iola, WI 54990, website: www.collect.com (entertainment cards).

Mercator's World (MAG), 845 Willamette St., Eugene, OR 97401, e-mail: gturley@asterpub.com, website: www.mercatormag.com (modern and historic maps, globes, atlases, charts and the stories behind them).

Non-Sport Update (MAG), 4019 Green St., Harrisburg, PA 17110, e-mail: rtoser@nonsportupdate.com, website: www.nonsportupdate.com.

Paper Collectors' Marketplace (MAG), PO Box 128, Scandinavia, WI 54977-0128, e-mail: pcmpaper@gglbbs.com, website: www.pcmpaper.com.

Paper Pile Quarterly (MAG), PO Box 337, San Anselmo, CA 94979-0337, e-mail: apaperpile@aol.com.

Remember That Song (NL), 5623 N. 64th Ave., Glendale, AZ 85301, e-mail: rtslois@yahoo.com.

ARCHIVES & MUSEUMS

Heritage Map Museum, PO Box 412, Lititz, PA 17543, 717-626-5002, fax: 717-626-8858, website: www.carto.com.

The Museum of Printing, 800 Massachusetts Ave., North Andover, MA 01845, 978-686-0450, website: www.museumofprinting.org.

The Museum of Printing History, 1324 W. Clay St., Houston, TX 77019, 713-522-4652, fax: 713-522-5694, website: www.printingmuseum.org.

Women's Sheet Music Collection, Mills Music Library, University of Wisconsin, 728 State St., Madison, WI 53706-1494, 608-263-1884, website: www.library.wisc.edu/libraries/Music/wsmc.

APPRAISERS

Many of the auctions and repair services listed in this section will also do appraisals. *See also* the general list of "Appraisal Groups" on page 483.

AUCTIONS

↬ SEE ALSO "SELLING THROUGH AUCTION HOUSES," PAGE 485.

Alexander Autographs, Inc., 100 Melrose Ave., Suite 100, Greenwich, CT 06830, 203-622-8444, fax: 203-622-8765, e-mail: info@alexautographs.com, website: www.alexautographs.com. Auctions of historic documents and manuscripts. Mail, phone, fax, and e-mail bids accepted. Buyer's premium 15%. Catalog $20. Prices realized on website. Appraisals.

America West Archives, PO Box 100, Cedar City, UT 84721, 435-586-9497, fax: 435-586-9497, e-mail: awa@netutah.com, website: www.america westarchives.com. Auctions of historical old documents from the Old West period. Mail and phone bids accepted. Buyer's premium 10%. Prices realized available in following catalog. Catalog $3; yearly subscription $15 for 6 issues. Appraisals.

Cohasco, Inc., PO Drawer 821, Yonkers, NY 10702, 914-476-8500, fax: 914-476-8573, e-mail: dpc@dpc.nu, website: cohasco.com. Historical documents, manuscripts, and collectibles. Mail and phone bids accepted. Buyer's premium 12½%. Catalogs 2 for $10. Prices realized for specific lots mailed after auction. Appraisals.

EAC Gallery, 99 Powerhouse Rd., Suite 204, Roslyn Heights, NY 11577, 516-484-6280, fax: 516-484-6278, e-mail: eac@eacgallery.com, website: www.eacgallery.com. Specializing in historical documents, fine art, and sports memorabilia. Mail and phone bids accepted. Buyer's premium 15%. Free catalog. Prices realized mailed after auction. Appraisals.

Kit Barry Auctions, 88 High St., Brattleboro, VT 05301, 802-254-3634, fax: 802-254-3634, e-mail: kbarry@surfglobal.net. Nineteenth- and early twentieth-century ephemera. Mail, phone, and fax bids accepted. Buyer's premium 10%. Catalogs $10–$20. Prices realized mailed after auction. Appraisals.

Old World Auctions, PO Box 2224, 270 Hillside Ave., Sedona, AZ 86339, 928-282-3944 or 800-664-7757, fax: 928-282-3945, e-mail: marti@old worldauctions.com, website: oldworldauctions.com. Specializing in antique maps and related travel and exploration books and graphics. Mail, phone, and Internet bids accepted. Buyer's premium 12%. Catalogs $25 per year. Prices realized available on website and mailed in next catalog.

Paul Riseman Auctions, 2205 S. Park Ave., Springfield, IL 62704-4335, 217-787-2634, fax: 217-787-0062, e-mail: riseman@riseman.com, website: www.riseman.com. Absentee auctions of collectible ephemera, popular sheet music, and entertainment-related memorabilia. Mail, phone, fax, and e-mail bids accepted. No buyer's premium. Prices realized mailed after auction. Free catalogs. Appraisals.

PBA Galleries, 133 Kearny St., 4th Floor, San Francisco, CA 94108, 415-989-2665 or 866-999-7224, fax: 415-989-1664, e-mail: pba@pba galleries.com, website: www.pbagalleries.com. Auctioneers and appraisers of rare and antiquarian books and works on paper. Buyer's premium 15%. Mail, phone, and Internet bids accepted. Prices realized mailed after auction and available on website. Catalog $15, yearly subscription $175.

Victorian Images, Box 284, Marlton, NJ 08053, 856-354-2154, fax: 856-354-9699, e-mail: rmascieri@aol.com, website: tradecards.com/vi. Absentee auctions of trade cards, ephemera, nineteenth-century advertising. Mail, phone, and Internet bids accepted. Buyer's premium 13%. Prices realized mailed after auction and available on website. Catalog $18; yearly subscription $90. Appraisals.

Vintage Cover Story, PO Box 975, Burlington, NC 27215, 336-570-2810, e-mail: BobNews@aol.com. Historic newspapers. Mail, phone, and e-mail bids accepted. Buyer's premium 20%. Prices realized mailed upon request. Appraisals.

Waverly Auctions, Inc., 4931 Cordell Ave., Bethesda, MD 20814, 301-951-8883, fax: 301-718-8375, e-mail: waverly1660@earthlink.net, website: waverlyauctions.com. Auctions of maps, prints, autographs, and used and rare books. Mail, phone, and Internet bids accepted. Buyer's premium 15%. Prices realized mailed after auction and available on website. Catalog $7; yearly subscription $38. Appraisals.

REPAIRS, PARTS & SUPPLIES

➤ SEE ALSO "CONSERVATORS & RESTORERS," PAGE 520.

Andrea Pitsch Paper Conservation, 212-594-9676, Mon.–Fri., fax: 212-268-4046, e-mail: apnyc@interport.net. Conservation and restoration of paper-based objects: art, architectural drawings and blueprints, manuscripts and documents, maps, oil and acrylic paintings on paper, watercolors and gouaches, drawings, posters, prints, and ephemera. Consultation on condition of paper collections, prospective purchases, storage, and handling. Brochure $1 and SASE. By appointment only.

AntiqueConservation.com, Div. of Ponsford Ltd., 5441 Woodstock Rd., Acworth, GA 30102, 770-924-4848, fax: 770-529-2278, e-mail: GordonPonsford@AntiqueConservation.com, website: www.Antique Conservation.com. Conservation and restoration of fine art and antiques, frames and gilding, paintings, paper, and more. Appraisals.

Archival Conservation Center, Inc., 8225 Daly Rd., Cincinnati, OH 45231, 513-521-9858, fax: 513-521-9859. Repair and restoration of works of art on paper, including engravings, lithographs, watercolors, old maps, newspapers, Oriental scrolls, parchment documents, posters, books, and family Bibles. Smoke odor removal. Freeze drying of water-damaged materials. Free brochure available upon request.

Bags Unlimited, 7 Canal St., Rochester, NY 14608, 800-767-BAGS or 716-436-9006, fax: 716-328-8526, e-mail: info@bagsunlimited.com, website: www.bagsunlimited.com. Products for storing, displaying, and shipping collectibles. Specializing in products for comics, magazines, and many miscellaneous items. Archival materials sold: polyethylene, polypropylene, Mylar, acid-free boards and storage boxes. High-clarity, recyclable, 100% polyethylene bags. Three grades of backing boards, several sizes of storage boxes and divider cards.

Bill Cole Enterprises, Inc., PO Box 60, Dept. RK1, Randolph, MA 02368-0060, 781-986-2653, fax: 781-986-2656, e-mail: bcemylar@cwbusiness.com, website: www.bcemylar.com. Manufacturers and distributors of archival supplies to protect paper documents from turning yellow. Acid-free boards and boxes. Mylar sleeves for baseball cards, comic books, movie posters, paper money, and other paper collectibles.

Boston Art Conservation, Paul Messier, Paper Conservator, 9 Station St., Brookline, MA 02146, 617-738-1126, 9:00 A.M.–5:00 P.M., e-mail: admin@bosartconserv.com, website: bosartconserv.com. Conservation of works of art on paper, Asian paintings (scrolls and screens), photographs, art/artifacts on paper, and textiles. Collection surveys. Consultations on proper storage and display. Free brochure.

Chicago Conservation Center, 730 N. Franklin, Suite 701, Chicago, IL 60610, 312-944-5401, fax: 312-944-5479, e-mail: chicagoconservation @yahoo.com, website: chicagoconservation.com. Restoration of works of art on paper.

Conservation of Art on Paper, Inc., 2805 Mount Vernon Ave., Alexandria, VA 22301, 703-836-7757, fax: 703-836-8878, e-mail: capi@erols.com. Conservation treatments for art and historic artifacts on paper, including historic artifacts, memorabilia, fine prints, watercolors, drawings, pastels, rare posters, collages, scrapbooks, manuscripts, and documents. Vault storage, classes and lectures, publications about caring for art on paper, collection surveys, insurance reports.

Dieu Donne Papermill, Inc., 433 Broome St., New York, NY 10013, 212-226-0573, fax: 212-226-6088, e-mail: info@papermaking.org, website: www.papermaking.org. Not-for-profit hand papermaking studio. Conservation papermaking. Custom order papers. Colors, fibers, texture, and sizes matched. On-site workshops. Papermaking supplies.

Dobson Studios, 810 N. Daniel St., Arlington, VA 22201, 703-243-7363, e-mail: ddobson@dobson-studios.com, website: www.dobson-studios.com. Conservation of Oriental woodblock prints, screens, scrolls, Western paper and parchment, including watercolors, documents, drawings, photographs, pictures, etchings, prints, woodblock prints, certificates, posters, and oil paintings on various supports, including glass and silk. Most paper objects are washed and deacidified, if needed. All work and materials are reversible.

Document Preservation Center, PO Drawer 821, Yonkers, NY 10702, 914-476-8500, fax: 914-476-8573, e-mail: cohascodpc@earthlink.net, website: dpc.nu. Acid-free products for preservation and storage of paper collectibles, including many sizes of protectors for paper items. Slipcases, binders, acid-free Ultrafilm on rolls, archival sealing tapes, acid-free tissue and mat boards, acid-free mounting corners and repair tape, acid-free paste, pocket pages, deacidification solution, acid-free storage boxes in a variety of sizes, and more. Brochure $1.

G.M. Wylie Co., PO Box AA, Washington, PA 15301-0660, 800-747-1249, fax: 724-225-0741, e-mail: info@gmwylie.com, website: gmwylie.com. Safe long-term storage supplies for paper collectibles. Products include acid-free binders, albums, boxes, envelopes, folders, map folders, marking pens, mounting corners, newspaper storage boxes, preservation supplies, repair tape, wrapping paper, and much more. Order by mail, phone, or e-mail. Catalog $1.50 or visit the website.

Graphic Conservation Co., 329 W. 18th St., Suite 701, Chicago, IL 60616, 312-738-2657, fax: 312-738-3125, e-mail: info@graphicconservation.com, website: www.graphicconservation.com. Preservation of works of art on paper, including prints, drawings, watercolors, pastels, maps, globes, posters, manuscripts, architectural process prints, wallpaper, historical documents, billboard advertising, and paper memorabilia. Dry cleaning, stain reduction, flattening, deacidification, inpainting, tear repairs and fills. Archival matting. Free brochure.

Hollinger Corporation, PO Box 8360, Fredericksburg, VA 22404, 800-634-0491, 8:30 A.M.–5:00 P.M., e-mail: hollingercorp@erols.com, website: www.hollingercorp.com. Archival print boxes, envelopes, folders, tubes, photographic storage materials, acid-free papers, plastic sleeves, and products to store documents, books, photographs, maps, and more. Free catalog.

Intermuseum Laboratory, 83 N. Main St., Allen Art Bldg., Oberlin, OH 44074, 440-775-7331, 9:00 A.M.–5:00 P.M., fax: 440-774-3431, e-mail: sandra.williamson@oberlin.edu, website: www.oberlin.edu/~ica. A nonprofit, regional art conservation center that provides preservation and conservation services and education for member and nonmember museums and institutions, as well as private and corporate collectors. Conservation of paper-based materials, paintings, murals, frames, and more.

Linda A. Blaser, 9200 Hawkins Creamery Rd., Gaithersburg, MD 20882, e-mail: blaser@erols.com. Conservation of books and flat paper items. Collection condition surveys. Speaker services.

Metal Edge, Inc., 6340 Bandini Blvd., Commerce, CA 90040, 800-862-2228 or 213-721-7800; fax: 888-822-6937, e-mail: info@metaledgeinc.com, website: www.metaledgeinc.com. Storage, conservation, and identification supplies. Binders, boxes, bags, folders, document cases, boards, and paper. Book storage boxes, book and document repair supplies and more. Free catalog.

Museum Shop, Ltd., Richard Kornemann, conservator, 20 N. Market St., Frederick, MD 21701, 301-695-0424. Restoration of paper, including documents, etchings, lithographs. Free brochure.

New Orleans Conservation Guild, Inc., 3301 Chartres St., New Orleans, LA 70117, 504-944-7900, fax: 504-944-8750, e-mail: info@art-restoration.com, website: www.art-restoration.com. Restoration and conservation of fine art and antiques, including paper. Appraisals and research searches. Call or write for brochure.

Northeast Document Conservation Center, 100 Brickstone Sq., Andover, MA 01810-1494, 978-470-1010, fax: 978-475-6021, e-mail: nedcc@nedcc.org, website: www.nedcc.org. Nonprofit regional conservation center specializing in treatment of art and artifacts on paper, including books, documents, maps, photographs, posters, prints, works of art on paper, baseball cards, board games, cartoon cels, globes, and very large paper objects. Free brochure. Open 8:30 A.M.–4:30 P.M., Mon.–Fri.

Old World Restorations, Inc., 5729 Dragon Way, Cincinnati, OH 45227, 513-271-5459, fax: 513-271-5418, e-mail: info@oldworldrestorations.com, website: www.oldworldrestorations.com. Restoration and conservation of art and antiques, including paper, documents, and more. Specialized packing and shipping. Nationwide service. Send or e-mail photos for preliminary estimates. Free brochure.

Paper-Backed, 44 Medway Rd., San Anselmo, CA 94960, 415-453-3189, e-mail: marrrr@aol.com. Preservation and restoration of posters and linen backing. Movie one sheets, travel and advertising posters restored.

Philadelphia Print Shop, Ltd., 8441 Germantown Ave., Philadelphia, PA 19118, 215-242-4750, fax: 215-242-6977, e-mail: philaprint@philaprint shop.com, website: www.philaprintshop.com. Conservation services for art on paper. Handcrafted binding and refurbishing of rare and special books. Appraisals and research.

Richard C. Baker Conservation, 1712 (rear) S. Big Bend Blvd., St. Louis, MO 63117, 314-781-3035, e-mail: baker@RichardCBaker.com, website: www.RichardCBaker.com. Conservation services for books and printed works on paper and parchment. Treatments include binding restoration, facsimile binding, adhesive tape removal, stain reduction, washing, aqueous and nonaqueous deacidification, lining, mending, and inpainting.

Rosine Green Associates, Inc., 89 School St., Brookline, MA 02446, 617-277-8368, fax: 617-731-3845, e-mail: rga@ix.netcom.com. Conservation and restoration of fine art, including paper.

Scott K. Kellar/Bookbinding & Conservation, 2650 Montrose Ave., Chicago, IL 60618-1507, 773-478-2825, fax: 801-760-6843, e-mail: skkellar @earthlink.net. Conservation of rare books and printed material. Deacidification and archival encapsulation of documents, maps, and posters.

The2Buds.com, 462 W. Silver Lake Rd. N., Traverse City, MI 49684, 888-270-0552, Mon.–Fri. 9:00 A.M.–5:00 P.M., e-mail: postcards@the 2buds.com, website: www.the2buds.com. Archival supplies for storing and displaying vintage postcards, comics, trading cards, and other collectibles. Products include postcard sleeves, newspaper bags, comic bags, rigid sleeves, storage boxes, albums, binder pages, and much more. Internet sales only.

University Products, Inc., 517 Main St., PO Box 101, Holyoke, MA 01040, 800-628-1912; fax: 800-532-9281, fax: 800-532-9281, e-mail: info@ universityproducts.com, website: www.universityproducts.com. Specialized storage for baseball cards, comics, magazines, and other collectibles. Archival supplies for conservation, restoration, repair, storage, and display. Archival storage boxes, paper and plastic enclosures, acid-free board and papers, adhesives, albums, preservation framing supplies, tools, equipment, chemicals, and other materials. Free catalog.

Wei T'o Associates, Inc., 21750 Main St., Unit #27, Matteson, IL 60443-3702, 708-747-6660, fax: 708-747-6639, e-mail: weito@weito.com, website: www.weito.com. Deacidification sprays and solutions used to protect paper against deterioration and discoloring. "Wei T'o, an ancient Chinese god, protects books against destruction from fire, worms, and insects, and robbers, big or small," according to the company.

Williamstown Art Conservation Center, 225 South St., Williamstown, MA 01267, 413-458-5741, fax: 413-458-2314, e-mail: wacc@clark.williams.edu, website: www.williamstownart.org. Conservation of paper and other materials. Analytical services.

PAPERWEIGHTS

The media are always reporting the high prices of antique French paperweights. For many years, the value was rising so quickly that paperweights were considered a better investment than stocks or real estate. Unfortunately, few of us will ever discover the rare antique paperweight in fine condition that would sell for over $258,500 (a record price set in 1990). The paperweights we might own could be average-to-good antique French, English, or American weights, modern weights, or Chinese or Italian copies of old weights. They could also be some of the many paperweights that are not all glass: the snow weights, advertising weights, and others.

The *Paperweight Collectors Association Newsletter* had these words for members: "Fortunate indeed is the collector whose heir will enjoy and continue to develop the collection. Many families are faced with the problem of disposing of a collection. One collector told me that he enjoyed his paperweights so much that he was going to take them with him when he went, but he never gave me the secret of how he proposed to do this. Another collector, who has since learned the wisdom of his words, said that he had never seen a U-Haul trailer behind a hearse."

The newsletter continues with good advice:

> If you want to sell a collection for the highest dollars, you must find a collector who wants each weight, and sell it directly. Of course, this is time-consuming, if not impossible. Consider donating the weights to a museum and taking the tax deduction. This has been done by several well-known paper-weight collectors and the collections can be seen by those who want to learn how to recognize a fine old weight of value.
>
> Auctions are a good method, but don't expect the high prices announced for the best weights. A minor difference in color, design, or any flaws can alter the value. If you have rare weights, the auction, even with the seller's fees and other costs, is a good way to sell. The rare weights are advertised to a worldwide group of collectors with money and an interest in buying more weights. You might want to sell to a paperweight dealer. There are a few who sell both old and new weights, but many specialize. Some will buy the weights outright, some will take your collection on consignment and send you the money as the weights are sold.

A list of dealers can be found through the *Paperweight Collectors Association Newsletter*. Some advertise in the antiques publications. Modern weights are sold by gift shops as well as antiques dealers, and some of these shops may be willing to sell your weights on consignment.

Chinese and Italian paperweights were made in the twentieth century to look like older, better weights. These can be very confusing for a novice. Ask an expert in paperweights, preferably a dealer, appraiser, or auctioneer who sells fine paperweights. An expert will be glad to show you what characteristics of the glasswork are important.

In general, if the weight is made of small "canes" that look like hard candy, the canes should be very crisp and clear, with no blurring of color or distortion of edges. The clear glass should be perfect, with no bubbles, flaws, or discoloration. The bottom should be ground flat. If there are flowers or animals inside, these too should be made with precision, with no blurred edges or blurred color. Flowers and insects should be lifelike. If you remember that each color is made from a single strand of glass that has been worked by hand, you can understand the artistry in a single paperweight.

Advertising weights, small metal figural weights, snowdomes (clear plastic domes with figurines and "snow" inside), and other collectible but not artistic weights sell through regular antiques dealers and auction houses, the Internet, flea markets, and sales. Because weights are small, you can take them to these sales and discreetly try to sell them to dealers who have some others in stock. Remember, the best way to sell any antique or collectible is to find someone who has already shown an interest in and a knowledge of the item. Any dealer who sells an antique has to buy that antique from someone.

REPAIR

A slightly nicked or scratched paperweight can be restored. The glass can be repolished to remove scratches and nicks. Cracks cannot be repaired. It is important to be sure the condition of the paperweight is good. Repolishing scratched glass will not lower the value of the item, but if there is a large nick and removing it changes the overall shape of the weight, the value is lowered.

◆▸ SEE ALSO GLASS

REFERENCE BOOKS

The Art of the Paperweight, Lawrence Selman (Paperweight Press, 123 Locust St., Santa Cruz, CA 95060, 1988).
Glass Paperweights of the Bergstrom-Mahler Museum, Geraldine J. Casper (U.S. Historical Society Press, Richmond, VA, 1989).

PRICE BOOKS

Advertising Paperweights: Figural, Glass, Metal, Richard Holiner and Stuart Kammerman (Collector Books, Paducah, KY, 2002).
The Charlton Standard Catalogue of Caithness Paperweights, Colin Terris (Charlton Press, Toronto, 1999).
Old English Paperweights, Robert G. Hall (Schiffer, Atglen, PA, 1998).

CLUBS & THEIR PUBLICATIONS

Caithness Glass Paperweight Collectors Society, *Caithness Report* (NL), *Reflections* (MAG), 141 Lanza Ave., Bldg. 12, Garfield, NJ 07026, e-mail: caithglas@aol.com, website: www.caithnessglass.co.uk.

Friends of Degenhart, *Heartbeat* (NL), PO Box 186, Cambridge, OH 43725, e-mail: degmus@clover.net.

International Paperweight Society, *IPS Newsletter* (NL), 123 Locust St., Santa Cruz, CA 95060, e-mail: lselman@got.net, website: paperweight.com.

Paperweight Collectors Association, Inc., *Paperweight Collectors Association Newsletter* (NL), *Bulletin of the Paperweight Collectors Association* (MAG), PMB 130, 274 Eastchester Dr. #117, High Point, NC 27262, e-mail: pca@paperweight.org, website: www.paperweight.org.

Perthshire Paperweight Collectors Club, *PPCC Newsletter* (NL), 123 Locust St., Santa Cruz, CA 95060, e-mail: club@perthshire.com, website: paperweight.com.

ARCHIVES & MUSEUMS

Berstrom-Mahler Museum, 165 N. Park Ave., Neenah, WI 54956-2994, (920) 751-4658, e-mail: info@paperweightmuseum.com, website: www.paperweightmuseum.com.

APPRAISERS

The auction and many of the repair services listed in this section will also do appraisals. *See also* the general list of "Appraisal Groups" on page 483.

AUCTIONS

➸ **SEE ALSO "SELLING THROUGH AUCTION HOUSES," PAGE 485.**

L.H. Selman Ltd., 123 Locust St., Santa Cruz, CA 95060, 800-538-0766 or 831-427-1177, fax: 831-427-0111, e-mail: lselman@got.net, website: theglassgallery.com. Paperweight auctions. Mail, phone, fax, and e-mail bids accepted. Buyer's premium 10%. Catalog $25; annual subscription $60 for 3 catalogs. Prices realized mailed after auction and on website. Restoration and conservation services. Appraisals.

REPAIRS, PARTS & SUPPLIES

➸ **SEE ALSO "CONSERVATORS & RESTORERS," PAGE 520.**

Andrew H. Dohan, 20 Mystic Ln., Malvern, PA 19355, 610-722-5800, fax: 610-647-5476, e-mail: dohan@juno.com. Free paperweight evaluation questionnaire. Advice on where to get restoration based on the object and its value. *Dictionary of Paperweight Signature Canes—Identification & Dating,* $30; supplement $10.

George N. Kulles, 13441 Little Creek Dr., Lockport, IL 60441, 708-301-0996. Glass paperweights restored. Appraisals.

Herb Rabbin, PO Box 421205, Los Angeles, CA 90042, 323-258-1776, 10:00 A.M.–7:00 P.M., e-mail: hrabbin@earthlink.net, website: home.earthlink.net/~hrabbin. Repairs, restores, and reconstructs broken snowdomes. Glass or plastic, old or new, whole or damaged. Fabricates one-of-a-kind or limited production runs. Please call first.

L.H. Selman Ltd., 123 Locust St., Santa Cruz, CA 95060, 800-538-0766 or 831-427-1177, fax: 831-427-0111, e-mail: lselman@got.net, website: theglassgallery.com. Restoration and conservation services. Appraisals.

➛ PEWTER, SEE METALS

PHONOGRAPHS

Phonographs, phonograph records, radios, and even television sets are popular collectibles. Early phonographs are stocked in some shops, but later models are often ignored. The item must be in good working condition to be of value. "Crossover" examples, those wanted by collectors of another type of antique, are worth more than might be suspected and are worth restoring. For instance, Barbie's Vanity Fair record player is worth over $700. An RCA Little Nipper record display sells for around $500.

RECORDS

Enrico Caruso was a great opera singer, but in spite of the stories you hear, his records are not all worth thousands of dollars. One very early European record has a high value. The others are worth only a few dollars. Price is determined by demand. Today's collectors are more interested in "My Bonnie" by Tony Sheridan and the Beat Brothers (early Beatles) on the 1961 Decca label than they are in Bing Crosby singing "White Christmas." Probably the rarest record is "Stormy Weather" by the Five Sharps, which auctioned for $3,800 in 1977. It's worth much more today—if you can find one. Still, just a very few rare records are selling for over $1,000.

Sad but true: most 78s (a standard size after 1926, but almost completely replaced by 1957) and unusual-looking early records are not of great value. Cylinder discs for pre-1906 phonographs are usually worth just a few dollars in the shops; flat, one-sided records (made until 1923) are also of limited interest to collectors. The 33 RPM record was developed in 1930 but was not popular until 1948, the same year the 45 RPM record was introduced. Picture records, those with a picture showing on the plastic record, are collected, but most sell for under $50.

Most records sell for low prices, if they can be sold at all. Condition is important, and any record that has overwhelming surface noises, a label in poor condition, cracks, chips, or deep scratches is not salable to anyone. Records in mint (never played) to very good condition can be sold. Try playing the record before you sell it, unless you are sure it has never been played.

The picture sleeve is important and adds to the value. The value of albums is sometimes determined partially by the picture on the album cover. Even empty album covers with important artwork or graphics are sold.

Pricing records can be difficult because it is not just the artist and song but also the label that determine the value. The best price books about records include pictures of the labels, so you should have no problem identifying what you have.

The most valued 78 RPM records were made between 1915 and 1935. Unfortunately, if the same record was reissued on a 33 or 45 RPM disc, the earlier record is of less value. Some Enrico Caruso records are now available in reissue with enhanced sound quality, so the 78s do not sell well. Some combinations of artists are treasured, but were recorded without listing all of the artists' names on the record; some artists are valued highly only on particular labels (Al Jolson on Columbia or Brunswick); and some artists recorded under many names. Many 45s have been bootlegged or illegally copied, and these copies are not of great value. These factors show that it will take real study to know your records and to set a sensible price. The library and the price books will help.

Collectors specialize, so your records can be sold not only by artist and song, but also by type of music: rock, jazz, big band, blues, country and western, etc. If you plan to sell the records yourself at a show or house sale, be sure to sort them into separate boxes to make it easier for people to find the type of music they are interested in. Like other collectibles, records are easily sold on Internet auction sites.

If you have some rare records, perhaps the best way to sell them is through the dealers who specialize in records. You can find them in the Yellow Pages under "Compact Disc, Cassette Tapes & Records" or look for record convention ads in your local newspaper. Compact discs and cassette tapes have some resale value, too. If you just have a pile of old records in poor condition, you may find it doesn't pay to spend the time researching and selling them. Most accumulations of old records found at house sales and rummage sales are of little, if any, value. They are not even welcomed at some thrift shops.

➥ SEE ALSO CELEBRITY MEMORABILIA, MOVIE MEMORABILIA

PHONOGRAPHS

We are constantly asked the value of old phonographs. The early type with the large horn is probably the most valuable. Least desirable are the floor-standing phonographs from the 1910s to 1950s. They may play, but they are not attractive and the quality of the music from the old records is poor. Phonographs are listed in *Kovels' Antiques & Collectibles Price List* and in several special price lists devoted to phonographs.

The general rule is to check carefully if the machine has an exposed horn or unusual turntable arrangement with obvious pulleys and belts. Lower your expectations for enclosed machines, even if they are floor models. Many of the old phonographs are found with records, and if the records are unusual in size or shape—cylinders or "fat," one-sided, flat records—you probably own an old machine. A collector may want it if it is unusual and still in working condition. Even if it is not working, a collector able to fix your phonograph might be willing to buy it, but prices are generally below $150.

REPAIR

Phonograph repairs can be expensive, slow, and sometimes impossible. If you are able to fix this type of collectible, you can usually make a good buy. Repairs can often cost more than the value of a phonograph in very good condition.

Early phonograph records include many types. There are price books that list thousands of phonograph records, but many record titles are still unlisted. Records cannot be restored and have value only if they are in good playing condition.

PRICE BOOKS

Antique Phonograph Gadgets, Gizmos & Gimmicks, Timothy C. Fabrizio and George F. Paul (Schiffer, Atglen, PA, 1999).

Beatle Mania: An Unauthorized Collector's Guide, Courtney McWilliams (Schiffer, Atglen, PA, 1998).

The Beatles Digest, Goldmine magazine, editors (Krause, Iola, WI, 2000).

Discovering Antique Phonographs, 1877–1929, Timothy C. Fabrizio and George F. Paul (Schiffer, Atglen, PA, 2000).

Forever Lounge: A Laid-Back Price Guide to the Languid Sounds of Lounge Music, John Wooley, Thomas Conner, and Mark Brown (Antique Trader Books, Dubuque, IA, 1999).

Girl Groups: Fabulous Females That Rocked the World, John Clemente (Krause, Iola, WI, 2000).

Goldmine 45 RPM Picture Sleeve Price Guide, Charles Szabla (Krause, Iola, WI, 1998).

Goldmine British Invasion Record Price Guide, Tim Neely and Dave Thompson (Krause, Iola, WI, 1997).

Goldmine Christmas Record Price Guide, Tim Neely (Krause, Iola, WI, 1997).

Goldmine Country and Western Record Price Guide, Tim Neely (Krause, Iola, WI, 2001).

Goldmine Heavy Metal Record Price Guide, Martin Popoff (Krause, Iola, WI, 2000).

Goldmine Jazz Album Price Guide, Tim Neely (Krause, Iola, WI, 2000).

Goldmine Price Guide to 45 RPM Records, 3rd edition, Tim Neely (Krause, Iola, WI, 2001).

Goldmine Promo Record & CD Price Guide, 2nd edition, Fred Heggeness (Krause, Iola, WI, 1998).

Goldmine Record Album Price Guide, 2nd edition, Tim Neely (Krause, Iola, WI, 2001).

Goldmine Records and Prices, Tim Neely, editor (Krause, Iola, WI, 2002).

Goldmine Standard Catalog of American Records, 1950 to 1975, Tim Neely (Krause, Iola, WI, 2002).

Goldmine Standard Catalog of American Records, 1976–present, Tim Neely (Krause, Iola, WI, 2001).

Official Price Guide to Elvis Presley Records and Memorabilia, 2nd edition, Jerry Osborne (House of Collectibles, New York, 1998).

Official Price Guide to Records, 15th edition, Jerry Osborne (House of Collectibles, New York, 2001).

Official Price Guide to the Beatles Records and Memorabilia, 2nd edition, Perry Cox (House of Collectibles, New York, 1999).

Phonographs with Flair: A Century of Style in Sound Reproduction, Timothy C. Fabrizio, George F. Paul (Schiffer, Atglen, PA, 2001).

CLUBS & THEIR PUBLICATIONS

American Bandstand Fan Club, *Bandstand Boogie* (MAG), PO Box 131, Adamstown, PA 19501, e-mail: popfrosty@webtv.net, website: fiftiesweb.com.

Association for Recorded Sound Collections, *ARSC Journal* (MAG), PO Box 543, Annapolis, MD 21404-0543, e-mail: shambarger@sprynet.com, website: www.arsc-audio.org.

International Association of Jazz Record Collectors, *IAJRC Journal* (MAG), 1443 Red Oak Ln., Port Charlotte, FL 33948, e-mail: admiral@ewol.com, website: www.geocities.com/BourbonStreet/3910/index.html.

OTHER PUBLICATIONS

Disc Collector (NL), PO Box 315, Cheswold, DE 19936.

DISCoveries (NP), *Goldmine* (MAG), 700 E. State St., Iola, WI 54990-0001, e-mail: info@krause.com, website: www.krause.com.

New Amberola Graphic (MAG), 213 Caledonia St., St. Johnsbury, VT 05819, e-mail: mfb@together.net (phonographs and records made before 1935).

Record Finder (NP), 8508 Sanford Dr., Richmond, VA 23228, e-mail: sales1@RecordFinders.com, website: RecordFinders.com.

ARCHIVES & MUSEUMS

Johnson Victrola Museum, Delaware State Museum, PO Box 1401, Dover, DE 19903, 302-739-5316, fax: 302-739-6712, website: www.destatemuseums.org/jvm.

Rock and Roll Hall of Fame and Museum, One Key Plaza, Cleveland, OH 44114, 800-493-ROLL, e-mail: curatorial@rockhall.com, website: www.rockhall.com.

USEFUL SITES

The Internet Museum of Flexi/Cardboard/Oddity Records, www.wfmu.org/MACrec.

APPRAISERS

Many of the auctions and repair services listed in this section will also do appraisals. *See also* the general list of "Appraisal Groups" on page 483.

AUCTIONS

➜ **SEE ALSO "SELLING THROUGH AUCTION HOUSES," PAGE 485.**

Antique Phonograph Center, PO Box 2574, Hwy. 206, Vincentown, NJ 08088, 609-859-8617, e-mail: fsi491160@aol.com. Mail and phone bids accepted. No buyer's premium. Restoration and conservation. Appraisals.

Jerry Madsen, 4624 W. Woodland Rd., Edina, MN 55424-1553, 612-926-7775, e-mail: jerryclare@aol.com. Auction lists of Berliners, Zonophones, Nipper items, records, cylinders, etc. Send first-class stamp for lists and photos.

REPAIRS, PARTS & SUPPLIES

➜ **SEE ALSO "CONSERVATORS & RESTORERS," PAGE 520.**

Antique Phonograph Books, Allen Koenigsberg, 502 E. 17th St., Brooklyn, NY 11226, 718-941-6835, e-mail: allenamet@aol.com, website: www.phonobooks.com. Books, catalogs, manuals, and patents on antique phonographs and records. Will answer questions relating to repair, history, maintenance, identification, patents, etc. Send first-class stamp for brochure.

Antique Phonograph Center, PO Box 2574, Hwy. 206, Vincentown, NJ 08088, 609-859-8617, e-mail: fsi491160@aol.com. Restoration and conservation of antique Victor, Edison, and Columbia phonographs. Appraisals.

Antique Phonograph Supply Co., Rt. 23, Box 123, Davenport Center, NY 13751-0123, 607-278-6218, fax: 607-278-5136, e-mail: apsco@antiquephono.com, website: www.antiquephono.com. Repairs, parts, and services for all windup phonographs. Steel mainsprings, steel needles, record sleeves, horns, accessories, and books. Comprehensive rebuilding of motors and reproducers. International business welcomed. Catalog $3.

Bags Unlimited, 7 Canal St., Rochester, NY 14608, 800-767-BAGS or 716-436-9006, fax: 716-328-8526, e-mail: info@bagsunlimited.com, website: www.bagsunlimited.com. Products for storing, displaying, and shipping collectibles. Specializing in products for records and many miscellaneous items. Archival materials sold. Acid-free storage boxes and divider cards.

Cabco Products, 3481 N. High St., Columbus, OH 43214, 614-267-8468, fax: 614-267-8468, e-mail: jproto1@aol.com. Record collectors' supplies, including jackets, sleeves, protectors, storage boxes; video protection, cassette tape supplies, CD and jewel box supplies, etc. Free catalog.

Chet Ramsay Antiques, 2460 Strasburg Rd., Coatesville, PA 19320-4339, 610-384-0514. Restoration of all types and makes of phonographs, 1912 and older. Shop and showroom open by appointment. Call 10:00 A.M.–6:00 P.M.

Childhood Radios, 13853 Mountain View Place, 818-362-8888, e-mail: ronmansfield@earthlink.net, website: www.ronmansfield.com. Specializing in the restoration of collectible cold war electronics from the 1950s and 1960s, including vintage hi-fi gear, test equipment, and tube stereo.

Dan Reed, PO Box 169, Victorville, CA 92393, 760-242-5748. Phonographs, gramophones, and Victrolas repaired. Parts available.78s and cylinder records.

Donley's Wild West Town, 8512 S. Union Rd., Union, IL 60180, 815-923-9000, 10:00 A.M.–6:00 P.M. Phonograph parts and repair service.

Far West Record Supply, PO Box 3027, San Dimas, CA 91773, 626-335-5544. Paper and polypropylene sleeves for LPs, 45s, and 78s. Resealable sleeves for 12-inch, 10-inch, and 7-inch records and CDs. Steel needles for windup phonographs. Free brochure.

French Lace Antiques and Restoration, 120 N. Market St., Paxton, IL 60957, 217-379-4140, fax: 217-379-4140, e-mail: phonoman1960@prairieinet.net, website: www.frenchlace.us. Restoration of windup phonographs (Victrolas), tube radios, and record players. Always looking for parts.

G.M. Wylie Co., PO Box AA, Washington, PA 15301-0660, 800-747-1249, fax: 724-225-0741, e-mail: info@gmwylie.com, website: gmwylie.com. Record storage boxes, sleeves, and much more. Order by mail, phone, or e-mail. Catalog $1.50 or visit the Web page.

Hawthorn's Antique Audio, 77 Columbia Ave., Roseville, CA 95678, 916-773-4727, fax: 916-773-4727, e-mail: hawthorn@vfr.net, website: www.vfr.net/~hawthorn. Repair of all types of hand-wound phonographs. Victrola needles; record sleeves and albums for 78s; other supplies available by mail. Professional appraisals of record collections for tax or insurance purposes. Research and information on most types of phonographs and records.

Jerry Madsen, 4624 W. Woodland Rd., Edina, MN 55424-1553, 612-926-7775, e-mail: jarryclare@aol.com. Phonograph reproducers, gramophone toys, needle tins, and other items having to do with old phonographs. Send stamp for free lists and photos.

Kim Gutzke, 7134 15th Ave. S., Minneapolis, MN 55423, 612-869-4963, fax: 612-798-4169, e-mail: kgutzke@mn.rr.com. Wurlizter jukebox grille screens and Popperette Popcorn decals. Makes 45 RPM and 78 RPM records and 10-inch picture discs for jukeboxes and phonographs.

The Magic Barn, Dawson's Antiques, 516 N. Ave. B, Washington, IA 52353, 319-653-5043, e-mail: radio4me@hotmail.com. Restoration of mechanical music, including phonographs.

Metal Edge, Inc., 6340 Bandini Blvd., Commerce, CA 90040, 800-862-2228 or 213-721-7800; fax: 888-822-6937, e-mail: info@metaledgeinc.com, website: www.metaledgeinc.com. Storage for records, audio reels, and more. Free catalog.

Mike Zuccaro—Antique Electronics Repair, 8795 Corvus St., San Diego, CA 92126-1920, 858-271-8294, e-mail: mjzuccaro@aol.com. Repair and restoration of vintage hi-fi equipment from the 1920s through the 1970s.

The Musical Wonder House & The Merry Music Box, Attention: Repairs, 18 High St., PO Box 604, Wiscasset, ME 04578, 207-882-7163, fax: 207-882-6373, e-mail: musicbox@musicalwonderhouse.com, website: www.musicalwonderhouse.com. Repair and restoration of antique and contemporary spring-wound phonographs, singing birds, and whistling figures. The Musical Wonder House is a museum of mechanical musical instruments, open Memorial Day weekend through October 15. Appraisals. Mail order all year. Brochure $1.

Randle Pomeroy, 54 12th St., Providence, RI 02906, 401-272-5560, after 6:00 P.M. Antique phonographs cleaned and repaired, specializing in reproducer work.

Something Special Enterprises, PO Box 74, Allison Park, PA 15101-0074, 412-487-2626, e-mail: SSEorder@hotmail.com. Supplies for storing records, cassettes, compact discs, and other collectibles. CD jewel cases, storage boxes, mailers, record sleeves. Free flyer.

The2Buds.com, 462 W. Silver Lake Rd. N., Traverse City, MI 49684, 888-270-0552, Mon.–Fri. 9:00 A.M.–5:00 P.M., e-mail: postcards@the 2buds.com, website: www.the2buds.com. Archival supplies for storing and displaying collectibles. Sleeves for 45s RPM records and 3 RPM albums. Internet sales only.

University Products, Inc., 517 Main St., PO Box 101, Holyoke, MA 01040, 800-628-1912; fax: 800-532-9281, e-mail: info@universityproducts.com, website: www.universityproducts.com. Archival supplies and materials for storage, specializing in storage for records. Conservation tools and equipment; books and videos. Free catalog.

The Victrola Man, 17024 Frazier Road, Plano, IL 60545, 630-552-1558, e-mail: victrolman@aol.com. Old windup phonographs repaired. Many original and new replacement parts and related items such as steel replacement needles, records, memorabilia items.

Victrola Repair Service, 206 Cliff St., St. Johnsbury, VT 05819, 800-239-4188 anytime, e-mail: victrola@together.net, website: homepages. together.net/~victrola. Repair of all brands of windup phonographs. Antique phonograph parts, including mainsprings, needles, reproduction phonograph dancing dolls, record cleaning products, restoration supplies, books, manuals, and more. Worldwide service.

Wyatt's Musical Americana, PO Box 601, Lakeport, CA 95453, 707-263-5013, fax: 707-263-8823, website: www.wyattsmusical.com. Original and reproduction parts and repair services for all makes of windup phonographs and gramophones. Catalog, 64 pages, $4 in U.S., $6 outside U.S.

Yesterday Once Again, PO Box 6773, Huntington Beach, CA 92615, 714-963-2474, telephone hours Mon.–Fri. 7:00 A.M.–9:30 A.M. and 4:30 P.M.–6:30 P.M., fax: 714-963-1558, e-mail: yesterdayonceagain@yahoo.com. Antique and vintage phonograph repair service. Parts and accessories, mainsprings, reproducers, books, and reprints of instruction manuals. Mail order worldwide. Free brochure.

PHOTOGRAPHY

CAMERAS

Any old camera has a value. So do stereo viewers and cards, screens, darkroom equipment, most professional photographs, sports photos, and amateur photos taken before 1918 that show everyday life or historic events. Even some snapshots or news pictures taken more recently will sell. Most working old cameras can be sold online through an Internet auction site, which is a better place than an antiques shop to try to sell a camera. You might be able to trade in an old camera for a new one, but camera shops are becoming less willing to buy and sell used equipment.

The Internet attracts photography buffs, too. Search for specific sites dedicated to NIKON or BROWNIE, or look for general sites where cameras are bought, sold, and traded. For information about old photographs and photography galleries, try association sites, like www.icp.org (the International Center of Photography).

There are camera and photography clubs in most large cities. The members of these clubs buy many types of cameras, photographs, and photographic equipment. Call some local camera stores, the museum or historical society, or search online for information on local camera clubs. Then call a member and describe what you have for sale. Often the members will help you price the items, will offer to buy them, or will tell you about dealers who might want them. Most large cities have camera and photography shows, and you can find customers for all types of photography-related items. Even film boxes, tripods, lenses, slide mounts, darkroom equipment, screens, and other photographica are wanted.

A working 35-mm camera made after 1950 can be sold to most pawnbrokers. More unusual cameras probably cannot. There are publications for the photography collector with interests in cameras, vintage pictures, 3-D, or other related subjects. Most of these publications have buy and sell ads and wanted lists. It is always best to read these for information on prices and possible customers. Cameras and exceptional pictures, daguerreotypes and daguerreotype cases, stereo viewers and stereo pictures (3-D), glass plate slides, and twentieth-century photographs by well-known photographers are often sold by antiques and art auction houses. Fine photographs by name artists are often sold in art galleries or at antiques auctions.

We have found that information about old cameras and photographs spreads well by word of mouth. If you have time to wait to sell your items, try this subtle form of advertising. Go to flea markets and the shows, and tell your local camera store and friends exactly what you have to offer for sale. Give them a list of the items, including brand names, condition, and identifying numbers. When describing a camera, include the manufacturer's name, serial number, words written near the lens, type and condition of case, and any instruction books, lenses, or other parts that are included. Even the original bill and box are important. The word will be spread to other collectors, and one day you will receive a phone call from an unknown collector searching for just the items you have.

Any camera that seems unusual to you may have a value. Very old cameras, pre-1900, are of special interest. Unusual shapes, even a Mickey Mouse–shaped camera, extra-large or extra-small cameras, and of course cameras of exceptional quality sell well. Condition is important. Wear, scratches, and minor repairable problems lower the price by 25 to 50 percent.

EQUIPMENT

Once at a house sale we watched a teenage friend of our son buy a strange metal and glass object for a quarter. He told us later that he took it to a camera store and sold it for $50. He had recognized the close-up lens for a special make of camera. At the same sale we saw a happy collector buy an old wooden tripod, oak cases for slides, and other 1910 paraphernalia. He wanted it to decorate a room. Anything connected with photography will sell. There is new interest in old magazines and trade catalogs on photography. Collectors will buy it all. Your job is to find the true collector of photographica.

PHOTOGRAPHS

Early photographs, daguerreotypes (silver images on glass), ambrotypes (glass negatives backed with dark paper), tintypes (photos printed on black tin), and other pictures that were not printed on paper have a special group of customers. Some want to add to their "country look" decorating. Some want pictures for historical reasons and search for street views, war views, pictures of soldiers, miners, or people in other occupations, children with toys or buggies, or interior shop scenes. Some seek the most artistic photographs by the often nameless but early skilled photographers. All early daguerreotypes and ambrotypes sell unless they are badly damaged. Restoration is next to impossible.

Cartes de visite (2-by-4-inch photographs on card stock), cabinet cards (4-by-7-inch photographs on card stock), album photos of grandparents, and other Victorian pictures also sell, but often for low prices.

MODERN PHOTOGRAPHS

Wallace Nutting "prints" are really hand-tinted photographs taken in the early 1900s. They picture views of early homes, landscapes, and interiors. Mr. Nutting sold hundreds of thousands of these pictures, each signed with his name. Collectors rediscovered them in the early 1980s. The highest price paid for a Nutting print was $8,910 for *Old Mother Hen* in 2002. Modern art photographs by artists like **ANSEL ADAMS**, **MARGARET BOURKE-WHITE**, or **DIANE ARBUS** sell for high prices in galleries. There has been some speculation that the price structure at auctions has been unduly influenced by some pre-planned bidding, but whatever the reason for the ups and downs of this market, your picture will have a value if it is an original.

ODDITIES

Some collectors are interested in the oddities, the photos printed on porcelain dishes or enameled on plaques for tombstones. Stanhopes are tiny pictures seen through peepholes in canes or charms. Wide pictures, 36 inches or more, taken with a special camera also interest a few collectors. The subjects are usually large groups of people or city views. These and other older oddities also have a market.

STEREO VIEWS

Stereo view cards are often found in boxes. Sets from the 1920s were often sold with a photograph of the family who bought them. There was one picture of some children, then boxes and boxes of educational scenes. These are of very low value. The stereo card has two almost identical pictures mounted on a piece of cardboard. When viewed through the stereoscope, the pictures look 3-D. The cardboard corners of the rectangular cards were square from 1854 to 1870 and sometimes the cardboard was colorful. Round corners were favored from 1868 to 1882. The curved cardboard mounts used after 1880 were usually buff, gray, or black. Thin cardboard was introduced about 1900. Colored pictures were made from 1900 to 1929.

Prices vary with age and subject. Views sell best near the area they picture. It may pay to try to sell out-of-state views by mail or Internet. Dealers at flea markets and postcard shows, as well as general antiques dealers, sell stereo views, so any of them might buy yours.

REPAIR

Prices of photographs have risen into the thousands of dollars for choice pictures, so conservation, restoration, and storage have become very important. Many types of photographs can be included in the collector's world. Movies are one special type. The old nitrate film is combustible and dangerous to store. If you are fortunate enough to find or own some early movies, have them copied on modern film. The American Film Institute at the Kennedy Center for the Performing Arts, Washington, DC 20566, can help you with this problem.

All types of photographs, from daguerreotypes and glass-plate slides to stereopticon slides, cartes de visite, and modern pictures, are important as art as well as history. Do not try a home-remedy restoration. Many old pictures can be saved if the work is done by an expert.

Old cameras can be restored, but once again expertise is required. Sometimes a local camera shop can have the camera repaired, but most old cameras need special parts that are no longer available. Modern photography club members are often interested in antique cameras and photographic equipment, and it is helpful to check with a local professional photographer to see if there is someone in your area who likes to work with old cameras.

➻ SEE ALSO COMIC ART, MOVIE MEMORABILIA, PAPER COLLECTIBLES

PRICE BOOKS

Collecting Picture and Photo Frames, Stuart Schneider (Schiffer, Atglen, PA, 1998).

Collector's Guide to Early Photographs, 2nd edition, O. Henry Mace (Krause, Iola, WI, 1999).

Photographic Cases: Victorian Design Sources, 1840–1870, Adele Kenny (Schiffer, Atglen, PA, 2001).

Stereo Views: An Illustrated History and Price Guide, 2nd edition, John Waldsmith (Krause, Iola, WI, 2002).

Wallace Nutting Pictures: Identification & Values, Michael Ivankovich (Collector Books, Paducah, KY, 1997, values 2001).

CLUBS & THEIR PUBLICATIONS

American Photographic Historical Society, *Photographica in Focus* (MAG), 1150 Ave. of the Americas, New York, NY 10036.

American Society of Camera Collectors Inc., 7952 Genesta Ave., Van Nuys, CA 91406.

The Daguerreian Society, *The Daguerreian Society Newsletter* (NL), 3045 W. Liberty Ave., Suite 9, Pittsburgh, PA 15216-2460, e-mail: DagSocPgh@aol.com, website: www.daguerre.org.

International Stereoscopic Union (ISU), *Stereoscopy* (MAG), 6320 SW 34th Ave., Portland, OR 97201, e-mail: shab@easystreet.com.

Leica Historical Society of America, *Viewfinder* (MAG), PO Box 7607, Louisville, KY 40257-0607, e-mail: admin@lhsa.org, website: www.lhsa.org.

Magic Lantern Society of the United States and Canada, *Magic Lan-*

tern Gazette (NL), 3321 114th St., Gig Harbor, WA 98332, e-mail: rbtdhall@aol.com, website: www.magiclanternsociety.org.

National Stereoscopic Association, *Stereo World* (MAG), N.S.A. Membership, PO Box 86708, Portland, OR 97286, e-mail: larryhiker@yahoo.com, website: www.stereoview.org.

Nikon Historical Society, *Nikon Journal* (MAG), PO Box 3213, Munster, IN 46321, e-mail: rotoloni@msn.com, website: www.nikonhs.org.

Photographic Historical Society of Canada, *Photographic Canadiana* (MAG), Box 54620, RPO Avenue-Fairlawn, Toronto, ON M5M 4N5, Canada, e-mail: PHSC@onramp.ca, website: web.onramp.ca/phsc.

Photographic Historical Society of New England, *Photographic Historical Society of New England Journal* (MAG), PO Box 65189, West Newton, MA 02465-0189, website: phsne.org.

Stereoscopic Society of America (SSA), *SSA Yearbook,* 6320 SW 34th Ave., Portland, OR 97201, e-mail: shab@easystreet.com.

Wallace Nutting Collectors Club, *Wallace Nutting Collectors Club Newsletter* (NL), PO Box 22475, Beachwood, OH 44122, e-mail: ghhamann@ earthlink.net.

Zeiss Historical Society, *Zeiss Historica* (MAG), 300 Waxwing Dr., Cranbury, NJ 08512, e-mail: mzubatkin@att.net (Zeiss cameras & binoculars).

OTHER PUBLICATIONS

Art on Paper (MAG), 39 E. 78th St., Suite 501, New York, NY 10021, e-mail: info@artonpaper.com, website: www.artonpaper.com.

CameraShopper (MAG), PO Box 1086, New Canaan, CT 06840, e-mail: camshop@aol.com, website: www.camera-shopper.com.

Military Images Magazine (MAG), PO Box 2391, Southeastern, PA 19399-2391, e-mail: milimage@yahoo.com, website: civilwar-photos.com.

The Photo Review (MAG), *The Photograph Collector* (NL), 140 E. Richardson Ave., Suite 301, Langhorne, PA 19047, e-mail: info@photoreview.org, website: www.photoreview.org.

ARCHIVES & MUSEUMS

George Eastman House, International Museum of Photography and Film, 900 East Ave., Rochester, NY 14607, 585-271-3361, fax: 585-271-3970, website: www.eastman.org.

International Center of Photography, 1133 Avenue of the Americas, New York, NY 10036, 212-857-0000, e-mail: info@icp.org, website: www.icp.org.

Magic Lantern Castle Museum, 1419 Austin Hwy., San Antonio, TX 78209, 210-805-0011, fax: 210-822-1226, website: www.magiclanterns.org.

USEFUL SITES

Canon Camera Museum, www.canon.com/camera-museum.

APPRAISERS

Many of the auctions and repair services listed in this section will also do appraisals. *See also* the general list of "Appraisal Groups" on page 483.

AUCTIONS

•→ SEE ALSO "SELLING THROUGH AUCTION HOUSES," PAGE 485.

Auction Team Köln, 4025 Cattlemen Rd., PMB 108, Sarasota, FL 34233, 941-925-0385, fax: 941-925-0487, e-mail: auction@breker.com, website: www.breker.com. Specialty auctions of all kinds of old technology, including photographica. Mail and phone bids accepted. Buyer's premium 20%. Prices realized available on website after auction. Catalog $58 per year.

Be-Hold, Inc., 78 Rockland Ave., Yonkers, NY 10705, 914-423-5806, fax: 914-423-5802, e-mail: behold@be-hold.com, website: www.be-hold.com. Specializing in nineteenth- and twentieth-century photographs. Catalogs are available on the website, as well as in printed form. Subscription $50 per year, 3 catalogs. Mail, phone, fax, e-mail, and Internet bids accepted. No buyer's premium. Prices realized mailed and posted on website after auction. Appraisals.

Cowan Auctions, 673 Wilmer Ave., Terrace Park, OH 45226, 513-871-1670, fax: 513-871-8670, e-mail: info@historicamericana.com, website: www.historicamericana.com. Early photography, Americana, Civil War, and American Indian collectibles. Mail, phone, fax, and e-mail bids accepted. Buyer's premium 15%. Catalogs $25–$30. Prices realized mailed after auction and available on website. Appraisals.

Michael Ivankovich Auction Co., Inc., PO Box 1536, Doylestown, PA 18901, 215-345-6094, fax: 215-345-6692, e-mail: ivankovich@wnutting.com, website: www.wnutting.com. Auctions of Wallace Nutting, hand-colored photography, early twentieth-century prints. Mail, phone, and Internet bids accepted. Buyer's premium 10%. Catalogs free on website. Prices realized mailed after auction and available on website. Restoration and conservation. Appraisals.

Page & Bryan Ginns, Stereographica, 2109 Rt. 21, Valatie, NY 12184, 518-392-5805, fax: 518-392-7925, e-mail: The3dman@aol.com, website: www.stereographica.com. Absentee auctions: mail, phone, and Internet bids accepted. No buyer's premium. Catalog $20. Prices realized mailed and available on website after auction.

R.M. Smythe & Co., 26 Broadway, Suite 973, New York, NY 10004-1703, 800-622-1880 or 212-943-1880, fax: 212-908-4670, e-mail: info@smytheonline.com, website: www.smytheonline.com. Auctions of photographs and historic Americana. Mail, phone, fax, and Internet bids accepted. Buyer's premium varies with amount of sale, 10%, 12%, and 15%. Prices realized mailed after auction. Catalog $25, subscription $87.50. Appraisals.

Swann Galleries, Inc., 104 E. 25th St., New York, NY 10010, 212-254-4710, fax: 215-979-1017, e-mail: swann@swanngalleries.com, website: www.swanngalleries.com. Auctions of photographs. Buyer's premium varies. Mail, phone, and fax bids accepted. Catalogs.

REPAIRS, PARTS & SUPPLIES

⇢ SEE ALSO "CONSERVATORS & RESTORERS," PAGE 520.

AntiqueConservation.com, Div. of Ponsford Ltd., 5441 Woodstock Rd., Acworth, GA 30102, 770-924-4848, fax: 770-529-2278, e-mail: GordonPonsford@AntiqueConservation.com, website: www.Antique Conservation.com. Conservation and restoration of photographs. Can remove tears, cuts, scratches, and holes in photos, rebuild areas that have faded, and replace areas that have been lost.

Atlantic Camera Repair Corp., 276 Higbie Ln., West Islip, NY 11795, 631-587-7959, 8:30 A.M.–5:30 P.M., fax: 631-587-7750. Repair, service, and restoration of all photographic equipment, including 8 mm, Super 8, and 16-mm sound and silent movie equipment. Antique cameras restored. Bellows, shutters, lenses, video cameras, projectors, meters, and other photographic equipment repaired. Send SASE to request information.

Boston Art Conservation, 9 Station St., Brookline, MA 02146, 617-738-1126, 9:00 A.M.–5:00 P.M., e-mail: admin@bosartconserv.com, website: bosartconserv.com. Conservation of photographs and works of art on paper. Consultations on proper storage and display. Free brochure.

Century Business Solutions, PO Box 2393, Brea, CA 92822, 800-767-0777, fax: 800-786-7939, website: www.centurybusinesssolutions.com. Products for organizing and storing photographs, slides, film, and other collectibles. Photo albums and pages.

Devashan, 445 S. Canyon, Spearfish, SD 57783, 605-722-5355, e-mail: dollmaker@mato.com, website: www.devashan.com. Photo restoration, both on the picture and with a computer. Send SASE for brochure.

Dobson Studios, 810 N. Daniel St., Arlington, VA 22201, 703-243-7363, e-mail: ddobson@dobson-studios.com, website: www.dobson-studios.com. Conservation of photographs.

Eugene R. Groves, PO Box 2471, Baton Rouge, LA 70821-2471, 225-381-0256, fax: 225-346-8049, e-mail: gene@tpbp.com. Restoration of daguerreotypes and ambrotypes for families and historical societies to preserve these images for future generations. Services performed free of charge or for a nominal charge. Send a copy of the photograph or photocopy of your image for further information.

Exposures, 1 Memory Ln., PO Box 3615, Oshkosh, WI 54903-3615, 800-222-4947 orders, 800-572-575, fax: 888-345-3702, e-mail: csr@exposures online.com, website: www.exposuresonline.com. Archival supplies, albums, frames, boxes, storage and display items. Free catalog.

G.M. Wylie Co., PO Box AA, Washington, PA 15301-0660, 800-747-1249, fax: 724-225-0741, e-mail: info@gmwylie.com, website: gmwylie.com. Safe long-term storage supplies for photos and other paper collectibles. Products include acid-free binders, albums, boxes, envelopes, folders, map folders, marking pens, photo mounting corners, preservation supplies, repair tape, and much more. Order by mail, phone, or e-mail. Catalog $1.50 or visit the website.

Hollinger Corporation, PO Box 8360, Fredericksburg, VA 22404, 800-634-0491, 8:30 A.M.–5:00 P.M., e-mail: hollingercorp@erols.com, website: www.hollingercorp.com. Archival print boxes, envelopes, folders, tubes, photographic storage materials, acid-free papers, plastic sleeves, and products to store photographs, negatives, and more. Free catalog.

Light Impressions, PO Box 787, Brea, CA 92822-0787, 800-828-6216, 714-441-4539 for international calls, fax: 800-828-5539, 714-441-4564 for international faxes, e-mail: Liwebsite@impressions.com, website: www.lightimpressionsdirect.com. Archival supplies, including photo albums, frames, mat board; slide, negative, film, and print storage; portfolios, storage boxes and bags, scrapbooking supplies, and more. Free catalog.

Metal Edge, Inc., 6340 Bandini Blvd., Commerce, CA 90040, 800-862-2228 or 213-721-7800; fax: 888-822-6937, e-mail: info@metaledgeinc.com, website: www.metaledgeinc.com. Storage for slides, negatives, photos, microfilm, and more. Free catalog.

Northeast Document Conservation Center, 100 Brickstone Sq., Andover, MA 01810-1494, 978-470-1010, fax: 978-475-6021, e-mail: nedcc@nedcc.org, website: www.nedcc.org. Nonprofit regional conservation center specializing in treatment of art and artifacts on paper, including photographs. Preservation microfilming, duplication of historical photographs, preservation planning surveys, disaster assistance, technical leaflets. Free brochure. Open Mon.–Fri. 8:30 A.M.–4:30 P.M.

Old World Restorations, Inc., 5729 Dragon Way, Cincinnati, OH 45227, 513-271-5459, fax: 513-271-5418, e-mail: info@oldworldrestorations.com, website: www.oldworldrestorations.com. Restoration and conservation of art and antiques, including photographs. Specialized packing and shipping. Nationwide service. Free brochure.

Painted Light Photos, 5301 N. Clark St., Chicago, IL 60640, 773-728-5301, e-mail: blaing1065@aol.com. Restoration, duplication, and hand-tinting of black and white photographs. Conservation framing and shadow box framing. Send SASE for brochure.

Peter J. Dugan, Fine Art Restoration, 1300 Coventry Cir., Vernon Hills, IL 60061, 847-367-0561, e-mail: pdugan6439@aol.com. Restoration of photos and frames.

Poor Richard's Restoration & Preservation Studio Workshop, 101 Walnut St., Montclair, NJ 07042, 973-783-5333, fax: 973-744-1939, e-mail: jrickford@webtv.com, website: www.rickford.com. Restoration, conservation, and archival and preservation services for photographs and other objects. Restoration of family memorabilia and keepsakes. By appointment, Tues.–Fri. noon–5:00 P.M., Sat. noon–3:00 P.M.

Romney, PO Box 806, Williamsburg, NM 87942, 505-894-4775, e-mail: eromney@zianet.com, website: www.edromney.com. Antique camera repair manuals, tools, and supplies. Free brochure.

Russell Norton, PO Box 1070, New Haven, CT 06504-1070, 203-281-0066. Archival polypropylene sleeves in 13 sizes for antique photographs and postcards. Send SASE for more information.

The2Buds.com, 462 W. Silver Lake Rd. N., Traverse City, MI 49684, 888-270-0552, Mon.–Fri. 9:00 A.M.–5:00 P.M., e-mail: postcards@the 2buds.com, website: www.the2buds.com. Archival supplies for storing and displaying photographs and other collectibles. Storage boxes, albums, and more. Internet sales only.

Tommy Boy Grfx, 2025 W. Cris Ave. Anaheim, CA 92804, 714-774-0888, fax: 714-774-0888, e-mail: tsyr3tt@hotmail.com. Scanning, retouching, and restoring of family pictures.

University Products, Inc., 517 Main St., PO Box 101, Holyoke, MA 01040, 800-628-1912; fax: 800-532-9281, fax: 800-532-9281, e-mail: info @universityproducts.com, website: www.universityproducts.com. Specialized storage for photos, including albums, light boxes, and storage. Archival supplies for conservation, restoration, repair, storage, and display of collectibles. Free catalog.

➡➡ **PICTURE FRAMES, SEE FRAMES & MIRRORS**

PLASTIC

Objects made of all types of plastics, from Parkesine to Lucite, are now being collected. Plastic is fragile, and a scratched or cracked piece is lower in value. Some types of plastic fade or discolor in sunlight, scorch if overheated, or are stained by alcohol or other materials. Plastic should be washed with a solution of soap and warm water and a soft cloth. Very hot water and detergents may remove the shine. Never use scouring powder or any form of abrasive. Do not put plastic dishes in the dishwasher unless they are marked "dishwasher safe." They will eventually become dull and, if decorated, may lose the color in the decoration.

Removing the old adhesive from price-tag labels can be a problem. Use turpentine, not alcohol, acetone (nail polish remover), or lighter fluid. Novus II is a plastic cleaner that can be found in some stores. Check the stores listed in the conservation section of this book.

Plastic that is cracked or badly scratched or stained cannot be restored. Some types of plastic, especially "tortoiseshell," will gradually deteriorate and melt.

A word of warning: celluloid is flammable and must be stored in a well-ventilated area where the temperature is never over 120 degrees Fahrenheit. If the celluloid in a favored old toy is decomposing, it may help to soak it in washing soda (sodium carbonate). After it is dry, coat the item with clear nail polish.

➠ **PLASTIC PIECES ARE LISTED IN THIS BOOK BY SHAPE**

➠ **SEE ALSO ADVERTISING COLLECTIBLES, DOLLS, FURNITURE, JEWELRY, KITCHEN PARAPHERNALIA, LIGHTING DEVICES, TOYS**

PRICE BOOKS

1950s Plastics Design: Everyday Elegance, 2nd edition, Holly Wahlberg (Schiffer, Atglen, PA, 1999).

Celluloid: Collectibles from the Dawn of Plastics, Robert Brenner (Schiffer, Atglen, PA, 1999).

Celluloid: Collector's Reference and Value Guide, Keith Lauer and Julie Robinson (Collector Books, Paducah, KY, 1999).

Collecting Plastics: A Handbook and Price Guide, 2nd edition, Jan Lindenberger (Schiffer, Atglen, PA, 1999).

Halloween Favorites in Plastic, Charlene Pinkerton (Schiffer, Atglen, PA, 1998).

Kovels' Depression Glass & Dinnerware Price List, 7th edition, Ralph and Terry Kovel (Three Rivers Press, New York, 2001), includes plastic dinnerware.

Melmac Dinnerware, Gregory R. Zimmer and Alvin Daigle Jr. (L-W Book Sales, Gas City, IN, 1997).

Plastic Cup Collectibles, Bryan Meccariello (Schiffer, Atglen, PA, 1998).

REPAIRS, PARTS & SUPPLIES

➠ **SEE ALSO "CONSERVATORS & RESTORERS," PAGE 520.**

Chem-Clean Furniture Restoration, Bucks County Art & Antiques Co., 246 W. Ashland St., Doylestown, PA 18901, 215-345-0892, e-mail: iscsusn@att.net. Plastics repaired and renewed. Research. Appraisals. Free brochure.

➠ **PLAYER PIANOS, SEE MUSICAL INSTRUMENTS**

➠ **PLUMBING, SEE ARCHITECTURAL ANTIQUES**

POLITICAL MEMORABILIA

Every fourth year, when a presidential race is filling the minds and newspapers of Americans, the price of political ephemera rises. The political buttons, banners, and oddities are suddenly discovered by a new group of collectors. Of course, there are many serious collectors who seek political items every year. The hobby has a national club, publication, shows, and a built-in publicity possibility that encourages new collectors and higher prices regularly. To a collector, there are two kinds of political memorabilia: authentic items and "brummagems." The brummagems are the tourist-trap pieces, made because they will sell. They are not official pieces from a national party. Most of the buttons with off-color or insulting slogans were made to be sold by hucksters, and they are not true political pieces.

In the back of the drawer at your grandfather's house, you found a treasure trove that includes some John Kennedy campaign buttons, a cake of soap shaped like a baby but labeled McKinley, a pencil that says "Win with Willkie," "I Like Ike" cigarettes, a newspaper proclaiming the "election of Dewey," and a Teddy Roosevelt bandanna. Are they really political items? Are they rare and valuable?

The record price for a campaign button, set in 1991, was $49,700 for a Cox-Roosevelt metal pinback button. It is one of only four known. It is a type known to the trade as a "jugate," a button picturing two candidates. A jugate is priced higher than a button for a single candidate. In general, a jugate is also of much more value than a button with just the names of the candidates. Buttons promoting a candidate for mayor or senator are of interest locally, but if your candidate eventually ran for president, the button may be high priced. Buttons for candidates for the smaller parties like the Socialist Labor Party are often high priced because they are rare. Buttons that promote both a local candidate for Senate or Congress and a national candidate for president also have a good value. Foreign-language buttons are scarce and sell well.

There are many books about political memorabilia. They include a set of three books on buttons, one on textiles, and several on the general subject. Most of these books include prices. Unfortunately, since the general price guides do not have room for complete descriptions and pictures, they are of limited use. The buttons are priced differently for slightly different print style, color, size, photo, or other feature. The American Political Items Collectors, whose membership represents the serious political buyers in the country, publishes material on real and fake political pieces. If you have rarities, this group's members are your best prospective customers.

Buttons are small and easy to store, so most collectors have many. Other items are often rarer and bring high prices. Political bandannas, jewelry, knives, cigars, trays, dishes, dolls, umbrellas, canes, and posters are all collected. Anything that pictures a candidate running for office is salable. Anything that pictures an elected president or vice president is in demand among regular political collectors and other groups of collectors. In recent years there has been active interest in campaign material for women who ran for office or the wives of elected officials. Older items are usually of more value than newer ones. Never discard anything that mentions a politician. It can be sold.

But what about your grandfather's treasures? Most of the Kennedy buttons and the Willkie pencil and Ike cigarettes are probably worth under $20; the baby-shaped soap with the original box is worth over $125; the bandanna is worth $100. The newspaper about Dewey's "election" is worth about $400.

REPRODUCTIONS

The purist collector only saves buttons and other items that were made for an actual campaign and not those produced for a gift or novelty shop afterward. The American Political Items Collectors (APIC), PO Box 1149, Cibolo, TX 78108, carefully documents actual campaign material each year in the publications sent to its members. Reproductions have been made of many early campaign items. Kleenex had a national promotion in the 1970s that included reproductions of many old campaign buttons. Several other similar promotions have offered repros since then. These buttons are marked on the edge with information about the reproduction year and company. Even these are now worth a few dollars. Check in other sections for restorers of political memorabilia that's made of glass, metals, or textiles.

PRICE BOOKS

100 Years of Political Campaign Collectibles, Mark Warda (Sphinx Publishing, PO Box 25, Clearwater, FL, 34617, 1996).

All for the Cause: Campaign Buttons for Social Change, 1960s–1990s, William A. Sievert (Splash Inc., PO Box 155, Rehoboth Beach, DE 19971, 1997).

Noble's Catalog and Price Guide of National Political Convention Tickets and Other Convention Ephemera, Edward Krohn, editor (David G. Phillips Publishing, PO Box 611388, N. Miami, FL 33161, 1996).

Political Campaign Stamps, Mark Warda (Krause, Iola, WI, 1998).

CLUBS & THEIR PUBLICATIONS

American Political Items Collectors, *Keynoter* (MAG), PO Box 1149, Cibolo, TX 78108, e-mail: apic@texas.net.

OTHER PUBLICATIONS

Political Collector (NP), PO Box 5171, York, PA 17405.

Rail Splitter: A Journal for the Lincoln Collector (NL), PO Box 275, New York, NY 10044, e-mail: splitter@rcn.com, website: www.railsplitter.com.

USEFUL SITES

HarpWeek, www.harpweek.com. Online archives of *Harper's Weekly* cartoons and commentaries with explanations.

The Political Graveyard, www.politicalgraveyard.com

The White House, www.whitehouse.gov. Click on resources link for list of presidential libraries.

APPRAISERS

Many of the auctions listed in this section will also do appraisals. *See also* the general list of "Appraisal Groups" on page 483.

AUCTIONS

•• SEE ALSO "SELLING THROUGH AUCTION HOUSES," PAGE 485.

David Quintin, PO Box 800861, Dallas, TX 75380-0861, 972-625-7189, fax: 972-985-4911, e-mail: dqtexas@aol.com. Political campaign items, including presidential, gubernatorial, and congressional. Mail, phone, fax, and e-mail bids accepted. Buyer's premium 10%. Catalogs, 5 issues for $10. Prices realized available after auction.

Gallery of History Auctions, 3601 W. Sahara Ave., Promenade Suite, Las Vegas, NE 89102-5822, 800-GALLERY (800-425-5379) or 702-364-1000 for international calls, fax: 702-364-1285, e-mail: galleryofhistory @galleryofhistory, website: www.galleryofhistory.com. "History for Sale" absentee auctions six times a year. Mail, phone, fax, and Internet bids accepted. Buyer's premium 15%. Catalogs by mail or on website. Prices realized published in next auction catalog and on website. Framing services.

Hake's Americana & Collectibles, PO Box 1444, York, PA 17405-1444, 717-848-1333, Mon.–Fri. 10:00 A.M.–5:00 P.M., fax: 717-852-0344, e-mail: hake@hakes.com, website: www.hakes.com. Twentieth-century nostalgia collectibles, including political Americana. Mail, phone, and Internet bids accepted. No buyer's premium. Catalog $7; yearly subscription $30. Sample catalog free. Appraisals.

Slater's Americana, 5335 N. Tacoma Ave., Suite 24, Indianapolis, IN 46220, 317-257-0863, Mon.–Fri. 9:00 A.M.–1:00 P.M. only, e-mail:

info@slatersamericana.com, website: www.slatersamericana.com. Vintage presidential and political campaign memorabilia. Mail, phone, and fax bids accepted. Buyer's premium 15%. Prices realized available after auction. Appraisals.

POSTCARDS

The first postal card with a printed stamp was issued in Austria in 1869. The idea proved to be so profitable for the government, it was quickly copied by many other countries. The United States issued its first government postcard in May 1873. (A card dated May 12 or 13, 1873, would be a very high-priced rarity.) These early cards had printed messages. Personal messages were charged first-class rates. It was not until May 19, 1898, that private postcards were charged at a lower rate. A postal card has a preprinted stamp. A postcard has a space for an adhesive stamp.

It seems as if everyone's elderly aunt saved boxes of picture postcards sent to her by friends and relatives. A card can sell for anywhere from 5 cents to over $500. It pays to study before you take an offer for the whole box. First examine the stamps and check on the value of any unusual ones. The postmark and amount of postage will help to date the card. Look for any unusual stickers. Christmas seals, parcel post stamps, TB or Red Cross stickers, Easter seals, and

SEVEN PERIODS OF POSTCARDS FOR A COLLECTOR

1. *The Pioneer Era Cards* (1893–1898) are the oldest available and bring high prices.
2. *Private Mailing Cards* (1898–1901) have the words "Private Mailing Card— Authorized by Act of Congress" printed on the back. These cards sell for premium prices.
3. *The Undivided Back* period (1902–1907). These cards also sell for premium prices.
4. *The Divided Back* era (1907–1915).
5. *The White Border* period (1915–1930) featured many printed cards of poor quality with white borders.
6. *Linen Cards* (1920–1950) were printed on paper with a linen-textured surface. These were often bright-colored cards with cartoons or jokes.
7. *The Photochrome Cards or Chrome Cards* (1939 to present) are those seen today. Color film was available for these glossy cards.

other extra stamps can add to the value of your card. There are collectors who want just stickers.

Some collectors seek postcards made of unusual materials. Birch bark, woven silk, leather, feathers, fur, peat moss, mother-of-pearl, celluloid, real hair, fabrics, wood, and paper were used for cards. Some cards, called "mechanicals," were made with a metal spring to produce some action. A donkey tail might wag or a head nod. A few double cards were made that squeaked when pressed. Foldout, see-through, hold-to-light, and puzzle cards were also made. All these novelty cards should be priced higher than a regular card made after 1915. Condition for these cards and all others is very important. A very worn card is of little value.

Manufacturers and artists with famous names add to the value of your cards. Look for **RAPHAEL TUCK**, **ELLEN CLAPSADDLE**, **BERTHA CORBETT**, **HOWARD CHANDLER CHRISTY**, **LOUIS WAIN**, **HARRISON FISHER**, **LANCE THACKEREY**, **GENE CARR**, and **FRANCES BRUNDAGE**. Add to your price if the card pictures coins, stamps, famous or infamous people, Kewpies, blacks, advertising, disasters, animals dressed like people, fruits or vegetables that look like people, World's Fairs, expositions, or holidays. The best holidays are Halloween and Christmas, especially any card that includes a full-length picture of Santa Claus. All types of patriotic cards, including those featuring Fourth of July and political events, are in demand. Early planes, early autos, fire equipment, and other types of transportation are always wanted. The larger the picture of the car, the better; the largest are the so-called close-up transportation cards. Photograph cards of the streets filled with stores, advertising, people, ads, or special events are collected. Extra-large cards or sets of cards bring a premium. Unpopular cards include views of woods, parks, rivers, mountains, churches, hospitals, residential street scenes, and other scenery with few buildings or people.

SETTING PRICES

After you have some idea of the value of your postcards, you have several options for selling them. A private collector may want your cards. Expect to get 50 to 75 percent of the published retail value. If private collectors were to pay 100 percent, they could buy it retail from any dealer's stock. If you sell just a few to a collector, you may find you are left with a relatively unsalable collection.

There are many postcard and paper ephemera shows. Collectors and dealers usually pay well for rare cards. Go to a show and mention your collections. Decide if you want to sell single cards or the whole box. Make that decision before you sell the best ten items and then find that no one wants the rest. If you have time, you can sell the ordinary cards at any flea market or house sale. They can often be sold from a box labeled "All cards one price." Dealers tell us to use the prices 5 cents, 10 cents, 25 cents, 50 cents, etc. Never price at $1.25. There is a psychology to pricing merchandise, and for some reason, postcards sell best for one coin or bill; 45¢ or $1.25 are just not good prices.

Most serious dealers sort the cards by subject and state and display them in boxes or plastic mounts. Most collectors only want a special type of card and won't look through too big a pile.

If you don't want to work at selling each postcard, offer them as a lot to a dealer. There is a rule of thumb. A dealer will usually pay you 50 to 75 percent of the retail value of a card worth $1 or more, but will pay only 25 percent or less for the less expensive cards. The work involved in mounting, showing, and carrying is the same, and most dealers prefer selling the better cards.

You might send the postcards to a mail-order or Internet auction that specializes in postcards. These auctions sell the best cards individually and the others in groups or lots. You will be paid for the lots that are sold and all the unsold items will be returned to you. It can take from three to six months to get your money after you send the collection to a mail-order auction. There is usually a 20 to 30 percent fee charged. The postcard publications list many possible places to sell cards.

The best advice we've heard regarding the pricing of cards came

HOW TO TALK "POSTCARD"

Artist-Signed—The artist's signature (full name or initials)
Chromes—Full-color photographic image reproduced as a halftone on modern presses
Continental size—A postcard approximately 4 x 6 in.
Deltiology—The hobby of collecting postcards
Greeting—A postcard sent as a holiday greeting
Hold-to-Light—A postcard that shows a hidden image when held to the light
Novelty—Postcards that have moving parts or are made of odd material such as leather, wood, or metal
Standard size—A postcard approximately $3\frac{1}{2}$ x $5\frac{1}{2}$ in.

from a dealer who said, "Ask yourself, which would the customer prefer to have in his pocket, the card or the money?" The value is not like the value of gold or silver; it is a matter of demand. The value is in the eye of the buyer. Look at the price books, but they are only guides.

REPAIR

Most postcards are made of paper and have all of the storage and care problems of any other paper collectible. They should be kept out of the heat and away from strong sunlight and damp air. Most of all, they should never be glued or taped. Slight soil can be cleaned off postcards with an art-gum eraser. Bent cards can sometimes be ironed flat. If postcards are glued into an album, it may be possible to soak them free. This requires care and time.

➝ SEE ALSO PAPER COLLECTIBLES

PRICE BOOKS

Black Postcard Price Guide, J.L. Mashburn (Colonial House, Enka, NC, 1999).
The Postcard Price Guide, 4th edition, J.L. Mashburn (Colonial House, Enka, NC, 2001).
Propaganda Postcards of World War II, Ron Menchine (Krause, Iola, WI, 2000).
Sports Postcard Price Guide, J.L. Mashburn (Colonial House, PO Box 609, Enka, NC, 1998).

CLUBS & THEIR PUBLICATIONS

Curt Teich Postcard Archives, *Image File* (MAG), Lake County Discovery Museum, 27277 Forest Preserve Dr., Wauconda, IL 6008, e-mail: teicharchives@co.lake.il.us, website: www.lcfpd.org/teich_archives.
Philip Boileau Collectors' Society, *Philip Boileau Collectors' Society Newsletter* (NL), 1025 Redwood Blvd., Redding, CA 96003-1905, e-mail: pboileaucc@aol.com or gamlin@aol.com, website: hometown. aol.com/PBoileauCC/index.html.
Postcard History Society, *The Journal* (NL), 1795 Kleinfeltersville Rd., Stevens, PA 17578-9669, e-mail: midcreek@ptd.net.

OTHER PUBLICATIONS

Barr's Postcard News (NP), 70 S. Sixth St., Lansing, IA 52151, e-mail: bpcn@rconnect.com, website: www.bpcn.com.
Gloria's Corner (NL), PO Box 507, Denison, TX 75021-0507, e-mail: gmj@texoma.net.
Picture Postcard Monthly (MAG), 15 Debdale Ln., Keyworth, Nottinghamshire NG12 5HT, UK, e-mail: reflections@argonet.co.uk, website: www.postcardcollecting.co.uk.

Postcard Collector (MAG), 700 E. State, Iola, WI 54990, e-mail: info @krause.com, website: www.krause.com.

APPRAISERS

Many of the auctions and repair services listed in this section will also do appraisals. *See also* the general list of "Appraisal Groups" on page 483.

AUCTIONS

➡ SEE ALSO "SELLING THROUGH AUCTION HOUSES," PAGE 485.

Jim Mehrer's Postal History, 2405 30th St., Rock Island, IL 61201, 309-786-6539, fax: 309-786-4840, e-mail: mehrer@postal-history.com, website: www.postal-history.com. Mail, phone, and Internet bids. No buyer's premium. Catalogs free to regular bidders, otherwise $2 U.S., $4.50 foreign; yearly subscription $12 U.S., $30 foreign.

VintagePostcards.com, 60-C Skiff St., Suite 116, Hamden, CT 06517, 203-248-6621, fax: 203-281-0387, e-mail: quality@vintagepostcards.com, website: www.vintagepostcards.com. Postcard auctions. Mail, phone, and Internet bids accepted. No buyer's premium. Catalog $15. Appraisals.

Virginia Mail Auction, John McClintock, PO Box 1765, Manassas, VA 20108, 703-368-2757. Postcard auctions. Mail and phone bids accepted. Send SASE for free catalog. Send SASE for prices realized. Appraisals.

REPAIRS, PARTS & SUPPLIES

➡ SEE ALSO "CONSERVATORS & RESTORERS," PAGE 520.

Bags Unlimited, 7 Canal St., Rochester, NY 14608, 800-767-BAGS or 716-436-9006, fax: 716-328-8526, e-mail: info@bagsunlimited.com, website: www.bagsunlimited.com. Postcard storage boxes and sleeves. Archival products for storing, displaying, and shipping collectibles.

G.M. Wylie Co., PO Box AA, Washington, PA 15301-0660, 800-747-1249, fax: 724-225-0741, e-mail: info@gmwylie.com, website: gmwylie.com. Safe long-term storage supplies for postcards and other paper collectibles. Order by mail, phone, or e-mail. Catalog $1.50 or visit the website.

Jim Mehrer's Postal History, 2405 30th St., Rock Island, IL 61201, 309-786-6539, fax: 309-786-4840, e-mail: mehrer@postal-history.com, website: www.postal-history.com. Pre-1930 U.S. postal history and related reference literature and supplies, including sleeves, albums, boxes, and dividers.

RN Products, 39 Monmouth St., Red Bank, NJ 07701-1613, 732-741-0626, fax: 732-741-0479, e-mail: mostco@monmouth.com. Complete line of postcard supplies. Aluminum dealer display cases. Send SASE for brochure.

Russell Norton, PO Box 1070, New Haven, CT 06504-1070, 203-281-0066.

Archival polypropylene sleeves in 13 sizes for antique photographs and postcards. Send SASE for more information.

The2Buds.com, 462 W. Silver Lake Rd. N., Traverse City, MI 49684, 888-270-0552, Mon.–Fri. 9:00 A.M.–5:00 P.M., e-mail: postcards@the 2buds.com, website: www.the2buds.com. Archival supplies for storing and displaying vintage postcards. Postcard sleeves, storage boxes, albums, and more. Internet sales only.

University Products, Inc., 517 Main St., PO Box 101, Holyoke, MA 01040, 800-628-1912; fax: 800-532-9281, fax: 800-532-9281, e-mail: info @universityproducts.com, website: www.universityproducts.com. Specialized storage for postcards. Archival supplies for conservation, restoration, repair, storage, and display. Free catalog.

➻ **POSTERS, SEE PRINTS**

POTTERY & PORCELAIN

An aunt left you her household belongings representing fifty or more years of accumulation, including figurines, a cabinet with her collection of cups, lamps, kitchen mixing bowls, pottery crocks that held pickles, flower vases, dresser sets, ashtrays, three sets of dishes, and serving pieces. How would you sell everything for the best total price? Age and quality of ceramics do influence price, but a 1950 Hall pottery pitcher could be worth more than an 1850 German bowl. The whims of collectors determine the value, and sometimes the fashion of the day makes originally inexpensive pieces more important. The stoneware crocks that were cheap food-storage containers during the 1800s, yellowware, Art Deco dishes of the 1920s, nineteenth-century R.S. Prussia pieces decorated with voluptuous women, and some recent art pottery and California studio pottery sell for higher prices than fine wares from the eighteenth and early nineteenth centuries.

If you are fortunate enough to have a close friend who understands antiques and collecting, ask for help. Few collectors are experts in everything, but many of them can make good guesses about what might have value. A collector has been to the shops and shows and absorbs much information about what sells.

If you have a few dishes, spend a little time and do the research to be sure that you are not selling a treasure for 50 cents at your garage sale. If you have a houseful of dishes, you may have to sell them through a dealer or auction gallery or Internet sale and hope to get the best price for everything. Even the experts miss a few of the best items at times.

How do you tell if you own a piece by an important factory in high demand by collectors? Look in the general price guides under the names you might find on your dishes. For example, **R.S. PRUSSIA, NIPPON, ROYAL DOULTON, WEDGWOOD, SUSIE COOPER, HALL, HULL, MCCOY, ROSEVILLE, WELLER, ROYAL BAYREUTH, HAVILAND, MINTON, LOTUS, NORITAKE, ROYAL COPENHAGEN,** and many others are listed by name. If the factory is listed by name, collectors are buying it. Some types are listed but not marked, so look at the shows and in the books until you can recognize **SATSUMA, BANKO, SUMIDA GAWA, CHINESE EXPORT PORCELAIN, STAFFORDSHIRE, GOUDA, YELLOWWARE, SPATTERWARE, STONEWARE, IRONSTONE, PÂTE-SUR-PÂTE,** and **MAJOLICA.** The collectors also look for the names of countries, such as **OCCUPIED JAPAN** and **CZECHOSLOVAKIA.** Research prices for these best-sellers.

WHERE TO SELL

If the task of identification seems overwhelming, you might want to send the contents to a consignment shop. These shops sell good-quality items and usually charge about 25 to 35 percent commission. The shop knows the highest retail price to ask, and even if a few things do not sell, you will have most of your money in a few months with very little work on your part. If you consign your dishes, be sure the shop has insurance. Get a signed contract describing the items (including any damage) and stating the terms of sale and the commission you will be charged.

You could also sell your items through your own house or garage

QUICK CLUES FOR DATING YOUR DISHES

- If the name of the country of origin, such as "Spode, England," appears, the dishes were probably made after 1891.
- The words "made in England" or "made in France" have been favored since about World War I. The term "Ltd." as part of a company name for English companies was used after 1880. "RD" in a diamond-shaped cartouche was used in England from 1842 to 1883. The letters "RD" followed by numbers were in use after 1884.
- The words "22 carat gold" and "ovenproof" were used after the 1930s.
- "Made in Occupied Japan" was used only from 1945 to 1952.
- "Dishwasher proof" was used after 1955.
- "Microwave safe" first appeared in the 1970s.

sale, or through an ad in the local paper. If you are offering the items on your own, be sure to follow the sensible rules of safety: never admit a stranger when you are alone in the house; take only cash and not checks; and watch for theft when strangers are inside. It might be wise to put all "for sale" items in the garage and let no one enter your house.

If you sell most of the items to an antiques shop, you face the problem of what price to ask. To decide, you need a knowledgeable friend, a book like *Kovels' New Dictionary of Marks—Pottery & Porcelain*, a few good price books, and a working idea of the going prices in the gift and china shops. A simple rule of thumb is to compare your prices against those for similar pieces of new china. Most buyers will never pay more than 50 percent of china store prices and usually pay only 30 percent of retail prices. Many new sets of dishes can now be purchased for less than retail at discount stores.

Antiques dealers are interested in what sells quickly, so they want attractive, undamaged figurines, lamps, vases, and the currently "hot" items like FIESTA (bright-colored pottery of the 1930s), CALIFORNIA figurines of the 1950s, SHELLEY dishes in Chintz pattern, country-look crocks and bowls, cookie jars, and marked art pottery. In the late 1990s imported novelty wares like HOLT-HOWARD, lady head vases, and cookie jars became very popular and pricey.

Pottery and porcelain are available just about everywhere you look on the Internet. Pieces are often offered through online auctions. Search for names like FIESTA or RUSSEL WRIGHT and you'll probably come up with more sites than you need. All of the Internet antiques malls (see Part III for a list) have pottery dealers, and many dealers have their own individual sites. Look for collectors associations on the Web, too. Many club sites feature classified ads or links to dealers.

An auction house offers another way to sell a house filled with ceramics. It is a good method if you can't take the time to separate the good from the bad. The good pieces will be sold separately. The best pieces may even be pictured and described in a brochure or catalog. There is a charge to have your piece pictured in the catalog. Sets of dishes sell, but for low prices. Odd dishes can be placed into box lots and sold, but prices will be low. The auction house pays within three to six months, and its employees do all the work. Be sure to get a signed contract before leaving your merchandise. Have a written description of the items, including damage and repairs, and all terms of the sale. Try to set the date for the sale. Be sure your pieces are insured by the auction house while on its premises. Check to see if the auction house keeps your money in escrow.

SPECIAL CASES

Sets of dishes can be sold to a matching service. There are many dealers throughout the country who make a living by selling matching pieces for sets of dishes, silver, or glassware. Most are listed in this book, and many advertise in antiques publications and decorating magazines. These dealers always have customers waiting for dishes. Most dishes sell for low prices, but if your set is a popular pattern that is in demand, you can sell the set for a good price. Send a description and a photograph or photocopy of a plate, front and back, and indicate the colors. Offer your set for sale. Be sure to include a self-addressed, stamped envelope.

FIESTA and other modern dishes sell easily through newspaper ads, Internet ads, garage sales, and flea markets, or to dealers. Only perfect pieces can be sold. Chips and scratches make a difference. If the piece of pottery is twentieth-century and common, a chip lowers the value by 90 to 100 percent. If the piece is rare (a Rookwood vase decorated with an Indian), a chip lowers the value only 10 to 20 percent. Prices are easy to find in the general price guides. AUTUMN LEAF pattern, AZALEA pattern, WILLOW WARE, and LENOX china also sell easily. Anything by CLARICE CLIFF or SHELLEY brings high prices.

Lamps are always hard to sell. If the ceramic base is not by a well-known art pottery or a name artist, it will sell simply as secondhand furniture.

➻ SEE ALSO LIGHTING DEVICES

Figurines of top quality from the eighteenth and early nineteenth centuries sell well, but perhaps not as high as you may hope. Look for the crossed swords mark of MEISSEN, the anchor of CHELSEA, or other symbols. Art Deco figures are popular now. Names worth extra money are WEINER WERKSTATTE, GOLDSCHEIDER, and ROBJ. Staffordshire figurines of dogs or unidentifiable people, romantic bisque Victorian men and women, and copies of eighteenth-century pieces also sell for less than most people think. We often hear descriptions like "I know it is of value because every fingernail can be seen." This is not always true. You can often see every fingernail on a poor-quality figurine. The very best figurines do sell for thousands of dollars, however, and it might pay to take a clear picture or the actual figurines to an auction house, dealer, or appraiser to learn the value.

"Country look" pieces are the most confusing to a novice. Grandmother's yellowware mixing bowl or blue spatter butter jar can be worth hundreds of dollars to the right collector or dealer. You must go to the shows and see the types of wares that are now popular and high priced. Stoneware crocks get publicity because examples with cobalt blue decorations of birds, people, or animals sell for thousands of dollars. Plain crocks are not expensive. The modern-shaped, bright red, cream, or blue pottery dishes made during the 1940s to store water or leftovers in the refrigerator sell well. So do some of the salt and pepper sets, cookie jars, and canister sets of the 1920s to the 1980s.

Ashtrays don't sell well unless marked with a famous maker's name. Plain bowls, trays, and candy dishes sell for low prices unless they are by big makers. Beer steins of any type sell well; best are those by **METTLACH**.

Novelty items, like figurines with nodding heads, open-mouthed monsters that are toothpick holders, fairings, trinket boxes, **GOSS** souvenirs, small figurines of blacks, and "pink pig with green basket" figures, are all in demand.

Art pottery from the United States and England has become popular since the 1970s. Prices are steadily rising. The best of **ROOKWOOD** can sell for thousands of dollars. Record price in 1991 was $198,000 for a Rookwood vase with an electroplated copper fish swimming under a sea-green glaze. It was made in 1900 by Kataro Shirayamadani. There are many books about art pottery, including *Kovels' American Art Pottery,* that list names, patterns, and marks. The art pottery that many collect today was the florist's flower container of yesterday. An art pottery vase, filled with chicken wire so it could hold flowers, may still be in your grandmother's basement. Books have now made dealers and collectors into experts, and they are willing to pay top prices for good pieces. If the original cover for an art pottery or other type of ceramic jar is noticeably missing (some jars are made to be complete in appearance without a cover), deduct 50 percent. If a vase is decorated with, or shaped like, a pig or a snake, add 25 to 100 percent. The **ROYAL DOULTON** and **HUMMEL** figurine craze has cooled since the 1980s. Prices may not be as high as you hope. Royal Doulton dinnerwares sell like any other sets of dishes. They sell quickly to dealers or at auction. The Royal Doulton price books give retail prices, so you can easily price figures and jugs by name or HN number. Anything marked "Goebel Hummel" sells, although collectors prefer pieces with the old marks. If two figurines look exactly alike, the value may be different because of the small black V and Bee on the bottom. Marks, figurines, plates, and values are easy to find in the general price books or on the Internet.

Anything Asian sells. If the marks are Chinese or Japanese characters, they are a mystery to most of us. Not only are they hard to read, but they were also often copied and put on the bottom of later porcelain pieces. It is said that 80 percent of Chinese porcelains have "retrospective" marks (for example, an eighteenth-century copy with a sixteenth-century mark). An unmarked piece is usually of more value than a piece with an earlier, but retrospective, mark. The very old pieces (old is over 250 years old) sell to museums and serious collectors. This type of porcelain should be sold through a major auction house or top-priced dealer. Only experts can recognize the difference between old and more recent Oriental pieces. Since the 1970s, quantities of average-quality blue and white nineteenth-century china have been shipped from China and Hong Kong for sale to collectors. These pieces are salable as decorative items, and they should be priced accordingly.

Chinese export porcelain includes not only dishes made in China in the eighteenth and nineteenth centuries to be sold in America and Europe, but also twentieth-century pieces. Some of the early dishes can be very valuable. Their gray-blue color can be easily recognized. Important tureens or platters with elaborate decorations or with a famous owner's initials can sell for thousands of dollars. A plain cup and saucer could be worth at least $100. If you have any export dishes, have them appraised before offering them for sale. Other Asian wares are also popular. The early, sophisticated Satsuma and the cruder twentieth-century pottery and porcelain made in Occupied Japan after World War II, and almost any other Asian porcelains sell quickly and for more money than comparable English or American pieces. Try to find someone to identify your pieces, and then check the prices in the general guides.

Blue and white dishes seem to be a favorite of collectors. Staffordshire "flow blue" was made in many patterns. Look for pieces without the word "England." They are usually older and should be worth more. If the center design is an American or Canadian architectural or historical scene, it is part of what collectors call "historic blue," and it can be worth a high price. The more common, fanciful Oriental scenes, flowers, or other center designs sell for average prices. Platters, pitchers, and service bowls sell well because so few can be found. A soup tureen with an American view would be the best of all. It would sell for thousands of dollars. There are auctions and dealers who handle historic Staffordshire exclusively or it can be sold in a sale of different types of antiques.

ROWLAND AND MARSELLUS made a similar twentieth-century blue and white ware that is gaining in value. They made "rolled edge" plates with views of towns and cities for the local tourist trade. Collectors want all of the hundreds of different examples. Other popular blue and white patterns are IVANHOE, GIBSON GIRL, and the special plates made for colleges and universities by WEDG-WOOD. In 1976 a grocery store giveaway was a set of dishes called LIBERTY BLUE. These also sell well today.

In the past eight years the California pottery of the 1930s to 1960s has suddenly become popular. Pieces by BAUER, WEIL, KAY FINCH, FRANCISCAN, METLOX, CATALINA, SASCHA BRASTOFF, FLORENCE, HEDI SCHOOP, TWIN WINTON, and VERNON now sell quickly, especially on the Internet. Other American wares, including RED WING, GLIDDEN, HOLT-HOWARD, PURINTON, PFALTZGRAFF, and LADY HEAD PLANTERS, are also in demand.

Limited editions include many types of newer collectibles. The designation "limited edition" first became popular during the 1960s, even though the first dated plate produced for one year was the Bing & Grondahl Christmas plate of 1895. Many types of porcelains and silver were made in limited quantities, but the idea of stating the limits before offering the collectible was new. Some pieces are limited to an announced number, some to the number made before a particular date. Limited editions can include plates, figurines, eggs, bells, forks, spoons, plaques, boxes, steins, mugs, urns, Christmas ornaments, paperweights, bottles, thimbles, and more.

It is difficult to sell limited edition plates, figurines, etc., at a profit, though a few have gained in value. There is a small resale market for most of them. A few dealers buy plates at a set percent less than their original price. Advertising for limited editions often stresses the "investment" potential. In the real world, there is almost never a gain in dollar value to the retail buyer. When reselling a limited piece, it is necessary to have the original box and certifying paper to get a good price. Because of the demand for the original box, some dealers will gladly pay for the rare empty box. Look in the limited edition collectors' magazines for prices and dealers who buy plates. Talk to the local gift shops that sell plates or to those that handle what is known as "secondary market" plates. A few matching services sell the best of the limited edition plates. Go to the shows. There is a huge swap meet at each national plate collectors convention; if you can't sell your plates, perhaps you can trade them.

REPAIR

Dishes, figurines, lamp bases, flowerpots, crocks, and garden ornaments may be made of ceramics—pottery or porcelain. To care for and repair them properly, it is necessary to have some idea of the difference between pottery and porcelain.

Pottery is usually heavier than porcelain. It is opaque and chips more easily. Because it is more porous, it may become stained by dark-colored food or dirt. Porcelain is translucent; if it is held in front of a strong light, the light will show through. If it is chipped, the break will be shell-like in shape. Pottery usually cracks on a line. Porcelain is thinner, lighter, more durable, and usually more expensive than pottery. The names stoneware, delft, bone china, majolica, and ironstone all refer to either pottery, porcelain, or similar wares with similar problems.

If your pottery or porcelain dishes are stained, as a last resort it is possible to bleach them using Biz laundry stain remover. This will eventually damage the dishes. If dishes are cracked or chipped, repairs are possible. Invisible waterproof glues are available in most hardware, art-supply, drug, and building-supply stores. For a simple break, glue is the best method of repair. If there is further damage and a hole or crack must be filled or if repainting is required, it can still be a do-it-yourself job, but special equipment and instructions are necessary.

Repairs to limited editions are almost useless if you are concerned with value. The slightest chip, crack, or imperfection lowers the value considerably, and almost any repair will cost more than the value of the repaired piece. The only exception might be for very rare figurines.

FILL IN A SET

Many old sets of dishes have, say, only eleven dinner plates, ten cups and saucers, and twelve of everything else. It is possible to buy the same pattern of old dishes to fill in the set. HAVILAND, CASTLE-TON, FRANCISCAN, LENOX, NORITAKE, OXFORD, SYRACUSE, and other makes are sold through matching services, which are listed in Part III. To sell to or order from a service, you must know the pattern of the dish. Hundreds of patterns are listed in books at your library.

Many of the patterns have names included on the back of the dish as part of the mark. Identify the pattern name from this information or use this easy method: Place a plate facedown on a photocopying machine and copy the front and the back. Indicate the colors that appear on the plate and send the photocopies to an appropriate matching service listed in this book.

To properly identify makers, it may be necessary to check the marks in a special book of marks. For example, "H & Co" is one of the marks used by the famous Haviland Company of France that can be matched through services. Some patterns are still being made and can be replaced through special orders. Firms such as **WEDG-WOOD**, **ROYAL DOULTON**, **SPODE**, and **ROYAL WORCESTER** offer this service for a limited number of their patterns.

•→ SEE ALSO ADVERTISING COLLECTIBLES, HOLIDAY COLLECTIBLES

REFERENCE BOOKS

Pottery & Porcelain—American
General books on American ceramics are listed below. Ask your librarian about the books on specific U.S. manufacturers.

American Art Pottery, David Rago (Knickerbocker, New York, 1997).

American Art Tile, 1876–1941, Norman Karlson (Rizzoli, NY, 1998).

American Ceramics: 1876 to the Present, revised edition, Garth Clark (Abbeville, New York, 1987).

American Painted Porcelain, Dorothy Kamm (Antique Trader Books, Dubuque, IA, 1999).

American Porcelain, 1770–1920, Alice Cooney Frelinghuysen (Harry N. Abrams, New York, 1989).

American Stonewares: The Art and Craft of Utilitarian Potters, Georgeanna H. Greer (Schiffer, Atglen, PA, 1981).

A Century of Ceramics in the United States, Garth Clark and Margie Hughto (E. P. Dutton, New York, 1979).

China and Glass in America 1880–1980, Charles L. Venable et al. (distributed by Harry N. Abrams, New York, 2000).

Dictionary Guide to United States Pottery & Porcelain, 19th and 20th Century, Jenny B. Derwich and Mary Latos (Jenstan, Franklin, MI, 1984).

Glidden Pottery, Margaret Carney (Schein-Joseph International Museum of Ceramic Art, Alfred, NY, 2001).

Kovels' *American Art Pottery,* Ralph and Terry Kovel (Crown, New York, 1993).

Pottery & Porcelain—Asian
Chinese Trade Porcelain, Michael Beurdeley (Charles E. Tuttle, Rutland, VT, 1962).

Japanese Porcelain, 1800–1950, Nancy Schiffer (Schiffer, Atglen, PA, 1986).
Noritake: Jewel of the Orient, Bob Page, Dale Frederiksen, and Dean Six (Replacements, Ltd., 1089 Knox Rd., Greensboro, NC 27420, 2001).

Pottery & Porcelain—British

General books are listed below. Ask your librarian about the books on specific British manufacturers, including Coalport, Crown Devon, Davenport, Goss, Mason's, Minton, Moorcroft, New Hall, Poole, Rockingham, Royal Doulton, Spode, Sunderland, Wade, Wedgwood, and Worcester.

A Collector's History of British Porcelain, John and Margaret Cushion (Antique Collectors' Club, Wappingers Falls, NY, 1992).
British Pottery: An Illustrated Guide, Geoffrey A. Godden (Harmony Books, New York, 1975).
The Charlton Standard Catalogue of Chintz, 3rd edition, Linda Eberle and Susan Scott (Charlton, Birmingham, MI, 1999).
The Concise Encyclopedia of English Pottery and Porcelain, Wolf Mankowitz and Reginald G. Haggar (Hawthorn, New York, 1957).
The Dictionary of Minton, Maureen Batkin and Paul J. Atterbury (Antique Collectors' Club, Wappingers Falls, NY, 1999).
The Dictionary of Worcester Porcelain, 1751–1851, Volume 1, John Sandon (Antique Collectors' Club, Wappingers Falls, NY, 1993).
Doulton Lambeth Wares, Desmond Eyles (Hutchinson, London, 1975).
Flow Blue China and Mulberry Ware: Similarity and Value Guide, Petra Williams (Fountain House East, Jeffersontown, KY, 1981).
Flow Blue China: An Aid to Identification, 2 volumes, Petra Williams (Fountain House East, Jeffersontown, KY, 1971, 1981).
Historical Staffordshire: An Illustrated Check-List and First Supplement, David and Linda Arman (Arman Enterprises, Danville, VA, 1974, 1977).
Royal Crown Derby, 3rd edition, John Twitchett and Betty Bailey (Antique Collectors' Club, Wappingers Falls, NY, 1988).
Royal Doulton, 1815–1965: The Rise and Expansion of the Royal Doulton Potteries, Desmond Eyles (Hutchinson, London, 1965).
Royal Doulton Figures Produced at Burslem, Staffordshire, Desmond Eyles, Louise Irvine, and Valerie Baynton (Richard Dennis, Shepton Beauchamp, Somerset, UK, 1994).
Royal Worcester Porcelain from 1862 to the Present Day, Henry Sandon (Clarkson N. Potter, New York, 1973).
The Sandon Guide to Royal Worcester Figures, 1900–1970, David, John, and Henry Sandon (Alderman Press, Edmonton, UK; distributed by Seven Hills, Cincinnati, 1987).
Staffordshire Romantic Transfer Patterns: Cup Plates and Early Victorian China, 2 volumes, Petra Williams (Fountain House East, Jeffersontown, KY, 1978, 1986).
Victorian Art Pottery, E. Lloyd Thomas (Guildart, London, 1974).

Victorian Ceramic Tiles, Julian Barnard (New York Graphic Society, Boston, 1972).

Victorian Staffordshire Figures, 1835–1875, Books 1 and 2, A. & N. Harding (Schiffer, Atglen, PA, 1998).

Wedgwood Ceramics, 1846–1959, Maureen Batkin (Richard Dennis, London, 1982).

Pottery & Porcelain—Dinnerware

Art Deco Tableware, Judy Spours (Rizzoli, New York, 1988).

China Identification Kit (Replacements Ltd., PO Box 26029, Greensboro, NC 27420, 1996).

Pottery & Porcelain—Majolica

Majolica, Nancy Kenmore (Crown, New York, 1990).

Majolica: A Complete History and Illustrated Survey, Marilyn Karmason and Joan Stacke (Harry Abrams, New York, 2002).

Majolica: American and European Wares, Jeffrey B. Snyder and Leslie Bockol (Schiffer, Atglen, PA, 2000).

Victorian Majolica, Leslie Bockol (Schiffer, Atglen, PA, 1999).

Pottery & Porcelain—Marks

British Studio Potters' Marks, Eric Yates-Owen and Robert Fournier (A & C Black, London, 1999).

Directory of European Porcelain, Ludwig Danckert (N.A.G. Press, London, 1981).

The East Liverpool, Ohio, Pottery District: Identification of Manufacturers and Marks, Ronald L. Michael, editor (Society for Historical Archaeology, Washington, DC, 1982).

Encyclopedia of Marks on American, English, and European Earthenware, Ironstone, and Stoneware, 1780–1980, Arnold A. and Dorothy E. Kowalsky (Schiffer Publishing, Atglen, PA, 1999).

Guide to the Patterns and Markings on the Backs of United States Ceramic Tiles, 1870s–1930s, Micahel Padwee (Tile Heritage Foundation, Healdsburg, CA, 1997).

New Handbook of British Pottery & Porcelain Marks, Geoffrey A. Godden (Barrie & Jenkins, North Pomfret, VT, 2000).

Keramik-Marken Lexikon: Porzellan und Keramik Report, 1885–1935, Dieter Zühlsdorff (Arnoldsche, Stuttgart, Germany; distributed by Hayden & Fandetta, New York, 1994). In German (porcelain and pottery marks of the world).

Kovels' Dictionary of Marks: Pottery and Porcelain, 1650 to 1850, Ralph and Terry Kovel (Crown, New York, 1995).

Kovels' New Dictionary of Marks: Pottery & Porcelain, 1850 to the Present, Ralph and Terry Kovel (Crown, New York, 1986).

Lehner's Encyclopedia of U.S. Marks on Pottery, Porcelain & Clay, Lois Lehner (Collector Books, Paducah, KY, 1988).

Les Porcelaines Françaises (Tardy, Paris, 1950). In French (French porcelain marks).

Les Potteries Françaises, 3 volumes (Tardy, Paris, 1949). In French (French pottery marks).

Marks on German, Bohemian and Austrian Porcelain, 1710 to the Present, Robert E. Röntgen (Schiffer, Atglen, PA, 1997).

Pottery & Porcelain—Miscellaneous

General books on ceramics are listed below. There are also books on specific items, such as salt and pepper shakers, cookie jars, and limited editions.

Belleek Irish Porcelain, Marion Langham (Quiller, London, 1993).

Ceramica: Mexican Pottery of the 20th Century, Amanda Thompson (Schiffer, Atglen, PA, 2001).

Collector's Encyclopedia of R.S. Prussia, 4 volumes, Mary Frank Gaston (Collector Books, Paducah, KY, 1995).

Haviland China: A Pattern Identification Guide, 2 volumes, Gertrude Tatnall Jacobson (Wallace-Homestead/Krause, Iola, WI, 1979).

Hungarian Ceramics from the Zsolnay Manufactory, 1853–2001, Eva Csenkey and Agota Steinert (Yale University Press, New Haven, CT, 2002).

An Illustrated Dictionary of Ceramics, George Savage and Harold Newman (Thames and Hudson, New York, 1985).

Luckey's Hummel Figurines & Plates, 12th edition, Carl F. Luckey (Krause, Iola, WI, 2002).

Mettlach Book, Gary Kirsner (Glentiques, PO Box 8807, Coral Springs, FL 33075, 1987).

Nineteenth Century Pottery and Porcelain in Canada, Elizabeth Collard (McGill University Press, Montreal, 1967).

The No. 1 Price Guide to M.I. Hummel Figurines, Plates, Miniatures, & More . . . , 7th edition, Robert Miller (Portfolio, Huntington, NY, 1998).

Scandinavian Art Pottery: Denmark and Sweden by Robin Hecht (Schiffer, Atglen, PA, 2000).

PRICE BOOKS

The 2000 Price Guide to Crested China, Nicholas Pine (Milestone Publications, Horndean, England, 2000).

The ABC's of ABC Ware, Davida and Irving Shipkowitz (Schiffer, Atglen, PA, 2002).

Adams Ceramics: Staffordshire Potters and Pots, 1779–1998, David A. Furniss, J. Richard Wagner, and Judith Wagner (Schiffer, Atglen, PA, 1999).

America by Pfaltzgraff, Vicki Quint, editor (Pfaltzgraff America Collectors Club, 2536 Quint La., Columbia, IL 62236, 2000).

The American Art Pottery Price Guide: Ohio (Treadway, Cincinnati, OH, 2000).

American Painted Porcelain, Dorothy Kamm (Antique Trader Books, Dubuque, IA, 1999).

American Stonewares: The Art and Craft of Utilitarian Potters, 3rd edition, Georgeanna H. Greer (Schiffer, Atglen, PA, 1999).

Anglo-American Ceramics, Part I: Transfer Printed Creamware and Pearlware for the American Market, 1760–1860, David and Linda Arman (Oakland Press, Portsmouth, RI, 1998).

Antique Limoges at Home, Debby DuBay (Schiffer, Atglen, PA, 2002).

Antique Trader American and European Art Pottery Price Guide, 2nd edition, Kyle Husfloen, editor (Krause, Iola, WI, 2002).

Antique Trader Pottery & Porcelain Ceramics Price Guide, 3rd edition, Kyle Husfloen, editor (Krause, Iola, WI, 2000).

The Arts & Crafts Price Guide: Ceramics, A Decade of Auction Results, Treadway Gallery in association with John Toomey Gallery (Treadway, Cincinnati, OH, 1998).

Beautiful Bauer: A Pictorial Study with Prices, Jeffrey B. Snyder (Schiffer, Atglen, PA, 2000).

Best of Blue Ridge Dinnerware, Betty and Bill Newbound (Collector Books, Paducah, KY, 2003).

Blue Ridge China Traditions, Frances and John Ruffin (Schiffer, Atglen, PA, 1999).

Bohemian Decorated Porcelain, James D. Henderson (Schiffer, Atglen, PA, 1999).

British Art Deco Ceramics, Colin Mawston (Schiffer, Atglen, PA, 2000).

Catalina Island Pottery and Tile, 1927–1937: Island Treasures, Carole Coates (Schiffer, Atglen, PA, 2001).

The Charlton Standard Catalogue of Beswick Animals, 4th edition, Diana and John Callow and Marilyn and Peter Sweet (Charlton Press, Toronto, 1999).

The Charlton Standard Catalogue of Beswick Pottery, 2nd edition, Diana and John Callow (Charlton Press, Toronto, 1999).

The Charlton Standard Catalogue of Chintz, 3rd edition, Susan Scott (Charlton Press, Birmingham, MI, 1999).

The Charlton Standard Catalogue of Coalport Collectibles, Alf Willis (Charlton Press, Toronto, 2000).

The Charlton Standard Catalogue of Coalport Figurines, 2nd edition, Tom Power (Charlton Press, Toronto, 1999).

The Charlton Standard Catalogue of Hagen-Renaker, 3rd edition, Gayle Roller (Charlton Press, Birmingham, MI, 2003).

The Charlton Standard Catalogue of Lilliput Lane Cottages, 3rd edition, Annette and Tom Power (Charlton Press, Toronto, 2000).

The Charlton Standard Catalogue of Royal Doulton Animals, 3rd edition, Jean Dale (Charlton Press, Birmingham, MI, 2002).

The Charlton Standard Catalogue of Royal Doulton Beswick Figurines, 6th edition, Jean Dale (Charlton Press, Birmingham, MI, 1998).

The Charlton Standard Catalogue of Royal Doulton Beswick Jugs, 5th edition, Jean Dale (Charlton Press, Birmingham, MI, 1999).

The Charlton Standard Catalogue of Royal Doulton Beswick Storybook Figurines, 6th edition, Jean Dale (Charlton Press, Palm Harbor, FL, 2000).

The Charlton Standard Catalogue of Royal Doulton Bunnykins, Jean Dale and Louise Irvine (Charlton Press, Birmingham, MI, 1999).

The Charlton Standard Catalogue of Royal Doulton Figurines, 8th edition, Jean Dale (Charlton Press, Palm Harbor, FL, 2002).

The Charlton Standard Catalogue of Royal Worcester Animals, John Edwards (Charlton Press, Palm Harbor, FL, 2001).

The Charlton Standard Catalogue of Royal Worcester Figurines, 2nd edition, Anthony Cast and John Edwards (Charlton Press, Palm Harbor, FL, 2000).

The Charlton Standard Catalogue of Wade: General Issues, Volume 1, 3rd edition, Pat Murray (Charlton Press, Birmingham, MI, 1999).

The Charlton Standard Catalogue of Wade: Liquor Products, Volume 4, 3rd edition, Pat Murray (Charlton Press, Birmingham, MI, 1999).

The Charlton Standard Catalogue of Wade Whimsical Collectables, 5th edition, Pat Murray (Charlton Press, Toronto, 2000).

Chintz Ceramics, 3rd edition, Jo Anne P. Welsh (Schiffer, Atglen, PA, 2000).

Collectible Cups and Saucers, Books I & II, Jim and Susan Harran (Collector Books, Paducah, KY, Book I 1997, prices 2001; Book II 2000).

Collectible Kay Finch, Devin Frick, Jean Frick, and Richard Martinez (Collector Books, Paducah, KY, 1997).

Collectible Teapots: A Reference and Price Guide, Tina Carter (Krause, Iola, WI, 2000).

Collectibles Market Guide and Price Index, Collectors' Information Bureau (available from Krause, Iola, WI, 2000).

Collectibles Price Guide and Directory to Secondary Market Dealers, 9th edition (Collectors' Information Bureau, Barrington, IL, 1999).

Collecting Blue Willow, M.A. Harman (Collector Books, Paducah, KY, 2001).

Collecting Carlton Ware, David Serpell (Francis Joseph, London, 1999).

Collecting Fiesta, Lu-Ray & Other Colorware, Mark Gonzalez (L-W Book Sales, Gas City, IN, 2000).

Collecting Hull Pottery's Little Red Riding Hood, Mark and Ellen Supnick (L-W Book Sales, Gas City, IN 46933, 1998).

Collecting Lladró, Peggy Whiteneck (Krause, Iola, WI, 2001).

Collecting Noritake, A to Z: Art Deco & More, David Spain (Schiffer, Atglen, PA, 1999).

Collecting Poole Pottery, Robert Prescott-Walker (Francis Joseph, London, England, 2000).

Collecting Shawnee Pottery, Mark E. Supnick (L-W Book Sales, Gas City, IN, 2000).

Collecting Sylvac Pottery, Stella Ashbrook (Francis Joseph, London, England, 2000).

Collector's Encyclopedia of Bauer Pottery: Identification & Values, Jack Chipman (Collector Books, Paducah, KY, 1998).

Collector's Encyclopedia of Blue Ridge Dinnerware, Volume 2, Betty and Bill Newbound (Collector Books, Paducah, KY, 1998).

Collector's Encyclopedia of California Pottery, 2nd edition, Jack Chipman (Collector Books, Paducah, KY, 1999).

Collector's Encyclopedia of English China, Mary Frank Gaston (Collector Books, Paducah, KY, 2002).

Collector's Encyclopedia of Fiesta: Plus Harlequin, Riviera, and Kitchen Kraft, 9th edition, Bob and Sharon Huxford (Collector Books, Paducah, KY 2001).

Collector's Encyclopedia of Hall China, 3rd edition, Margaret and Kenn Whitmyer (Collector Books, Paducah, KY, 2001).

Collector's Encyclopedia of Howard Pierce Porcelain, Darlene Hurst Dommel (Collector Books, Paducah, KY, 1998).

Collector's Encyclopedia of Lefton China, Books 1 and 2, Loretta DeLozier (Collector Books, Paducah, KY, 1995, 1997; Book 1 values update, 1998).

Collector's Encyclopedia of Limoges Porcelain, 3rd edition, Mary Frank Gaston (Collector Books, Paducah, KY, 2000).

Collector's Encyclopedia of Muncie Pottery, Jon Rans and Mark Eckelman (Collector Books, Paducah, KY, 1999).

The Collector's Encyclopedia of Niloak, 2nd edition, David Edwin Gifford (Collector Books, Paducah, KY, 2001).

Collector's Encyclopedia of Nippon Porcelain, 7th series, Joan F. Van Patten (Collector Books, Paducah, KY, 2002).

Collector's Encyclopedia of Red Wing Art Pottery, B. L. and R. L. Dollen (Collector Books, Paducah, KY, 2001).

Collector's Encyclopedia of Rosemeade Pottery, Darlene Hurst Dommel (Collector Books, Paducah, KY, 2000).

Collector's Encyclopedia of Roseville Pottery, Volume 1, revised edition, Sharon and Bob Huxford and Mike Nickel (Collector Books, Paducah, KY, 2001).

Collector's Encyclopedia of Roseville Pottery, Volume 2, Sharon and Bob Huxford and Mike Nickel (Collector Books, Paducah, KY, 2001).

Collector's Encyclopedia of Russel Wright, 3rd edition, Ann Kerr (Collector Books, Paducah, KY, 2002).

Collector's Encyclopedia of Stangl Dinnerware, Robert C. Runge Jr. (Collector Books, Paducah, KY, 2000).

Collector's Encyclopedia of Van Briggle Art Pottery, Richard Sasicki and Josie Fania (Collector Books, Paducah, KY, 1993, values 2002).

Collector's Guide to Feather Edge Ware, Lisa S. McAllister (Collector Books, Paducah, KY, 2001).

The Collector's Guide to Lady Figurine Planters, Pat and Keith Armes (Schiffer, Atglen, PA, 2000).

Collector's Guide to Made in Japan Ceramics, Book 3, Carole Bess White (Collector Books, Paducah, KY, 1998).

Collector's Guide to Souvenir China: Keepsakes of a Golden Era, Laurence W. Williams (Collector Books, Paducah, KY, 1998).

Collector's Guide to Trenton Potteries, Thomas L. Rago (Schiffer Atglen, PA, 2001).

A Collector's Guide to Willow Ware, Jennifer A. Lindbeck (Schiffer, Atglen, PA, 2000).

Collector's Mart Price Guide to Limited Edition Collectibles, 8th edition, Mary L. Sieber, editor (Krause, Iola, WI, 2002).

Collector's Value Guide: Precious Moments by Enesco, 2nd edition, Jeff Mahony, editor (CheckerBee, Middletown, CT, 1999).

The Complete Cookie Jar Book, 2nd edition, Mike Schneider (Schiffer, Atglen, PA, 1999).

The Concise Encyclopaedia and Price Guide to Goss China, 2nd edition, Nicholas Pine (Milestone Publications, Waterlooville, Hampshire, UK, 1999).

Conta and Boehme Porcelain, Janice and Richard Vogel (4720 S.E. Fort King St., Ocala, FL 34470-1501, 2001).

Cumbow China of Abingdon, Virginia, Richard Foil (319 Bogey Dr., Abingdon, VA, prices 2001).

Czechoslovakian Pottery: "Czeching" Out America, Sharon Bowers, Sue Closser, and Kathy Ellis (Glass Press, Marietta, OH, 1999).

The Decorative Art of Limoges Porcelain and Boxes, Keith and Thomas Waterbrook-Clyde (Schiffer, Atglen, PA, 1999).

Depression Pottery, Jeffrey B. Snyder (Schiffer, Atglen, PA, 1999).

Dresden Porcelain Studios, Jim and Susan Harran (Collector Books, Paducah, KY, 2002).

Fiesta: The Homer Laughlin China Company's Colorful Dinnerware, 3rd edition, Jeffrey B. Snyder (Schiffer, Atglen, PA, 2000).

Fiesta, Harlequin, and Kitchen Kraft Dinnerwares, Homer Laughlin China Collectors Association (Schiffer, Atglen, PA, 2000).

Flow Blue: A Collector's Guide to Patterns, History, and Values, 3rd edition, Jeffrey B. Snyder (Schiffer, Atglen, PA, 1999).

Franciscan: An American Dinnerware Tradition, Bob Page and Dale Frederiksen (Replacements, Ltd., PO Box 26029, Greensboro, NC 27420, 1999).

Franciscan Dining Services, 2nd edition, Jeffrey B. Snyder (Schiffer, Atglen, PA, 2002).

Frankoma and Other Oklahoma Potteries, 3rd edition, Phyllis and Tom Bess (Schiffer, Atglen, PA, 2000).

Goebel Figurines and Prints by Charlot Byj, Rocky Rockholt (Schiffer, Atglen, PA, 2001).

Greenbook Guide to Department 56 Villages (56 Freeway Dr., Cranston, RI 29290, 2002).

Greenbook Guide to Department 56 Snowbabies (56 Freeway Dr., Cranston, RI 29290, 2002).

Head Vases Etc.: The Artistry of Betty Lou Nichols, Maddy Gordon (Schiffer, Atglen, PA, 2002).

Historical Staffordshire: American Patriots and Views, 2nd edition, Jeffrey B. Snyder (Schiffer, Atglen, PA, 2000).

Homer Laughlin: A Giant Among Dishes, 1873–1939, Jo Cunningham (Schiffer, Atglen, PA, 1998).

Homer Laughlin China, 1940s and 1950s, Jo Cunningham (Schiffer, Atglen, PA, 2000).

Homer Laughlin: Decades of Dinnerware, Bob Page, Dale Frederiksen, and Dean Six (Replacements, Ltd., 1089 Knox Rd., Greensboro, NC 27420, 2003).

The House of Haeger, 1914–1944: The Revitalization of American Art Pottery, Joe and Joyce Paradis (Schiffer, Atglen, PA, 1999).

Hull Pottery: Decades of Design, Jeffrey B. Snyder (Schiffer, Atglen, PA, 2001).

Introducing Roseville Pottery, Mark Bassett (Schiffer, Atglen, PA, 1999).

Josef Originals, 2nd edition, Dee Harris and Jim and Kay Whitaker (Schiffer, Atglen, PA, 1999).

Josef Originals: Figurines of Muriel Joseph George, Jim and Kaye Whitaker (Schiffer, Atglen, PA, 2000).

Kenton Hills Porcelains Inc.: The Story of a Small Art Pottery, 1939–1944, Nick and Marilyn Nicholson (9418 Mapletop Lane, Loveland, OH 45140, 1998).

Kovels' Depression Glass & Dinnerware Price List, Ralph and Terry Kovel (Three Rivers Press, New York, 2001).

Lefton China Old and New: More Lefton China, Ruth McCarthy (Schiffer, Atglen, PA, 2001, 2000).

Lefton China Price Guide, Loretta DeLozier (Collector Books, Paducah, KY, 1999).

Living with Limoges, Debby DuBay (Schiffer, Atglen, PA, 2001).

The Lladró Authorized Reference Guide, (Lladró Society, Moonachie, NJ, 1998).

McCoy Pottery, Jeffrey B. Snyder (Schiffer, Atglen, PA, 1999).

McCoy Pottery: Collector's Reference and Value Guide, Volumes 2 and 3, Margaret Hanson, Bob Hanson, and Craig Nissen (Collector Books, Paducah, KY, 1999, 2002).

Mustache Cups: Timeless Victorian Treasures, Glenn Erardi and Pauline C. Peck (Schiffer, Atglen, PA, 1999).

Napco, Kathleen Deel (Schiffer, Atglen, PA, 1999).

The No. 1 Price Guide to M.I. Hummel Figurines, Plates, Miniatures, & More, 8th edition, Robert L. Miller (Portfolio Press, Huntington, NY, 2000).

Noritake Dinnerware: Identification Made Easy, Robin Brewer (Schiffer, Atglen, PA, 1999).

Noritake for Europe, Pat Murphy (Schiffer, Atglen, PA, 2001).

Occupied Japan for the Home, Florence Archambault (Schiffer, Atglen, PA, 2000).

Official Price Guide to Collector Plates, 7th edition, Rinker Enterprises (House of Collectibles, NY, 1999).

Pacific Pottery: Tableware from the 1920s, '30s, '40s . . . and More, Jeffrey B. Snyder (Schiffer, Atglen, PA, 2001).

Pocket Guide to Occupied Japan, Monica Lynn Clements and Patricia Rosser Clements (Schiffer, Atglen, PA, 1999).

Popular Souvenir Plates, Monica Lynn Clements and Patricia Rosser Clements (Schiffer, Atglen, PA, 1998).

Post 86 Fiesta, Richard Racheter (Collector Books, Paducah, KY, 2001).

Price Guide to Holt-Howard Collectibles and Related Ceramicwares of the '50s & '60s, Walter Dworkin (Krause, Iola, WI, 1998).

Quimper Pottery: A Guide to Origins, Styles, and Values, Adela Meadows (Schiffer, Atglen, PA, 1998).

R.S. Prussia: The Art Nouveau Years, Leland and Carol Marple (Schiffer, Atglen, PA, 1998).

The Ransburg Collection: Hand-Painted Stoneware and Decorated Metalware, Dave Ransburg (Converse Publishing, 1125 Main St., Peoria, IL 61606, 2000).

Red Wing Art Pottery, Volume 2, Ray Reiss (Property Publishing, Chicago, 2000).

Redware: America's Folk Art Pottery, 2nd edition, Kevin McConnell (Schiffer, Atglen, PA, 1999).

Rookwood Pottery: Bookends, Paperweights, Animal Figurals, Nick and Marilyn Nicholson and Jim Thomas (Collector Books, Paducah, KY, 2002).

Roseville in All Its Splendor, Jack and Nancy Bomm (L-W Book Sales, Gas City, IN, 1998, values 2003).

Roseville Pottery Collector's Price Guide, 9th edition, Gloria and James Mollring (PO Box 22754, Sacramento, CA 95822, 2003).

Roseville Pottery Price Guide, No. 12, Sharon and Bob Huxford (Collector Books, Paducah, KY, 2001).

R.S. Prussia: The Art Nouveau Years, Leland and Carol Marple (Schiffer, Atglen, PA, 1998).

R.S. Prussia: The Early Years, Leland and Carol Marple (Schiffer, Atglen, PA, 1997).

Russel Wright: Dinnerware, Pottery and More, Joe Keller and David Ross (Schiffer, Atglen, PA, 2000).

Sanfords Guide to Peters and Reed, Martha and Steve Sanford (Adelmore Press, 230 Harrison Ave., Campbell, CA 95008, 2000).

Sanfords Guide to the Robinson Ransbottom Pottery Co., Sharon and Larry

Skillman (Martha Sanford, 230 Harrison Ave., Campbell, CA 95008, 2001).

Scandinavian Art Pottery: Denmark and Sweden, Robin Hecht (Schiffer, Atglen, PA, 2000).

Scandinavian Ceramics and Glass, 1940s to 1980s, George Fischler and Barrett Gould (Schiffer, Atglen, PA, 2000).

Scottish Ceramics, Henry E. Kelly (Schiffer, Atglen, PA, 1999).

Spongeware, 1835–1935: Makers, Marks, and Patterns, Henry E. Kelly, and Arnold A. and Dorothy E. Kowalsky (Schiffer, Atglen, PA, 2001).

Staffordshire Animals, Adele Kenny (Schiffer, Atglen, PA, 1998).

Sumida . . . According to Us, Herbert Karp and Gardner Pond (KarPond, PO Box 250709, Atlanta, GA 30325, 2001).

Treasure or Not? How To Compare and Value American Art Pottery, David Rago and Suzanne Perrault (Octopus Publishing Group, London, England, 2001).

Twentieth Century Lefton China and Collectibles, Karen Barton (Schiffer, Atglen, PA, 2001).

Uhl Pottery, Anna Mary Feldmeyer and Kara Holtzman (Collector Books, Paducah, KY, 2001).

Understanding Roseville Pottery, Mark Bassett (Schiffer, Atglen, PA, 2002).

Universal Dinnerware and Its Predecessors, Timothy J. Smith (Schiffer, Atglen, PA, 2000).

Wade Miniatures, Donna Baker (Schiffer, Atglen, PA, 2000).

Warwick China, John R. Rader, Sr. (Schiffer, Atglen, PA, 2000).

Weller, Roseville and Related Zanesville Art Pottery and Tiles, Betty Ward and Nancy Schiffer (Schiffer, Atglen, PA, 2000).

White Ironstone China: Plate Identification Guide, 1840–1890, Ernie and Deb Dieringer (Schiffer, Atglen, PA, 2001).

Willow Ware Made in the U.S.A.: An Identification Guide, Connie Rogers (1733 Chase Ave., Cincinnati, OH 45223,1996, prices 2000).

The World of Ceramics, Pat and Larry Aikins (L-W Book Sales, Gas City, IN, 2000).

The World of Kreiss Ceramics, Pat and Larry Aikins (L-W Book Sales, Gas City, IN, 1999).

Zanesville Stoneware Company, Jon Rans, Glenn Ralston, and Nate Russell (Collector Books, Paducah, KY, 2002).

Zsolnay Ceramics: Collecting a Culture, Federico Santi and John Gacher (Schiffer, Atglen, PA, c1998).

CLUBS & THEIR PUBLICATIONS

Abingdon Pottery Collectors, *Abingdon Pottery Collectors Newsletter* (NL), 210 Knox Hwy. 5, Abingdon, IL 61410.

American Art Pottery Association, *Journal of the American Art Pottery Association* (MAG), PO Box 834, Westport, MA 02790-0697, e-mail: patspots@ma.ultranet.com, website: www.amartpot.org.

American Ceramic Circle, *American Ceramic Circle Journal* (MAG), *Newsletter* (NL), 520 16th St., New York, NY 11215, e-mail: nlester@earthlink.net.

Amphora Collectors Club International, *Amphora Files* (NL), 10159 Nancy Dr., Meadville, PA 16335.

Belleek Collectors' International Society, *Belleek Collector* (MAG), PO Box 1498, Great Falls, VA 22066, e-mail: info@belleek.com, website: www.belleek.ie.

Blue & White Pottery Club, *Blue & White Pottery Club* (NL), 224 12th St. NW, Cedar Rapids, IA 52405.

Butter Pat Patter Association, *Butter Pat Patter* (NL), 265 Eagle Bend Dr., Bigfork, MT 59911-6235.

Calendar Plate Collectors Club, *The Calendar* (NL), 710 N. Lake Shore Dr., Tower Lakes, IL 60010, e-mail: agumtow@aol.com.

Carlton Ware Collectors International, *Carlton Times* (MAG), PO Box 161, Sevenoaks, Kent TN15 6GA, UK, e-mail: cwciclub@aol.com, website: www.carltonwarecollectorsinternational.com.

CAS Collectors, PO Box 46, Madison, WI 53701-0046, 608-241-9138, fax: 608-241-8770, website: www.cascollectors.com (Ceramic Arts Studio collectors).

China Students' Club, Inc., *Shards* (NL), 76 Hunnewell St., Needham, MA 02494, e-mail: abhomer@hotmail.com.

Clarice Cliff Collectors Club, *Clarice Cliff Collectors Club: The Review* (MAG), Fantasque House, Tennis Dr., The Park, Nottingham NG7 1AE, UK, e-mail: information2@claricecliff.com, website: www.claricecliff.com.

Collecting Doulton & Beswick Collectors Club, *Collecting Doulton & Beswick Collectors Club* (MAG), PO Box 310, Richmond, Surrey TW10 7FU, UK.

Cornish Collectors Club, *Cornish Pixie* (NL), PO Box 58, Buxton, Derbyshire SK17 0FH, UK, e-mail: cornish@btconnect.com.

Currier & Ives Dinnerware Collectors, *Collectors' Newsletter* (NL), 29470 Saxon Rd., Toulon, IL 61483, e-mail: unclebud@eastadmin.bhc.edu, website: www.royalchinaclub.com.

Dedham Pottery Collectors Society, *Dedham Pottery Collectors Society Newsletter* (NL), 248 Highland St., Dedham, MA 02026, e-mail: dpcurator@aol.com, website: www.dedhampottery.com.

ENESCO Precious Moments Collectors' Club, *Goodnewsletter* (NL), PO Box 219, Itasca, IL 60143-0219, website: www.enesco.com.

Eva Zeisel Collectors Club, *Eva Zeisel Times* (NL), 695 Monterey Blvd., # 203, San Francisco, CA 94127, e-mail: PatMoore@EvaZeisel.org, website: www.evazeisel.org.

Florence Ceramics Collectors Society, *The Floraline* (NL), 1971 Blue Fox Dr., Lansdale, PA 19446, e-mail: FlorenceCeramics@aol.com.

Flow Blue International Collector's Club, *Blue Berry Notes* (NL), PO Box 6664, Leawood, KS 66206, website: www.flowblue.org.

Franciscan Collectors Club, *Franciscan Newsletter* (NL), 500 S. Farrell, Unit

S-114, Palm Springs, CA 92264, e-mail: newsletter@gmcbl.com, website: www.gmcb.com.

Frankoma Family Collectors Association, *Pot & Puma* (NL), *Prairie Green Sheet* (NL), PO Box 32571, Oklahoma City, OK 73123-0771, e-mail: fcca4nancy@aol.com, website: www.frankoma.org.

Friar Tuck Collectors Club, *Friar Tuck Collectors Club Newsletter* (NL), 136 North Shore Rd., Derry, NH 03038, e-mail: bondfarm@attbi.com.

The Friends of Blue, *Friends of Blue* (NL), PO Box 122, Didcot D.O., Oxford OX11 0YN, UK, website: www.fob.org.uk (blue & white pottery).

Gonder Collectors, *Gonder Collector's Newsletter* (NL), 917 Hurl Dr., Pittsburgh, PA 15236-3636, e-mail: gondernut@aol.com.

Goss & Crested China Club, *Goss & Crested China Club Newsletter* (NL), 62 Murray Rd., Horndean, Hampshire PO8 9JL, UK, e-mail: info@goss chinaclub.demon.co.uk, website: www.gosschinaclub.demon.co.uk.

Haeger Pottery Collectors of America, *HPCA News* (NL), 5021 Toyon Way, Antioch, CA 94509, e-mail: lanettec@colorspot.com.

Hall China/Jewel Tea Collector's Club, *Hall China Collector's Newsletter* (NL), PO Box 361280, Cleveland, OH 44136, e-mail: chandler-10@msn.com, website: www.chinaspecialties.com.

Harbour Lights Collectors Society, *Lighthouse Legacy* (NL), 1000 N. Johnson Ave., El Cajon, CA 92020, e-mail: HarbourLights@HarbourLights.com, website: www.HarbourLights.com.

Haviland Collectors Internationale Foundation, *Haviland Collectors Internationale Quarterly Newsletter* (NL), PO Box 271383, Fort Collins, CO 80527, e-mail: HCIF@mwci.net, website: www.havilandcollectors.com.

Homer Laughlin China Collectors Association, *The Dish* (MAG), PO Box 26021, Crystal City, VA 22215-6021, e-mail: info@hlcca.org, website: www.hlcca.org.

Houghton-Dalton Collector's Society, 1801 N. Main St., Findlay, OH 45840, e-mail: jdmmh@aol.com.

Hummel Collector's Club, Inc., *Hummel Collector's Club, Inc.* (NL), Dorothy Dous, 1261 University Dr., Yardley, PA 19067-2857, e-mail: customer service@ hummels.com, website: hummels.com.

International Association of R.S. Prussia Collectors, Inc., *International Association of R.S. Prussia Collectors* (NL), PO Box 446, Mount Joy, PA 17552, e-mail: chocset@aol.com, website: www.rsprussia.com.

International Nippon Collectors Club, *INCC Journal* (MAG), *INCC News* (NL), 1531 Independence Ave. SW, Washington, DC 2000, website: www.nipponcollectorsclub.com.

International Willow Collectors, 503 Chestnut St., Perkasie, PA 18944, e-mail: willowpd@enter.net, website: www.willowcollectors.org.

Lladró Society, *Expressions* (MAG), *Lladró Antique News* (NL), 1 Lladro Dr., Moonachie, NJ 07074-9835, website: www.lladro.com.

M.I. Hummel Club, *Insights* (NL), PO Box 11, Pennington, NJ 08534-0011, website: www.mihummel.com.

Majolica International Society, *Majolica Matters* (NL), 1275 First Ave., PMB 103, New York, NY 10021, e-mail: majolica@pobox.com, website: www.majolicasociety.com.

Moorcroft Collectors Club (MCC), *Moorcroft Collectors Club Newsletter* (NL), Moorcroft, Sandbach Rd., Burslem, Stoke-on-Trent ST6 2DQ, UK, e-mail: cclub@moorcroft.com, website: www.moorcroft.com.

National Autumn Leaf Collectors Club, *N.A.L.C.C.* (NL), PO Box 900968, Palmdale, CA 93590-0968, e-mail: downing@hpnc.com, website: nalcc.org.

National Shelley China Club, *National Shelley China Club Newsletter* (NL), 591 W. 67th Ave., Anchorage, AK 99518, e-mail: imahart@alaska.net, website: www.nationalshelleychinaclub.com.

Noritake Collectors' Society, *Noritake News* (NL), 1237 Federal Ave. E., Seattle, WA 98102, e-mail: spain1237@yahoo.com.

North American Torquay Society, *Torquay Collector* (MAG), 214 N. Ronda Rd., McHenry, IL 60050, e-mail: rxmanlee@mc.net.

North Dakota Pottery Collectors Society, *North Dakota Pottery Collectors Society Newsletter* (NL), Box 14, Beach, ND 58621, e-mail: csshortnd@mcn.net, website: www.ndpcs.com.

O.J. Club, *Upside Down World of an O.J. Collector* (NL), 29 Freeborn St., Newport, RI 02840-1821, e-mail: florence@aiconnect.com (Occupied Japan).

Official International Wade Collectors Club, *Official Wade Club Magazine* (MAG), Westport Rd., Burslem, Stoke-on-Trent, Staffordshire ST6 4AP, UK, e-mail: wade9908@aol.com, website: www.wade.co.uk/wade.

Old Sleepy Eye Collectors Club of America, Inc., *Sleepy Eye Newsletter* (NL), PO Box 5445, Rockford, IL 61125.

Oyster Plate & Collectibles Society International, *Oyster Plate & Collectibles Society Newsletter* (NL), PO Box 632, Brigantine, NJ 08203, e-mail: AbsoluteOyster@aol.com, website: www.geocities.com/Heartland/Bluffs/1570.

Pfaltzgraff America Collectors Club, *The America Messenger* (NL), PO Box 648, Columbus, IN 47202, e-mail: zubba@iquest.net, website: groups.yahoo.com/group/pfaltzgraffamericacollectors.

Phoenix Bird Collectors of America, *Phoenix Bird Discoveries* (NL), 685 S. Washington, Constantine, MI 49042 (Phoenix bird dinnerware).

Pickard Collector's Club, *Pickard Collector's Club Newsletter* (NL), 300 E. Grove St., Bloomington, IL 61701, e-mail: joyluke@aol.com, website: www.pickardcollectors.org.

Pilkington's Lancastrian Pottery Society, *Pilkington's Lancastrian Pottery Society Newsletter* (NL), c/o Wendy Stock, Sullom Side, Barnacre Garstang, Preston, Lancs. PR3 1GH, UK, website: www.pilkpotsoc. freeserve.co.uk.

Poole Pottery Collectors Club, *Poole Pottery Collectors Club Magazine*

(MAG), Sopers Ln., Poole, Dorset BH17 7PP, UK, website: www.poole pottery.co.uk.

Quimper Club International, *Quimper Club International Newsletter* (NL), 5316 Seascape Ln., Plano, TX 75093, e-mail: join@quimperclub.org, website: www.quimperclub.org.

Red Wing Collectors Society, *Red Wing Collectors Newsletter* (NL), PO Box 50, Red Wing, MN 55066, e-mail: rwcs1@win.bright.net, website: www.redwingcollectors.org.

Royal Bayreuth Collectors' Club, Inc., *RBCC, Inc.* (NL), Mary McCaslin, Secretary, 6887 Black Oak Ct. E., Avon, IN 46123, e-mail: maryjack @indy.rr.com.

Royal Doulton International Collectors Club, *Gallery* (MAG), *Royal Doulton International Collectors Club Newsletter* (NL), 701 Cottontail Ln., Somerset, NJ 08873, e-mail: icc@royal-doulton.com, website: www.royal-doulton.com.

RumRill Society, PO Box 2161, Hudson, OH 44236, e-mail: phenabs @aol.com.

Southern Folk Pottery Collectors Society, *Southern Folk Pottery Collectors Society Newsletter* (NL), 220 Washington St., Bennett, NC 27208.

The Spode Society, *The Spode Society Review* (NL), PO Box 1812, London NW4 4NW, UK, e-mail: spodemuseum@spode.co.uk, website: www.spode.co.uk.

Stangl/Fulper Collectors Club, *Stangl/Fulper Times* (NL), PO Box 538, Flemington, NJ 08822, e-mail: stanglovers@rcn.com, website: www.stanglfulper.com.

Stein Collectors International, *Prosit* (MAG), PO Box 342, Stevens Point, WI 54481-0342, e-mail: rcress@cscpub.com, website: www.stein collectors.org.

Tea Leaf Club International, *Tea Leaf Readings* (NL), PO Box 377, Belton, MO 64012-0377, e-mail: TeaLeafClubIntl@cs.com, website: www.tealeaf club.com (Tea Leaf and other luster-trimmed ironstone).

Tile Heritage Foundation, *Tile Heritage: A Review of American Tile History* (MAG), *Flash Point* (NL), PO Box 1850, Healdsburg, CA 95448, e-mail: foundation@tileheritage.org, website: www.tileheritage.org.

Tiles & Architectural Ceramics Society, *Glazed Expressions* (MAG), *TACS Journal*, 36 Friars Ave., Stone, Staffordshire ST15 0AF, UK, e-mail: alanswale@clara.co.uk, website: www.tilesoc.org.uk.

Transferware Collectors Club, *T.C.C. Bulletin* (NL), PMB 541, 1500A East College Way, Mount Vernon, WA 98273, website: www.trans collectorsclub.org.

Uhl Collectors Society, *Uhl Family Happenings* (NL), 3535 W. 630 S,- Huntingburg, IN 47542, e-mail: ckugler@psci.net, website: www.uhl collectors.org.

Watt Collectors Association, *Watt's News* (NL), PO Box 507, Linwood, NC

27299-0507, e-mail: wattcollectors@yahoo.com, website: server34. hypermart.net/wattcollectors/watt.htm.

Wedgwood Society of Boston, *Wedgwood Society of Boston* (NL), Frazier at D.H.S./Wedgwood, Box 215, Dedham, MA 02027-0215, e-mail: wedgwood@hotmail.com, website: www.angelfire.com/ma/wsb.

Wedgwood Society of New York, *Ars Ceramica* (MAG), 5 Dogwood Ct., Glen Head, NY 11545, e-mail: bstarr1264@aol.com.

White Ironstone China Association, Inc., *White Ironstone Notes* (NL), PO Box 855, Fairport, NY 14450-0855, e-mail: dieringer1@aol.com, website: www.whiteironstonechina.com.

OTHER PUBLICATIONS

Collector's Mart Magazine (MAG), 700 E. State St., Iola, WI 54990-0001, e-mail: info@krause.com, website: www.krause.com.

Cowan Pottery Journal (NL), Cowan Pottery Museum of Rocky River Public Library, 1600 Hampton Rd., Rocky River, OH 44116-2699, website: www.cowanpottery.org.

The Crazed Collector (NL), PO Box 2635, Dublin, CA 94568, e-mail: crazedcollctr@aol.com (Chintz and other collectibles).

Dorothy Kamm's Porcelain Collector's Companion (NL), PO Box 7460, Port St. Lucie, FL 34985-7460, e-mail: dorothy.kamm@usa.net.

Fiesta Collector's Quarterly (NL), PO Box 471, Valley City, OH 44280, website: www.chinaspecialties.com/fiesta.html.

Head Hunters Newsletter (NL), PO Box 83 H, Scarsdale, NY 10583, e-mail: maddy.gordon@worldnet.att.net.

McCoy Lovers' NMXpress (NL), 8934 Brecksville Rd., Suite 406, Brecksville, OH 44141-2318, e-mail: nmxpress@aol.com, website: www.nmxpress.com.

National Blue Ridge Newsletter (NL), 144 Highland Dr., Blountville, TN 37617-5404.

Old Quimper Review (MAG), Box 377, East Greenwich, RI 02818.

Prussia Collectors (NL), PO Box 446, Mount Joy, PA 17552, e-mail: chocset@aol.com, website: www.rsprussia.com.

Purinton News & Views (NL), PO Box 153, Connellsville, PA 15425, e-mail: jmcmanus@hhs.net.

Tea Talk (NL), PO Box 860, Sausalito, CA 94966, e-mail: TeaTalk@aol.com.

The Village Chronicle Magazine (MAG), 56 Freeway Dr., Cranston, RI 02920, website: www.villagechronicle.com (Dept. 56).

The Wade Watch Newsletter (NL), Collector's Corner, 8199 Pierson Ct., Arvada, CO 80005, e-mail: wadewatch@wadewatch.com, website: www.wadewatch.com.

Willow Review (NL), PO Box 41312, Nashville, TN 37204, e-mail: willowware@aol.com.

ARCHIVES & MUSEUMS

The Bennington Museum, W. Main St., Bennington, VT 05201, 802-447-1571, fax: (802) 442-8305, website: www.benningtonmuseum.com.

Cowan Pottery Museum of Rocky River Public Library, 1600 Hampton Rd., Rocky River, OH 44116-2699, 440-333-7610, ext. 214, website: www.rrpl.org/rrpl_cowan.stm.

Jones Museum of Glass and Ceramics, Douglas Mountain Rd., Douglas Hill, ME 04204, 207-787-3370, fax: 207-787-2800.

Museum of Ceramics of East Liverpool, 400 E. 5th St., East Liverpool, OH 43920, 330-386-6001, websites: www.novaord.com/CeramicsMuseum and www.ohiohistory.org/places/ceramics.

Ohio Ceramic Center, P.O. Box 200, Crooksville, OH 43731, 740-697-7021, website: www.ohiohistory.org/places/ohceram.

Ross C. Purdy Museum of Ceramics, American Ceramic Society, 735 Ceramic Place, Westerville, OH 43081, 614-890-4700, fax: 614-899-6109, e-mail: info@acers.org, website: www.acers.org/acers/museum.asp.

Schein-Joseph International Museum of Ceramic Art, New York State College of Ceramics at Alfred University, Alfred, NY 14802, 607-871-2421, website: nyscc.alfred.edu/mus.

Tile Heritage Foundation, P.O. Box 1850, Healdsburg, CA 95448, 707-431-TILE (8453), fax: 707-431-8455, website: www.tiles.org/pages/tileorgs/thfinfo.htm.

USEFUL SITES

American Dinnerware Identification, www.ohioriverpottery.com.

Ohiopottery.com, www.ohiopottery.com.

Roseville Pottery Exchange, www.ohioriverpottery.com/roseville_exchange/roseville.html.

Stoke-on-Trent Potteries, www.thepotteries.org.

Wingtips, www.redwingnet.com. Information on Red Wing pottery.

APPRAISERS

Many of the auctions and repair services listed in this section will also do appraisals. *See also* the general list of "Appraisal Groups" on page 483 and Matching Services, page 537.

Gift Music Book + Collectibles Secondary Market Dealer + Worldwide Search & Appraisal Service, 708-755-7622, fax: 208-275-5014, e-mail: jntschulte@rocketmail.com, website: www.tias.com/stores/gift. Appraisals of name-brand limited edition plates, dolls, ornaments, steins, houses, figurines, and more (not antiques); $15 for 1 item, prorated for a collection. Send all specific info from item (name, date, artist, series, #, edition, box, certificate, and size) along with hardcopy or digital pictures, especially of back/bottom. All credit cards & Paypal accepted.

AUCTIONS

↦ SEE ALSO "SELLING THROUGH AUCTION HOUSES," PAGE 485.

Andre Ammelounx, PO Box 136, Palatine, IL 60078, 847-991-5927, fax: 847-991-5947, e-mail: aapo136@aol.com, website: tsaco.com. Antique beer steins and drinking vessels. Mail and fax bids accepted. Buyer's premium 15%. Catalog $30 per year. Prices realized mailed after auction. Appraisals.

BBR Auctions, Elsecar Heritage Centre, Barnsley, S. Yorkshire S74 8HJ, UK, 011-44-1226-745156, fax: 011-44-1226-351561, e-mail: sales@bbrauctions.co.uk, website: www.bbrauctions.co.uk. Doulton, Wade, Beswick, pub jugs, and more. Mail and phone bids accepted. Buyer's premium 10%. Prices realized mailed after auction. Restoration and conservation. Appraisals.

Bruce and Vicki Waasdorp Stoneware Auctions, PO Box 434, Clarence, NY 14031, 716-759-2361, fax: 716-759-2397, e-mail: waasdorp@antiques-stoneware.com, website: www.antiques-stoneware.com. American utilitarian pottery and decorated stoneware absentee auctions. Mail, phone, e-mail, and Internet bids accepted. Buyer's premium 10%. Prices realized mailed and available on website after auction. Catalog $20. Appraisals.

Collector's Sales & Services, PO Box 6, Pomfret Center, CT 06259-0006, 860-974-7008, e-mail: collectors@AntiqueChina.com, website: www.antiqueglass.com. Auctions of china. Mail and phone bids accepted. Buyer's premium 10%. China cleaning and restoration services. Appraisals.

David Rago Auctions, Inc., 333 N. Main St., Lambertville, NJ 08530, 609-397-9374, fax: 609-397-9377, e-mail: info@ragoarts.com, website: www.ragoarts.com. In person, mail and phone bids accepted. Buyer's premium 15%. Prices realized available on website after auction. Appraisals.

McAllister Auctions, PO Box 294, Paradise, MI 49768, 800-746-6604 phone/fax, e-mail: mmcall1872@aol.com. Cataloged art pottery auctions held across the country. Free online catalogs. Absentee bids accepted.

NSA Auctions, Newton-Smith Antiques, 88 Cedar St., Cambridge, ON N1S 1, Canada, 519-623-6302, e-mail: info@nsaauctions.com, website: www.nsaauctions.com. Pottery and stoneware auctions. Mail, phone, and Internet bids accepted. No buyer's premium. Catalog price varies. Prices realized mailed after auction and available on website. Appraisals.

Smith & Jones, 12 Clark Ln., Sudbury, MA 01776, 978-443-5517, fax: 978-443-2796, e-mail: smthjones.gis.net, website: www.smithandjonesauctions.com. Absentee auctions of American and European art pottery. Mail, phone, fax, and Internet bids. Buyer's premium 10%. Catalogs and prices realized available.

Southern Folk Pottery Collectors Society, 220 Washington St., Bennett, NC 27208, 336-581-4246, fax: 336-581-4247, e-mail: sfpcs@rtmc.net. Biannual absentee auctions of southern pottery. Mail and phone bids accepted. Catalog prices vary; call for price. Prices realized mailed after auction.

Strawser Auctions, PO Box 332, Wolcottville, IN 46795, 260-854-2859, fax: 260-854-3979, e-mail: michael@strawserauctions.com, website: strawserauctions.com. Majolica and Fiesta. Mail bids accepted. Buyer's premium none to 10%. List of prices realized mailed after auction. Appraisals.

Web Wilson's Online Auctions, PO Box 506, Portsmouth, RI 02871, 800-508-0022, fax: 401-683-1644, e-mail: hww@webwilson.com, website: www.webwilson.com. Antique tiles and more. Phone, fax, and e-mail bids accepted. Buyer's premium 10%. Catalog posted on website or by mail. Prices realized posted on website after auction. Appraisals.

Woody Auction, PO Box 618, Douglass, KS 67039, 316-747-2694, fax: 316-747-2145, e-mail: woodyauction@earthlink.net, website: www.woody auction.com. R.S. Prussia. In person, mail, fax, and e-mail bids accepted. No buyer's premium. Catalogs available in print and online. Prices realized mailed after auction. Free catalogs.

REPAIRS, PARTS & SUPPLIES

➠ **SEE ALSO "CONSERVATORS & RESTORERS," PAGE 520.**

A. Ludwig Klein & Son, Inc., PO Box 145, Harleysville, PA 19438, 215-256-9004 or 800-379-2929, fax: 215-256-9644, website: www.aludwig klein.com. Conservation and restoration of porcelain, dolls, statuary, monuments, and more. Professional cleaning. Appraisals, insurance claims. Worldwide. By appointment. Free brochure.

Albert Post Gallery, 2291 Newbury Dr., West Palm Beach, FL 33414, 561-333-7740, fax: 561-333-7740, e-mail: apostgallery@aol.com. Restoration and conservation of porcelain. Appraisals.

Allan B. Mittelmark, 366 Clinton Ave., Cedarhurst, NY 11516, 561-733-4801, fax: 561-740-1164, e-mail: amsco366@aol.com. Restoration of porcelain, including Boehm, Lladro, Goebel, Hummel, and other manufacturers.

Antique & Art Restoration by Wiebold, 413 Terrace Pl., Terrace Park, OH 45174, 800-321-2541, 513-831-2541, fax: 513-831-2815, e-mail: wiebold @eos.net, website: www.wiebold.com. Fine art restoration and conservation: art pottery, porcelain, collectible figurines, bisque dolls, and more. Missing parts replaced.

Antique China Restorations by MyJolie Hutchings, 1941 Wolfsnare Rd., Virginia Beach, VA 23454-3544, 757-425-1807. Restorations of antiques and contemporary ceramics, china, porcelain, terra-cotta, majolica, bisque, marble, soapstone, lamps, Hummel, Lladro, Roseville, etc. Invisible repairs and replacement of missing parts, finials, handles, fingers, etc.

Antique Restoration Co., 440 E. Centre Ave., Newtown, PA 18940, 215-968-2343, fax: 215-860-5465. Porcelain repaired. Free brochure.

Antique Restoration Service, 521 Ashwood Dr., Flushing, MI 48433, 810-659-5582, 810-659-0505, e-mail: sshch@aol.com. Invisible restoration of all kinds of pottery and china. Restoration of frames, lamps, and other objects. Soldering and wiring, if necessary. Missing parts reconstructed.

Antique Restorations, 1313 Mt. Holly Rd., Burlington, NJ 08016-3773, 609-387-2587, Mon.–Sat., 9:00 A.M.–6:00 P.M., fax: 609-387-2587, e-mail: ronaiello@comcast.net. Restorations of china, porcelain, pottery, dolls' heads, and art objects. Specializes in the restoration of Royal Doulton, Wedgwood, Meissen, Roseville, Fulper, Nippon, Hummel, Lladro, Boehm, Cybis, David Winter Cottages, Dept. 56, and others. Restoration supplies. Private restoration lessons. Free restoration supply catalog on request.

AntiqueConservation.com, Div. of Ponsford Ltd., 5441 Woodstock Rd., Acworth, GA 30102, 770-924-4848, fax: 770-529-2278, e-mail: Gordon Ponsford@AntiqueConservation.com, website: www.AntiqueConservation.com. Conservation and restoration of fine art and antiques, including porcelain and sculpture. Appraisals.

Antiques Etc., 1270 Autumn Wind Way, Henderson, NV 89052, 702-270-9910, e-mail: jimchel@ix.netcom.com. Restoration and appraisals of porcelain.

The Art of Fire at Chaerie Farm, 7901 Hawkins Creamery Rd., Laytonsville, MD 20882, 301-253-6642, e-mail: artofire@bellatlantic.net, website: www.artoffire.com. Porcelain and pottery restoration. Open 7 days a week. Please call ahead on weekdays.

Artwork Restoration, 30 Hillhouse Rd., Winnipeg, MB R2V 2V9, Canada, 204-334-7090, e-mail: morry@escape.ca. Restoration of vases, figurines, lamps, antique dolls, Lladro, Hummel, picture frames, Inui soapstone carvings, and more. Missing parts replaced.

Attic Unlimited, 22435 E. LaPalma Ave., Yorba Linda, CA 92887, 714-692-2940, fax: 714-692-2947, e-mail: atticunlimited@aol.com, website: www.atticunlimited.com. Restoration of Lladros, Hummels, Armanie, porcelain, pottery, and any objects of art.

Beverly Standing Designs, 1026 Elizabeth St., Pasadena, CA 91104, 626-798-2306, fax: 626-798-3529, e-mail: bubbs120@aol.com. Restoration of fine porcelain. By appointment only.

Broken Art Restoration, 1841 W. Chicago Ave., Chicago, IL 60622, 312-226-8200 or 815-472-3900, fax: 815-472-3930. Restoration of porcelain, pottery, and ceramics. By appointment. Free brochure.

The Brushstroke, 4250 Van Cortlandt Pk. E., #1B, Bronx, NY 10470, 718-

994-5989, e-mail: art_restoration@usa.com. Conservation and restoration of porcelain, ceramics, and other objects of art. Pickup and delivery service within 50-mile radius in tristate NYC area. Free estimates.

Carl "Frank" Funes, 57 Maplewood Ave., Hempstead, NY 11550, 516-483-6712. Restoration of porcelain.

Carolyn Henegan, 7760 Southern Blvd., West Palm Beach, FL 33411, 561-793-9386, e-mail: chenegan@yahoo.com. Restoration and conservation of porcelains, earthenware (faience), and stoneware. Photos of previous work available upon request.

Cerami-Cure Restoration Studio, 3919 Magazine Street, New Orleans, LA 70115, 504-250-2276, e-mail: ceramicureit@hotmail.com. Restoration and conservation of pottery and porcelain antiques and objects. Partial or full restoration, including creation of handles and lost areas; retouching and airbrushing. Research services available.

Ceramic Restorations of Westchester, Inc., 8 John Walsh Blvd., Suite 412, Peekskill, NY 10566, 914-734-8410, fax: 914-762-1719, e-mail: siegmar@aol.com, website: www.collectorsresources.com. Repair and restoration of art objects, collectibles, and antiques made from ceramics, porcelain, china, stone, plaster, cold cast, and resin. M.I. Hummel repair specialist.

Ceramic Restorations, Inc., 224 W. 29th St., 12th Floor, New York, NY 10001, 212-564-8669, 9:00 A.M.–6:00 P.M. fax: 212-843-3742. Restoration and conservation of antique and contemporary ceramics, including porcelain, terra-cotta, bisque, and faience. Invisible or museum-style repairs, reconstruction, and replacement of missing elements.

Ceramicare, PO Box 1812, Corrales, NM 87048, 505-898-2728, fax: 505-899-2976, e-mail: agoldschmidt@earthlink.net, website: home.earth link.net/~agoldschmidt/wizzg.html. Repair and restoration of antiquities and art ceramics

China and Crystal Clinic, 1808 N. Scottsdale Rd., Tempe, AZ 85281, 800-658-9197, fax: 480-945-1079, e-mail: VictorColeman@earthlink.net. Restoration of porcelain, china, pottery, and many related materials.

The China Mender, Savage, MD 20763, 301-498-9423, e-mail: china mender@aol.com. Restoration and conservation of pottery and porcelain, specializing in Roseville, stoneware, utilitarian pottery, majolica, and early ceramics. Stain and mineral deposits removed. Serving collectors and dealers in the Washington, DC/Baltimore metro area. Photos, references, and brochure available upon request. Reasonable turnaround time. By appointment only.

Collectible Restorations International, 309 Rt. 17M, PO Box 933, Harriman, NY 10926, 845-783-4438, fax: 845-783-4438 *47, e-mail: fredi@fredi-boese.com, website: www.frediboese.com. Specializing in the repair and restoration of M.I. Hummel figurines and all Goebel products.

Collector's Sales & Services, PO Box 6, Pomfret Center, CT 06259-

0006, 860-974-7008, e-mail: collectors@AntiqueChina.com, website: www.antiqueglass.com. China cleaning and restoration services. Appraisals.

David Smith, 1142 S. Spring St., Springfield, IL 62704, 217-523-3391, fax: 217-523-0478, e-mail: davemarble@msn.com. Pottery restorations. Broken or chipped pieces fixed. Brochure 50 cents. Open Mon.–Fri. 10:00 A.M.–5:00 P.M.

Dean's China Restoration, 324 Guinevere Ridge, Cheshire, CT 06410, 800-669-1327 or 203-271-3659, e-mail: DSandAssociates@aol.com. Invisible restoration of all types of china, porcelain, pottery, and figurines. Pieces can be brought to the studio or sent from anywhere. Free estimates. Free brochure.

Devashan, 445 S. Canyon, Spearfish, SD 57783, 605-722-5355, e-mail: dollmaker@mato.com, website: www.devashan.com. Porcelain and ceramic repair. Send SASE for brochure.

Dunhill Restoration, c/o All Makes Vacuum, 2309 Lee Rd., Cleveland Heights, OH 44118, 216-291-1771. Restoration of broken porcelain and pottery. Replacement of missing pieces. Work guaranteed. Black-light proof.

The Eclectic Crone's Nest, Ophelia, VA 22530, 703-739-5832 (weekdays) or 804-453-3379 (weekends), e-mail: grnponds@aol.com. Restores and repairs pottery, art pottery, statues, figurines, ceramics, and porcelain. No dishware.

European Restorations, Inc., 915 NW 1st Ave., Apt. H2501, Miami, FL 33136, 305-373-5358, fax: 305-373-5358, e-mail: jstenson@bellsouth.net. Porcelain, ceramics, and pottery restorations. Classes available.

Excalibur Restorations, 7605 Carleton Dr., Spring Grove, IL 60081, 815-675-0223, e-mail: excaliburrestorations@rsg.org, website: excalibur restorations.com. Porcelain and pottery restoration using reversible techniques and materials.

Final Touch, Inc., 34 Ranch Rd., Woodbridge, CT 06525, 203-389-5485, fax: 203-389-5553, e-mail: FinalTh@optonline.net. Repair of ceramics. Appraisals.

Fine Wares Restoration, PO Box 753, Bridgton, ME 04009, 207-647-2093, e-mail: sharonsmithabbott@yahoo.com. Ceramic conservation services for museum and private collections. Written estimates and suggested treatment provided at no cost.

Flo-Blue Shoppe, 22860 W. Thirteen Mile Rd., Birmingham, MI 48025, 248-433-1933, fax: 248-433-3878. Flow Blue matching service. Restoration services available. Appraisals.

Gepetto Restoration, 31121 Via Colinas, Suite 1003, Westlake Village, CA 91362, 818-889-0901, fax: 818-889-8922, e-mail: barrykorngiebel@mail city.com. Fine porcelain repair, specializing in porcelain figurines. Appraisal of objects of art, specializing in European porcelains.

Gerlinde Kornmesser, 1705 Glenview Rd., Glenview, IL 60025, 847-

724-3059 or 847-375-8105, e-mail: gkantiques@cs.com, website: www.gkrestoration.com. Pottery and porcelain restoration classes, summer only, Lawrence University, Appleton, Wisconsin.

Give Me A Break, PO Box 5553, Napa, CA 94581, 707-226-2924, e-mail: joan@fixeschina.com, website: www.fixeschina.com. Invisible china and porcelain restoration, specializing in Florence Ceramics, porcelain lace restoration, Roseville Pottery, cookie jars, and chalkware.

Glass Studio, 5412A Dickson, Houston, TX 77007, 713-880-1090, fax: 713-880-3544, e-mail: nfwassef@msn.com. Pottery and porcelain repair. Figurines repaired.

Goodbye Mrs. Chips, 425-558-9142, e-mail: debbie@goodbyemrs chips.com, website: www.goodbyemrschips.com. Pottery and porcelain repair, restoration, and cleaning. No cost or obligation for quotes.

Grady Stewart—Expert Porcelain Restoration, 2019 Sanson St., Philadelphia, PA 19103, 215-567-2888. Restoration of fine antique porcelain and pottery.

Grashe Fine Art Restorers, 35 148th Ave. SE, #9, Bellevue WA 98007, 425-644-7500, fax: 425-644-7582, e-mail: art@grashe.com, website: www.grashe.com. Specializes in the restoration and conservation of porcelain, ceramics, pottery, and terra-cotta.

Gusten's Restoration Studio, 336 923-2647, e-mail: gusten@ix.net com.com, website: www.gustensrestoration.com. Restoration of fine porcelain and art pottery, specializing in reversible restoration that does no further damage to the object. Missing pieces replicated and replaced. Work done on a full range of art objects, including American Art Pottery, European and Asian Porcelain, as well as figurines of all types and makers. By appointment only.

Hadley Restorations, 4667 Third St., La Mesa, CA 91941-5529, 619-462-5290, e-mail: cphadcearthlink.net, website: www.assoc-restorers.com. Restoration of china, porcelain, pottery (both earthenware and stoneware), and chalkware. Free brochure. China restoration classes in La Mesa; demonstrations, lectures on china restoration.

Hamlin's Restoration Studio, 14640 Manchester Rd., Ballwin, MO 63011, 636-256-8579, e-mail: hamlinsrestoration@msn.com, website: www.hamlinsrestoration.com. Repair and restoration of fine china, porcelain, and pottery, specializing in Capo-di-Monte, Meissen, Hummel, Boehm, Lladro, Wedgwood, and other fine antiques.

Heart Broken Jewelry, 1325 McKinley Ave., South Bend, IN 46617, 574-287-1615, e-mail: valerie@HeartBrokenJewelry.com. Custom jewelry made from pieces of broken china or glass. Several pieces of jewelry can be made from one broken piece of china.

Heimbolds, 2950 SW Persimmon Ln., Dunnellon, FL 34431, 352-465-0756. Conservation and restoration of pottery and porcelain. Free estimates. Free brochure.

Herbert F. Klug Conservation & Restoration, Box 28002 #16, Lakewood,

CO 80228, 303-985-9261, e-mail: hgklug@qadas.com. Conservation and restoration of classical antiquities, Oriental porcelains, European porcelains, and limited edition figurines such as Boehm, Cybis, Kaiser, Lladro, and Hummel. By appointment only.

A Home Design, 5220 Veloz Ave., Los Angeles, CA 91356, 818-757-7766, fax: 818-708-3722, e-mail: homedesign@mail.com. Fine arts restoration. Operating in the southern California area.

Hummel Collectors' Club, Inc.—Dorothy Dous, Inc., 261 University Dr., Yardley, PA 19067-2857, 888-548-6635 or 215-493-6204, fax: 215-321-3367, e-mail: customerservice@hummels.com, website: www.hummels.com. CrazeMasters representative. Hummel figurines decrazed.

J & H China Repairs, 8296 St. George St., Vancouver, BC V5X 3S5, Canada, 604-321-1093, fax: 604-321-1093. Restoration of porcelain, ceramics, figurines, and sculptures.

James Davidson, 928 Independence St., New Orleans, LA 70117-5738, 504-944-0545, fax: 504-944-0545, e-mail: cjd9440545@netscape.net. Restoration of porcelain and pottery, specializing in gilding techniques on porcelain.

Joan Walton, 3646 Pershing Ave., San Diego, CA 92104, 619-291-6539. Restoration of fine European porcelain and American art pottery, specializing in Lladro. Services cover all of southern California. Shipping available.

John Edward Cunningham, 1525 E. Berkeley, Springfield, MO 65804, 417-889-7702. Porcelains restored. Restoration of Boehm and Royal Worcester. Missing parts replaced. Hours by appointment.

Jonathan Mark Gershen, 1463 Pennington Rd., Ewing Township, NJ 08618, 609-882-9417. Repair and restoration of porcelain and pottery. Missing parts fabricated, shattered pieces restored, historically accurate reconstruction of decorative art objects. Send for information on how to ship your items for evaluation. Worldwide service. Free brochure.

Just Enterprises—Art & Antique Restoration, 2790 Sherwin Ave., # 10, Ventura, CA 93003, 805-644-5837, fax: 805-644-5837, e-mail: justenterprises vc@yahoo.com, website: justenterprisesvc.com. Art and antique restoration, including porcelain.

kariel_creations, 5631 E. Marina Dr., Dania, FL 33312, 954-967-6029, fax: 954-967-6029, e-mail: karic8888@msn.com. Restoration and repair of pottery, porcelain, and collectibles of all kinds.

Kay Marsden Gilpin, 2218 Bohler Rd. NW, Atlanta, GA 30327, 404-355-6394, 11:00 A.M.–7:00 P.M. e-mail: ggilpin@sprynet.com. Ceramics restoration.

Keller China Restoration, 4825 Windsor Dr., Rapid City, SD 57702, 605-342-6756, e-mail: KellerChina@rapidnet.com. Restoration of porcelain, ceramics, and pottery. Figurines restored, including Hummel, Lladro, and Precious Moments; dolls repaired. Chips and hairline cracks repaired; missing parts reproduced. Free brochure.

Ken Marshall, 2424 N. Wishon #7, Fresno, CA 93704, 559-243-0655. Restoration of porcelain.

Kingsmen Antique Restoration Inc., 19 Passamore Ave., Unit 28, Scarborough, ON Canada M1V 4T5, 416-291-8939, fax: 416-291-8939, e-mail: kingsmen@sprint.ca. Invisible mending of art objects. Restoration of porcelain, pottery, soapstone, and more. Service worldwide. Call for information on sending objects for estimates.

Kistner's Full Claims Service, Inc., 520 20th St., Rock Island, IL 61201, 309-786-5868, fax: 309-794-0559, e-mail: kistners1@home.com, website: www.kistners.com. Restoration of porcelain, figurines, life-size statues, and other objects. Serving eastern Iowa and northwestern Illinois. Free brochure.

KLM Studios, 9525 Kenwood Rd., Suite 16-226, Cincinnati, OH 45242, 513-652-9216, e-mail: info@klmstudios.com, website: www.klm studios.com. Art restoration services for ceramics.

Larsen's Collectibles, 757 120th St., Hampton, IA 50441-7555, 641-866-6733. Lids, handles, and spigots for stoneware crocks and jugs. Handles that will fit most rolling pins.

Leak Enterprises, 12500 SE Hwy. 301, Belleview, FL 34420-4410, 352-245-8862, e-mail: jleak@leakenterprises.com, website: www.leak enterprises.com. Restoration of Lladro, Hummel, Boehm, Roseville, and other American pottery; Meissen, Cybis, Orientalia, and any other quality porcelain and ceramics.

Leatherman Restoration, 509 Mairo St., Austin, TX 78748, 512-282-1556, fax: 512-282-1562, e-mail: rondl@juno.com, website: leatherman services.com. Repair and restoration of pottery, ceramics, statues, figurines, tiles, and miscellaneous items.

Legacy Art Restorations & Design Int'l. Inc., 4221 N. 16th St., Phoenix, AZ 85016-5318, 602-263-5178, fax: 602-263-6009, e-mail: restoration @legacyintlinc.com, website: legacyintlinc.com. Restoration of fine art and collectibles, including porcelain and ceramics. Conservator and restorer of Lladro and Belleek.

MAC Enterprises, 122 Miro Adelante, San Clemente, CA 92673, 949-361-9528, e-mail: macrestor@aol.com. Restoration of porcelain, ceramics, pottery, and collectibles. Registered Hummel restorer. Ship UPS or call for information. Send SASE for brochure.

Marye Anne, Porcelain Doctor, Reno, NV, 775-851-3340. China mending, restoration, and stain removal.

Meeting House Furniture Restoration, 87 Waterman Hill, Quechee, VT 05059, 802-295-1309, fax: 802-296-5911. Porcelain and china repair.

Mike Meshenberg, 2571 Edgewood Rd., Beachwood, OH 44122, 216-464-2084. Ceramic repairs, specializing in figurines, including Lladro.

N Pieces, 219 Virginia Rd., Excelsior Springs, MO 64024, e-mail: frog-mom2@epsi.net. Repair of all types of art pottery, porcelain, and stoneware, including Roseville, Van Briggle, Weller, Rookwood, R.S. Prussia, Flow Blue, Lladro, and Hummel.

New Orleans Conservation Guild, Inc., 3301 Chartres St., New Orleans, LA 70117, 504-944-7900, fax: 504-944-8750, e-mail: info@art-restoration.com, website: www.art-restoration.com. Restoration and conservation of fine art and antiques, including porcelain and ceramics. Appraisals and research searches. Call or write for brochure.

Old World Restorations, Inc., 5729 Dragon Way, Cincinnati, OH 45227, 513-271-5459, fax: 513-271-5418, e-mail: info@oldworldrestorations.com, website: www.oldworldrestorations.com. Restoration and conservation of porcelain, art, and antiques. Specialized packing and shipping. Nationwide service. Send or e-mail photos for preliminary estimates. Free brochure.

Past & Present, 14851 Avenue 360, Visalia, CA 93292, 559-798-0029, fax: 559-798-1415, e-mail: P-P@ix.netcom.com, website: www.pastpresent.net. Discontinued china. Appraisals and restoration.

Peter Dale, Restorer, 9773 N. Cin. Col. Rd., Waynesville, OH 45068, 513-897-2665. Restoration of pottery, porcelain, chalkware, and composition. Missing parts molded on dolls, figurines, nodders, etc. Stained objects cleaned. Workbook, *How to Restore or Mend Pottery, China, etc.* Lessons on repair and restoration.

Peter J. Dugan, Fine Art Restoration, 1300 Coventry Cir., Vernon Hills, IL 60061, 847-367-0561, e-mail: pdugan6439@aol.com. Restoration of porcelain.

Pick Up The Pieces, 711 W. 17th St., Unit C-12, Costa Mesa, CA 92627, 800-824-6967, fax: 949-645-8381, e-mail: johnnce@yahoo.com, website: www.pickupthepieces.com. Fine art and collectible repair and restoration. Specializing in repair of Lladro, Hummels, Boehm, Meissen, Royal Doulton, Armani, Dresden, Disney Classics, Capo-di-Monte, and other manufacturers.

Pleasant Valley Restoration, 1725 Reed Rd., Knoxville, MD 21758, 301-432-2721, 9:00 A.M.–7:00 P.M. e-mail: PVRfixit@aol.com. Restoration of porcelain, Hummels, and other art and antique objects. Custom color matching and airbrush work. Previous restorations detected and verified.

Poor Richard's Restoration & Preservation Studio Workshop, 101 Walnut St., Montclair, NJ 07042, 973-783-5333, fax: 973-744-1939, e-mail: jrickford@webtv.com, website: www.rickford.com. Restoration, conservation, preservation, and archival services. By appointment, Tues.–Fri. noon–5:00 P.M., Sat. noon–3:00 P.M.

Professional Restoration Studio, PO Box 435, N. 5th St., Highland, NC 28741, 828-526-4064, fax: 828-526-4064, e-mail: crystalstudio@earth link.net. Restoration of porcelain, including Boehm, Dresden, Hummel, Lalique, Meissen, Rosenthal, Waterford, and more. Missing pieces rebuilt.

Rafail & Polina Golberg, Golberg Restoration Co., Polina & Rafail Gol-berg, 411 Westmount Dr., Los Angeles, CA 90048, 310-652-0735, fax: 310-274-3770, e-mail: info@restorationworld.com, website: www.restoration world.com. Restoration and conservation of antiques and objects of art, including porcelain and pottery. Free estimates via the Internet.

Renaissance Restoration, Main PO Box 562, Purchase, NY 10577, 877-734-8233, fax: 877-734-8277. Porcelain restoration.

Restoration Services, 1417 Third St., Webster City, IA 50595, 515-832-1131, e-mail: repair@netins.net, website: www.Restorationmaterials. safeshopper.com. Restoration services for china, pottery, porcelain, ceramics, and most other materials. Replacement parts fabricated. Supplies, videos, home study course, classes available. Mini manuals, "Repairing China, Pottery & Figurines" and "Color Matching Guide."

Restoration Studio, PO Box 3440, Glens Falls, NY 12801, 518-743-9416, e-mail: anna98@nycap.rr.com. Restoration and conservation of ceramic objects of art, including bone china, pottery, stoneware, ironstone, and related wares. Restoration lessons given at the studio. Free estimates. Free brochure.

Restorations by Maureen, PO Box 187, Rancho Cordova, CA 95741-0187, 916-366-1899, e-mail: mdmdecker@starband.net. Restoration of porcelain, pottery, ceramics, and figurines.

Restorations by Patricia, 420 Centre St., Nutley, NJ 07110, 973-235-0234. Restoration and repair of religious statuary (5 inches to 5 feet), plaster statues and collectibles, porcelain, pottery, cold cast porcelain, bisque dolls, and figurines, specializing in Hummel, Lladro, Boehm, Herend, Royal Doulton, Meissen, etc. Can personalize hair, eyes, and clothing on statues and figurines, bride and groom, etc.

Restorations Unlimited, 3009 W. Genesee St., Syracuse, NY 13219, 315-488-7123, fax: 315-488-7123, e-mail: d64curtin@aol.com. Repair of bisque and porcelain, including Hummel, Lladro, David Winter, Dept. 56, and Harbour Lights.

Restorer Supplies, Inc., PO Box 387, Golden CO 80402-0387, 303-384-9121, e-mail: sales@RestorerSupplies.com, website: www.Restorer Supplies.com. Porcelain and ceramic restoration supplies. Supplies for every step of restoration: mending, filling, impression materials, casting, sanding, painting, glazing, and polishing. Distributors of the Cold-Glaze system from Europe. Will answer restoration-related questions.

Restorite Systems, PO Box 7096-A, West Trenton, NJ 08628, 609-530-1526. Products for restoring porcelain and pottery. Repair kit for restoring broken or chipped china. Includes supplies necessary to mend dozens of pieces and illustrated instruction book. Mail order only. Free brochure.

Richard Beggs, Pottery Restoration, 9553 White Tail Tr., Kernersville, NC 27284, e-mail: rtbeg@webtv.net. Specializes in the restoration of

American art pottery and southern pottery. Please call for further information before shipping item to be restored.

Richford's Restoration, 147 Michigan Ave., Daytona Beach, FL 32114, 386-239-0939, fax: 386-252-1700, e-mail: srich4d@bellsouth.net. Restoration of porcelain and pottery, specializing in Roseville, Weller, and stoneware crocks and jugs. Repair and cleaning of all types of porcelain, including Flow Blue, Royal Doulton, Hummel, etc. Will teach classes at your location. Call for information.

Robert E. DiCarlo, PO Box 616222, Orlando, FL 32861, 407-886-7423, e-mail: rollybob@cs.com. Restoration of porcelain, china, pottery, and collectible figurines, including Boehm, Cybis, Armani, Goebel, etc.

Rock Scherzer, Restorer, 11200 Gratiot, Saginaw, MI 48609, 989-249-0827, fax: 989-781-4426, e-mail: scherzer@concentric.net. Pottery and porcelain restoration.

Rosine Green Associates, Inc., 89 School St., Brookline, MA 02446, 617-277-8368, fax: 617-731-3845, e-mail: rga@ix.netcom.com. Conservation and restoration of fine art, including porcelain and objects of art. Custom display cases.

Sano Studio, 767 Lexington Ave. at 60th St., New York, NY 10021, 212-759-6131, fax: 212-759-6131. Restoration of antique pottery and porcelain.

Sharlan Restorations, Beachwood, Ohio 44122, 216-464-3434, e-mail: Sharlan1@msn.com (only for inquiries from prospective customers), website: rtantiques.com/sharlan.htm. Restoration and repair of ceramic, porcelain, pottery, and china collectibles.

Sharon Carabajal, 9424 Halidon Way, Sacramento, CA 95839, 916-688-8667, e-mail: bcarabajal@aol.com. Porcelain restoration, primarily horse figurines. Free estimates. Hours 9:00 A.M. PST–6:00 P.M.

The Sisters, 4163 Danamar Dr., Pensacola, FL 32504, 850-484-0975 or 850-476-7513, e-mail: sjtrimble@worldnet.att.net. General restoration of porcelain, marble, jade, alabaster, Dresden lace, and more. Lladro restoration. Free brochure.

Specialized Repair Co., 12101 S. 1390 W., Riverton, UT 84065, 801-254-2777, fax: 801-254-3513, e-mail: SpecRep@SoftSolutions.com. Porcelain and figurine repair. Specializing in claim service for moving companies.

Studio 2000—The Porcelain Clinic, Chicago Suburbs, 847-487-4768, e-mail: ifixchina@porcelainclinic.com, website: www.porcelain clinic.com. European and American methods of porcelain restoration. Invisible repairs, complete reversibility. Hummel, Limoges, majolica, Meissen, Nippon, Rookwood, Roseville, Weller, and others. Specializing in the restoration of American art pottery. Classes and apprentice programs available.

Swan Restorations, 2627 Montrose Ave., Abbotsford, BC V2S 3TS, Canada, 604-855-6694, fax: 604-855-1720. Restoration of antiques and collectibles, including porcelain, pottery, and china. Free written estimates. Hours Mon.–Fri. 10:00 A.M.–5:00 P.M., or by appointment. Call before sending item to be repaired.

T.S. Restoration—J.M. Denson, 2015 N. Dobson Rd., Suite 4, PMB 59B, Chandler, AZ 85224, 480-963-3148, website: www.assoc-restorers.com. Restoration supplies, graphic lessons, and videos, concentrating on the restoration of porcelain and ceramic art objects. Mail order. Send LSASE for information.

Tile Restoration Center, Inc., 3511 Interlake N., Seattle, WA 98103, 206-633-4866, fax: 206-633-3489, e-mail: trc@tilerestorationcenter.com, website: www.tilerestorationcenter.com. On-site restoration of tile installations. Reproduction of Arts and Crafts period tiles. Specializing in reproductions of Batchelder and Claycraft tiles. Custom design, custom color matching. Catalog $10.

Tindell's Restoration, 825 Sandburg Pl., Nashville, TN 37214, 615-885-1029, fax: 615-391-0712, e-mail: info@ATindellsRestorationSchools.com, website: www.TindellsRestorationSchools.com. Restoration services, seminars, training, and products. Can restore porcelain, pottery, ceramics, and much more. Appraisals. Free brochure.

Vasedoktor, website: www.heirloompotteryrepair.com. Repair and restoration of American art pottery, specializing in Roseville, Weller, Hull, Peters and Reed, Newcomb College, and some Frankoma.

Venerable Classics, 645 4th St., Suite 208, Santa Rosa, CA 95404, 800-531-2891 or 707-575-3626, fax: 707-575-4913 call first, website: www.venerableclassics.com. Restoration of porcelain and many other fragile decorative objects. Restoration of ceramic clock cases, Lladro, Hummels, dolls, and more. Please call with questions. Free brochure.

Zorella Restoration, 1936 Mt. Royal Terr., Baltimore, MD 21217, 410-225-2141, fax: 410-462-2135, e-mail: szorella@aol.com. Restoration of porcelain, ceramics, and art objects; Rose Medallion, Canton Ware, etc.

PRINTS

It is difficult to sell black-and-white prints, etchings, and engravings. They are not popular now, and only very special prints in excellent condition by known artists will bring good money. Many prints that are attractive if framed have no antiques value. Some are just pages taken from old books. It takes an art expert to evaluate art prints. Your local museum may be able to help you identify the artist and age. The research needed to determine how to price the print is the same as the research needed to price a fine painting. (See Paintings section.)

There are many terms whose meanings are familiar only to an

expert. You don't need to know the meaning of first strike, restrike, foxing, edition, steel engraving, etc., unless you plan to go into the business of selling prints. The subtleties of these terms are complicated.

Japanese woodblock prints are popular and sell quickly. Some old, rare prints were available immediately after World War II for only a few dollars each, and many soldiers brought them home. Today, some of the old prints in fine condition are worth thousands of dollars. The colors should be bright, the paper untorn and without stains. If the print has been glued to a backing, it has lost its value. Several books are available to help you identify these prints, but once again it takes an expert to know whether the woodblock print is worth a few hundred or a few thousand dollars. If you have had the prints for over thirty years, it would be wise to have an appraisal by an expert.

Movie, travel, and other posters are listed in price books and are easier to identify than prints. The only hazards are the reproductions, since many old posters have been reissued and reproduced. There are clues to look for, however, especially for movie posters, and research in the library will help.

Travel posters and circus posters sell at highest prices as decorative pictures. A Yosemite Winter Sports poster from the 1930s sold for $6,325 in 2001. Large, colorful posters with interesting subjects sell quickly if in very good condition. Torn, faded posters do not sell. French posters by well-known artists, advertising posters, and posters printed by important companies are bought by specialists who will pay more than the average poster price. Check the value in a general price book or look in the catalogs sent out by mail-order or Internet poster dealers. These dealers also have to buy more posters, so they could be your customers.

Calendar art—the pictures printed for the tops of wall-hung paper calendars—is a new area of collecting. Pinup-girl prints by **PETTY**, **VARGAS**, and other artists working after 1940 are in demand. Sentimental pictures of children by early 1900s artists like **BESSIE PEASE GUTMANN** or **ROSE O'NEILL** sell well. Landscapes by **R. ATKINSON FOX** or Art Deco prints by **MAXFIELD PARRISH** are also desirable.

Old **CURRIER & IVES** prints have always been popular. Action scenes and outdoor scenes are priced the highest; religious subjects, vases of flowers, and portraits of children are priced low. Be careful, because there have been many reproductions. Look in *Currier & Ives Prints: An Illustrated Check List* by Frederic A. Conningham for the exact size of the original of your print. Then look up the value in the general price books.

Hand-colored bird prints by **JOHN GOULD** or **JOHN JAMES AUDUBON**, botanical prints, interior room views, architectural drawings, military scenes, and many other prints removed from nineteenth-century books are sold by special dealers at most large antiques shows. These may be the dealers who will buy your prints.

REPAIR

Restoration of any type of paper is difficult. It is possible to carefully clean dust from a print by using wallpaper cleaner, wadded fresh white bread, or an art-gum eraser. Creases can be carefully ironed out with a very cool iron. More ambitious repairs should always be done by a restorer. Do not tape or glue any paper item: the acids in the adhesive will eventually cause damage. Marks from old tape can sometimes be removed by a restorer.

↝ SEE ALSO PAINTINGS, PAPER COLLECTIBLES

PRICE BOOKS

American and European Postcards of Harrison Fisher, Illustrator, Naomi Welch (Images of the Past, 309 Playa Blvd., La Selva Beach, CA 95076).

Bessie Pease Gutmann: Over Fifty Years of Published Art, Karen A. Choppa (Schiffer, Atglen, PA, 1998).

Collector's Value Guide to Japanese Woodblock Prints, Sandra Andacht (Krause, Iola, WI, 2000).

Collectors Guide to Early Twentieth Century American Prints, Michael Ivankovich (Collector Books, Paducah, KY, 1998).

The Complete Works of Harrison Fisher, Illustrator, Naomi Welch (Images of the Past, 309 Playa Blvd., La Selva Beach, CA 95076).

Currier & Ives Lithographs Value Guide, George Cohenour (4301 Beaumont Road, Dover, PA 17315, www.currierprints.com, 2001).

R. Atkinson Fox and William M. Thompson: Identification and Price Guide, 2nd edition, Patricia L. Gibson (Collectors Press, Portland, OR, 2000).

R. Atkinson Fox: His Life & Work, Rita C. Mortenson (L-W Book Sales, Gas City, IN, 1991, prices revised 1999).

CLUBS & THEIR PUBLICATIONS

American Historical Print Collectors Society, *Imprint* (MAG), PO Box 201, Fairfield, CT 06430, e-mail: rbraun724@optonline.net, website: www.ahpcs.org.

Philip Boileau Collectors' Society, *Philip Boileau Collectors' Society Newsletter* (NL), 1025 Redwood Blvd., Redding, CA 96003-1905, e-mail:

pboileaucc@aol.com or gamlin@aol.com, website: hometown.aol. com/PBoileauCC/index.html.

OTHER PUBLICATIONS

Art on Paper (MAG), 39 E. 78th St., Suite 501, New York, NY 10021, e-mail: info@artonpaper.com, website: www.artonpaper.com (fine art prints, drawings & photography).

Journal of the Print World (NP), PO Box 978, Meredith, NH 03253-0978, e-mail: sophia@cyberportal.net, website: www.JournalofthePrintWorld.com.

APPRAISERS

Some of the repair services listed in this section will also do appraisals. *See also* the general list of "Appraisal Groups" on page 483.

J.K. Flynn Company, 471 Sixth Ave., Park Slope, Brooklyn, NY 11215, 718-369-8934, fax: 718-369-8934, e-mail: jkflynncompany@aol.com. Fine art appraising and consulting. Specializing in the appraisal of American and European paintings, but also include sculpture, prints, drawings, and other mixed media works on paper. Free lists of services.

Liros Gallery, PO Box 946, 14 Parker Point Rd., Blue Hill, ME 04614, 207-374-5370, fax: 207-734-5370, e-mail: liros@lirosgallery.com, website: www.lirosgallery.com. Appraisals of paintings, prints, and icons. Free brochure.

AUCTIONS

➠ **SEE ALSO "SELLING THROUGH AUCTION HOUSES," PAGE 485.**

Last Moving Picture Co., Kirtland Antique Mall, 10535 Chillicothe Rd., Kirtland, OH 44094, 440-256-3660, fax: 440-256-3431, e-mail: lastmo@aol.com, website: vintagefilmposters.com. Movie poster auctions. Mail, phone, and Internet bids accepted. Buyer's premium 15%. Catalog $10. Prices realized available on website after auction. Some appraisals.

Old World Auctions, PO Box 2224, 270 Hillside Ave., Sedona, AZ 86339, 928-282-3944 or 800-664-7757, fax: 928-282-3945, e-mail: marti@old worldauctions.com, website: oldworldauctions.com. Specializing in antique maps and related travel and exploration books and graphics. Mail, phone, and Internet bids accepted. Buyer's premium 12%. Catalogs $25 per year. Prices realized available on website and mailed in next catalog.

Poster Auctions International, Inc., 601 W. 26th St., New York, NY 10001, 212-787-4000, fax: 212-604-9175, e-mail: info@posterauctions.com, website: www.posterauctions.com. Poster auctions. Mail, phone, fax, and e-mail bids accepted. Buyer's premium 15%. Catalogs $50. Prices realized mailed after auction and available on website. Appraisals.

Swann Galleries, Inc., 104 E. 25th St., New York, NY 10010, 212-254-

4710, fax: 215-979-1017, e-mail: swann@swanngalleries.com, website: www.swanngalleries.com. Auctions of prints, posters, and other art on paper. Buyer's premium varies. Mail, phone, and fax bids accepted. Catalogs.

Waverly Auctions, Inc., 4931 Cordell Ave., Bethesda, MD 20814, 301-951-8883, fax: 301-718-8375, e-mail: waverly1660@earthlink.net, website: waverlyauctions.com. Auctions of prints, maps, and used and rare books. Mail, phone, and Internet bids accepted. Buyer's premium 15%. Prices realized mailed after auction and available on website. Catalog $7; yearly subscription $38. Appraisals.

William Morford Auctions, RR #2, Cazenovia, NY 13035, 315-662-7625, fax: 315-662-3570, e-mail: morf2bid@aol.com, website: morfauction.com. Absentee auctions of Maxfield Parrish prints. Mail, phone, and Internet bids accepted. Buyer's premium 10%. Prices realized mailed after auction and available on website. Catalog $12; yearly subscription $20. Restoration and conservation. Appraisals.

REPAIRS, PARTS & SUPPLIES

➤ SEE ALSO "CONSERVATORS & RESTORERS," PAGE 520.

Andrea Pitsch Paper Conservation, 212-594-9676, Mon.–Fri., fax: 212-268-4046, e-mail: apnyc@interport.net. Conservation and restoration of paper-based objects: art, including posters and prints. Consultation on condition of paper collections, prospective purchases, storage, and handling. Brochure $1 and SASE. By appointment only.

Bags Unlimited, 7 Canal St., Rochester, NY 14608, 800-767-BAGS or 716-436-9006, fax: 716-328-8526, e-mail: info@bagsunlimited.com, website: www.bagsunlimited.com. Products for storing, displaying, and shipping collectibles. Archival materials sold: polyethylene, polypropylene, Mylar, acid-free boards and storage boxes. High-clarity, recyclable, 100% polyethylene bags. Three grades of backing boards, several sizes of storage boxes and divider cards.

Bill Cole Enterprises, Inc., PO Box 60, Dept. RK1, Randolph, MA 02368-0060, 781-986-2653, fax: 781-986-2656, e-mail: bcemylar@cwbusiness.com, website: www.bcemylar.com. Manufacturers and distributors of archival supplies to protect paper documents from turning yellow. Acid-free boards, and boxes. Mylar sleeves for movie posters and other paper collectibles.

Conservation of Art on Paper, Inc., 2805 Mount Vernon Ave., Alexandria, VA 22301, 703-836-7757, fax: 703-836-8878, e-mail: capi@erols.com. Conservation treatments for art and historic artifacts on paper, including fine prints and rare posters. Vault storage, classes and lectures, publications about caring for art on paper, collection surveys, insurance reports.

Dobson Studios, 810 N. Daniel St., Arlington, VA 22201, 703-243-7363, e-mail: ddobson@dobson-studios.com, website: www.dobson-studios.com. Conservation of Oriental woodblock prints, screens, scrolls, Western paper, and parchment. Most paper objects are washed and deacidified, if needed. All work is reversible.

Graphic Conservation Co., 329 W. 18th St., Suite 701, Chicago, IL 60616, 312-738-2657, fax: 312-738-3125, e-mail: info@graphicconservation.com, website: www.graphicconservation.com. Preservation of works of art on paper, including prints, posters, and architectural process prints. Dry cleaning, stain reduction, flattening, deacidification, inpainting, tear repairs, and fills. Archival matting. Free brochure.

Hollinger Corporation, PO Box 8360, Fredericksburg, VA 22404, 800-634-0491, 8:30 A.M.–5:00 P.M., e-mail: hollingercorp@erols.com, website: www.hollingercorp.com. Archival print boxes, envelopes, folders, tubes, acid-free papers, plastic sleeves, and products to store prints and more. Free catalog.

Museum Shop, Ltd., 20 N. Market St., Frederick, MD 21701, 301-695-0424. Restoration of paper, including etchings and lithographs. Free brochure.

Northeast Document Conservation Center, 100 Brickstone Sq., Andover, MA 01810-1494, 978-470-1010, fax: 978-475-6021, e-mail: nedcc @nedcc.org, website: www.nedcc.org. Nonprofit regional conservation center specializing in treatment of art and artifacts on paper, including posters, prints, and works of art on paper. Preservation microfilming, preservation planning surveys, disaster assistance, technical leaflets. Free brochure. Open Mon.–Fri. 8:30 A.M.–4:30 P.M.

Philadelphia Print Shop, Ltd., 8441 Germantown Ave., Philadelphia, PA 19118, 215-242-4750, fax: 215-242-6977, e-mail: philaprint@philaprint shop.com, website: www.philaprintshop.com. Conservation services for art on paper. Appraisals and research.

Scott K. Kellar, Bookbinding & Conservation, 2650 Montrose Ave., Chicago, IL 60618-1507, 773-478-2825, fax: 801-760-6843, e-mail: skkellar @earthlink.net. Conservation of rare books and printed material. Deacidification and archival encapsulation of posters.

➻ **PURSES, SEE FASHION**

RADIO & TV

RADIO

The streamlined, colored-plastic creations of the 1930s are the most wanted radios. More recent figural radios, especially those patterned on Disney characters, are selling for high prices. The blue mirror–covered **EMERSON** or **SPARTON** is worth money, even if it is not in working order. Brown plastic-cased radios, wooden radios, and large elaborate floor models made after 1935 are of limited value even if they are in working order. Some floor models are considered furniture, and the insides are removed and replaced with a stereo. If your radio is the proper size and shape for this, it has some sale value. Sets with added value are **FADA**, **EMERSON**, and **CRYSTAL SETS**.

In the 1990s a new group of collectors started looking for transistor radios. These must work and have an unusual or high-style case to sell. These collectors are found on the Internet.

Radios have gained in interest since the 1970s. Old tubes and other parts are hard to find, but there are dealers, publications, and clubs that make the search a little easier. The slightest crack or scratch in the surface of an expensive colored plastic or Art Deco radio will lower the value by over 50 percent. This type of damage cannot be repaired.

TELEVISIONS

Early TV sets, those made before 1950 with screens of two inches or less, are of some interest to collectors. These early sets worked on a chemical battery that requires maintenance. Chances are your ordinary-looking old TV has very little value, especially if it is not working. Television sets that are wanted are in the most modern styles of the '50s. They include those with round picture tubes above the rectangular set or other unusual designs. These can often be repaired by an old-time TV serviceman, but many of the parts are out of production and difficult to locate. Most of these sets do not sell for thousands of dollars, and it is difficult to find the right collector.

Do not plug in the radio or TV to test it. You may cause damage or a fire. Just look for obviously missing parts. The serious collector will be able to judge value better than you. Even the tubes could be of use to repair other sets.

PRICE BOOKS

Classic TVs, Pre-War thru 1950s, Scott Wood, editor (L-W Book Sales, Gas City, IN, 1997 reprint of 1992 book).

Collector's Guide to Antique Radios, 5th edition, John Slusser (Collector Books, Paducah, KY, 2001).

The Complete Price Guide to Antique Radios: Pre-War Consoles, Mark V. Stein (Radiomania, Baltimore, MD, 2000).

The Complete Price Guide to Antique Radios: Tabletop Radios, (formerly *Machine Age to Jet Age*), 3 volumes (master index and 2002 prices in Volume 1), Mark V. Stein (Radiomania, Baltimore, MD, 1997–2002).

Genuine Plastic Radios of the Mid-Century, Ken Jupp and Leslie Piña (Schiffer, Atglen, PA, 1998).

Radio & TV Premiums: A Guide to the History and Value of Radio and TV Premiums, Jim Harmon (Krause, Iola, WI, 1997).

Radios by Hallicrafters, Chuck Dachis (Schiffer, Atglen, PA, 1996).

Saturday Morning TV Collectibles, '60s, '70s, '80s, Dana Cain (Krause, Iola, WI, 2000).

Television's Cowboys, Gunfighters & Cap Pistols, Rudy A. D'Angelo (Antique Trader Books, Dubuque, IA, 1999).

Transistor Radios, 1954–1968, Norman Smith (Schiffer, Atglen, PA, 1998).

TV Toys and the Shows That Inspired Them, Cynthia Boris Liljeblad (Krause, Iola, WI, 1996).

Zenith Radio: The Early Years, 1919–1935, Harold N. Cones and John H. Bryant (Schiffer, Atglen, PA, 1997).

Zenith Transistor Radios: Evolution of a Classic, Norman Smith (Schiffer, Atglen, PA, 1998).

CLUBS & THEIR PUBLICATIONS

Antique Wireless Association, Inc., *Old Timer's Bulletin* (MAG), PO Box E, Breesport, NY 14816, e-mail: awapeckham@aol.com, website: antique wireless.org.

Dark Shadows Fan Club, *Dark Shadows Announcement* (MAG), PO Box 69A04, Dept. K, West Hollywood, CA 90069, e-mail: gayboyloca @hotmail.com, website: surf.to/darkshadows.

Friends of Old-Time Radio, *Hello Again* (NL), Box 4321, Hamden, CT 06514, e-mail: jayhick@aol.com.

Southern California Antique Radio Society, *SCARS Gazette* (MAG), 9301 Tex-homa Ave., Northridge, CA 91325, e-mail: bbschoen@att.net, website: www.antiqueradios.org.

Tube Collectors Association, *Tube Collector* (MAG), PO Box 1181, Medford, OR 97501-0143, e-mail: bobshir@uswest.com, website: www.tube collectors.org.

OTHER PUBLICATIONS

Antique Radio Classified (MAG), PO Box 2, Carlisle, MA 01741, e-mail: arc@antiqueradio.com, website: www.antiqueradio.com.

ARCHIVES & MUSEUMS

Library of American Broadcasting, Hornbake Library, University of Maryland, College Park, MD 20742, 301-405-9160, fax: 301-314-2634, website: www.lib.umd.edu/UMCP/LAB.

The Museum of Television & Radio, 25 West 52 St., New York, NY 10019, 212-621-6600, and 465 North Beverly Dr., Beverly Hills, CA 90210, 310-786-1000, website: www.mtr.org.

APPRAISERS

Many of the repair services listed in this section will also do appraisals. *See also* the general list of "Appraisal Groups" on page 483.

Waves, 110 W. 25th Ave., 10th Floor, New York, NY 10001, 212-989-9284, fax: 201-461-7121, e-mail: clwave@aol.com, website: www.wavesradio.com. Radios, TVs, phonographs, etc., appraised.

REPAIRS, PARTS & SUPPLIES

➽ SEE ALSO "CONSERVATORS & RESTORERS," PAGE 520.

Antique Electronic Supply, 6221 S. Maple Ave., Tempe, AZ 85283, 480-820-5411, fax: 480-820-4643, e-mail: info@tubesandmore.com, website: www.tubesandmore.com. Vacuum tubes and parts for antique radio restoration: transformers, sockets, speakers, capacitors, resistors, crystal radio kits and parts, cabinet restoration materials, wire, grille cloth, tools, books, literature, and more. Free catalog, online or in print.

Antique Radio Grille Cloth Headquarters, 624 Cedar Hill Rd., Ambler, PA 19002, e-mail: john@grilleclothcom, website: www.grillecloth.com. Reproduction grille cloth for radios from 1920 to 1940. Complete set of samples is available for $3.

Antique Radio Restoration & Repair, 20 Gary School Rd., Pomfret Center, CT 06259, 860-928-2628, fax: 860-928-2628, e-mail: bob@oldradio doc.com, website: www.oldradiodoc.com. Restoration of old radios. Service for all tube-type antique American, German, Canadian, and Dutch radios. Complete overhauls, cabinet refinishing.

Atom Radio/The Kays, 5 Fiske St., Worcester, MA 01602-2922, 508-755-4880, Mon.–Fri. Antique radios rebuilt. Tube radios repaired, rebuilt, and restored.

Childhood Radios, 818-362-8888, website: www.ronmansfield.com. Specializes in the restoration of collectible cold war electronics from the 1950s and 1960s—transistor radios, crystal sets, Heathkits, vintage hi-fi gear, test equipment, tube stereos. Service manuals, restoration, parts, and repair help. Radio restoration video.

Eric Wrobbel, 20802 Exhibit Ct., Dept. K, Woodland Hills, CA 91367-5205, 818-884-2282, 9:00 A.M.–5:00 P.M. e-mail: ewrobbel@aol.com, website: members.aol.com/ewrobbel/pubpage.htm. Books and videos on transistor radios and toy crystal radios. Photo guides for several major brands of collectible transistor radios—all entries are pictured. Call or see website for details.

French Lace Antiques and Restoration, 120 N. Market St., Paxton, IL 60957, 217-379-4140, fax: 217-379-4140, e-mail: phonoman1960@prairieinet.net, website: www.frenchlace.us. Restoration of tube radios. Always looking for parts.

George Bursor, 977 Kings Rd., Schenectady, NY 12303, 518-346-3713, e-mail: jukebox950@aol.com. Restoration of tube radios. Send SASE for free brochure.

The Magic Barn, Dawson's Antiques, 516 N. Ave. B, Washington, IA 52353,

319-653-5043, e-mail: radio4me@hotmail.com. Restoration of antique radios.

Maurer Vintage Radios, 29 S. Fourth St., Lebanon, PA 17042, 717-272-2481, e-mail: dmradios@aol.com, website: members.aol.com/dmradios. Radio parts and repair. New and old radio and TV tubes. Send tube numbers and LSASE for price quotes and availability. Radio books, magazines, service manuals. Send LSASE for book list. Mail order only.

Mike Zuccaro—Antique Electronics Repair, 8795 Corvus St., San Diego, CA 92126-1920, 858-271-8294, e-mail: mjzuccaro@aol.com. Repair and restoration of antique radios from the 1920s through the 1970s.

The Neon Radio, 503 E. Market St., Lockhart, TX 78644, 512-398-7777, fax: 425-977-8212, e-mail: stephen@neonradio.com, website: neon radio.com. Antique and vintage tube radios repaired. Schematic diagrams for vintage radios available. Free valuation of old radios.

Olde Tyme Radio Co., 2445 Lyttonsville Rd., Suite 317, Silver Spring, MD 20910, 301-587-5280, 10:00 A.M.–10:00 P.M., e-mail: oldetymeradio @juno.com. Electronic restoration of chassis of all American radios. Parts, including capacitors, resistors, tubes, transformers, dial lamps, etc. Data packages on American radios from 1920 to 1960. A-B-C battery-regulated power supply made to order. Send double-stamped LSASE for brochure.

Richies TV, Radio, & Coin-Op Repairs, New Jersey, 973-694-6374 evenings, e-mail: radiorich1@yahoo.com, website: radiorich1.freeyellow.com. Repair and restoration of antique radios, TVs, and coin-operated machines. Service and parts.

Romney, PO Box 806, Williamsburg, NM 87942, 505-894-4775, e-mail: eromney@zianet.com, website: www.edromney.com. Radio repair manuals, tools, and supplies. Free brochure.

Tom's Antique Radio & TV, 8 Howe Ln., Millbury, MA 01527, 508-865-6293. Repair and restoration of pre-1960 tube radios, pre-1960 television sets, and Predicta TVs. Free brochure.

•• RECORDS, SEE PHONOGRAPHS

RUGS

Everyone knows that Oriental rugs have value, but it is almost impossible to determine the value unless you are a rug expert. If you inherit a large, old Oriental, get it appraised by a rug dealer or sell it through an auction gallery. Never ask a rug dealer to "make an offer." If you were in the business of selling old rugs, wouldn't you offer as little as possible so that you could make a larger profit? The actual worth of the rug and the offer may have little in common. It is better to pay for an appraisal from a competent person and then try to sell it elsewhere. If you sell it as part of a house sale, be sure to learn the proper name for the rug, and be sure you have an expert set the price. Many things affect rug prices: the condition (no worn spots, stains, or missing fringe), the color (unfaded), the number of knots to the inch, the material (silk or wool is best), and the design and overall quality. Size is also important. Room-size rugs and stair runners sell quickly. Very large rugs, 18 by 30 feet or larger, can bring good prices only at a well-advertised auction or from a major rug dealer.

Chinese rugs, especially those with Art Deco designs and pleasing colors (purple and chartreuse are hard to sell), any type of pictorial rag rug, needlepoints, dhurries, Navajo rugs, and almost any other type of usable floor coverings sell for good prices. If you have no guidelines and your rug is in good condition, measure it, determine the number of square yards, and price it at a little more than good new carpeting.

REPAIR

Oriental rugs should always be kept clean and in good repair. Repairs should be done by a professional, although some minor work can be accomplished at home. A worn spot can be covered temporarily by coloring the exposed beige backing with crayon or colored ink. A full fringe adds to the value of a rug and should never be trimmed or replaced unless absolutely necessary. There are rug dealers in large department stores or in shops in large cities who can do repairs. If a local restorer is not available, a rug can be shipped to another city.

➺ **SEE ALSO TEXTILES**

BOOKS ON REPAIR

Oriental Rugs Care and Repair, Majid Amini (Van Nostrand Reinhold, New York, 1981).

PRICE BOOKS

Hooked Rug Treasury, Jessie A. Turbayne (Schiffer, Atglen, PA, 1997).

APPRAISERS

Two of the repair services listed in this section will also do appraisals. *See also* the general list of "Appraisal Groups" on page 483.

REPAIRS, PARTS & SUPPLIES

➻ SEE ALSO "CONSERVATORS & RESTORERS," PAGE 520.

A.E. Runge, Jr., Oriental Rugs, 108 Main St., Yarmouth, ME 04096, 207-846-9000, website: www.rungerugs.com. Specializes in decorative pre–World War II Persian village rugs and carpets. Hand washing, repair, and restoration. Appraisals.

Sylvia J. Dole, Sugarwood Rd., Plainfield, VT 05667, 802-454-7184, e-mail: sugar1@together.net, website: www.paxp.com/doles. Restoration of hooked rugs. Will finish a hooked rug that has been started or hook a rug on commission.

David Zahirpour, 4922 Wisconsin Ave. NW, Washington, DC 20016, 202-338-4141, e-mail: zahirpour@aol.com. Restoration, cleaning, and appraisals of Oriental rugs. Lecturer and consultant.

➻ SCALES, SEE SCIENTIFIC COLLECTIBLES

SCIENTIFIC COLLECTIBLES

Antique microscopes, telescopes, medical apparatus, and much more are included in scientific collectibles. Of special interest are quack medical machines. These all require special restoration and repair. Sometimes a local expert who works with modern microscopes or telescopes can help.

There is not much that can be done about the weather, but for centuries people have wanted to know when storms are approaching. The barometer was invented by Evangelista Torricelli in Florence, Italy, in the 1640s. It measures the change in air pressure and helps indicate changes in weather. Many eighteenth- and nineteenth-century barometers still exist and, like all sensitive scientific instruments, often need repair by a specialist. Some repair specialists are listed here. All early barometers sell for hundreds or even thousands of dollars.

MEDICAL & DENTAL

The best customers for medical and dental antiques are doctors and dentists. Strange-looking old tools, dental chairs, examining tables, advertising cards, catalogs, medicine bottles, and anything else related to medicine has a market. Dental and barber items like shaving mugs, razors, barbershop signs (the old-time dentist and barber were the same man), extraction tools, and even false teeth are collected, usually by dentists. All early pharmaceutical collectibles can be sold easily. A small local shop or drugstore will often buy pieces for use in window displays. Decorative bottles (see Bottles), cabinets, and early medicine labels and packets sell easily to general collectors. Quack medicine items like electric-shock machines to cure rheumatism are of special interest to many. A different group of people will buy any drug-related items like medicine bottles labeled "cocaine" or "marijuana."

There are special dealers who once or twice a year conduct mail-order auctions of medical, dental, and drug-related collectibles. You can locate them through the ads in general antiques publications. If you have a large collection, it would be profitable to take an ad in a professional magazine of interest to doctors, dentists, or lawyers. Locate these with the help of your local librarian.

SCALES

All types of scales are collected, from nineteenth-century balance scales used to weigh gold or letters or drugs to twentieth-century drugstore scales. Old ones are of value, but there are only a few experts who can advise you. However, there is a scale collectors' society with an informative newsletter, and the members may be able to help. Twentieth-century drugstore scales in working order sell for hundreds to thousands of dollars. The large figural cast-iron Mr. Peanut scale is worth over $15,000.

REPAIR

Information about repair of scales is scarce, although there are a few books and articles to help you solve problems with early scales. Sometimes a large, spring-operated scale can be repaired by a local shop that fixes scales for grocery stores and commercial businesses. Search for these through the "Business to Business" Yellow Pages if that is how your phone books are divided, or look under "Scales" in the regular Yellow Pages.

PRICE BOOKS

Scales: A Collector's Guide, Bill and Jan Berning (Schiffer, Atglen, PA, 1999).

CLUBS & THEIR PUBLICATIONS

Antique Telescope Society, *Journal of the Antique Telescope Society* (MAG), 1878 Robinson Rd., Dahlonega, GA 30533, 706-864-8207, e-mail: whbreyer@syclone.net, website: www.irhino.com/oldscope.

International Society of Antique Scale Collectors, *Equilibrium* (NL), 3616 Noakes St., Los Angeles, CA 90023, e-mail: tdooley@macnexus.org, website: www.isasc.org.

Medical Collectors Association, *Medical Collectors Association Newsletter* (NL), Montefiore Medical Park, 1695A Eastchester Rd., Bronx, NY 10461, e-mail: blaufox@aecom.yu.edu.

Ophthalmic Antiques International Collectors' Club, *Ophthalmic Antiques* (NL), 6 Grammar School Rd., North Walsham, Norfolk NR28 9JH, UK.

Oughtred Society, *Journal of the Oughtred Society* (MAG), PO Box 99077, Emoryville, CA 94662, website: www.oughtred.org.

Scientific Instrument Society, *Bulletin of the Scientific Instrument Society* (MAG), 31 High St., Stanford in the Vale, Faringdon, Oxon SN7 8LH, UK, website: www.sis.org.uk.

OTHER PUBLICATIONS

American Artifacts: Scientific Medical & Mechanical Antiques (MAG), PO Box 412, Taneytown, MD 21787, e-mail: smma@americanartifacts.com, website: www.americanartifacts.com/smma.

Veterinary Collectibles Roundtable (NL), 7431 Covington Hwy., Lithonia, GA 30058, e-mail: Petvet@mindspring.com, website: petvet.home. mindspring.com/VCR (antique veterinary patent medicines and advertising collectibles).

ARCHIVES & MUSEUMS

Dittrick Medical History Center, Case Western Reserve University, Allen Memorial Library, 11000 Euclid Ave., Cleveland, OH 44106-1714, 216-368-3648 (archives), website: www.cwru.edu/artsci/dittrick/home.htm.

National Museum of Civil War Medicine, PO Box 470, Frederick, MD 21705, 301-695-1864, fax: 301-695-6823, website: www.civilwarmed.org.

USEFUL SITES

Medical Antiques.com, www.medicalantiques.com.

APPRAISERS

Many of the auctions and repair services listed in this section will also do appraisals. *See also* the general list of "Appraisal Groups" on page 483.

AUCTIONS

➟ **SEE ALSO "SELLING THROUGH AUCTION HOUSES," PAGE 485.**

Auction Team Köln, 4025 Cattlemen Rd., PMB 108, Sarasota, FL 34233, 941-925-0385, fax: 941-925-0487, e-mail: auction@breker.com, website: www.breker.com. Specialty auctions of all kinds of old technology, including photographica, office technology, clocks, and toys. Mail and phone bids accepted. Buyer's premium 20%. Prices realized available on website after auction. Catalog $58 per year.

Maritime Antiques & Auctions, PO Box 322, York, ME 03909-0322, 207-363-

4247, fax: 207-363-1416, e-mail: nautical@cybertours.com, website: www.maritiques.com. Specializes in scientific instruments, maritime antiques, and firehouse memorabilia. Mail and phone bids accepted. Buyer's premium 15%. Prices realized mailed after auction. Appraisals.

Mike Smith's Patent Medicine Auction, 7431 Covington Hwy., Lithonia, GA 30058, 770-482-5100, fax: 770-484-1304, e-mail: petvetmike@mind spring.com. Absentee auctions of veterinary antiques and collectibles. Mail, phone, and Internet bids accepted. Buyer's premium 10%. Prices realized mailed after auction and available on website. Appraisals.

Veterinary Collectibles Roundtable, 7431 Covington Hwy., Lithonia, GA 30058, 770-482-5100 (days), fax: 770-484-1304, e-mail: Petvet@mind spring.com, website: petvet.home.mindspring.com/VCR. Twice yearly consignment/phone bid auctions of antique veterinary patent medicines and associated advertising. Color catalogs and prices realized are available for $10 per auction.

REPAIRS, PARTS & SUPPLIES

➼ **SEE ALSO "CONSERVATORS & RESTORERS," PAGE 520.**

The Barometer Shop, HC 68, Box 130-L, Cushing, ME 04563, 207-354-8055, fax: 207-354-2687, e-mail: barometershop@earthlink.net, website: www.barometershop.net. Repair and restoration of barometers of all types. Various parts available.

Barometer World & Museum, Quicksilver Barn, Merton, Okehampton, Devon, England EX20 3DS, 011-44-1805-603443, fax: 011-44-1805-603344, e-mail: barometers@barometerworld.co.uk, website: www.barometer world.co.uk. Antique barometers restored, cases repaired and repolished, fitments cleaned, parts replaced if needed. Send photo of barometer first before sending it to be repaired.

European Watch & Casemakers, Ltd., PO Box 1314, Highland Park, NY 08904-1314, 732-777-0111, 10:00 A.M.–6:00 P.M., e-mail: horology@ webspan.net. Restoration of scientific instruments. Consulting and appraisal; expert testimonies in civil and criminal lawsuits. Free brochure.

Medford Clock & Barometer, 3 Union St., Medford, NJ 08055, 609-953-0014, fax: 609-953-0411, e-mail: medclock@aol.com, website: www.medfordclock.com. Antique mercury barometers repaired and restored. New mercury barometer tubes hand-blown on site.

Tele-Optics, 630 E. Rockland Rd., PO Box 6313, Libertyville, IL 60048, 847-362-7757, fax: 847-362-7757. Service and repairs on all makes and models of binoculars, telescopes, and rifle scopes. Aneroid-type barometers repaired. No mercurial (glass tube) type. Free brochure.

➼ **SCRIMSHAW, SEE IVORY**
➼ **SHEET MUSIC, SEE PAPER**

SILVER & SILVER PLATE

An old sterling silver teaspoon is never worth less than its melt-down value, which is the weight of the spoon multiplied by the going price of silver bullion. The number is reported in the daily newspapers on the stock quotation pages. If a dime is old enough to be made of a silver alloy, it could be worth more than 10 cents in meltdown value based on the price of silver.

Most antique silver is worth more than the meltdown value, but the value is often calculated from that figure. Some appraisers weigh old silver and multiply the result by two to four times the meltdown; some use other formulas. Jewelry stores, coin shops, and "Gold, Silver, and Platinum Dealers" are listed in the phone book, and they will weigh and buy for the meltdown value. This is actually the lowest price you should receive for your pieces. Don't forget that some pieces of old silver, especially candlesticks, are "weighted." There is a heavy material in the base that keeps the candlestick from tipping. The meltdown buyers are interested in what the thin sterling shell weighs after the weight is removed.

Makers' names and hallmarks are important in determining value. The names **GEORG JENSEN**, **TIFFANY**, **MARTELÉ**, **LIBERTY**, or the initials of famous English silversmiths, like **PAUL STORR** or **PAUL DE LAMERIE**, add to the value of a piece of silver. The English hallmark system of four or five small marks looks like this 🔲 🔲 🔲 🔲. If the king's head looks to the right, the piece was made before 1850 and probably has added value. Queen Victoria's head faces left. Queen Elizabeth II's head faces left. The lion is an indication of sterling quality.

The showiest pieces of silver, such as tea sets, punch bowls,

GOOD MELTDOWN VALUE

- Coin, Sterling, and 925 are all marks indicating solid silver.
- The number "925" means 925 parts silver for every 1,000 parts of metal. It is marked on what is called "sterling silver."
- The word "coin" is stamped on nineteenth-century pieces that were made from melted coins. The silver content varies from 800 to 925 parts of silver.
- "800" is marked on many European silver pieces. All these pieces are wanted for meltdown.

epergnes, and large candelabra, always have a good resale value. Elaborate English pieces dating from 1850 to 1900 are usually "ball-park" priced from five to seven times the meltdown value. If the work is exceptional, if the silversmith is well known, or if the history ties the silver to a famous family or event, it could be worth ten to twelve times the meltdown price or more. The condition is always important. There should be no dents, broken handles, or alterations.

Tea sets of any description usually can be sold, even in poor condition. Twentieth-century plated or sterling sets should be priced at less than half the modern department-store prices. Sterling sets must be priced with the weight considered. Earlier sets are worth more than modern sets. The price is determined by age, artistic value, and the maker. Silver tea services sell best at important house sales or auctions. Contact local house-sale managers to see if you can have it sold by them at someone else's house. Silver-plated trays, small dishes, and flatware have a very low resale value, especially if they are not in mint condition.

Ordinary silver made after 1900 usually sells for about twice the meltdown price. If the decorations are lavish or if the piece is a desirable shape, such as a punch bowl, it might sell for four times the meltdown. Very large or very decorative pieces can bring up to ten times meltdown. Pieces with a special meaning, such as Jewish religious items or historic pieces, sell for even more. Commemorative silver medals and modern limited edition sets usually sell for meltdown.

Very ornate Victorian silver is back in fashion, and "more is better" when it comes to pricing. All sterling serving spoons, forks, asparagus servers, fish servers, grape shears, and other large serving pieces sell at prices comparable to modern examples or for even more. Very small pieces, like nut picks or pickle forks, do not sell as well. Pieces with elaborate, crisp, bright-cut designs sell well. Those with worn bright cutting are not in much demand. Figural napkin rings, picture frames, and souvenir spoons have a special value to collectors, so the meltdown value is in no way related to the price.

Sterling silver flatware in good condition is always worth more than meltdown. Sell it through an auction or offer it at a house sale at a price from 30 to 50 percent less than the department store price for a similar set. It can also be sold to a silver matching service by mail or Internet. (To find matching services, visit large antiques shows or check the Matching Services section in Part III.) Send a photocopy of the front and back of a spoon or fork if you don't know the pattern name. Include a list of pieces and a stamped, self-addressed envelope.

A monogram will lower the value on a set of silver less than 100 years old, but a crest or elaborate monogram on eighteenth-century or early nineteenth-century silver adds to the value. You do not have to remove a monogram; doing so is expensive and can cause damage. Use it and tell friends the silver belonged to your great-aunt. The market for silver flatware is multileveled. If the retailer, department store, or gift shop gets $5,000 for a new set of silver, a discount store might get 25 percent less, or $3,750. The antiques shop or auction gallery would probably ask 50 percent of retail, or $2,500, for a used set. The meltdown would be half of that, $1,250 or even less. You determine your price by where you plan to sell the set. Silver-plated flatware is also collected and can be matched, but it sells for low prices.

PLATED SILVER

Early Sheffield plated silver, made before 1840 by rolling a thin layer of silver on a copper base, has a special value for collectors. Good pieces are worth thousands of dollars. If the copper shows because the top layer of silver is worn, the value is at least 50 percent less. If a piece of early rolled Sheffield is replated, deduct 90 percent.

If a piece of electroplated silver made after 1840 needs resilvering, deduct 50 percent. If the handle of a piece has been replaced, the feet redone, or any other part totally replaced, deduct 75 percent. If the piece has been reworked (a stein made from a vase), the result is worth meltdown value plus about 10 percent.

REPAIR

Silver should be kept clean. Use any good commercial polish, and if you keep the silver on display, use a tarnish-retarding polish. For storage, tarnish-retarding cloths and papers are also available.

POOR MELTDOWN VALUE

- "Silver plate," "A1," "EPNS," "triple plate," and other similar marks mean that the piece is made of a base metal and is covered with a thin layer of silver.
- The world "Sheffield" has several meanings. If it is stamped on the bottom of your piece, you probably have an item that is silver plated. None of the plated pieces have a good meltdown value.

Never use household scouring powder or instant silver polish on your silver. Never store silver in a nonporous plastic wrap, because the wrap may melt or moisture may collect between the silver and the wrap. Never wrap with rubber bands. Silver will tarnish more quickly if displayed on latex-painted shelves, in oak furniture, or near oak trees. If you use camphor (mothballs) to prevent tarnish, don't let the camphor touch the silver.

Knife blades may separate from hollow handles if they are stored in a hot attic or washed in a dishwasher. They can be repaired by using a nonmelting filler. An expert should do this.

Silver that is kept on display and never used for eating, such as a large candelabrum, can be lacquered. This will keep the piece clean almost indefinitely. Any good plating company can lacquer a piece. Look for a local company in your phone book.

Antique plated silver may "bleed" (the copper underneath shows through the silver). This is not totally objectionable. Resilvering may lower the value, so check on the age and type of silver plate before you replate. Very early "rolled-on" silver on copper Sheffield pieces should rarely be replated. Late nineteenth- and twentieth-century plated silver that was originally electroplated can be replated with no loss of value. These pieces are usually marked "silver plate." The handles and feet were often made of Britannia metal and will appear black when the silver plate wears off. Local platers are listed in your phone company's Yellow Pages under "Plating."

There is a new product on the market that adds a thin layer of silver to worn pieces. The silver liquid is applied with a cloth. This is a temporary "repair," but it does improve the appearance of worn silver plate.

➻ **SEE THE MATCHING SERVICES LIST IN PART III.**
➻ **SEE ALSO JEWELRY, METALS**

REFERENCE BOOKS

American Silverplate, revised edition, Dorothy T. Rainwater and H. Ivan (Schiffer, Atglen, PA, 1988).

Book of Old Silver, Seymour B. Wyler (Crown, New York, 1937).

Book of Sheffield Plate, Seymour B. Wyler (Crown, New York, 1949).

Directory of Gold & Silversmiths, Jewellers & Allied Traders, 1838–1914, from the London Assay Office Registers, 2 volumes, John Culme (Antique Collectors' Club, Wappingers Falls, NY, 1987).

Encyclopedia of American Silver Manufacturers, 4th edition revised, Dorothy T. Rainwater and Judy Redfield (Schiffer, Atglen, PA, 1998).

Georg Jensen: A Tradition of Splendid Silver, Janet Drucker (Schiffer, Atglen, PA, 1997).

International Hallmarks on Silver (Tardy, Paris, 1981).

Jackson's Silver & Gold Marks of England, Scotland & Ireland, 3rd edition revised, Ian Pickford, editor (Antique Collectors' Club, Wappingers Falls, NY, 1989).

Kovels' American Silver Marks, 1650 to the Present, Ralph and Terry Kovel (Crown, New York, 1989).

Silver Curios in the Home, Dorothy Rainwater and Beryl Frank (Schiffer, Atglen, PA, 1999).

Stainless Flatware Guide (Replacements, Ltd., Greensboro, NC, 1998).

PRICE BOOKS

Collectible Souvenir Spoons: The Grand Tour, Book 2, Wayne Bednersh (Collector Books, Paducah, KY, 2001).

Collector's Encyclopedia of Stangl Artware, Lamps, and Birds by Robert C. Runge Jr. (Collector Books, Paducah, KY, 2002).

Georg Jensen: A Tradition of Splendid Silver, 2nd edition, Janet Drucker (Schiffer, Atglen, PA, 2001).

Miller's Buyer's Guide: Silver and Plate, Daniel Bexfield, editor (Miller's Tenterden, Kent, England, 2002).

Silver Novelties in the Gilded Age, 1870–1910, Deborah Crosby (Schiffer, Atglen, PA, 2001).

Sterling Flatware: An Identification and Value Guide, 2nd edition, Tere Hagan (L-W Book Sales, Gas City, IN, 1999).

Sterling Silver Flatware for Dining Elegance, 2nd edition, Richard Osterberg (Schiffer, Atglen, PA, 1999).

Sterling Silver, Silverplate and Souvenir Spoons, with revised prices (L-W Book Sales, Gas City, IN, 1987, prices 1999).

CLUBS & THEIR PUBLICATIONS

American Spoon Collectors, *The Spooners Forum* (NL), 510 SE Bayberry Ln., Lee's Summit, MO 64063-4355, e-mail: spoonerbill@aol.com.

Northeastern Spoon Collectors Guild, *The NSCG Cauldron* (NL), PO Box 12072, Albany, NY 12212, e-mail: bownor@aol.com, website: souvenir spoons.com/nscg.

Society of American Silversmiths, PO Box 72839, Providence, RI 02907, e-mail: sas@silversmithing.com, website: www.silversmithing.com.

OTHER PUBLICATIONS

Silver (MAG), Silver Magazine, PO Box 9690, Rancho Santa Fe, CA 92067, e-mail: silver@silvermag.com, website: www.silvermag.com.

USEFUL SITES

American Souvenir Spoons, www.souvenirspoons.com.

The Online Encyclopedia of American Silver Marks, www.silver collecting.com.

APPRAISERS

Many of the repair services listed in this section will also do appraisals. *See also* the general list of "Appraisal Groups" on page 483. *See also* "Matching Services" on page 537.

National Association of Jewelry Appraisers, PO Box 6558, Annapolis, MD 21401-0558, 410-897-0889. Appraisal services on silver hollowware, silver flatware, and jewelry. Appraisers throughout the United States.

AUCTIONS

➼ SEE ALSO "SELLING THROUGH AUCTION HOUSES," PAGE 485.

Kraus Antiques, Ltd., PO Box 12537, Ft. Pierce, FL 34979, 772-465-0770, fax: 772-468-9020, e-mail: sterling@silverauctions.net, website: www.silverauctions.net. Sterling silver flatware absentee auctions. Mail, phone, and Internet bids accepted. No buyer's premium. Prices realized mailed after auction. Free catalog. Call, write, or e-mail your request for illustrated catalog.

REPAIRS, PARTS & SUPPLIES

➼ SEE ALSO "CONSERVATORS & RESTORERS," PAGE 520.

Many of the silver matching services listed on page 537 also do restoration and repair. *See also* "Conservators & Restorers," page 520.

Abercrombie & Co., 9159A Brookeville Rd., Silver Spring, MD 20910, 800-585-2385 or 301-585-2385, fax: 301-587-5708, e-mail: abernco@erols.com, website: www.silverplaters.com. Silver plating, polishing, and repair. Dents smoothed or removed; handles, hinges, lids, and spouts repaired; garbage-disposal-damaged flatware repaired; new blades, brushes, combs, and mirrors fitted.

Al Bar-Wilmette Platers, 127 Green Bay Rd., Wilmette, IL 60091, 847-251-0187, fax: 847-251-0281, e-mail: info@albarwilmette.com, website: www.albarwilmette.com. Silver repaired and restored; silver plating. Restoration of metal finishes; missing parts furnished.

Antique & Art Restoration by Wiebold, 413 Terrace Pl., Terrace Park, OH 45174, 800-321-2541, 513-831-2541, fax: 513-831-2815, e-mail: wiebold @eos.net, website: www.wiebold.com. Fine art restoration and conservation of silver and other objects. Missing parts replaced. Silver plating.

Blue Crystal (Glass), Ltd., Units 6-8, 21 Wren St., London WC1X 0HF, UK, 011-44-20-7278-0142, fax: 011-44-20-7278-0142, e-mail: bluecrystal glass@aol.com, website: www.bluecrystalglass.co.uk. Blue glass liners and other colors for silver salt and mustard pots; stoppers and bottles for silver cruet stands; claret bottles for silver mounts; hand-cut dishes for epergne stands, etc.

Classic Restoration Co., 10800 Carnegie Ave., Cleveland, OH 44106, 216-791-9050, 10:00 A.M.–6:00 P.M. Repairs of silver hollowware and flatware and other metal objects. Missing parts reproduced.

David Warther Carving Museum, 2561 Crestview Dr. NW, Dover, OH 44622-7405, e-mail: ivorybuyer@adelphia.net, website: www.ivorybuyer.com. Ivory insulators and finials for sterling hollowware. Free brochure.

Facets, 107 Boundary Rd. Leyton, London, UK E17 8NQ, 011-44-208-520-3392, e-mail: repairs@facetsglass.co.uk, website: www.facetsglass.co.uk. Glass and antique restoration company offering a wide range of services, including cleaning the inside of decanters, scent bottles, and vases; repair of antique combs, brushes, cutlery; replating and repolishing; replacement of tea and coffeepot handles.

Fleming's Lighting & Silver Restoration, 24 Elm St., Cohasset Village, MA 02025, 781-383-0684. Silver repair and replating. Free brochure.

Grashe Fine Art Restorers, 35 148th Ave. SE #9, Bellevue WA 98007, 425-644-7500, fax: 425-644-7582, e-mail: art@grashe.com, website: www.grashe.com. Specializes in the restoration and conservation of silver and other objects.

Hamlin's Restoration Studio, 14640 Manchester Rd., Ballwin, MO 63011, 636-256-8579, e-mail: hamlinsrestoration@msn.com, website: www.hamlinsrestoration.com. Repair and restoration of silver and other fine antiques.

Hiles Plating Co., Inc., 2028 Broadway, Kansas City, MO 64108, 816-421-6450, fax: 816-421-1132, e-mail: hilespl@aol.com, website: www.hilesplating.com. Antique silver restoration. Repairs; parts supplied. Repairs on sterling silver, silver plate, coin silver, pewter, copper, and brass. Plating in silver, gold, brass, nickel, and copper. Some prices given over the phone.

Jeffrey Herman, PO Box 704, Chepachet, RI 02814, 800-584-2352 or 401-567-7800, fax: 401-567-7801, e-mail: restoration@silversmithing.com, website: www.silversmithing.com/jherman. Restoration, conservation, and refinishing of sterling and pewter hollowware and flatware. Dents and monograms removed, disposal-damaged flatware refurbished, silver soldering, rebuilding, knife blades installed, etc. Hand-finishing a specialty. Price list and museum references available.

Martin M. Fleisher, Silversmith, PO Box 305, Copiague, NY 11726-0305, 631-842-2927, e-mail: mfleishe@suffolk.lib.ny.us. Silver restoration service.

Martines' Antiques, 516 E. Washington, Chagrin Falls, OH 44022, 440-247-6421, fax: 216-397-1048, e-mail: martines-silver@e2grow.com, website: martines-silver.e2grow.com. Silver repair.

McBuffers, 1420 Dille Rd., Unit F, Euclid, OH 44117, 216-486-6696, fax: 216-486-4152. Silver repair and replating. Cleaning, buffing, and polishing. Silverware refinished. Brochure.

Memphis Plating Works, 682 Madison Ave., Memphis, TN 38103, 901-526-3051. Repairing and refinishing of metals, including silver.

MidweSterling Flatware, 4311 NE Vivion Rd., Kansas City, MO 64119-2890, 816-454-1990, fax: 816-454-9341, e-mail: info@silverwarehouse.com, website: silverwarehouse.com. Sterling silver, silver plate, and stainless repair. Garbage-disposal damage fixed, knife blades replaced, professional polishing. Appraisals.

New England Country Silver, Inc., 25859 Wellington Rd., Crisfield, MD 21817, 410-968-3060, 9:00 A.M.–3:00 P.M. fax: 410-968-2810, e-mail: necsilver@aol.com, website: www.silverrestoring.com. Complete restoration service for silver plate and sterling silver. Missing parts duplicated. New stainless knife blades, combs, brushes, and mirrors. Velvet backing for picture frames. Engraving.

Oexning Silversmiths, 320 Hwy. 197 S., Bakersville, NC 28705, 828-688-9998 or 800-332-6857, fax: 828-688-9976, e-mail: oexning@aol.com, website: www.oexningsilversmiths.com. Silver restoration, replating, and repair. Sterling refinishing. Dent removal. Missing parts cast, including feet, handles, and ornate work. New brushes and combs; steel blades, meat forks, knife sharpeners, nail sets, letter openers. New insulators for coffee sets.

Orum Silver Co., Inc., 51 S. Vine St., Meriden, CT 06450-0805, 203-237-3037, fax: 203-237-3037, e-mail: orum.silver@snet.net, website: orumsilver.com. Repairing and replating of old silver and antiques. Brushes, combs, and mirrors for dresser sets. Restoration of church goods, chalices, Bible stands, etc. Free brochure.

Past & Present, 14851 Avenue 360, Visalia, CA 93292, 559-798-0029, fax: 559-798-1415, e-mail: P-P@ix.netcom.com, website: www.pastpresent.net. Restoration of silver tableware.

Patrick J. Gill & Sons, 9 Fowle St., Woburn, MA 01801, 781-933-3275, fax: 781-933-3751, e-mail: joe@patrickgillco.com, website: patrickgillco.com. Metal repair, refinishing, and replating. Flatware, hollowware, dresser sets, and other metal objects replated. Repair of broken or damaged parts; knife blades replaced. Jewelry repaired and restored, silver plate or gold plate.

Peninsula Plating Works, 1083 Americas, San Carlos, CA 94070, 650-326-7825, fax: 650-593-2650. Repairing, polishing, and plating of silver and other metal items. Repair of silver flatware and hollowware. Free brochure.

Replacements, Ltd., PO Box 26029, 1089 Knox Rd., Greensboro, NC 27420-6029, 800-REPLACE (800-737-5223), fax: 336-697-3100, e-mail: inquire@replacements.com, website: www.replacements.com. Silver repair, restoration, cleaning, and polishing.

Restoration & Design Studio, 249 E. 77th St., New York, NY 10021, 212-517-9742, fax: 212-517-9742. Repair and restoration of silver. Ivory insulators for tea or coffee pots.

Robben Restoration, 5628 Cheviot Rd., Cincinnati, OH 45247, 877-257-0596 toll free or 513-741-3619, e-mail: RRsilver1@aol.com. Metal restoration, specializing in silver repair. Fabrication, plating, soldering, dent removal, part replacement, etc. Wicker handle replacements, blade replacements, hand-carved ebony and ivory insulators and handles. Dresser sets restored. Silver–plate lamp restoration. Free brochure.

Senti-Metal Co., 1919 Memory Ln., Columbus, OH 43209, 800-323-9718, fax: 614-252-4602, e-mail: bronzeinfo@bronshoe.com, website: www.resilver.com. Silver restoration. Repair and replating of silver plate and hollowware. Restoration and polishing of sterling silver. Free catalog.

Stephen Smithers, Silversmith, 1057 Hawley Rd., Ashfield, MA 01330, 413-625-2994, e-mail: stevesmithers@stevesmithers.com, website: www.stevesmithers.com. Period silver restoration and conservation. Making of missing or additional pieces for tea, coffee, or serving sets with matching forms or details. Custom hand-hammered hollowware and flatware.

Sterling Buffet, PO Box 1665, Mansfield, OH 44901, 800-537-5783 or 419-529-0505, Fax: 419-529-0506, e-mail: info@sterlingbuffet.com, website: www.sterlingbuffet.com. Flatware chests, drawer liners, custom drawer liners, tarnish resistant wraps, and silver polish.

Swan Restorations, 2627 Montrose Ave., Abbotsford, BC V2S 3TS, Canada, 604-855-6694, fax: 604-855-1720. Restoration of antiques and collectibles. Silver cleaning service; jewelry cleaning. Free written estimates. Hours Mon.–Fri. 10:00 A.M.–5:00 P.M., or by appointment. Call before sending item to be repaired.

Thome Silversmiths, 49 W. 37th St., 4th Floor, New York, NY 10018, 212-764-5426 or 570-426-7480, fax: 212-391-8215 or 570-426-7481, e-mail: robert378@cs.com. Restoration of objects of art and Judaica. Silver repaired. Jewelry boxes relined; velvet backs for picture frames. Silver plating. Cleaning and polishing of flatware and hollowware; hand engraving.

Tindell's Restoration, 825 Sandburg Pl., Nashville, TN 37214, 615-885-1029, fax: 615-391-0712, e-mail: info@ATindellsRestorationSchools.com, website: www.TindellsRestorationSchools.com. Restoration services, seminars, training, and products. Restoration of silver and much more. Appraisals. Free brochure.

Virginia Silversmiths, Inc., 532 Oakley Ave., Lynchburg, VA 24501, 804-845-0062 days, 804-845-1958, e-mail: Slvrspoke@aol.com, website: www.SilverRestoration.com. Silversmith, restoration, repair, and resilvering services. Difficult as well as simple repairs.

Vroman's Silver Shop, 442A Fleetwood Pl., Glendora, CA 91740, 800-824-5174, fax: 626-963-1402, e-mail: vrosilver@aol.com. Silver repair and restoration; knives rebladed, tea sets replated, water pitchers dedented, Victorian silver plate restored, etc.

WTC Associates, Inc., 2532 Regency Rd., Lexington, KY 40503, 859-278-4171, fax: 859-277-5720. Sterling silver repairs, including replacement of missing parts. Silver plating; silver plate and sterling repairs; gold plating and gold leaf; mirrors resilvered.

Zophy's Fine Silver Plating, 4702 Park St., Box 10, Peterboro, NY 13134, 315-684-3062, fax: 315-684-3494. Silver plating. Sterling repair. Mon.–Fri. 7:00 A.M.–3:00 P.M.

➥ **SLOT MACHINES, SEE COIN-OPERATED MACHINES**

SMOKING COLLECTIBLES

Tobacco, like beer, seems to be a popular collecting area for men. Anything that has a picture of tobacco or that has held tobacco has a market. Labels, ads, tobacco cards, felts, tins, pipes, tags, cigar cutters, and other smoking memorabilia sell well to general antiques dealers or in any of the usual ways one sells antiques. (See Advertising Collectibles.) A large collection of tobacco-related material might do well at auction or on the Internet. A small collection could be sold quickly at flea markets and shows.

A nonsmoker is amazed that old pipes sell for high prices to men who want to use them or display them. Lighters, cigar clippers, tobacco stamps, and cigar and cigarette cases are wanted for use and display. These are items that also sell well to friends who are smokers. Even ashtrays are gaining popularity. Prices can be found in the general price books. Matchbooks have been a popular collectible since the advertising matchbook was introduced in 1889. They were given free at good restaurants and hotels, but now fewer can be found.

Cigarette and cigar lighters have been made since the late nineteenth century, but collectors search for unusual pocket lighters made since the 1940s and the earlier large electric-spark or kerosene cigar lighters that were kept on store counters. The store lighters should be sold to those interested in advertising.

Remember those silver-plated Ronson lighters that everyone received as a wedding gift in the 1950s? They were unsalable until about 1985, when 1950s decor was being revived by avant-garde collectors and the lighter was needed as a table ornament. Now all types of figural lighters are in demand. The bartender-behind-the-bar lighter of the 1930s, the Coca-Cola bottle lighter of the 1950s, or the dueling-pistol lighter of the 1960s all sell well. Any lighter with an ad or an unusual shape will usually sell to a collector or flea market dealer. This is an international market with many buyers from Europe and Japan, and it is very active on the Internet.

The common urn-shaped Ronson table lighters do not sell well because there are so many of them. Silver and gold pocket lighters, some with precious jewels, should be sold like jewelry. Look for RONSON, figurals, the Kool cigarettes plastic penguin, and large, figural, cigar-store lighters.

REPAIR

It is now possible to have old lighters repaired. Matchbooks should be stored in scrapbooks, but first carefully remove the staple and the matches. The staple may rust and the matches are a fire hazard. Pipes can be restored by any dealer in modern pipes. You will probably want a new, unused stem if you plan to smoke the pipe.

REFERENCE BOOKS

The Legend of the Lighter, Ad Van Weert (Abbeville, New York, 1995).

PRICE BOOKS

American Tobacco Cards: Price Guide & Checklist, Robert Forbes and Terence Mitchell (Tuff Stuff Publications, Richmond, VA, 1999).

Antique Cigar Cutters & Lighters, Jerry Terranova and Douglas Congdon-Martin (Schiffer, Atglen, PA, 1996).

The Art of the Smoke: A Pictorial History of Cigar Box Label Art, Jero L. Gardner (Schiffer, Atglen, PA, 1998).

Camel Cigarette Collectibles: The Early Years, 1913–1963, Douglas Congdon-Martin (Schiffer, Atglen, PA, 1996).

Camel Cigarette Collectibles, 1964–1995, Douglas Congdon-Martin (Schiffer, Atglen, PA, 1997).

Cigar Box Labels: Portraits of Life, Mirrors of History, Gerard S. Petrone (Schiffer, Atglen, PA, 1998).

Cigarette Card Values: 1999 Catalogue of Cigarette and Other Trade Cards (Murray Cards Ltd., London, England, 1999).

Cigarette Lighters, Stuart Schneider and George Fischler (Schiffer, Atglen, PA, 1996).

Collectible Match Holders for Tabletops and Walls, Jean and Franklin Hunting (Schiffer, Atglen, PA, 1998).

Collecting Antique Meerschaum Pipes: Miniature to Majestic Sculpture, Ben Rapaport (Schiffer, Atlgen, PA, 1999).

The Collector's Guide to Vintage Cigarette Packs, Joe Giesenhagen (Schiffer, Atglen, PA, 1999).

A Complete Guide to Collecting Antique Pipes, 2nd edition, Benjamin Rapaport (Schiffer, Atglen, PA, 1998).

Great Cigar Stuff for Collectors, Jerry Terranova and Douglas Congdon-Martin (Schiffer, Atglen, PA, 1997).

The Handbook of Vintage Cigarette Lighters, Stuart Schneider and Ira Pilossof (Schiffer, Atglen, PA, 1999).

The International Collectors' Book of Cigarette Packs, Fernando Righini and Marco Papazonni (Schiffer, Atglen, PA, 1998).

The Matchcover Collector's Price Guide, 2nd edition, Bill Retskin (Antique Trader Books, Dubuque, IA, 1997).

Pocket Matchsafes: Reflections of Life & Art, 1840–1920, W. Eugene Sanders Jr. and Christine C. Sanders (Schiffer, Atglen, PA, 1997).

Tobacco Containers from Canada, United States, and the World, Norman Carlson (New Antique Ventures, Medicine Hat, Alberta, Canada, 2002).

The Viet Nam Zippo: 1933–1975, Jim Fiorella (Schiffer, Atglen, PA, 1998).

Zippo: The Great American Lighter, David Poore (Schiffer, Atglen, PA, 1997).

CLUBS & THEIR PUBLICATIONS

American Matchcover Collecting Club, *Front Striker Bulletin* (NL), PO Box 18481, Asheville, NC 28814-0481, e-mail: bill@matchcovers.com, website: www.matchcovers.com.

Badgerstate Matchcover Club, *Badgerstate Bulletin* (NL), N9032 E. Miramar Dr., East Troy, WI 53120, e-mail: evelyntiger@aol.com.

British Matchbox Label & Booklet Society, *Match Label News* (MAG), 122 High St., Melbourn, Cambridgeshire SG8 6AL, UK, website: enterprise.shv.hb.se/~match/bml&bs.

Cigarette Pack Collectors Association, *Brandstand* (NL), 61 Searle St., Georgetown, MA 01833, e-mail: cigpack@aol.com, website: home town.aol.com/cigpack.

International Match Safe Association, *International Match Safe Association Newsletter* (NL), PO Box 791, Malaga, NJ 08328-0791, e-mail: mrvesta1@aol.com, website: www.matchsafe.org.

London Cigarette Card Co. Ltd., *Card Collectors News* (NL), Sutton Rd., Somerton, Somerset TA11 6QP, UK, e-mail: cards@londoncigcard.co.uk, website: www.londoncigcard.co.uk.

On the LIGHTER Side, International Lighter Collectors, *OTLS: On the LIGHTER Side* (NL), PO Box 1733, Quitman, TX 75783-1733, website: otls.com.

Pocket Lighter Preservation Guild and Historical Society, *Flint & Flame* (NL), 380 Brooks Dr., Suite 209A, Hazelwood, MO 63042, e-mail: plpg3@aol.com.

Rathkamp Matchcover Society, *R.M.S. Bulletin* (NL), 1509 S. Dugan Rd.,

Urbana, OH 43078-9209, e-mail: trowerms.@main-net.com, website: www.matchcover.org.

Society of Tobacco Jar Collectors, *Tobacco Jar Newsletter* (NL), 1705 Chanticleer Dr., Cherry Hill, NJ 08003, e-mail: agurst@aol.com, website: www.tobaccojarsociety.com.

Universal Coterie of Pipe Smokers, *Pipe Smoker's Ephemeris* (NL), 20-37 120th St., College Point, NY 11356-2128.

Windy City Matchcover Club, *Bulletin* (NL), 1307 College Ave., Apt. 12, Wheaton, IL 60187, e-mail: LTLB1T@aol.com.

Zippo Click, *Zippo Click Newsletter* (NL), Zippo Manufacturing Co., 1932 Zippo Dr., Bradford, PA 16701, website: www.zippoclick.com.

OTHER PUBLICATIONS

Card Times (MAG), 70 Winifred Ln., Aughton, Ormskirk, Lancashire L39 5DL, UK, e-mail: david@cardtimes.co.uk, website: www.cardtimes.co.uk (cigarette cards, trading cards, sports and nonsports cards, phone cards, printed ephemera).

Cigar-Label Gazette (NL), PO Box 3, Lake Forest, CA 92630, e-mail: ed@cigarlabelgazette.com, website: www.cigarlabelgazette.com.

Pipes & Tobaccos (MAG), 3000 Highwoods Blvd., Suite 300, Raleigh, NC 27604, e-mail: subscribe@pt-magazine.com, website: www.pt-magazine.com.

ARCHIVES & MUSEUMS

Museum of Tobacco Art and History, 800 Harrison St., Nashville, TN 37203, 615-271-2349.

National Lighter Museum, 5715 S. Sooner Rd., Guthrie, OK 73044, 405-282-3025, website: www.natlitrmus.com.

Zippo/Case Museum, 1932 Zippo Dr., Bradford, PA 16701, 888-442-1932, website: www.zippo.com/about/museum/index.html.

REPAIRS, PARTS & SUPPLIES

↔ SEE ALSO "CONSERVATORS & RESTORERS," PAGE 520.

Authorized Sales & Service, 30 W. 57th St., New York, NY 10019, 212-586-0947, fax: 212-586-1296, e-mail: info@antiquelighters.com, website: www.vintagelighters.com. Restoration and repair of all types of cigarette lighters.

Zippo Repair Clinic, Zippo Manufacturing Co., 1932 Zippo Dr., Bradford, PA 16701, website: www.zippo.com/about/repairclinic/index.html. Zippo lighters repaired at no charge. The inside lighting mechanism replaced with a new mechanism; hinges repaired. Lighters that cannot be repaired are replaced. Located in the Zippo/Case Museum. Clinic hours Mon.–Fri. 9:00 A.M.–3:30 P.M.

SPORTS COLLECTIBLES

BASEBALL CARDS

Baseball cards and other sports cards have been collected since they were first distributed in the 1880s. The first cards were placed in packs of cigarettes or tobacco as free advertising promotion pieces. From 1910 to 1915 the cards were made by the millions; then only a few were made until the 1930s. The second period of baseball cards came with their use by candy and gum companies. The modern baseball card started in 1933 with the Goudey Gum Company. World War II caused paper shortages and baseball cards were not made. In 1948 the Bowman and Leaf companies made cards. Topps Gum Company cards were introduced in 1951.

Baseball cards are the favorites of collectors, but there are cards for other sports, such as hockey, football, or basketball. Value is determined by condition, rarity, and the popularity of the player pictured. Collectors also save gum wrappers, Dixie cup lids, and other paper items that picture sports stars. They even save the empty boxes that held the gum packs in the store.

There are special shows, auctions, and publications for sports card collectors, but much of the buy-sell activity is on the Internet.

There are many price books and publications for collectors. Most are available in public libraries and bookstores because baseball card collecting is a popular pastime for millions. Our son first entered the world of collecting when he was in second grade. He started saving baseball cards. His cards were traded, carried in a cramped pocket, "flipped" in a then-popular game, and finally stored in a shoebox. When one of his friends moved to Australia, he was given the treasure trove of baseball cards that belonged to the friend and his older brothers. A few years ago we rediscovered the cards, which had been stored in our attic. Many were rare, but they were all in poor condition, with scuffed pictures and ragged edges, and their value appeared to us to be low. He asked us to sell them. After checking with experts, we sold the box of 237 cards for over $2,000.

Sort your cards by date and manufacturer. Match up the sets and put the cards in numerical order. Look at a current price book from your bookstore or library, and make a list of the cards you own and their approximate value. Always consider the condition when pricing a card. Note which sets are complete. Watch for error cards.

The price books will comment on these. If you find a card that does not seem to be in the price book, look again. You may be looking in the gum card section and have cards that came with breakfast cereal.

There are several unique pricing rules. The earlier in a player's career the card was printed, the more it is worth. This means that rookie cards for famous players are high-priced. Cards sell for more on the two coasts than in the middle of the country (so do many other collectibles). Cards sell best near the hometown of the team or player. Cards were numbered as they were printed; high numbers were released late in the season.

Although for most antiques the lowest or earliest numbers are most wanted, for baseball cards it is the opposite. The high numbers bring the highest prices. This is because there were usually fewer high-numbered cards printed. In general, the first and last card in a set are the most expensive because sets were often kept in a pack held with a rubber band. The front and back cards were the most likely to be damaged.

Another odd pricing fact: if you add the price book prices for each card in a set, the total is more than the listed price for the complete set. This is probably because buyers are more interested in completing a set than in buying a full one. Buyers will pay extra for a single card if they need it.

Take your list to a local baseball card show or check the Internet. Shows can be found in all parts of the country. If you can't find one, check the ads in the publications listed here.

Talk to the dealers. Show your inventory list and the cards. Be careful not to give a box of cards to a dealer and offer to sell a part of them. Hold out for an offer for all of them unless you want to set up your own booth to sell the collection individually. Good cards sell quickly. The others are worth very little and can be difficult to sell. Remember that a dealer is trying to sell and not just buy at a show.

The rules of etiquette say you must never try to start selling your items to a busy dealer. Don't interrupt any ongoing conversations in a booth—wait until the dealer is free. You will find that stories spread quickly, and dealers and collectors will soon look for you and the possible treasure that might be in your baseball card collection. Expect to get less than half the price book value for a card, and remember to judge condition accurately. If you are unsure, examine other cards. Never throw out a baseball card. Give it to a young friend.

Sports collectibles are big business on the Internet. Live auctions, e-mail auctions, and online catalogs offer thousands of cards for sale. Don't be afraid to go to a site and send an e-mail message describing your cards. General Internet antique malls have jumped on the bandwagon, too, and many of the same dealers you'd see at sports shows are online there.

RELATED BASEBALL MEMORABILIA

Anything that looks like a baseball card or pictures a ballplayer or sports figure has a value. This includes cigarette cards (often from England), as well as small felt or silk pictures of players, bobbin' heads, candy boxes, bread wrappers, labels, plastic cups with a player and an ad, ads cut from comic pages, figures picturing players, and many other items. Some of these collectibles sell for good prices—over $100 for the right empty box, over $500 for a cardboard sign advertising a cigarette and picturing a ballplayer. Most of the cards sell for under $2 each, but a box of hundreds has enough value to make it worth the effort. The dream of every collector is to find an old box with the fabled Honus Wagner card. (But be careful about finding the card of your dreams; the Wagner card has been faked in recent years.) Game-worn jerseys, home run balls, and special game-used bats are expensive one-of-a-kind collectibles. Seats, signs, and even infield grass from a stadium that is being demolished can get big prices.

SPORTS OTHER THAN BASEBALL

Don't overlook other sports-related items. Football, golf, tennis, hunting, fishing, bowling, skiing, billiards, Olympic events, soccer, and many other sports have fans who are serious collectors. Anything that pictures a sports activity, is used to play a sport (golf clubs or tennis rackets), or is associated with an important player or winning team (photos, autographed footballs, Olympic medals, programs) is collectible. Even uniforms, children's games, and toys are wanted by the right collector. Baseball enthusiasts gather at baseball card shows. Football cards and other sports cards can also be found there. The specialty auction offering sports items developed in the 1980s. There are sales that include wooden-handled golf clubs, odd-shaped gut-strung tennis rackets, and even cricket bats. They also include boxing gloves, dishes picturing sports, figural whiskey bottles that are sports-related, and oddities like nodders with team logos or plastic figurines of players. Some of these auctions are advertised in the general antiques publications or on the Internet, while some are part of the auction schedule of the major auction galleries or special large sports auctions. Every item offered for sale belonged to someone like you who wanted cash instead of an old football. Other potential buyers of sports memorabilia are local sports enthusiasts and members of sports-related collecting clubs.

Don't forget the importance of college sports. The pennants, programs, team photos, and souvenirs are cherished by many alumni. Talk to the university librarian or coaches to see if they have any sort of sports trophy display. One family found their father's autographed baseball from a 1914 university team. Instead of including it in the house sale after his death, they gave it to the school sports department. It is displayed in the case with an appropriate tag mentioning their father, the winning pitcher. They also got a tax deduction for the estate.

REPAIR

Cards should be stored so that they will be dirt and insect free. Plastic holders made to hold the cards are sold through shows and publications. Little can be done to restore cards, except for dusting or a simple cleaning with an art-gum eraser. Rare cards can be restored by a conservation expert, but this is expensive. Condition is important in determining price. Bent corners might be ironed straight; use a cool iron and protect the card with a thin piece of fabric. Never trim a card.

If you want to fix a tennis racket, see a pro at a tennis shop. You may have trouble getting old materials such as gut for stringing, but it can be done.

↦ SEE PAPER COLLECTIBLES

PRICE BOOKS

2003 *Baseball Card Price Guide,* 17th edition (Sports Collectors Digest, Iola, WI, 2003).

2003 *Standard Catalog of Baseball Cards,* 12th edition, Robert F. Lemke, editor (Krause, Iola, WI, 2002).

2003 *Standard Catalog of Basketball Cards,* editors of *Tuff Stuff* magazine (Krause, Iola, WI, 2002).

2003 *Standard Catalog of Football Cards,* 6th edition, editors of *Tuff Stuff* magazine (Krause, Iola, WI, 2002).

Antique Golf Collectibles, 2nd edition, Chuck Furjanic (Kruase, Iola, WI, 1999).

Baseball Bat Price Guide, No. 2, Dave Bushing and Joe Phillips (The Glove Collector, 14057 Rolling Hills Lane, Dallas, TX 75240-3807, 1999).

Beckett Official 2003 Price Guide to Baseball Cards, 23rd edition, James Beckett (House of Collectibles, NY, 2003).

Beckett Official 2003 Price Guide to Basketball Cards, 11th edition, James Beckett (House of Collectibles, NY, 2002).

Beckett Official 2003 Price Guide to Football Cards, 22nd edition, James Beckett (House of Collectibles, NY, 2002).

Collecting Sports Memorabilia, Michael McKeever (Alliance, Brooklyn, NY, 1996).

Collectors' Guide to Sports Illustrated and Sports Publications, 2nd edition (P & R Publications, Las Vegas, NV, $19.95, 1997).

Instant Expert: Collecting Fishing, Carl Caiati (Alliance, Brooklyn, NY, 1997).

Instant Expert: Collecting Fly Fishing, Carl Caiati (Alliance, Brooklyn, NY, 1997).

The Negro Leagues Autograph Guide, Kevin Keating and Michael Kolleth (Tuff Stuff Publications, Richmond, VA, 1999).

Old Fishing Lures and Tackle, 6th edition, Carl F. Luckey (Krause, Iola, WI, 2002).

Standard Catalog of Sports Memorabilia, 2nd edition, Dennis Tuttle and Dennis Thornton, editors (Krause, Iola, WI, 2001).

Top of the Line Fishing Collectibles, Donna Tonelli (Schiffer, Atglen, PA, 1997).

Top of the Line Hunting Collectibles, Donna Tonelli (Schiffer, Atglen, PA, 1998).

Tuff Stuff's Baseball Memorabilia Price Guide, 2nd edition, Larry Canale, editor (Antique Trader, Iola, WI, 2001).

Tuff Stuff's Baseball Postcard Collection, Ron Menchine (Antique Trader, Iola, WI, 1999).

Tuff Stuff's Complete Guide to Starting Lineup: A Pictorial History of Kenner Starting Lineup Figures, Jim Warren II (Tuff Stuff Books, Richmond, VA, 1997).

Vintage Baseball Glove Pocket Price Guide, No. 7, Dave Bushing and Joe Phillips (The Glove Collector, 14507 Rolling Hills Ln., Dallas, TX 75240, 2000).

Wood Shafted Golf Club Value Guide, 4th edition, Pete Georgiady (Airlie Hall Press, Greensboro, NC, 1999).

CLUBS & THEIR PUBLICATIONS

Antique Snowmobile Club of America, *Iron Dog Tracks* (NL), 32832 Cty. Rd. 39, Pequot Lakes, MN 56472, e-mail: ascoa921@uslink.net, website: www.ascoa.org.

Cricket Memorabilia Society, *Cricket Memorabilia Society News* (NL), 4 Stoke Park Ct., Stoke Rd., Bishops Cleeve, Cheltenham, Gloucestershire

GL52 8US, UK, e-mail: cms@cricinfo.com, website: www.cricket.org/link_to_database/.

Ducks Unlimited, Inc., *Ducks Unlimited Magazine* (MAG), One Waterfowl Way, Memphis, TN 38120, e-mail: webmaster@ducks.org, website: www.ducks.org.

Florida Antique Tackle Collectors, Inc., *Florida Antique Tackle Collectors, Inc., Newsletter* (NL), PO Box 420703, Kissimmee, FL 34742-0703, e-mail: rkgast@cfl.rr.com, website: www.fatc.net.

Golf Collectors' Society, *Bulletin* (NL), PO Box 241042, Cleveland, OH 44124, e-mail: kkuhl67615@aol.com, website: www.golfcollectors.com.

National Cap & Patch Association, *c.a.p.* (NL), 1521 240th St., Emerald, WI 54012.

National Fishing Lure Collectors Club, *National Fishing Lure Collectors Club Magazine* (MAG), *N.F.L.C.C. Gazette* (NL), 197 Scottsdale Circle, Reeds Spring, MO 65737, e-mail: nflcc.com, website: www.nflcc.com.

North American Trap Collectors Association, *Traps* (NL), PO Box 94, Galloway, OH 43119 (trading, researching, and preserving steel traps).

Olympin Collector's Club, *Olympin Collector's Club Newsletter* (NL), 1386 Fifth St., Schenectady, NY 12303, e-mail: dbigsbyl@nycap.rr.com.

Tennis Collectors' Society, *Tennis Collector* (NL), Guildhall, Great Bromley, Colchester, Essex C07 7TU, UK.

Washington Senators Historical Baseball Association, *Save the Senators* (NL), 11417 St. Rd. 535, Orlando, FL 32836, e-mail: RSB173@aol.com.

OTHER PUBLICATIONS

Baseball Weekly (NP), 7950 Jones Branch Dr., McLean, VA 22108-0605, website: www.usatoday.com/bbwfront.htm.

Beckett Baseball Card Monthly (MAG), *Beckett Basketball Card Monthly* (MAG), *Beckett Football Card Monthly* (MAG), *Beckett Hockey Collector* (MAG), *Beckett Racing Collector* (MAG), *Beckett Vintage Sports Collectibles* (MAG), PO Box 7647, Red Oak, IA 51591-0644, website: www.beckett.com.

Boxing Collectors' News (NL), 7571 Raleigh Ln., Jonesboro, GA 30236-2623, e-mail: askbcn@boxingcollectors.com, website: boxingcollectors.com.

Canadian Sports Card Collector (MAG), Trajan Publishing Corporation, 103 Lakeshore Rd., Suite 202, St. Catharines, ON L2N 2T6, Canada, e-mail: sports@cscmag.ca, website: www.cscmag.ca.

Card Times (MAG), 70 Winifred Ln., Aughton, Ormskirk, Lancashire L39 5DL, UK, e-mail: david@cardtimes.co.uk, website: www.cardtimes.co.uk (a magazine about cigarette cards, trading cards, sports and nonsports cards, phone cards, printed ephemera).

Glove Collector Newsletter (NL), 14057 Rolling Hills Ln., Dallas, TX 75240-3807, e-mail: glovecol@onramp.com.

Hunting & Fishing Collectibles (MAG), PO Box 40, Lawsonville, NC 27022, e-mail: hfcollectibles@aol.com, website: www.hfcollectibles.com.

On Target! The Newsletter for Collectors of Target Balls (NL), 34007 Hillside Ct., Farmington Hills, MI 48335-2513, e-mail: rfinch@detnews.com.

Sports Collectors Digest (NP), *Tuff Stuff* (MAG), 700 E. State St., Iola, WI 54990-0001, e-mail: info@krause.com, website: www.krause.com.

Sports Market Report (NL), 510-A So. Corona Mall, Corona, CA 92879-1420, e-mail: dbtogi@aol.com, website: www.SportsMarketReport.com.

Sweet Spot (NL), 816 Congress, Suite 1280, Austin, TX 78701, e-mail: chuck-kaufman@hotmail.com, website: www.sweetspotnews.com.

ARCHIVES & MUSEUMS

American Museum of Fly Fishing, PO Box 42, 3657 Main St., Manchester, VT 05254, 802-362-3300, website: www.amff.com.

Golf House, United States Golf Association, PO Box 708, Far Hills, NJ 07931, 908-234-2300, website: www.usga.org/golfhouse.

National Baseball Hall of Fame, Inc., 25 Main St., Cooperstown, NY 13326, 888-425-5633, website: www.baseballhalloffame.org.

National Football Museum, Inc., 2121 George Halas Dr. NW, Canton OH 44708, 330-456-8207, website: www.nationalfootballmuseum.com.

APPRAISERS

Many of the auction and repair services listed in this section will also do appraisals. *See also* the general list of "Appraisal Groups," page 483.

Professional Sports Authentication (PSA), PO Box 6180, Newport Beach, CA 92658, 800-325-1121 or 714-833-8824; e-mail: info@psacard.com, website: www.psacard.com. Grading and authentication of baseball, football, basketball, hockey, and other sports and nonsports cards. Service available to members of PSA or through authorized dealers. PSA/DNA provides signed-in-the-presence autograph authentication.

AUCTIONS

➺ SEE ALSO "SELLING THROUGH AUCTION HOUSES," PAGE 485.

All-American Collectibles, Inc., 31-00 Broadway, 3rd Floor, Fair Lawn, NJ 07410, 800-872-8850, 201-797-2555, e-mail: all-american-collectibles @worldnet.att.net. Baseball memorabilia and Americana. Mail bids accepted. Buyer's premium 10%.

EAC Gallery, 99 Powerhouse Rd., Suite 204, Roslyn Heights, NY 11577, 516-484-6280, fax: 516-484-6278, e-mail: eac@eacgallery.com, website: www.eacgallery.com. Specializes in sports memorabilia. Mail and phone bids accepted. Buyer's premium 15%. Free catalog. Prices realized mailed after auction. Appraisals.

Greg Manning Auctions, Inc., 775 Passaic Ave., West Caldwell, NJ 07006-6409, 800-221-0243 or 973-882-0004, fax: 973-882-3499, e-mail: gmauction@aol.com, website: gmaiweb2.gregmanning.com. Sports cards. Internet, interactive telephone, and simulcast Internet and live auctions. Mail, phone, and fax bids accepted. Buyer's premium 10%. Prices realized mailed after auction. Appraisals.

Grey Flannel Auctions, 549 Middle Neck Rd., Great Neck, NY 11023, 516-446-5533, fax: 516-446-5592, e-mail: GFCSports@aol.com, website: www.greyflannel.com. Game-used jerseys, bats, autographs, etc. Mail, phone, and Internet bids accepted. Buyer's premium 15%. Free catalogs. Prices realized mailed after auction and available on website. Appraisals.

Ingrid O'Neil's Olympic Auctions, PO Box 872048, Vancouver, WA 98687, 360-834-5202, fax: 360-834-2853, e-mail: auctions@ioneil.com, website: www.ioneil.com. Absentee auctions of Olympic Games memorabilia. Mail, phone, fax, and e-mail bids accepted. Buyer's premium 15%. Catalog $15; yearly subscription $30. Prices realized mailed after auction. Appraisals.

Just Kids Nostalgia, 310 New York Ave., Huntington, NY 11743, 516-423-8449, fax: 631-423-4326, email: info@justkidsnostalgia.com, website: www.justkidsnostalgia.com. Sports memorabilia. Mail, phone, fax, and e-mail bids accepted. Prices realized mailed after auction and available on website.

Lang's Sporting Collectibles, Inc., 665 Pleasant Valley Rd., Waterville, NY 13480, 315-841-4263, e-mail: LangsAuction@aol.com. Mail and phone bids accepted. Buyer's premium 13% with 3% discount for cash or check. Prices realized mailed after auction. Appraisals.

Leland's, 3947 Merrick Rd., Seaford, NY 11783, 516-409-9700, fax: 516-409-9797, e-mail: info@lelands.com, website: www.lelands.com. Specializes in auctions of vintage sports memorabilia and sports and nonsports cards. Mail and phone bids accepted. Buyer's premium 15%. Prices realized mailed after auction. Appraisals.

MastroNet, Inc., 1511 W. 22nd St., Suite 125, Oak Brook, IL 60523, phone: 630-472-1200, fax: 630-472-1201, website: www.mastronet.com. Auctions of sports memorabilia. Buyer's premium 15%. Prices realized available after auction. Sports catalog subscription (3–4) $75 per year.

Past Tyme Pleasures, 2491 San Ramon Valley Blvd., PMB 204, San Ramon, CA 94583, 925-484-4488, fax: 925-484-2551, e-mail: pasttyme1 @attbi.com, website: www.pasttyme1.com. Antique hunting and fishing collectibles. Mail, phone, fax, and e-mail bids accepted. Buyer's premium 10%. Prices realized mailed after auction and available on website. Appraisals.

Slater's Americana, 5335 N. Tacoma Ave., Suite 24, Indianapolis, IN 46220, 317-257-0863, Mon.–Fri. 9:00 A.M.–1:00 P.M. only, fax: 317-254-9167, email: info@slatersamericana.com, website: www.slatersamericana.com. Vintage sports memorabilia. Mail, phone, and fax bids accepted. Buyer's premium 15%. Prices realized available after auction. Appraisals.

SoldUSA Auctions, 1418 Industrial Rd., Box 11, Matthews, NC 28105, 704-815-1500, fax: 704-844-6436, e-mail: croberts@soldusa.com, website: soldusa.com. Hunting and fishing collectibles, fine firearms, and western collectibles. Mail, phone, fax, and e-mail bids accepted. Buyer's premium 10%. Catalog $24. Prices realized on website and in following catalog. Restoration. Appraisals.

Superior Galleries, 9478 W. Olympic Blvd., Beverly Hills, CA 90212, 877-782-6773 or 310-203-9761, fax: 310-203-8037, e-mail: alan@superior-stamps.com, website: www.superiorstamps.com. Sports memorabilia and other collectibles. Mail, phone, fax, and e-mail bids accepted. Buyer's premium 15%. Catalog $5. Yearly subscription $20. Prices realized available after auction on website. Appraisals.

Teletrade, Inc., 27 Main St., Kingston, NY 12401-3853, 800-232-1132 or 914-339-2900, e-mail: bradj@teletrade.com or pauls@teletrade.com, website: www.teletrade.com. Absentee auctions of sports cards. Phone and Internet bids only. Buyer's premium 10%. Prices realized mailed and available on website after auction.

REPAIRS, PARTS & SUPPLIES

➻ SEE ALSO "CONSERVATORS & RESTORERS," PAGE 520.

Bill Cole Enterprises, Inc., PO Box 60, Dept. RK1, Randolph, MA 02368-0060, 781-986-2653, fax: 781-986-2656, e-mail: bcemylar@cwbusiness.com, website: www.bcemylar.com. Manufacturers and distributors of archival supplies to protect paper documents from turning yellow. Acid-free boards and boxes. Mylar sleeves for baseball cards.

Northeast Document Conservation Center, 100 Brickstone Sq., Andover, MA 01810-1494, 978-470-1010, fax: 978-475-6021, e-mail: nedcc@nedcc.org, website: www.nedcc.org. Nonprofit regional conservation center specializing in treatment of art and artifacts on paper, including baseball cards. Free brochure. Open Mon–Fri. 8:30 A.M.–4:30 P.M.

Seitz and Co., 1772 Selby Ave., St. Paul, MN 55104-6030, 651-646-3659. Wood and metal stands for ballpark and stadium box seat chairs allow you to use the seat as a chair without bolting it to the floor or wall. Free advice on identification and authenticity of seats. Free catalog.

The2Buds.com, 462 W. Silver Lake Rd. N., Traverse City, MI 49684, 888-270-0552, Mon.–Fri. 9:00 A.M.–5:00 P.M., e-mail: postcards@the2buds.com, website: www.the2buds.com. Archival supplies for storing and displaying vintage collectibles including trading cards and pennants. Sleeves, bags, storage boxes, albums, binder pages, and more. Internet sales only.

STAMPS

There have been stamp collectors since 1840, when the first postage stamp was introduced by Sir Rowland Hill of England. It is a highly specialized field. Stamps should be examined by a dealer in stamps or an auction house that knows that market. A large, serious collection requires an expert.

Condition, rarity, and demand determine prices. A stamp should have its original bright color, a centered design, and wide margins. There should be no defects, full gum on the back, no hinge marks, and only a light, clear cancellation mark if used. It should have no tears, dirt, creases, pinholes, or uneven perforations. The average child's collection is rarely valuable, but it should always be checked.

The post office sells corner blocks of stamps to collectors every day. These have been put away as an investment by many casual collectors who have little understanding of the market. Most of the blocks under thirty years old sell only for face value or less. Check with a stamp dealer. If the stamps have no value to collectors, then use them on letters. Many sheets of commemoratives are equally unsalable for more than the face value. If you have blocks, sheets, or sets of stamps, be sure you determine the value before you split them up or use them.

Don't ignore the stamps on old postcards and letters. Even printed stamps on postal cards could give extra value to the card. First-day covers have a special value, and the stamp should not be removed. The cover is printed with a special drawing and is used the first day of issue of the stamp. Sell the entire envelope. Envelopes with stamps postmarked before 1900 should be checked for value. Those dating from before the Civil War should be appraised by an expert. Letters mailed without stamps for special reasons (during the Civil War) can be very valuable. Never remove a stamp from an envelope to sell it. Sell the envelope and stamp together.

The best way to value or to sell stamps is with the help of experts. You may want a formal appraisal before you decide whether the collection should be auctioned or sold to a dealer. Dealers are listed in the Yellow Pages of the telephone book. It is rarely a good idea to break up a collection and sell the stamps yourself unless you are a serious collector who has purchased through clubs and shows. The stamps are too small and too fragile to be handled over and over.

Sometimes the stamp is more valuable as part of a "cover" (the special stamped envelope). Unusual cancellation marks, postal marks, written information, hand stamps, or decorations on the envelope make a cover valuable. First-day covers should always be left intact. If you send a collection of stamps or an album to an appraiser, dealer, or prospective buyer, photocopy each page first. This will give you a record of the collection in case of a later disagreement.

NONPOSTAL, OR CINDERELLA, STAMPS

A "Cinderella" stamp is any stamp not produced by a government to be used as postage. Christmas seals, Easter seals, and other charity stamps are used to raise money and show support for various organizations. The first Christmas seals were created in 1904 by a Danish postal worker to raise money to cure and prevent tuberculosis. Another nonpostal stamp is the poster stamp. Mainly used as an advertising and propaganda device, the stamps are miniature posters that were collected and sometimes pasted into scrapbooks. Collectors often had to continue to buy certain products to complete their books. Tax stamps, telegraph stamps, and grocery store trading stamps are also collected. Unaffixed stamps are more desirable.

REPAIR AND STORAGE

Stamp collectors know that condition and storage are important considerations. Most stamps are kept in albums and mounted with either hinges or mounts. Never tape or glue a stamp into an album. Inexpensive or used stamps may be "hinged" using special stamp hinges made with gum that will not harm the stamps. High-priced and mint, unused stamps should be mounted with stamp mounts, small corners that hold the stamp in place. Hinges, mounts, and albums can be found at your local stamp stores or through mail-order companies listed in stamp publications.

Sometimes you will want to soak a stamp off an envelope. If the envelope is colored or there is ink writing or heavy postmarks, you must test to be sure nothing will fade or run. Brightly colored envelopes from Christmas cards should not be soaked; the color could run and ruin the stamps. Soak white envelopes with stamps in a large dish of warm (room temperature, not hot) water. Stir gently. The stamps will float away from the paper. Sometimes a drop of detergent should be added to the water. Gently rub the back of the stamp with your fingers to remove any remaining glue.

Never leave a stamp in the water for more than an hour. Dry the stamps on white absorbent paper or terry cloth towels. When almost dry, press the stamps flat under a heavy weight or place them in a drying book made of blotters. Let the stamps dry at least four days before you mount them as part of your collection.

There are products that remove marks made by tape or adhesives, ink, grease, and other disfiguring blotches. There are also experts who restore stamps, but only rare and valuable stamps make the expenditure worthwhile.

Store stamps in a dry place that is not too warm and is out of direct sunlight. Do not remove the selvage around a mint or used stamp. Especially important is a selvage with plate numbers and markings. Don't tear stamp groups apart. Blocks and sets are collected in a different way than single stamps. Check your local library for books on stamps. Many contain information on care and conservation.

REFERENCE BOOKS

The International Encyclopaedic Dictionary of Philatelics, 3rd edition, R. Scott Carlton (Krause Publications, Iola, WI, 1997).

PRICE BOOKS

2003 Brookman United States, United Nations & Canada Stamps & Postal Collectibles, David S. MacDonald, editor (Krause, Iola, WI, 2002).

2003 Catalog of Errors on U.S. Postage Stamps, Stephen R. Datz (Krause, Iola, WI, 2003).

Krause-Minkus Standard Catalog of U.S. Stamps 2003, 6th edition, Maurice D. Wozniak, editor, (Krause, Iola, WI, 2002).

Scott 2003 Standard Postage Stamp Catalogue, 4 volumes, James E. Kloetzel, editor (Scott Publishing Co., New York, 2003).

The Official 2003 Blackbook Price Guide of United States Postage Stamps, 25th edition, Marc and Tom Hudgeons (House of Collectibles, New York, 1998).

CLUBS & THEIR PUBLICATIONS

American Air Mail Society, *Airpost Journal* (MAG), *Jack Knight Air Log* (MAG), PO Box 5367, Virginia Beach, VA 23471-0367, e-mail: AAMSInformation @aol.com, website: ourworld.compuserve.com/homepages/aams.

American Philatelic Society, *American Philatelist* (MAG), PO Box 8000, State College, PA 16803-8000, e-mail: flsente@stamps.org, website: www.stamps.org.

American Topical Association, *Topical Time* (MAG), PO Box 50820, Albuquerque, NM 87181-0820, e-mail: ATAstamps@junocom, website: home.prcn.org/~pauld/ATA.

Christmas Seal and Charity Stamp Society, *Seal News* (NL), PO Box 18615, Rochester, NY 14618-8615, e-mail: FHW-33@worldnet.att.net.

Collectors of Religion on Stamps Society, *COROS Chronicle* (MAG), 425 N. Linwood Ave., #110, Appleton, WI 54914-3476, website: www.powernet online.com/~corosec/coros1.htm.

Confederate Stamp Alliance, *Confederate Philatelist* (MAG), 19450 Yuma St., Castro Valley, CA 94546, e-mail: FastOffshore@aol.com, website: www.csalliance.org.

Dogs on Stamps Study Unit, *DOSSU Journal* (NL), 202A Newport Rd., Monroe Twp., NJ 08831, website: www.dossu.org.

International Stamp Collectors Society, *InterStamps* (NL), PO Box 854, Van Nuys, CA 91408, e-mail: iibick@aol.com, website: www.bick.net.

Israel Stamp Collectors Society, *Israstamps* (NL), PO Box 854, Van Nuys, CA 91408, e-mail: iibick@aol.com, website: www.bick.net.

Junior Philatelists of America, *The Philatelic Observer* (NL), PO Box 2625, Albany, OR 97321, e-mail: exec.sec@jpastamps.org, website: www.jpastamps.org.

Korea Stamp Society, Inc., *Korean Philately* (NL), PO Box 6889, Oak Ridge, TN 37831, e-mail: jtalmage@usit.net, website: www.pennfamily.org/KSS-USA.

Military Postal History Society, *Military Postal History Society Bulletin* (MAG), 5410 Fern Loop, West Richland, WA 99353, e-mail: kinsley@owt.com, website: homepage.mac.com/mphs/index.html (soldier campaign covers, patriotics, prisoner-of-war mail, naval mail, occupation and internment covers, picture postcards of a military nature, etc.).

Post Mark Collectors Club, *PMCC Bulletin* (NL), 23381 Greenleaf Blvd., Elkhart, IN 46514-4504, e-mail: bob.milligan@prodigy.net, website: www.postmarks.org.

United States Philatelic Classics Society, *Chronicle of the U.S. Classic Postal Issues* (MAG), Mark D. Rogers, PO Box 80708, Austin, TX 78708, e-mail: mrogers23@austin.rr.com, website: www.uspcs.org (19th-century philately).

United States Stamp Society, *The Specialist* (MAG), PO Box 6634, Katy, TX 77491-6634, website: www.usstamps.org.

Universal Ship Cancellation Society, *USCS Log* (MAG), 747 Shard Ct., Fremont, CA 94539, e-mail: shaymur@flash.net, website: www.uscs.org.

Zeppelin Collectors Club, *Zeppelin Collector* (NL), PO Box A3843, Chicago, IL 60690-3843 (aerophilatelic).

OTHER PUBLICATIONS

Canadian Stamp News (NP), Trajan Publishing Corporation, 103 Lakeshore Rd., Suite 202, St. Catharines, ON L2N 2T6, Canada, e-mail: newsroom@trajan.com, website: www.canadianstampnews.ca.

Linn's Stamp News (NP), PO Box 29, Sidney, OH 45365, e-mail: subscribe@linns.com, website: www.linns.com.

Mekeel's & Stamps Magazine (MAG), *U.S. Stamp News* (MAG), PO Box 5050,

White Plains, NY 10602, e-mail: stampnews@aol.com, website: www.stampnews.com/page7.htm.

Scott Stamp Monthly (MAG), PO Box 828, Sidney, OH 45365, e-mail: ssm@scottonline.com, website: www.scottonline.com.

Stamp Collector (NP), 700 E. State St., Iola, WI 54990-0001, e-mail: info@krause.com, website: www.krause.com.

ARCHIVES & MUSEUMS

National Postal Museum, 2 Massachusetts Ave. NE, Washington, DC 20560, 202-357-2991, e-mail: NPMem004@sivm.si.edu, website: www.si.edu/postal.

Spellman Museum of Stamps & Postal History, 235 Wellesley St., Weston, MA 02193, 781-768-8367, fax: 781-768-7332, e-mail: info@spellman.org, website: www.spellman.org.

APPRAISERS

Many of the auctions and repair services listed in this section will also do appraisals. *See also* the general list of "Appraisal Groups," page 483.

Professional Stamp Experts (PSE), PO Box 6170, Newport Beach, CA 92658, 877-782-6788, fax: 949-567-1187, e-mail: psa@collectors.com, website: www.psestamp.com. Rare and collectible stamp authentication and grading. Service available to members of PSE or through authorized dealers.

AUCTIONS

➤➤ **SEE ALSO "SELLING THROUGH AUCTION HOUSES," PAGE 485.**

Greg Manning Auctions, Inc., 775 Passaic Ave., W. Caldwell, NJ 07006-6409, 800-221-0243 or 973-882-0004, fax: 973-882-3499, e-mail: gmauction@aol.com, website: gmaiweb2.gregmanning.com. Stamp auctions. Internet, interactive telephone, and simulcast Internet and live auctions. Mail, phone, and fax bids accepted. Buyer's premium 15% on stamps and 10% on sports. Prices realized mailed after auction. Appraisals.

Jim Mehrer's Postal History, 2405 30th St., Rock Island, IL 61201, 309-786-6539, fax: 309-786-4840, e-mail: mehrer@postal-history.com, website: www.postal-history.com. Pre-1930 U.S. postal history and related reference literature and supplies. Mail, phone, and Internet bids. No buyer's premium. Catalogs free to regular bidders, otherwise $2 U.S., $4.50 international; yearly subscription $12 U.S., $30 international.

Superior Galleries, 9478 W. Olympic Blvd., Beverly Hills, CA 90212, 877-782-6773 or 310-203-9761, fax: 310-203-8037, e-mail: alan@superior stamps.com, website: www.superiorstamps.com. Stamps and other collectibles. Mail, phone, fax, and e-mail bids accepted. Buyer's premium 15%. Catalog $5. Yearly subscription $20. Prices realized available after auction on website. Appraisals.

REPAIRS, PARTS & SUPPLIES

➻ SEE ALSO "CONSERVATORS & RESTORERS," PAGE 520.

Century Business Solutions, PO Box 2393, Brea, CA 92822, 800-767-0777, fax: 800-786-7939, website: www.centurybusinesssolutions.com. Products for organizing and storing stamps and other collectibles.

RN Products, 39 Monmouth St., Red Bank, NJ 07701-1613, 732-741-0626, fax: 732-741-0479, e-mail: mostco@monmouth.com. Complete line of stamp supplies. Aluminum dealer display cases. Send SASE for brochure.

University Products, Inc., 517 Main St., PO Box 101, Holyoke, MA 01040, 800-336-4847, fax: 800-532-9281, e-mail: info@universityproducts.com, website: www.universityproducts.com. Archival supplies for conservation, restoration, repair, storage, and display. Specialized storage for stamps and other collectibles. Archival storage boxes, paper and plastic enclosures, acid-free board and papers, adhesives, albums, preservation framing supplies, tools, equipment, chemicals, and other materials. Free catalog.

STOCKS & BONDS

It seems that everyone who survived the stock market crash of 1929 had some stocks or bonds that, although worthless, were saved. Today there are two possible values for these old stocks. A few might have value due to a merger or acquisition. The worthless company or mine may have merged, been sold, struck gold, or become part of a valuable company in some other way. To learn if you own stocks or bonds of value, first try your library. Look in *The Directory of Obsolete Securities* (Financial Information, Inc.), *The Capital Changes Daily* (Commerce Clearing House), or even try tracking mergers through the Standard & Poor's or Moody's directories. It is also possible to use a company that will research your stock for a fee. Some are listed at the end of this chapter.

If your stocks have no value as part of a company, they still have a value for collectors who specialize in the scripophily market (that's the formal name for the collecting of stocks and bonds). Old certificates were decorated with elaborately engraved vignettes. Some were fanciful pictures of Liberty or other symbols, some pictured the industry with oil wells or smokestacks, and some were a combination of these. These certificates are sometimes framed and sold as gifts to collectors. For example, a picture of an oil well may intrigue a car collector. Railroads, mines, airplanes, and automobiles are favored. If the certificate is signed by a famous person, such as Thomas Edison or John D. Rockefeller, the price is higher. Some certificates have revenue stamps, and rare ones are purchased by stamp collectors. Old stock certificates are bought and sold regularly on the Internet. A founder's stock certificate for Standard Oil signed by John D. Rockefeller sold for a record $61,000. Condition is always important; clean, crisp certificates are worth more than creased, worn examples. Hole-punched cancel marks lower the value. Other fiscal paper, such as mortgages, checks, and legal documents, may also have value.

⇢ SEE PAPER COLLECTIBLES

REPAIR

Take care of your stocks and bonds like other paper items. Never use glue or tape to mount the paper unless you feel the item is of minimal value. Old stock certificates used as wallpaper can rarely be removed and sold.

CLUBS & THEIR PUBLICATIONS

International Bond & Share Society, *Scripophily* (MAG), U.S.A. Chapter, PO Box 430, Hackensack, NJ 07602-0430, e-mail: IBSS@scripophily.org, website: www.scripophily.org.

Old Certificates' Collectors Club, *Old Certificates' Collectors Club* (NL), 4761 W. Waterbuck Dr., Tucson, AZ 85742, e-mail: ssi@stocksearchintl.com, website: stocksearchintl.com (old stock and bond certificates).

OTHER PUBLICATIONS

Friends of Financial History (MAG), Museum of American Financial History, 26 Broadway, New York, NY 10004-1763, website: www.financialhistory.com.

ARCHIVES & MUSEUMS

The Museum of American Financial History, 28 Broadway, New York, NY 10004, 212-908-4519, 800-98-FINANCE, fax: 212-908-4601, website: www.financialhistory.com.

REPAIRS, PARTS & SUPPLIES

⇢ SEE ALSO "CONSERVATORS & RESTORERS," PAGE 520.

R.M. Smythe, 26 Broadway, Suite 973, New York, NY 10004-1703, 800-622-1880 or 212-943-1880, fax: 212-908-4670, website: www.rm-smythe.com.

Research on inactive, unlisted, and obscure securities. Information on how to redeem them.

Stock Search International Inc., 4761 W. Waterbuck Dr., Tucson, AZ 85742, 800-537-4523 or 520-579-5635, fax: 520-579-5639, e-mail: ssi@stock searchintl.com, website: www.stocksearchintl.com. Research and fund-recovery services. Conducts stock searches to establish the worth of bond or share certificates as investments. Will also evaluate their potential value as collectible items. Free brochure.

STOVES

Antique cooking and heating stoves have gained popularity in recent years and all types can be sold. The problem is that they are large and heavy, so try to sell them through an ad in your local paper. Be sure that your stove, as well as your chimney, is in safe working condition if you plan to use it. Many old stoves must be vented to the outside. Old parts are available through many of the dealers who sell antique stoves. New parts can be purchased or made for most old stoves.

An amateur should never restore or install an old stove that is to be used. Many communities have strict fire-code laws that require permits plus an inspection of any working stove after installation. Always call a professional to safely install your stove. The name of a company that can install a stove can be found in the Yellow Pages of your phone directory.

CLUBS & THEIR PUBLICATIONS

Antique Stove Association, 469 Long Hwy., Little Compton, RI 02837, e-mail: Help@AntiqueStoveAssoc.org, website: www.AntiqueStove Assoc.org.

OTHER PUBLICATIONS

Antique Stove Exchange (NL), PO Box 2101, Waukesha, WI 53187, website: www.theantiquestovexchng.com.

REPAIRS, PARTS & SUPPLIES

➡ **SEE ALSO "CONSERVATORS & RESTORERS," PAGE 520.**

Antique & Vintage Stoves, 21595 Windstove Way, Perris, California 92570, 909-657-9998, e-mail: sales@vintagestoves.com, website: www.vintagestoves.com. VintageStoves.com specializes in antique gas stoves from the 1940s and 1950s; provides repair and restoration services as well as sales.

Antique Stove Information Clearinghouse, 421 N. Main St., Monticello, IN 47960-1932, 574-583-6465. Archive of over 2,000 stove manufacturers' catalogs dating from 1860 to 1937. Photocopies available, $3 per stove. Manufacturers' original catalogs bought, sold, located, and reprinted. The Clearinghouse puts buyers and sellers of antique stoves (1930s and earlier) and stove parts together and offers restoration consultation, parts search advice, catalogs, and books on antique stoves. Call for free consultation or send SASE for information.

Barnstable Stove Shop, Inc., Box 472, Rt. 149, West Barnstable, MA 02668, 508-362-9913, 9:00 A.M.–4:30 P.M.. Antique wood, coal, and gas stoves restored. Large parts inventory, mostly coal and wood stoves. Brochure $1.

Brunelle Enterprises, Inc., 203 Union Rd., Wales, MA 01081, 413-245-7396, e-mail: bob@oldstoves.com, website: oldstoves.com. Restoration of antique coal and wood kitchen and parlor stoves.

Bryant Stove & Music, Inc., 27 Stovepipe Alley, Thorndike, ME 04986, 207-568-3665, e-mail: bryants@ uninet.net, website: www.uninet.net/~bryants. Stove parts for sale; replacement grates and liners. Trim renickeled. Museum. Free brochure.

Buckeye Appliance & Antiques, 714 W. Fremont, Stockton, CA 95203-9643, 209-464-9643, fax: 209-464-9643, e-mail: calbuck@aol.com. Service and restoration of vintage gas stoves.

J.E.S. Enterprises & The Old Appliance Club, PO Box 65, Ventura, CA 93002-0065, 805-643-3532, fax: 805-643-3532, e-mail: jes@west.net, website: www.theoldapplianceclub.com. Vintage stove restoration service and products. Vintage thermostat and electric oven element rebuilding. Safety systems for antique ranges; reproduction and original parts. Sign up at www.theoldapplianceclub.com to receive "The Old Appliance Communique" free of charge. Catalog $3.

Johnny's Appliances & Classic Ranges, 17549 Sonoma Hwy., PO Box 1407, Sonoma, CA 95476-1407, 707-996-9730. Restoration and parts for classic ranges from the 1950s and older. Oven thermostats recalibrated, valves rebuilt and adjusted, door hinges and springs repaired, porcelain panels redone, nickel and chrome replated. Send SASE for free brochure.

Kustom Khrome, 1680 E. 4th St., Colby, KS 67701, 785-462-7617. Antique stove restoration, including sandblasting, painting, plating, welding, etc.

Lehman Hardware, One Lehman Circle, PO Box 41, Kidron, OH 44603-0041, 330-857-5757, fax: 330-857-5785, e-mail: info@lehmans.com, website: www.lehmans.com. Stove accessories and supplies, including stove paint, isinglass, flue-hole covers, and stove door gaskets. Old-fashioned hard-to-find items for nonelectric living. Tools; books. Catalog $3.

Macy's Texas Stove Works, 5515 Almeda Rd., Houston, TX 77004-7443, 713-521-0934, fax: 713-521-0889, website: www.macysclassicstoveworks.com. Restoration, parts, and services for vintage and antique stoves and ranges. Clocks and timers rebuilt; thermostats rebuilt and calibrated; safeties repaired or replaced. Knobs, handles, thermostats, and other parts available.

R.J. Pattern Services, c/o R.J. Hoerr, 1212 W. Detroit St., New Buffalo, MI 49117, 616-469-7538, fax: 616-469-8554, e-mail: mhoerr@starband.net. Cast iron, aluminum, and brass castings. Wood and plastic (foundry) patterns and models. Antique stove and range replacement parts. Classic gas range knobs, dials, and handles. Castings for antique tractor restoration. Antique toy and salesman sample stove restoration.

Van Dyke's Restorers, PO Box 278, Woonsocket, SD 57385, 605-796-4425, 800-558-1234 order, fax: 605-796-4085, e-mail: restoration@cabelas.com, website: www.vandykes.com.

Woodman's Parts Plus, PO Box 186, East Wakefield, NH 03830-0186, phone: 603-522-8216, 9:00 A.M.–5:00 P.M., fax: 603-522-3007. Parts for wood and coal cook stoves, kerosene lamps, gas grills. Custom-made wrought iron accessories.

→ TELEPHONE CARDS, SEE NUMISMATIC COLLECTIBLES

TELEPHONE COLLECTIBLES

If you have anything old that has the word *telephone* or the familiar bell symbol, it can be sold. Everything from telephone booths to telephones to telephone insulators are collected. The highest-priced phones are those that look old and can be altered to actually work on today's phone lines. Blue glass paperweights, banks, enameled signs, and anything else marked with the Bell Telephone logo are purchased. Prices can be found in the general price books.

Telephone and telegraph insulators have been collected since the 1960s by serious collectors who know the makers, use, and patent histories of the insulators. Insulators are the usually dome-shaped glass objects once perched at the top of all U.S. telephone poles. Now they are rarely used in this country except along railroad lines. Most insulators are found today by digging in dumps or at the base of old poles. Railroad lines are private property and you need permission to dig there. Be careful about trying to remove insulators from abandoned poles. You could get electrocuted. Selling is usually done at special insulator shows or at bottle shows. Only unusual or rare insulators in perfect condition sell for over a few dollars. Insulators are priced in many general price books, but it takes some knowledge to recognize a treasure. If you have a basket of old insulators, take them to a show and talk to the collectors. They may be able to tell you what the insulators are worth, and the show is the best place for you to dispose of them. Be careful. Some old insulators are being radiated to change their color to deep purple or other bright colors. The color does not add to the low value.

Never attempt to remove an insulator from a pole. There are often power lines on the poles and collectors have been electrocuted.

REPAIR

Many types of old telephones can be repaired and used. Old dial phones can even be converted to push-button phones through the addition of an extra box or by another method. Contact your local phone company for exact information about the types of equipment that will work. Replacement parts and reproduction phones are available.

Old phones often require more power to ring the bell, and sometimes too many phones on one line can prevent all of them from working. We learned about this the hard way when we tried to install an extra old phone. A normal house line can handle "five ringers," we were told; most new phones are only "half ringers," but old phones can be more than "one ringer."

Insulators can be repaired by specialists and by those listed in other sections of this book who do glass and ceramic work. Invisible repairs with new plastics are being done.

PRICE BOOKS

Collectible Novelty Phones (If Mr. Bell Could See Me Now . . .), Jim David Davis (Schiffer, Atglen, PA, 1998).

The Definitive Guide to Colorful Insulators, Mike Bruner (Schiffer, Atglen, PA, 2000).

CLUBS & THEIR PUBLICATIONS

Antique Telephone Collectors Association, *ATCA Newsletter* (NL), PO Box 94, Abilene, KS 67410, website: www.atcaonline.com.

National Insulator Association, *Drip Points* (NL), 1315 Old Mill Path, Broadview Heights, OH 44147-3276, e-mail: drippoints@insulators.com, website: www.nia.org.

Telephone Collectors International, *Singing Wires* (NL), 3207 E. Bend Dr., Algonquin, IL 60102-9664, e-mail: membership@singingwires.org, website: www.singingwires.org.

OTHER PUBLICATIONS

Crown Jewels of the Wire (MAG), 1560 Hugo Rd., Merlin, OR 97532, e-mail: hbanks@grantspass.com, website: www.crownjewelsofthewire.com (insulators).

ARCHIVES & MUSEUMS

The Museum of Communications, 7000 E. Marginial Way S, Seattle, WA 98108, 206-767-3012, website: www.scn.org/tech/telmuseum.

Telephone Pioneer Communication Museum of San Francisco, 1515 19th Ave., San Francisco, CA 94122, 415-542-0182, fax: 415-661-1077.

USEFUL SITES

Cyber Telephone Museum, www.museumphones.com.

REPAIRS, PARTS & SUPPLIES

↦ SEE ALSO "CONSERVATORS & RESTORERS," PAGE 520.

Billard's Old Telephones, 21710 Regnart Rd., Cupertino, CA 95014, 408-252-2104. Parts for old telephones. Catalog $1.

Chicago Old Telephone Co., 327 Carthage St., Sanford, NC 27330-4206, 919-774-6625, fax: 919-774-7666, e-mail: marsh45@earthlink.net, website: www.chicagooldtelephone.com. Antique telephone parts and restoration. Rental of old telephones as theater props.

House of Telephones, 2677 E. Valley Dr., San Angelo, TX 76905-8303, 915-482-0101, fax: 915-655-5681, e-mail: olevrier@aol.com. Antique telephone parts and supplies. Reproduction cloth cords made to any length; dials, mouthpieces, transmitter arms, cranks, nameplates, etc. Mail order worldwide. Free brochure.

Mahantango Manor Inc., PO Box 170, Dalmatia, PA 17017, 800-642-3966 or 570-758-8000, Mon.–Thurs. 7:00 A.M.–5:00 P.M., fax: 570-758-6000. Replacement parts for antique telephones. Parts for wooden wall phones, candlestick phones, cradle phones, and modern wooden decorator wall phones with handsets. Mouthpieces, receivers, cords, crank handles, door locks, books, and more. Catalog $2, with coupon for $2 off next purchase.

Phone Wizard, 23 S. Berlin Pike, Lovettsville, VA 20180, 540-822-4730, fax: 540-822-4733, e-mail: bruce@phonewizard.net. Repair and restoration of antique telephones. Antique telephone parts and supplies. Conversions. Can make any antique telephone work without affecting its value. Free catalog.

TEXTILES

The women's movement sparked an interest in the work of women from past centuries. That seems to have started the amazing rise in the price of old quilts, woven coverlets, samplers, and other examples of feminine handiwork from the past. Country decorating magazines added to the interest, and it wasn't long before collectors wanted open shelves piled high with examples of quilts and homespun cloth. Quilts are hung like huge pictures on the walls behind beds heaped with white-work pillows and covers. Paisley shawls become tablecloths. All of this means that any type of old textile that exhibits some handiwork can be sold.

People who collect fabrics also buy woven silk pictures, including Stevengraphs, good examples of needlepoint and Berlin work, and the many tools used in sewing, lacework, and other needlework. If you find an old, filled sewing basket, you have a treasure. There are buyers for thimbles, tape measures, buttons, trim, half-finished embroideries, and even the sewing basket.

SAMPLERS

The sampler originated in England. It was literally a sample of needlework done by a young girl. Every well-to-do girl was expected to weave and sew enough for her future home. It was considered an important part of her dowry. Hand-loomed sheets, covers, towels, and underclothes were expensive. In the legal accountings after a death, the linens were among the most valuable items in an eighteenth-century home. Each item was embroidered with letters and numbers as part of an inventory system. Samplers had the alphabet, numbers, some symbolic pictures, and perhaps a motto or favorite saying. It was then proudly signed and dated by the girl who had stitched it.

Samplers were made on homespun fabric, and the thread was often home-dyed. These materials discolor and fade, so condition is very important. A sampler with clear colors and a light background is worth from five to ten times as much as a similar sampler that is brown and faded. American and Canadian samplers are priced higher than English examples. You can sometimes identify the country of origin from the wording and designs. Crowns usually indicate an English sampler.

Seventeenth-century samplers are long and thin. In the eighteenth century, the sampler became more rectangular. Nineteenth-century samplers have pictorial and memorial designs. Some "darning" samplers were made. Holes were cut and then darned. These were often from Holland. Italian samplers were frequently fringed instead of hemmed, and they often featured religious motifs. German samplers favored very small designs, often made with wool thread. Spanish samplers were almost always square, with a center design and borders. American samplers from the 1920s to the 1950s usually had a motto and lots of white space. Many were black and white. These sell for $25 to $100 for ordinary examples.

Age can influence the price. The older the better, provided the condition is good. Repairs lower the value of a sampler, so you should never repair an old one before selling it. Leave that to an expert. The history of the maker's family always adds to the value. If your sampler was made by a distant relative, write down all the information you know, including the name, birthplace, and birth date of the maker. Attach the history to the back of the frame. The sampler would be even more valuable if your great-great-aunt had been part of a presidential family or had roomed with Nellie Bly. Any verifiable facts that connect the sampler to local or national history add to the price.

Eighteenth-century American samplers sell for very high prices. If you are selling, try to have an appraisal by an expert before setting the price. Early nineteenth-century samplers are also high-priced; the handiwork of a 1920s child, however, is of a limited value.

QUILTS

If you can call it a quilt, you can sell it. The newspapers often report sales of quilts for thousands of dollars, but these quilts are exceptional. Record price in 1991 was $264,000 for an appliquéd quilt dated November 18, 1867, depicting the reconciliation between the North and the South. Age influences the price, but the most important factor is skill. The better the quilt design and stitching, the higher the price. Quilts are judged like fine paintings. Experts look for good design, originality, and unusual fabrics, as well as condition and age.

There are several kinds of quilts. Some are pieced with many small patches stitched together. This large composite piece is used as the top layer of a sandwich with a plainer bottom layer and a cotton filling. The three layers are then quilted together into one useful covering. Small stitches and attractive curved patterns in the almost invisible quilting are the key to a top-quality quilt. The very late or very simple quilt "sandwiches" may only be held together with knotted strings placed at intervals.

The earliest quilts had a large center design. By the Civil War, it had become fashionable to use overall repetitive designs that are known by names like Four-Patch, Log Cabin, Pineapple, and Sunburst. Machine-stitched quilts were made in the late nineteenth century and after.

Many fine quilts can still be found today in attic trunks. The mountain areas of West Virginia and Kentucky seem to furnish an endless quantity to the "pickers" who supply the best shops with antiques. The Amish from all areas make quilts of geometric blocks and dark colors; these quilts have become fashionable and expensive. Beware, as there are still skilled needleworkers making Amish and other quilts. The fabrics are probably the best guide to age, although old fabrics are being used in some new quilts.

Libraries are filled with books about quilts and quilt values. Quilts are considered "folk art" and sell quickly. There will be quilts of all qualities at almost every antiques show. We went to a tailgate show in Indiana one weekend, and a single dealer had 150 quilts hanging on a fence.

The supply seems endless, but there is a real shortage of top-quality pieces. They sell well everywhere, but sell for the most money at the trendy New York shops. If you find twenty quilts made over eighty years ago by a very talented relative, it might pay to take them to New York.

COVERLETS AND HOMESPUN

Early fabrics were often completely handmade, from the growing of the cotton or flax to the cleaning, clipping, spinning, dyeing, and weaving of the finished thread. Homespun cloth was usually made in subdued shades of blue, green, brown, or red. Checked or striped patterns gained in favor and price during the 1980s when the faded, country look was "in." Modern copies of the fabrics are being made, but collectors will always pay a premium for the real thing. Prices are standard and are easy to determine from a careful look at an antiques show. If your homespun is of similar size and condition, it should sell to a dealer for about half the retail price asked at a show.

Woven coverlets are more complicated to price because the condition, design, and maker's signature are equally important. Many coverlets have a name and date woven into the corner. These names can be checked in *Checklist of American Coverlet Weavers* by the Colonial Williamsburg Foundation, published in 1980. Coverlets by some weavers and coverlets with special borders, such as a train, boat, or building design, are popular and expensive. Check in the price books and at the shows to learn more about their value; books list coverlets by maker or pattern. Coverlets sell well at shows, online, and auctions or to private collectors.

PRINTED TEXTILES

Antique printed textiles sell to a small group of collectors. An old textile, such as a piece of drape, bedspread, or valance that is over one hundred years old, is sometimes valuable because the print is historically interesting. Scenes of the death of Washington, fabrics used in political campaigns, World's Fair mementos, or important, early, roller-printed fabrics are high-priced. They sell best in pieces that can be framed and hung as pictures or used to make pillows. The entire repeat of the pattern should be included.

Some newer fabrics are in demand for use as upholstery materials for curtains or pillows. Art Deco and Art Nouveau designs, bark cloth and free-form patterns of the 1950s, or bright Hawaiian Deco prints sell to the right person. The fabrics probably have a lower value if there is not sufficient yardage for at least one chair. These fabrics sell best on the Internet or at specialized antiques shops.

Some collectors want historical handkerchiefs to frame for pictures. A good fabric "picture" is worth hundreds of dollars. Look in the library for books that picture old roller-printed fabrics. Many modern reproductions have been made, but if you are selling fabric found in an old attic trunk, you probably know if it is old or new. The dealer buying it will certainly know. Just remember, don't throw away any fabrics before you try to sell them.

LACE

There are probably fewer experts on old lace than in almost any field of collecting. Pieces of very old lace, such as collars, cuffs, or bits of trim, sell for thousands of dollars in Europe, where lace has been recognized and appreciated. Few collectors or dealers in the United States are interested in lace of that quality. Only the museums seem to be knowledgeable.

If you have a box of your mother's old lace, chances are it is not over fifty years old and is of value only in the places where vintage clothing is bought and sold. If your mother made lace, or came from Europe and possibly saved the lace from her own or her grandmother's wedding dress, you might have some valuable pieces. Take the lace to be appraised by an auction gallery, if possible. Ask the gallery's experts if they sell much lace and what prices they seem to get. If they can't identify old lace, ask for the expert at your local museum. The museum won't give a price, but an expert can tell you if your lace is old, handmade, and rare.

Large lace pieces might sell for good prices to the vintage clothing shops that sell elaborate, redesigned lace blouses or wedding dresses. If you have lace that a museum identifies as made before 1750, contact a major auction gallery.

We have tried to understand lace for years. We are able to tell handmade from machine-made and good from bad, but we still are not able to distinguish great from good. It takes an expert with experience. Pricing is even more difficult, so if you have any suspicion that your lace treasures are old and handmade, take them to an expert dealer, appraiser, museum curator, or auction gallery for an opinion.

ARTS AND CRAFTS EMBROIDERY

The interest in bungalows and the Arts and Crafts furnishings of the early 1900s has also created a demand for the embroidered tablecloths and bed linens of the period. The coarse fabric and large embroidered designs are easy to recognize and to sell.

REPAIR

Textiles include everything from rugs, coverlets, and quilts to lace and needlework. Care is especially important for all of these, as they are perishable. The greatest harm to a fabric can come from strong sunlight and dirt.

A small piece of fabric can be successfully displayed if it is washed and stitched to unbleached muslin with unbleached pure cotton thread. It should be mounted on acid-free backing and framed under glass. Never hang it in full sunlight. Information about textiles may be found at some museums with vintage costume collections.

It is often safer to wash or clean a quilt than to store it as found. Proper washing and hanging are important if you plan to display the quilt on a wall. Be sure that the quilt is hung from a rod held by a tunnel of cloth that supports the entire weight of the quilt and does not cause tears. The Abby Aldrich Rockefeller Folk Art Center, PO Box 1776, Williamsburg, VA 23187, identifies quilts and sells books about their care and display.

It is possible to do an almost undetectable restoration on a quilt if you can find the proper fabric. If you have some minor damage on a quilt, you might check on the cost and quality of repairs before you sell. The usual rule for antiques is never to repair before you sell, but if the quilt is to be sold at auction, it will probably pay to have it in usable condition.

Many modern quilt makers will repair old quilts. Some even have supplies of old fabrics. Sources of the many types of supplies needed are listed in the book *Considerations for the Care of Textiles and Costumes* by Harold Maitland (Indianapolis: Indianapolis Museum of Art, 1980). If not in your local library, it should be available through interlibrary loan.

Rugs can also be hung. The same method of display is used for rugs and quilts. Stitch support pieces of undyed, unbleached fabric to the back of the piece, add a "tunnel" of fabric, then slide a rod through the tunnel.

Lace should be laundered, stretched, repaired, and either used or framed. Stores that sell old clothing may be able to help with repairs.

Cleaning a rug or quilt requires care and the proper supplies. Use Orvus WA Paste (found at stores that have supplies for horses and farm animals) or Woolite. Always test the colors first to be sure that they will not run. Rinse thoroughly, dry, and either use or store on rolls. This is not too difficult a project for the careful amateur, but be sure to follow directions.

Most rug dealers also clean and repair rugs, so you may be able to find a local expert by checking the Yellow Pages of your local telephone book.

→ SEE ALSO FOLK ART

REFERENCE BOOKS

American Coverlets and Their Weavers: Coverlets from the Collection of Foster and Muriel McCarl, Clarita S. Anderson (Colonial Williamsburg Foundation, Williamsburg, VA, 2002).

Checklist of American Coverlet Weavers (Colonial Williamsburg Foundation, Abby Aldrich Rockefeller Folk Art Center, Williamsburg, VA, 1978).

Legacy of Lace: Identifying, Collecting, and Preserving American Lace, Kathleen Warnick and Shirley Nilsson (Crown, New York, 1988).

Needlework Tools and Accessories, Molly G. Proctor (B.T. Batsford, London; distributed by Trafalgar Square, North Pomfret, VT, 1990).

The Quilt I.D. Book, Judy Rehmel (Prentice Hall, New York, 1986).

Red & White: American Redwork Quilts, by Deborah Harding (Rizzoli, New York, 2000).

The Secrets of Real Lace, Elizabeth M. Kurella (The Lace Merchant, PO Box 222, Plainwell, MI 49080; 1994).

Threads of History: Americana Recorded on Cloth, 1775 to the Present, Herbert Ridgeway Collins (Smithsonian Institution, Washington, DC, 1979). (Fabrics related to historical events, including political bandannas, and printed textiles.)

PRICE BOOKS

Antique & Collectible Buttons, Volume 2, Debra J. Wisniewski (Collector Books, Paducah, KY, 2002).

Beacon Blankets Make Warm Friends, Jerry and Kathy Brownstein (Schiffer, Atglen, PA, 2001).

A Century of American Sewing Patterns: 1860–1959, Lori Hughes (C&B Press, PO Box 5595, Concord, CA 94524, 1998).

Chenille: A Collector's Guide, Judith Ann Greason and Tina Skinner (Schiffer, Atglen, PA, 2002).

The Collectible 70s: A Price Guide to the Polyester Decade, Michael Jay Goldberg (Krause, Iola, WI, 2001).

Collecting Household Linens and *Collecting More Household Linens,* Frances Johnson (Schiffer, Atglen, PA, 1997).

The Complete Guide to Vintage Textiles, Elizabeth Kurella (Schiffer, Atglen, PA, 1999).

Official Price Guide to Vintage Fashion and Fabrics, Pamela Smith (House of Collectibles, NY, 2001).

Sewing Tools & Trinkets, 2 volumes, Helen Lester Thompson (Collector Books, Paducah, KY, 1997, 2002).

The Story of Antique Needlework Tools, Bridget McConnel (Schiffer, Atglen, PA, 1999).

The Story of the Thimble: An Illustrated Guide for Collectors, Bridget McConnel (Schiffer, Atglen, PA, 1997).

Terrific Tablecloths from the '40s & '50s, Loretta Smith Fehling (Schiffer, Atglen, PA, 1998).

Treasure or Not? How To Compare and Value American Quilts, Stella Rubin (Octopus Publishing Group, London, England, 2001).

Vintage Quilts: Identifying, Collecting, Dating, Preserving & Valuing, Bobbie Aug, Sharon Newman, and Gerald Roy (Collector Books, Paducah, KY, 2002).

Vintage White Linens: A to Z, Marsha Manchester (Schiffer, Atglen, PA, 1997).

CLUBS & THEIR PUBLICATIONS

Colonial Coverlet Guild of America, *CCGA News* (NL), 5617 Blackstone, LaGrange, IL 60525, e-mail: lifsr8@cs.com.

International Sewing Machine Collectors Society, *ISMACS News* (MAG),

5701 S. 112th St., Lincoln, NE 68526, e-mail: USRep@ismacs.net, website: www.ismacs.net.

Stevengraph Collectors' Association, *Stevengraph Collectors' Association Quarterly Newsletter* (NL), 29 War Bonnet Rd., Canaan, NH 03741, e-mail: stevengraph@yahoo.com.

Thimble Collectors International, *TCI Bulletin* (NL), 3230 E. Upper Hayden Lake Rd., Hayden, ID 83835, e-mail: thimbletree@aol.com, website: www.thimblecollectors.com.

OTHER PUBLICATIONS

Hali (MAG), Hali Publications Ltd., St. Giles House, 50 Poland St., London W1F 7NF, UK, e-mail: hali@centaur.co.uk, website: www.hali.com (carpets, textiles, and Islamic art).

Thimble Guild (NL), PO Box 381807, Duncanville, TX 75138-1807, e-mail: thimble_guild@msn.com.

Vintage Gazette (NL), 194 Amity St., Amherst, MA 01002, e-mail: merrylees@aol.com.

ARCHIVES & MUSEUMS

American Textile History Museum, 491 Dutton St., Lowell, MA 01854-4221, 978-441-0400, fax: 978-441-1412, website: www.athm.org.

The Fabric Workshop and Museum, 1315 Cherry St., 5th Floor, Philadelphia, PA 19107, 215-568-1111, fax: 215-568-8211, website: www.fabricworkshop museum.org.

The Lace Museum, 552 S. Murphy Ave., Sunnyvale, CA 94086, 408-730-4695, website: www.thelacemuseum.org.

Museum of the American Quilter's Society, 215 Jefferson St., Paducah, KY 42001, 270-442-8856, fax: 270-442-5448, website: www.quilt museum.org.

San Jose Museum of Quilts and Textiles, 110 Paseo de San Antonio, San Jose, CA 95112-3639, 408-971-0323, fax: 408-971-7226, website: www.sjquiltmuseum.org.

Textile Museum, 2320 S St. NW, Washington, DC 20008-4008, e-mail: info@textilemuseum.org, website: www.textilemuseum.org.

APPRAISERS

Many of the repair services listed in this section will also do appraisals. *See also* the general list of Appraisal Groups, page 483.

Koch & Associates Appraisals, 2306 Main St., Newberry, SC 29108, phone: 1-877-488-4730, website: kochappraisal.hypermart.net. Online and on-site appraisal services in central South Carolina. Specialist in eighteenth-century accessories, clothing, and textiles.

REPAIRS, PARTS & SUPPLIES

↦ SEE ALSO "CONSERVATORS & RESTORERS," PAGE 520.

American Textile History Museum, 491 Dutton St., Lowell, MA 01854-4221, 978-441-1198, fax: 978-441-1412, website: www.athm.org. The Textile Conservation Center (TCC), a nonprofit regional conservation center, is a department of the American Textile History Museum. Conservation services include cleaning, stabilization, display systems, and documentation. On-site examination and treatment of textiles too fragile or too large to travel is available. Lectures, workshops, and consultations. Free brochure. Call or write for additional information before sending textiles.

Boston Art Conservation, 9 Station St., Brookline, MA 02146, 617-738-1126, 9:00 A.M.–5:00 P.M., e-mail: admin@bosartconserv.com, website: bosartconserv.com. Conservation of textiles and other objects. Collection surveys. Consultations on proper storage and display. Free brochure.

Cherish, PO Box 941, New York, NY 10024-0941, 212-724-1748, fax: 212-724-1748 call first, e-mail: smarx@I2000.com. Organizing and fitting closets or cabinets to house collections, using only inert materials to create a safe storage environment. Designs and all materials are available. Acid-free boxes, tissues, padded hangers, Orvus paste, and more. Free brochure.

Chicago Conservation Center, 730 N. Franklin, Suite 701, Chicago, IL 60610, 312-944-5401, fax: 312-944-5479, e-mail: chicagoconservation @yahoo.com, website: chicagoconservation.com. Restoration of textiles.

Evelyn of Sewtique, 391 Long Hill Rd., PO Box 1293, Groton, CT 06340-1293, 800-332-9122 or 860-464-2001, fax: 860-445-1448, e-mail: Sewtique @aol.com, website: members.aol.com/sewtique/home.htm. Cleans, repairs, restores, and preserves laces, linens, fur, leather, quilts, tapestries, and wedding and special-event apparel. Removes spots and stains from contemporary and vintage textiles and costumes. Written appraisals for textiles and apparel; expert witness. Free brochure.

G.M. Wylie Co., PO Box AA, Washington, PA 15301-0660, 800-747-1249, fax: 724-225-0741, e-mail: info@gmwylie.com, website: gmwylie.com. Safe long-term storage supplies for textiles and other collectibles. Textile storage boxes, wrapping paper, and much more. Order by mail, phone, or e-mail. Catalog $1.50 or visit the website.

Hollinger Corporation, PO Box 8360, Fredericksburg, VA 22404, 800-634-0491, 8:30 A.M.–5:00 P.M. e-mail: hollingercorp@erols.com, website: www.hollingercorp.com. Archival storage materials, boxes, tubes, acid-free papers, and other products to store textiles and other collectibles. Free catalog.

The Laundry at Linens Limited, Inc., 240 N. Milwaukee St., Milwaukee,

WI 53202, 800-637-6334 or 414-223-1123, fax: 414-223-1126, e-mail: linenslimited@msn.com, website: www.thelaundryat.com. European hand laundry service, specializing in cleaning fine and antique linens: bed linens, table linens, and heirloom pieces such as baptismal gowns and wedding dresses. Nationwide service. Free brochure.

Mini-Magic, 3910 Patricia Dr., Columbus, OH 43220, 614-457-3687, toll-free order number 888-391-0691, fax: 614-459-2306, e-mail: minimagic @mini-magic.com, website: www.mini-magic.com. Fabrics and trim for doll clothes, sewing, and craft projects. French fashion patterns and kits. Doll stands, washing paste, acid-free boxes and tissue, muslin, buckles, buttons, hat supplies, and more.

Poor Richard's Restoration & Preservation Studio Workshop, 101 Walnut St., Montclair, NJ 07042, 973-783-5333, fax: 973-744-1939, e-mail: jrickford@webtv.com, website: www.rickford.com. Restoration, conservation, archival, and preservation services for textiles and other objects. Restoration of family memorabilia and keepsakes. By appointment, Tues.–Fri. noon–5:00 P.M., Sat. noon–3:00 P.M.

Rocky Mountain Quilts, 130 York St., York Village, ME 03909, 800-762-5940 or 207-363-6800, fax: 207-351-3381, e-mail: rockymtnquilts @cybertours.com, website: rockymountainquilts.com. Textile washing and restoration, using same date or older fabrics. Work guaranteed. Antique fabrics for sale.

Sharon's Antiques Vintage Fabrics, e-mail: sharon@rickrack.com, website: www.rickrack.com. Vintage and antique fabrics supplied for quilt and textile restoration.

Stephen & Carol Huber Inc., 40 Ferry Rd., Old Saybrook, CT 06475, 860-388-6809, fax: 860-434-9809, e-mail: hubers@antiquesamplers.com, website: www.antiquesamplers.com. Conservation, repair, and appraisals of samplers.

Stillwater Textile Conservation Studio, 603-938-2310, fax: 603-938-2455, e-mail: stillwaterstudio@conknet.com, website: www.stillwater studio.org. Textile conservation. Consultation, storage design and planning, custom dyeing of fabric and yarns, and framing.

Textile Conservation Workshop, 3 Main St., South Salem, NY 10590, 914-763-5805, e-mail: textile@bestweb.net, website: www.rap-arcc.org/ welcome/tcwsite2.htm. Conservation and restoration of antique textiles. Condition surveys with recommendations for storage, exhibition, and treatment. Lectures, discussions, and information about new techniques. Informational handouts available on the website.

Tina Kane, 8 Big Island Rd., Warwick, NY 10990, 845-986-8522, e-mail: tinakane@pair.com, website: textileconservator.pair.com. Conservation and restoration of all flat textiles. Reproduction of upholstery panels, tapestry, and needlepoint.

Tinsel Trading Co., 47 W. 38th St., New York, NY 10018, 212-730-1030, e-mail: TinselTrading@juno.com, website: tinseltrading.com. Vintage flowers, buttons, tassels, ribbons, and metallic fabrics trims.

➻ **TINS, SEE ADVERTISING COLLECTIBLES**
➻ **TOKENS, SEE NUMISMATIC COLLECTIBLES**

TOOLS

Decorating magazines often show a few tools hung on the wall as sculptural decorations. Old tools can be sold to any friend or antiques dealer. There are also many serious tool collectors who specialize in one type of tool, such as wrenches or planes, or who have large general collections. Some collectors even buy the toolbox. If you have a toolbox filled with old hand tools, it would pay to try to find the dealers who specialize in tools or to contact the members of a tool-collecting club. Some auction houses have special tool sales a few times a year. If you have only one item, it is probably best to sell it locally. Many old-looking tools have minimal value, but some special tools are worth hundreds or even thousands of dollars.

Look for the name **STANLEY**. It adds to the value, and there are several specialized price books for Stanley tools. Also look for **KEEN KUTTER, WINCHESTER**, and stamped names and locations that were sometimes put on the early handmade tools by the makers. The most popular tools seem to be axes, planes, and rulers.

REPAIR

There is a disagreement among collectors about the desired condition of tools. Some clean and wax the wood and clean the metal. Others will not buy a tool that has been newly waxed or varnished. It won't hurt to remove the major dirt with a quick washing, but don't wax, scour, or use rust remover. Let the new owner make that decision. If you do it, you are taking a chance of losing a sale.

The restoration of tools requires the knowledge of a woodworker, a metalworker, and an expert on tools. Local shops dealing with tools may be able to help, but many antique tools are beyond the skill and knowledge of the modern toolworker.

Tools should be kept clean and in working condition. Metal parts should be rust-free and usually require oil or another preservative.

REFERENCE BOOKS

A Diderot Pictorial Encyclopedia of Trades and Industry, 2 volumes, Denis Diderot (Dover, New York, 1959).

Dictionary of Woodworking Tools: c.1700–1970, revised edition, R.A. Salaman (Astragal Press, Mendham, NJ, 1997).

PRICE BOOKS

The 2002 Stanley Tools Pocket Guide, John Walter, annual (The Tool Merchant, PO Box 227, Marietta, OH 45750, e-mail: toolmerchant @sprynet.com, website: www.thetoolmerchant.com, 2003).

Antique & Collectible Stanley Tools: Guide to Identity & Value, John Walter (The Tool Merchant, PO Box 227, Marietta, OH 45750, e-mail: tool merchant@sprynet.com, website: www.thetoolmerchant.com, 2003).

The Antique Tool Collector's Guide to Value, Ronald S. Barlow (L-W Book Sales, Gas City, IN, 1991, values 2002).

The Catalogue of Antique Tools, Martin J. Donnelly (Antique Tools, 31 Rumsey St., Bath, NY 14810, 1998).

Early 20th Century Stanley Tools, Jack P. Wood (L-W Book Sales, Gas City, IN, 2000, values 2002).

A Price Guide to Antique Tools, 3rd edition, Herbert P. Kean (Astragal Press, Mendham, NJ, 2001).

Town-Country Old Tools, Locks, Keys, Closures, 6th edition, Jack Wood (L-W Book Sales, Gas City, IN, 1997, values 2001).

Unauthorized Guide to Snap-on Collectibles, 1920–1998, Caroline M. Schloss (Schiffer, Atglen, PA, 1999).

CLUBS & THEIR PUBLICATIONS

American Precision Museum Association, Inc., *Tools & Technology* (MAG), PO Box 679, Windsor, VT 05089, e-mail: apm@sover.net, website: www.americanprecision.org.

American Printing History Association, *APHA Newsletter* (NL), PO Box 4922, Grand Central Station, New York, NY 10163-4922, website: www.printinghistory.org.

Antique & Collectible Tools, Inc., *Fine Tool Journal* (NL), 27 Fickett Rd., Pownal, ME 04069, e-mail: CEB@FineToolJ.com, website: www.Fine ToolJ.com.

Blow Torch Collectors Association, *The Torch* (NL), 3328 258th Ave. SE, Issaquah, WA 98029, e-mail: roncarr@prodigy.net, website: communities.msn.com/BlowTorchCollectorsAssociation.

Collectors of Rare and Familiar Tools Society (CRAFTS), *Tool Shed* (NL), 38 Colony Ct., Murray Hill, NJ 07974, e-mail: jmwhelwdpl@aol.com, website: www.craftsofnj.org.

Early American Industries Association, Inc., *Chronicle* (MAG), 167 Bakerville Rd., South Dartmouth, MA 02748, website: www.eaiainfo.org.

The Hardware Companies Kollectors Klub, *The Winchester, Keen Kutter, Diamond Edge Chronicles* (NL), 432 S. Gore Ave., St. Louis, MO 63119, e-mail: duhn@earthlink.net, website: www.thckk.org.

Mid-West Tool Collectors Association, *Gristmill* (MAG), PO Box 8016, Berkeley, CA 94707-8016, website: www.mwtca.org.

Ohio Tool Collectors Association, *Ohio Tool Box* (NL), PO Box 261, London, OH 43140-0261.

The Old Lawnmower Club, *Grassbox* (NL), Membership Secretary, Milton Keynes Museum, McConnell Dr., Wolverton, Milton Keynes MK12 5EL, UK, e-mail: olc@artizan.demon.co.uk, website: www.artizan.demon. co.uk/olc.

Tool Group of Canada, *Yesterday's Tools* (NL), 15 Chudleigh Ave., Toronto, ON M4R 1T1, Canada, e-mail: gt_wright@yahoo.com, website: www.thetoolgroupofcanada.com.

OTHER PUBLICATIONS

Tool Ads (NP), Box 1795, Hamilton, MT 59840, e-mail: airgunads@bitterroot.net.

USEFUL SITES

Museum of Woodworking Tools, www.antiquetools.com.

AUCTIONS

➥ **SEE ALSO "SELLING THROUGH AUCTION HOUSES," PAGE 485.**

Tool Shop Auctions, Tony Murland, 78 High St., Needham Market, Suffolk IP6 8AW, UK, 011-44-1449-272992, fax: 011-44-1449-722683, e-mail: tony@antiquetools.co.uk, website: www.antiquetools.co.uk. Specializes in auctions of antique hand tools. Mail, phone, and Internet bids accepted. Buyer's premium 11.75%. Catalog $10 general sale, $35 international; yearly subscription $65. Prices realized mailed to subscribers and available on website. Appraisals.

REPAIRS, PARTS & SUPPLIES

➥ **SEE ALSO "CONSERVATORS & RESTORERS," PAGE 520.**

Artisans of the Valley, 103 Corrine Dr., Pennington, NJ 08534, 609-637-0450, fax: 609-637-0452, e-mail: woodworkers@artisansofthe valley.com, website: www.artisansofthevalley.com. Restoration on antique tools, farm equipment, military equipment, etc. Consultation services to architects, contractors, and curators. Free catalog.

TOYS

Don't discard any old toys. Even a Barbie doll's girdle has value to a collector. The best-selling toys are antique dolls, teddy bears, nineteenth-century iron toys, banks, robot and space toys, pedal cars, battery-operated toys, and scale-model autos and trains. Games, game boards, celebrity items, and farm toys are good sellers. Any toy that is out of production and mint-in-the-box has a resale value to collectors.

Any old toy in good condition has value. Most badly worn toys are of little value except for use as parts for repairs.

Toy and doll shows are the best places to sell old toys. Dealers at these special shows have serious collectors for customers, so they can sell for the highest prices and can usually afford to pay the highest prices. General antiques dealers buy many types of toys. Look around in the shops and offer your toys to the dealer with toys like yours.

It may be embarrassing to think that your childhood toys are collectible, but age is not the only factor determining value. The most desirable robots and space toys from the 1960s sell for hundreds of dollars. Big isn't necessarily better. Size doesn't determine the value. Lead and even plastic soldiers sell well if they are rare and in good condition. Look for the name **BRITAINS**.

TRAINS

Special train collector shows in many cities provide the best place to sell an old train and its accessories. Even the houses, lampposts, trees, and figures made for elaborate train landscapes are selling well. Names that add value to trains and accessories include **LIONEL, AMERICAN FLYER, CARLISLE AND FINCH, DORFAN, REVELL INC., MECCANO**, and **PLASTICVILLE**.

CARS

All sorts of small and large automotive toys are wanted, from miniatures to pedal cars large enough for a child to ride. Look for the names **BUDDY L, TOOTSIETOY, DINKY TOY, CORGI, HUBLEY, GREY, KENTON, MANOIL**, and **ARCADE**.

MANUFACTURERS OF IMPORTANCE

Some very well-known toy-makers produced a great variety of toys for many years: wooden, iron, battery-operated, tin, slush-cast models, and windups. Collectors recognize the most famous of these companies and sometimes specialize in their products. This means there is added value to early toys marked **MARX**, **BING**, **CHEIN**, **FISHER-PRICE**, **IVES**, **LINEOL**, **LEHMANN**, **MARKLIN**, **SCHUCO**, **STRAUSS**, and **STEPHENS AND BROWN**.

BANKS

Bank collectors search for old mechanical banks and iron still (nonmechanical) banks. The highest price paid for a mechanical bank is $426,000 for "The Old Woman in the Shoe." A mechanical bank usually moves when a lever is pressed. Many of these have been reproduced and some reproductions have the words "Book of Knowledge" on the bottom. Other reproductions are unmarked. Even the reproduction can be sold, but for a low price. There are books that tell which banks have been made recently, how to tell a fake by checking the bottom marking, and other clues.

If there are indications that your bank has been altered on the bottom, it is probably a recent copy. "Recent" means after 1930. The "age of mechanical banks" was from the late 1890s to World War I. Some mechanical banks have sold for hundreds to thousands of dollars since the 1970s, so collectors have now started to buy iron still banks. Several specialized price books picture and price hundreds of these banks. Repainted banks are worth much less than examples with old, worn paint. New paint might hide identification marks of a recent copy.

TEDDY BEARS

Condition is important when selling old toys, games, or dolls, but collectors do not seem to mind how worn-out a teddy bear may be. The only toy that can be tattered and torn and still worth big money is a teddy bear over fifty years old. Collectors seem to think it proves the bear was "loved." Poor condition lowers value a little, but not as much as it does for any other type of antique. We have seen teddy bears with no eyes, worn "fur," and arms missing or hanging sell at auction to a dealer for over $300.

The first teddy bear was made in 1902. Early teddy bears often have longer noses than the new ones. Some have added features like electrically lit eyes or internal music boxes. There seems to be no explanation for the teddy bear mania of today. Any bear made before 1950 is worth over $100. Some are worth thousands.

There has been so much interest in teddy bears that there are clubs, calendars, contests, newspapers, magazines, and books on the subject. If you have an old bear, everyone will want to buy it. Try to find a trusted collector friend or a qualified appraiser who will know if you own one worth a fortune or just a nice bear. Look for the name STEIFF (and a tag in the ear), for long noses, and for unfamiliar types of fur. Other stuffed toys are collected but nothing compares to the value of teddy bears.

GAMES

Games have a special appeal for collectors. If you are lucky enough to have an early baseball board game, it may be of more value to a baseball memorabilia collector than to a game collector. The Lindbergh games based on his airplane flight, the games with ads for products like Coca-Cola, and the celebrity or TV-related games like Star Trek sell for more money to the specialist than to the game collector. If **LITTLE ORPHAN ANNIE, JACK ARMSTRONG, CHARLIE CHAPLIN, HOPALONG CASSIDY,** or **DISNEY** characters are on the game or box, you have a high-priced item.

Collectors divide games into types. "Name games" are those that are collected for their association with well-known events, people, places, or collecting areas. The theme of the game is important. Remember, the collector is not buying the game to play it but rather to display it. The graphics of the board, the box, and the shape of the playing pieces add to the value. Look for anything that includes pictures of airplanes, animals, automobiles, bicycles, blacks, cartoons, circus themes, fortune-tellers, motorcycles, movies, political themes, radios, Santa Claus, sports, the Statue of Liberty, TV, and war battles.

Game collectors also want what one expert calls "game games." These games are collected for their graphics, their parts, or their historic value. Unless early (pre-1910) or exceptionally decorated, "game games" do not sell as well as "name games." The companies that made these games are important. Those marked **MILTON BRADLEY, MCLOUGHLIN BROTHERS, IVES, PARKER BROTHERS, SELCHOW & RIGHTER, BLISS, E.I. HORSMAN, CLARK & SOWDON,** and **WEST & LEE** are popular and usually high priced.

The first board game, "Mansion of Happiness," was manufactured in 1843 by W. & S. B. Ives. Other "Mansion of Happiness" games were made by Parker Brothers in 1894 and by McLoughlin in 1895, but they are not as valuable as the Ives example. A rare game may not be more valuable, because collectors prefer games by well-known companies.

Games were bought for children. They were usually loved, used, abused, and eventually damaged. Condition is important. A pristine game is always more valuable. A large piece torn from the graphics on the front of a box can lower the value by 30 percent. Metal games are worth more than lithographed paper and wooden games, with the exception of the very rare and very early examples. Wood is worth more than cardboard. A few games have playing pieces made of metal, Bakelite or other plastics, ceramics, or even ivory. Pewter pieces are worth more than wooden pieces. Modern plastic is of no extra value.

Sometimes the playing pieces are of special interest because they are small toys or marbles that have a resale value even when separated from the game board. Unusual spinners, ivory dice, play money, and uncommon designs on the playing cards add value. Unusual playing cards over fifty years old have special buyers and clubs.

All these are just hints. The market for games is ruled strictly by supply and demand. A collector eager for everything ever made about the Dionne quintuplets will pay a premium for the right game picturing the babies. You must price your games with this intangible in mind. It is often not the age or beauty alone that determines the price of a game. In the late 1970s, the country-look decorating magazines began to show rooms with checkerboards and backgammon boards hung like rare paintings. Today, no old wooden game board is too shabby or too crude to demand a high price as "folk art." Don't discard any type of game board; it will sell.

SLEDS

Another toy that has found favor as folk art is the wooden sled. The best example we have seen brought over $30,000 at auction. Most ordinary sleds sell for under $100. It pays to check the market. Old sleds should have hand-wrought iron runners and painted wooden bodies. A date as part of the decoration is a plus. Other toys

IS BIG BETTER FOR ELECTRIC MODEL TRAINS?

The most popular are the O gauge (1¼ inches between the rails). Others are Standard Gauge (twice as wide as O gauge), HO gauge (half as wide as O gauge), OO gauge (about ⅜ inches between the rails), and S gauge (⅞ inches between the rails). N and Z gauge trains (about ⅜ inch and ¼ inch between the rails, respectively) are gaining in popularity.

that have gained in value from the "folk art" tag are decorated drums, whirligigs, painted wooden toys, rag dolls (especially black and Amish examples), and doll quilts.

AND MORE

There are specialists who want almost every type of toy or game. Try to find the right dealers, collectors, and clubs. Marbles, sports-related toys, celebrity toys, puzzles, magic tricks, cars, military toys, farm toys, wooden pull toys, even toys in special shapes, like dogs, cats, or particular breeds, are bought by these specialists.

Windups, tin toys, character toys, and trains are popular Internet collectibles. If you have action figures in your attic (even those less than five years old), search for the manufacturer's name, like **KENNER** or **GALOOB**. There are sites devoted to one kind of toy, and sites devoted to toys in general. Internet antiques malls always have toy dealers. Online auctions (see Part III for a list) offer free ads to sellers.

It is difficult to discuss toy sales, because absolutely every toy older than five years is wanted by someone. Sometimes there is a quick interest in new toys like Cabbage Patch dolls, Hot Wheels, or Beanie Babies. Even early computer-type games are collected (they have to work). Tin windup toys are wanted, but prices are 75 to 90 percent lower if they have a broken spring. If you have boxes of toys in the attic, be sure to check carefully on their possible value before you sell.

REPAIR

It is not advisable for the amateur to make many types of repairs on toys. Remember, too, that many toys have been reproduced. Be sure you understand the differences between old and new toys before you spend money on repairs. Libraries are filled with books on this subject. If you want a cast-iron bank that looks like a new one, buy a reproduction, but don't paint an old one.

Never repaint or restore a metal toy if there is any way to avoid it. Don't repaint, restore, or redress an old toy before you sell it. You could destroy all the value for a collector. If an iron or tin toy is repainted, deduct 75 percent. If a small piece is missing, such as a driver of a wagon, the wheel of a car, or an arm from a figure in the Dogpatch band, deduct only 20 percent. These missing pieces can be found. It is now possible to find reproduced parts for old toys, especially cars and trucks. Decals, wheels, and other parts are available. An old toy that is missing its paint is usually worth more than a toy from the same period that has been repainted. The exception to this rule seems to be pedal cars. Collectors of these, just like collectors of full-size cars, seem to prefer a "new" look. A fine restoration will add to the value.

The working parts of old toys are difficult to replace unless you are mechanically inclined. Key-wind mechanisms and power sources for trains are complicated and must often be replaced.

The battery-driven mechanical toys of the 1950s that featured a cigarette-smoking bartender or monkey can be made to smoke again if you add a drop of oil.

➜ SEE ALSO DOLLHOUSES, DOLLS, MOVIE MEMORABILIA, MUSICAL INSTRUMENTS

➜ FOR BICYCLES, SEE TRANSPORTATION

REFERENCE BOOKS

A sampling of toy and doll reference books is below. Ask your librarian for other books. Schiffer Publishing, Atglen, PA, has a series on miniature cars, such as Corgi, Dinky, Lledo, Matchbox, etc. Hobby House, Cumberland, MD, and Theriault's Gold Horse Publishing, Annapolis, MD, have many books on dolls; and Kalmbach Publishing, Waukesha, WI, publishes books on toy train companies in its Greenberg series.

The Art of the Tin Toy, David Pressland (Crown, New York, 1976).

The Golden Age of Toys, Remise and Jean Fondin (New York Graphic Society, Boston, MA, 1967).

Greenberg's Guide to Lionel Trains, 8 volumes, Bruce Greenberg (Kalmbach, Waukesha, WI, 1985–1994).

PRICE BOOKS

A World of Bus Toys & Models, Kurt M. Resch (Schiffer, Atglen, PA, 1999).

Action Figures of the 1960s and *Action Figures of the 1980s,* John Marshall (Schiffer, Atglen, PA, 1998).

America's Standard Gauge Electric Trains, Peter H. Riddle (Antique Trader Books, Norfolk, Va, 1998).

American Games: Comprehensive Collector's Guide, Alex G. Malloy (Krause, Iola, WI, 2000).

Battery Toys: The Modern Automata, 2nd edition, Brian Moran (Schiffer, Atlgen, PA, 1999).

The Bean Family Pocket Guide 1999, Shawn Brecka (Antique Trader Books, Dubuque, IA, 1998).

The Beanie Family Album and Collector's Guide, Shawn Brecka (Antique Trader Books, Dubuque, IA, 1998).

The Big Bear Book, Dee Hockenberry (Schiffer, Atglen, PA, 2000).

Big Book of Little Bears, Shawn Brecka (Krause, Iola, WI, 2000).

Care Bears Collectibles, Jan Lindenberger (Schiffer, Atglen, PA, 1997).

Cast Iron Automotive Toys, Myra Yellin Outwater, Eric B. Outwater, and Stevie and Bill Weart (Schiffer, Atglen, PA, 2000).

Characters of R. John Wright, Shirley Bertrand (Hobby House Press, Grantsville, MD, 2000).

Cherished Teddies, 3rd edition, Jeff Mahony, editor (CheckerBee, Middletown, CT, 1999).

Coin Banks by Banthrico, James L. Redwine (Schiffer, Atglen, PA, 2001).

The Collectible GI Joe by Derryl DePriest (Running Press, Philadelphia, 1999).

Collecting American-Made Toy Soldiers, 3rd edition, Richard O'Brien (Krause, Iola, WI, 1997).

Collecting Antique Marbles, 3rd edition, Paul Baumann (Krause, Iola, WI, 1999).

Collecting Dinky Toys, Mike Richardson (Francis Joseph, London, England, 2001).

Collecting Foreign-Made Toy Soldiers: Identification and Value Guide, Richard O'Brien (Krause, Iola, WI, 1997).

Collecting Monster Toys, John Marshall (Schiffer, Atglen, PA, 1999).

Collecting Pokémon, Jeffrey B. Snyder (Schiffer, Atglen, PA, 2000).

Collecting Star Wars Toys, 1977–Present, 2nd edition, Jeffrey B. Snyder (Schiffer, Atglen, PA, 1999).

Collecting Toy Premiums: Bread, Cereal, Radio, James L. Dundas (Schiffer, Atglen, PA, 2001).

Collecting Yo-Yos, James L. Dundas (Schiffer, Atglen, PA, 2000).

Collector Steiff Values, 2nd edition, Peter Consalvi Sr. (Hobby House Press, Grantsville, MD, 2000).

Collector's Digest Price Guide to Pull Toys (L-W Book Sales, Gas City, IN, 1996).

Collector's Guide to Banks: Pottery, Porcelain, Composition, Jim and Beverly Mangus (Collector Books, Paducah, KY, 1998).

Collector's Guide to Battery Toys, 2nd edition, Don Hultzman (Collector Books, Paducah, KY, 2002).

Collector's Guide to Glass Banks, Charles V. Reynolds (Collector Books, Paducah, KY, 2001).

Collector's Guide to My Merry, Fred Diehl (Hobby House Press, Grantsville, MD, 2001).

Collector's Guide to Tootsietoys, 2nd edition, David E. Richter (Collector Books, Paducah, KY, 1996).

Collector's Guide to TV Toys and Memorabilia, 1960s and 1970s, 2nd edition, Greg Davis and Bill Morgan (Collector Books, Paducah, KY, 1999).

Collector's Value Guide: Boyds Bears & Friends, 4th edition, Jeff Mahony, editor (CheckerBee Publishing, Middletown, CT, 1999).

Collector's Value Guide: Boyds Plush Animals, 4th edition, Jeff Mahony, editor (CheckerBee Publishing, Middletown, CT, 1999).

Collector's Value Guide: Ty Beanie Babies, 6th edition, Jeff Mahony, editor (CheckerBee Publishing, Middletown, CT, 1999).

Comic Book Hero Toys, John Marshall (Schiffer, Atglen, PA, 1999).

The Complete Encyclopedia to GI Joe, 3rd edition, Vincent Santelmo (Krause, Iola, WI, 2001).

Composition & Wood Dolls and Toys: A Collector's Reference Guide, Michele Karl (Antique Trader Books, Dubuque, IA, 1998).

Corgi Toys, 3rd edition, Edward Force, revised by Bill Manzke (Schiffer, Atglen, PA, 1997, values 2000).

Cracker Jack Toys: The Complete, Unofficial Guide for Collectors, Larry White (Schiffer, Atglen, PA, 1997).

Cribbage Boards, 1863–1998, Bette L. Bemis (Schiffer, Atglen, PA, 2000).

Dinky Toys, 4th edition, Edward Force (Schiffer, Atglen, PA, 1999).

The Encyclopedia of Marx Action Figures, Tom Heaton (Krause, Iola, WI, 1999).

The Encyclopedia of Matchbox Toys, 2nd edition, Charlie Mack (Schiffer, Atglen, PA, 1999).

Evolution of the Pedal Car, Volumes 4 and 5, Neil S. Wood, editor (L-W Book Sales, Gas City, IN, 1999, 2000).

Fast Food Toys, 3rd edition, Gail Pope and Keith Hammond (Schiffer, Atglen, PA, 1999).

Fisher-Price Toys: A Pictorial Price Guide to the More Popular Toys, Brad Cassity (Collector Books, Paducah, KY, 2000).

Fisher-Price: Historical, Rarity, and Value Guide, 1931–Present, 3rd edition, Bruce R. Fox and John J. Murray (Krause, Iola, WI, 2002).

Flexible Flyer and Other Great Sleds for Collectors, Joan Palicia (Schiffer, Atglen, PA, 1997, values 2001).

Funny Face: An Amusing History or Potato Heads, Block Heads, and Magic Whiskers, Mark Rich and Jeff Potocsnak (Krause, Iola, WI, 2002).

GI Joe: Official Identification and Price Guide, 1964–1999, Vincent Santelmo (Krause, Iola, WI, 1999).

G-Men and FBI Toys and Collectibles, Harry and Jody Whitworth (Collector Books, Paducah, KY, 1998).

The Golden Age of Automotive Toys, 1925–1941: Identification & Value Guide, Ken Hutchison and Greg Johnson (Collector Books, Paducah, KY, 1997).

Greenberg's Guide: American Flyer 1946–2003 Pocket Price Guide (Kalmbach Publishing, Waukesha, WI, 2002).

Greenberg's Guide: Lionel Trains 1901–2003 Pocket Price Guide, Kent J. Johnson and Linda Wenzel, editors (Kalmbach Publishing, Waukesha, WI, 2002).

Greenberg's Guide to Aurora Model Kits, Thomas Graham (Kalmbach Publishing, Waukesha, WI, 1998).

Greenberg's Guide to Gilbert Erector Sets, 2 volumes, William M. Bean (Kalmbach Publishing, Waukesha, WI, 1993, 1998).

Greenberg's Pocket Price Guide: Marx Trains, 8th edition, Kent J. Johnson and Julie Lafountain, editors (Kalmbach Publishing, Waukesha, WI, 2002).

Hake's Price Guide to Character Toys, 4th edition, Ted Hake (Avon, New York, 2002).

Heuser's Quarterly Price Guide to Official Diecast Collectible Banks, Custom Imprinted Replicas and 1/18 Scale "American Muscle Cars" by Ertl, Richard L. Heuser (Heuser Publishing, PO Box 300, West Winfield, NY 13491, 2002).

Holiday Plastic Novelties: The Styrene Toys, Charlene Pinkerton (Schiffer, Atglen, PA, 1999).

Hot Wheels: The Ultimate Redline Guide, 1968–1977, Jack Clark and Robert P. Wicker (Collector Books, Paducah, KY, 2003).

Hubley Toy Vehicles, 1946–1965, Steve Butler (Schiffer, Atglen, PA, 2001).

J. Chein & Co.: A Collector's Guide to an American Toymaker, Alan Jaffe (Schiffer, Atglen, PA, 1997, values 2002).

Japanese Toys: Amusing Playthings from the Past, William C. Gallagher (Schiffer, Atglen, PA, 2000).

Kenton Toys: The Real Thing in Everything But Size, Charles M. Jacobs (Schiffer, Atglen, PA, 1996).

Lesley's Matchbox Toys: The Superfast Years, 1969–1982 and *Universal's Matchbox Toys: The Universal Years, 1982–1992*, 2nd edition, Charlie Mack (Schiffer, Atglen, PA, 1999).

Marbles Illustrated: Prices at Auction, Robert Block (Schiffer, Atglen, PA, 1999).

Marbles, 3rd edition, Robert Block (Schiffer, Atglen, PA, 1999).

Marionettes and String Puppets Collector's Reference Guide, Daniel E. Hodges (Antique Trader Books, Dubuque, IA, 1998).

Marx Toys Sampler: A History and Price Guide, Michelle L. Smith (Krause, Iola, WI, 2000).

Matchbox Toys: 1947 to 1998, 3rd edition, Dana Johnson (Collector Books, Paducah, KY, 1999).

Mego Action Figure Toys, 2nd edition, John Bonavita (Schiffer, Atglen, PA, 2000).

Miller's American Insider's Guide to Toys and Games, Tim Luke (London, England, 2002).

Miller's Teddy Bears: A Complete Collector's Guide, Sue Pearson (Octopus Publishing Group, London, England, 2001).

More Board Games, Desi Scarpone (Schiffer, Atglen, PA, 2000).

O'Brien's Collecting Toy Cars & Trucks, 3rd edition, Elizabeth A. Stephan, editor (Krause, Iola, WI, 2000).

O'Brien's Collecting Toy Trains, 5th edition, Elizabeth A. Stephan, editor (Krause, Iola, WI, 1999).

O'Brien's Collecting Toys, 10th edition, Elizabeth A. Stephan, editor (Krause, Iola, WI, 2001).

The Official Hake's Price Guide to Character Toys, 4th edition, Ted Hake (Gemstone, NY, 2002).

Official Price Guide to Action Figures, 2nd edition, Stuart W. Wells III and Jim Main (House of Collectibles, New York, 1999).

Ohio Art: The World of Toys, Lisa Kerr with Jim Gilcher (Schiffer, Atglen, PA, 1998).

Penny Banks around the World, Don Duer (Schiffer, Atglen, PA, 1997, values 2000).

Playtime Pottery & Porcelain from Europe and Asia, Lorraine Punchard (Schiffer, Atglen, PA, 1996).

The Penny Bank Book: Collecting Still Banks, revised edition, Andy and Susan Moore (Schiffer, Atglen, PA, 1997).

The Raggedy Ann & Andy Family Album, Susan Ann Garrison (Schiffer, Atglen, PA, 1989, prices 1998).

Renwal: World's Finest Toys, Charles F. Donovan Jr. (L-W Book Sales, Gas City, IN, 1999).

Sand Pail Encyclopedia, Karen Horman and Polly Minick (Hobby House Press, Grantsville, MD, 2002).

Schroeder's Collectible Toys: Antique to Modern, 8th edition, Sharon and Bob Huxford, editors (Collector Books, Paducah, KY, 2001, values 2002).

Squeaky Toys: A Collector's Handbook and Price Guide, L.H. MacKenzie (Schiffer, Atglen, PA, 1998).

Standard Catalog of Die-Cast Vehicles, Dan Stearns, editor (Collector Books, Paducah, KY, 2002).

Standard Catalog of Farm Toys, Elizabeth A. Stephan and Dan Stearns, editors (Krause, Iola, WI, 2001).

Steam Toys: A Symphony in Motion, Morton A. Hirschberg (Schiffer, Atglen, PA, 1996, values 2000).

Stock Car Model Kit Encyclopedia and Price Guide, Bill Coulter (Krause, Iola, WI, 1999).

Sulphide Marbles, Stanley A. Block and M. Edwin Payne (Schiffer, Atglen, PA, 2001).

Teddy Bear Figurines Price Guide, Jesse Murray (Hobby House Press, Grantsville, MD, 1996).

Television's Cowboys, Gunfighters and Their Cap Pistols, Rudy D'Angelo (Antique Trader, Iola, WI, 1999).

Today's Hottest Die-Cast Vehicles, Elizabeth A. Stephan, editor (Krause, Iola, WI, 2000).

Toy Buildings, 1880–1980, Patty Cooper and Dian Zillner (Schiffer, Atglen, PA, 2000).

Toy Crystal Radios and *Toy Walkie Talkies,* Eric Wrobbel (20802 Exhibit Ct., Woodland Hills, CA 91367, 1997, 2001, values 2002).

Toy Shop's Action Figure Price Guide, Elizabeth A. Stephan, editor (Krause, Iola, WI, 2000).

Toys and Prices 2003, annual, Sharon Korbeck and Elizabeth A. Stephan, editors (Krause, Iola, WI).

Toys That Shoot and Other Neat Stuff, James L. Dundas (Schiffer, Atglen, PA, 1998).

Ty Plush Animals, 3rd edition, Jeff Mahony, editor (CheckerBee, Middletown, CT, 2000).

The Unauthorized Encyclopedia of Corgi Toys, Bill Manzke (Schiffer, Atglen, PA, 1997).

The Unofficial Guide to Transformers, 1980s through 1990s, J.E. Alvarez (Schiffer, Atglen, PA, 1999).

Vintage Toys: Robots and Space Toys, Jim Bunte, Dave Hallman, and Heinz Mueller (Krause, Iola, WI, 1999).

White Knob Wind Up Collectibles Toys, Robert E. Birkenes (Schiffer, Atglen, PA, 1998).

CLUBS & THEIR PUBLICATIONS

1/87 Vehicle & Equipment Club, *1/87 Vehicle & Equipment Club* (NL), 102 Plymouth Park S/C Box #168, Irving, TX 75061, e-mail: info@1-87 vehicles.org, website: 1-87vehicles.org.

52 Plus Joker, *Clear the Decks* (MAG), 670 Carlton Dr., Elgin, IL 60120-4008, e-mail: illhawkeye@msn.com, website: www.52plusjoker.org (playing cards).

A.C. Gilbert Heritage Society, *A.C. Gilbert Heritage Society Newsletter* (NL), 1440 Whalley Ave., PMB 252, New Haven, CT 06515, e-mail: hedbergc @aol.com, website: www.acghs.org.

American Yo-Yo Association, *American Yo-Yo Association Newsletter* (NL), PO Box 797, Valrico, FL 33595, website: www.ayya.net.

Antique Engine, Tractor & Toy Club, Inc., *Antique Engine, Tractor & Toy Club, Inc. Quarterly Newsletter* (NL), 5731 Paradise Rd., Slatington, PA 18080-4028.

Association of Game and Puzzle Collectors, *Game & Puzzle Collectors Quarterly* (NL), PMB 321, 197M Boston Post Rd. W., Marlborough, MA 01752, e-mail: agca@agca.com, website: www.agpc.org,.

Chess Collectors International, *Chess Collector* (NL), PO Box 166, Commack, NY 11725, e-mail: lichess@aol.com.

Chicago Playing Card Collectors Inc., *Chicago Playing Card Collectors Inc.* (NL), 1319 E. Sanborn, Palatine, IL 60067, e-mail: Dohabe@aol.com, website: cpccinc.org.

Club of Anchor Friends, *Medelingenblad* (MAG), c/o George Hardy, 1670 Hawkwood Ct., Charlottesville, VA 22901, e-mail: Georgeh@mail.rlc.net, website: www.ankerstein.org.

Corgi Collector Club, *Corgi Collector* (MAG), PO Box 323, Swansea, South Wales SA1 1BJ, UK, e-mail: info@corgi.co.uk, website: www.corgi.co.uk.

Cribbage Board Collectors Society, *Members of the Board* (NL), PO Box 170, Carolina, RI 02812-0170, e-mail: bbemis@home.com, website: www.cribbage.org.

Dinky Toy Club of America, *Dinky Toy Club of America Newsletter* (NL), PO Box 11, Highland, MD 20777, e-mail: mndinky@erols.com, website: www.erols.com/dinkytoy.

English Playing Card Society, *English Playing Card Society Newsletter* (NL), 11 Pierrepont St., Bath, Somerset BA1 1LA, UK, e-mail: srpls@cwco.net, website: www.wopc.co.uk/epcs/index.html.

Figures Collectors Club, *FCC* (NL), 11174 Hunts Corner Rd., Clarence, NY 14031, e-mail: bripvc@toyline.com, website: www.figurescollectors club.org.

Fisher-Price Collectors Club, *Gabby Goose* (NL), 1442 N. Ogden, Mesa, AZ 85205, e-mail: fpclub@aol.com.

G.I. Joe Collectors' Club, *G.I. Joe Collectors' Club* (NL), 225 Cattle Baron Parc Dr., Fort Worth, TX 76108, e-mail: lisa@mastercollector.com, website: www.mastercollector.com.

G.I. Joe International Collectors Club, *G.I. Joe International Collectors Club Newsletter* (NL), 150 S. Glenoaks Blvd., #9204, Burbank, CA 91502, e-mail: gijoe@gijoeinformation.com, website: gijoeinformation.com.

International Playing-Card Society, *Playing-Card* (MAG), 3570 Delaware Common, Indianapolis, IN 46220, e-mail: brsw@iquest.net.

Lionel Collectors Club of America, *Lion Roars* (MAG), *Interchange Track* (NL), PO Box 479, La Salle, IL 61301-0479, website: www.lionelcollectors.org.

Lionel Operating Train Society, *Switcher* (MAG), *Track Changes* (NL), PO Box 62240, Cincinnati, OH 45262-0240, e-mail: businessoffice@lots-trains.org, website: www.lots-trains.org.

Marble Collectors Society of America, *Marble Mania* (NL), PO Box 222, Trumbull, CT 06611, e-mail: BlocksChip@aol.com, website: www.block site.com/mcsa/index.htm.

Marble Collectors Unlimited, *Marble Mart/Newsletter* (NL), PO Box 206, Northboro, MA 01532, e-mail: marblesbev@aol.com.

Marklin Club, *Insider* (MAG), PO Box 510851, New Berlin, WI 53151-0851, e-mail: club@marklin.com, website: www.marklin.com.

Matchbox International Collectors Association (MICA), *MICA* (MAG), PO Box 28072, Waterloo, ON N2L 6J8, Canada.

Mechanical Bank Collectors of America, *Banker* (NL), PO Box 13323, Pittsburgh, PA 15243, e-mail: raytoys@aol.com, website: mechanical banks.org.

National Marble Club of America, *National Marble Club of America Newsletter* (NL), 1250 Harbourtowne Dr., Myrtle Beach, SC 29577.

National Model Railroad Association, Inc., *NMRA Bulletin* (MAG), 4121 Cromwell Rd., Chattanooga, TN 37421, e-mail: hq@hq.nmra.org, website: www.NMRA.org.

Ohio Art Collector's Club, *Ohio Art Beat* (NL), 415 Rosemont Ave., Bryan, OH 43506, e-mail: milimiller@adelphia.net, website: www.geocities. com/ohioartcollectors.

Original Omnibus Co. Club, *Bus Route* (NL), PO Box 323, Swansea, South Wales SA1 1BJ, UK.

Schoenhut Collectors' Club, *Schoenhut Newsletter* (NL), 1003 W. Huron, Ann Arbor, MI 48103-4217, e-mail: aawestie@provide.net.

Southern California Meccano & Erector Club, *Southern California Meccano & Erector Club Newsletter* (NL), PO Box 7653, Northridge, CA 91327-7653, website: www.erector.webnexus.com.

Still Bank Collectors Club, *Penny Bank Post* (NL), 4175 Millersville Rd., Indianapolis, IN 46205, e-mail: egelhoffl@juno.com, website: stillbank club.com.

Toy Car Collectors Association, *Toy Car Collector* (MAG), c/o Dana Johnson Enterprises, PO Box 1824, Bend, OR 97709-1824, e-mail: toynutz @teleport.com, website: www.toynutz.com.

Toy Gun Collectors of America, *Toy Gun Collectors of America Newsletter* (NL), 3009 Oleander Ave., San Marcos, CA 92069.

Toy Train Operating Society, *Toy Train Operating Society (T.T.O.S.) Bulletin* (MAG), *TTOS Order Board* (MAG), 25 W. Walnut St., Suite 308, Pasadena, CA 91103-3634, e-mail: ttos@ttos.org, website: www.ttos.org.

Train Collectors Association, *Train Collectors Quarterly* (MAG), PO Box 248, Strasburg, PA 17579-0248, e-mail: toytrain@traincollectors.org, website: www.traincollectors.org.

Treasures for Little Children, *Tiny Times* (NL), 8201 Pleasant Ave. S., Bloomington, MN 55420, e-mail: postmaster@treasuresforlittlechildren.com, website: treasuresforlittlechildren.com (children's dishes, toy glass, miniature furniture, dollhouses, and related toys).

Winchester/Shenendoah Valley Hot Wheels Club, *Wheels Are Spinning* (NL), 118 Deer Hill Ct., Stephens City, VA 22655, e-mail: hwdan2@earthlink.net.

Winross Collectors Club of America, *Winross Model Collectors* (NL), PO Box 444, Mount Joy, PA 17552, e-mail: wccainc@aol.com, website: wccaonline.com.

OTHER PUBLICATIONS

Antique Toy World (MAG), PO Box 34509, Chicago, IL 60634.

Classic Toy Trains (MAG), PO Box 1612, Waukesha, WI 53187-1612, e-mail: editor@classtrain.com, website: www.classtrain.com.

Die Cast Digest (MAG), PO Box 12510, Knoxville, TN 37912-0510, website: www.diecastdigest.com.

Gamers Alliance Report (NL), PO Box 197-K, East Meadow, NY 11554, e-mail: gamers@gamersalliance.com, website: www.gamersalliance.com.

Glass Bank Collector Newsletter (NL), PO Box 155, Poland, NY 13431.

Hobby Horse News (MAG), 14 Garraux St., Greenville, SC 29609, e-mail: thhn2000@aol.com, website: www.hobbyhorsenews.com (Information about new and retired model horses from all manufacturers, including Breyer, Stone, Hagen Renaker, and more).

HO-USA (MAG), 435½ S. Orange St., Orange, CA 92866-1911, e-mail: rb.housa@ix.netcom.com, website: pages.prodigy.com/housa.

Hot Wheels Newsletter (NL), 26 Madera Ave., San Carlos, CA 94070-2937, e-mail: hwnewsltr@aol.com, website: hometown.aol.com/hwnewsltr.

Kit Collectors Clearinghouse (MAG), 3213 Hardy Dr., Edmond, OK 73013-5319, e-mail: cheersjb@swbell.net.

KitBuilders Magazine (MAG), 320 S. Jefferson St., Woodstock, IL 60098, e-mail: reznhedz@enteract.com.

Lee's Action Figure News & Toy Review (MAG), PO Box 322, Monroe, CT 06468.

LGN Telegram (MAG), PO Box 332, Hershey, PA 17033, e-mail: Stationmaster@LGBTelegram.com, website: www.LGBTelegram.com.

Master Collector (NL), 225 Cattle Baron Parc Dr., Fort Worth, TX 76108, e-mail: brian@mastercollector.com, website: www.mastercollector.com.

Matchbox U.S.A. (NL), 62 Saw Mill Rd., Durham, CT 06422, e-mail: mtchboxusa@aol.com, website: www.charliemackonline.com.

Mini Soldier Gazette (MAG), PO Box 15, Eatontown, NJ 07724, e-mail: minisoldier@minisoldier.com, website: www.minisoldier.com.

Model Collector (MAG), IPC Media Subscriptions, Freepost CY 1061, PO Box 272, Haywards Heath,W. Sussex RH16 3FS, UK, e-mail: modelcollector@ipcmedia.com.

O Gauge Railroading (MAG), 65-69 S. Broad St., PO Box 239, Nazareth, PA 18064-0239, e-mail: publisher@ogaugerr.com, website: www.ogaugerr.com.

Old Toy Soldier (MAG), PO Box 13324, Pittsburgh, PA 15243-0324, e-mail: raytoy@aol.com, website: oldtoysoldier.com.

One-Inch Warrior (MAG), 65 Walton Ct., Woking, Surrey GU21 5EE, UK, e-mail: editor@plasticwarrior.freeserve.co.uk, website: www.zyworld.com/PlasticWarrior (20/25/30/35 mm plastic figures).

Plastic Warrior (MAG), 65 Walton Ct., Woking, Surrey GU21 5EE, UK, e-mail: editor@plasticwarrior.freeserve.co.uk, website: www.zyworld.com/PlasticWarrior (54/60 mm plastic figures).

Pressed Steel Toys Monthly (MAG), PO Box 1289, McAfee, NJ 07428-1289, e-mail: pedalcar@netrom.com, website: pedalcar.net.

S Gaugian (MAG), 7236 W. Madison St., Forest Park, IL 60130, website: www.heimburgerhouse.com.

Spectacular News (NL), SpecCast, 428 6th Ave. NW, Dyersville, IA 52040, e-mail: info@speccast.com, website: www.speccast.com.

Teddy Bear Review (MAG), PO Box 5000, Iola, WI 54945-5000.

Teddy Bear Times (MAG), 208 Fourth St. SW, Kasson, MN 55944, website: www.teddybeartimes.com.

Tomart's Action Figure Digest (MAG), 3300 Encrete Ln., Dayton, OH 45439-1944, website: tomart.com.

Toy Cars & Models (MAG), 700 E. State St., Iola, WI 54990-0001, e-mail: info@krause.com, website: www.krause.com.

Toy Farmer (MAG), *Toy Trucker & Contractor* (MAG), 7496 106th Ave. SE, LaMoure, ND 58458-9404, website: www.toyfarmer.com.

Toy Shop (NP), 700 E. State St., Iola, WI 54990-0001, e-mail: info@krause.com, website: www.krause.com.

Toy Soldier & Model Figure (MAG), Ashdown Publishing, 208 Fourth St. SW, Kasson, MN 55944, e-mail: ashdown@ashdown.co.uk, website: www.toy-soldier.com.

Toy Soldier Review (MAG), e-mail: bill@vintagecastings.com, website: www.vintagecastings.com/tsronline.htm. Formerly a print magazine, currently available online.

Tractor Classics: Canadian Toy Magazine (MAG), Box 489, Rocanville, SK S0A 3L0, Canada, e-mail: ctmtoys@sk.sympatico.ca.

Traders' Horn (NL), 1903 Schoettler Valley Dr., Chesterfield, MO 63017-5203, e-mail: brcitsa@bluerhino.com.

Trainmaster (NL), 5001-B NW 34th St., Gainesville, FL 32605 (Lionel O gauge trains).

Wheel Goods Trader (MAG), PO Box 435, Fraser, MI 48026-0435, e-mail: wheelgoodstrader@ameritech.net, website: wgtpub.com (pedal cars).

Yo-Yo Times (NL), PO Box 1519-RTK, Herndon, VA 22070, e-mail: yoyotime@aol.com, website: www.yoyotimes.com.

ARCHIVES & MUSEUMS

Delaware Toy & Miniature Museum, P.O. Box 4053, Rte. 141, Wilmington, DE 19807, 302-427-TOYS (8697), fax: 302-427-8654, e-mail: toys@thomes.net, website: www.thomes.net/toys.

National Farm Toy Museum, 1110 16th Ct. Ave. SE, Dyersville, IA 52040, 319-875-2727, website: www.nftmonline.com.

The National Toy Train Museum, The Train Collectors Association, PO Box 248, Paradise Lane, Strasburg, PA 17579, 717-687-8623, fax: 717-687-0742, website: www.traincollectors.org/toytrain.html.

National Yo-Yo Museum, 320 Broadway, Chico, CA 95928, website: www.nationalyoyo.org.

Shelburne Museum, Inc., PO Box 10, Shelburne, VT 05842, 802-985-3346, 800-253-0191, fax: 802-985-2331, website: www.shelburnemuseum.com.

Space Farms Zoo & Museum, Rte. 519, Sussex, NJ 07461, 973-875-5800, website: www.spacefarms.com.

Spinning Top Museum, *Spin-offs* (NL), 533 Milwaukee Ave., Burlington, WI 53105.

Strong Museum, One Manhattan Square, Rochester, NY 14607, 585-263-2700, fax: 585-263-2493, website: www.strongmuseum.org.

The Teddy Bear Museum, 2511 Pine Ridge Rd., Naples, FL 34109, 239-

598-2711, 800-681-BEAR, fax: 239-598-9239, website: www.teddy
museum.com.

Washington Dolls' House & Toy Museum, 5236 44th St. NW, Washington,
DC 20015, 202-244-0024 or 202-363-6400.

USEFUL SITES

Toynutz, www.toynutz.com.

APPRAISERS

Many of the auctions and repair services listed in this section will
also do appraisals. *See also* the general list of "Appraisal Groups" on
page 483.

David Claxton, 2952 Lynn Ave., Billings, MT 59102-6640, 406-656-0949,
e-mail: mtslots@att.net. Appraisals of Lionel and American Flyer
train sets.

AUCTIONS

➜ **SEE ALSO "SELLING THROUGH AUCTION HOUSES," PAGE 485.**

The AuctionBlocks, PO Box 2321, Shelton, CT 06484, 203-924-2802, fax:
203-924-2802, e-mail: auctionblocks@aol.com, website: www.auction
blocks.com. Absentee and Internet marble auctions. Mail, phone, fax,
and e-mail bids accepted. No buyer's premium. Printed catalog $20;
yearly subscription $135. Prices realized mailed and available on web-
site after the auction.

Auctions Unlimited Inc., PO Box 1162, Port Ewen, NY 12466, 914-706-0171,
fax: 561-264-0487, e-mail: sal@Auctions-Unlimitedinc.com, website:
www.auctions-unlimited.com. Auctions of toys and collectibles. Mail,
phone, fax, e-mail, and Internet bids accepted. No buyer's premium.
Prices realized mailed and available on website after auction.

Bertoia Auctions, 2141 DeMarco Dr., Vineland, NJ 08360, 856-692-1881,
fax: 856-692-8697, e-mail: bill@bertoiaauctions.com, website:
www.bertoiaauctions.com. Specializes in auctions of antique toys,
banks, dolls, trains, soldiers, doorstops, and folk art. On-site auctions;
live on Internet also. Mail, phone, and fax bids accepted. Buyer's premium 10%. Prices realized mailed after auction. Catalog $35.

Greenberg Auctions, 1393 Progress Way, Suite 907, Eldersburg, MD 21784,
410-795-7448, e-mail: bwimperis@greenbergshows.com, website:
greenbergshows.com. Specialized train auctions held live in Sykesville, Maryland. Online catalogs, auction dates, and absentee bidding
information are available at auctions@greenbergshows.com. Printed
catalogs are available for $5 each. Call for catalog and consigning
information.

Henry/Peirce Auctioneers, 1456 Carson Ct., Homewood, IL 60430, 708-
798-7508, fax: 708-799-3594, e-mail: mhenry89@attbi.com, website:

www.henrypeirce.com. Specializing in auctions of mechanical and still banks. Mail bids accepted. No phone bids. Buyer's premium 10%. Prices realized mailed after auction. Catalog prices vary. Appraisals.

Howard B. Parzow, PO Box 3464, Gaithersburg, MD 20885-3464, 301-977-6741, fax: 301-208-8947, e-mail: hparzow@aol.com, website: www.hbparzowauctioneer.com. Mail and phone bids accepted. Buyer's premium 10%. Appraisals.

Just Kids Nostalgia, 310 New York Ave., Huntington, NY 11743, 516-423-8449, fax: 631-423-4326, e-mail: info@justkidsnostalgia.com, website: www.justkidsnostalgia.com. Auctions of old toys, movie posters, TV and comic characters, advertising, sports, rock 'n' roll, and other pop culture memorabilia. Mail, phone, fax, and e-mail bids accepted. Prices realized mailed after auction and available on website.

Lloyd Ralston Gallery, 350 Long Beach Blvd., Stratford, CT 06615, 203-386-9399, fax: 203-386-9519, e-mail: lrgallelry@aol.com, website: www.lloydralstontoys.com. Specializing in auctions of trains, toy soldiers, and die-cast vehicles. Mail and phone bids accepted. Buyer's premium 10%. Catalogs $20–$25. Prices realized mailed after auction and available on website.

Martin Auction Co., Inc., Rt. 51 S., Clinton, IL 61727, 217-935-3245, e-mail: info@martinauction.com, website: www.martinauction.com. Auctions of toys and antiques. Catalogs for toy auctions are posted on the website the week before the auction.

New England Auction Gallery, Box 764, Middleton, MA 01949, 978-304-3140, e-mail: markrim@attbi.com, website: www.old-toys.com. Auctions of toys, games, and character collectibles. Mail, phone, fax, and e-mail bids accepted. Buyer's premium 5%. Catalos $10 in U.S., $15 foreign; first catalog free. Yearly subscription $30. Appraisals. Prices realized in next catalog after auction. Appraisals.

Noel Barrett Antiques, Carversville Rd., Box 300, Carversville, PA 18923, 215-297-5109, e-mail: toys@noelbarrett.com, website: noelbarrett.com. Auctions of vintage toys. Mail, phone, fax, and e-mail bids accepted. Buyer's premium 10%. Prices realized mailed after auction and available on website. Catalog $35. Appraisals.

Randy Inman Auctions, PO Box 726, Waterville, ME 04903-0726, 207-872-6900, fax: 207-872-6966, e-mail: inman@inmanauctions.com, website: www.inmanauctions.com. Toys and related items. Mail and phone bids accepted. Buyer's premium 10%. Prices realized available after auction. Appraisals.

Richard Opfer Auctioneering Inc., 1919 Greenspring Dr., Timonium, MD 21093, 410-252-5035, fax: 410-252-5863, e-mail: info@opferauction.com, website: www.opferauction.com. Buyer's premium 10%. Mail and phone bids accepted. Prices realized mailed and available on website after some auctions. Catalog prices vary from $3 to $35, depending on sale. Referrals given for restoration and conservation. Appraisals.

Running Rabbit Auctions, PO Box 701, Waverly, TN 37185, 931-296-3600, e-mail: marbles@waverly.net, website: runningrabbit.com. Absentee auctions of marbles. Mail, phone, fax, and e-mail bids accepted. Buyer's premium 10%. Print catalogs and video catalogs $25 each, $40 for both. Prices realized mailed after auction.

Smith House Toys, PO Box 336, Eliot, ME 03903, 207-439-4614, fax: 207-439-8554, e-mail: smithtoys@aol.com, website: www.smithhouse toys.com. Toys from 1900 to 1970. Mail, phone, fax, e-mail, and Internet bids accepted. Buyer's premium 10%. Catalog $15, subscription $35 for three issues. Prices realized mailed after auction. Appraisals.

REPAIRS, PARTS & SUPPLIES

➼ SEE ALSO "CONSERVATORS & RESTORERS," PAGE 520.

Antique Marble Restoration, 467 Sunday Dr., Altoona, WI 54720, 715-834-8630, e-mail: clearwater@charter.net, website: www.clearwater agate.com. Old and antique glass marbles restored.

Art 'n' Things, 135 S. Anderson Ave., Fairview, NJ 07022, 201-943-2288. Reproduction boxes for robots and other toys from the turn of the century through the 1950s; reproduction boxes for monster, superhero, and TV-related figure kits of the 1960s. Reproductions of original Aurora instruction sheets. Free catalog.

Blue Diamond Classics, PO Box 81906, Lincoln, NE 68501, 402-323-3220, e-mail: bdc@inebraska.com, website: www.bluediamondclassics.com. Pedal car parts and graphics. Wheels, tires, hub caps, windshields, steering wheels, lights, hood ornaments, etc.

Buddy-K Toys, 20 Durham St., Hellertown, PA 18055, 610-838-6505 anytime. Repair and enhancement or total restoration of large pressed steel toys of the 1920s through 1940s. Decals, parts, and accessories available for Buddy L, Keystone, Steelcraft, American National, Sturditoy, Son-ny, and others. Showroom open by appointment. Insured UPS delivery and COD orders. Parts and decals catalog $10.

Cap Gun Repairs, PO Box 3192, Oshkosh, WI 54903, 920-231-5362, fax: 920-231-5810, e-mail: toys@athenet.net, website: www.toyrepair.com. Cast-iron and die-cast parts for toy cap guns. Cap guns, battery-operated toys, tin windup toys, and electric or windup trains repaired. Cap gun parts catalog $10.

Captain Bob's Antique Toy Repair, 9 Mohawk Dr., Hampden, MA 01036, 413-566-5109, 9:00 A.M.–7:00 P.M. Antique toy repair: battery-operated toys, windups, mechanical, friction, and clockwork toys. Worldwide service.

Charlie's Trains, PO Box 158-K, Hubertus, WI 53033, 262-628-1544. Lionel trains: repair and restoration, parts, wire, and bulbs, principally for 1945–1970 equipment. Send $2 for 18-page catalog.

Chrome-Tech USA, 2314 Ravenswood Rd., Madison, WI 53711, 608-274-

9811, e-mail: chrometechusa@charter.net, website: www.chrometech usa.com. Chrome plating service for plastic toy restoration. Send SASE for free brochure.

Classic Tin Toy Co., PO Box 81, Sheboygan, WI 53015, 920-693-8417, fax: 920-693-8189, e-mail: toys@classictintoy.com, website: www.classic tintoy.com. Repair and restoration of tin toys; also pressed steel toys, aluminum trucks and toys, tricycles, pedal cars, and toy trains. Replacement parts for toys and trains, including windup motors, replacement tires, tracks for tanks, reproduction parts for robots, and more.

"Club Hair" for G.I. Joe, Craig Blankenship, PO Box 2141, Yakima, WA 98907-2141, 509-965-5920, fax: 509-972-1022, e-mail: ToyBroker @aol.com, website: www.clubhairforgijoe.com. G.I. Joe repair, restringing, and part replacement. Specializing in hair reflocking. G.I. Joe accessories and replica parts.

Cowboys & Kidillacs, 1709 Santa Cecilia, Kingsville, TX 78363, 361-595-1015, fax: 361-595-5026, e-mail: kidillac@swbell.net. Complete line of pedal car, wagon, scooter, and tricycle parts. Custom tire service for riding toys. Catalog $5.

Crooked Herman's, 2924 Bonacum Dr., Lincoln, NE 68502, 402-431-4441 daytime only, e-mail: info@crookedherman.com, website: crooked herman.com. Parts for pedal cars and airplanes made from 1910 to the present. Replacement parts, reconstruction, duplication of hard-to-find parts; tire service. Research and identification. Catalog $3.50.

D & S Pedal Car Restorations, 15257 S 24th St., Phoenix, AZ 85048, 480-759-5131, fax: 480-704-9637, e-mail: dspedalcars@earthlink.net, website: dspedalcarrestorations.com. Restorations of all types of pedal cars and electric-powered promotional vehicles. Nationwide services, ranging from simple restorations to wild customs, appraisals, and restoration tips.

Dan Latina, 29 Wheeler Dam Rd., Salem, NH 03079, 603-898-2191, after 7:00 P.M. ET, e-mail: dlatina@aol.com, website: www.danlatina.com. Original antique toy parts for tin windups, battery-operated toys, friction vehicles, plastic toys, toy trains, and more. Lists available on website, by e-mail, or send LSASE for brochure.

David or Debbie Sharp, 6449 W. 12th St., Indianapolis, IN 46214, 317-243-3172, e-mail: vetteford@yahoo.com. Replacement and reproduction parts and decals for Tonka toys, 1950–1970. Mail order only, no phone orders. Catalog $1.

David Smith, 1142 S. Spring St., Springfield, IL 62704, 217-523-3391, fax: 217-523-0478, e-mail: davemarble@msn.com. Glass marbles restored: grinding and buffing the glass. Glass, china, and pottery restorations. Broken or chipped pieces fixed. Brochure 50 cents. Open Mon.–Fri. 10:00 A.M.–5:00 P.M.

Doll & Bear's Paradise, 855½ N. Cedar, Laramie, WY 82072, 307-742-3429, e-mail: dolls2fix@fiberpipe.net. Repair and restoration of dolls and stuffed animals. Composition, plastic, bisque, porcelain, cloth, leather, and metal dolls restored, restrung, and cleaned. Wigs; hair rerooting. Doll clothes made to order. Doll clothes hand washed. Stuffed animals cleaned and mended; fabric and features replaced.

Donald R. Walters, Rt. 1 Box 51A, Curtiss, WI 54422, 715-654-5440. Toy refinishing, repair, and painting.

Eastern Pedal Products, Inc., 31874 Tappers Corner Rd., Cordova, MD 21625, 410-364-5490, fax: 410-364-5402, e-mail: gandrew@easternpedal products.com, website: www.easternpedalproducts.com. Parts for die-cast pedal tractors. Catalog $2.

Eccles Brothers, Ltd., 5875 Madison Ave., Burlington, IA 52601, 319-752-3840 days; 319-753-1179, fax: 319-753-5933. Repair parts, paints, tin helmets, and accessories for toy soldiers. Propellers, antennas, replacement tires, and other parts for Arcade, Tootsietoy, Hubley, and other toys. Send SASE for free repair parts & accessories brochure. Illustrated catalog of soldiers, cars, racers, trucks, airplanes, and civilian figures made from original toy factory molds, $3.

Edinburgh Imports, Inc., PO Box 340, Newbury Park, CA 91319-0340, 805-376-1700, fax: 805-376-1711, e-mail: rblock@edinburgh.com, website: www.edinburgh.com. Supplies, patterns, and kits for making and repairing teddy bears and stuffed animals. Mohair, alpaca, wool, and rayon plush fabrics, including the original Steiff mohair by Schulte. Patterns and kits. Worldwide shipping. Advice and guidance, no charge. Fabric catalog $2, supplies $2, patterns and kits $2.

Egli Toy Salvage, 1750 Udall Ave., Manson, IA 50563, 712-469-3949. Restoration and parts for most farm toys. Specializing in hard-to-find toys and parts. Bodies for custom builders. Send SASE (60 cents postage) for parts list. Call for more information, evenings.

Ernest Rudsill, Rudy, 2605 SW 49th St., Corvallis, OR 97333-1326, 541-753-7891, e-mail: rudy@proaxis.com. Damaged marbles refinished.

H & R Tire, 970 Ray St., Huntington, IN 46750-1246, 260-356-5414, 8:00 A.M.–9:00 P.M. Hard rubber tires for bicycles, tricycles, and wagons.

Heimbolds, 2950 SW Persimmon Ln., Dunnellon, FL 34431, 352-465-0756. Art conservation restorers: pottery and porcelain, glass, dolls, toys, signs, paintings, stone or organic carvings, etc. Free estimates. Free brochure.

Iron Man Toys, 434 N. School St., Lodi, CA 95240, 209-334-6101, 8:00 A.M.–6:00 P.M. e-mail: ironman45@softcom.net. Restoration of cast-iron toy cars, trucks, airplanes, trains, mechanical banks, etc. Custom parts cast in bronze, brass, and cast iron; paint matched.

Juvenile Automobiles, 291 High St., Woonsocket, RI 02895, 401-762-9661, e-mail: vaz185@aol.com. Replacement parts for pedal cars, specializing in tires to fit all wheel goods. Catalog $6.

Log Cabin Train Shop, 600 Rochester Rd., Pittsburgh, PA 15237-1704, 412-366-7060, fax: 412-366-7060, e-mail: logcabintrainshop@att.net. Parts and repairs for Lionel trains. Send $2 for 44-page parts catalog.

Long Island Doll Hospital, 45395 Main Rd., PO Box 1604, Southold, NY 11971, 631-765-2379, e-mail: jadav@suffolk.lib.ny.us, website: www.jandavisantiques.com. Dolls, Steiff, and other stuffed animals repaired. Appraisals. Free brochure.

Manny Fernandez, 2922 Cotton Gum, Garland, TX 75044, 972-530-9115, e-mail: res03F5d@gte.net. Restoration of pedal cars, old bikes, trikes, Buddy L, Steelcraft, Keystone, Smith-Miller, and similar toys. Complete stripping of all paint and rust. Old colors matched.

Marc Olimpio's Antique Toy Restoration Center, PO Box 477, Springvale, ME 04083, 207-636-3772, fax: 207-636-3772, e-mail: mojo1@psouth.net. Restoration of early American tin and cast-iron toys c.1840–1900: mechanical banks, still banks, and other hand-painted toys of the period.

MIB Toy Restoration, 1021 Dare Road Yorktown, VA 23692, 757-898-8647, e-mail: mibrestoration01@aol.com. Restoration and/or repair of pressed steel toys: Tonka, Buddy L, Nylint etc; pedal cars, wagons, tricycles, bicycles, and other riding toys.

Michael Sabatelle, Box 040136, Brooklyn, NY 11204-0006, 718-236-1278, e-mail: mdrews69@hotmail.com. Replacement and original parts for Lionel trains, postwar (1945–1969) and MPC (1970–1988). Repairs. Mail order. Catalog $1.

New York Doll Hospital, Inc., 787 Lexington Ave., New York, NY 10021, 212-838-7527. Repairs, restorations, and appraisals of antique dolls and animals.

Northeast Document Conservation Center, 100 Brickstone Sq., Andover, MA 01810-1494, 978-470-1010, fax: 978-475-6021, Mon.–Fri. 8:30 A.M.–4:30 P.M., e-mail: nedcc@nedcc.org, website: www.nedcc.org. Nonprofit regional conservation center specializing in treatment of art and artifacts on paper, including board games. Preservation microfilming, duplication of historical photographs, preservation planning surveys, disaster assistance, technical leaflets. Free brochure.

Obsessions Toy Restorations, 7315 Rain Bow Ln., Indianapolis, IN 46236, 317-823-0033, fax: 317-826-7566, e-mail: obessed@ori.net. Toy truck parts catalog covering 1920s through 1940s Buddy L, Keystone, Sturditoy, American National, Kelmet, Kingsbury, Steelcraft, Sonny, and others. Catalog $7 plus $2 postage. Restoration, enhancement, and repair.

Pandy's Collectibles, 16 Palmer St., Medford, MA 02155, 781-395-5569, 8:00 A.M.–9:00 P.M., e-mail: Pandyscol@aol.com, website: www.pandys.com. Restoration of A.C. Gilbert Erector sets. Original and reproduction parts, boilers, part cans, labels, and manuals available. Mail order worldwide.

Pedal Car Graphics by Robert, 1207 Charter Oak Dr., Taylors, SC 29687, 864-244-4308. Pedal car decals, pedal car reference books. Catalog, 80+ pages, $5 plus $1 postage.

Pedal Car Parts, 2536 Willow Dr., Arnold, MO 63010-2829, 636-296-5908. Pedal car parts and repair. Bumpers, front ends, hood ornaments, pedals, wheels, bells, and more. Complete undercarriages for pedal cars built. Books on pedal cars and restoration. Free brochure.

Pedal Car Specialties, Inc., 38 Oak Ridge Rd., Newfoundland, NJ 07435, 973-697-4982 days; 973-209-2032, e-mail: pedalcar@netrom.com. Toy restoration, specializing in pedal car and pressed steel cars and trucks. Parts for most pressed steel toys.

Pedal Cars, 111 W. Walnut, Anamosa, IA 52205, 319-462-4754. Pedal car restoration. Appraisals.

Portell Restorations, 1574 Saddle Dr., Festus, MO 63028, 314-931-8192, fax: 636-937-8192. Complete restorations and parts for American-made pedal cars. Sheet metal and suspension fabrication. Catalog $4.

Puppetry Arts Institute, 11025 E. Winner Rd., Independence, MO 64052, 816-252-7248, 9:00 A.M.–10:00 P.M., e-mail: pai@att.net, website: www.hazelle.org. Hazelle marionette parts; vinyl heads for hand puppets and finger puppets. Free brochure.

Quality First Antique Toy Restoration Inc., Randy's Toy Shop, 165 N. 9th St., Noblesville, IN 46060, 317-776-2220, 8:00 A.M.–5:00 P.M., fax: 317-776-9007, e-mail: randy@randystoyshop.com, website: www.randystoyshop.com. Antique toy restoration and repair. Reproduction parts for tin, celluloid, and plastic toys; paint touch-up; mechanisms repaired. Can match parts for most American, German, and Japanese toys. Box restoration. Mail order or UPS shipment. Brochure $5.

Quarterhorse Investments, Inc., 336 W. High St., Elizabethtown, PA 17022, 717-295-9188. Restoration supplies for rocking horses. Send SASE for brochure.

R.F. Giardina Co. Inc., PO Box 562, Oyster Bay, NY 11771, 516-922-1364, fax: 516-922-4601, website: www.rfgco.com. Repair services for all types of trains. Reproduction American Flyer parts, repair and rebuilding kits, special repair tools, operating books, manuals, and more. Plasticville, Tootsietoy, Mini-Toy, Renwal parts. Catalog $4.

R.J. Pattern Services, c/o R.J. Hoerr, 1212 W. Detroit St., New Buffalo, MI 49117, 616-469-7538, fax: 616-469-8554, e-mail: mhoerr@starband.net. Antique toy and salesman sample stove restoration.

Restoration Train Parts, 135 Richwood Dr., Gloversville, NY 12078, 518-725-4446, 11:00 A.M.–3:00 P.M. Replacement parts for toy trains, including American Flyer, AMT, Ives, Lionel, Varney HO trains. Ignition engine replacement parts for antique model airplanes. American Flyer, Lionel, Ives parts catalogs $20 postpaid; Varney HO parts catalog $15 postpaid; model airplane ignition engine/glow parts catalog $18 postpaid.

Rockinghorse Antiques, 111 St. Helena Ave., Dundalk, MD 21222, 410-

285-0280. Restoration of carousel horses and related items, rocking horses, and antique wicker carriages. Appraisals, identification, and value. Free brochure.

Samuelson Pedal Tractor Parts, 234 First Ave. East, PO Box 346, Dyersville, IA 52040, 563-875-6222, fax: 563-875-6126, e-mail: pedalparts @aol.com, website: www.pedaltractorparts.com/parts.html. Parts for pedal cars and tricycles. Pedal car tires, rims, pedals, grills, seats, steering wheels. Tricycle wheels and tires.

Sottung's Service Center, 808 Girard Ave., Croydon, PA 19021, 215-788-5353, after 5:00 P.M. Reproduction parts for Plasticville houses and buildings. Repairs and restorations on toy trains. Send 8½-by-11-in. envelope with 83 cents postage for brochure.

Specialty Castings, 19 Mill Rd., Boxford, MA 01921, 978-887-9783, e-mail: specialty@gis.net, website: www.gis.net/~specialty. Replicas of cast-iron, brass, bronze, aluminum, and pewter parts. Lost wax casting. Shrinkage compensation. Mold making. Plastic and rubber parts. New complete piece made from broken pieces. Call or write; send samples, photos, or drawings of part needed. Catalog $5.

Stan Orr's Train Parts, Box 97, Stormville, NY 12582-0097, 845-221-7738, 9:00 A.M.–9:00 P.M., e-mail: info@stanorrtrainparts.com, website: www.stanorrtrainparts.com. Lionel train parts. Catalog $2 plus LSASE.

Sy Schreckinger, PO Box 104, East Rockaway, NY 11518, 516-536-4154, 9:00 A.M.–9:00 P.M. Invisible repairs made on mechanical banks and toys; restoration and repainting. Repairs made in all metals. No welding or brazing. Bank and toy cleaning.

Teddy Bear Doctor, Dick Roenspies, 9980 Exchange Rd., Prairie du Sac, WI 53578, 608-544-5006, e-mail: roenspie@midplains.net. Restoration of antique teddy bears and stuffed animals, specializing in Steiff and Schuco.

Thomas Toys, Inc., PO Box 405, Fenton, MI 48430, 810-629-8707, fax: 810-714-6097. Custom reproduction parts and tires for old toys. Wheels, ladders, racks, steering wheels, grilles, decals, etc. Cast iron and aluminum parts. Catalog $7 postpaid.

Tin Toy Works, 1313 N. 15th St., Allentown, PA 18102, 610-439-8268, fax: 610-439-1288, e-mail: tintoyworks@enter.net. Antique tin toys restored, missing parts manufactured, mechanisms repaired. Tin and composition figures, lifeboats, masts, go-rounds, figures for Lionel boats and race cars, tin and composition auto figures, etc.

Tony Orlando, 6661 Norborne, Dearborn Heights, MI 48127-2076, 313-561-5072, 9:00 A.M.–5:00 P.M. Conservation and restoration of carousel figures, rocking horses, and cigar store figures. References furnished.

The Toy Doctor, R.R. 1, Box 202, Eades Rd., Red Creek, NY 13143, 315-754-8846, fax: 315-754-6238, e-mail: repair@thetoydoctor.com, website: www.thetoydoctor.com. Repair of battery-operated toys, windups, friction toys, and automatons. Robots and space toys a specialty.

Toy Surgeon, Jerry Shook, 6528 Cedar Brook Dr., New Albany, OH 43054-7796, 614-855-7796, fax: 614-855-7796, e-mail: surgeontoy@aol.com. Plastic part reproductions for most toys. Send original (insured) for duplication; mold will be made and original returned and quote sent. Send SASE and $2 for illustrated parts list.

Toys & More, PO Box 3192, Oshkosh, WI 54903, 920-231-5362, fax: 920-231-0491, e-mail: toys@athenet.net, website: www.toyrepair.com. Cap gun replacement parts, including grips, hammers, latches, triggers, springs, bullets, etc., for cap guns made from 1940 to 1960. Parts catalog $10. Repair of cap guns, battery-operated toys, tin windups, celluloid toys, talker toys, and toy trains.

Toys of Yesteryears, PO Box 59, Nipomo, CA 93444, 805-929-4835, fax: 805-929-1936. Restoration of vintage pedal cars, by appointment. Parts.

TrainRepairParts.com, 287 Main Street, PO Box 2170, New Britain, CT 06051, 860-223-0600, website:trainrepairparts.com. Original and reproduction repair parts for postwar Lionel and American Flyer trains. Reproduction stickers for American Flyer. Repair manuals. Mail order worldwide. Catalog $4.

Vod Varka Springs, 1251 U.S. Rt. 30, PO Box 170, Clinton, PA 15026-0170, 724-695-3268. Custom-made springs and wire forms. Flat-type springs for clocks. Made to order per print or sample. Can make almost anything out of wire or flat stock.

West Virginia Railroad Co., 118 Chestnut Hill Rd., Hanover, PA 17331, 717-359-8392, e-mail: mytrains@supernet.com. Toy train repair and restoration. Lionel, Flyer, and Marx tinplate parts. Glass bead blasting. Free train list with SASE.

Wickering Heights, Jim and Judy Sikorski, 401 Superior St., Rossford, OH 43460, 419-666-9461, e-mail: jamest@accesstoledo.com. Restoration of antique wicker. Carriages and doll buggies a specialty. Color match, restaining, touch-up, and hardware cleaning. Send photo for estimate.

TRANSPORTATION

VINTAGE CARS

The larger an antique, the harder it is to sell to an out-of-town customer. That is the general rule, but for cars this rule does not hold. A car in working condition can be driven or hauled to its new home with a minimum of problems. This means that antique and classic automobiles have a national market. To get the best price for a car, first check the guides used by automobile dealers and wholesalers when they make an offer on your secondhand car. After you have established these prices, get a copy of *Hemmings Motor News,* the newspaper for car collectors, and check further.

There are car swap meets and sales in every area of the country. Any old-car owner can tell you how to find these rallies. This is the best place to sell a car if you know the value. If you don't, it may pay to visit a rally and ask for some opinions from collectors. They are always happy to help.

An ad in your local paper sells classic autos just as well as it sells used cars. If you own a desirable antique auto or an expensive classic, it will sell well at an antique car auction. They are listed in *Hemmings* or in the other car publications found in your library.

The smaller automotive collectibles, such as taillights, paint, floor mats, hubcaps, hood ornaments, instruction books, or anything else needed for a car, sell well through the regular antiques dealers and shows, as well as at special car meets. A car meet usually has tables for dealers or collectors who want to swap or sell parts. You can sell your items at the meet to dealers or collectors. Don't forget old license plates and gasoline station memorabilia like gas pump globes or even full-size gas pumps.

There is an abundance of websites devoted to classic cars. You can find tires for your vintage Jaguar, a new grille for your GTO, or sell either car. Sites like www.classiccars.net act like an online swap meet. Even the *Kelley Blue Book* is online at www.kbb.com. There are more than cars on the Internet—look for sites related to railroad memorabilia, too.

BICYCLES AND MOTORCYCLES

In 1839, when roads were rough and the way long, a Scottish blacksmith named Kirkpatrick MacMillan invented the bicycle. It weighed fifty-seven pounds and sported a carved horsehead at its front. The years have seen many improvements, including steering, rubber tires, and motors. Collectors of vintage motorcycles and bicycles often ride the antique models. Parts can be found in commercial bicycle and motorcycle shops and at huge automobile flea markets. There are special clubs and publications for motorcycle collectors and some crossover with the car-collecting organizations.

TRAIN MEMORABILIA

Railroads have a charm that never fades. Collectors are interested in toy railroads (see Toys) as well as real ones. You can buy dining-car silverware or dishes or even whole train cars if you wish. Full-size trains—and airplanes, boats, and farm machinery—present problems. They are huge, difficult to transport, and of limited interest. Sometimes they can be sold to a town restoration, a large outdoor village museum, or an amusement park. An ad in an antiques paper, a specialized publication, or even a local newspaper might bring results. The best customer for you is someone who has previously purchased a full-size vehicle.

OTHER TRANSPORTATION COLLECTIBLES

The lure of the sea remains as romantic today as it has for centuries. Many collectors search for memorabilia about whaling, steamships, famous sinkings, sailboats, fishing, and other specialties. All these are included in maritime antiques.

Transportation memorabilia such as railroad bells, uniforms, menus, china, replicas of trains, ads, boating brochures, spark plugs, motors, makers' nameplates, and farm machinery parts (especially cast-iron seats) are easily sold if you locate the right collectors. Toys related to all these collections also sell well through the meets and publications and at regular toy shows. The same rules apply for large horse-drawn carriages, sleighs, popcorn wagons, or any of the over-size riding antiques.

Horse-drawn vehicles, like carriages and sleds, are collected by a small, earnest group with space and, probably, horses. To learn more about horse-drawn vehicles, read the special publications on the subject. Meets, restoration problems, and history are discussed. There are still a few working wheelwrights in rural America who can put an iron band on a wooden wheel and do other repairs. To locate one requires ingenuity and determination. Try calling a local farm paper and ask if they can help. Talk to the stables and riding schools in your area. We met a midwestern wheelwright doing demonstrations at a local "living history" fair.

There are meets for owners of farm equipment, especially steam-powered equipment, and for train, boat, motorcycle, firefighting, and airplane enthusiasts. Locate the meets, attend (if possible), and explain what you have to sell. Farm area newspapers usually list these events.

REPAIR

There are many collectors of old automobiles, automobile parts, instruction books, and memorabilia. Many professional restorers work in all parts of the country. Local collectors can tell you about nearby restoration shops. Parts can be found through ads in automobile-related publications or your local newspaper. Word-of-mouth advertising through other collectors and dealers is also successful. Huge auto collectors' flea markets are held throughout the country. Almost every type of part—old or reproduction—can be found. Collectors often go to shows looking like walking billboards with lists of wants written in large letters on a shirt or sign. After a day of walking through miles of dealers' and collectors' booths and asking questions, you will probably get the answer about where to find your car part. Check at your library for more information about local clubs and events.

PRICE BOOKS

Auto Racing Memorabilia and Price Guide, Mark Allen Baker (Krause, Iola, WI, 1996).

Automobilia, Leila Dunbar (Schiffer, Atglen, PA, 1998).

Bicycle Collectibles, Dan Gindling (Van der Plas, San Francisco, 2001).

Encyclopedia of Petroliana: Identification and Price Guide, Mark Anderton (Krause, Iola, WI, 1999).

Gasoline Treasures, Mike Bruner (Schiffer, Atglen, PA, 1996, values 2000).

Hemmings' Collector Car Almanac (Hemmings Motor News, Bennington, VT, 2001).

License Plates of the United States: A Pictorial History, 1903 to the Present, Bob and Chuck Crisler (Interstate Directory Publishing, 420 Jericho Turnpike, Jericho, NY 11753, 1997).

Miller's 2002 Classic Motorcycles Price Guide, Valerie Lewis, editor (Antique Collectors' Club, Wappingers Falls, NY, 2001).

Miller's 2002 Collectors Cars Price Guide, Robert Murfin, editor (Antique Collectors' Club, Wappingers Falls, NY, 2001).

Motorcycle Collectibles and *More Motorcycle Collectibles,* Leila Dunbar (Schiffer, Atglen, PA, 1996, 1997).

Ocean Liner Collectibles, Myra Yellin Outwater (Schiffer, Atglen, PA, 1998).

Petroleum Collectibles, Rick Pease (Schiffer, Atglen, PA, 1997, values 2000).

Promotionals 1934–1983: Dealership Vehicles in Miniature, Steve Butler (L-W Book Sales, Gas City, IN, 1997).

Railroadiana, Bill and Sue Knous (RRM Publishing, 1903 S. Niagara St., Denver, CO 80224, 2000).

CLUBS & THEIR PUBLICATIONS

20th Century Railroad Club, *The Fast Mail* (NL), 329 W. 18th St., Suite 902, Chicago, IL 60616, website: 20thcentury.org.

American Driving Society, *The Whip Newsletter* (NL), PO Box 160, Metamora, MI 48455, e-mail: info@americandrivingsociety.org, website: www.americandrivingsociety.org.

American Station Wagon Owners Association, *Wagon Roundup* (NL), 8922 Butternut Ct., Indianapolis, IN 46260, e-mail: ASWOA@aol.com, website: www.ASWOA.com.

American Truck Historical Society, *Wheels of Time* (MAG), PO Box 901611, Kansas City, MO 64190-1611, e-mail: aths@mindspring.com, website: www.aths.org.

Antique & Classic Boat Society, Inc., *Rudder* (NL), 422 James St., Clayton, NY 13624, e-mail: hqs@acbs.org, website: www.acbs.org.

Antique Airplane Association, Inc., *Antique Airplane Digest* (MAG), *Antique Airplane Association News* (NL), *Airpower Museum Bulletin* (MAG), 22001 Bluegrass Rd., Ottumwa, IA 52501-8569, website: www.aaa-apm.org.

Antique Automobile Club of America, Inc., *Antique Automobile* (MAG), PO Box 417, Hershey, PA 17033, website: www.aaca.org.

Antique Caterpillar Machinery Owners Club, *A Quarterly Magazine of the Antique Caterpillar Machinery Owners Club* (MAG), PO Box 2220, East Peoria, IL 61611, website: www.acmoc.org.

Antique Motorcycle Club of America, *Antique Motorcycle* (MAG), PO Box 310, Sweetser, IN 46987, e-mail: amc@comteck.com, website: antiquemotorcycle.org.

Antique Truck Club of America, Inc., *Double Clutch* (MAG), PO Box 97, Apollo, PA 15613, e-mail: bpowell@kiski.net, website: www.atca-inc.net.

Automobile License Plate Collectors Association, Inc., *ALPCA Newsletter* (NL), 7365 Main St., #214, Stratford, CT 06614-1300, e-mail: membership@alpca.org, website: www.alpca.org.

Carriage Association of America Inc., *Carriage Journal* (MAG), 177 Pointers-Auburn Rd., Salem, NJ 08079, e-mail: carrassc@mindspring.com, website: www.caaonline.com.

Cast Iron Seat Collectors Association, *Seat Newsletter* (NL), 40874 231st Ave., Le Center, MN 56057, e-mail: gctrax@vclear.lakes.com, website: www.castironseatclub.org.

Chesapeake & Ohio Historical Society, Inc., *Chesapeake & Ohio Historical Magazine* (MAG), PO Box 79, Clifton Forge, VA 24422, e-mail: cohs@cfw.com, website: www.cohs.org.

Chris Craft Antique Boat Club, Inc., *Brass Bell* (NL), 217 S. Adams St., Tallahassee, FL 32301-1708, e-mail: wwright@nettally.com, website: www.chris-craft.org.

Contemporary Historical Vehicle Association Inc., *Action Era Vehicle* (MAG), PO Box 493398, Redding, CA 96049-3398, website: www.classicar.com/clubs/chva/chva.htm.

Cushman Club of America, *Cushman Club of America Magazine* (MAG), PO Box 661, Union Springs, AL 36089, e-mail: ccoa@ustconline.net.

EAA Vintage Aircraft Association, *Vintage Airplane* (MAG), PO Box 3086, Oshkosh, WI 54903-3086, e-mail: vintageaircraft@eaa.org, website: www.vintageaircraft.org.

Farm Machinery Advertising Collectors, *Farm Machinery Advertising Collectors* (NL), 10108 Tamarack Dr., Vienna, VA 22182-1843, e-mail: schnakenbergdd@erols.com, website: farmmachineryadvertise.com.

Historical Construction Equipment Association, *Equipment Echoes* (NL), 16623 Liberty Hi Rd., Bowling Green, OH 43402, e-mail: info@hcea.net, website: www.hcea.net.

Horseless Carriage Club of America, *Horseless Carriage Gazette* (MAG), 49239 Golden Oak Loop, Oakhurst, CA 93644, e-mail: office@hcca.org, website: www.hcca.org.

International Stationary Steam Engine Society, *I.S.S.E.S. Bulletin* (MAG), 178 Emerson Pl., Brooklyn, NY 11205, website: www.steamengine society.org.

Lincoln Highway Association, *The Lincoln Highway Forum* (MAG), PO Box 308, Franklin Grove, IL 61031, e-mail: lnchwyhq@essex1.com, website: www.lincolnhighwayassoc.org.

Military Transport Association of New Jersey, *Motor Pool Messenger* (NL), 12 Indian Head Rd., Morristown, NJ 07960, e-mail: MVehicle@aol.com, website: hometown.aol.com/MVehicle/home.htm.

Military Vehicle Preservation Association, *Army Motors* (MAG), *Supply Line* (NL), PO Box 520378, Independence, MO 64052-0378, 816-737-5111, fax: 816-737-5423, website: www.mvpa.org.

Model A Restorers Club, *Model A News* (MAG), 24800 Michigan Ave., Dearborn, MI 48124-1713, e-mail: membership@modelaford.org, website: www.modelaford.org.

Nautical Research Guild, *Nautical Research Journal* (MAG), 12012 Kerwood Rd., Silver Spring, MD 20904-2815, website: www.Naut-Res-Guild.org.

New York Central System Historical Society, Inc., *Central Headlight* (MAG), PO Box 81184, Cleveland, OH 44181-0184, website: www.nycshs.org.

Oceanic Navigation Research Society, Inc., *Ship to Shore* (MAG), PO Box 8797, Universal City, CA 91618-8005, e-mail: ONRS@earthlink.net.

Railroadiana Collectors Association, Inc., *Railroadiana Express* (MAG), 550 Veronica Pl., Escondido, CA 92027-2869, e-mail: rcaisec@home.com, website: railroadcollectors.org.

Rolls-Royce Foundation, *The Flying Lady* (MAG), *The Hyphen* (NL), 191 Hempt Rd., Mechanicsburg, PA 17055, e-mail: rroc.hq@rroc.org, website: www.rroc.org.

The Silver Cloud and Bentley 'S' Society, *Post "55"* (MAG), 7621 Kingsbury Rd., Alexandria, VA 22315, e-mail: hallambert@erols.com.

Society for the Preservation and Appreciation of Motor Fire Apparatus in America, *Enjine Enjine* (NL), 5420 S. Kedvale Ave., Chicago, IL 60632, e-mail: bconnors@spaamfaa.org, website: www.spaamfaa.org.

Spark Plug Collectors of America, *The Ignitor* (NL), *Hot Sheet* (NL), 9 Heritage Ln., Simsbury, CT 06070-2132.

Steamship Historical Society of America, Inc., *Steamboat Bill* (MAG), 300 Ray Dr., Suite 4, Providence, RI 02906, website: www.sshsa.org.

Texas Date Nail Collectors Association, *Nailer News* (NL), 501 W. Horton, No. 10, Brenham, TX 77833, e-mail: oaks@uindy.edu.

Titanic International, Inc., *Voyage* (MAG), PO Box 7007, Freehold, NJ 07728, website: www.TitanicInternational.org.

Tucker Automobile Club of America, Inc., *Tucker Topics* (NL), 9509 Hinton Dr., Santee, CA 92071-2760, e-mail: tuckerclub@aol.com, website: www.tuckerclub.org.

Two-Cylinder Club, *Two-Cylinder* (MAG), PO Box 430, Grundy Center, IA 50638-0430, website: www.two-cylinder.com.

The Veteran Motor Car Club of America, *Bulb Horn* (MAG), 4441 W. Altadena Ave., Glendale, AZ 85304-3526, e-mail: rwr1022@juno.com, website: www.vmcca.org.

The Wheelmen, *The Wheelmen* (MAG) & (NL), 14 Mulford Lane, Montclair, NJ 07042-1719, website: www.thewheelmen.org (restoration and riding of early cycles, 1918 or earlier).

World Airline Historical Society, *Captain's Log* (MAG), PO Box 660583, Miami Springs, FL 33266, e-mail: information@wahsonline.com, website: www.wahsonline.com.

World War I Aeroplanes, Inc., *Skyways* (MAG), *WW I Aero* (MAG), 15 Crescent Rd., Poughkeepsie, NY 12601, website: www.aviation-history.com/wwwiaero.htm (*WWI Aero*, airplanes made from 1900–1919; *Skyways* airplanes made from 1920–1940).

Zeppelin Collectors Club, *Zeppelin Collector* (NL), PO Box A3843, Chicago, IL 60690-3843.

OTHER PUBLICATIONS

Aero Trader (MAG), *Aero Trader and Chopper Shopper* (MAG), 100 W. Plume St., Norfolk, VA 23510, e-mail: sherrill@traderonline.com, website: aerotraderonline.com.

Antique Power (MAG), PO Box 500, Missouri City, TX 77459, e-mail: antique@antiquepower.com, website: www.antiquepower.com (antique tractors, new tractor toys, and collectibles).

Automobile Quarterly (MAG), PO Box 1950, New Albany, IN 47151-9902, e-mail: info@autoquarterly.com, website: www.Autoquarterly.com.

Belt Pulley (MAG), 20114 Illinois Rt. 16, Nokomis, IL 62075, e-mail: beltpulley@mcleodusa.net, website: www.beltpulley.com (antique tractors and other farm equipment).

Cars & Parts (MAG), *Cars & Parts Corvette* (MAG), PO Box 482, Sidney, OH 45365-0482, website: www.carsandparts.com.

Check The Oil! (MAG), PO Box 937, Powell, OH 43065-0937, e-mail: ctomagazine@aol.com.

Classic & Mororcycle Mechanics (MAG), *Classic Bike* (MAG), *Classic Bike Guide* (MAG), *Classic MotorCycle* (MAG), *Classic Racer* (MAG), *Offroad Review* (MAG), *Old Bike Mart* (NP), Motorsport, 31757 Honey Locust Rd., Jonesburg, MO 63351-9600, e-mail: motorsport@socket.net.

Classic Boating Magazine (MAG), 280 Lac La Belle Dr., Oconomowoc, WI 53066-1648, website: www.classicboatingmagazine.com.

Classic Chevy World (MAG), 8235 N. Orange Blossom Tr., Orlando, FL 32810, e-mail: info@classicchevy.com, website: www.classicchevy.com.

Collectible Automobile (MAG), PO Box 482, Mt. Morris, IL 61054, e-mail: collectibleautomobile@pubint.com.

Disabled Veterans' Keychain Tag & Chauffeur's Badge Collectors Newsletter (NL), c/o Dr. Edward Miles, 888 Eighth Ave., New York, NY 10019, e-mail: emiles33@aol.com.

Farm Collector (MAG), 1503 SW 42nd St., Topeka, KS 66609, e-mail: farmcollector@cjnetworks.com, website: www.farmcollector.com (antique tractors, farm implements, and other antique farm equipment).

Fire Apparatus Journal (MAG), PO Box 141295, Staten Island, NY 10314-1295, e-mail: fireappjnl@aol.com, website: www.fireapparatusjournal.com.

Fordson Tractor Club, 250 Robinson Rd., Cave Junction, OR 97523.

Gas Engine Magazine (MAG), 1503 SW 42nd St., Topeka, KS 66609, e-mail: rbackus@ogdenpubs.com, website: www.gasenginemagazine.com (tractors and stationary gas engines).

Green Magazine (MAG), 2652 Davey Rd., Bee, NE 68314, e-mail: info@greenmagazineonline.com, website: www.greenmagazineonline.com (John Deere tractors and machinery, toys, models, etc.).

Hemmings Motor News (MAG), Box 100, Bennington, VT 05201, e-mail: hmnmail@hemmings.com, website: www.hemmings.com.

Iron-Men Album Magazine (MAG), 1503 SW 42nd St., Topeka, KS 66609, e-mail: rbackus@ogdenpubs.com, website: www.ironmenalbum.com (steam tractor engines).

Key, Lock and Lantern (MAG), 35 Nordhoff Pl., Englewood, NJ 07631, e-mail: keylocklantern@aol.com, website: www.klnl.org.

Military Vehicles (MAG), 700 E. State St., Iola, WI 54990-0001, website: www.krause.com/static/militaria.htm.

Old Allis News (MAG), 10925 Love Rd., Bellevue, MI 49021, e-mail: allisnews@aol.com (Allis-Chalmers tractors and equipment).

Old Cars Weekly (NP), *Old Cars Price Guide* (MAG), 700 E. State St., Iola, WI 54990-0001, e-mail: info@krause.com, website: www.krause.com.

Petroleum Collectibles Monthly (MAG), PO Box 556, LaGrange, OH 44050-0556, e-mail: scottpcm@aol.com, website: www.pcmpublishing.com (service station items, signs, gas pumps, pump globes, cans, toys, trinkets, virtually everything relating to gasoline filling stations).

PL8S: The License Plate Collectors Hobby Magazine (MAG), PO Box 222, East Texas, PA 18046, e-mail: drew@pl8s.com, website: www.pl8s.com.

Rural Heritage (MAG), 281 Dean Ridge Ln., Gainesboro, TN 38562, e-mail: editor@ruralheritage.com, website: www.ruralheritage.com (in support of farming and logging with horses, mules, and oxen).

Signpost (NL), PO Box 41381, St. Petersburg, FL 33743, e-mail: gobucs13@aol.com (highway signs).

This Old Truck (MAG), PO Box 500, Missouri City, TX 77459, e-mail: antique@antiquepower.com, website: www.antiquepower.com.

Walneck's Classic Cycle—Trader (MAG), PO Box 420, Mt. Morris, IL 61054-8388, e-mail: sherrill@traderonline.com, website: www.walnecks.com.

Wheel Goods Trader (MAG), PO Box 435, Fraser, MI 48026-0435, e-mail: wheelgoodstrader@ameritech.net, website: wgtpub.com (bicycles and pedal cars).

ARCHIVES & MUSEUMS

Antique Gas & Steam Engine Museum, 2040 North Santa Fe Ave., Vista, California 92083, 760-941-1791, 800-5-TRACTOR, websites: members. aol.com/maxbrother/maxdir/test.html and www.ziggyworks.com/ ~museum.

Bicycle Museum of America, 7 W. Monroe St., New Bremen, Ohio 45869, 419-629-9249, website: www.bicyclemuseum.com.

Henry Ford Museum and Greenwich Village, 20900 Oakwood Blvd., PO Box 1970, Dearborn, MI 48121-1970, 313-982-6001, website: www.hfmgv.org.

Indian Motorcycle Museum, 33 Hendee St., PO Box 90003, Mason Square Station, Springfield, MA 01139, 413-797-2624, website: www.sidecar. com/indian.

National Bicycle History Archive of America, PO Box 28242, Santa Ana, CA 92799, 714-647-1949, e-mail: oldbicycle@aol.com, website: members. aol.com/oldbicycle.

National Railroad Museum, 2285 S. Broadway St., Green, Bay WI 54304, 920-437-7623, fax: 920-437-1291, website: www.nationalrr museum.org.

Virginia Museum of Transportation, 303 Norfolk Ave., Roanoke, VA 24016, 540-342-5670, website: www.vmt.org.

USEFUL SITES

The Aviation History Online Museum, www.aviation-history.com

Primarily Petroliana, www.oldgas.com.

APPRAISERS

Many of the auctions and repair services listed in this section will also do appraisals. *See also* the general list of Appraisal Groups, page 483.

Col. Glenn Larson, Inc. 4415 Canyon Dr., Amarillo, TX 79110, 806-358-9797, fax: 775-306-8292, e-mail: colonel@arn.net. Appraisals of collector cars.

International Automotive Appraisers Association, PO Box 338, Montvale, NJ 07645, 201-391-3251, fax: 201-782-0663 or 978-383-4776, website: www.auto-appraisers.com. Will provide names and addresses of member appraisers to individuals needing an automotive appraisal.

AUCTIONS

➻ SEE ALSO "SELLING THROUGH AUCTION HOUSES," PAGE 485.

Copake Auction, Box H, 266 Rte. 7A, Copake, NY 12516, 518-329-1142, fax: 518-329-3369, e-mail: info@copakeauction.com, website: www.copake auction.com. Bicycle and Americana auctions. Mail, phone, and on-site bids accepted. Buyer's premium 10%. Prices realized mailed after auction. Appraisals.

Kruse International, 5540 County Rd. 11A, PO Box 190, Auburn, IN 46706, 260-925-5600 or 800-968-4444, fax: 260-925-5467, e-mail: info@kruse international, website: www.kruse.com. Online and live auctions of vehicles. Mail, phone, and online bids accepted. Buyer's premium varies. Free catalogs. Prices realized posted on website. Appraisals.

Maritime Antiques & Auctions, PO Box 322, York, ME 03909-0322, 207-363-4247, fax: 207-363-1416, e-mail: nautical@cybertours.com, website: www.maritiques.com. Specializing in maritime antiques and paintings and firehouse memorabilia. Mail and phone bids accepted. Buyer's premium 15%. Prices realized mailed after auction. Appraisals.

New England Events Mgt., PO Box 678, Wolfeboro, NH 03894-0678, 603-569-0000, e-mail: dragonflies@metrocast.net. Auctions of antique and classic boats. Mail bids accepted. Phone bids taken until 5:00 P.M. the night before the auction, not during the auction. Buyer's premium 10%. Prices realized available by request. Appraisals.

REPAIRS, PARTS & SUPPLIES

➻ SEE ALSO "CONSERVATORS & RESTORERS," PAGE 520.

American Alloy Foundry, 112-120 S. Eden St., Baltimore, MD 21231, 410-276-1930, fax: 410-276-1947. Brass, bronze, and aluminum castings in the sand mold method. Can reproduce from originals to make exact copies. Antique car parts, boat parts, airplane parts, etc. Brochure $1.

Brass 'n Bounty, 68 Front St., Marblehead, MA 01945, 781-631-3864, fax: 781-631-6204, e-mail: bnb@brassandbounty.com, website: www.brass andbounty.com. Antique boat hardware and gear.

Bumper Boyz, 2435 E. 54th St., Los Angeles, CA 90058, 800-815-9009 or 323-587-8976, fax: 323-587-2013. Vintage classic bumpers, specializing in Ford, GMC, and Chrysler bumpers. Will rechrome bumpers, grilles, guards, moldings, and miscellaneous parts.

Gensys Inc., 104 E. Ave K-4, Suite A, Lancaster, CA 93536, 661-726-9525, fax: 661-726-9525, e-mail: id.denham@verizon.net, website: www.gensys inc.net. Gensys Inc. represents E-Z Way Restoration Products, refinishing products that eliminate methylene chloride and remove paint, varnish, and other coatings. Products for coating metal and wood. Free restoration course. Complete package for care and restoration of boats, aircraft, and industrial parts. "Free Restoration Primer" available on website.

Little Century, H. Thomas & Patricia Laun, 215 Paul Ave., Syracuse, NY 13206, 315-437-4156 (winter) or 315-654-3244 (summer), e-mail: tlaun @twcny.rr.com. Fire department antiques and collectibles repaired. Brass lantern parts; fire truck bells and parts sold, made, and repaired.

Memory Lane Classics, 24516 Third St., Grand Rapids, OH 43522, 419-832-3040, fax: 419-832-2015, e-mail: info@memorylane-classics.com, website: www.memorylane-classics.com. Antique and classic bicycle parts and accessories, 1920s through the 1970s. Catalog $4.

Memphis Plating Works, 682 Madison Ave., Memphis, TN 38103, 901-526-3051. Repairing and refinishing of metals. Refinishing chrome on antique and show cars.

Military Vehicle Preservation Association, PO Box 520378, Independence, MO 64052-0378, 816-737-5111, fax: 816-737-5423, website: www.mvpa.org. Restoration services, parts, and supplies.

National Bicycle History Archive of America, Leon Dixon, PO Box 28242, Santa Ana, CA 92799, 714-647-1949, e-mail: oldbicycle@aol.com, website: members.aol.com/oldbicycle. Archive of classic bicycle information. Over 30,000 catalogs, books, and photos from the 1860s to the 1970s. Their website is devoted to identifying, cataloging, and restoration advice.

R.J. Pattern Services, c/o R.J. Hoerr, 1212 W. Detroit St., New Buffalo, MI 49117, 616-469-7538, fax: 616-469-8554, e-mail: mhoerr@starband.net. Castings for antique tractor restoration. Cast-iron, aluminum, and brass castings. Wood and plastic (foundry) patterns and models.

Time Passages, Ltd., Scott Anderson, PO Box 65596, West Des Moines, IA 50265, 515-223-5105, fax: 515-223-5149, e-mail: timepass@netins.net, website: www.time-pass.com. Gasoline pump restoration parts and supplies; reproduction decals and ID tags. Historical consultation and appraisals. Catalog $4, or free with purchase.

Vod Varka Springs, 1251 U.S. Rt. 30, PO Box 170, Clinton, PA 15026-0170, 724-695-3268. Custom-made springs and wire forms. Made to order per print or sample. Can make almost anything out of wire or flat stock.

TRUNKS

Nineteenth-century trunks sell to people who want to use them as tables or toy chests. All kinds sell—humpback, flat, leather-covered, or wooden. In bad condition, the price is low, but since many people want to restore the trunk as a do-it-yourself project, almost any trunk sells. In the 1990s old doctor bags, twentieth-century hard-sided suitcases, alligator or other attractive leather suitcases, and steamer trunks started to sell. These must be in good usable condition. Watch for any by VUITTON. These sell for hundreds of dollars.

REPAIR

Leather requires special care. Use only accepted leather cleaners and preservatives. Never use general-purpose waxes and polishes. Most department, furniture, and hardware stores sell suitable leather cleaners. Products such as neat's-foot oil and mink oil, sold in shoe stores, leather shops, shoe repair shops, and saddleries, are made especially for use on leather.

Old trunks should be restored to their original condition. If they are in very poor condition, they can be refinished in some decorative manner, but this will change the piece from an old trunk to a decorative accessory. There are many books about modern decorations for trunks but very few on correct restoration. Parts, including hardware, leather handles, and trim, are available by mail.

One major problem with old trunks is that they may smell musty. To remove the odor, wash the interior of the trunk and let it dry in a sunny spot. If the odor persists, try storing some charcoal, crumpled newspaper, clay Kitty Litter, or other absorbent material in the closed trunk for a few days.

PRICE BOOKS

Trunks, Traveling Bags, and Satchels, Roseann Ettinger (Schiffer, Atglen, PA, 1998).

REPAIRS, PARTS & SUPPLIES

A & H Brass & Supply, 126 W. Main St., Johnson City, TN 37604, 423-928-8220. Trunk supplies. Complete line of restoration hardware. Catalog $3.

Antique Trunk Co., 3706 W. 169th St., Cleveland, OH 44111-5726, 216-941-8618 or 440-835-9619, e-mail: thebuda@msn.com. Trunk restoration. Full line of hard-to-find trunk parts, including corners, coverings, handles, locks, nails, and straps; repair books, plans, and more. Free catalog of over 300 items.

C & H Supply, 5431 Mountville Rd., Adamstown, MD 21710, 301-663-1812, Mon.–Fri. 9:00 A.M.–5:00 P.M., e-mail: CandHSupplyCo@aol.com. Replacement trunk parts. Reproduction brass hardware. Paint and varnish removers, stains, and lacquers. Most orders shipped within 24 hours. Catalog $4.

Charolette Ford Trunks, Box 50368, Amarillo, TX 79159, 806-372-3061 or 800-553-2649, fax: 806-379-7932, website: www.charolletteford trunks.com. Trunk repair supplies. Locks, hinges, drawbolts, handles, nails, leather straps, and more. Books on trunk identification and restoration. Trunk restoration video $29.95. Illustrated parts catalog $2.95. Hours 8:00 A.M.–5:00 P.M.

Constantines Wood Center, 1040 E. Oakland Park Blvd., Ft. Lauderdale, FL 33334, 954-561-1716, fax: 954-565-8149, website: www.constantines.com. Woodworkers supplies, including hardwoods, tools, and hardware. Free catalog. Hours: Mon.–Fri. 8:30 A.M.–5:30 P.M., Sat. 9:00 A.M.– 4:00 P.M. (October 1–May 31); Mon.–Fri. 8:30 A.M.–5:30 P.M., Sat. 9:00 A.M.– 1:00 P.M. (June 1–September 30).

Heirloom Restorations, 267 Sherry Ln, East Peoria, IL 61611-9410, 309-694-0960, e-mail: heirloom-restorations@insightbb.com. Trunk restoration. Original finish replaced, including gold faux; trunk interiors restored. Brass and copper cleaning and buffing.

Just Trunks, 110 Sugarberry Dr., New Castle, DE 19720, 302-834-8408. Trunk restorations, parts, and supplies. Mon.–Sat. 9:00 A.M.–5:00 P.M.

Muff's Antiques, 135 S. Glassell St., Orange, CA 92866, 714-997-0243, fax: 714-997-0243, e-mail: muffs@earthlink.net, website: www.muffs hardware.com. Antique restoration hardware. Hard-to-find hardware for trunks and more. Old-fashioned locks and keys. Mail order worldwide. Catalog free online, $5 in print. Tues.–Sat. 11:00 A.M.–5:00 P.M., Sun. 1:30 P.M.–4:00 P.M.

Original Woodworks, 4631 Lake Ave., White Bear Lake, MN 55110, 651-429-2222, e-mail: orgwood@iaxs.net, website: originalwoodworks.com. Antique trunk conservation and restoration.

Phyllis Kennedy, 10655 Andrade Dr., Zionsville, IN 46077, 317- 873-1316, fax: 317-873-8662, e-mail: philken@kennedyhardware.com, website: www.kennedyhardware.com. Hardware and parts for trunks. Wholesale catalog $3.

Scott's Beckers' Hardware, Inc., 1411 S. 3rd St., Ozark, MO 65721, 417-581-6525, 888-991-0151 orders, fax: 417-581-4771, website: www.scot beckhdw.com. Antique hardware, trunk parts. Catalog online and in print. Retail showroom open Mon.–Fri. 8:30 A.M.–5:00 P.M., Sat. 9:00 A.M.– 3:00 P.M.

Van Dyke's Restorers, PO Box 278, Woonsocket, SD 57385, 605-796-4425, 800-558-1234 orders, fax: 605-796-4085, e-mail: restoration @cabelas.com, website: www.vandykes.com. Brass hardware of all kinds, trunk parts. Special parts designed to duplicate the original pieces. Mail order worldwide. Catalog.

•◆ TYPEWRITERS, SEE WRITING UTENSILS

WESTERN ARTIFACTS

Anything representative of the Old West is easily sold. Spurs, saddles, photographs, carvings, furniture, snowshoes, even old boots sell well. All American Indian-made pieces are in demand, both old and new. This includes blankets, rugs, beadwork, pottery, baskets, clothing, and special crafts like quillwork.

There are some legal restrictions on the sale of Indian pieces. Federal law currently prohibits selling anything using an eagle feather. Sometimes the feathers appear on kachina dolls or ceremonial headpieces. A few animal furs may also cause trouble. Religious items may be reclaimed by the Indian tribes, so these are not sold through an open auction or show. Mexican Indian pieces of importance are, by law, kept in Mexico, and smuggled items will be confiscated in both the United States and Mexico. Eskimo items may include ivory that cannot be sold. Discreet conversations with dealers in Indian items may make it possible for you to donate the piece to a museum or quietly sell it to another private collector. But remember, this may be illegal.

Many baskets, dolls, and beaded pieces were made by the Indians to sell to tourists in the early 1900s. These all sell quickly at reasonable prices, and you can learn the values through the general price books. It is the unusual items, like a carved figure or ceremonial pipe, that are very high priced.

Arrowheads dug up on your land should be sold to nearby specialists. Any Indian item sells best closest to its point of origin, if that is known. If you have a collection of baskets, clothing, or carvings assembled from many sources, you should contact a southwestern or major eastern dealer or gallery. A large collection or an important piece should be appraised by a competent expert on Indian art, a rarity in most cities. It will be of no help to go to the average appraiser of fine arts for values. Ask for references and be sure the appraiser has appraised Indian art before.

Cowboy hats, even if in poor condition, boots, cowgirl shirts, skirts, and scarves are collected and worn. Look in *The Indian Trader* or other publications about Indian art. Dealers and shows will be listed, and if you live far away you can offer your pieces by mail with pictures. Rarity, artistic value, condition, history, and age determine the price of an Indian artifact.

Indian objects, including tourist baskets and Navajo rugs; cowboy equipment, including elaborate boots and belts; and prints, paintings, and bronzes depicting horses and horsemen of the West, all came into favor in the 1960s, and prices have continued rising. Don't underestimate the value of any collectible that pictures a cowboy or western scene. Even a child's wastebasket picturing a horse can be worth $75.

The best place to sell western pieces is in the West, where the decorators search for the unusual. If you live in another section of the country, you may have to sell your pieces at a lower price to a dealer who goes to the western shows. Top-quality, authentic, old pieces sell well at auction houses in any part of the country.

Anything from the Old West is saved, including barbed wire, saddles, bits, stirrups, watches, guns, and posters. The first barbed wire was patented by Lucien Smith of Kent, Ohio, in 1867. More than 1,500 different varieties of barbed wire are known. Collectors prefer pieces that are eighteen inches in length.

REPAIR

Perfect pieces of American Indian pottery are so rare that the slightly damaged and repaired piece is in demand. If you break a piece of cut glass in half, then glue it together, the resale value drops to about 10 percent of the original value. If you repair a broken piece of American Indian pottery, the resale value is from 50 to 75 percent of the original value. So if you drop your vase by the famous Indian potter Maria, save the pieces and have the vase professionally restored.

Many western pieces are listed elsewhere in this book, so be sure to look in Dolls; Fashion; Folk Art; Jewelry; Pottery & Porcelain; Rugs; Textiles; and Wicker, Rattan & Basketry sections.

PRICE BOOKS

Collecting Indian Knives, 2nd edition, Lar Hothem (Krause, Iola, WI, 2000).
Collecting the Old West, Jim and Nancy Schaut (Krause, Iola, WI, 1999).
Cowboy Culture: The Last Frontier of American Antiques, 2nd edition, Michael Friedman (Schiffer, Atglen, PA, 1999).
The Four Winds Guide to Indian Trade Goods & Replicas, Preston E. Miller and Carolyn Corey (Schiffer, Atglen, PA, 1998).
Native American Fetishes, Kay Whittle (Schiffer, Atglen, PA, 1998).
North American Indian Artifacts, 6th edition, Lar Hothem (Krause, Iola, WI, 1998).
North American Indian Jewelry and Adornment, Lois Sherr Dubin (Harry N. Abrams, NY, 1999.

The Overstreet Indian Arrowheads Identification and Price Guide, 6th
   edition, Robert Overstreet (Avon, NY, 1999).
Warman's Native American Collectibles: A Price Guide & Historical Reference,
   John A. Shuman III (Krause, Iola, WI, 1998).

CLUBS & THEIR PUBLICATIONS
American Barbed Wire Collector's Society, *Wire Collector News* (NL), 1023
   Baldwin Rd., Bakersfield, CA 93304-4203, e-mail: barbedwirejohn
   @bak.rr.com.
National Association for Outlaw and Lawman History, Inc., *NOLA Quarterly*
   (NL), 1917 Sutton Place Tr., Harker Heights, TX 76548-6043, e-mail:
   millrpaula@aol.com, website: www.outlawlawman.com.
National Bit, Spur & Saddle Collectors Association, *Bit, Spur & Saddle* (NL),
   PO Box 12183, Casa Grande, AZ 85230-2183.
New Mexico Barbed Wire Collectors Association, *Wire Barb & Nail* (NL), PO
   Box 102, Stanley, NM 87056, e-mail: nsowle@aol.com.

OTHER PUBLICATIONS
American Cowboy (MAG), PO Box 54555, Boulder, CO 80323-4555, e-mail:
   cowboy@cowboy.com, website: www.americancowboy.com.
American Indian Art Magazine (MAG), 7314 E. Osborn Dr., Scottsdale, AZ
   85251.
Barbed Wire Collector (MAG), Devil's Rope Museum, 100 Kingsley St., PO
   Box 290, McClean, TX 79057, e-mail:
   barbwiremuseum@centramedia.net, website: www.barbwire
   museum.com.
Cowboy Collector Network (NL), PO Box 7486, Long Beach, CA 90807,
   e-mail: hoppyccn@aol.com.
Cowboys & Indians (MAG), PO Box 538, Mt. Morris, IL 61054, e-mail:
   mail@cowboysindians.com, website: www.cowboysindians.com.
Indian Artifact Magazine (MAG), Fogelman Publishing, 245 Fairview Rd.,
   Turbotville, PA 17772, e-mail: iam@uplink.net, website: indian-
   artifacts.net.
Indian Trader (MAG), PO Box 1421, Gallup, NM 87305, e-mail: trader
   @cia-g.com, website: www.cia-g.com/~trader/index.htm.
TrueWest (MAG), 6702 E. Cave Creek Rd., Cave Creek, AZ 85331, website:
   www.truewestmagazine.com.
Whispering Wind (MAG), PO Box 1390, Folsom, LA 70437-1390, e-mail:
   whiswind@i-55.com, website: whisperingwind.com.

ARCHIVES & MUSEUMS
Autry Museum of Western Heritage, 4700 Western Heritage Way,
   Griffith Park, Los Angeles, CA 90027, 213-667-2000, website:
   www.autry-museum.org (Gene Autry memorabilia).

Indian Center Museum, 650 North Seneca, Wichita, KS 67203, 316-262-5221, fax: 316-262-4216, website: www.theindiancenter.com.

Kansas Barbed Wire Museum, 120 W. First St., PO Box 578, La Crosse, KS 67548-0578, 785-222-9900, website: www.rushcounty.org/barbedwire museum.

Museum of Indian Arts and Culture/Laboratory of Anthropology, 710 Camino Lajo, PO Box 2087, Santa Fe, NM 87504, 505-476-1250, website: www.miaclab.org.

Museum of the Great Plains, 601 NW Ferris Ave., Lawton, OK 73507, 580-581-3460, fax: 580-581-3458, website: www.museumgreatplains.org.

National Cowboy and Western Heritage Museum, 1700 NE 63rd St., Oklahoma City, OK 73111, website: www.cowboyhalloffame.org.

National Cowgirl Museum and Hall of Fame, 1720 Gendy St., Fort Worth, TX 76107, 817-336-4475, website: www.cowgirl.net.

National Museum of the American Indian, 4220 Silver Hill Rd., Suitland, MD 20746, 301-238-6624 and One Bowling Green, New York, NY 10004, 212-514-3700, website: www.nmai.si.edu.

APPRAISERS

The auctions listed in this section will also do appraisals. *See also* the general list of "Appraisal Groups," page 483.

AUCTIONS

➤➤ **SEE ALSO "SELLING THROUGH AUCTION HOUSES," PAGE 485.**

Allard Auctions, Inc., PO Box 460, St. Ignatius, MT 59865, 800-314-0343 or 406-745-0500, fax: 406-745-0502, e-mail: info@allardauctions.com, website: www.allardauctions.com. Specializes in Indian artifacts, art, jewelry, and collectibles. Mail, phone, fax, e-mail, and Internet bids accepted. Buyer's premium 10% (15% for Internet bids). Prices realized mailed after auction and available on website. Catalog $30; yearly subscription $75. Appraisals.

Cowan Auctions, 673 Wilmer Ave., Terrace Park, OH 45226, 513-871-1670, fax: 513-871-8670, e-mail: info@historicamericana.com, website: www.historicamericana.com. American Indian collectibles, early photography, Americana, Civil War, and decorative arts. Mail, phone, fax, and e-mail bids accepted. Buyer's premium 15%. Catalogs $25–$30. Prices realized mailed after auction and available on website. Appraisals.

Four Winds Indian Auction, PO Box 580, St. Ignatius, MT 59865-0580, 406-745-4336, fax: 406-745-3595, e-mail: 4winds@bigsky.net. Absentee auctions of Indian goods. Mail, phone, and fax bids accepted. No buyer's premium. Catalog $18. Prices realized mailed after auction. Some restoration and conservation. Appraisals.

SoldUSA Auctions, 1418 Industrial Rd., Box 11, Matthews, NC 28105, 704-

815-1500, fax: 704-844-6436, e-mail: croberts@soldusa.com, website: soldusa.com. Western collectibles. Mail, phone, fax, and e-mail bids accepted. Buyer's premium 10%. Catalog $24. Prices realized on website and in following catalog. Restoration. Appraisals.

Witherell's, 300 20th St., Sacramento, CA 95814, 916-446-6490, e-mail: brian@witherells.com, website: www.witherells.com. Specializes in investment-grade nineteenth- and early twentieth-century western Americana, firearms, and American furniture. A written guarantee and a full description and condition report attesting to an object's authenticity accompany all objects. Mail and phone bids accepted. Buyer's premium 15%. Prices realized mailed after auction. Appraisals.

REPAIRS

Reversen Time Inc., 6005 Bunchberry Ct., Raleigh, NC 27616-5454, 919-981-7323, e-mail: hamblest@mindspring.com, website: www.mindspring.com/~hamblesl/index.html. Ethnographic conservation of Pacific Northwest artifacts.

WICKER, RATTAN & BASKETRY

All baskets, from Indian and Nantucket baskets to Chinese sewing baskets, are popular. The price is determined by quality, design, maker, variety, use, and condition. Miniatures under two inches high and very large baskets always command premium prices. Amateurs have a hard time pricing baskets. New African, Chinese, Filipino, South American, Korean, Taiwanese, and other baskets are often made as exact replicas of old baskets. Since natural materials are used, the design is copied exactly, and the work is by hand. It takes great knowledge to tell the old from the new. As a seller, you are only worried about getting as much as possible. If you know the basket has been in your family for fifty years, you know it is old, so you can price it accordingly. If you bought it at a house sale last year, you may not have a valuable basket, and pricing could be difficult. Good auction houses and dealers in baskets can tell the difference.

Prices are often listed by the maker in general price books. The most desirable baskets are by the Shakers, American Indians, or the Nantucket Lightship makers. Added features like potato-stamp designs, feathers or beads incorporated in the basket, or a strong history of maker and ownership will add to the price. Remember, baskets are of many shapes and sizes, from laundry baskets to toys to oriental flower containers.

REPAIR

Wicker and rattan baskets, furniture, and other objects should be kept away from direct heat and sunny windows. Pieces should be washed occasionally or wiped with a damp sponge. Moisture will keep wicker from becoming dry and brittle. Repairs can be made. There are several books that include pictures and simple descriptions of how to fix a leg or mend a bit of snagged wicker. There are "wicker hospitals" for repairs to valuable pieces.

➻ **SEE ALSO FURNITURE**

BOOKS ON REPAIR

Caner's Handbook, Bruce W. Miller and Jim Widess (Van Nostrand Reinhold, New York, 1983).

Old New England Splint Baskets, John E. McGuire (Schiffer, Atglen, PA, 1985).

Successful Restoration Shop, Thomas Duncan (Sylvan Books, Syracuse, IN, 1985).

Techniques of Basketry, Virginia I. Harvey (Van Nostrand Reinhold, New York, 1974).

Wicker Furniture: A Guide to Restoring & Collecting, Richard Saunders (Crown, New York, 1990).

REPAIRS, PARTS & SUPPLIES

➻ **SEE ALSO "CONSERVATORS & RESTORERS," PAGE 520.**

A & H Brass & Supply, 126 W. Main St., Johnson City, TN 37604, 423-928-8220. Caning supplies, replacement seats. Howard's products. Catalog $3.

Able to Cane, 439 Main St., PO Box 429, Warren, ME 04864, 207-273-3747, fax: 207-774-6481, e-mail: boz@midcoast.com, website: abletocane.net. Restoration of antique furniture. Natural rush seating, Shaker taping, French caning, wicker repair. Caning and basketry supplies. Instruction available. Catalog upon request.

Cane & Basket Supply Co., 1238 S. Cochran Ave., Los Angeles, CA 90019, 323-939-9644, fax: 323-939-7237, e-mail: info@caneandbasket.com, website: www.caneandbasket.com. Hand caning, French caning, blind caning, press caning, rush seating, natural and fiber. Wicker repair. Weaving. Shaker tape weaving, rawhide weaving. Supplies for the do-it-yourselfer. Free catalog.

Caning Shop, 926 Gilman St., Dept. KOV, Berkeley, CA 94710-1494, 800-544-3373, fax: 510-527-7718, e-mail: Kovel@caning.com, website: www.caning.com. Complete selection of chair caning, basketry supplies, books, and tools. Cane, webbing spline, reed, rattan poles, sea grass, ash splints, hickory bark, rawhide, shaker tape, gourds, basketry dyes, hoops and handles, pressed fiber seats, raffia, waxed linen threads, etc. Classes. Free brochure.

Connecticut Cane & Reed Co., PO Box 762, Manchester, CT 06040, 860-646-6586, fax: 860-649-2221, e-mail: canereed@ntpix.net, website: www.caneandreed.com. Chair seating and basketry supplies. Free catalog.

Frank's Cane & Rush Supply, 7244 Heil Ave., Huntington Beach, CA 92647, 714-847-0707, fax: 714-843-5645, e-mail: franks@franksupply.com, website: www.Franksupply.com. Chair caning and seat weaving supplies; wicker repair and upholstery supplies; basketry and fiber arts supplies; raffia and hat-making supplies; videos and instruction books.

H.H. Perkins Co., 222 Universal Dr., North Haven, CT 06473, 800-462-6660, e-mail: HPerkinsco@HHPerkins.com, website: www.HHPerkins.com. Basketry and seat weaving supplies, including cane, rush, splint, basket reeds, hoops, handles, dyes. Furniture kits, repair and restoration products, tools, stains and finishes, books, patterns, and videos. Free catalog.

Nate's Nantuckets, 17 Waterloo St., Warner, NJ 03278, 603-456-2126. Basket maker's supplies, including cane, brass hardware, bone and ivory findings, kits, and publications. Classes. Discount basket supply catalog.

Price House Antiques, 137 Cabot St., Beverly, MA 01915, 978-927-5595. Chair caning, pressed and hand caning; porch weaving; wicker repair and restoration. Rush and most natural weaving materials.

Reversen Time Inc., 6005 Bunchberry Ct., Raleigh, NC 27616-5454, 919-981-7323, e-mail: hamblest@mindspring.com, website: www.mindspring.com/~hamblesl/index.html. Ethnographic conservation of Pacific Northwest artifacts.

Rockinghorse Antiques, 111 St. Helena Ave., Dundalk, MD 21222, 410-285-0280. Restoration of antique wicker carriages. Appraisals, identification, and value. Free brochure.

Scott's Beckers' Hardware, Inc., 1411 S. 3rd St., Ozark, MO 65721, 417-581-6525 or 888-991-0151 orders, fax: 417-581-4771, website: www.scotbeckhdw.com. Refinishing supplies, caning supplies, and more. Catalog online and in print. Retail showroom open Mon.–Fri. 8:30 A.M.–5:00 P.M., Sat. 9:00 A.M.–3:00 P.M.

Wicker Fixer, 924 Prairie Ridge Rd., Ozark, MO 65721, 417-581-6148, e-mail: wckerfxr@gte.net, website: wickerfixer.com. Wicker repairs and restoration. Minor to major surgery, painting, and cleaning. Get your dog-chewed, cat-clawed, bird-pecked wicker fixed. Tip and care information on wicker available, $5.

The Wicker Fixers, 1900 Stoney Ridge Rd., Cumming, GA 30041, 770-887-8518 e-mail: dottym@mindspring.com. Chair caning, including laced (French) and pressed cane, split oak, binder cane, sea grass,

Shaker tape; all types of caning. Complete wicker restoration and repair, including bamboo, rattan, and reed.

The Wicker Woman, 531 Main St., PO Box 61, 507-753-2006, e-mail: cathryn@wickerwoman.com, website: www.wickerwoman.com. Wicker restoration and seat weaving specialist since 1975. Restoration of all types of wicker furniture to include 1890s–1930s wicker, chair caning, paper fiber and natural rush, oak, ash, reed, and hickory splint, Danish Modern, and sea grass.

Wicker Workshop, Larry Cryderman and Shoshana Enosh, 18744 Parthenia St., #1, Northridge, CA 91324, 818-886-4524 or 818-692-4999, fax: 818-886-0115, e-mail: shoshenosh@aol.com. Restoration and repair of wicker, cane, rattan, rush, Danish lace, split reed, cord sea grass, and herringbone. Spindles and rockers made. Wood furniture repaired. Custom finishes and paint; parts made.

Wickering Heights, Jim and Judy Sikorski, 401 Superior St., Rossford, OH 43460, 419-666-9461, e-mail: jamest@accesstoledo.com. Restoration of antique wicker. Carriages and doll buggies a specialty. Color match, restaining, touch-up, and hardware cleaning. Send photo for estimate.

●▸ **WINDOW & DOOR PARTS, SEE GLASS**

●▸ **WOODCUTS, SEE PRINTS**

WRITING UTENSILS

Pens, automatic pencils, ink bottles, inkwells, typewriters, and many other devices connected with writing are being collected. In the 1980s, early pens and the plastic-cased pens of the 1920s through the 1950s became of interest to collectors. The problems associated with old fountain pens are stiff or leaky ink sacs or dirty pen points, which can be fixed carefully at home if the proper parts are purchased. There are also some specialists in pen repairs listed in this chapter.

Typewriters have been difficult to sell unless they are very old and unusual, but a new group of collectors emerged in the 1990s. There are several auctions each year for rare typewriters. The most important auctions are in Germany. But most machines made after 1920 are of minimal value.

●▸ **FOR INKWELLS AND INK BOTTLES, SEE ALSO BOTTLES, GLASS, POTTERY & PORCELAIN**

REFERENCE BOOKS

Fountain Pens and Pencils: The Golden Age of Writing Instruments, George Fischler and Stuart Schneider (Schiffer, Atglen, PA, 1990).

The Book of Fountain Pens and Pencils, Stuart Schneider and George Fischler (Schiffer, Atglen, PA, 1992).

Ink Bottles and Inkwells, William E. Covill Jr. (William S. Sullwold, Taunton, MA, 1971).

PRICE BOOKS

Antique Typewriters & Office Collectibles, Darryl Rehr (Collector Books, Paducah, KY, 1997).

Antique Typewriters from Creed to QWERTY, Michael Adler (Schiffer, Atglen, PA, 1997).

The Incredible Ball Point Pen, Henry Gostony and Stuart Schneider (Schiffer, Atglen, PA, 1998).

Pens & Pencils: A Collector's Handbook, Regina Martini (Schiffer, Atglen, PA, 1996).

Victorian Pencils: Tools to Jewels, Deborah Crosby (Schiffer, Atglen, PA, 1998).

The Write Stuff: Collector's Guide to Inkwells, Fountain Pens, and Desk Accessories, Ray and Bevy Jaegers (Krause, Iola, WI, 2000).

CLUBS & THEIR PUBLICATIONS

American Pencil Collectors Society, *The Pencil Collector* (NL), 3351 Jeffrey Ln., Eau Claire, WI 54703.

Antique Typewriter Collector's Club, *Typex* (NL), PO Box 52607, Philadelphia, PA 19115, e-mail: Typex1@aol.com, website: freenet.tlh.fl.us/~curtis7 (antique typewriters and other vintage office equipment).

Early Typewriter Collectors Association, *ETCetera* (MAG), PO Box 286, Southboro, MA 01772, e-mail: etcetera@writeme.com, website: typewriter.rydia.net/etcetera.htm.

Pen Collectors of America, Inc., *The Pennant* (MAG), PO Box 447, Fort Madison, IA 52627-0447, e-mail: info@pencollectors.com, website: www.pencollectors.com.

Writing Equipment Society, *Journal of the Writing Equipment Society* (MAG), 22 Strathmore Ave., Hull HU6 7HJ, UK, e-mail: nigel@writesociety.freeserve.co.uk.

OTHER PUBLICATIONS

Float About (NL), 1676 Millsboro Rd., Mansfield, OH 44906-3374, e-mail: DiAndra@FloatAbout.com, website: www.FloatAbout.com (float pencils).

Pen World International (MAG), PO Box 6037, Kingwood, TX 77339, e-mail: info@penworld.com, website: www.penworld.com.

Ribbon Tin News (NL), 28 The Green, Watertown, CT 06795, e-mail: rtn.hoby@snet.net.

REPAIRS, PARTS & SUPPLIES

➥ SEE ALSO "CONSERVATORS & RESTORERS," PAGE 520.

Classic Fountain Pens, PO Box 46723, Los Angeles, CA 90046, 323-655-2641, Mon.–Sat. 9:00 A.M.–5:00 P.M., fax: 323-651-0265, e-mail: John@nibs.com, website: www.nibs.com. Fountain pen nib repairs and restoration, modification, and customization. Regrinding, retipping any size nib, repairs to nib cracks and splits, bladder and diaphragm replacement, imprint restoration, ink flow adjustment.

Fountain Pen Hospital, 10 Warren St., New York, NY 10007, 800-253-7367 or 212-964-0580, fax: 212-227-5916, e-mail: info@FountainPen Hospital.com, website: www.FountainPenHospital.com. Antique pens repaired. Tools and supplies for pen repair. If you would like your pen repaired, pack it in a hard box, include a note with your name, address, and phone number and a description of the problem, and send it insured to the Repair Department at Fountain Pen Hospital.

Howard Levy, 2567 Sherwood Rd., Bexley, OH 43209, 614-351-9988, Mon.–Fri. 6:00 P.M.–10:00 P.M., weekends 9:00 A.M.–10:00 P.M., fax: 614-351-9989, e-mail: bexlevy@aol.com. Repair and restoration of antique and modern fountain pens.

Pen Fancier's Club, 1169 Overcash Dr., Dunedin, FL 34698, 727-734-4742, 10:00 A.M.–9:00 P.M., fax: 727-738-0476, e-mail: penfanc@aol.com. Pens and pen parts. Repair manuals for fountain pens and mechanical pencils. Quarterly catalog $15 per year. Sample issue $4.

Vintage Fountain Pens, 3481 N. High St., Columbus, OH 43214, 614-267-8468, fax: 614-267-8468, e-mail: jproto1@aol.com. Pen repair and restoration, specializing in gold point adjusting and repair.

ALL THE REST

Over thirty-five years ago we wrote: "There is a time in everyone's life when you must decide what to do with an attic, basement, or even a drawer full of odd bits of small 'junk.' Don't throw anything away. More good antiques have been lost because of overeager housekeeping than by all other ways combined. Open all boxes and sort the contents. Stop for a moment and think, study, read, and ask lots of questions. There is a collector for almost anything. We have known of individuals and organizations that want matchboxes, playing cards, racetrack betting tickets, theater ticket stubs, theater programs, postmarks, Masonic items, erotica, gambling chips, trunks, Christmas seals, funeral invitations, old valentines and greeting cards, ads, trading cards, military insignia, railroad passes, coffin markers, newspapers, sheet music, comic books, magazines, almost anything (including the box it came in). Be patient! No item loses value with age. If, after looking around, you can find no value for the items, give them to a collector, historical society, or even a neighbor's young child. They will go into another box of 'junk' to be saved for another generation of collectors. Maybe in twenty-five years it will have a value, and for the next twenty-five it will give joy to the child who received it."

The advice was good then, and still is. Notice that many of the things we mentioned then that were considered worthless, such as greeting cards, ads, and comic books, are valued today, some even worth thousands of dollars. It's impossible to mention everything you might have that could be sold through the antiques market. We have tried to discuss selling most types of collectibles. A few other specialized collecting interests that are important enough to have created a club or publication include animal license tags, lightning rods, badges, bells, buttons, buckles, fans, flags, ships in bottles, the Statue of Liberty, miniature key chain tags, fireworks, Boy Scout memorabilia, and World's Fair and exposition items.

One word of pessimism: there are a few things that are poor sellers. They are often not worth the time required to find a buyer. These include most old Bibles, encyclopedias and dictionaries, forty-eight- to fifty-star flags, and sewing machines (unless very old). In a book we wrote over thirty years ago, we listed things the country store collectors were ignoring. Included were brooms, turkey-feather dusters, and soapstone foot warmers—all still not too easy to sell. But we wish we had the rest of the things on the list: bathtubs, candy-making tools, early electrical equipment, egg carriers, egg-beaters, flour sifters, gas mantles, glass rolling pins, graniteware (enamel on metal dishes), iceboxes, ice-cream makers, ice-cream scoops, needle cases, peanut butter pails, and pencil sharpeners.

Our last bit of advice about selling is the "Damn Fool Theory": "REMEMBER, IF I WAS DAMN FOOL ENOUGH TO BUY THIS ANTIQUE, SOMEWHERE THERE IS ANOTHER DAMN FOOL WHO WILL BUY IT FOR MORE MONEY." So don't throw anything away. A buyer is out there somewhere; it just takes time and effort.

PRICE BOOKS

1001 Salt & Pepper Shakers, Larry Carey and Sylvia Tompkins (Schiffer, Atglen, PA, 1994); 1002 Salt & Pepper Shakers, 1995; 1003 Salt & Pepper Shakers, 1996; 1004 Salt & Pepper Shakers: Nursery Rhymes, Literary Characters, 1998.

19th Century Wooden Boxes, Arene Wiemers Burgess (Schiffer, Atglen, PA, 1997).

A Collector's Guide to Cast Metal Bookends, Gerald P. McBride (Schiffer, Atglen, PA, 1997).

A Collector's Guide to Salem Witchcraft & Souvenirs, Pamela E. Apkarian-Russell (Schiffer, Atglen, PA, 1998).

American Nutcrackers: A Patent History and Value Guide, James Rollband (Off Beat Books, 1345 Poplar Ave., Sunnyvale, CA 94087-3770, 1996).

The American Pickle Castor: A Comprehensive Photo and Price Guide to the Victorian Pickle Castor, 1865–1900, Bernice Thach (Poor House Antiques, Wichita, KS, 2000).

Annotated Bibliography: World's Columbian Exposition, Chicago 1893, Supplement, G.L. Dybwad and Joy V. Bliss (The Book Stops Here, 1108 Rocky Point Court NE, Albuquerque, NM 87123, 1999).

ANRI Woodcarvings: Handcarved in Italy, Philly Rains and Donald Bull (Schiffer, Atglen, PA, 2001).

Antique Toothbrush Holders, John, Nancy, and Brooke Smith (Schiffer, Atglen, PA, 2002).

Bookend Revue, Robert Seecof, Donna Seecof, and Louis Kuritzky (Schiffer, Atglen, PA, 1996).

Breyer Molds & Models: Horses, Riders, & Animals, 1950–1995, Nancy Atkinson Young (Schiffer, Atglen, PA, 1997).

British Royalty Commemoratives, 2nd edition, Dougles H. Flynn and Alan H. Bolton (Schiffer, Atglen, PA, 1999).

Celluloid Treasures of the Victorian Era, Joan Van Patten and Elmer & Peggy Williams (Collector Books, Paducah, KY, 1999).

Collectible Ashtrays, Jan Lindenberger (Schiffer, Atglen, PA, 2000).

Collectible Bells: Treasures of Sight and Sound, Donna S. Baker (Schiffer, Atglen, PA, 1998).

Collectibles for the Kitchen, Bath and Beyond, 2nd edition, Ellen Bercovici, Bobbie Zucker Bryson, and Deborah Gillham (Krause, Iola, WI, 2001).

Collecting Flashlights, Stuart Schneider (Schiffer, Atglen, PA, 1996).

Collecting Salt & Pepper Shaker Series, Irene Thornburg (Schiffer, Atglen, PA, 1998).

Collector's Digest Price Guide to Cowboy Cap Guns and Guitars, Jerrell Little (L-W Book Sales, Gas City, IN, 1996).

Collector's Guide to Bubble Bath Containers, Greg Moore and Joe Pizzo (Collector Books, Paducah, KY, 1999).

Collector's Guide to Letter Openers, Everett Grist (Collector Books, Paducah, KY, 1998).

Collector's Guide to Lunchboxes: Metal, Vinyl, Plastic, Carole Bess White and L.M. White (Collector Books, Paducah, KY, 2001).

Collector's Guide to PEZ, Shawn Peterson (Krause, Iola, WI, 2000).

Dog Antiques and Collectibles, Patricia Robak (Schiffer, Atglen, PA, 1999).

Dreamsicles: Secondary Market Price Guide & Collector Handbook, 2nd edition (CheckerBee, Meriden, CT, 1998).

Flashlights: Early Flashlight Makers and the First 100 Years of Eveready, Billy T. Utley (ArrowPoint Press, PO Box 4095, Tustin, CA 92781, 2001).

Florida Kitsch, Myra and Eric Outwaterc (Schiffer, Atglen, PA, 1999).

Flower Frogs for Collectors, Bonnie Bull (Schiffer, Atglen, PA, 2001).

Flue Covers: Collector's Value Guide, Jim Meckley II (Collector Books, Paducah, KY, 1998).

The Galaxy's Greatest Star Wars Collectibles Price Guide, Stuart W. Wells III (Antique Trader Books, Dubuque, IA, 1998).

Guide to Tarzan Collectibles, Glenn Erardi (Schiffer, Atglen, PA, 1998).

Hawaiiana: The Best of Hawaiian Design, Mark Blackburn (Schiffer, Atglen, PA, 1996).

The Illustrated Encyclopedia of Metal Lunch Boxes, 2nd edition, Allen Woodall and Sam Brickell (Schiffer, Atglen, PA, 1999).

The Investor's Guide to Vintage Character Collectibles, Rex Miller (Krause, Iola, WI, 1999).

Judaica, Myra Yellin Outwater (Schiffer, Atglen, PA, 1999).

Law Enforcement Memorabilia, Monty McCord (Krause, Iola, WI, 1999).

The Lightning Rod Collectibles Price Guide, Russell Barnes (PO Box 141994, Austin, TX 78714, 1997).

Miniature Metal Souvenir Buildings from Germany, "Doc and The Magic Lady" (Ronald R. Hendrickson, Stolzenauer Str. 7, 28207 Bremen, Germany, 1997).

Monumental Miniatures: Souvenir Buildings from the Collection of Ace Architects, Margaret Majua and David Weingarten (Antique Trader Books, Dubuque, IA, 1999).

More PEZ for Collectors, 3rd edition, Richard Geary (Schiffer, Atglen, PA, 2000).

Neptune's Treasures, Carole and Richard Smyth (Carole Smyth Antiques, PO Box 2068, Huntington, NY 11743, 1998) (shell work).

New York World's Fair Collectibles: 1964–65, Joyce Gran (Schiffer, Atglen, PA, 1999).

PEZ Collectibles, 3rd edition, Richard Geary (Schiffer, Atglen, PA, 1999).

Popular Arts of Mexico, 1850–1950, Donna McMenamin (Schiffer, Atglen, PA, 1996).

Science Fiction Collectibles, Stuart W. Wells III (Krause, Iola, WI, 1999).

Standard Price Guide to U.S. Scouting Collectibles, George Cuhaj (Krause, Iola, WI, 1998).

Star Wars Collector's Pocket Companion, Stuart W. Wells III (Krause, Iola, WI, 2000).

Strawberry Shortcake Collectibles: An Unauthorized Handbook and Price Guide, Jan Lindenberger (Schiffer, Atglen, PA, 1998).

String Along with Me: A Collector's Guide to Stringholders, Sharon Ray Jacobs (L-W Book Sales, Gas City, IN, 1996).

Unauthorized Guide to Ziggy Collectibles, Andrea Campbell (Schiffer, Atglen, PA, 1999).

Vintage Bar Ware, Stephen Visakay (Collector Books, Paducah, KY, 1997).

World War II Homefront Collectibles, Martin Jacobs (Krause, Iola, WI, 2000).

World's Fair Collectibles: Chicago 1933 and New York 1939, Howard M. Rossen (Schiffer, Atglen, PA, 1998).

CLUBS & THEIR PUBLICATIONS

American Bell Association, *Bell Tower* (MAG), ABA Membership Chairman, 7210 Bellbrook Dr., San Antonio, TX 78227-1002, e-mail: aba-ron @juno.com, website: www.collectoronline.com/club-ABA.html.

Angel Collectors' Club of America, *Halo Everybody!* (NL), 16342 W. 54th Ave., Golden, CO 80403, e-mail: YoAngelPres@cs.com.

Antique & Art Glass Salt Shaker Collectors Society, *Pioneer* (NL), 130 Pine Ave., Bryan, OH 43506, e-mail: antiques@wmis.net, website: www.cbantiques.com/ssc.

Bookend Collector Club, *Bookend Collector Club Newsletter* (NL), 4510 NW 17th Pl., Gainesville, FL 32605, e-mail: lkuritzky@aol.com.

Brewster Society, *News Scope* (NL), PO Box 1073, Bethesda, MD 20817, e-mail: cozybaker1@aol.com, website: www.brewstersociety.com (organization for designers and collectors of kaleidoscopes).

Butter Pat Patter Association, *Butter Pat Patter* (NL), 265 Eagle Bend Dr., Bigfork, MT 59911-6235.

Cat Collectors, *Cat Talk* (NL), PO Box 150784, Nashville, TN 37215-0784, e-mail: musiccitykitty@yahoo.com, website: www.catcollectors.com.

Circus Historical Society, *Bandwagon* (MAG), 1954 Old Hickory Blvd., Brentwood, TN 37027-4014.

Commemorative Collectors Society, *Journal of the Commemorative Collectors Society* (MAG), Lumless House, Gainsborough Rd., Winthorpe, Newark Notts. NG24 2NR, UK.

Corn Items Collectors Association Inc., *The Bang Board* (NL), 9288 Poland Rd., Warrensburg, IL 62573, e-mail: bob@burrusseed.com.

Cupid Collectors Club, *Cupid Capers* (NL), 920 Newton, Waterloo, IA, e-mail: ingles12@home.com, website: www.cupidcollectors.com.

Czech Collectors Association (CCA), *Journal of Czech Decorative Arts* (MAG), *Czech Collectors Association Newsletter* (NL), Box 137, Hopeland, PA 17533, e-mail: info@czechcollectors.org, website: www.czechcollectors.org.

Egg Cup Collectors' Club of Great Britain, *Egg Cup World* (MAG), Mrs. Sue Wright, Subscriptions Secretary, Bryn Hywel, Llangranog Rd., Ceredigion, Wales SA44 5JL UK, e-mail: suewright@suecol.freeserve.co.uk, website: www.eggcupworld.co.uk.

Elephant Collectors, *Jumbo Jargon* (NL), 1002 W. 25th St., Erie, PA 16502-2427.

Fire Mark Circle of the Americas, *FMCA Journal* (MAG), *FMCA Newsletter* (NL), 2859 Marlin Dr., Chamblee, GA 30341-5119, e-mail: ghartleysr

@aol.com, website: www.firemarkcircle.org (origin and history of insurance companies, their firemarks, fire brigades and fire fighting equipment, firemen's badges, medals, and tokens and old insurance company signs).

Flashlight Collectors of America, *Beacon Newsletter* (NL), PO Box 4095, Tustin, CA 92781, e-mail: flashlight1@home.com.

Global Lottery Collector's Society, *Global News* (NL), 14 Tenth St., Plum Island, MA 01951-1913, e-mail: Kluffer@aol.com, website: Lotology.com.

Happy Pig Collectors Club, *Happy Pig* (NL), 4542 N. Western Ave., Chicago, IL 60625, e-mail: happypigclub@ameritech.net, website: members. iquest.net/~drdan/index.html.

Historical Society of Early American Decoration, Inc., *The Decorator* (MAG), c/o Lois Tucker, PO Box 429, North Berwick, ME 03906, e-mail: lois@gwi.net, website: www.hsead.org.

Horn & Whistle Enthusiasts Group, *Horn & Whistle* (NL), 1403 Halpin Rd., Middlebury, VT 05753, e-mail: efagen@sover.net, website: hornand whistle.com.

The Ice Screamers, *The Ice Screamer* (NL), PO Box 465, Warrington, PA 18976, e-mail: smoothsail@aol.com, website: www.icescreamers.com (ice cream and soda fountain memorabilia).

International Coalition of Art Deco Societies, 1 Murdoch Terr., Brighton, MA 02135, website: www.deco-echoes.com/society.html (lists of local and regional Art Deco societies are on the website).

International Frog Collectors Club, *Beyond the Pond* (NL), PO Box 201413, Bloomington, MN 55420, e-mail: LMFrogLady@aol.com, website: www.frogcollectors.com.

International Gnome Club, *Gnome News* (NL), 6740 Duncan Ln., Carmichael, CA 95608-2817, e-mail: gnomegnet@aol.com, website: www.gnomereserve.co.uk/club.

International Netsuke Society, *International Netsuke Society Journal* (MAG), PO Box 833272, Richardson, TX 75083-3272, e-mail: kevinw@net port.com, website: www. netsuke.org.

International Scouting Collectors Association (ISCA), *ISCA Journal* (MAG), c/o Doug Krutilek, 9025 Alcosta Blvd, #230, San Ramon, CA 94583, e-mail: noacman@aol.com, website: www.scouttrader.org.

International Society of Animal License Collectors, *Paw Prints* (NL), 928 SR 2206, Clinton, KY 42031, e-mail: tagman@ibm.net.

International Wood Collectors Society, *World of Wood* (MAG), 2300 W. Rangeline Rd., Greencastle, IN 46135-7875, e-mail: cockrell@tds.net, website: www.woodcollectors.org.

Judaica Collectors Society, *Judaica News* (NL), PO Box 854, Van Nuys, CA 91408-0854, e-mail: iibick@aol.com, website: www.bick.net.

Magic Collectors' Association, *Magicol: Quarterly Journal of the MCA* (MAG), PO Box 511, Glenwood, IL 60425.

Mauchline Ware Collectors Club, *Mauchline Ware Collectors Club* (MAG), PO

Box 3780, New York, NY 10185, e-mail: enquires@mauchlineclub.org, website: www.mauchlineclub.org. Mauchline wooden ware.

National Association of Soda Jerks, *Fiz Biz* (NL), PO Box 115, Omaha, NE 68101-0115, e-mail: director@omahahistory.org.

National Toothpick Holder Collectors Society, *Toothpick Bulletin* (NL), PO Box 852, Archer City, TX 76351, e-mail: tpinfo@glass-works.com, website: www.collectoronline.com/club-NTHCS.html.

New England Society of Open Salt Collectors, *Salt Talk* (NL), PO Box 177, Sudbury, MA 01776-0177, e-mail: mimiahw@aol.com, website: www.opensalts.info.

North American Vexillogical Association, *NAVA News* (NL), PMB 225, 1977 N. Olden Ave. Ext., Trenton, NJ 08618-2193, e-mail: pres@nava.org, website: www.nava.org. Flags and symbols.

Novelty Salt & Pepper Shakers Club, *Novelty Salt & Pepper Shakers Club Newsletter* (NL), PO Box 677388, Orlando, FL 32867-7388, e-mail: dmac925 @yahoo.com, website: members.aol.com/spclub1234/index.htm.

Nutcracker Collectors' Club, *Nutcracker Collectors' Club Newsletter* (NL), 12204 Fox Run Dr., Chesterland, OH 44026, e-mail: nutsue@core.com.

Open Salt Seekers of the West, *Open Salt Seekers of the West* (NL), 1067 Salvador, Costa Mesa, CA 92626.

Rin Tin Tin Fan Club, *Rinty's News* (NL), PO Box 1505, Rosenberg, TX 77471, e-mail: Rinty@RinTinTinl.com, website: www.RinTinTin.com.

Roycrofters-at-Large Association, *Roycroft Campus Chronicle* (NL), PO Box 417, East Aurora, NY 14052, e-mail: asleep220@aol.com, website: www.roycrofter.com/rala/rala.html.

The Society of Arts and Crafts, 175 Newbury St., Boston, MA 02116, e-mail: societycraft@earthlink.net, website: www.societyofcrafts.org (publishes *MassCrafts,* a guide to crafts in Massachusetts and central New England).

Souvenir Building Collectors Society, *Souvenir Building Collector* (NL), 9917 Essex Dr., Omaha, NE 68114, e-mail: info@SBCollectors.org, website: www.SBCollectors.org.

Squirrel Lovers Club, *In a Nutshell* (NL), 318 W. Fremont Ave., Elmhurst, IL 60126, e-mail: sqrlman@mediaone.net, website: members.aol.com/ sqrllovers.

Statue of Liberty Collectors' Club, *Statue of Liberty Collectors' Club Newsletter* (NL), 26601 Bernwood Rd., Cleveland, OH 44122, e-mail: lbrtyclub @aol.com, website: www.statueoflibertyclub.com.

Stockyard Collectors Club, *The Stockyard Collector* (NL), 5 Seneca W., Hawthorn Woods, IL 60047 (dedicated to the preservation of stockyard history and collectibles).

Thermometer Collector's Club of America, *Thermometer Facts & Fiction* (NL), 6130 Rampart Dr., Carmichael, CA 95608, e-mail: jockobwca @aol.com.

World's Fair Collectors' Society, Inc., *Fair News* (NL), PO Box 20806, Sarasota, FL 34276-3806, e-mail: WFCS@aol.com, website: hometown. aol.com/bbqprod/wfcs.html.

OTHER PUBLICATIONS

Charmed I'm Sure (NL), 24 Seafoam St., Staten Island, NY 10306, e-mail: zacherly24@excite.com (bubble gum charms).

Daruma (MAG), c/o Ms. Takeguchi Momoko, Amagasaki, Mukonoso Higashi 1-12-5, Japan 661-0032, e-mail: momoko@gao.ne.jp, website: www.darumamagazine.com (English-language magazine devoted to Japanese art and antiques).

Echoes (MAG), 107 W. Van Buren, Suite 204, Chicago, IL 60605, e-mail: hey@deco-echoes.com, website: www.deco-echoes.com (focusing on design from the Art Deco era through the 1970s).

The Equine Image (MAG), PO Box 4750, Lexington, KY 40544-4750, website: www.equineimages.com.

Great Scots Magazine (MAG), 1028 Girard NE, Albuquerque, NM 87106, e-mail: scottie@tartanscottie.com, website: www.tartanscottie.com (scottish terrier collectibles).

Holly Hobbie Collectors Gazette (NL), Donna Stultz, 1455 Otterdale Mill Rd., Taneytown, MD 21787-3032, e-mail: hhgazette@hotmail.com.

Honey Pots International (NL), 4455 Nevada St., Salem, OR 97305, e-mail: bettybee@cyberis.net (honey pots and beekeeping memorabilia).

Lighthouse Digest (MAG), PO Box 1690, Wells, ME 04090, e-mail; lhdigest@lhdigest.com, website: www.lhdigest.com.

Orientalia Journal (NL), PO Box 94, Little Neck, NY 11363, e-mail: orientalia@aol.com, website: members.aol.com/Orientalia.

Orientations (MAG), 17th Floor, 200 Lockhart Rd., Hong Kong, e-mail: info @Orientations.com.hk, website: www.orientations.com.hk (Asian art).

PEZ Collector's News (NL), PO Box 14956, Surfside Beach, SC 29587, e-mail: peznews@juno.com, website: www.pezcollectorsnews.com.

Police Collectors News (NP), 2392 US Hwy. 12, Baldwin, WI 54002, e-mail: pcnews@scecnet.net, website: www.p-c-news.com (police insignia and memorabilia).

Prehistoric Times (MAG), 145 Bayline Circle, Folsom, CA 95630-8077, e-mail: pretimes@aol.com, website: www.prehistorictimes.com (reviews of model kits, toy figures and books; interviews with artists and scientists; and news and information about prehistoric life).

Salty Comments (NL), 401 Nottingham Rd., Newark, DE 19711, e-mail: desaltbox@cs.com (open salts only).

Scottie Sampler (MAG), PO Box 450, Danielson, CT 06239-0450, e-mail: dbohnlein@snet.net, website: www.campbellscotties.com/ index2.htm (scottish terrier collectibles).

Scout Memorabilia (MAG), Lawrence L. Lee Scouting Museum, PO Box 1121, Manchester, NH 03105-1121, e-mail: adminstrator@scouting museum.org, website: www.scoutingmuseum.org.

Scout Stuff (NP), PO Box 1841, Easley, SC 29671, e-mail: cjensen@streamwood.net, website: www.streamwood.net.

Spinning Wheel Sleuth (NL), PO Box 422, Andover, MA 01810, e-mail: ffw@netway.com, website: www.spwhsl.com.

Strawberryland Gazette (NL), 138 E. Main Cross, Greenville, KY 42345, website: www.strawberrybonkers.com (Strawberry Shortcake).

Style: 1900 (MAG), 333 N. Main St., Lambertville, NJ 08530, e-mail: style1900@ragoarts.com, website: www.ragoarts.com.

Tomb with a View (NL), PO Box 24810, Lyndhurst, OH 44124-0810, e-mail: TombView@aol.com, website: hometown.aol.com/TombView/twav.html (cemetery art, history, heritage, social customs, and preservation).

Windmillers' Gazette (NL), PO Box 507, Rio Vista, TX 76093-0507, website: www.windmillersgazette.com.

ARCHIVES & MUSEUMS

American Computer Museum, 234 E Babcock St., Bozeman, MT 59715-4765, 406-587-7545, fax: 406-587-9620, e-mail: americancomputermuseum@computer.org, website: www.compustory.com/index.htm.

The Blair Museum of Lithophanes, Toledo Botanical Garden, 5403 Elmer Dr., Toledo, OH 43615, 419-245-1356.

Computer Museum of America, 640 C St., San Diego, CA 92101, 619-235-8222, website: www.computer-museum.org (adding machines and typewriters are also in the collection).

Lawrence L. Lee Scouting Museum, PO Box 1121, Manchester, NH 03105-1121, 603-669-8919, fax: 603-541-6436, e-mail: adminstrator@scoutingmuseum.org, website: www.scoutingmuseum.org.

Shaker Museum and Library, 88 Shaker Museum Road, Old Chatham, NY 12136, 518-794-9100, website: www.shakermuseumoldchat.org.

USEFUL SITES

American Computer Museum, www. compustory.com

About Inventors, inventors.about.com

Bad Fads Museum, www.badfads.com.

The Dance Card Museum, www.drawrm.com/dance.htm.

Dead Media Project, www.deadmedia.org. Odd inventions and antiquated devices.

Edisonian Museum, www.edisonian.com.

REPAIRS, PARTS & SUPPLIES

➥ **SEE ALSO "CONSERVATORS & RESTORERS," PAGE 520.**

American Marine Model Gallery, Inc., 12 Derby Sq., Salem, MA 01970-3704, 978-745-5777, fax: 978-745-5778, e-mail: wall@shipmodel.com, website: www.shipmodel.com. Restoration of ship models, including hull, sails, rigging, and fittings. Display units, lighting, custom models, and appraisals. Hours Tues.–Sat., 10:00 A.M.–4:00 P.M. or by appointment. Catalog $10.

Antique Aquariums & Pet Related Items, Gary Bagnall, 3100 McMillan Rd., San Luis Obispo, CA 93401, 805-542-9988, fax: 805-542-9295, e-mail: bag@zoomed.com. Repair of antique aquariums, terrariums, fish bowl stands, etc. Reproduction hand-blown crystal fish bowls, from original molds. Antique pet items, including bird cages, pet advertising and paper ephemera, dog and cat products, etc. Appraisals. Catalog $3.

August Restorations and Sales, 44 Cambridge Dr., Mashpee, MA 02649, 508-477-4169. Ship models repaired and restored, specializing in "basket case" wrecks or models that need extensive repair. Send photo for estimate.

Decorative Arts Studio, 36 Peel Rd., Danby, VT 05739, 802-293-5775, Mon.––Fri. 9:00 A.M.–5:00 P.M., fax: 802-293-5775. Stencils, historic to contemporary; brushes and related supplies. Restoration services of stenciling in your home; stencils created from your tracings. Seminars and private lessons. Catalog $4.

James S. Giuffre, 38 S. Ugstad Rd., Proctor, MN 55810, 218-624-3893, 8:00 A.M.–9:00 P.M. Collectible restoration. Authorized Harbour Lights repair and restoration, from touch-up painting to total refabrication.

Lights to Go!, PO Box 533, Derby, KS 67037, 316-304-3051, fax: 316-788-4911, e-mail: ltg@trafficlights.com, website: www.trafficlights.com. Traffic light control sequencers for antique and collectible traffic lights. Control circuit converts your light into a stand-alone, working unit. Circuits for traffic lights, railroad crossing traffic lights, School Zone markers, Walk/Don't Walk lights, and almost any electric light display.

Norman L. Sandfield, Netsuke, Oriental Art, 3150 N. Sheridan Rd., Chicago, IL 60657-4, 773-327-1733, fax: 773-327-1791, e-mail: norman@sanfield.org, website: www.internetsuke.com. Japanese inro cord in several colors. Ojime Miseru, silver or gold hangers that allow you to wear an ojime (Japanese slide fastener bead) on a chain or cord. Available in five standard sizes or custom made. "The Inro Knot: A Step-by-Step Illustrated Guide to Tying Different Knots for Hanging Medicine Boxes," including sample cord, $5; "The Cheat Sheet," a pocket-size reference to 102 common Japanese characters found in netsuke signatures, $2.

Rasa Arbas Design, 306 22nd St., Santa Monica, CA 90402, 310-828-3761, 9:00 A.M.–5:00 P.M., fax: 310-828-8235. Stencil designs with an emphasis on botanicals. Custom stenciling on site; color consulting; botanical paintings on a commissioned basis. Send SASE for price sheet.

Reversen Time Inc., Lee Hambleton, objects conservator, 6005 Bunchberry Ct., Raleigh, NC 27616-5454, 919-981-7323, e-mail: hamblest@mind spring.com, website: www.mindspring.com/~hamblesl/index.html. Ethnographic conservation of Pacific Northwest artifacts and Ukranian *pysanka* (Easter eggs).

Part III

GENERAL INFORMATION & SOURCE LISTS

GENERAL INFORMATION FOR COLLECTORS

Many books list prices of antiques and collectibles. These range from general books, like the annual *Kovels' Antiques & Collectibles Price List,* with 50,000 prices and more than 500 photos and drawings, to specialized small pamphlets that picture and price Uhl pottery, Popeye collectibles, or key-wind coffee tins. Specialized price books are listed in each chapter.

Many of the small specialized books are not found in the average bookstore or library. They can be ordered using the information listed here. Privately printed books include a complete address. Books that are listed here without the address can be located at your library or bookstore through Books in Print. Many books can be found on Internet sites, such as www.amazon.com or barnesand noble.com.

The most current price information is found in our monthly newsletter, available to subscribers and at many libraries. For information about the newsletter, send a double-stamped envelope to *Kovels on Antiques and Collectibles,* PO Box 22200, Beachwood, OH 44122.

REFERENCE BOOKS

The Aesthetic Movement: Prelude to Art Nouveau, Elizabeth Aslin (Frederick A. Praeger, New York, 1969) (decorative arts from 1855 to 1885).

Americans at Home: From the Colonists to the Late Victorians, Harold L. Peterson (Charles Scribner's Sons, New York, 1971) (pictures of rooms).

"The Art That is Life": The Arts & Crafts Movement in America, 1875–1920, Wendy Kaplan (New York Graphic Society, Boston, MA, 1987).

American Art Nouveau, Diane Chalmers Johnson (Harry N. Abrams, New York, 1979).

Art Deco, Victor Arwas (Harry N. Abrams, New York, 1980).

Design 1935–1965: What Modern Was, Martin P. Eidelberg, editor (Harry N. Abrams, New York, 1991).

Encyclopedia of Art Deco, Alastair Duncan (E.P. Dutton, New York, 1988).

Finnish Modern Design, Marianne Aav and Nina Stritzler-Levine (Yale University Press, New Haven, CT, 1998).

In Pursuit of Beauty: Americans and the Aesthetic Movement, Doreen Bolger Burke et al. (Rizzoli, New York, 1986) (decorative arts from 1860 to 1885).

Kovels' Know Your Antiques, revised edition, Ralph and Terry Kovel (Crown, New York, 1990) (general guide to antiques from 1700s to 1890s).

Kovels' Know Your Collectibles, revised edition, Ralph and Terry Kovel (Crown, New York, 1981, 1992) (general guide to collectibles from 1870s to 1950s).

Marks and Monograms of the Modern Movement, 1875– 1930, Malcolm Haslam (Charles Scribner's Sons, New York, 1977).

Official Identification and Price Guide to Arts and Crafts, Bruce Johnson (House of Collectibles, New York, 1988).

Random House Collector's Encyclopedia: Victoriana to Art Deco (Random House, New York, 1974).

Tasteful Interlude: American Interiors through the Camera's Eye, 1860–1917, 2nd edition, William Seale (American Association for State and Local History, Nashville, TN, 1981).

PRICE BOOKS

The 1950s/Modern Price Guide: Decorative Objects (Treadway, Cincinnati, OH, 2000).

2002 Collector's Mart Price Guide to Limited Edition Collectibles, Mary L. Sieber, editor (Krause, Iola, WI, 2001).

Affordable Art Deco, Ken Hutchison and Greg Johnson (Collector Books, Paducah, KY, 1999).

Antique Trader Antiques & Collectibles Price Guide, annual, Kyle Husfloen, editor (Krause, Iola, WI).

Antique Trader's Country Americana Price Guide, 2nd edition, Kyle Husfloen, editor (Krause, Iola, WI, 2000).

The Arts & Crafts Price Guide: Decorative Objects, A Decade of Auction Results, Treadway Gallery in association with John Toomey Gallery (Treadway, Cincinnati, OH, 1998).

California's Best: Old West Art and Antiques, Brad and Brian Witherell (Schiffer, Atglen, PA, 1999).

The Collectible '70s: A Price Guide to the Polyester Decade, Michael Jay Goldberg (Krause, Iola, WI, 2001).

Collectibles Market Guide and Price Index, 17th edition (Collectors' Information Bureau, Barrington, IL, 1999).

Collectibles Price Guide & Directory to Secondary Market Dealers, 9th edition (Collector's Information Bureau, Barrington, IL, 1999).

Fabulous Fifties: Designs for Modern Living, 2nd edition, Sheila Steinberg and Kate Dooner (Schiffer, Atglen, PA, 1999).

Flea Market Trader, 13th edition, Sharon and Bob Huxford, editors (Collector Books, Paducah, KY, 2002).

Floridiana: Collecting Florida's Best, Myra Yellin Outwater and Eric B. Outwater (Schiffer, Atglen, PA, 2000).

Fun Collectibles from the 1950s, 1960s, and 1970s, 2nd edition, Jan Lindenberger (Schiffer, Atglen, PA, 2000).

Garage Sale and Flea Market Annual, 11th edition (Collector Books, Paducah, KY, 2003).

Kovels' Antiques & Collectibles Price List, annual, Ralph and Terry Kovel (Crown, Inc./Three Rivers Press, New York).

Lyle Official Antiques Review 2000, Anthony Curtis, editor (Perigee, NY, 1999).

Lyle: 1,001 More Antiques Worth a Fortune, Anthony Curtis (Berkley, NY, 1999).

Miller's Price Guide 2002/3: Collectibles, Volume 14, Madeleine Marsh, editor (Octopus Publishing, London, England, 2002).

Miller's International Antiques Price Guide 2002, Volume 23, Lisa Norfolk, editor (Octopus Publishing Group, London, England, 2001).

Official Price Guide to Antiques and Collectibles, 18th edition, Harry L. Rinker (House of Collectibles, New York, 2000).

Official Price Guide to Country Antiques and Collectibles, 4th edition, Dana G. Morykan (House of Collectibles, New York, 1999).

Official Guide to Flea Market Prices, Harry L. Rinker (House of Collectibles, New York, 2001).

Official Rinker Price Guide to Collectibles, Post-1920s Memorabilia, 4th edition, Harry L. Rinker (House of Collectibles, New York, 2000).

Schroeder's Antiques Price Guide, 21st edition, Sharon and Bob Huxford, editors (Collector Books, Paducah, KY, 2003).

Today's Hottest Collectibles, 3rd edition, Dan Stearns, editor (Krause, Iola, WI, 2000).

Wallace-Homestead Price Guide to American Country Antiques, 16th edition, Don and Carol Raycraft (Krause, Iola, WI, 1999).

Warman's Americana & Collectibles, 10th edition, Ellen T. Schroy, editor (Krause, Iola, WI, 2001).

Warman's Antiques and Collectibles Price Guide, 35th edition, Ellen T. Schroy, editor (Krause, Iola, WI, 2001).

Warman's Country Antiques Price Guide, Don and Elizabeth Johnson (Krause, Iola, WI, 2001).

Warman's Flea Market Price Guide, 2nd edition, Don Johnson and Ellen T. Schroy (Krause, Iola, WI, 2001).

Warman's Antiques and Collectibles Price Guide, 36th edition, Ellen T. Schroy, editor (Krause, Iola, WI, 2002)

Old auction catalogs may have useful price information. It is possible to buy catalogs from past sales with lists of prices realized from the auction houses. Several dealers specialize in selling old catalogs at the antique shows or by mail.

The Catalog Kid, Andy Rose, PO Box 2194, Ocean, NJ 07712-2194, 800-258-2056; 732-502-9153 outside the U.S., fax: 732-502-9156, e-mail: catalogs@catalogkid.com, website: www.catalogkid.com. Post-auction catalogs from Christie's, Sotheby's, Phillips, Treadway, Rago, Fontaines, Antiquorum, Icon20, etc. Catalogs from the 1970s to the present.

BUYER BOOKS

Maloney's Antiques & Collectibles Resource Directory, 6th edition, David J. Maloney Jr. (Antique Trader Books, Dubuque, IA, 2001).

CLUBS & THEIR PUBLICATIONS

Antique Collectors' Club, *Antique Collecting* (MAG), 91 Market St. Industrial Park, Wappingers Falls, NY 12590, e-mail: info@antiquecc.com, website: www.antiquecc.com.

International Coalition of Art Deco Societies, 1 Murdock Terr., Brighton, MA 02135, 617-787-2637, fax: 617-782-4430, website: www.deco-echoes.com/society.html (write or check the website for a list of clubs in your area).

Museum of Early Southern Decorative Arts, *Journal of Early Southern Decorative Arts* (MAG); *Luminary* (NL), MESDA Membership, PO Box F, Salem Station, Winston-Salem, NC 27108, 336-721-7344, fax: 336-721-7335, e-mail: galbert@oldsalem.org, website: www.mesda.org.

National Trust for Historic Preservation, *Preservation* (MAG), 1785 Massachusetts Ave. NW, Washington, DC 20036, 800-944-6847, 202-588-6000, fax: 202-588-6266, e-mail: members@nthp.org, website: nthp.org.

Ohio Historical Society, *Timeline* (MAG), 1982 Velma Ave., Columbus, OH 43211-2497.

Roycrofters-At-Large Association, *Roycroft Campus Chronicle* (NL), PO Box 417, East Aurora, NY 14052, 716-655-1565; 716-655-0571, fax: 716-655-0562, e-mail: asleep220@aol.com, website: www.roycrofter.com/rala/rala.html.

OTHER PUBLICATIONS

American Antiquities Exchange (NP), 126 E. High St., Springfield, OH 45502, e-mail: mail@americanantiquities.com, website: www.americanantiquities.com.

Antique & Collectables (NP), PO Box 12589, El Cajon, CA 92022, e-mail: antiqunews@aol.com.

Antique & Collectible News (NP), PO Box 529, Anna, IL 62906, e-mail: reppert@midwest.net.

Antique & Collectors Reproduction News (NL), PO Box 12130, Des Moines, IA 50312-9403, e-mail: acrn@repronews.com, website: www.repronews.com.

The Antique Dealer (MAG), 115 Shaftesbury Ave., London WC2H 8AD, UK, e-mail: info@theantiquedealer.co.uk.

Antique Dealer and Collectors Guide (MAG), Esco Business Services Ltd., PO

Box 935, Finchingfield, Braintree, Essex CM7 4LN, UK, e-mail: marypayne@esco.co.uk, website: www.antiquecollectorsguide.co.uk.

Antique Journal (NP), 2329 Santa Clara Ave., Suite 207, Alameda, CA 94501, e-mail: antiquejrl@aol.com.

Antique Register (NP), *The Country Register* (NP), PO Box 84345, Phoenix, AZ 85071, e-mail: barbara@countryregister.com, website: www.countryregister.com (published alternately; advertising and promotion of country and Victorian shops, tearooms, bed-and-breakfasts, etc.)

Antique Review (NP), 700 E. State St., Iola, WI 54990, e-mail: info@krause.com, website: www.krause.com.

Antique Shoppe (NP), PO Box 2175, Keystone Heights, FL 32656, e-mail: antshoppe@aol.com, website: www.antiqnet.com/antiqueshoppe.

Antique Showcase (MAG), 103 Lakeshore Rd., Suite 202, St. Catharines, ON L2N 2T6, Canada, e-mail: office@trajan.com.

Antique Trader (NP), 700 E. State St., Iola, WI 54990-0001, e-mail: info@krause.com, website: www.krause.com.

Antique-ing Trip Planner (MAG), PO Box 219K, Western Springs, IL 60558-0219, website: www.antique-ing.com.

The Antiquer (MAG), PO Box 2054, New York, NY 10159-2054, e-mail: info@theantiquer.net, website: theantiquer.net.

Antiques & Art Around Florida (MAG), PO Box 2481, Fort Lauderdale, FL 33303-2481, e-mail: aarf@shadow.net, website: aarf.com.

Antiques and Art Independent (MAG), e-mail: antiquesnews@hotmail.com, website: www.antiquesnews.co.uk.

Antiques & Auction News (NP), PO Box 500, Mount Joy, PA 17552, e-mail: dsater7650@aol.com.

Antiques & Collectibles Magazine (NP), PO Box 33, Westbury, NY 11590, e-mail: savannah@slip.net, website: www.goodtimesmag.com.

Antiques & Collecting (MAG), 1006 S. Michigan Ave., 5th Floor, Chicago IL 60605, e-mail: acm@interaccess.com.

Antiques and The Arts Weekly (NP), Newtown Bee Publishing Co., PO Box 5503, Newtown, CT 06470-5503, e-mail: subscriptions@thebee.com, website: www.antiquesandthearts.com.

Antiques Gazette (NP), PO Box 305, Hammond, LA 70404, e-mail: gazette@i-55.com, website: theantiquesgazette.com.

Antiques Info (MAG), PO Box 93, Broadstairs, Kent CT10 3YR, UK, website: www.antiques-info.co.uk.

Antiques Roadshow Insider (NL), PO Box 338, Mount Morris, IL 61054-8076.

Antiques Trade Gazette (NP), 34 E. 64th St., New York, NY 10021-7351, e-mail: subscriptions@antiquestradegazette.com, website: www.antiquestradegazette.com.

AntiqueWeek (NP), 27 N. Jefferson St., PO Box 90, Knightstown, IN 46148, e-mail: Antiquewk@aol.com, website: www.antiqueweek.com or www.mayhill-publications.com (published in two editions, Eastern and Central).

Apollo Magazine Ltd. (MAG), PO Box 47, N. Hollywood, CA 91603-0047, e-mail: ApolloUSA@aol.com, website: apollomagazine.com.

Architectural Digest (MAG), PO Box 59061, Boulder, CO 80328-9061, e-mail: subscriptions@archdigest.com, website: www.archdigest.com.

Art & Antiques (MAG), 2100 Powers Ferry Rd., Atlanta, GA 30339, website: www.artantiquesmag.com.

Art & Auction (MAG), PO Box 3085, Langhorne, PA 19047-9185, e-mail: edit@artandauction.com, website: www.artandauction.com (includes reviews of important auctions throughout the U.S., Europe, Latin America, and Asia).

Auction Exchange and Collectors News (NP), PO Box 67, 929 Industrial Pkwy., Plainwell, MI 49080-0057, e-mail: info@eauctionexchange.com, website: www.eauctionexchange.com.

BBC Homes & Antiques (MAG), BBC Worldwide Ltd., Homes & Antiques Subscriptions, PO Box 279, Sittingbourne, Kent ME9 8DF, UK, e-mail: homes&antiques@galleon.co.uk, website: www.beeb.com/homesandantiques.

Cape Cod Antiques & Arts (NP), 5 Namskaket Rd., Orleans, MA 02653.

Cape Cod Antiques Monthly (NP), PO Box 546, Farmington, NH 03835, e-mail: tumeroll@s-way.com.

CIB Collectibles Report (NL), Collectors' Information Bureau, 77 W. Washington St., Suite 1716, Chicago, IL 60602, e-mail: askcib@collectorsinfo.com., website: www.collectorsinfo.com

Collect it! (MAG), The Tower, Phoenix Square, Colchester, Essex CO4 9PE, UK, e-mail: info@essentialpublishing.co.uk., website: www.collectit.co.uk.

Collectibles Canada (MAG), 103 Lakeshore Rd.. Suite 202, St. Catharines, ON L2N 2T6, Canada, e-mail: newsroom@trajan.com, website: www.trajan.com.

Collector (NP), PO Box 148, Heyworth, IL 61745, e-mail: collinc@davesworld.net.

Collector Editions (MAG), PO Box 306, Grundy Center, IA 50638.

Collector Magazine (MAG), Southern California Collectors Association, 436 W. 4th St., #222, Pomona, CA 91766, e-mail: Icollect@aol.com.

Collector Magazine & Price Guide (MAG), 700 E. State St., Iola, WI 54990, e-mail: info@krause.com, website: www.krause.com.

Collectors' Classified (NL), PO Box 347, Holbrook, MA 02343-0347, e-mail: ccmay1975@aol.com.

Collectors Journal (NP), PO Box 601, Vinton, IA 52349-0601, e-mail: antiquesCJ@aol.com, website: www.collectorsjournal.com.

Collector's Mart Magazine (MAG), 700 E. State St., Iola, WI 54990-0001, e-mail: info@krause.com, website: www.krause.com.

Collectors News (MAG), PO Box 306, Grundy Center, IA 50638, e-mail: collectors@collectors-news.com, website: collectors-news.com.

Cotton & Quail/Antique Gazette (NP), 700 E. State St., Iola, WI 54990, e-mail: info@krause.com.

Country Collectibles (MAG), 1115 Broadway, New York, NY 10010-0397, e-mail: nyjacksier@aol.com.

Discover Mid-America (NP), 104 E. 5th St., Suite 201, Kansas City, MO 64106, e-mail: kkweyand@discoverypub.com, website: discoverypub.com (articles on day trips and overnight trips to discover antiques, collectibles, and heritage crafts at shops and shows in a nine-state area).

Early American Life (MAG), PO Box 420235, Palm Coast, FL 32142-0235, website: www.earlyamericanlife.com.

Farm and Dairy (NP), PO Box 38, Salem, OH 44460, e-mail: subscribe @farmanddairy.com, website: www.farmanddairy.com (includes Antique Collector and Auction Guide section).

Flea Market Shopper's Guide (NP), PO Box 8, La Habra, CA 90633, e-mail: dennis@rgcshows.com, website: www.rgcshows.com.

Georgian Antique Digest (MAG), 22 Louisa St. E., PO Box 429, Thornbury, ON N0H 2P0, Canada, e-mail: gad@georgian.net.

Great Lakes Trader (NP), 132 S. Putnam, Williamston, MI 48895, e-mail: GLTrader@aol.com.

House & Garden (MAG), PO Box 37618, Boone, IA 50037-4618, e-mail: subscriptions@house-and-garden.com, website: www.house-and-garden.com.

Indiana Antique Buyers News (NP), PO Box 213, Silver Lake, IN 46982, e-mail: IABN@hoosierlink.net, website: www.indianaantique.com.

Journal America (NP), PO Box 459, Hewitt, NJ 07421, e-mail: journal @warwick.net.

Journal of Antiques and Collectibles (NP), PO Box 950, Sturbridge, MA 01566, e-mail: JMJY2@aol.com, website: www.journalofantiques.com.

Journal of Decorative and Propaganda Arts (MAG), 1001 Washington Ave., Miami Beach, FL 33139, e-mail: dapa@thewolf.fiu.edu, website: www.wolfsonian.fiu.edu/education/publications.

Journal of Early Southern Decorative Arts (MAG), *Luminary* (NL), Museum of Early Southern Decorative Arts, MESDA Membership, PO Box F Salem Station, Winston-Salem, NC 27108, e-mail: galbert@oldsalem.org, website: www.mesda.org.

Kovels on Antiques and Collectibles (NL), PO Box 420347, Palm Coast, FL 32142-0347, website: www.kovels.com.

Magazine Antiques (MAG), PO Box 37009, Boone, IA 50037-0009.

Maine Antique Digest (NP), Box 1429, Waldoboro, ME 04572-1429, e-mail: mad@maine.com, website: www.maineantiquedigest.com.

MidAtlantic Antiques Magazine (NP), PO Box 5040, Monroe, NC 28111, e-mail: maeditor@TheEJ.com.

Modernism Magazine: 20th Century Art & Design (MAG), 333 N. Main St., Lambertville, NJ 08530, e-mail: Modernist@Ragoarts.com, website: www.ragoarts.com.

Mountain States Collector (NP), PO Box 2525, Evergreen, CO 80437-2525, e-mail: spreepub@aol.com, website: mountainstatescollector.com.

New England Antiques Journal (NP), PO Box 120, Ware, MA 01082, e-mail: visit@antiquesjournal.com, website: www.antiquesjournal.com.

New Hampshire Antiques Monthly (NP), PO Box 546, Farmington, NH 03835, e-mail: tumeroll@s-way.com.

New York Antique Almanac (NP), PO Box 2400, New York, NY 10021, e-mail: nyantique@aol.com.

New York-Pennsylvania Collector (NP), 73 Buffalo St., Canandaigua, NY 14424, e-mail: Collector@MPNewspapers.com, website: www.NY-PACollector.com.

Northeast (NP), PO Box 37, Hudson, NY 12534, e-mail: nejournal @mhonline.net, website: www.northeastjournal.com.

Ohio Collectors' Magazine (MAG), PO Box 1522, Piqua, OH 45356, e-mail: tonyafb@yahoo.com.

Old Stuff (NP), PO Box 1084, McMinnville, OR 97128, e-mail: millers@oldstuffnews.com, website: oldstuffnews.com.

Renninger's Antique Guide (NP), PO Box 495, Lafayette Hill, PA 19444.

Smithsonian (MAG), Smithsonian Institution, PO Box 420311, Palm Coast, FL 32142-0311, website: www.smithsonianmag.si.edu.

Southeastern Antiquing and Collecting Magazine (MAG), PO Box 510, Acworth, GA 30101-0510, e-mail: antiquing@go-star.com, website: go-star.com.

Southern Antiques (NP), PO Drawer 1107, Decatur, GA 30031-1107, e-mail: southernantiques@msn.com.

Thompsons Antiques Gazette (NP), Marianne Thompson, 50-39026 Rg Rd 275, Red Deer County, AB T4S 2A9, Canada, e-mail: mdthompson @shaw.ca.

Tradicion Revista (MAG), Paul Rhetts, 925 Salamanca Way, Albuquerque, NM 87107-5647, e-mail: info@nmsantos.com, website: www.nmsantos.com (art and culture of the Hispanic Southwest).

Treasure Chest (NP), PO Box 1120, Attleboro, MA 02703, e-mail: treasurechest@thesunchronicle.com.

Unravel the Gavel (NP), 14 Hurricane Rd., #1, Belmont, NH 03220, e-mail: gavel96@worldpath.net, website: www.thegavel.net (antiques and auctions in New Hampshire and northern New England).

Upper Canadian (NP), PO Box 653, Smiths Falls, ON K7A 4T6, Canada, e-mail: uppercanadian@recorder.ca, website: www.upper canadian.com.

Vermont Antique Times (NP), 2434 Depot St., PO Box 1880, Manchester Center, VT 05255, e-mail: vat@sover.net (covers Connecticut, Massachusetts, New Hampshire, and Vermont).

Victoria (MAG), PO Box 7150, Red Oak, IA 51591-2578, e-mail: victoriamag
@hearst.com, website: www.victoriamag.com.

West Coast Peddler (NP), PO Box 5134, Whittier, CA 90607, e-mail: west
coastpeddler@earthlink.net, website: www.WestCoastPeddler.com.

World of Interiors (MAG), Tower House, Lathkill St., Market Harborough,
Leics. LE16 9EF, UK, website: www.worldofinteriors.co.uk.

Yesteryear (NP), PO Box 2, Princeton, WI 54968, e-mail: yesteryear
@vbe.com.

ARCHIVES & MUSEUMS

There are local archives, historical societies, and museums in
every state that can help you learn more about regional collectibles.
Here are a few with a national focus.

Library of Congress, Washington, DC 20540, 202-707-5000, fax: 202-
707-5844, website: lcweb.loc.gov.

National Trust for Historic Preservation, 1785 Massachusetts Ave. NW,
Washington, DC 20036, 800-944-6847, 202-588-6000, fax: 202-
588-6266, e-mail: members@nthp.org, website: nthp.org.

Smithsonian Institution, 900 Jefferson Dr. SW, Rm. 2410, MRC 421, Washington, DC 20560, 202-357-2700, fax: 202-786-2515, website: www.si.edu.

The Wolfsonian, 1001 Washington Ave., Miami Beach, FL 33139, 305-531-
1001, fax: 305-531-2133, website: www.wolfsonian.fiu.edu.

USEFUL SITES

Antiquestrade.com, online price guide of items sold in England.

Art Fact, www.artfact.com. Subscription-based online price guide.

Collectors.org, www.collectors.org.

The History Net, www.thehistorynet.com.

Library of Congress, www.loc.gov.

Making of America, moa.umdl.umich.edu.

Old-Paper.com, www.old-paper.com. Vintage catalogs, brochures, and
advertisements.

Pennsylvania Historical and Museum Commission, www.state.pa.us/
PA_Exec/Historical_Museum/DAM/psa.htm.

APPRAISAL GROUPS

The major antiques appraisal associations are listed below. Most
have lists of members and will send you a complete list or the names
of local appraisers. You can also check their websites for information
on how to find an appraiser in your area. Appraisers usually include
their membership information in their advertising in the Yellow

Pages of the telephone book. Many of those listed in the sections on auction houses, matching services, and repair also appraise.

Tell the appraiser what you want the appraisal for: insurance purposes, selling value, or estate valuation. Be sure to ask what the charge is for the appraisal. A written appraisal will cost more than a verbal appraisal.

American Society of Appraisers (ASA), PO Box 17265, Washington, DC 20041, 800-272-8258 or 703-478-2228, fax: 703-742-8471, e-mail: asainfo@apo.com, website: www.appraisers.org. *Directory of Accredited Personal Property Appraisers* lists tested and accredited members, geographically, in the U.S. and abroad. Information on the appraisal profession, questions and answers about appraising. Single copy free.

Antique Appraisal Association of America (AAAA), 11361 Garden Grove Blvd., Garden Grove, CA 92843, 714-530-7090. Newsletter for members.

Appraisers Association of America, Inc. (AAA), 386 Park Ave. S., Suite 2000, New York, NY 10016, 212-889-5404, fax: 212-889-5503, e-mail: aaal@rcn.com, website: www.appraisersassoc.org. Free referral service of personal property appraisers. Searchable database on website.

Appraisers National Association (ANA), 25602 Alicia Parkway, PMB 245, Laguna Hills, CA 92653, 949-349-9179, e-mail: info@ana-appraisers.org, website: www.ana-appraisers.org. Nonprofit professional association of personal property appraisers. Referral to a qualified appraiser. Educational seminars and activities relating to personal property appraising.

Art Dealers Association of America (ADAA), 575 Madison Ave., New York, NY 10022, 212-940-8590, fax: 212-940-6484, e-mail: adaa@art dealers.org, website: www.artdealers.org. Appraisal of works of fine art being donated to museums or other nonprofit organizations if an appraisal is needed for income tax purposes. Membership directory.

International Society of Appraisers (ISA), 16040 Christensen Rd., Suite 102, Seattle, WA 98188-2929, 888-472-5762 toll free or 206-241-0359, fax: 206-241-0436, e-mail: isahq@isa-appraisers.org, website: www.isa-appraisers.org. Personal property appraisals. Free referrals.

New England Appraisers Association (NEAA), 5 Gill Terrace, Ludlow, VT 05149, 802-228-7444, fax: 802-228-7444, e-mail: llt44@ludl.tds.net, website: www.newenglandappraisers.net. *The Appraisers Standard,* quarterly newsletter, $20 per year. Referral service nationwide. Send request by e-mail or regular mail.

SELLING THROUGH AUCTION HOUSES

Most antiques can be sold through an auction gallery. It is best to show the actual antique to the gallery, but if distance makes that impossible, the mail will help. Write a letter about the antique, giving its size and a description of all its flaws. Copy any markings as closely as possible. It is necessary to send a clear photograph for most items. Some things, like plates, fabrics, books, and other flat objects, can be placed on the glass of a photocopy machine and "pictured" in this way. Be sure to describe the colors if you are sending a black-and-white image, and include a stamped, self-addressed envelope and a letter explaining where you live, how many items you wish to sell, and any history of the antique.

Ask for a contract from the gallery outlining its sales policies and charges. Ask if the money from any sale will be kept in an escrow account. Reread the advice in Part I of this book before you sign a contract. Never ship merchandise without a contract. All items should be sent by mail or a delivery service with insurance and a return-receipt request. If you are shipping a large piece of furniture by truck, be sure you have insurance and a receipt that states the value and includes a full description, including condition.

Remember, the antique is yours until you have proof it has been received by the auction house. If it is lost or damaged on the way to the sale, your insurance is expected to pay the claim. We once shipped a large sideboard with gilt-bronze ormolu and a porcelain plaque on the front cabinet door. The porcelain was removed by the movers and packed separately. When the piece arrived, the two small gold-headed screws that held the plaque in place were missing. The movers paid the claim of more than $100 for these small items because we could prove that the replacements had to be exact or the value of the sideboard would be lowered.

There are many regional auction houses. Those listed here advertise nationally and will sell you a catalog and sale results through the mail or the Internet. Most accept bids by mail, phone, fax, e-mail, or the Internet. We have seen the advertising and catalogs from these auction galleries and have attended many of their sales. Every auction house listed here has been contacted. We list only auctions that send enough information before the sale to make it possible for an out-of-town bidder to participate. We have not listed auction houses that would be available only to those who travel to the location of the sale. Do not take inclusion in this list as any form of endorsement. To those who may have been omitted, we apologize. The lack of listing is an oversight and is not a lack of endorsement.

Most of these auction houses hold on-site, live auctions and sell all types of antiques and collectibles. A few sell just specialty items, such as coins or dolls. We have indicated some of these.

A-1 Auction Service, 2042 N. Rio Grand Ave., Suite E, Orlando, FL 32854, 407-839-0004, fax: 407-839-0004, e-mail: dwhite500@cfl.rr.com, website: www.a-1auction.net. Mail and phone bids accepted. Buyer's premium 10%. Appraisals.

A-Plus Auctions, N. Hwy. 1, Cocoa, FL 32926, 321-639-4440, fax: 321-636-9809, e-mail: info@aplusauctions.com, website: www.aplusauctions.com. Mail, phone, and Internet bids accepted. Buyer's premium 10%. Prices realized mailed after auction. Appraisals.

Albrecht Auction Service, PO Box 50, Vassar, MI 48768, 989-823-8835, fax: 989-823-2543, e-mail: info@albrechtauction.com, website: www.albrechtauction.com. Antiques, collectibles, estates, and consignments. Mail, phone, and Internet bids accepted. No buyer's premium. Prices realized mailed or e-mailed after auction. Free catalog. Appraisals.

Alderfer Auction Co., 501 Fairgrounds Rd., Hatfield, PA 19440, 215-393-3000, fax: 215-368-9055, e-mail: info@alderferauction.com, website: www.alderferauction.com. Specializes in antiques, fine art, decorative accessories, coins, and firearms. Mail and pre-arranged phone bids accepted. Buyer's premium 10%. Catalog $25; yearly subscription $80.

Alexander Autographs, Inc., 100 Melrose Ave., Suite 100, Greenwich, CT 06830, 203-622-8444, fax: 203-622-8765, e-mail: info@alexautographs.com, website: www.alexautographs.com. Auctions of historic

INITIALS AND ACRONYMS AFTER AUCTIONEERS' NAMES

AARE—Accredited Auctioneer of Real Estate. The auctioneer has met certain requirements set by the Auction Marketing Institute.

CAGA—Certified Appraisers Guild of America. The auctioneer has met certain requirements set by the Missouri Auction School.

CAI—Certified Auctioneers Institute. The auctioneer has met certain requirements set by the Auction Marketing Institute.

GPPA—Graduate Personal Property Appraiser. The auctioneer has met certain requirements set by the Auction Marketing Institute.

NAA—the auctioneer belongs to the National Auctioneers Association, a professional organization of more than 6,000 auctioneers.

documents and manuscripts. Mail, phone, fax, and e-mail bids accepted. Buyer's premium 15%. Catalog $20. Prices realized on website. Appraisals.

All-American Collectibles, Inc., 31-00 Broadway, 3rd Floor, Fair Lawn, NJ 07410, 800-872-8850, 201-797-2555, e-mail: all-american-collectibles @worldnet.att.net. Americana, baseball memorabilia, and cartoon art. Mail bids accepted. Buyer's premium 10%.

Allard Auctions, Inc., PO Box 1030, St. Ignatius, MT 59865-1030, 888-314-0343 or 406-745-0500, fax: 406-745-0502, e-mail: info@allard auctions.com, website: www.allardauctions.com. Specializes in Indian artifacts, art, jewelry, and collectibles. Mail, phone, fax, e-mail, and Internet bids accepted. Buyer's premium 10% (15% for Internet bids). Prices realized mailed after auction and available on website. Catalog $30; yearly subscription $75. Appraisals.

America West Archives, PO Box 100, Cedar City, UT 84721, 435-586-9497, fax: 435-586-9497, e-mail: awa@netutah.com, website: www.america westarchives.com. Auctions of historical old documents from the Old West period. Mail and phone bids accepted. Buyer's premium 10%. Prices realized available in following catalog. Catalog $3; yearly subscription $15 for 6 issues. Appraisals.

American Historical Auctions, 24 Farnsworth St., Suite 605, Boston, MA 02210, 617-443-0033, fax: 617-443-0789. Mail, phone, and fax bids accepted. Buyer's premium 15%. Prices realized mailed to successful bidders. Appraisals.

American Social History and Social Movements, PO Box 203, Tucker, GA 30085, 678-937-1835, fax: 678-937-1835, e-mail: ashsm@bellsouth.net, website: www.ashsm.com. Specializes in auctions of social history items. Mail, fax, phone, and Internet bids accepted. Buyer's premium 10%–15%. Catalog $12; yearly subscription $30.

Anderson Auction, PO Box 644, Troy, OH 45373, 937-339-0850, fax: 937-339-8620, e-mail: aaauction@erinet.com, website: www.erinet.com/ aaauctn. Absentee auctions of political and historical memorabilia, four auctions per year. Phone, fax, and e-mail bids accepted. Catalog subscription, three issues $25; $35 international. Write or e-mail for a complimentary copy.

Andre Ammelounx, PO Box 136, Palatine, IL 60078, 847-991-5927, fax: 847-991-5947, e-mail: aapo136@aol.com, website: tsaco.com. Antique beer steins and drinking vessels, Swiss (Black Forest) woodcarvings. Mail and fax bids accepted. Buyer's premium 15%. Catalog $30 per year. Prices realized mailed after auction. Appraisals.

Antique Helper/Dan Ripley Antiques, 907 E. Michigan St., #102, Indianapolis, IN 46202, 317-955-5900, fax: 253-322-5430, e-mail: sales@antiquehelper.com, website: www.antiquehelper.com. Online and live auctions. Mail, phone, fax, e-mail, and live eBay bids accepted. Buyer's premium 10%. Prices realized mailed after auction. Catalog $12. Free verbal appraisals.

Antique Phonograph Center, PO Box 2574, Hwy. 206, Vincentown, NJ 08088, 609-859-8617, e-mail: fsi491160@aol.com. Mail and phone bids accepted. No buyer's premium. Restoration and conservation. Appraisals.

Antiquorum Auctioneers, 609 Fifth Ave., Suite 503, New York, NY 10017, 212-750-1103, fax: 212-750-6127, e-mail: newyork@antiquorum.com, website: www.antiquorum.com. Auctions of important collector's watches, wristwatches, and clocks about eight times a year, three of which are held in Geneva, one in Hong Kong, and three to four sales in New York. Buyer's premium 15% up to $50,000, 10% over $50,000. Prices realized mailed on request. Appraisals.

Apple Tree Auction Center, 1616 W. Church St., Newark, OH 43055, 740-344-4282, fax: 740-344-3673, e-mail: info@appletreeauction.com, website: www.appletreeauction.com. Auctions of general antiques, fine art, Heisey glass, and Oriental rugs. Mail, phone, and Internet bids. Prices realized available on website after auction. Appraisals.

Arte Primitivo, Howard S. Rose Gallery, 3 E. 65th St., #2, New York, NY 10021, 212-570-6999, fax: 212-570-1899, e-mail: info@arteprimitivo.com, website: www.arteprimitivo.com. Specializes in absentee auctions of pre-Columbian art, classical and Egyptian antiquities, Asian antiquities and antiques, and ethnographic art. Mail, phone, fax, e-mail, Internet, and in person bids accepted. Buyer's premium 15%. Catalogs $15 U.S., $20 international.

Arthur Auctioneering, 563 Reed Rd., Hughesville, PA 17737, 800-278-4873 or 717-584-3697. Mail bids accepted. No phone bids. Buyer's premium 10%. Prices realized mailed after auction. Appraisals.

Aspireauctions.com, 12730 Larchmere Blvd., Cleveland, OH 44120, 216-231-5515, fax: 216-231-5530, e-mail: cynthia@aspireauctions.com, website: aspireauctions.com. Online auctions. Buyer's premium 15%. Gallery open by appointment only, except during preview. Preview hours 11:00 A.M.–6:00 P.M. beginning on Mondays until the last lot has closed. Free appraisals.

Aston Macek Auction Co., 2825 Country Club Rd., Endwell, NY 13760, 607-785-6598, fax: 607-785-6598, e-mail: astonmacek@stny.rr.com, website: www.astonmacek.com. No buyer's premium. Prices realized mailed after auction. Catalog price varies.

Auction Team Köln, 4025 Cattlemen Rd., PMB 108, Sarasota, FL 34233, 941-925-0385, fax: 941-925-0487, e-mail: auction@breker.com, website: www.breker.com. Specialty auctions of all kinds of old technology, including photographica, office technology, clocks, and toys. Mail and phone bids accepted. Buyer's premium 20%. Prices realized available on website after auction. Catalog $58 U.S. per year.

Auction under the Big Top, 7 Cooks Glen Rd., Spring City, PA 19745, 610-469-6331, e-mail: barbmgr@aol.com, website: carousel.com. Carousel auctions. Mail and phone bids accepted. Buyer's premium 10%. Free catalog. Appraisals.

The AuctionBlocks, PO Box 2321, Shelton, CT 06484, 203-924-2802, fax: 203-924-2802, e-mail: auctionblocks@aol.com, website: www.auction blocks.com. Absentee and Internet marble auctions. Mail, phone, fax, and e-mail bids accepted. No buyer's premium. Printed catalog $20; yearly subscription $135. Prices realized mailed and available on website after the auction.

Auctionblocks.net, e-mail: admin@auctionblocks.net, website: auction blocks.net. Online auctions. Buy and sell in thousands of listing categories. No listing fees.

Auctions Unlimited Inc., PO Box 1162, Port Ewen, NY 12466, 914-706-0171, fax: 561-264-0487, e-mail: sal@Auctions-Unlimitedinc.com, website: www.auctions-unlimited.com. Auctions of toys and collectibles. Mail, phone, fax, e-mail, and Internet bids accepted. No buyer's premium. Prices realized mailed and available on website after auction.

Autopia Advertising Auctions, 19937 NE 154th St., #C2, Woodinville, WA 98072-5629, 425-883-7653, fax: 425-867-5568, e-mail: win@Autopia Auctions.com, website: www.AutopiaAuctions.com. Mail and phone bids accepted. Buyer's premium 10%. Prices realized mailed after auction. Appraisals.

Balfour & Wessels Framefinders Inc., 454 E. 84th St., New York, NY 10028, 212-396-3896, fax: 212-396-3899, e-mail: framefinders@aol.com, website: framefinders.com. Auctions of antique frames. Mail, phone, and e-mail bids accepted. Buyer's premium 15%. Catalog $10. Prices realized mailed after auction. Appraisal services; restoration and conservation.

Baltimore Book Company, 2114 N. Charles St., Baltimore, MD 21218, 410-659-0550. Books, autographs, maps, and photographs. Mail bids accepted. Buyer's premium 15%. Catalog $5, $25 for eight issues. Prices realized mailed after auction. Appraisals.

Barridoff Galleries & Auction House, Box 9715, Portland, ME 04104, 207-772-5011, fax: 207-772-5049, e-mail: fineart@barridoff.com, website: www.barridoff.com. Mail, phone, and fax bids accepted. Buyer's premium 15% up to $100,000, 10% over $100,000. Catalog $35 in U.S. and Canada, $60 elsewhere. Prices realized available after auction.

BBR Auctions, Elsecar Heritage Centre, Barnsley, S. Yorkshire S74 8HJ, UK, 011-44-1226-745156, fax: 011-44-1226-351561, e-mail: sales@bbr auctions.co.uk, website: www.bbrauctions.co.uk. Bottles, pub jugs, breweriana, Doulton, Wade, Beswick, and more. Mail and phone bids accepted. Buyer's premium 10%. Prices realized mailed after auction. Restoration and conservation. Appraisals.

Be-Hold, Inc., 78 Rockland Ave., Yonkers, NY 10705, 914-423-5806, fax: 914-423-5802, e-mail: behold@be-hold.com, website: www.be-hold.com. Specializes in nineteenth- and twentieth-century photographs. Catalogs are available on the website and in printed form. Subscription $50 per year, three catalogs. Mail, phone, fax, e-mail, and online bids accepted. No buyer's premium. Prices realized mailed and posted on website after auction. Appraisals.

Bertoia Auctions, 2141 DeMarco Dr., Vineland, NJ 08360, 856-692-1881, fax: 856-692-8697, e-mail: bill@bertoiaauctions.com, website: www.bertoiaauctions.com. Specializes in auctions of antique toys, banks, doorstops, dolls, trains, soldiers, and folk art. On-site auctions, live on Internet also. Mail, phone, and fax bids accepted. Buyer's premium 10%. Prices realized mailed after auction. Catalog $35.

Bob, Chuck & Rich Roan, Inc., RR #4, Box 118, Cogan Station, PA 17728, 800-955-ROAN or 570-494-0170, fax: 570-494-1911, e-mail: roaninc@uplink.net, website: www.roaninc.com. General collections, estates, lamps, firearms, etc. Mail, phone, fax, and e-mail bids accepted. Buyer's premium 10%. Catalogs and prices realized for specialty auctions; listings for other auctions. Appraisals.

Bonhams, Montpelier Street, Knightsbridge, London SW7 1HH, UK, 011-44-20-7629-6602, fax: 011-44-20-7629-8876, e-mail: info@bonhams.com, website: www.bonhams.com. Auctions of pictures, silver, furniture, ceramics, jewelry, books, clocks, watches, rugs, coins, medals, stamps, motor cars, and collectors' items. Mail, phone, and Internet bids accepted. Buyer's premium 10%–17.5%. Catalog prices vary. Appraisals.

Bonhams & Butterfields, 220 San Bruno Ave., San Francisco, CA 94103, 415-861-7500, fax: 415-861-8951, e-mail: info@butterfields.com, website: www.butterfields.com. Mail, phone, fax, and e-mail bids accepted. All major sales are online. Online bids are accepted if preregistered. Buyer's premium 17.5%. Cost of catalogs and subscriptions vary. Prices realized mailed after auction and available on website. Appraisals for estates, taxes, and insurance. Second location: 7601 Sunset Blvd., Los Angeles, CA 90046; 323-850-7500; fax: 323-850-5843.

Bradford Auction Gallery, Box 160, Rte. 7, Sheffield, MA 01257, 413-229-6667, fax: 413-229-3278, e-mail: info@bradfordauctions.com, website: www.bradfordauctions.com. General antiques auctions. Mail, phone, fax, and e-mail bids accepted. Buyer's premium 12%. Catalog $3 by mail. Prices realized available after auction.

Braswell's at the Stamford Auction Gallery, 737 Canal St., Stamford, CT 06902, 203-327-2227, e-mail: staff@braswellgalleries.com, website: www.braswellgalleries.com. Phone, fax, and e-mail bids accepted. Buyer's premium 15%. Prices realized mailed after auction. Free catalogs.

Bruce and Vicki Waasdorp Stoneware Auctions, PO Box 434, Clarence, NY

14031, 716-759-2361, fax: 716-759-2397, e-mail: waasdorp@antiques-stoneware.com, website: www.antiques-stoneware.com. American utilitarian pottery and decorated stoneware absentee auctions. Mail, phone, e-mail, and Internet bids accepted. Buyer's premium 10%. Prices realized mailed and available on website after auction. Catalog $20. Appraisals.

Brunk Auctions, PO Box 2135, Asheville, NC 28802, 828-254-6846, fax: 828-254-6845, e-mail: auction@brunkauctions.com, website: www.brunk auctions.com. Mail, phone, fax, and e-mail bids accepted. Buyer's premium 10%. Free color brochure for each auction. Catalogs $20–$25. Appraisals for estates going to auction.

Buffalo Bay Auction Co., 5244 Quam Circle, St. Michael, MN 55376, 763-428-8480, e-mail: buffalobayauction@hotmail.com, website: www.buffalo bayauction.com. Internet auctions of advertising and country store collectibles. Mail, phone, e-mail and Internet bids accepted. Buyer's premium 10%. Prices realized available on website after auction.

C & D Gale, 2404 Berwyn Rd., Wilmington, DE 19810-3525, 302-478-0872, fax: 302-478-6866, e-mail: cdgale@dol.net, website: www.cdgale.com/catalog/exonumia.htm. Auctions of nineteenth-century U.S. tokens. Mail, phone, and Internet bids accepted. Buyer's premium 10%. Catalog free online; text-only hard copy catalog $5 for one-year subscription. Prices realized mailed after auction, $1.

Carlsen Gallery, Inc., 5098 Rt. 81, Greenville, NY 12083, 518-634-2466 or 518-966-5068, fax: 518-634-2467, e-mail: info@carlsengallery.com, website: www.carlsengallery.com. Mail, phone, fax, and e-mail bids accepted. No catalog; flyers and website list items to be sold. Buyer's premium 12.5%. Prices realized available after auction. Appraisals.

Castner's Auction & Appraisal Service, 6 Wantage Ave., Branchville, NJ 07826, 973-948-3868, fax: 973-948-3919, e-mail: castner@garden.net, website: www.castnerauctions.com. General estate auctions. Phone bids accepted. Buyer's premium 10%. Catalog $1 with registration. Some prices realized available on website after auction. Referral to restoration and conservation sources. Appraisals.

Charlton Hall Galleries, Inc., 912 Gervais St., Columbia, SC 29201, 803-779-5678, fax: 803-733-1701, e-mail: info@charltonhallauctions.com, website: www.charltonhallauctions.com. Buyer's premium 15%. Catalog subscription $115 per year, four catalogs. Appraisals.

Christie's New York, 20 Rockefeller Plaza, New York, NY 10020, 212-636-2000, fax: 212-636-2399, e-mail: info@christies.com, website: www.christies.com. Mail, phone, fax, and Internet bids accepted. Catalog prices and buyer's premiums vary. Locations in London and other cities around the world.

Cigar Label Art, PO Box 3902, Mission Viejo, CA 92691-6036, 949-582-7686, fax: 949-582-7947, e-mail: wayne@cigarlabelart.com, website: www.cigarlabelart.com. Absentee auctions of cigar labels. Mail, phone, fax, and e-mail bids accepted. High bid prices updated on website daily. No buyer's premium.

Cincinnati Art Galleries, 225 E. Sixth St., Cincinnati, OH 45202, 513-381-2128, fax: 513-381-7527, e-mail: info@cincinnatiartgalleries.com, website: www.cincinnatiartgalleries.com. Art pottery and art glass auctions. Mail and phone bids accepted. Buyer's premium 15%. Prices realized mailed after auction and available on website. Appraisals.

Cohasco, Inc., PO Drawer 821, Yonkers, NY 10702, 914-476-8500, fax: 914-476-8573, e-mail: dpc@dpc.nu, website: cohasco.com. Historical documents, manuscripts, and collectibles. Mail and phone bids accepted. Buyer's premium 12½%. Catalogs two for $10. Prices realized for specific lots mailed after auction. Appraisals.

Col. Glenn Larson, Inc., 4415 Canyon Dr., Amarillo, TX 79110, 806-358-9797, fax: 775-306-8292, e-mail: colonel@arn.net. General and antiques auctions approximately once a month. Buyer's premium 10%. Prices realized available after auction. Appraisals of collector cars.

Collection Liquidators, 341 Lafayette St., Suite 2007, New York, NY 10012, 212-505-2455, fax: 212-505-2455, e-mail: coliq@erols.com, website: www.collectionliquidators.com. Absentee auctions of Black Americana and KKK memorabilia. Mail, phone, fax, and e-mail bids accepted. Buyer's premium 10%. Prices realized mailed after auction and available on website. Catalogs $10; yearly subscription $26. Restoration and conservation. Appraisals.

Collectors Auction Services, RR2 Box 431 Oakwood Rd., Oil City, PA 16301, 814-677-6070, fax: 814-677-6166, e-mail: director@caswel.com, website: www.caswel.com. Mail and phone bids accepted. Buyer's premium 10%. Prices realized mailed after auction. Appraisals.

Conestoga Auction Co., 768 Graystone Rd., PO Box 1, Manheim, PA 17545, 717-898-7284, fax: 717-898-6628, e-mail: ca@conestogaauction.com, website: www.conestogaauction.com. Mail and phone bids accepted. Buyer's premium 10%. Prices realized mailed after auction if catalog is purchased. Appraisals.

Copake Auction, Box H, 266 Rte. 7A, Copake, NY 12516, 518-329-1142, fax: 518-329-3369, e-mail: info@copakeauction.com, website: www.copake auction.com. Americana and bicycle auctions. Mail and phone bids accepted. Buyer's premium 10%. Prices realized mailed after auction. Appraisals.

Cowan Auctions, 673 Wilmer Ave., Terrace Park, OH 45226, 513-871-1670, fax: 513-871-8670, e-mail: info@historicamericana.com, website: www.historicamericana.com. Early photography, Americana, decorative arts, Civil War, and American Indian collectibles. Mail, phone, fax, and e-mail bids accepted. Buyer's premium 15%. Catalogs $25–$30. Prices realized mailed after auction and available on website. Appraisals.

Craftsman Auctions, 1485 W. Housatonic, Pittsfield, MA 01201, 800-448-

7828 or 609-397-9374, fax: 609-397-9377, website: www.ragoarts.com. Arts and Crafts auctions held in Pittsfield, Massachusetts, and Lambertville, New Jersey. Absentee and phone bids accepted. Buyer's premium 15%. Prices realized available on website after auction. Appraisals.

Cyr Auction Company, PO Box 1238, 100 Lewiston Rd., Gray, ME 04039, 207-657-5253, fax: 207-657-5256, e-mail: info@cyrauction.com, website: www.cyrauction.com. Cataloged and uncataloged auctions. Buyer's premium 10% for uncataloged auctions, 15% for cataloged auctions. Catalog prices vary. Prices realized available on website after cataloged auctions.

Dargate Auction Galleries, 214 N. Lexington Blvd., Pittsburgh, PA 15208, 412-362-3558, e-mail: dargate@dargate.com, website: www.dargate.com. Mail, phone, and e-mail bids accepted. Buyer's premium 17.5%. Catalogs usually $3. Prices realized available on website after auction. Appraisals.

Dave Beck Auctions, PO Box 435, Mediapolis, IA 52637, 319-394-3943, fax: 319-394-3943, e-mail: adman@mepotelco.net. Specializes in auctions of advertising watch fobs. Mail, phone, fax, and e-mail bids accepted. No buyer's premium. Prices realized mailed after auction. Free catalogs. Yearly subscription $15.

David Rago Auctions, 333 N. Main St., Lambertville, NJ 08530, 609-397-9374, fax: 609-397-9377, e-mail: info@ragoarts.com, website: www.ragoarts.com. In person, mail, phone, fax, and online bids accepted. Buyer's premium 15%. Prices realized available on website after auction. Craftsman-Lambertville auctions include Arts and Crafts pottery, metalwork, lighting, and other decorative objects. David Rago Modern Auctions include sales of 20th Century Modern: Art Nouveau, Art Deco, Weiner Werkstatte, Mid-Century Modern, op, pop, Memphis, and more. Appraisals.

Davis Auction Service, e-mail: kdrd123@winco.net, website: www.biddersandbuyers.com/davis. Antiques, collectibles, farm equipment, farm primitives, farm toys, and tool auctions. Specializes in stoneware, primitives, art pottery, ephemera, hunting related items.

Dawson's Auctioneers & Appraisers, 128 American Rd., Morris Plains, NJ 07950, 973-984-6900, e-mail: info@dawsons.org, website: www.dawsons.org. General auctions. Phone, fax, and e-mail bids accepted. Live auction simulcast on eBay. Buyer's premium 17%. Catalogs and prices realized on website. Appraisals.

Decoys Unlimited, 2320 Main St., W. Barnstable, MA 02668, 508-362-2766, e-mail: tsharmon@attbi.com, website: www.decoysunlimitedinc.com. Decoy auctions. Mail and phone bids accepted. Buyer's premium 10%. Prices realized available after auction. Restoration and conservation services. Appraisals.

DeFina Auctions, 1591 State Rte. 45 South, Austinburg, OH 44010, 440-

275-6674, fax: 440-275-2028, e-mail: info@definaauctions.com, website: www.definaauctions.com. In-person and absentee bids accepted. Buyer's premium 10%; 15% for online bids.

Douglas Auctioneers, Rt. 5, South Deerfield, MA 01373, 413-665-2877, fax: 413-665-2877, e-mail: doug@douglasauctioneers.com, website: www.douglasauctioneers.com. Mail, phone, and Internet bids accepted. Buyer's premium 15%. Free catalog. Restoration and conservation. Appraisals.

Doyle New York, 175 E. 87th St., New York, NY 10128, 212-427-2730, fax: 212-369-0892, e-mail: info@DoyleNewYork.com, website: www.DoyleNewYork.com. Mail, phone, fax, and Internet bids accepted. Buyer's premium varies. Catalog free on website; print catalog price varies. Appraisals. Walk-in appraisals on Tuesday mornings.

DuMouchelle's Art Galleries Co., 409 E. Jefferson, Detroit, MI 48226, 313-963-0248, fax: 313-963-8199, e-mail: info@dumouchelles.com, website: www.dumouchelles.com. Mail, phone, and fax bids accepted. Buyer's premium 15%. Prices realized mailed after auction. Appraisals.

EAC Gallery, 99 Powerhouse Rd., Suite 204, Roslyn Heights, NY 11577, 516-484-6280, fax: 516-484-6278, e-mail: eac@eacgallery.com, website: www.eacgallery.com. Specializes in historical documents, fine art, and sports memorabilia. Mail and phone bids accepted. Buyer's premium 15%. Free catalog. Prices realized available after auction. Appraisals.

Early American History Auctions, PO Box 3341, La Jolla, CA 92038, 858-459-4159, fax: 858-459-4373, e-mail: history@earlyamerican.com, website: www.earlyamerican.com. Autographs, coins, currency, and Americana. Absentee auctions. Mail, fax, phone, and e-mail bids accepted. Buyer's premium 15%.

Early Auction Company, 123 Main St., Milford, OH 45150, 513-831-4833, fax: 513-831-1441. Mail and phone bids accepted. Buyer's premium 10%. Prices realized mailed after auction. Appraisals.

Fink's Off The Wall Auctions, 108 E. 7th St., Lansdale, PA 19446-2622, 215-855-9732, fax: 215-855-6325, e-mail: lansbeer@finksauctions.com, website: www.finksauctions.com. Breweriana auctions. Mail, phone, and e-mail bids accepted. Buyer's premium 10%. Catalog $15. Prices realized mailed after auction and available on website. Appraisals.

Fontaine's Auction Gallery, 1485 W. Housatonic St., Pittsfield, MA 01201, 413-448-8922, fax: 413-442-1550, e-mail: fontaine@taconic.net, website: www.fontaineauction.com. Mail, phone, fax, and Internet bids accepted. Buyer's premium 12%. Prices realized mailed after auction. Catalogs are free, but there is a charge for priority postage: $28 for three years.

Four Winds Indian Auction, PO Box 580, St. Ignatius, MT 59865-0580, 406-745-4336, fax: 406-745-3595, e-mail: 4winds@bigsky.net. Absentee auctions of Indian goods. Mail, phone, and fax bids accepted. No buyer's premium. Catalog $18. Prices realized mailed after auction. Some restoration and conservation. Appraisals.

Frank H. Boos Gallery, 420 Enterprise Ct., Bloomfield Hills, MI 48302-0386, 248-332-1500, fax: 248-332-6370, e-mail: artandauction@boos gallery.com, website: www.boosgallery.com. Mail and phone bids accepted. Buyer's premium 15% up to $50,000, 10% over $50,000. Catalog $25 postpaid. Yearly subscription $90. Appraisals.

Frank's Antiques, PO Box 516, 2405 N. Kings Rd., Hilliard, FL 32046, 904-845-2870, e-mail: franksauct@aol.com. Mail, phone, and fax bids accepted. Buyer's premium 10%.

Freeman's, Samuel T. Freeman & Co., 1808 Chestnut St., Philadelphia, PA 19103, 215-563-9275, fax: 215-563-8236, e-mail: info@freemans auction.com, website: www.freemansauction.com. Mail, phone, and fax bids accepted. Buyer's premium varies. Prices realized available on website after auction. Appraisals.

Galerias Louis C. Morton, Monte Athos # 179, Lomas Virreyes de Chapultepec CP 11000, 011-520-5005, e-mail: subastas@lmorton.com, website: www.lmorton.com. Auctions of antiques, modern and contemporary art, books, documents, jewelry, etc. Phone and fax bids accepted. Buyer's premium 15%. Catalog $40, yearly subscription $400. Prices realized available after auction. Appraisals.

Gallery of History Auctions, 3601 W. Sahara Ave., Promenade Suite, Las Vegas, NE 89102-5822, 800-GALLERY (800-425-5379) or 702-364-1000 for international calls, fax: 702-364-1285, e-mail: galleryofhistory @galleryofhistory, website: www.galleryofhistory.com. "History for Sale" absentee auctions six times a year. Mail, phone, fax, and Internet bids accepted. Buyer's premium 15%. Catalogs by mail or on website. Prices realized published in next auction catalog and on website. Framing services.

Garth's Auctions, Inc., PO Box 369, 2690 Stratford Rd., Delaware, OH 43015, 740-362-4771, fax: 740-363-0164, e-mail: info@garths.com, website: www.garths.com. Mail, phone, fax, and Internet bids accepted. Buyer's premium 10%. Catalog $18, yearly subscription $145. Prices realized mailed after auction and available on website. Appraisals.

Gary Kirsner Auctions, PO Box 8807, Coral Springs, FL 33075, 944-344-9856, fax: 944-344-4421, e-mail: gkirsner@garykirsnerauctions.com, website: garykirsnerauctions.com. Specializes in auctions of beer steins. Mail, fax, and e-mail bids accepted. Buyer's premium 15%. Catalog subscription $30. Prices realized mailed after auction and available on website. Appraisals.

Gary Metz's Muddy River Trading Co., PO Box 18185, Roanoke, VA 24014, 540-344-7333, fax: 540-344-3014, e-mail: metz@rbnet.com, website: www.muddyrivertrading.com. Antique advertising auctions. Mail, phone, and Internet bids accepted. Buyer's premium 12.5%. Prices realized mailed after auction and available on website.

Gene Harris Antique Auction Center, Inc., PO Box 476, 203 S. 18th Ave., Marshalltown, IA 50158, 800-862-6674 or 641-752-0600, fax: 641-753-0226, e-mail: ghaac@marshallnet.com, website: www.geneharris auctions.com. Prearranged mail and phone bids accepted. Buyer's premium 10%. Free catalog. Prices realized mailed after auction and available on website. Appraisals.

Glass-Works Auctions, Box 180, East Greenville, PA 18041, 215-679-5849, fax: 215-679-3068, e-mail: glswrk@enter.net, website: www.glswrk-auction.com. Absentee auctions of antique bottles and glass barbershop memorabilia. Mail, phone, and fax bids accepted. Buyer's premium 12%. Prices realized mailed after auction.

Glasses, Mugs & Steins, PO Box 207, Sun Prairie, WI 53590, 608-837-4818, fax: 608-825-4205, e-mail: pkroll@charter.net, website: www.gmskroll.com. Beer glasses, mugs, and steins. Mail, phone, and Internet bids accepted. Buyers premium 10% for items $201 and above, 5% for items $101–$200, and none for items selling for $100 or less. Prices realized mailed after auction and available on website. Catalog $13 bulk mail, yearly subscription $25 for two issues.

Great Gatsby's, 5070 Peachtree Industrial Blvd., Atlanta, GA 30341, 800-428-7297 or 770-457-1903, fax: 770-457-7250, e-mail: internet @greatgatsbys.com, website: www.greatgatsbys.com. Live auctions in Atlanta in February, May, and October. Catalogs $10 for one-year subscription. Mail and phone bids accepted. Buyer's premium. Online auctions continuously on the website. Appraisals.

Green Valley Auctions Inc., Rt. 2, Box 434-A, Mt. Crawford, VA 22841, 540-434-4260, fax: 540-434-4532, e-mail: gvai@shentel.net, website: www.greenvalleyauctions.com. Early American glass, lighting, eighteenth- and nineteenth-century ceramics, Southern decorative arts. Mail, phone, fax, and e-mail bids accepted. Catalog price varies. Prices realized mailed after auction. Appraisals.

Greenberg Auctions, 1393 Progress Way, Suite 907, Eldersburg, MD 21784, 410-795-7448, e-mail: bwimperis@greenbergshows.com, website: greenbergshows.com. Specialized train auctions held live in Sykesville, Maryland. Online catalogs, auction dates, and absentee bidding information are available at auctions@greenbergshows.com. Printed catalogs are available for $5 each. Call for catalog and consigning information.

Greg Manning Auctions, Inc., 775 Passaic Ave., W. Caldwell, NJ 07006-6409, 800-221-0243 or 973-882-0004, fax: 973-882-3499, e-mail: gmauction@aol.com, website: gmaiweb2.gregmanning.com. Coins, stamps, and sports cards. Internet, interactive telephone, and simulcast Internet and live auctions. Mail, phone, and fax bids accepted.

Buyer's premium 15% on stamps and 10% on sports. Prices realized mailed after auction. Appraisals.

Greg Martin Auctions, 660 Third St., Suite 100, San Francisco, CA 94107, 415-522-5708, fax: 415-522-5706, e-mail: info@gmartin-auctions.com, website: www.gmartin-auctions.com. Auctions of firearms and armor, historical memorabilia. Phone and Internet bids accepted. Buyer's premium 12%. Catalog $40. Prices realized mailed and available on website after auction. Appraisals.

Grey Flannel Auctions, 549 Middle Neck Rd., Great Neck, NY 11023, 516-446-5533, fax: 516-446-5592, e-mail: GFCSports@aol.com, website: www.greyflannel.com. Game-used jerseys, bats, autographs, etc. Mail, phone, and Internet bids accepted. Buyer's premium 15%. Free catalog. Prices realized available after auction. Appraisals.

Guernsey's, 108 E. 73rd St., New York, NY 10021, 212-794-2280, fax: 212-744-3638, e-mail: auctions@guernseys.com, website: www.guernseys.com. Auctions of large specialized collections, from the Civil War to Elvis Presley's Graceland. Mail, phone, and Internet bids accepted. Buyer's premium 17.5% up to $100,000; 10% thereafter. Catalog price varies. Appraisals.

Guyette & Schmidt, Inc., PO Box 522, West Farmington, ME 04992, 207-778-6256, fax: 207-778-6501, e-mail: decoys@guyetteandschmidt.com, website: www.guyetteandschmidt.com. Decoy auctions, three per year. Specializes in antique duck decoys and shorebird decoys, fish decoys, fish carvings, waterfowl paintings and prints, duck calls, and ammunition advertising. Mail and phone bids accepted. Buyer's premium 10%. Catalog $36, subscription $108 per year. Prices realized mailed after auction. Free appraisals of antique waterfowl art and related items.

Hake's Americana & Collectibles, PO Box 1444, York, PA 17405-1444, 717-848-1333, fax: 717-852-0344, e-mail: hake@hakes.com, website: www.hakes.com. Twentieth-century nostalgia collectibles from comic characters to advertising and political Americana. Mail, phone, and Internet bids accepted. No buyer's premium. Catalog $7; yearly subscription $30. Sample catalog free. Appraisals.

Hart Galleries, 2301 S. Voss Rd., Houston, TX 77057, 713-266-3500, fax: 713-266-1013, e-mail: general@hartgalleries.com, website: www.hart galleries.com. European and American antiques, art, and Oriental rugs. Mail, phone, and Internet bids accepted. Buyer's premium 15%. Prices realized mailed after auction. Catalog $25. Auction brochures, $20 per year.

Harvey Clars Estate Auction Gallery, 5644 Telegraph Ave., Oakland, CA 94609, 510-428-0100, fax: 510-568-9917, e-mail: info@harveyclar.com, website: www.harveyclar.com. Fine art, decoratives, jewelry, rugs, and antiques. Phone bids accepted only if in excess of $1,000. Absentee bids may be faxed. Buyer's premium 15%. Prices realized mailed after auction and available on website. Free catalogs for some auctions. Appraisals.

HCA (Historical Collectible Auctions), 24 Northwest Court Square, Suite 201, Graham, NC 27253, 336-570-2803, fax: 336-570-2748, e-mail: hcaauction@aol.com, website: www.hcaauctions.com. Americana historical items. Mail, phone, fax, and e-mail bids accepted. Buyer's premium 15%. Catalog $12, free to recent buyers. Prices realized mailed after auction. Appraisals.

Henry/Peirce Auctioneers, 1456 Carson Ct., Homewood, IL 60430, 708-798-7508, fax: 708-799-3594, e-mail: mhenry89@attbi.com, website: www.henrypeirce.com. Specializes in auctions of mechanical and still banks. Mail bids accepted. No phone bids. Buyer's premium 10%. Prices realized mailed after auction. Catalog prices vary. Appraisals.

Hesse Galleries, 350 & 385 Main St., Otego, NY 13825, 607-988-2523, fax: 607-988-2523, e-mail: info@hessegalleries.com, website: www.hesse galleries.com. Absentee and phone bids accepted. Buyer's premium 10%. Prices realized mailed after auctions. Catalogs $20. Appraisals.

Holiday Auction, 4027 Brooks Hill Rd., Brooks, KY 40109, 502-955-9238, fax: 502-957-5027, e-mail: holauction@aol.com, website: members.aol.com/holauction/index.html. Absentee auctions of holiday collectibles only. Mail, phone, fax, and e-mail bids accepted. Buyer's premium 10%. Catalog $10. Prices realized mailed after auction.

House of David Auctions, 220 North 7th St., Haines City, FL 33844, 800-248-4389 or 863-422-1679, fax: 863-422-9560, e-mail: control@house ofdavidauctions.com, website: www.HouseOfDavidAuctions.com. Art, antiques, collectibles, and estate auctions. Regularly scheduled auctions are held the first Friday of every month. Online previews and auction dates are available at www.HouseOfDavidAuctions.com.

Howard B. Parzow, PO Box 3464, Gaithersburg, MD 20885-3464, 301-977-6741, fax: 301-208-8947, e-mail: hparzow@aol.com, website: www.hbparzowauctioneer.com. Americana, advertising and country store, drug and apothecary, coin-operated machines, toys. Mail and phone bids accepted. Buyer's premium 10%. Appraisals.

Ingrid O'Neil's Olympic Auctions, PO Box 872048, Vancouver, WA 98687, 360-834-5202, fax: 360-834-2853, e-mail: auctions@ioneil.com, website: www.ioneil.com. Olympic games memorabilia. Absentee bids only: mail, phone, fax, and e-mail bids accepted. Buyer's premium 15%. Catalog $15; yearly subscription $30. Prices realized mailed after auction. Appraisals.

Ivey-Selkirk Auctioneers, 7447 Forsyth Blvd., St. Louis, MO 63105, 314-726-5515, fax: 314-726-9908, website: www.iveyselkirk.com. Check the website for upcoming auctions, online catalogs, and prices realized.

J.C. Devine, Inc., PO Box 413, Milford, NH 03055, 603-673-4967, fax: 603-672-0328, e-mail: jcdevine@empire.net, website: www.jcdevine.com. Catalog prices vary. Mail, phone, and fax bids accepted. Buyer's premium varies.

Jackson's Auctioneers & Appraisers, 2229 Lincoln St., Cedar Falls, IA 50613, 319-277-2256, fax: 319-277-1252, e-mail: marketing@jacksons auction.com, website: www.jacksonsauction.com. Fine art and antiques auction and appraisal services. Mail and phone bids accepted. Buyer's premium 15%. Catalogs $25–$30. Subscription $150. Prices realized mailed after auction and available on website. Restoration and conservation services. Appraisals.

James D. Julia, Inc., PO Box 830, Rt. 201, Skowhegan Rd., Fairfield, ME 04937, 207-453-7125, fax: 207-453-2502, e-mail: julia@juliaauctions.com, website: www.juliaauctions.com. Catalog prices vary. Mail and phone bids accepted. Buyer's premium 15%. Prices realized mailed after auction and available on website.

Jerry Madsen, 4624 W. Woodland Rd., Edina, MN 55424-1553, 612-926-7775, e-mail: jerryclare@aol.com. Auction lists of Berliners, Zonophones, Nipper items, records, cylinders, etc. Send first-class stamp for lists and photos.

Jim Mehrer's Postal History, 2405 30th St., Rock Island, IL 61201, 309-786-6539, fax: 309-786-4840, e-mail: mehrer@postal-history.com, website: www.postal-history.com. Pre-1930 U.S. postal history and related reference literature and supplies. Mail, phone, and Internet bids. No buyer's premium. Catalogs free to regular bidders, otherwise $2 U.S., $4.50 international; yearly subscription $12 U.S., $30 international.

Joel Markowitz, Box 10, Old Bethpage, NY 11804, 516-249-9405, fax: 516-249-9405, e-mail: smctr@sheetmusiccenter.com, website: www.sheetmusiccenter.com. Mail order auctions of sheet music. Mail, phone, and e-mail bids accepted. No buyer's premium. Catalog on website.

John McInnis Auctioneers, 76 Main St., Amesbury, MA 01913, 800-822-1417 or 978-388-0400, fax: 978-388-8863, e-mail: contact@JohnMcInnis Auctioneers.com, website: www.johnmcinnisauctioneers.com. Mail and phone bids accepted. Buyer's premium 10%. Appraisals.

John R. Pastor Antique & Bottle Glass Auction, 7288 Thorncrest Dr. SE, Ada, MI 49301, 616-285-7604. Mail and phone bids accepted. Buyer's premium 10%. Prices realized mailed after auction. Appraisals.

John Toomey Gallery, 818 North Blvd., Oak Park, IL 60301, 708-383-5234, fax: 708-383-4828, e-mail: info@johntoomeygallery.com, website: www.treadwaygallery.com. Arts and Crafts, midcentury modern, and paintings. Mail, phone, fax, and e-mail bids accepted. Buyer's premium 15%. Catalog $35. Prices realized on website after auction.

Joseph DuMouchelle International Auctioneers, 5 Kercheval Ave., Grosse

Pointe Farms, MI 48236-3601, 313-884-4800 ext. 23 or 800-475-, fax: 313-884-7662, e-mail: joe@dumouchelleauction.com, website: www.dumouchelleauction.com. Specializes in jewelry auctions. Mail and phone bids accepted. Buyer's premium 15%. Prices realized mailed after auction. Appraisals.

Joy Luke Auction Gallery, 300 E. Grove St., Bloomington, IL 61701, 309-828-5533, fax: 309-829-2266, e-mail: robert@joyluke.com, website: www.joyluke.com. Mail, phone, fax, and Internet bids accepted. Buyer's premium 12½%. Prices realized mailed after auction. Appraisals.

July 4th Antiques, 31 Cactus Ct., Parachute, CO 81635, 970-285-7041, fax: 970-285-1302, e-mail: J4Antiques@aol.com. Old firecracker and fireworks labels, packs, boxes, and catalogs. Internet and cataloged auctions. Mail, phone, fax, and e-mail bids accepted. No buyer's premium. Free appraisals; always buying.

Just Kids Nostalgia, 310 New York Ave., Huntington, NY 11743, 516-423-8449, fax: 631-423-4326, e-mail: info@justkidsnostalgia.com, website: www.justkidsnostalgia.com. Auctions of old toys, movie posters, TV and comic characters, advertising, sports, rock 'n' roll, and other pop culture memorabilia. Mail, phone, fax, and e-mail bids accepted. Prices realized available after auction.

Ken Farmer Auctions and Appraisals, 105 Harrison St., Radford, VA 24141, 540-639-0939, fax: 540-639-1759, e-mail: info@kfauctions.com, website: kfauctions.com. Phone, fax, and e-mail bids accepted. Buyer's premium 10%–15%. Free catalogs. Prices realized available on website after auction. Appraisals.

Kenneth S. Hays & Associates, Inc., 120 S. Spring St., Louisville, KY 40206, 502-584-4297, fax: 502-585-5896, e-mail: kenhays@haysauction.com, website: www.haysauction.com. Specializes in Victorian antiques, antique dolls, and clocks. Mail and phone bids accepted. No buyer's premium. Prices realized mailed after some auction. Appraisals.

Kit Barry Auctions, 88 High St., Brattleboro, VT 05301, 802-254-3634, fax: 802-254-3634, e-mail: kbarry@surfglobal.net. Nineteenth- and early twentieth-century ephemera. Mail, phone, and fax bids accepted. Buyer's premium 10%. Catalogs $10–$20. Prices realized mailed after auction. Appraisals.

Kraus Antiques, Ltd., PO Box 12537, Ft. Pierce, FL 34979, 772-465-0770, fax: 772-468-9020, e-mail: sterling@silverauctions.net, website: www.silverauctions.net. Sterling silver flatware absentee auctions. Mail, phone, and Internet bids accepted. No buyer's premium. Prices realized mailed after auction. Free catalog. Call, write, or e-mail your request for illustrated catalog.

Kruse International, 5540 County Rd. 11A, PO Box 190, Auburn, IN 46706, 260-925-5600 or 800-968-4444, fax: 260-925-5467, e-mail: info@kruseinternational, website: www.kruse.com. Online and live auctions of vehicles. Mail, phone, and online bids accepted. Buyer's premium varies. Free catalogs. Prices realized posted on website. Appraisals.

Lang's Sporting Collectables, Inc., 663 Pleasant Valley Rd., Waterville, NY 13480, 315-841-4623, e-mail: LangsAuction@aol.com. Mail and phone bids accepted. Buyer's premium 13% with 3% discount for cash or check. Prices realized mailed after auction. Appraisals.

Last Moving Picture Co., Kirtland Antique Mall, 10535 Chillicothe Rd., Kirtland, OH 44094, 440-256-3660, fax: 440-256-3431, e-mail: lastmo@aol.com, website: vintagefilmposters.com. Movie poster auctions. Mail, phone, and Internet bids accepted. Buyer's premium 15%. Catalog $10. Prices realized available on website after auction. Some appraisals.

Leland's, 3947 Merrick Rd., Seaford, NY 11783, 516-409-9700, fax: 516-409-9797, e-mail: info@lelands.com, website: www.lelands.com. Specializes in auctions of vintage sports memorabilia, sports and nonsports cards, and specialized collections of rock 'n' roll and entertainment memorabilia. Mail and phone bids accepted. Buyer's premium 15%. Prices realized mailed after auction. Appraisals.

Lincoln Galleries, 225 Scotland Rd., Orange, NJ 07050, 973-672-8301, fax: 973-676-0129, website: www.lincolngalleries.com. Mail and phone bids accepted. Buyer's premium 15%. Prices realized mailed after auction upon request. Catalog $3. Restoration and conservation services. Appraisals.

Lloyd Ralston Gallery, 350 Long Beach Blvd., Stratford, CT 06615, 203-386-9399, fax: 203-386-9519, e-mail: lrgallelry@aol.com, website: www.lloydralstontoys.com. Specializes in auctions of trains, toy soldiers, and die cast vehicles. Mail and phone bids accepted. Buyer's premium 10%. Catalogs $20–$25. Prices realized mailed after auction and available on website.

Los Angeles Modern Auctions, PO Box 462006, Los Angeles, CA 90046, 323-904-1950, fax: 323-904-1954, e-mail: info@lamodern.com, website: lamodern.com. Specializes in twentieth-century decorative arts. Mail, phone, fax, and e-mail bids accepted. Buyer's premium 17.5%. Prices realized mailed by request. Appraisals by appointment only.

Malter Galleries Inc., 17003 Ventura Blvd., Suite 205, Encino, CA 91316, 818-784-7772, fax: 818-784-4726, e-mail: mike@maltergalleries.com, website: www.maltergalleries.com. Specializes in Greek, Roman, and Egyptian coins and artifacts. Mail, phone, and Internet bids accepted. Buyer's premium 15%. Free catalogs. Prices realized available after auctions. Restoration and conservation services. Appraisals.

Manion's International Auction House, Inc., PO Box 12214, Kansas City, KS 66112, 913-299-6692, fax: 913-299-6792, e-mail: collecting@manions.com, website: www.manions.com. Auctions of antiques and collectibles of historical interest. Mail, phone, fax, and e-mail bids accepted. Manion's has three types of auctions: Gold Auctions have printed catalogs and are also on the website; Silver Auctions are on the website only; Bronze Auctions are self-service auctions—members may post items to be auctioned.

Mapes Auctioneers & Appraisers, 1729 Vestal Parkway West, Vestal, NY 13850, 607-754-9193, fax: 607-786-3549, e-mail: info@mapes auction.com, website: www.mapesauction.com. Antiques, fine art, decorative arts, and estate auctions. Mail, phone, fax, and e-mail bids accepted. Buyer's premium 10% for specialty auctions, none on weekly household auctions. Free catalogs. Prices realized mailed after auction. Appraisals.

Maritime Antiques & Auctions, PO Box 322, York, ME 03909-0322, 207-363-4247, fax: 207-363-1416, e-mail: nautical@cybertours.com, website: www.maritiques.com. Specializes in maritime antiques and paintings, firehouse memorabilia, and scientific instruments. Mail and phone bids accepted. Buyer's premium 15%. Prices realized mailed after auction. Appraisals.

Martin Auction Co., Inc., Rt. 51 South, Clinton, IL 61727, 217-935-3245, e-mail: info@martinauction.com, website: www.martinauction.com. Auctions of toys and antiques. Catalogs for toy auctions are posted on the website the week before the auction.

Martone's Gallery, 699 New London Turnpike, W. Greenwich, RI 02817, 401-885-3880, e-mail: jack@martonesgallery.com, website: www.martonesgallery.com. Phone bids accepted. Buyer's premium 10%. Catalogs. Prices realized mailed after auction on request.

MastroNet, Inc., 1511 W. 22nd St., Suite 125, Oak Brook, IL 60523, 630-472-1200, fax: 630-472-1201, website: www.mastronet.com. Auctions of sports and Americana. Buyer's premium 15%. Prices realized available after auction. Catalog subscriptions: $100 for all catalogs (5–7 per year); sports catalogs (3–4) $75 per year; Americana catalogs (2–3) $50 per year.

McAllister Auctions, PO Box 294, Paradise, MI 49768, 800-746-6604, phone/fax, e-mail: mmcall1872@aol.com. Cataloged art pottery auctions held across the country. Free online catalogs. Absentee bids accepted.

McLendon Auctions & Realty Company, PO Box 2331-Morganton, NC 28680, 828-437-9257, fax: 828-437-9257, e-mail: mclendonauctions @msn.com, website: www.mclendonauctions.com. General auctioneers of personal and business properties and real estate.

McMasters Harris Auction Co., PO Box 1755, Cambridge, OH 43725, 740-432-7400, fax: 740-432-3191, e-mail: info@mcmastersharris.com, website: mcmastersharris.com. Antique dolls, vintage Barbies, and collectibles. Mail, fax, phone, and Internet bids accepted. No buyer's premium. Catalog $30; yearly subscription $99. Prices realized mailed after auction and available on website.

McMurray Antiques & Auctions, PO Box 393, Kirkwood, NY 13795, 607-775-5972, fax: 607-775-2321. Specializes in drugstore, apothecary, patent medicines, and advertising. Three auctions per year. Mail and phone bids accepted. Buyer's premium 10%. Catalog $15. Prices realized mailed after auction. Appraisals.

Meisner's Auction Service, PO Box 115, Rt. 20 & 22, New Lebanon, NY 12125, 518-766-5002, fax: 518-794-8073, e-mail: auction115@aol.com, website: www.meissnersauction.com. Antiques and dolls. Mail, phone, and e-mail bids accepted. Buyer's premium 10%. Prices realized available after auction. Appraisals.

Michael Ivankovich Auction Co., Inc., PO Box 1536, Doylestown, PA 18901, 215-345-6094, fax: 215-345-6692, e-mail: ivankovich@wnutting.com, website: www.wnutting.com. Auctions of Wallace Nutting, hand-colored photography, and early twentieth-century prints. Mail, phone, and Internet bids accepted. Buyer's premium 10%. Catalogs free on website. Prices realized mailed after auction and available on website. Restoration and conservation. Appraisals.

Midwest Auction Galleries, 13015 Larchmere Blvd., Shaker Heights, OH 44120, 216-421-9742, e-mail: auction@midwestauctiongalleries.com, website: www.midwestauctiongalleries.com. Online auctions of fine art and antiques.

Mike Smith's Patent Medicine Auction, 7431 Covington Hwy., Lithonia, GA 30058, 770-482-5100, fax: 770-484-1304, e-mail: petvetmike @mindspring.com. Veterinary antiques and collectibles. Absentee bids only: mail, phone, and Internet bids accepted. Buyer's premium 10%. Prices realized mailed after auction and available on website. Appraisals.

Mohawk Arms, Inc., PO Box 157, Bouckville NY 13310, 315-893-7888 or 315-893-7889, fax: 315-893-7707, e-mail: mohawk@militaryrelics.com, website: www.militaryrelics.com. Militaria, all periods. Mail and phone bids accepted. Buyer's premium varies depending on value of item. Catalog $19.50 in U.S. and Canada; yearly subscription, two catalogs, $39. Prices realized mailed after auction. Appraisals.

Monsen and Baer, PO Box 529, Vienna, VA 22183, 703-938-2129, fax: 703-242-1357, e-mail: monsenbaer@erols.com. Perfume bottle auctions. Mail and phone bids accepted. Buyer's premium 10%. Prices realized mailed after auction.

The Mouse Man Ink, 11 Trumbull Ave., Wakefield, MA 01880, 781-246-3876, fax: 781-246-3876, e-mail: mouse_man@rcn.com, website: www.mouseman.com. Bimonthly Internet auctions of Disneyana collectibles. Will evaluate Disney items made from the 1930s to the mid-1970s for a fee, $5 for the first item, $2 for each additional item. Does not evaluate cels or animation art.

Neal Auction Co., 4038 Magazine St., New Orleans, LA 70115, 504-899-5329 or 800-467-5329, fax: 504-897-3808, e-mail: customer service@nealauction.com, website: www.nealauction.com. Mail and phone bids accepted. Buyer's premium varies. Prices realized available on website after auction. Catalogs $35 in U.S., $55 international. Yearly subscription $125 in U.S., $325 international.

New England Absentee Auctions, Inc., 16 Sixth St., Stamford, CT 06905, 203-975-9055, fax: 203-323-6407, e-mail: NEAAuction@aol.com. Absentee auctions of antiques and collectibles.

New England Auction Gallery, Box 764, Middleton, MA 01949, 978-304-3140, e-mail: markrim@attbi.com, website: www.old-toys.com. Auctions of toys, games, and character collectibles. Mail, phone, fax, and e-mail bids accepted. Buyer's premium 5%. Catalogs $10 in U.S., $15 international; first catalog free. Yearly subscription $30. Appraisals. Prices realized in next catalog after auction. Appraisals.

New England Events Mgt., PO Box 678, Wolfeboro, NH 03894-0678, 603-569-0000, e-mail: dragonflies@metrocast.net. Auctions of antique and classic boats. Mail bids accepted. Phone bids taken until 5:00 P.M. the night before the auction, not during the auction. Buyer's premium 10%. Prices realized available by request. Appraisals.

New Hampshire Auctions.com, Hill, New Hampshire, 603-770-2647, fax: 603-934-6998, e-mail: nha@worldpath.net, website: www.new hampshireauctions.com. Site designed to give the collector, buyer, or vacationer to New Hampshire one central location to find the auctions, auctioneers, and their specialties in the state.

New Hampshire Book Auctions, PO Box 678, Wolfeboro, NH 03894-0678, 603-569-0000, e-mail: dragonflies@metrocast.net. Mail bids accepted. Phone bids taken until 5:00 P.M. the night before the auction, not during the auction. Buyer's premium 10%. Prices realized available by request. Appraisals.

New Orleans Auction Galleries, Inc., 801 Magazine St., New Orleans, LA 70130, 800-501-0277 or 504-566-1849, fax: 504-566-1851, e-mail: info@neworleansauction.com, website: www.neworleansauction.com. Mail and phone bids accepted. Buyer's premium 10%. Prices realized mailed to subscribers upon request. Appraisals.

Noel Barrett Antiques, Carversville Rd., Box 300, Carversville, PA 18923, 215-297-5109, e-mail: toys@noelbarrett.com, website: noelbarrett.com. Auctions of vintage toys. Mail, phone, fax, and e-mail bids accepted. Buyer's premium 10%. Prices realized mailed after auction and available on website. Catalog $35. Appraisals.

Norman C. Heckler & Co., 79 Bradford Corner Rd., Woodstock Valley, CT 06282, 860-974-1634, fax: 860-974-2003, e-mail: heckler@neca.com, website: www.hecklerauction.com. Bottles, flasks, early glass, stoneware, and related items. Both absentee and live sales. Mail, phone, and fax bids accepted. Buyer's premium 12%. Catalog $25; yearly subscription $100. Appraisals.

Northeast Auctions, 93 Pleasant St., Portsmouth, NH 03801, 603-433-8400, fax: 603-433-0415, website: www.northeastauctions.com. General, marine, Chinese export, folk art, and American furniture auctions. Phone and fax bids accepted. Buyer's premium 15% up to $50,000, 10% over $50,000. Catalog $20; yearly subscription $125 for 5–10 catalogs. Prices realized mailed after auction and available on website. Appraisals.

Norton Auctioneers of Michigan, Inc., 50 W. Pearl, Coldwater, MI 49036-1967, 517-279-9063, fax: 517-279-9191, e-mail: nortonsold@cbpu.com, website: www.nortonauctioneers.com. Unique collections, carousels, amusement parks, museums. Buyer's premium varies. Appraisals.

Nostalgia Publications, Inc., Allan Petretti, PO Box 4175, River Edge, NJ 07661, 201-488-4536, fax: 201-883-0938, e-mail: nostpub@webtv.net. Soda pop mail, phone, and fax auctions. No buyer's premium. Catalog $10; subscription $25 for three auctions. Two auctions per year. Prices realized printed in the next catalog. Appraisals.

NSA Auctions, Newton-Smith Antiques, 88 Cedar St., Cambridge, ON N1S 1, Canada, 519-623-6302, e-mail: info@nsaauctions.com, website: www.nsaauctions.com. Early glass, bottles, pottery, and stoneware auctions. Mail, phone, and Internet bids accepted. No buyer's premium. Catalog price varies. Prices realized mailed after auction and available on website. Appraisals.

O'Gallerie, Inc., 228 NE 7th Ave., Portland, OR 97232, 888-238-0202 or 503-238-0202, fax: 503-236-8211, e-mail: info@ogallerie.com, website: www.ogallerie.com. Mail and phone bids accepted. Buyer's premium 12%. Prices realized available on website free, or mailed after auction, $2. Catalog $10 by mail; yearly subscription $95.

Old Barn Auction, 10040 St. Rt. 224 W., Findlay, OH 45840, 419-422-8531, fax: 419-422-5321, e-mail: auction@oldbarn.com, website: www.oldbarn.com. Specializes in Indian artifacts, guns, Civil War, toys, candy containers. Mail and phone bids accepted. Buyer's premium 10%. Prices realized mailed after auction. Catalog $15; yearly subscription $45. Appraisals.

Old World Auctions, PO Box 2224, 270 Hillside Ave., Sedona, AZ 86339, 928-282-3944 or 800-664-7757, fax: 928-282-3945, e-mail: marti@old worldauctions.com, website: oldworldauctions.com. Specializes in antique maps and related travel and exploration books and graphics. Mail, phone, and Internet bids accepted. Buyer's premium 12%. Catalogs $25 per year. Prices realized available on website and mailed in next catalog.

Pacific Glass Auctions, 1507 21st. St., Suite 203, Sacramento, CA 95814, 800-806-7722, fax: 916-443-3199, e-mail: info@pacglass.com, website: pacglass.com. Mail and phone bids accepted. Buyer's premium 12%. Prices realized mailed after auction. Appraisals.

Page & Bryan Ginns, Stereographica, 2109 Rt. 21, Valatie, NY 12184, 518-392-5805, fax: 518-392-7925, e-mail: The3dman@aol.com, website: www.stereographica.com. Absentee auctions: mail, phone, and Internet bids accepted. No buyer's premium. Catalog $20. Prices realized mailed and available on website after auction.

Page Auctioneers & Appraisers, 5596 E. Main St., Batavia, NY 14020, 585-343-2934, fax: 585-343-2814, e-mail: info@pageauction.com, website: www.pageauction.com. Antiques and collectibles. Mail, phone, fax, Internet, and in-person bids. Buyer's premium 10%. Prices realized mailed after auction. Free catalog. Appraisals.

Park City Auction Service, PO Box 6314, Bridgeport, CT 06606, 203-333-5251, fax: 203-333-5251, e-mail: prkcityauct@aol.com, website: www.parkcityauction.com. Mail and phone bids accepted. Buyer's premium 10%. Prices realized mailed after auction. Appraisals.

Past Tyme Pleasures, 2491 San Ramon Valley Blvd., PMB 204, San Ramon, CA 94583, 925-484-4488, fax: 925-484-2551, e-mail: pasttyme1 @attbi.com, website: www.pasttyme1.com. Antique advertising, hunting and fishing, general store, tobacco, soda, and breweriana. Mail, phone, fax, and e-mail bids accepted. Buyer's premium 10%. Prices realized mailed after auction and available on website. Appraisals.

Paul Riseman Auctions, 2205 S. Park Ave., Springfield, IL 62704-4335, 217-787-2634, fax: 217-787-0062, e-mail: riseman@riseman.com, website: www.riseman.com. Absentee auctions of collectible popular sheet music, entertainment-related memorabilia, ephemera, and autographs. Mail, phone, fax, and e-mail bids accepted. No buyer's premium. Prices realized mailed after auction. Free catalogs. Appraisals.

PBA Galleries, 133 Kearny St., 4th Floor, San Francisco, CA 94108, 415-989-2665 or 866-999-7224, fax: 415-989-1664, e-mail: pba@pba galleries.com, website: www.pbagalleries.com. Auctioneers and appraisers of rare and antiquarian books and works on paper. Buyer's premium 15%. Mail, phone, and Internet bids accepted. Prices realized mailed after auction and available on website. Catalog $15, yearly subscription $175.

Pence Auction Co., 1409 Woodbury Ln., Liberty, MO 64068-1266, 816-781-4218, fax: 816-781-9201, e-mail: penceauction@msn.com, website: www.penceauction.com. Antiques and estate auctions. Mail bids accepted. No buyer's premium. Prices realized mailed after auction. Free catalog. Appraisals.

Pennypacker-Andrews Auction Centre, Inc., PO Box 558, Shillington, PA 19607-0558, 610-777-6121, fax: 610-777-3751, e-mail: cpa88@aol.com, website: www.pennypackerandrewsauction.com. Antique furniture, glassware, china, artwork, folk art, jewelry, and estate work. Mail, phone, fax, and e-mail bids accepted. Buyer's premium 10%. Free catalogs. Appraisals.

Philip Weiss Auctions, 1 Neil Ct., Oceanside, NY 11572, 516-594-0731, fax: 516-594-9414, e-mail: auction22@aol.com, website: www.philipweiss auctions.com. Collectibles, toys, trains, dolls, rare books, etc. Mail, phone, fax, and e-mail bids accepted. Buyer's premium 10%. Catalog on website. Free appraisals.

Phillips, de Pury & Luxembourg, 450 W. 15 St., New York, NY 10011, 212-940-1200, fax: 212-688-1647, website: phillips-dpl.com. Mail and phone bids accepted. Prices realized mailed after auction. Appraisals.

Pook & Pook Inc., PO Box 268, Downingtown, PA 19335, 610-269-0695, fax: 610-269-9274, e-mail: info@pookandpook.com, website: www.pookandpook.com. Specializes in eighteenth- and nineteenth-century American, English, and continental furniture, fine art, textiles, folk art, metalware, pottery, and porcelain. Mail, phone, fax, and e-mail bids accepted. Buyer's premium varies. Prices available on website after auction. Catalog $35; yearly subscription $160. Appraisals.

Poster Auctions International, Inc., 601 W. 26th St., New York, NY 10001, 212-787-4000, fax: 212-604-9175, e-mail: info@posterauctions.com, website: www.posterauctions.com. Poster auctions. Mail, phone, fax, and e-mail bids accepted. Buyer's premium 15%. Catalogs $50. Prices realized mailed after auction and available on website. Appraisals.

R & R Enterprises, 3 Chestnut Dr., Bedford, NH 03110, 603-471-0808, fax: 603-471-2844, e-mail: bid@rrauction.com, website: www.rrauction.com. Auctions of vintage and contemporary autographs. Mail, phone, fax, and e-mail auctions. Buyer's premium 17%. Catalog $20; yearly subscription $199.

R.M. Smythe & Co., 26 Broadway, Suite 973, New York, NY 10004-1703, 800-622-1880 or 212-943-1880, fax: 212-908-4670, e-mail: info@smythe online.com, website: www.smytheonline.com. Auctions of coins, currency, stocks and bonds, autographs, photographs, and historic Americana. Mail, phone, fax, and Internet bids accepted. Buyer's premium varies with amount of sale, 10%, 12%, and 15%. Prices realized mailed after auction. Catalog $25, subscription $87.50. Appraisals.

Rafael Osona, PO Box 2607, Nantucket, MA 02584, 508-228-3942, fax: 508-228-8778, e-mail: osona@aol.com, website: www.nantucketon line.com/antiques/osona. Americana, Nantucket art, baskets, and marine memorabilia. Phone and fax bids accepted. Buyer's premium 12%. Catalog subscription $27 per year. Appraisals.

Randy Inman Auctions, PO Box 726, Waterville, ME 04903-0726, 207-872-6900, fax: 207-872-6966, e-mail: inman@inmanauctions.com, website: www.inmanauctions.com. Specializes in antique advertising, coin-operated machines, toys, and related items. Mail and phone bids accepted. Buyer's premium 10%. Prices realized available after auction. Appraisals.

Red Baron Auctions, 6450 Roswell Rd., Atlanta, GA 30328, 404-

252-3770, fax: 404-252-0268, e-mail: rbaron1@bellsouth.net, website: www.redbaronsantiques.com. Auctions of architectural elements, furniture, garden items, and fine art. Mail and phone bids accepted. Buyer's premium. Catalogs. Prices realized available after auction.

Richard Opfer Auctioneering Inc., 1919 Greenspring Dr., Timonium, MD 21093, 410-252-5035, fax: 410-252-5863, e-mail: info@opferauction.com, website: www.opferauction.com. Art, antiques and collectibles, estates, toys, and advertising. Buyer's premium 10%. Mail and phone bids accepted. Prices realized mailed and available on website after some auctions. Catalog prices varies from $3 to $35, depending on sale. Referrals given for restoration and conservation. Appraisals.

Richard W. Withington, Inc., 590 Center Rd., Hillsboro, NH 03244, 603-464-3232, fax: 603-464-4901, e-mail: withington@conknet.com, website: www.withingtonauction.com. Antiques and antique dolls. No mail or phone bids. Buyer's premium 10%. Prices realized mailed after auction. Doll catalogs $16. Free auction brochures. Appraisals.

Robert C. Eldred Co., Inc., PO Box 796, 1483 Rte. 6A, East Dennis, MA 02641, 508-385-3116, fax: 508-385-7201, e-mail: info@eldreds.com, website: www.eldreds.com. Mail, phone, and fax bids accepted. Buyer's premium 15%. Catalog price varies. Prices realized mailed after auction and available on website. Appraisals.

Running Rabbit Auctions, PO Box 701, Waverly, TN 37185, 931-296-3600, e-mail: marbles@waverly.net, website: runningrabbit.com. Absentee auctions of marbles. Mail, phone, fax, and e-mail bids accepted. Buyer's premium 10%. Print catalog and video catalogs $25 each, $40 for both. Prices realized mailed after auction.

Russ Cochran's Comic Art Auction, PO Box 469, 4 Court Sq., West Plains, MO 65775, 417-256-2224, fax: 417-256-5555, e-mail: ec@gemstone pub.com. Comic art auctions. Buyer's premium 10%. Mail, phone, and fax bids accepted.

Samuel Cottone Auctions, 15 Genesee, Mt. Morris, NY 14510, 716-658-3119, fax: 716-658-3152, e-mail: scottone@rochester.rr.com, website: www.cottoneauctions.com. Mail, phone, and fax bids accepted. Buyer's premium 10%. Prices realized mailed upon request and available on website.

Savoia's Auction, Inc., Rt. 23, S. Cairo, NY 12482, 518-622-8000, fax: 518-622-9453, e-mail: savoias@netheaven.com, website: www.savoias.com. American Arts and Crafts, twentieth-century design, sports collectibles, and estate auctions. Mail, phone, fax, and e-mail bids accepted. Buyer's premium 10%–15%. Catalogs online. Prices realized mailed after auction and available on website. Appraisals.

Schrager Auction Galleries, Ltd., PO Box 100043, 2915 N. Sherman Blvd., Milwaukee, WI 53210, 414-873-3738, fax: 414-873-5229, e-mail: askus@schragerauction.com, website: www.schragerauction.com.

Mail and phone bids accepted. No buyer's premium. Prices realized mailed and available on website after auction. Catalogs $7 to $10; subscription to mailing list $10. Appraisals.

Seeck Auctions, PO Box 377, Mason City, IA 50402, 641-424-1116, e-mail: JimJan@seeckauction.com, website: seeckauction.com. Mail and e-mail bids accepted. No buyer's premium. Prices realized on website after auction.

Shelley's Auction Gallery, 429 N. Main St., Hendersonville, NC 28792-4903, 828-698-8485, fax: 828-693-4305, e-mail: sag@shelleysauction.com, website: www.shelleysauction.com. Specializes in antiques, jewelry, and collectibles. Mail, phone, and Internet bids accepted. Buyer's premium 10%. Prices realized mailed after auction, $15; also available on website. Appraisals.

Shot Glass Exchange, PO Box 219K, Western Springs, IL 60558, 708-246-1559, fax: 708-246-1559. Mail bids only. Two auctions per year. Buyer's premium 10% on items over $50. Prices realized mailed after auction.

Skinner, Inc., 357 Main St., Bolton, MA 01740, 978-779-6241, fax: 978-779-5144, website: www.skinnerinc.com. Mail, phone, fax, and e-mail bids accepted. Buyer's premium 15% up to $50,000; 10% over $50,000. Second location at The Heritage on the Garden, 63 Park Plaza, Boston, MA 02116, 617-350-5400, fax: 617-350-5429. Appraisals.

Slater's Americana, 5335 N. Tacoma Ave., Suite 24, Indianapolis, IN 46220, 317-257-0863, Mon.–Fri. 9:00 A.M.–1:00 P.M. only, fax: 317-254-9167, e-mail: info@slatersamericana.com, website: www.slatersamericana.com. Vintage presidential and political campaign memorabilia, sports memorabilia, and Americana. Mail, phone, and fax bids accepted. Buyer's premium 15%. Prices realized available after auction. Appraisals.

Smith & Jones, 12 Clark Ln., Sudbury, MA 01776, 978-443-5517, fax: 978-443-2796, e-mail: smthjones@gis.net, website: www.smithandjones auctions.com. Absentee auctions of American and European art pottery. Mail, phone, fax, and Internet bids. Buyer's premium 10%. Catalogs and prices realized available.

Smith House Toys, PO Box 336, Eliot, ME 03903, 207-439-4614, fax: 207-439-8554, e-mail: smithtoys@aol.com, website: www.smith housetoys.com. Toys from 1900 to 1970. Mail, phone, fax, e-mail, and Internet bids accepted. Buyer's premium 10%. Catalog $15, subscription $35 for three issues. Prices realized mailed after auction. Appraisals.

SoldUSA Auctions, LLC, 1418 Industrial Rd., Box 11, Matthews, NC 28105, 704-815-1500, fax: 704-844-6436, e-mail: croberts@soldusa.com, website: soldusa.com. Hunting and fishing collectibles, fine firearms, and western collectibles. Mail, phone, fax, and e-mail bids accepted.

Buyer's premium 10%. Catalog $24. Prices realized on website and in following catalog. Restoration. Appraisals.

Sotheby's, 1334 York Ave., New York, NY 10021, 212-606-7000, website: www.sothebys.com. Mail, phone, fax, and e-mail bids accepted. Variable buyer's premium. Catalog prices vary. Sotheby's has locations in London, Paris, Geneva, Hong Kong, and other cities. Check the website for the addresses.

South Bay Auctions, PO Box 303, 485 Montauk Hwy., East Moriches, NY 11940, 631-878-2909, fax: 631-878-1863, e-mail: info@southbay auctions.com, website: www.southbayauctions.com. Period furniture and accessories, fine arts, silver, field and stream items, fine decorative items, toys, etc. Mail and phone bids accepted. Buyer's premium 15%. Highlights of prices realized available on website. Affiliated with Sothebys.com online auctions. Appraisals.

Stack's Coin Galleries, 123 W. 57th St., New York, NY 10019, 212-582-2580, fax: 212-582-1946, e-mail: info@stacks.com, website: www.stacks.com. Rare coins. United States, foreign, ancient, gold, and silver coins. Mail bids accepted. Buyer's premium 15%. Catalog $10. Appraisals.

Stanton Auctioneers, PO Box 146, 144 S. Main St., Vermontville, MI 49096, 517-726-0181, fax: 517-726-0060, e-mail: stantons@voyager.net, website: www.stantons-auctions.com. General property liquidations, antique phonographs, and music boxes. Mail, phone, fax, and e-mail bids accepted. No buyer's premium. Prices realized available following cataloged sales. Catalog price varies. Appraisals.

Strawser Auctions, PO Box 332, Wolcottville, IN 46795, 260-854-2859, fax: 260-854-3979, e-mail: michael@strawserauctions.com, website: strawserauctions.com. Majolica, Fiesta, antiques, and estates. Mail bids accepted. Buyer's premium none to 10%. List of prices realized mailed after auction. Appraisals.

Superior Galleries, 9478 W. Olympic Blvd., Beverly Hills, CA 90212, 877-782-6773 or 310-203-9761, fax: 310-203-8037, e-mail: alan@superior stamps.com, website: www.superiorstamps.com. Stamps, sports memorabilia, Hollywood memorabilia, and other collectibles. Mail, phone, fax, and e-mail bids accepted. Buyer's premium 15%. Catalog $5. Yearly subscription $20. Prices realized available after auction on website. Appraisals.

Swann Galleries, Inc., 104 E. 25th St., New York, NY 10010, 212-254-4710, fax: 215-979-1017, e-mail: swann@swanngalleries.com, website: www.swanngalleries.com. Over 20 rare book auctions per year. Also auctions of photographs, posters, prints, drawings, maps and atlases, and autographs. Buyer's premium varies. Mail, phone, and fax bids accepted. Catalogs.

Teletrade, Inc., 27 Main St., Kingston, NY 12401-3853, 800-232-1132 or 914-339-2900, e-mail: bradj@teletrade.com or pauls@teletrade.com, website: www.teletrade.com. Absentee auctions of rare coins and sports cards. Phone and Internet bids only. Buyer's premium 10%. Prices realized mailed and available on website after auction.

Tepper Galleries, Inc., 110 E. 25th St., New York, NY 10010, 212-677-5300, fax: 212-673-3686, e-mail: info@teppergalleries.com, website: www.teppergalleries.com. Phone bids accepted with prior approval. Buyer's premium 15%. Free catalogs. Prices realized mailed upon written request. Appraisals.

Theriault's, PO Box 151, Annapolis, MD 21404, 410-224-3655, fax: 410-224-2515, e-mail: info@theriaults.com, website: www.theriaults.com. Auctions of antique dolls and related items. On-site and online auctions. Mail, phone, fax, and e-mail bids accepted. Buyer's premium 10%. Catalog $49; yearly subscription $189. Prices realized mailed after auction and available on website. Appraisals.

Thomaston Auction Gallery, PO Box 300, Thomaston, ME 04861, 207-354-8141, fax: 207-354-9523, e-mail: barbara@kajav.com, website: www.thomastonauction.com. Auctions of antiques, paintings, coins, and ephemera. Mail and phone bids accepted. Buyer's premium 12%, 2% discount for cash or checks. Catalog $4. Prices realized available online. Restoration and conservation services. Appraisals.

Tim Isaac Antiques, 97 Prince William, St. John, NB E2L 2B2, Canada, 506-652-3222, fax: 506-652-9366, e-mail: isaacant@nbnet.nb.ca, website: www.timisaac.com. Fine art, New Brunswick furniture, and general auctions. No buyer's premium. Mail and phone bids accepted. Catalog online. Prices realized available after the auction. Appraisals.

Tool Shop Auctions, 78 High St., Needham Market, Suffolk 1P6 8AW, UK, 011-44-1449-272992, fax: 011-44-1449-722683, e-mail: tony@antique tools.co.uk, website: www.antiquetools.co.uk. Specializes in auctions of antique hand tools. Mail, phone, and Internet bids accepted. Buyer's premium 11.75%. Catalog $10 general sale, $35 international; yearly subscription $65. Prices realized mailed to subscribers and available on website. Appraisals.

Tradewinds Auctions, PO Box 249, Manchester, MA 01944-0249, 978-526-4085, fax: 978-526-3088, e-mail: taron@tradewindsantiques.com, website: tradewindsantiques.com. Auctions of antique canes and walking sticks only. Mail and phone bids accepted. Buyer's premium 12%. Catalog $40. Prices realized mailed after auction; partial list available on website. Appraisals.

Treadway Gallery, Inc., 2029 Madison Rd., Cincinnati, OH 45208, 513-321-6742, fax: 513-871-7722, e-mail: treadway2029@earthlink.net, website: www.treadwaygallery.com. Arts and Crafts, fine American and European paintings, and midcentury modern design. Mail, phone, and fax bids accepted. Buyer's premium 15%. Prices realized mailed after auction and available on website. Catalog $35; annual subscription $195. Restoration and conservation services. Appraisals.

US Amusement Auctions, PO Box 4819, Louisville, KY 40204, 502-

451-1263, fax: 502-897-7771, e-mail: webmaster@usamusement.com, website: www.usamusement.com. Auctions of video games, pinball machines, jukeboxes, darts, kiddie rides, pool tables, and redemption games; held in various locations. Buyer's premium 5%.

Veterinary Collectibles Roundtable, 7431 Covington Hwy., Lithonia, GA 30058, 770-482-5100 (days), fax: 770-484-1304, e-mail: Petvet@mind spring.com, website: petvet.home.mindspring.com/VCR. Twice yearly consignment phone-bid auctions of antique veterinary patent medicines and associated advertising. Full-color catalogs and postsale prices realized are available for $10 per auction.

Victorian Images, Box 284, Marlton, NJ 08053, 856-354-2154, fax: 856-354-9699, e-mail: rmascieri@aol.com, website: tradecards.com/vi. Absentee auctions of trade cards, ephemera, and nineteenth-century advertising. Mail, phone, and Internet bids accepted. Buyer's premium 13%; 10% for cash or check. Prices realized mailed after auction and available on website. Catalog $18; yearly subscription $90. Appraisals.

Vintage Cover Story, PO Box 975, Burlington, NC 27215, 336-570-2810, e-mail: BobNews@aol.com. Historic newspapers. Mail, phone, and e-mail bids accepted. Buyer's premium 20%. Prices realized mailed upon request. Appraisals.

VintagePostcards.com, 60-C Skiff St., Suite 116, Hamden, CT 06517, 203-248-6621, fax: 203-281-0387, e-mail: quality@vintagepostcards.com, website: www.vintagepostcards.com. Postcard auctions. Mail, phone, and Internet bids accepted. No buyer's premium. Catalog $15. Appraisals.

Waddington's, 111 Bathurst St., Toronto, ON M5V 2R1, Canada, 416-504-9100; toll free 877-504-5700, fax: 416-504-0033, e-mail: info@waddingtonsauctions.com, website: www.waddingtonsauctions.com. Specializes in Inuit and Canadian art. Mail, phone, and fax bids accepted. Absentee bids may also be left through icollector.com. Buyer's premium 15%. Prices realized mailed after auction and available on website. Appraisals.

Waverly Auctions, Inc., 4931 Cordell Ave., Bethesda, MD 20814, 301-951-8883, fax: 301-718-8375, e-mail: waverly1660@earthlink.net, website: waverlyauctions.com. Auctions of used and rare books, autographs, maps, and prints. Mail, phone, and Internet bids accepted. Buyer's premium 15%. Prices realized mailed after auction and available on website. Catalog $7; yearly subscription $38. Appraisals.

Web Wilson's Online Auctions, PO Box 506, Portsmouth, RI 02871, 800-508-0022, fax: 401-683-1644, e-mail: hww@webwilson.com, website: www.webwilson.com. Antique hardware, tiles, and more. Phone, fax, and e-mail bids accepted. Buyer's premium 10%. Catalog posted on website or available by mail. Prices realized posted on website after auction. Appraisals.

Weschler's, 909 E. St. NW, Washington, DC 20004, 800-331-1430 or 202-628-1281, fax: 202-628-2366, e-mail: info@weschlers.com, website: weschlers.com. Mail, phone, fax, and e-mail bids accepted. Buyer's premium 15%. Prices realized mailed after auction and available on website. Appraisals.

William "Pete" Harvey Gun Auctions, PO Box 280, Cataumet, MA 02534, 508-548-0660, fax: 508-457-0660, website: www.firearmsauctions.com. Firearms auctions only. Mail and phone bids accepted. Buyer's premium 10%. Prices realized mailed after auction. Catalog $35. Firearms appraised.

William Morford Auctions, RR #2, Cazenovia, NY 13035, 315-662-7625, fax: 315-662-3570, e-mail: morf2bid@aol.com, website: morfauction.com. Absentee auctions of antique advertising and Maxfield Parrish prints. Mail, phone, and Internet bids accepted. Buyer's premium 10%. Prices realized mailed after auction and available on website. Catalog $12; yearly subscription $20. Restoration and conservation. Appraisals.

Willis Henry Auctions, 22 Main St., Marshfield, MA 02050, 781-834-7774, fax: 781-826-3936, e-mail: wha@willishenry.com, website: www.willishenry.com. Shaker, Americana, and decorative arts auctions. Mail and phone bids accepted. Buyer's premium 15%. Prices realized mailed after auction. Prices of catalogs vary. Advice on restoration and conservation. Appraisals.

Winter Associates, PO Box 823, 21 Cooke St., Plainville, CT 06062, 800-962-2530 or 860-793-0288, fax: 860-793-8288, e-mail: info@winter associatesinc.com, website: winterassociatesinc.com. Estate liquidation and personal property appraisal. Mail and phone bids accepted. Buyer's premium 10%. Catalog $4. Appraisals.

Witherell's, 300 20th St., Sacramento, CA 95814, 916-446-6490, e-mail: brian@witherells.com, website: www.witherells.com. Specializes in investment-grade nineteenth- and early twentieth-century western Americana, firearms, and American furniture. A written guarantee and a full description and condition report attesting to an object's authenticity accompany all objects. Mail and phone bids accepted. Buyer's premium 15%. Prices realized mailed after auction. Appraisals.

Woody Auction, PO Box 618, Douglass, KS 67039, 316-747-2694, fax: 316-747-2145, e-mail: woodyauction@earthlink.net, website: www.woody auction.com. General auctions, carnival glass, and R.S. Prussia. In person, mail, fax, and e-mail bids accepted. No buyer's premium. Catalogs available in print and online. Prices realized mailed after auction. Free catalogs.

Wright Auctions, 1140 Fulton Ave., Chicago, IL 60607, 312-563-0020, website: www.wright20.com. Auctions of modern art and design. Phone and fax bids accepted. Buyer's premium 15%. Catalog prices vary.

York Town Auction, 1625 Haviland Rd., York, PA 17404, 717-751-0211, fax:

717-767-7729, e-mail: info@yorktownauction.com, website: www.york
townauction.com. Auctions of antiques, clocks, art, militaria, and
toys. Mail and phone bids accepted. Buyer's premium 12½%. Free listing of items to be auctioned. Fully illustrated catalogs available
online. Prices realized available online after auction. Appraisals.

CONSERVATION SUPPLIES

The best place to start looking for supplies is at your local hardware or art supply store. There are products to clean chandeliers still
in place on the ceiling, to tarnish-proof silver, replate silver, or
remove candle wax from tabletops. All types of metal polishes, polishes to match any shade of wood, marble polish, battery-powered
picture lights, felt pads to keep lamp bottoms from scratching furniture, dry cleaners for removing stains on cloth, linen wash to whiten
old damask napkins, and even special cleaners to remove crayon or
paint marks can be found. Dozens of new types of "instant" glue
and solder are available; some are clear for use on glass.

Some supplies needed for the proper care of antiques are difficult
to locate, including such products as acid-free paper-backing materials, special soaps, and special waxes. These are used primarily by
the professional restorer or conservator, but collectors often need
them as well. A list of sources for these parts and supplies follows.
Some of these companies sell only to wholesale accounts and will
not sell to individuals, but they will direct you to the store or dealer
nearest you that carries the products. Special items for use with one
type of antique, such as clock parts or doll eyes, are listed in the
appropriate sections.

There are mail-box rental stores that also pack and ship antiques.
Check your local phone book.

SOURCES

A & H Brass & Supply, 126 W. Main St., Johnson City, TN 37604, 423-928-
8220. Complete line of restoration hardware; reproduction furniture
hardware, veneers, caning supplies, replacement seats, Briwax,
Howard's products. Trunk supplies. Catalog $3. Separate catalog for
lamp parts.

Antique Hardware and Mirror Resilvering, 763 West Bippley Rd., Lake
Odessa, MI 48849, 616-374-7750, fax: 616-374-7752, e-mail: antiquehard
ware@robinsonsantiques.com, website: www.robinsonsantiques.com.
Original antique restoration hardware, door hardware, doorknobs, fur-

niture hardware, hinges, mirrors, locks, pulls, latches, registers, and more. Mirror resilvering. Original parts from 1650 to 1925. Free search. Free matching service.

Barfield Antiques, PO Box 575, Westcliffe, CO 81252, 719-783-0253, fax: 719-783-0253, e-mail: svs@ris.net, website: www.vintagesoak.com. Nancy's Vintage Soak, a whitener for antique linens, baby clothes, and laces. Removes age spots and yellowing. Safe for colorfast articles. Nontoxic.

Century Business Solutions, PO Box 2393, Brea, CA 92822, 800-767-0777, fax: 800-786-7939, website: www.centurybusinesssolutions.com. Products for organizing and storing photographs, slides, CDs, magazines, stamps, and coins. Binders, bags, envelopes, photo albums and pages, etc.

Competition Chemicals, Inc., PO Box 820, Iowa Falls, IA 50126, 641-648-5121, fax: 641-648-9816, website: www.simichromepolish.com. Distributor of Simichrome metal polish.

Conservation Resources International, 8000 H Forbes Pl., Springfield, VA 22151, 800-634-6932 or 703-321-7730, fax: 703-321-0629, e-mail: criusa@conservationresources.com, website: www.conservationre sources.com. Archival materials for long-term storage of collections. Boxes, envelopes, folders, and papers for archival storage. Chemicals and tools used in conservation treatments, including Renaissance Wax. Free catalog available.

Cutlery Specialties, 22 Morris Ln., Great Neck, NY 11024, 516-829-5899, fax: 516-773-8076, e-mail: dennis13@aol.com, website: www.restoration product.com. U.S. agent and distributor for Piecreator Enterprises Ltd. of London, manufacturer of Renaissance Wax/Polish and other restoration products. Vulpex Liquid Soap for cleaning feathers, leather, carpet, paintings, metal, shell, and practically everything from paper to stone, Quakehold Museum Wax for anchoring collectibles. De-Solv-it, an all-purpose cleaner. Zap-A-Dap-A-Goo, a flexible adhesive sealant.

Daniel Smith Artists' Materials, PO Box 84268, Seattle, WA 98124-5568, 206-224-0411, fax: 206-224-0406, e-mail: john.cogley@daniel smith.com, website: danielsmith.com. A complete line of fine-art materials, including drawing, painting, and print-making supplies; metal leafing supplies; framing and matting supplies.

Elaine Koronich, 14415 Caves Rd., Novelty, OH 44072, 440-338-1853, fax: 440-338-1853, e-mail: exsoaps@aol.com. Handcrafted soaps. Real soap flakes, not detergent, for laundering textiles. Mail order.

Epoxy Technology, Inc., 14 Fortune Dr., Billerica, MA 01821, 978-667-3805, fax: 978-663-9782, e-mail: salesinfo@epotek.com, website: www.epotek.com. Manufacturer of two-part, optically transparent epoxy systems with very low viscosities and room temperature cure.

Uses include restoration and repair of wood, glass, stone, porcelain, china, and other artifacts. The epoxy can be used to coat surfaces or to bond materials.

G.M. Wylie Company, PO Box AA, Washington, PA 15301-0660, 800-747-1249, fax: 724-225-0741, e-mail: info@gmwylie.com, website: gmwylie.com. Safe long-term storage supplies for paper collectibles, photos, postcards, and textiles. Products include acid-free binders, albums, boxes, envelopes, folders, map folders, marking pens, mounting corners, newspaper storage boxes, preservation supplies, repair tape, record storage boxes, sleeves, textile storage boxes, wrapping paper, and much more. Order by mail, phone, or e-mail. Catalog $1.50 or visit the website.

Gaylord Bros., PO Box 4901, Syracuse, NY 13221-4901, 800-448-6160, fax: 800-272-3412, website: www.gaylord.com. Archival storage materials and conservation tools, such as acid-free tissue, acid-free boxes, storage tubes for textiles, archival polyester enclosures for photos and documents, folders, and Vulpex and Orvus cleaners. Free catalog.

George Basch Company, Inc., PO Box 188, Freeport, NY 11520, 516-378-8100, 9:00 A.M.–3:00 P.M., fax: 516-378-8140, e-mail: mark@nevrdull.com, website: www.nevrdull.com. Nevr-Dull, a brand of treated cotton wadding cloth, cleans and polishes metal. Can be used on aluminum, brass, chromium, copper, gold, nickel, pewter, silver, and zinc. Cleans automotive trim, marine accessories and hardware, tools, cookware, and silverware.

Golden's Antique Supply, 8990 Main St., Woodstock, GA 30188, 888-202-1029 or 770-924-8528, fax: 770-924-8980, e-mail: wcgolden@antique supply.com, website: www.antiquesupply.com. Everything for the "antiqueholic" from testing equipment, restoration supplies, and archival supplies to display, hardware, books and videos.

Highland Hardware, 1045 N. Highland Ave., Atlanta, GA 30306, 800-241-6748, fax: 404-876-1941, e-mail: orderdept@highland-hardware.com, website: www.highland-hardware.com. Tools for fine woodworking. Hard-to-find hand tools: planes, chisels, saws, marking and measuring tools. Finishing supplies: dyes, stains, shellac, etc. Classes on all aspects of woodworking and finishing. Books on finishing and refinishing. Free catalog.

Hollinger Corporation, PO Box 8360, Fredericksburg, VA 22404, 800-634-0491, 8:30 A.M.–5:00 P.M., e-mail: hollingercorp@erols.com, website: www.hollingercorp.com. Archival print boxes, envelopes, folders, tubes, photographic storage materials, acid-free papers, plastic sleeves, and products to store documents, books, photographs, textiles, video and audio cassettes, maps, and more. Free catalog.

Howard Products. Inc., 560 Linne Rd., Paso Robles, CA 93446, 800-266-9545, fax: 805-227-1007, e-mail: custserv@howardproducts.com, website: www.howardproducts.com. Full line of wood-care products and metal polishes, available at retail stores. Dealers may call for samples. Free brochure.

Kramer's Best Antique Improver, PO Box 8715, Sugar Creek, MO 64054, 816-252-9512, fax: 816-252-9121, e-mail: kramer@kramerize.com, website: www.kramerize.com. Makers of Kramer's Best Antique Improver, an all-natural wood care and restoration product; Blemish Clarifier for heavy cleaning; and Wood Food Oyl for food-service items. Will answer questions over the phone. Send SASE for free flier. Instructions and uses booklet $1.95, free with purchase.

Lee Valley Tools, Ltd., 1090 Morrison Dr., Ottawa, ON K2H 1C2, Canada, 800-871-8158, fax: 800-513-7885, e-mail: customerservice@lee valley.com, website: www.leevalley.com. Fine woodworking and finishing tools and supplies for restoration and preservation. Free introductory catalog.

Light Impressions, PO Box 787, Brea, CA 92822-0787, 800-828-6216, 714-441-4539 for international calls, fax: 800-828-5539, 714-441-4564 for international faxes, e-mail: Liwebsite@impressions.com, website: www.lightimpressionsdirect.com. Archival supplies, including photo albums, frames, mat board; slide, negative, film, and print storage; portfolios, storage boxes and bags, scrapbooking supplies, and much more for photographs, artwork, and other valuable materials. Free catalog.

Marlyco Inc. dba Trevco Products, 445 Production St., San Marcos, CA 92078, 800-959-4053, 710-510-4969, fax: 710-510-4979, e-mail: Trevco@earthlink.net, website: www.Quakehold.com. Manufacturers of Quakehold safety fasteners, Crystalline Clear Museum Wax, Collectors Hold Museum Putty, and Clear Museum Gel for securing and anchoring collectibles.

Metal Edge, Inc., 6340 Bandini Blvd., Commerce, CA 90040, 800-862-2228 or 213-721-7800, fax: 888-822-6937, e-mail: info@www.metaledge inc.com, website: www.metaledgeinc.com. Storage, conservation, and identification supplies. Binders, boxes, bags, folders, document cases, board, and paper. Book storage boxes, book and document repair supplies; storage for slides, negatives, photos, records, audio reels, microfilm, and more. Free catalog.

Mini-Magic, 3910 Patricia Dr., Columbus, OH 43220, 614-457-3687, toll-free order number 888-391-0691, fax: 614-459-2306, e-mail: minimagic @mini-magic.com, website: www.mini-magic.com. Fabrics and trim for doll clothes, sewing, and craft projects. French fashion patterns and kits. Doll stands, washing paste, acid-free boxes and tissue, muslin, buckles, buttons, hat supplies, and more.

Mylan Enterprises, PO Box 971002, Dept. K, Boca Raton, FL 33497-1002, 561-852-0861, fax: 561-852-0862, e-mail: sales@mylanusa.com, website: www.mylanusa.com. Wrapping pads, bubble pac, and bubble bags for packing antiques and fragile items. Free brochure.

Pacific Engineering, PO Box 145, Farmington, CT 06034, fax: 860-674-8913, e-mail: blackwax@pewaxes.com, website: www.pewaxes.com. Manufacturers of Black Wax, a carnauba wax containing a mild abrasive for cleaning and polishing antiques and fine furniture; Crystal Wax, a paste wax; and Sienna Wax, a carnauba wax with brown pigment added to prevent the chalky effect sometimes left in cracks and carvings by wax residue.

Packaging Store Inc., 5675 DTC Blvd., Suite 280, Greenwood Village, CO 80111, 800-525-6309 or 303-741-6626, fax: 303-741-6653, e-mail: info@gopackagingstore.com, website: www.gopackagingstore.com. Custom packaging and shipping services, large, awkward, fragile, and valuable items. Crates, boxes, and packing materials. Check the website for the nearest store location.

Products Unlimited, 2836 N. Brookfield, Unit 2E, Brookfield, WI 53045, 262-821-6120 or 800-236-0136, fax: 262-821-6123, e-mail: products_jmp@yahoo.com. Wood refinisher's supplies, including paint and lacquer strippers, stains, finishes, stripping equipment, sandpapers, adhesives, and more. Distributor of national brand-name products. Sales and service in the upper Midwest.

Quill Hair & Ferrule, Ltd., PO Box 23927, Columbia, SC 29224, 800-421-7961, 803-788-4499, Mon.–Fri. 8:00 A.M.–5:00 P.M., fax: 803-736-4731, website: www.qhfonline.com. Specialty products and supplies. Paints, brushes, and hard-to-find supplies for sign restoration, faux finishing, and gold leaf.

Real Milk Paint, D.O. Siever Products, 618 California Rd., Quakertown, PA 18951, 800-339-9748 or 215-538-3886, fax: 215-538-5435, e-mail: dwayne@realmilkpaint.com, website: realmilkpaint.com. Real milk paint, 100% pure tung oil, waxes, crackle, ultrabond, dark raw tung oil, hide glue, and other restoration products. Free brochure.

The Refinishing Store, PO Box 498, Bath, OH 44210, 888-4-refinish, fax: 330-666-0586, e-mail: ann@refinish.com, website: www.refinish.com. Specialty products for professional and do-it-yourself restorers. Waxes, polishes, cleaners, fine finishes, repair items, resource books, and videos. Direct e-mail line to refinishing experts. Online catalog.

Restoration Services, 1417 Third St., Webster City, IA 50595, 515-832-1131, e-mail: repair@netins.net, website: www.Restorationmaterials.safeshopper.com. Restoration services and repair supplies for china, pottery, porcelain, ceramics, glass, ivory, jade, and most other materials. Videos, home study course, classes available. Glass chip filler, diamond hand pads for removing scratches, glass bonding resin, enamel glaze, stain remover, lacquers, milliput, less-toxic milliput substitute, flatner, and more. Mini manuals "Repairing China, Pottery & Figurines," "Color Matching Guide," and "Glass Cleaning & Repairing."

Restorite Systems, PO Box 7096-A, West Trenton, NJ 08628, 609-530-1526. Products for restoring porcelain, pottery, and glass. Repair kit for restoring broken or chipped china and glass. Includes supplies necessary to mend dozens of pieces and illustrated instruction book. Mail order only. Free brochure.

Solar Screen, 53-11 105th St., Corona, NY 11368, 800-347-6527 or 718-592-8223, fax: 888-271-0891 or 718-271-0891, website: www.solar-screen.com. Products that prevent fading caused by ultraviolet rays and help control glare and heat include Kool Vue window shades made of Mylar, Solar-Screen Transparent Sun Shades, transparent window covering material in sheets, E-Z Bond film for direct use on glass, and fluorescent bulb jackets. Decorative shade fabrics; printing on shade fabrics. Free brochures.

Talas, Division of Technical Library Service, Inc., 568 Broadway, Suite 107, New York, NY 10012, 212-219-0770, Mon.–Fri. 9:00 A.M.–5:30 P.M., fax: 212-219-0735, e-mail: info@talasonline.com, website: www.talasonline.com. Supplies for all areas of conservation, restoration, and storage. Archival storage, tissues, papers, boards, cleaners, bookbinding supplies, tools, and more. Catalog online and in print.

Tindell's Restoration, 825 Sandburg Pl., Nashville, TN 37214, 615-885-1029, fax: 615-391-0712, e-mail: info@ATindellsRestorationSchools.com, website: www.TindellsRestorationSchools.com. Restoration services, seminars, training, and products. Can restore porcelain, pottery, ceramics, crystal, glass, marble, oil paintings, frames, ivory, silver, bronze, and much more. Appraisals. Free brochure.

University Products, Inc., 517 Main St., PO Box 101, Holyoke, MA 01040, 800-336-4847, fax: 800-532-9281, e-mail: info@universityproducts.com, website: www.universityproducts.com. Archival supplies for conservation, restoration, repair, storage, and display. Archival storage boxes, paper and plastic enclosures, acid-free board and papers, adhesives, albums, preservation framing supplies, tools, equipment, chemicals, and other materials. Specialized storage for baseball cards, coins, comics, magazines, photos, postcards, stamps, and other collectibles. Free catalog.

Vaportek, Box 148, W226 N6339 Village Dr., Sussex, WI 53089, 262-246-5060, fax: 262-246-5065, e-mail: info@vaportek.com, website: www.Vaportek.com. Manufacturers of odor-neutralizing and air-purifying products that remove odors caused by cigarettes, mildew, pets, skunks, water damage, fire, smoke, etc. Free brochure.

Wm. Zinsser & Co., Inc., 173 Belmont Dr., Somerset, NJ 08875-1285, 732-469-4367, 8:30 A.M.–4:30 P.M., e-mail: bullseye@zinsser.com, website: www.zinsser.com. Mildew-proof exterior and interior paint, Jomax Mildew Killer & House Cleaner to remove mildew from siding, fences, etc.; paint additive to prevent mildew, wallcovering primer, Bulls Eye Shellac, and other products. Free catalog.

Wolman Wood Care Products, 2110 William Pitt Way., Pittsburgh, PA 15238,

800-556-7737, fax: 888-965-6261, e-mail: info@wolman.com, website: www.wolman.com. Wood-cleaning products, wood restoration and sealer products. Free brochure.

Woodcraft Supply Corp., PO Box 1686, Parkersburg, WV 26102-1686, 800-225-1153 for orders; 800-535-4482 for customer service; 800-535-4486 for technical service, e-mail: custserv@woodcraft.com, website: www.woodcraft.com. Woodworking tools, books, and supplies. Finishing products, glue, hardware, clamps, abrasives, etc. Clock supplies. Picture framing tools. Free catalog.

WSI Distributors, 405 N. Main St., St. Charles, MO 63301-2034, 636-946-5811, fax: 636-946-5832, e-mail: talk2us@wsidistributors.com, website: www.wsidistributors.com. Distributors of antique restoration supplies, primarily replacement and reproduction hardware, chair seat weaving supplies, trunk hardware, Hoosier cabinet hardware, wood veneers, and refinishing and touch-up supplies. Must be an antiques dealer, professional furniture restorer, or have a related business. Free catalog.

CONSERVATORS & RESTORERS

Listed here are restorers and conservators who work on a variety of objects. Others are listed in the appropriate sections of this book. But these are only partial listings of the conservators in America. For a more complete list, contact the American Institute for Conservation of Historic and Artistic works, listed below, which publishes a list of conservators and has a referral service. You can call or write, explain what you need, and receive a list of conservators in your area who specialize in your problem.

We have not seen the work done by many of the conservators listed here. Therefore, this listing does not represent a recommendation of quality. Be sure to check further if you decide to hire someone to restore a valuable work of art. Get a written receipt that includes a description of the piece and a value. Also, get a written statement about work to be done, length of time it will take, price, and details of insurance coverage. You may want to check your own insurance to be sure your valuable is properly insured against loss or damage. We sent an antique chair to be refinished and reupholstered. When the upholstery shop burned to the ground, a legal battle ensued to determine who would pay—the decorator, the department store, the upholsterer, or our insurance company.

ASSOCIATION & NEWSLETTER

Association of Restorers, *Restorers Update* (NL), 8 Medford Pl., New Hartford, NY 13413, e-mail: aorcca@adelphia.net, website: www.assocrestorers.com.

CONSERVATORS & RESTORERS

A Home Design, 5220 Veloz Ave., Los Angeles, CA 91356, 818-757-7766, fax: 818-708-3722, e-mail: homedesign@mail.com. Furniture and antiques touch-ups and restoration. Fabric and leather furniture repairs, cleaning, and reupholstering. Fine arts restoration, including items made from marble, wood carvings, glass, and mirrors. Repairs to real property, including flooring, cabinets, walls. Moving and damage claims, inspection and repair. Operating in the southern California area.

A. Ludwig Klein & Son, Inc., PO Box 145, Harleysville, PA 19438, 215-256-9004 or 800-379-2929, fax: 215-256-9644, website: www.aludwig klein.com. Conservation and restoration of glass, jade, porcelain, ivory, dolls, brass, bronze, pewter, silver, marble, frames, advertising, statuary and monuments, and more. Professional cleaning. Appraisals, insurance claims. Worldwide. By appointment. Free brochure.

American Institute for Conservation of Historic and Artistic Works, 1717 K Street, NW, Suite 301, Washington, DC 20006, 202-452-9545, fax: 202-452-9328, e-mail: info@aic-faic.org, website: aict.stanford.edu. Free conservation services referral system. In response to your inquiry, a computer-generated list of conservators will be compiled and grouped geographically, by specialization, and by type of service requested. Free brochures include "Guidelines for Selecting a Conservator" and "Caring for Your Treasures: Books to Help You."

Antique & Art Restoration by Wiebold, 413 Terrace Pl., Terrace Park, OH 45174, 800-321-2541, 513-831-2541, fax: 513-831-2815, e-mail: wiebold @eos.net, website: www.wiebold.com. Fine art restoration and conservation: art pottery, porcelain, collectible figurines, bisque dolls, oil paintings, gold leaf frames, silver, pewter, brass, glass, ivory, wood carvings. Missing parts replaced. Silver, gold, and brass plating.

Antique China Restorations by MyJolie Hutchings, 1941 Wolfsnare Rd., Virginia Beach, VA 23454-3544, 757-425-1807. Restorations of antiques and contemporary ceramics, china, porcelain, terra-cotta, majolica, bisque, marble, soapstone, wood, plaster, lamps, Hummel, Lladro, Roseville, etc. Invisible repairs and replacement of missing parts, finials, handles, fingers, etc.

Antique Hardware and Mirror Resilvering, 763 W. Bippley Rd., Lake Odessa, MI 48849, 616-374-7750, fax: 616-374-7752, e-mail: antiquehardware @robinsonsantiques.com, website: www.robinsonsantiques.com. Original antique restoration hardware, door hardware, doorknobs, furniture hardware, hinges, mirrors, locks, pulls, hinges, latches, registers, and more. Mirror resilvering. Original parts from 1650 to 1925. Free search. Free matching service.

Antique Restoration Co., 440 E. Centre Ave., Newtown, PA 18940, 215-968-2343, fax: 215-860-5465. Furniture stripping, repair, and refinishing. Cushions refilled and recovered; upholstery. Caning, rushing, and splint weave. Billiard tables restored, moved, and set up. Frames repaired. Porcelain repaired. Mirror resilvering; gold leafing; glass beveling. Metal polishing, plating, and lacquering. Free brochure.

Antique Restoration Service, 521 Ashwood Dr., Flushing, MI 48433, 810-659-5582, 810-659-0505, e-mail: sshch@aol.com. Restoration of porcelain, glass, wood, and ivory art objects. Restoration of frames and lamps. Soldering and wiring if necessary. Invisible restoration of all kinds of pottery and china. Missing parts reconstructed.

Antique Restorations, 1313 Mt. Holly Rd., Burlington, NJ 08016-3773, 609-387-2587, Mon.–Sat. 9:00 A.M.–6:00 P.M., fax: 609-387-2587, e-mail: ronaiello@comcast.net. Restorations of china, porcelain, pottery, dolls' heads, and art objects. Specializes in the restoration of Royal Doulton, Wedgwood, Meissen, Roseville, Fulper, Nippon, Hummel, Lladro, Boehm, Cybis, David Winter Cottages, Dept. 56, and others. Restoration supplies. Private restoration lessons. Free restoration supply catalog on request.

Antique Restorations, The Old Wheelwrights', Brasted Forge, Brasted, Kent TN16 1JL, UK, 011-44-1959-563863, fax: 011-44-1959-561262, e-mail: bfc@antique-restorations.org.co.uk, website: www.antique-restorations.org.uk. Complete range of antique and fine art services from furniture restoration and conservation to solutions for preserving your art collections and other valuables. Clock case restoration, brass castings and repair, polishing, upholstery, documentation service.

AntiqueConservation.com, Div. of Ponsford Ltd., 5441 Woodstock Rd., Acworth, GA 30102, 770-924-4848, fax: 770-529-2278, e-mail: GordonPonsford@AntiqueConservation.com, website: www.Antique Conservation.com. Conservation and restoration of fine art and antiques, frames and gilding, furniture, paintings, paper, photographs, porcelain, sculpture, stained glass, caning and weaving, and more. Can remove tears, cuts, scratches and holes in photos, rebuild faded areas, and replace areas that have been lost. Appraisals.

Appelbaum & Himmelstein, 444 Central Park W., New York, NY 10025, 212-666-4630, Mon.–Fri., fax: 212-316-1039, e-mail: aamdh@idt.net. Conservation treatment of paintings, objects, and textiles; collection surveys; consultation on collections care, including lighting, storage, and humidity control.

Archival Conservation Center, Inc., 8225 Daly Rd., Cincinnati, OH 45231,

513-521-9858, fax: 513-521-9859. Repair and restoration of works of art on paper, including engravings, lithographs, watercolors, old maps, newspapers, Oriental scrolls, parchment documents, posters, books and family Bibles. Smoke odor removal. Freeze drying of water-damaged materials. Free brochure available upon request.

Artisans of the Valley, 103 Corrine Dr., Pennington, NJ 08534, 609-637-0450, fax: 609-637-0452, e-mail: woodworkers@artisansofthe valley.com, website: www.artisansofthevalley.com. Specializes in conservation and restoration services and hand-crafted custom woodworking. Old finishes restored, missing carvings and moldings made, leather restored. Firearms, swords, and other military relics restored. Etched and stained glass work. Restoration on antique tools, farm equipment, military equipment, etc. Consultation services to architects, contractors, and curators. Free catalog.

Artwork Restoration, 30 Hillhouse Rd., Winnipeg, MB R2V 2V9, Canada, 204-334-7090, e-mail: morry@escape.ca. Restoration of vases, figurines, lamps, antique dolls, ivory carvings, Lladro, Hummel, picture frames, crystal, Inui soapstone carvings, and more. Missing parts replaced.

Attic Unlimited, 22435 E. LaPalma Ave., Yorba Linda, CA 92887, 714-692-2940, fax: 714-692-2947, e-mail: atticunlimited@aol.com, website: www.atticunlimited.com. Restoration of Lladros, Hummels, Armanie, porcelain, pottery, paintings, frames, glass religious statues and articles, antiques and collectibles, and any objects of art.

Beverly Standing Designs, 1026 Elizabeth St., Pasadena, CA 91104, 626-798-2306, fax: 626-798-3529, e-mail: bubbs120@aol.com. Restoration of fine porcelain and objects of art containing wood, glass, or marble. By appointment only.

Boston Art Conservation, 9 Station St., Brookline, MA 02146, 617-738-1126, 9:00 A.M.–5:00 P.M., e-mail: admin@bosartconserv.com, website: bosartconserv.com. Conservation of works of art on paper, Asian paintings (scroll and screens), photographs, art and artifacts on paper, and textiles. Collection surveys. Consultations on proper storage and display. Free brochure.

Bowthorpe Restorations, 320 Hudson Ln., Williamsburg, CO 81226, 719-784-0297, e-mail: usns@ris.net, website: www.bowthorpe-usa.com. Repairs broken porcelain, figurines, pottery, china, and all breakables, including Dresden, Hummel, Sitzendorf, McCoy, Roseville, and Hull.

Broken Art Restoration, 1841 W. Chicago Ave., Chicago, IL 60622, 312-226-8200 or 815-472-3900, fax: 815-472-3930. Restoration of porcelain, pottery, ceramics, wood, ivory, metal, stone, and art objects. By appointment. Free brochure.

The Brushstroke, 4250 Van Cortlandt Pk. E., #1B, Bronx, NY 10470, 718-994-5989, e-mail: art_restoration@usa.com. Conservation and restoration of oil paintings, porcelain, ceramics, ivory, jade, and other objects of art. Pickup and delivery service within 50-mile radius in tri-state NYC area. Free estimates.

Carl "Frank" Funes, 57 Maplewood Ave., Hempstead, NY 11550, 516-483-6712. Restoration of arms, armor, artifacts, ivory, metalwork, paintings, porcelain, and wood carvings. Rust removed from weapons. Metal objects cleaned and restored.

Ceramic Restorations, Inc., 24 W. 29th St., 12th Floor, New York, NY 10001, 212-564-8669, 9:00 A.M.–6:00 P.M., fax: 212-843-3742. Specializes in the restoration and conservation of antique and contemporary ceramics, including porcelain, terra-cotta, bisque, and faience. Invisible or museum-style repairs, reconstruction, and replacement of missing elements. Will also restore marble, ivory, stone, and plaster.

Chem-Clean Furniture Restoration, Bucks County Art & Antiques Company, 246 W. Ashland St., Doylestown, PA 18901, 215-345-0892, e-mail: iscsusn@att.net. Furniture repair and restoration; stripping, finishing, caning, reupholstery. Art restoration, frame repair, glass bending, glass beveling, gold leafing, lamp repair, marble repair, metal polishing, mirror resilvering, oil paintings restored, plastic repair. Research. Appraisals. Free brochure.

Chicago Conservation Center, 730 N. Franklin, Suite 701, Chicago, IL 60610, 312-944-5401, fax: 312-944-5479, e-mail: chicagoconservation @yahoo.com, website: chicagoconservation.com. Restoration of paintings, works of art on paper, frames, murals, sculptures, and textiles.

China and Crystal Clinic, 1808 N. Scottsdale Rd., Tempe, AZ 85281, 800-658-9197, fax: 480-945-1079, e-mail: jbenterprises2@earthlink.net, website: chinaandcrystalclinic.com. Restoration or conservation of porcelain, crystal, glass, jade, ivory, marble objects, pottery, bronze or metal figures, figurines, vases, goblets, porcelain dolls, porcelain clocks. Swarovski, Boehm, Agam art, Lladro, Hummel, Royal Doulton, Lalique, bisque, etc. Appraisals.

De Saram's Inc., 4504 Eden St., New Orleans, LA 70125, 504-827-2593, e-mail: Helen@desarams.com, website: www.desarams.com. Conservation and restoration of 3-D art. Specialist in decorative surfaces and patinas, including inlay work, polychrome, lacquer, traditional water gilding, and gold on porcelain. On-site conservation treatments for oversized art works and collections. Lectures, demonstrations, seminars and workshops on conservation concerns, treatments, traditional skills and materials.

Devashan, 445 S. Canyon, Spearfish, SD 57783, 605-722-5355, e-mail: dollmaker@mato.com, website: www.devashan.com. Porcelain and ceramic repair. Antique frames repaired and regilded. Glass chip removal. Restoration of composition dolls. Period doll clothes made.

Photo restoration, both on picture and with computer. Send SASE for brochure.

Dobson Studios, 810 N. Daniel St., Arlington, VA 22201, 703-243-7363, e-mail: ddobson@dobson-studios.com, website: www.dobson-studios.com. Conservation of Oriental woodblock prints, screens, scrolls, Western paper and parchment, including watercolors, documents, drawings, photographs, pictures, etchings, prints, woodblock prints, certificates, posters, and oil paintings on various supports, including glass and silk. Most paper objects are washed and deacidified, if needed. All work and materials are reversible.

European Watch & Casemakers, Ltd., PO Box 1314, Highland Park, NY 08904-1314, 732-777-0111, 10:00 A.M.–6:00 P.M., e-mail: horology@webspan.net. Restoration of unusual clocks, watches, scientific instruments, and objects of vertu, including Fabergé. Can make any part or restore any watch. Can forge alloys appropriate to the period of the object. Cases made for watch movements. Hard enameling. Consulting, appraisal; expert testimony in lawsuits. Free brochure.

Graphic Conservation Co., 329 W. 18th St., Suite 701, Chicago, IL 60616, 312-738-2657, fax: 312-738-3125, e-mail: info@graphicconservation.com, website: www.graphicconservation.com. Preservation of works of art on paper, including prints, drawings, watercolors, pastels, maps, globes, posters, manuscripts, architectural process prints, wallpaper, historical documents, billboard advertising, and paper memorabilia. Dry cleaning, stain reduction, flattening, deacidification, inpainting, tear repairs and fills. Archival matting. Free brochure.

Grashe Fine Art Restorers, 35 148th Ave. SE, #9, Bellevue WA 98007, 425-644-7500, fax: 425-644-7582, e-mail: art@grashe.com, website: www.grashe.com. Specializes in the restoration and conservation of artwork, heirlooms, and other possessions through the use of special techniques and materials. Paintings, porcelain, ceramics, pottery, terra-cotta, glass, ivory, marble, jade, bronze, and silver restored.

Hadley Restorations, 4667 Third St., La Mesa, CA 91941-5529, 619-462-5290, e-mail: cphadcearthlink.net, website: www.assoc-restorers.com. Restoration of china, porcelain, and pottery (both earthenware and stoneware), chalkware, marble, metal, and wood. Free brochure. China restoration classes in La Mesa; demonstrations, lectures on china restoration.

Harry A. Eberhardt & Son, Inc., 2010 Walnut St., Philadelphia, PA 19103, 215-568-4144, e-mail: artfix@magpage.com, website: eberhardts.com. Restoration of pottery, china, porcelain, glass, metal, marble, jade, stonework, chandeliers and lamps, and objects of art. Replacement parts for Lladro figurines.

Heimbolds, 2950 SW Persimmon Ln., Dunnellon, FL 34431, 352-465-0756. Art conservation restorers: pottery and porcelain, glass, dolls, toys, signs, paintings, stone or organic carvings, etc. Free estimates. Free brochure.

Herbert F. Klug Conservation & Restoration, Box 28002, #16, Lakewood, CO 80228, 303-985-9261, e-mail: hgklug@qadas.com. Conservation and restoration of classical antiquities, pre-Columbian art, Oriental porcelains, European porcelains, marble, ivory, Lalique glass, and limited edition figurines such as Boehm, Cybis, Kaiser, Lladro, and Hummel. By appointment only.

Heritage Restorations, 4233-F Howard Ave., Kensington, MD 20895-2419, 301-493-4458, fax: 301-530-8428, attention Stephen. Restoration of old world, European, continental, and American antiques.

Image Restoration Services, Inc., PO Box 489, Belvidere, IL 61008-0489, 815-547-5919, fax: 815-547-6413, e-mail: kummerowdl@aol.com. Complete restoration services of furniture, objects, and art.

Intermuseum Laboratory, 83 N. Main St., Allen Art Bldg., Oberlin, OH 44074, 440-775-7331, fax: 440-774-3431, e-mail: sandra.williamson @oberlin.edu, website: www.oberlin.edu/~ica. Nonprofit, regional art conservation center that provides preservation and conservation services and education for member and nonmember museums and institutions. Examination, documentation, and treatment of a wide range of cultural material of varying media, including paintings, works on paper, furniture, and decorative art objects. Conservation and preservation workshops, seminars, and internships.

Items of Value, Inc., 7419 Admiral Dr., Alexandria, VA 22307, 703-660-9380, fax: 703-660-9384. Restoration work for many different types of items. Restoration of wood, paintings, gesso, ivory, etc. Regilding, resilvering. Reproduction of brass hardware. Appraisals.

J & H China Repairs, 8296 St. George St., Vancouver, BC V5X 3S5, Canada, 604-321-1093, fax: 604-321-1093. Restoration of porcelain, ceramics, figurines, sculptures, dolls, stone, enamel, and picture frames.

James Davidson, 928 Independence St., New Orleans, LA 70117-5738, 504-944-0545, fax: 504-944-0545, e-mail: cjd9440545@netscape.net. Restoration of porcelain, pottery, marble, ivory, and jade art objects. Specializes in gilding techniques on porcelain.

James Lane, 8834 N. Virginia Ave., Palm Beach Gardens, FL 33418, 561-615-0622, e-mail: antiquef@bellsouth.net, website: www.antique restorers.com/LEATHER.htm. Desk-top leathers. Custom colors available.

John Edward Cunningham, 1525 E. Berkeley, Springfield, MO 65804, 417-889-7702. Porcelains, ivory, jade, gold leaf, oil paintings, and frames restored. Restoration of Boehm and Royal Worcester. Missing parts replaced. Specializes in carving elephant ivory parts for Art Deco, Oriental figurines, jewelry, and inlays. Hours by appointment.

Just Enterprises—Art & Antique Restoration, 2790 Sherwin Ave., #10, Ventura, CA 93003, 805-644-5837, fax: 805-644-5837, e-mail: justenterprisesvc@yahoo.com, website: justenterprisesvc.com. Art and antique restoration, specializes in porcelain doll repair (heads and parts). Please remove hair and eyes and head from doll before sending.

kariel_creations, 5631 E. Marina Dr., Dania, FL 33312, 954-967-6029, fax: 954-967-6029, e-mail: karic8888@msn.com. Restoration and repair of pottery, porcelain, gold, frames, and collectibles of all kinds.

Kingsmen Antique Restoration Inc., 19 Passamore Ave., Unit 28, Scarborough, ON M1V 4T5, Canada, 416-291-8939, fax: 416-291-8939, e-mail: kingsmen@sprint.ca. Invisible mending of art objects and oil paintings. Restoration of porcelain, pottery, glass, marble, jade, soapstone, ivory, cloisonné, papier-mâché, wood, bronze, pewter, brass, white metal, and more. Service worldwide. Call for information on sending objects for estimates.

Kistner's Full Claims Service, Inc., 520 20th St., Rock Island, IL 61201, 309-786-5868, fax: 309-794-0559, e-mail: kistners1@home.com, website: www.kistners.com. Complete furniture restoration, specializes in hand-rubbed finishes, European wax finishes, shellac finishes, and today's gallery finishes. Manufacture of new wooden parts; antique hardware replaced. Restoration of oil paintings, porcelain, figurines, life-size statues, model ships, and other objects. Serving eastern Iowa and northwestern Illinois. Free brochure.

Leatherman Restoration, 509 Mairo St., Austin, TX 78748, 512-282-1556, fax: 512-282-1562, e-mail: rondl@juno.com, website: leathermanservices.com. Repair and restoration of stone, pottery, marble, ceramic, and wood statues, figurines, tiles, and miscellaneous items. Restoration of damaged and incomplete fossils as well as ancient artifacts.

Legacy Art Restorations & Design Int'l. Inc., 4221 N. 16th St., Phoenix, AZ 85016-5318, 602-263-5178, fax: 602-263-6009, e-mail: restoration@legacyintlinc.com, website: legacyintlinc.com. Restoration of fine art and collectibles, including oil paintings, porcelain, ceramics, ivory, jade, alabaster, stone, and wood sculpture. Conservator and restorer of Lladro and Belleek.

MAC Enterprises, 122 Miro Adelante, San Clemente, CA 92673, 949-361-9528, e-mail: macrestor@aol.com. Restores porcelain, ceramics, pottery, frames, oil paintings, and collectibles. Registered Hummel restorer. Ship UPS or call for information. Send SASE for brochure.

Mike's Antiquary, 305 S. Main, PO Box 229, Almont, MI 48003, 810-798-3599, fax: 810-798-2042 call first, e-mail: jamm@ees.eesc.com. Refinishing, repair, and restoration. Furniture repaired: stripping, upholstery, caning, rushing, splinting. Metal polishing; silvering. Lamp restorations. Serving eastern U.S. Call for availability. Mon.–Fri. 10:00 A.M.–6:00 P.M., Sat. 10:00 A.M.–2:00 P.M.

New Orleans Conservation Guild, Inc., 3301 Chartres St., New Orleans, LA 70117, 504-944-7900, fax: 504-944-8750, e-mail: info@art-restoration.com, website: www.art-restoration.com. Restoration and conservation of fine art and antiques, including paintings, frames, furniture, porcelain and ceramics, glass, paper, and stone. Appraisals and research searches. Call or write for brochure.

Northeast Document Conservation Center, 100 Brickstone Sq., Andover, MA 01810-1494, 978-470-1010, fax: 978-475-6021, e-mail: nedcc @nedcc.org, website: www.nedcc.org. Nonprofit regional conservation center specializes in treatment of art and artifacts on paper, including books, documents, maps, photographs, posters, prints, and works of art on paper. They also treat baseball cards, board games, cartoon cels, globes, and very large paper objects. Preservation microfilming, duplication of historical photographs, preservation planning surveys, disaster assistance, technical leaflets. Free brochure. Open Mon.–Fri. 8:30 A.M.–4:30 P.M.

Old World Restorations, Inc., 5729 Dragon Way, Cincinnati, OH 45227, 513-271-5459, fax: 513-271-5418, e-mail: info@oldworldrestorations.com, website: www.oldworldrestorations.com. Restoration and conservation of art and antiques: paintings, frames, photographs, porcelain, glass, sculpture, statuary, stone, metals, paper, documents, and more. On-site architectural restorations of murals, frescoes, and gold leaf. Fire and water damage restoration. Specialized packing and shipping. Nationwide service. Send or e-mail photos for preliminary estimates. Free brochure.

Pick Up the Pieces, 711 W. 17th St., Unit C-12, Costa Mesa, CA 92627, 800-824-6967, fax: 949-645-8381, e-mail: johnnce@yahoo.com, website: www.pickupthepieces.com. Fine art and collectible repair and restoration. Porcelain, jade, marble, ivory, wood, bone, paintings, crystal, and glass. Specializes in repair of Lladro, Hummels, Boehm, Meissen, Royal Doulton, Armani, Dresden, Disney Classics, Capo-di-Monte, and other manufacturers.

Pleasant Valley Restoration, 1725 Reed Rd., Knoxville, MD 21758, 301-432-2721, 9:00 A.M.–7:00 P.M., e-mail: PVRfixit@aol.com. Restoration of porcelain, marble, glass, Hummels, and other art and antique objects. Custom color matching and airbrush work. Previous restorations detected and verified. Lamps rewired; power cords on old electrical devices replaced.

Poor Richard's Restoration & Preservation Studio Workshop, 101 Walnut St., Montclair, NJ 07042, 973-783-5333, fax: 973-744-1939, e-mail: jrickford@webtv.com, website: www.rickford.com. Restoration, conservation; archival and preservation services. Fine and decorative art, antiques, heirlooms, Bibles and other books, brass, ceramics, clocks, documents, dolls, furniture, glass, ivory, jewelry, photographs, silver, stone, textiles, and other objects. Restoration of family memorabilia and keepsakes. By appointment, Tues.–Fri. noon–5:00 P.M., Sat. noon–3:00 P.M.

Rafail & Polina Golberg, Golberg Restoration Co., 411 Westmount Dr., Los Angeles, CA 90048, 310-652-0735, fax: 310-274-3770, e-mail: info@restorationworld.com, website: www.restorationworld.com. Restoration and conservation of antiques and objects of art, including crystal, dolls, enamel, furniture, icons, ivory, marble, paintings, porcelain, pottery, screens, stone, wood, artifacts, etc. Custom-made parts. Free estimates via the Internet.

Restoration Resources, 822 E. Co. Rd. 1575 N., Gentryville, IN 47537, 812-937-2152, fax: 775-414-4966, e-mail: restore@psci.net, website: www.psci.net/restore. Restoration of antiques, primarily wooden objects, but will restore lamps, clocks, cast iron, and other types of mixed material objects. Specializes in salvage of "basket case" family heirlooms. Call between 9:00 A.M.–5:00 P.M. or leave a message. Free brochure.

Restoration Services, 1417 Third St. Webster City, IA 50595, 515-832-1131, e-mail: repair@netins.net, website: www.Restorationmaterials.safe shopper.com. Restoration services for china, pottery, porcelain, ceramics, glass, ivory, jade, and most other materials. Replacement parts fabricated. Supplies, videos, home study course, classes available. Glass chip filler, diamond hand pads for removing scratches, glass bonding resin, enamel glaze, stain remover, lacquers, milliput, less-toxic milliput substitute, flatner, and more. Mini manuals, "Repairing China, Pottery & Figurines," "Color Matching Guide," and "Glass Cleaning & Repairing."

Restorations by Patricia, 420 Centre St., Nutley, NJ 07110, 973-235-0234, weekdays. Specializes in the restoration, repair, and cleaning of antiques, pottery, porcelain, and plaster, including Hummel, Lladro, Meissen, etc. Restoration of plaster religious statuary, 6 inches to 6 feet, and Armani statues.

Reversen Time Inc., 6005 Bunchberry Ct., Raleigh, NC 27616-5454, 919-981-7323, e-mail: hamblest@mindspring.com, website: www.mind spring.com/~hamblesl/index.html. Clock case restoration and conservation; missing elements carved; clock movements repaired. Small art frame repairs; gilding. Ethnographic conservation of Pacific Northwest artifacts and Ukrainian *pasanke* (Easter eggs).

Richard C. Baker Conservation, 1712 (rear) S. Big Bend Blvd., St. Louis, MO 63117, 314-781-3035, e-mail: baker@RichardCBaker.com, website: www.RichardCBaker.com. Offers a full range of conservation services for books and printed works on paper and parchment. Treatments include binding restoration, facsimile binding, box making, adhesive tape removal, stain reduction, washing, aqueous and non-aqueous deacidification, lining, mending, and in-painting.

Rosine Green Associates, Inc., 89 School St., Brookline, MA 02446, 617-

277-8368, fax: 617-731-3845, e-mail: rga@ix.netcom.com. Conservation and restoration of fine art, including furniture, glass, porcelain, paintings, frames, Oriental lacquer, paper, and objets d'art.

Sheild Art & Hobby Shop, 4417 Danube Dr., King George, VA 22485-5707, 540-663-3711, fax: 540-663-3711 call first, e-mail: wsheild@crosslink.net. Complete carousel figure restoration with photo documentation. Wooden carved replacement pieces for damaged or missing parts; custom painting and appraisal included. Will complete carving and assist in finishing unfinished carousel figures purchased in "kit" form. Furniture restoration. Carved replacement pieces for various wooden items. Restoration of old religious and secular statues and reliefs made of plaster, wood, resin, and porcelain.

The Sisters, 4163 Danamar Dr., Pensacola, FL 32504, 850-484-0975 or 850-476-7513, e-mail: sjtrimble@worldnet.att.net. General restoration of porcelain, marble, jade, alabaster, Dresden lace, and more. Lladro restoration. Free brochure.

Sotheby's Restoration, 400 E. 111th St., 1st Floor, New York, NY 10029-3005, 212-894-1597, fax: 212-895-1605, e-mail: restorationNA@sothebys.com, website: www.sothebys.com. Will recommend restorers in the U.S. Restoration services are provided at Sotheby's in London.

Stewart's Restoration Studio, 2555 Goldenrod Dr., Bowling Green, KY 42104, 270-842-4580, fax: 270-842-4580, e-mail: stewartsrestore@aol.com. Restoration of porcelain, pottery, ceramics, glass, and marble antiques and collectibles.

Swan Restorations, 2627 Montrose Ave., Abbotsford, BC V2S 3TS, Canada, 604-855-6694, fax: 604-855-1720. Restoration of antiques and collectibles: porcelain, pottery, china, glass, crystal, ivory, jade, soapstone, and wood. Silver cleaning service; jewelry cleaning. Free written estimates. Hours Mon.–Fri. 10:00 A.M.–5:00 P.M., or by appointment. Call before sending item to be repaired.

Thome Silversmiths, 49 W. 37th St., 4th Floor, New York, NY 10018, 212-764-5426 or 570-426-7480, fax: 212-391-8215 or 570-426-7481, e-mail: robert378@cs.com. Restoration of objects of art and Judaica. Silver, gold, copper, brass, and pewter repaired. Jewelry boxes relined; velvet backs for picture frames. Brass and copper polishing and lacquering. Gold and silver plating. Cleaning and polishing of flatware and hollowware; hand engraving.

Tindell's Restoration, 825 Sandburg Pl., Nashville, TN 37214, 615-885-1029, fax: 615-391-0712, e-mail: info@ATindellsRestorationSchools.com, website: www.TindellsRestorationSchools.com. Restoration services, seminars, training, and products. Can restore porcelain, pottery, ceramics, crystal, glass, marble, oil paintings, frames, ivory, silver, bronze, and much more. Appraisals. Free brochure.

Tsondru Thangka Conservation, e-mail: tsondru@ns.sympatico.ca. Conservation of Tibetan thangkas, religious paintings on fabric used in meditation practices

Van Dyke's Restorers, PO Box 278, Woonsocket, SD 57385, 605-796-4425, 800-558-1234 order, fax: 605-796-4085, e-mail: restoration @cabelas.com, website: www.vandykes.com. Furniture components, including claw feet, table pedestals, legs, bentwood chair parts, reproduction pressed chair backs, seats, supports, leather desk-top pieces, and rolltop desk components. Brass hardware of all kinds, trunk parts, pie-safe tins, clock parts, curved-glass china cabinet parts, isinglass for stove doors, cane, reed, veneer, upholstery supplies, tools, stains, varnishes, brushes, modeling compounds. Special parts designed to duplicate the original pieces. Lamp parts for electric lamps and oil lamps, including Aladdin lamps. Shades and glass chimneys. Kitchen and bathroom plumbing supplies. Mail order worldwide. Catalog.

Venerable Classics, 645 Fourth St., Suite 208, Santa Rosa, CA 95404, 800-531-2891, 707-575-3626, fax: 707-575-4913 call first, website: www.venerableclassics.com. Restoration of porcelain, marble, crystal, jade, ivory, and many other fragile decorative objects. Restoration of ceramic clock cases, Lladro, Hummels, dolls, Swarovski crystal collectibles, and more. Please call with questions. Free brochure on request.

Williamstown Art Conservation Center, 225 South St., Williamstown, MA 01267, 413-458-5741, fax: 413-458-2314, e-mail: wacc@clark.williams.edu, website: www.williamstownart.org. Conservation of paintings, paper, three-dimensional objects, furniture, and frames. Analytical services. Painting conservation now offered in Atlanta at Atlanta Art Conservation Center, 6000 Peachtree Rd., Atlanta, GA 30341, 404-733-4589.

USEFUL SITES

Heritage Preservation, www.heritagepreservation.org.
Preservation Directory, www.preservationdirectory.com.

DISPLAYING COLLECTIBLES

Some special problems arise in displaying antiques properly. Rough porcelain or glass bases should not scratch furniture tops; picture hooks should be strong enough; and collectibles should be displayed to their greatest advantage.

Many display items can be purchased at local giftware, hardware, and art supply stores, but we have listed items that are not always found with ease. Other supplies can be found in the appropriate section in Part II or in Conservation Supplies in this section.

Art Display Essentials, 2 W. Crisman Rd., Columbia, NJ 07832, 800-862-9869, fax: 908-496-4956, e-mail: cmidkiff@artdisplay.com, website: www.artdisplay.com. Mail order company supplying collectors, galleries, and museums with display stands, easels, risers, bases, hangers, shelves, accessories, etc. Custom shop for fabricating customized stands. Catalog $2.

Bags Unlimited, 7 Canal St., Rochester, NY 14608, 800-767-BAGS or 716-436-9006, fax: 716-328-8526, e-mail: info@bagsunlimited.com, website: www.bagsunlimited.com. Products for storing, displaying, and shipping collectibles. Specializes in products for comics, magazines, postcards, and many miscellaneous items. Archival materials sold: polyethylene, polypropylene, Mylar, acid-free boards and storage boxes. High-clarity, recyclable, 100% polyethylene bags. Three grades of backing boards, several sizes of storage boxes and divider cards.

Button Images, 1317 Lynndale Rd., Madison, WI 53711-3370, 608-271-4566, fax: 608-271-4566, e-mail: buttonldy@aol.com, website: www.buttonimages.com. Supplies for cleaning, mounting, displaying, and storing buttons. Free catalog.

Collectors House, 710 New Brunswick Ave., Rahway, NJ 07065, 800-448-9298, fax: 732-845-3236, e-mail: info@collectorshouse.net, website: www.collectorshouse.net. Plate stands, postcard boxes and dividers, showcases, fitted table covers, riker mounts, dealer supplies. Free catalog.

marbleshowcase.com, 6936 N. Overhill Ave., Chicago, IL 60631, 773-594-9429, fax: 773-594-9479, e-mail: mikecoz@mc.net, website: www.marbleshowcase.com. Cases for display and storage of marbles and other small collectibles. Free brochure.

Roberts Colonial House, 15960 Suntone Dr., PO Box 308, South Holland, IL 60473, 800-234-0537 or 708-331-6233, fax: 800-640-7737 or 708-331-0538, e-mail: robertsdisplays@aol.com. Easels, plate hangers, dinnerware stands, risers, jewelry displays, acrylic domes, collectible display boxes. Christmas ornament holders and display stands. Free catalog and brochure.

Something Special Enterprises, PO Box 74, Allison Park, PA 15101-0074, 412-487-2626, e-mail: SSEorder@hotmail.com. Supplies for storing records, cassettes, compact discs, baseball cards, sheet music, comic books, magazines, and newspapers. CD jewel cases, storage boxes, mailers, record sleeves; baseball card holders; sheet music sleeves; bags for comic books and magazines; newspaper bags. Free flyer.

The Stand Man, PO Box 3005-TCB, West Orange, NJ 07052-3005, 973-325-2291, fax: 973-243-2454, e-mail: bela@TheStandman.com, website: TheStandman.com. Wide range of stands, racks, and hangers to display most antiques and collectibles. Free consultation service for anyone with questions or needing suggestions about their display needs. Catalog $5 with coupon, or $5 rebate with first $25 order.

Talsco of Florida, 5419 Crafts St., New Port Richey, FL 34652, 727-869-0662, fax: 727-869-0662. Display cases for antiques, dolls, ship models, and other collectibles. Free brochure.

The2Buds.com, 462 W. Silver Lake Rd. N., Traverse City, MI 49684, 888-270-0552, Mon.–Fri. 9:00 A.M.–5:00 P.M., e-mail: postcards@the 2buds.com, website: www.the2buds.com. Archival supplies for storing and displaying vintage postcards, comics, trading cards, and other collectibles. Postcard sleeves, newspaper bags, comic bags, record sleeves, rigid sleeves, storage boxes, albums, binder pages, and more. Internet sales only.

University Products, Inc., 517 Main St., PO Box 101, Holyoke, MA 01040, 800-336-4847, fax: 800-532-9281, e-mail: info@universityproducts.com, website: www.universityproducts.com. Archival supplies for conservation, restoration, repair, storage, and display. Archival storage boxes, paper and plastic enclosures, acid-free board and papers, adhesives, albums, preservation framing supplies, tools, equipment, chemicals, and other materials. Specialized storage for baseball cards, coins, comics, magazines, photos, postcards, stamps, and other collectibles. Free catalog.

Ziabicki Import Co., Inc., PO Box 081004, Racine, WI 53408, 262-633-7918, fax: 262-633-8711, e-mail: zimport@netwurz.net, website: www.ziabicki.com. Picture hangers: "Floreat" hangers in 10 lb. to 75 lb. sizes, sawtooth-type frame-hangs, D-ring hangers, and decorative hangers.

SHIPPING, INSURANCE & RECOVERY OF LOST ITEMS

SHIPPING

Packing antiques and collectibles to sell or to move can be a problem. Some items can be safely packed at home. Metal and wooden pieces can be wrapped in crumpled newspaper, then placed in a sturdy cardboard box with more crumpled paper stuffed between the items. Be sure nothing rattles or moves when you tape the box closed. China and glass is more difficult. Individual pieces can be wrapped in bubble wrap that is then held in place with bands of tape. Crumpled newspaper can be used, but the ink may stain some dishes.

To transport a box in your car, the pieces can be put in a box and wedged in place with more bubble wrap or paper. To ship the pieces or have them packed in a moving van, you should double-box them. Put the filled box inside a larger box and fill the space between the two boxes with foam "peanuts." Tape the inner and outer boxes shut and mark the package "Fragile, this side up." Never put a heavy iron doorstop in a box with a mixing bowl or any other breakable ceramic or glass. The heavy piece can be jostled and crush the bowl. Storage units, mailing services, moving companies, and home improvement stores often have boxes and other packing material for sale. There are special slotted boxes for pictures, and box dividers with squares the size of a wrapped cup. Plates should be wrapped individually and put in short stacks, about six plates to a pile. Too many plates will make too much weight on the bottom plates and they may crack. Plates, cups, and bowls should be upright in the box, never on an edge.

If you have odd-shaped or very valuable objects to ship, like a lamp with a glass shade, you might want to use a shipping service. Most mailing services pack and ship. They will even ship small pieces of furniture or a computer. Moving companies will pack the items they are moving. This is often advisable because if they pack it, their insurance should cover breakage. If you pack it, there could be a problem with a claim.

Large furniture can be handled by a mover or by one of the shipping companies that travel across the country. They will crate the piece if it is fragile (like a large mirror) or very valuable. Some also ship certain pieces with just a blanket wrap. We moved a small stone fountain that way. The shippers and packers should tell you the cost before the job is started. It is sometimes less expensive if there is no hurry about the delivery.

Listed here are some shippers and packers who offer nationwide service. Check your Yellow Pages for companies near you that ship locally.

Craters & Freighters, 800-736-3335, 9 A.M.–5:00 P.M. MT, e-mail: info @cratersandfreighters.com, website: www.cratersandfreighters.com. Packing, crating, and shipping service worldwide. Insured. Online quotes of cost of packing and shipping.

Graye Antique Transport Service, 17 Central St., Elkins, WV 26241, 304-637-2790, fax: 304-637-2791, e-mail: grayeantiqueser@meer.net. Consolidated shipper of antiques, art, and fine furniture serving the eastern half of the United States. Free brochure.

Period Antiques Delivery Service, Inc., PO Box 205, Millington, MD 21651, 800-962-1424 or 410-778-4357, fax: 410-778-7564, e-mail: pads@dmv.com, website: padsinc.com. Long-distance delivery of fine antiques and artwork, serving the eastern half of the United States, Maine to Florida, and west to Dallas, Houston, and Oklahoma City.

Transit Systems, Inc. (TSI), 999 Old Eagle School Rd., Suite 114, Wayne, PA

19087, 800-626-1257, fax: 800-228-8131, e-mail: johnt@harperreed.com. Will pack and ship large, fragile antiques and other items. Insurance coverage. Nationwide pickup and delivery.

INSURANCE

Special antiques and collections need special insurance that is not always easy to find. Many homeowners can add some of their antiques and collectibles to their existing policies. But larger collections and rare antiques may need more specific coverage. This is a list of companies that offer insurance policies for collectors. We list them as a service; we do not know if they have a history of settling claims to the satisfaction of their clients. If you plan to buy insurance from one of these firms, check with your state insurance board and other sources to determine the company's financial position and treatment of claims. Collectors can also find insurance through specialized clubs.

APS Insurance Plan, brokered by Hugh Wood, Inc., PO Box 414, Bowling Green Station, New York, NY 10274-0414, 888-APS-6494 (888-277-6496), fax: 212-509-4906, e-mail: insurance@stamps.org, website: www.stamps.org/services. Discounted insurance through Chubb for American Philatelic Society members.

American Collectors Insurance, Inc., 385 N. King's Hwy., PO Box 8343, Cherry Hill, NJ 08002-0343 or 800-360-2277, e-mail: info@american collectors.net, website: www.americancollectorins.com. Collectibles and vintage automobiles.

Antique and Collectible Association (ACA), PO Box 4389, Davidson, NC 28036, 800-287-7127, fax: 704-895-9088, e-mail: info@antiqueand collectible.com, website: antiqueandcollectible.com. Insurance for collectors, dealers, and shop owners.

AXA Art Insurance Corp., 4 W. 58th St., New York, NY, 10019, 212-415-8400 or 877-AXA-4ART (877-292-4278), website: www.axa-art.com. Fine art, rare books, antique weapons, vintage wine, jewelry, vintage automobiles, stamps, coins, and collectibles. Call or visit website to find an agent.

Chubb Group of Insurance Companies, Personal Insurance Division, 15 Mountain View Rd., Warren NJ 07059, 908-903-2000 or 866-324-8222, fax: 908-903-2027, website: www.chubb.com/personal. Historic homes and valuable possessions. Call or visit website to find an agent.

Collectibles Insurance, PO Box 1200, Westminster, MD 21158, 888-837-9537, fax: 410-876-9233, e-mail: info@insurecollectibles.com, website: www.collectinsure.com. Insurance for autographs, books, ceramics, comics, dolls, firearms, postcards, records, stamps, toys, and other collectibles.

Fireman's Fund Insurance Co., 777 San Martin Dr., Novato, CA 94998, 800-

227-1700, fax: 415-899-3600, website: www.firemansfund.com. Historic homes and scheduled valuable possessions. Call or visit website to find an agent.

Hagerty Insurance, PO Box 87, Traverse City, MI 49685, 800-922-4050, fax: 231-941-8227, e-mail: auto@hagerty.com, website: www.hagerty.com. Vintage automobiles.

Historic & Valuable Homeowners Insurance Program, MIMS International, 901 Dulaney Valley Rd., Suite 610, Towson, MD 21204, 410-296-1500 or 800-899-1399, fax: 410-296-1741, e-mail: bob@mimsintl.com, website: www.nationaltrust.org/historic_homeowner. Historic home and valuable possessions coverage in partnership with the National Trust for Historic Preservation and Chubb.

Thomson & Pratt Insurance Associates, Inc., 1223 Wilshire Blvd., Suite 590, Santa Monica, CA 90403, 310-394-5363 or 877-334-6327 (toll free), fax: 310-393-3532, e-mail: fineartguy @aol.com, website: www.fineart guy.com. Fine art insurance.

RECOVERY OF LOST ITEMS

Unfortunately, collectors may at one time or another have to face a loss caused by fire or theft. Correct procedures after the loss can help with the recovery of stolen pieces or an equitable settlement with their insurance company.

First contact local police or fire department officials. They will give you advice and often have leaflets that outline important steps to take. But recovery of antiques is very specialized and you need extra help. Consider hiring a "public" insurance adjuster, whose job it is to work on your behalf, not on behalf of your insurance company. To find a public insurance adjuster, look under "Insurance, Adjuster" in the Yellow Pages of your phone book.

Dealing with Disaster: How to Protect and Insure Your Collection from Theft, Fire, Flood, and Earthquake, and How to Handle Disaster If It Strikes, a special report by the Kovels (PO Box 22900, Beachwood, OH 44122, $15), is a good source for advice. Local appraisers, insurance adjusters, and claims experts can also help.

The Art Register, 20 E. 46th St., Suite 1402, New York, NY 10017, 212-297-0941, fax: 212-972-5091, e-mail: infol@alrny.com, website: www.artloss.com. Recovery and search services. International database of lost and stolen art, antiques, and collectibles.

International Foundation for Art Research, 500 Fifth Ave., Suite 1234, New York, NY 10110, 212-391-6234, fax: 212-391-8794, website: www.ifar.org. Information on authenticity, ownership, theft, and other artistic, legal, and ethical issues concerning art objects. Conferences, panels, and lectures; art authentication service.

Robert E. Spiel Associates, L.L.C., 855 Skokie Hwy., Suite N, Lake Bluff, IL 60044, 847- 234-1786, 847- 234-1784, e-mail: rob6960@aol.com or spiel@arttheft.com, website: www.arttheft.com. Safety and security. Lost collectible recoveries.

MATCHING SERVICES

Listed here are matching services for china, silver, and crystal patterns. When writing, include the name of your pattern and a clear photograph, photocopy, or sketch showing the design and any markings. It is important to include the manufacturer's name, if it appears. Do not send a piece of the china, silver, or crystal: you can obtain a usable image by placing a spoon or plate on a photocopy machine. Many companies selling Haviland china refer to the "Schleiger number." This is from a series of books written in 1950 by Arlene Schleiger, *Two Hundred Patterns of Haviland China,* 5 volumes. Your library may have a copy.

List the pieces you want, and be sure to include a stamped, self-addressed envelope for a reply. If you want to know that the service received your request, include a stamped, self-addressed postcard, too. Remember that your order may be kept on file for months until a matching piece is found. If you ask more than one service to search for a piece, let the others know if another service finds it. Manufacturers that are still in business, such as Waterford or Spode, sometimes take special orders for discontinued patterns. These orders are filled about once a year.

The dealers listed below have a general replacement line unless a specialty is indicated. The list is not an endorsement of any kind. It includes those services that sent us the requested information. There are probably many others we have not yet discovered. If you can suggest any additions, please let us know.

CHINA MATCHING SERVICES

5th Generation Antiques, 124 W. 8th Ave., Chico, CA 95926, 530-895-0813, fax: 530-895-0813, e-mail: fifthgenantq@sbcglobal.net. Specializes in Haviland matching.

A&A Dinnerware Locators, PO Box 50222, Austin, TX 78763-0222, 888-898-4202, fax: 512-264-2727, e-mail: info@aadinnerware.com, website: www.aadinnerware.com. Replacement of discontinued pieces of fine china, earthenware, and stoneware made by most major manufacturers.

Alice's Past & Presents Replacements, PO Box 465, Merrick, NY 11566, 516-379-1352, fax: 516-379-7302, e-mail: alicechina@aol.com, website: hometown.aol.com/alicechina/myhomepage/business.html. Discontinued tableware.

Ann Arbor Dinnerware, PO Box 6054, Ann Arbor, MI 48106-6054, 888-726-9693 or 734-663-5766, e-mail: aadinex@aadinex, website: www.aadinex.com. Specializes in Oneida stoneware and porcelain dinnerware.

Antiques, etc. by Jo C. Hancock, 621 S. Main St., Nashville, AR 71852-2707, 870-845-1070. Lenox china replacement service.

Auld Lang Syne Haviland Locating, 6321 Delta Ct., Magalia, CA 95954, 530-873-0693, e-mail: hollyzhit@aol.com. Haviland & Co., Theodore Haviland.

Beverly Hills Antique Center—Martin A. Pope, 24630 Hwy. 92, Platte City, MO 64079, 913-651-4972, e-mail: map007@juno.com. Specializes in matching Haviland china.

Bygone China Match, 1225 W. 34th N., Wichita, KS 67204, 316-838-6010, fax: 316-838-6010, e-mail: bygonchina@aol.com.

Cee Cee China, 3904 Parsons Rd., Chevy Chase, MD 20815, 800-619-6226, e-mail: ceeceechina@aol.com, website: www.ceeceechina.com. Matches Lenox, Oxford, Syracuse, and Gorham china.

China & Crystal Matchers Inc., 2379 John Glenn Dr., Suite 108-A, Chamblee, GA 30341, 800-286-1107 or 770-455-1162, fax: 770-452-8616, e-mail: chinacmi@bellsouth.net, website: www.chinaandcrystal.com. Matches most major manufacturers of china.

China & Crystal Replacements, 23714 Hwy. 7, Shorewood, MN 55331, 800-432-4448, fax: 952-474-8458, e-mail: thatchinashop@msn.com.

China and Crystal Match, 72 Longacre Rd., Rochester, NY 14621, 585-338-3781, fax: 585-338-3781, e-mail: chinamat@frontiernet.net. Specializes in matching Fitz & Floyd, Royal Doulton, Royal Worcester, and Wedgwood.

China Brokers, Ltd., 2723 SE 24th Ave., Cape Coral, FL 33904, 732-768-4145 or 941-242-4340, fax: 941-242-4340, e-mail: chinabrokers@world net.att.net.

China by Pattern, Inc., PO Box 1005, Pineville, NC 28134-1005, 704-846-9697, e-mail: ajdupre@msn.com. Patterns made by all American and European manufacturers and Noritake.

China Cabinet, PO Box 426, Clearwater, SC 29822, 800-787-1605 or 803-593-9655, fax: 803-593-9655, e-mail: thechinacabinet@aol.com. All discontinued or inactive patterns made by major manufacturers.

China Detectives, The Romany Centre, Suite F1, Wareham Rd., Holton Heath, Poole, Dorset BH16 6JL, UK, 011-44-1202-620466, fax: 011-44-1201-623839, e-mail: mike@chinadetectives.co.uk, website: www.chinadetectives.co.uk. Matching service for discontinued tableware patterns in china, pottery, and stoneware. Specializes in Denby, Royal Doulton, Poole, Wedgwood, and other U.K. potteries.

China Finders, 2823 Central Ave., St. Petersburg, FL 33713, 800-900-2557 or 727-328-0557, fax: 727-384-9317, e-mail: chinafinders@aol.com, website: www.chinafinders.com. Discontinued or obsolete dinnerware patterns made by most major manufacturers.

China House, 801 W. Eldorado, Decatur, IL 62522, 217-428-7212, fax: 217-864-4852, e-mail: apprreant@aol.com. Specializes in French and American Haviland. Appraisals.

China Matching Service, 56 Meadowbrook, Ballwin, MO 63011, 636-227-3444, e-mail: nackmanus@aol.com. Specializes in matching German, Austrian, Bavarian, and Czechoslovakian china and Lenox china. Appraisals.

China Replacements, PO Box 508, High Ridge, MO 63049, 800-562-2655, e-mail: chinarep@swbell.net, website: www.chinareplacements.com. Discontinued and hard-to-find patterns of china, porcelain, pottery, earthenware, and stoneware. All major manufacturers and many more.

The China Traders, PO Box 940700, Simi Valley, CA 93094, 800-638-9955, fax: 805-578-3803, e-mail: info@lloydmartin.com, website: www.chinatraders.com. Discontinued Lenox, Villeroy & Boch, Wedgwood, Franciscan, Noritake, and others. Appraisals.

Chinasearch, PO Box 1202, Kenilworth, Warwickshire CV8 2WW, UK, 011-44-1926-512402, fax: 011-44-1926-859311, e-mail: helen@china search.uk.com, website: www.chinasearch.uk.com. Discontinued china, specializes in Wedgwood, Royal Doulton, Royal Worcester, Denby. Sells only; cannot buy china from outside the United Kingdom. Brochure.

Clintsman International, 811 E. Geneva St., Elkhorn, WI 53121, 800-781-8900, fax: 262-723-1991, e-mail: findit@clintsmanint.com, website: www.clintsmanint.com. Patterns by all manufacturers. Pattern identification.

Coleman's Antiques, 3313 N. Sepulveda Blvd., Manhattan Beach, CA 90266, 310-545-6699, e-mail: jcruikshank@earthlink.net, website: www.colemansantiques.com. Specializes in pre-1930 French Haviland china patterns.

Country Oaks Antiques, 790 Roehampton Ct., Collierville, TN 38017, 901-854-6606, e-mail: frankttobey@cs.com. Specializes in Flow Blue.

Crystal Corner, PO Box 756, 317 Dyar Blvd., Boaz, AL 35957, 256-593-6169, fax: 256-593-6560, e-mail: ccorner@hiwaay.net, website: www.crystalcorner.com.

D & J Locations, 1601 E. Canal St., Tarboro, NC 27886, 800-818-5565 or 252-823-5333.

Dining Antiques, 6 Market Plaza, Reinholds, PA 17569, 888-346-4642, e-mail: diningan@ptd.net. Specializes in Syracuse China.

Dining Elegance, Ltd., PO Box 4203, St. Louis, MO 63163, 314-865-1408, e-mail: diningelegance@cs.com or info@diningelegance.com, website: www.diningelegance.com. Specializes in English china.

Dishes from the Past, 3701 Lovell Ave., Ft. Worth, TX 76107, 800-984-8801 or 817-717-6390, fax: 817-737-2282, e-mail: dishesfrompast@aol.com, website: dishesfromthepast.com. All major manufacturers.

Don's Antiques & Gifts, Heirloom Completions Division, 1620 Venice St., Granite City, IL 62040, fax: 618-931-4333, e-mail: questions @donsantiques.com, website: donsantiques.com.

Dunbar Antiques at Hillbrow, 3969 Waverly Rd., Owego, NY 13827, 607-687-5058 or 607-343-8320, fax: 607-687-5058, e-mail: dantiques @stny.rr.com. Franciscan matching service.

Dutch Village, Blue Delft Pottery, PO Box 1798, Holland, MI 49422, 616-396-1475, fax: 616-396-7534, website: www.bluedelft.com. Can help identify your Delft blue pottery from Holland and replace with something similar, if not the same.

Echo's Discontinued China & Silver, 1433 Lonsdale Ave., #121, North Vancouver, BC V7M 2H9, Canada, 800-663-6004, fax: 604-988-3611, e-mail: info@echoschina.com, website: www.echoschina.com. Specializes in matching English china. Appraisals of dinnerware. Brochure.

edish, 815 E. 2100 South, Salt Lake City, UT 84106, 888-768-8282, e-mail: questions@edish.com, website: www.edish.com. Dinnerware patterns by all major manufacturers available online or at two store locations. Second location: Antique Pavilion, 2311 Westheimer, Houston, TX 77098, 713-942-7171, fax: 713-521-2546.

Ferne & David Stephenson, 730 N. Fifth St., Hamburg, PA 19526, 610-562-4967, e-mail: fernd@ptd.com. Noritake Azalea.

Fiesta Plus, 380 Hawkins Crawford Rd., Cookeville, TN 38501, 931-372-8333, e-mail: fiestaplus@yahoo.com, website: www.fiestaplus.com. Fiesta, Harlequin, Riviera, and other Homer Laughlin patterns; Bauer, Franciscan, Johnson Brothers, LuRay, Metlox, Spode, Vernon Kilns, Vistosa.

Flo-Blue Shoppe, 22860 W. Thirteen Mile Rd., Birmingham, MI 48025, 248-433-1933, fax: 248-433-3878. Flow Blue matching service. Restoration services available. Appraisals.

Forget-Me-Not China, 17255 SE Licorice Way, Renton, WA 98059, 800-553-6693 or 425-254-0200, fax: 425-254-0239, e-mail: info@forgetme notchina.com, website: www.forgetmenotchina.com. Discontinued Lenox patterns.

Fulbreit China Locators, 607 Center Dr., Memphis, TN 38112, 901-327-3725, e-mail: chinas@midsouth.rr.com, website: www.fulbreitchina.com. Haviland and Homer Laughlin dinnerware.

Garbo, PO Box 41197, Los Angeles, CA 90041. Dinnerware matching service, selling only, no longer buying. Franciscan, Interpace, Noritake, Flintridge, Poppytrail, Mikasa, Vernonware, and Belora. Send SASE and information on the bottom of plates, items wanted, quantity, and measurements.

Glass Lady @ Kaleidoscope, 7501 Iron Bridge Rd., Richmond, VA 23237, 804-743-9811 or 804-743-9846, e-mail: glasslady8@aol.com.

Grace Graves—Haviland Matching Service, Ltd., 1610 N. Prospect Ave., #905, Milwaukee, WI 53202, 414-289-9710, fax: 414-291-9018, e-mail: hmsgraves@aol.com, website: www.graveshaviland.com. Specializes in matching Haviland china. Appraisals.

Grandpa's Trading Co., PO Box 1043, Tallevast, FL 34270-1043, 941-756-7337, e-mail: grandpas@earthlink.net, website: members.ebay.com/aboutme/grandpas. Replacement matching service for many types of midcentury china, including Blue Ridge, Corelle, Corningware, Fiesta, Harlequin, Homer Laughlin, Pennnsbury, Pfaltzgraff, Stangl, and more.

Haviland China Matching Service of Winona, 476 E. Fifth St., Winona, MN 55987-3923, 507-454-3283, e-mail: ahines@hbci.com. Specializes in matching French Haviland china.

Heritage China of Iowa, PO Box 243, Palo, IA 52324, 888-416-1595, fax: 319-227-7781, e-mail: dischina@aol.com, website: www.dish-china.com.

House of Serendipity, 645 Main St., Montevallo, AL 35115, 205-665-7996, e-mail: thehouseofserendipity@msn.com. American-made dinnerware.

Hugh Lackey Antiques and China Matching, 1816 Nacogdoches Rd., San Antonio, TX 78209, 210-829-5048, fax: 210-829-5048, e-mail: hlackey@texas.net.

Jacquelynn's China Matching Service, 219 N. Milwaukee St., Milwaukee, WI 53202, 800-482-8287, fax: 414-272-0361, e-mail: jchinams@cs.com, website: www.jchinareplacements.com. English and American china only.

Joanne Cone Matching Service, 34 Silverwood, Irvine, CA 92604, 949-551-3173, e-mail: jochina@aol.com, website: www.iadm.com. Specializes in Mikasa china. Appraisals.

Judy Giangiuli, RD 6, Box 292, New Castle, PA 16101, 724-924-1940, fax: 724-924-9211. Specializes in matching Castleton china.

Just China, PO Box 1401, Merrit Island, FL 32954, 800-5china1, 800-524-4621, e-mail: justchina@msn.com. Discontinued china patterns.

Larry Hamm, 2265 Hamilton-Middletown Rd., Hamilton, OH 45011, 513-892-0803, e-mail: larry_h45011@yahoo.com. Haviland china.

Lovers of Blue & White, Steeple Morden, Royston, Hertfordshire SG8 0RN, UK, 011-44-1763-853800, fax: 011-44-1763-853700, e-mail: china@blueandwhite.com, website: www.blueandwhite.com. English transferware and tableware. Free brochure. Appraisals.

Marian Church, RFD 6, Box 455, New Castle, PA 16101, 800-837-0145 or 724-924-2271. China replacements and collector plates. Lenox, Oxford, Franciscan, Castleton, and American Haviland patterns.

The Matchers, 181 Belle Meade, Memphis, TN 38117, 901-683-1337, e-mail: chinalady@earthlink.net. Specializes in Noritake, Lenox, Royal Doulton, Haviland, and other major factories. Appraisals.

Ms. China, PO Box 229, Monterey, CA 93942, 800-688-6807 or 831-655-9984, fax: 831-655-0198, e-mail: info@ms-china.com, website:

www.ms-china.com. Noritake matching service. For identification of unnamed Noritake patterns, send SASE and color photo. Appraisals.

Nora Travis, Haviland China Replacements, PO Box 6008, 13337 E. South St., #161, Cerritos, CA 90701, 714-521-9283, fax: 714-521-9283, e-mail: travishrs@aol.com, website: HavilandChinaReplace.com. French and American Haviland china replacements. Appraisals of Haviland only.

Old China Patterns Limited, 1560 Brimley Rd., Scarborough, ON M1P 3G9, Canada, 800-663-4533 or 416-299-8880, fax: 416-299-4721, e-mail: ocp@chinapatterns.com, website: www.chinapatterns.com. Dinnerware matching service. Inventory on website. Office/showroom hours Mon.–Thurs. 8:00 A.M.–5:00 P.M., Fri. 8:00 A.M.–4:00 P.M. Orders shipped worldwide. Appraisals.

Olympus Cove Antiques, 179 E. 300 South, Salt Lake City, UT 84111, 800-284-8046, e-mail: olympus@uswest.net, website: www.Olympus Cove.com.

Past & Present, 14851 Avenue 360, Visalia, CA 93292, 559-798-0029, fax: 559-798-1415, e-mail: P-P@ix.netcom.com, website: www.pastpresent.net. Discontinued china. Appraisals and restoration.

Pattern Finders Ltd., PO Box 206, Port Jefferson Station, NY 11776, 800-216-2446, fax: 631-928-5170, e-mail: apattern@aol.com, website: www.patternfinders.com. China matching. If not sure of your pattern name, mail, fax, or e-mail a photocopy of front and back of a dinner plate, with color notations.

Paul Church, 500 Oregon Ave., St. Cloud, FL 34769, 800-337-9075, e-mail: chinacrystal@juno.com, website: www.chinacrystalandmore.com. Lenox, Franciscan, and Castleton.

Popkorn, PO Box 1057, Flemington, NJ 08822, 908-782-9631, e-mail: popkornbob@netscape.net. Specializes in Stangl pottery. Appraisals.

Presence of the Past, 488 Main St., Old Saybrook, CT 06475, 860-388-9021, fax: 860-388-2025, e-mail: presencepast13@aol.com. Specializes in Haviland china matching. Appraisals.

Ralph Clifford/American Dinnerware, PO Box 5403, Berkeley, CA 94705, 510-843-9336. Specializes in Russel Wright and Franciscan.

Replacements, Ltd., PO Box 26029, 1089 Knox Rd., Greensboro, NC 27420-6029, 800-REPLACE (800-737-5223), fax: 336-697-3100, e-mail: inquire@replacements.com, website: www.replacements.com. Old and new china. Call the toll-free number, 8:00 A.M.–midnight, seven days a week, for free lists of pieces available in your pattern.

Retrospective Modern Design, PO Box 305, Manning, IA 51455, 888-301-6829, e-mail: retrodesign@earthlink.net, website: www.retrospective.net. American dinnerware from the 1940s–1960s, including Russel Wright, Ben Seibel, Eva Zeisel, Franciscan, Vernon Kilns, Metlox, Sascha Brastoff, and other potteries.

Robbins Nest, 124 Forrester Rd., Glasgow, KY 42141, 270-678-3661, fax: 270-678-3661, e-mail: robbinsnest@robbinsnest.com, website: www.robbinsnest.com. Specializes in Homer Laughlin.

Roundhill's, 6542 46th Ave. NE, Seattle, WA 98115, fax: 206-524-1252, e-mail: jwr8123@msn.com. American, English, and French china. Appraisals.

Schleiger's Haviland Connection, 1626 Crestview Rd., Redlands, CA 92374-6460, 909-798-0412, e-mail: davidaschleiger@hotmail.com, website: www.schleigerbooks.com. Haviland matching and Haviland books for identifying patterns.

Scott's Haviland Matching Service, 1911 Leland Ave., Des Moines, IA 50315, 800-952-7857, fax: 515-285-0744, e-mail: scottshaviland@worldnet.att.net, website: www.havilandchinabyscotts.com. Matching service for French Haviland, Robert Haviland and C. Parlon, Johann Haviland, Charles Field Haviland.

Search4Doulton, 19 Cloverdale Dr., Longwell Green, Bristol BS30 9XZ, UK, 011-44-117-932-5852, e-mail: enquiries@search4doulton.com, website: www.search4doulton.com. Matching service for Royal Doulton, Beswick, and Royal Crown Derby.

Shirley Stamen Matching Service, 9601 Arby Dr., Beverly Hills, CA 90210, 310-278-4040, e-mail: stajaf1@earthlink.net.

Sophia's China & Crystal, 141 Sedgwick Rd., Dept. RTK, Syracuse, NY 13203, 315-472-6834, e-mail: sophia@sophiaschina-crystal.com, website: www.sophiaschina-crystal.com.

Tabletop Designs, PO Box 448, Cheshire, CT 06410, 800-801-4084, e-mail: lenox@ntplx.net, website: www.tabletopdesigns.com. Discontinued patterns.

Tabletops Etc, 375 W. Cummings Park, Woburn, MA 01801, 888-242-0994 from U.S. or Canada, 781-932-9882 from other countries, e-mail: service@tabletopsetc.com, website: www.tabletopsetc.com. Online listing of dinnerware patterns available from a group of independent dealers. Many patterns are pictured.

Tablewhere? The Collector, 4 Queens Parade Close, Friern Barnet, London N11 3FY, UK, 011-44-20-8361-6111, fax: 011-44-20-8361-4143, e-mail: sales@tablewhere.co.uk, website: www.tablewhere.co.uk. Discontinued china patterns. Call toll free from U.S., 800-514-8176.

The Treasures of Limoges, 4059 N. Pennsylvania St., Indianapolis, IN 46205, 317-283-6192, fax: 317-926-7533, e-mail: caldwell@havilandmatcher.com, website: www.havilandmatcher.com. French and American Haviland only.

Unique Antiques, PO Box 15815, San Diego, CA 92175-5815, 619-281-8650, fax: 619-282-8407, e-mail: culrey@webcc.net. French and American Haviland. Appraisals.

CRYSTAL MATCHING SERVICES

5th Generation Antiques, 124 W. 8th Ave., Chico, CA 95926, 530-895-0813, fax: 530-895-0813, e-mail: fifthgenantq@sbcglobal.net.

A&A Dinnerware Locators, PO Box 50222, Austin, TX 78763-0222, 888-898-4202, fax: 512-264-2727, e-mail: info@aadinnerware.com, website: www.aadinnerware.com. Replacement of discontinued crystal made by most major manufacturers.

Alice's Past & Presents Replacements, PO Box 465, Merrick, NY 11566, 516-379-1352, fax: 516-379-7302, e-mail: alicechina@aol.com, website: hometown.aol.com/alicechina/myhomepage/business.html. Matching and locating service for discontinued tableware.

Antiques, etc. by Jo C. Hancock, 621 S. Main St., Nashville, AR 71852-2707, 870-845-1070. Lenox crystal.

Bygone China Match, 1225 W. 34th N., Wichita, KS 67204, 316-838-6010, fax: 316-838-6010, e-mail: bygonchina@aol.com.

Cee Cee China, 3904 Parsons Rd., Chevy Chase, MD 20815, 800-619-6226, e-mail: ceeceechina@aol.com, website: www.ceeceechina.com. Lenox crystal.

Charlotte's Glass Reflections, 1518A Florida Blvd., Bradenton, FL 34207, 941-756-4143, fax: 941-756-1940, e-mail: grmc@tampabay.rr.com, website: www.facets.net/glassreflections. Specializes in Fostoria. Also some Imperial, Cambridge, Heisey, and other American elegant glass companies.

China & Crystal Matchers Inc., 2379 John Glenn Dr., Suite 108-A, Chamblee, GA 30341, 800-286-1107 or 770-455-1162, fax: 770-452-8616, e-mail: chinacmi@bellsouth.net, website: www.chinaandcrystal.com. Matching most major manufacturers of crystal. Basic chip repair on stemware.

China & Crystal Replacements, 23714 Hwy. 7, Shorewood, MN 55331, 800-432-4448, fax: 952-474-8458, e-mail: thatchinashop@msn.com.

China and Crystal Match, 72 Longacre Rd., Rochester, NY 14621, 585-338-3781, fax: 585-338-3781, e-mail: chinamat@frontiernet.net. Specializes in Fostoria, Gorham, Lenox, Royal Doulton, and Tiffin crystal.

China Brokers, Ltd., 2723 SE 24th Ave., Cape Coral, FL 33904, 732-768-4145 or 941-242-4340, fax: 941-242-4340, e-mail: chinabrokers@worldnet.att.net.

China by Pattern, Inc., PO Box 1005, Pineville, NC 28134-1005, 704-846-9697, e-mail: ajdupre@msn.com. American and European manufacturers and Noritake.

China Cabinet, PO Box 426, Clearwater, SC 29822, 800-787-1605 or 803-593-9655, fax: 803-593-9655, e-mail: thechinacabinet@aol.com. All discontinued or inactive patterns made by major manufacturers.

China Finders, 2823 Central Ave., St. Petersburg, FL 33713, 800-900-2557 or

727-328-0557, fax: 727-384-9317, e-mail: chinafinders@aol.com, website: www.chinafinders.com. Discontinued or obsolete crystal patterns made by most major manufacturers.

China Replacements, PO Box 508, High Ridge, MO 63049, 800-562-2655, e-mail: chinarep@swbell.net, website: www.chinareplacements.com. Discontinued and hard-to-find patterns. All major manufacturers and many more.

Clintsman International, 811 E. Geneva St., Elkhorn, WI 53121, 800-781-8900, fax: 262-723-1991, e-mail: findit@clintsmanint.com, website: www.clintsmanint.com. Matching all manufactureres. Pattern identification.

Conner Antiques—Haviland Matching Service, 701 P St., Lincoln, NE 68508, fax: 402-435-4339. Fostoria.

Crystal Connection, 8661 Midland Dr., Greendale, WI 53129, 414-425-1321, e-mail: nskaja@execpc.com. Discontinued stemware patterns of Lenox, Fostoria, Cambridge, and Imperial crystal.

Crystal Corner, PO Box 756, 317 Dyar Blvd., Boaz, AL 35957, 256-593-6169, fax: 256-593-6560, e-mail: ccorner@hiwaay.net, website: www.crystal corner.com.

D & J Locations, 601 E. Canal St., Tarboro, NC 27886, 800-818-5565 or 252-823-5333.

Dining Elegance, Ltd., PO Box 4203, St. Louis, MO 63163, 314-865-1408, e-mail: diningelegance@cs.com or info@diningelegance.com, website: www.diningelegance.com.

Dishes from the Past, 3701 Lovell Ave., Ft. Worth, TX 76107, 800-984-8801 or 817-717-6390, fax: 817-737-2282, e-mail: dishesfrompast@aol.com, website: dishesfromthepast.com. All major manufacturers.

Don's Antiques & Gifts, Heirloom Completions Division, 1620 Venice St., Granite City, IL 62040, fax: 618-931-4333, e-mail: questions@dons antiques.com, website: donsantiques.com.

EAPG Inc, 1220 Monroe NE, Albuquerque, NM 87110, 505-268-0819, fax: 505-266-7204, e-mail: Elaine@patternglass.com, website: www.pattern glass.com. Matching service for Early American Pattern Glass (EAPG) tableware, c.1850–1910. Appraisals. Will refer to restoration services.

edish, 815 E. 2100 South, Salt Lake City, UT 84106, 888-768-8282, e-mail: questions@edish.com, website: www.edish.com. All major manufacturers. Available online or at two store locations. Second location: Antique Pavilion, 2311 Westheimer, Houston, TX 77098, 713-942-7171, fax: 713-521-2546.

Forget-Me-Not China, 17255 SE Licorice Way, Renton, WA 98059, 800-553-6693 or 425-254-0200, fax: 425-254-0239, e-mail: info@forgetme notchina.com, website: www.forgetmenotchina.com. Discontinued Lenox patterns.

Fostoria Crystal, Tom Bloom, 730 Charles St., Wellsburg, WV 26070, 304-737-2792, e-mail: trbcharles@aol.com. Fostoria.

Fostoria Registry, 1060 Crestline Dr., Crete, NE 68333, 402-826-2622, fax: 402-435-4339. Fostoria.

Fran Jay, PO Box 10, Lambertville, NJ 08530, e-mail: glasjay@erols.com, website: www.GlassShow.com. Depression and elegant glassware.

Glass Lady @ Kaleidoscope, 7501 Iron Bridge Rd., Richmond, VA 23237, 804-743-9811 or 804-743-9846, e-mail: glasslady8@aol.com. Matching service for glass. Glass repair.

Heritage China of Iowa, PO Box 243, Palo, IA 52324, 888-416-1595, fax: 319-227-7781, e-mail: dischina@aol.com, website: www.dish-china.com.

House of Serendipity, 645 Main St., Montevallo, AL 35115, 205-665-7996, e-mail: thehouseofserendipity@msn.com. American-made crystal.

Hugh Lackey Antiques and China Matching, 1816 Nacogdoches Rd., San Antonio, TX 78209, 210-829-5048, fax: 210-829-5048, e-mail: hlackey@texas.net.

Joanne Cone Matching Service, 34 Silverwood, Irvine, CA 92604, 949-551-3173, e-mail: jochina@aol.com, website: www.iadm.com. Specializes in Mikasa. Appraisals.

Judy Giangiuli, RD 6, Box 292, New Castle, PA 16101, 724-924-1940, fax: 724-924-9211. Fostoria.

Just China, PO Box 1401, Merrit Island, FL 32954, 800-5china1 (800-524-4621), e-mail: justchina@msn.com. Discontinued patterns.

Margaret Lane Antiques, 2 E. Main St., New Concord, OH 43762, 740-826-7414. Specializes in Cambridge glass and Heisey glass. Appraisals.

The Matchers, 181 Belle Meade, Memphis, TN 38117, 901-683-1337, e-mail: chinalady@earthlink.net. Specializes in most major factories. Appraisals.

Milbra's Crystal, PO Box 784, Cleburne, TX 76033, 817-645-6066, e-mail: longseat@flash.net. Specializes in Cambridge, Fostoria, Heisey, and Tiffin glass.

Nadine Pankow, 8825 W. 98th St., Palos Hills, IL 60465, e-mail: nadineglas@aol.com, website: members.aol.com/nadineglas. Depression glass matching service.

Old China Patterns Limited, 1560 Brimley Rd., Scarborough, ON M1P 3G9, Canada, 800-663-4533 or 416-299-8880, fax: 416-299-4721, e-mail: ocp@chinapatterns.com, website: www.chinapatterns.com. Discontinued crystal bought and sold. Inventory on website. Office/showroom hours Mon.–Thurs. 8:00 A.M.–5:00 P.M., Fri. 8:00 A.M.–4:00 P.M. Orders shipped worldwide. Appraisals.

Olympus Cove Antiques, 179 E. 300 South, Salt Lake City, UT 84111, 800-284-8046, e-mail: olympus@uswest.net, website: www.Olympus Cove.com.

Past & Present, 14851 Avenue 360, Visalia, CA 93292, 559-798-0029, fax: 559-798-1415, e-mail: P-P@ix.netcom.com, website: www.past present.net. Discontinued crystal. Appraisals and restoration.

Pattern Finders Ltd., PO Box 206, Port Jefferson Station, NY 11776, 800-216-2446, fax: 631-928-5170, e-mail: apattern@aol.com, website: www.patternfinders.com. If not sure of your pattern name, mail, fax, or e-mail a clear photo of a goblet for crystal identification.

Paul Church, 500 Oregon Ave., St. Cloud, FL 34769, 800-337-9075, e-mail: chinacrystal@juno.com, website: www.chinacrystalandmore.com. Lenox and Fostoria crystal.

Replacements, Ltd., PO Box 26029, 1089 Knox Rd., Greensboro, NC 27420-6029, 800-REPLACE (800-737-5223), fax: 336-697-3100, e-mail: inquire@replacements.com, website: www.replacements.com. Old and new crystal by most manufacturers. Crystal repair. Call the toll-free number, 8:00 A.M.–midnight, seven days a week, for free lists of pieces available in your pattern.

Retrospective Modern Design, PO Box 305, Manning, IA 51455, 888-301-6829, e-mail: retrodesign@earthlink.net, website: www.retrospective.net. Russel Wright glassware.

Roundhill's, 6542 46th Ave. NE, Seattle, WA 98115, 206-523-9710, fax: 206-524-1252, e-mail: jwr8123@msn.com. American, English, and French crystal. Appraisals.

Shirley Stamen Matching Service, 9601 Arby Dr., Beverly Hills, CA 90210, 310-278-4040, e-mail: stajaf1@earthlink.net.

Sophia's China & Crystal, 141 Sedgwick Rd., Dept. RTK, Syracuse, NY 13203, 315-472-6834, e-mail: sophia@sophiaschina-crystal.com, website: www.sophiaschina-crystal.com.

Tabletop Designs, PO Box 448, Cheshire, CT 06410, 800-801-4084, e-mail: lenox@ntplx.net, website: www.tabletopdesigns.com. Discontinued patterns.

Tabletops Etc, 375 W. Cummings Park, Woburn, MA 01801, 888-242-0994 from U.S. or Canada, 781-932-9882 from other countries, e-mail: service@tabletopsetc.com, website: www.tabletopsetc.com. Online listing of glassware patterns available from a group of independent dealers. Many patterns are pictured.

Unique Antiques, PO Box 15815, San Diego, CA 92175-5815, 619-281-8650, fax: 619-282-8407, e-mail: culrey@webcc.net. Lenox crystal matching. Appraisals.

SILVER MATCHING SERVICES

Alice's Past & Presents Replacements, PO Box 465, Merrick, NY 11566, 516-379-1352, fax: 516-379-7302, e-mail: alicechina@aol.com, website: hometown.aol.com/alicechina/myhomepage/business.html. Matching and locating service for discontinued tableware.

Ann Arbor Dinnerware LLC, PO Box 6054, Ann Arbor, MI 48106-6054, 888-726-9693 or 734-663-5766, e-mail: aadinex@aadinex, website: www.aadinex.com. Inactive stainless and sterling silver flatware.

Antique Cupboard Inc., 1936 MacArthur Rd., Wauwatosa, WI 53188,

800-637-4583 or 262-548-0556, e-mail: mail@antiquecupboard.com, website: www.antiquecupboard.com. Sterling silver, from rare antique silver patterns to current patterns. Search the website's online database of sterling silver flatware, silverplate, and hollowware silver patterns in stock.

As You Like It Silver Shop, 3033 Magazine St., New Orleans, LA 70115, 800-828-2311, fax: 504-897-6933, e-mail: ayliss@bellsouth.net, website: asyoulikeitsilvershop.com. Specializes in active, inactive, and obsolete sterling silver flatware patterns; hollowware.

Beverly Bremer Silver Shop, 3164 Peachtree Rd. NE, Atlanta, GA 30305, 404-261-4009, fax: 404-261-9708, e-mail: sterlingsilver@worldnet. att.net, website: www.beverlybremer.com. Sterling silver flatware and hollowware. Call or write for a free list of pieces in your sterling pattern. Open Mon.–Sat. 10:00 A.M.–5:00 P.M.

Beverly Hills Antique Center—Martin A. Pope, 24630 Hwy. 92, Platte City, MO 64079, 913-651-4972, e-mail: map007@juno.com. Specializes in matching silver-plated and sterling silver flatware.

Beverly Hills Pattern Matching Service, 270 N. Canon Dr., #1419, Beverly Hills, CA 90210, 800-443-1122, fax: 323-954-8501. Sterling silver, silver plate, and stainless steel flatware matching.

Buried Treasures, 3487 Arvin Dr., Clarksville, TN 37042, 931-431-5033, e-mail: antiquer@usit.net, website: www.rubylane.com/en/ shops/buriedtreasures. Sterling silver and silver plate flatware and hollowware.

Bygone China Match, 1225 W. 34th N., Wichita, KS 67204, 316-838-6010, fax: 316-838-6010, e-mail: bygonchina@aol.com. Matching services for silver.

Carman's Collectables, PO Box 238, Levittown, PA 19059, 215-946-9315, fax: 215-946-9451, e-mail: carmansc@aol.com, website: www.carmans collectables.com. Sterling silver and silver plate flatware and hollowware.

Cherishables—Sally A. Peelen, 1214 Matanzas Way, Santa Rosa, CA 95405, 707-579-2475, fax: 707-579-2475.

China Brokers, Ltd., 2723 SE 24th Ave., Cape Coral, FL 33904, 732-768-4145 or 941-242-4340, fax: 941-242-4340, e-mail: chinabrokers@world net.att.net.

China Cabinet, PO Box 426, Clearwater, SC 29822, 800-787-1605 or 803-593-9655, fax: 803-593-9655, e-mail: thechinacabinet@aol.com. All discontinued or inactive silver patterns by major manufacturers.

China Finders, 2823 Central Ave., St. Petersburg, FL 33713, 800-900-2557 or 727-328-0557, fax: 727-384-9317, e-mail: chinafinders@aol.com, website: www.chinafinders.com. Discontinued or obsolete flatware patterns by most major manufacturers.

China Replacements, PO Box 508, High Ridge, MO 63049, 800-562-2655, e-mail: chinarep@swbell.net, website: www.chinareplacements.com.

Discontinued and hard-to-find patterns of stainless, silver plate, and sterling silver. All major manufacturers and many more.

Clintsman International, 811 E. Geneva St., Elkhorn, WI 53121, 800-781-8900, fax: 262-723-1991, e-mail: findit@clintsmanint.com, website: www.clintsmanint.com. Matching all manufacturers of flatware. Pattern identification.

Crystal Corner, PO Box 756, 317 Dyar Blvd., Boaz, AL 35957, 256-593-6169, fax: 256-593-6560, e-mail: ccorner@hiwaay.net, website: www.crystalcorner.com. Stainless steel flatware.

Don's Antiques & Gifts, Heirloom Completions Division, 1620 Venice St., Granite City, IL 62040, fax: 618-931-4333, e-mail: questions@dons antiques.com, website: donsantiques.com. Sterling silver, silver plate, stainless steel, Dirigold, and Dirilyte flatware matching.

Echo's Discontinued China & Silver, 1433 Lonsdale Ave., #121, North Vancouver, BC V7M 2H9, Canada, 800-663-6004, fax: 604-988-3611, e-mail: info@echoschina.com, website: www.echoschina.com. Silver matching. Brochure.

edish, 815 E. 2100 South, Salt Lake City, UT 84106, 888-768-8282, e-mail: questions@edish.com, website: www.edish.com. Flatware locating service for stainless, silverplate, and sterling silver. Available online or at the two store locations. Second location: Antique Pavilion, 2311 Westheimer, Houston, TX 77098, 713-942-7171, fax: 713-521-2546.

Green Door Antiques, PO Box 18293, Rochester, NY 14618, 800-754-9633, fax: 716-381-4234, e-mail: AGreenDoor@aol.com, website: Green-DoorAntiques.com. Sterling and coin silver flatware.

Helen Lawler's Silver Service, 5400 E. County Rd. #2, Blytheville, AR 72315, 573-720-8502, e-mail: hlawler@missconet.com. Silver-plated flatware matching service; no sterling or stainless.

Hugh Lackey Antiques and China Matching, 1816 Nacogdoches Rd., San Antonio, TX 78209, 210-829-5048, fax: 210-829-5048, e-mail: hlackey @texas.net.

Imagination Unlimited, 4302 Alton Rd., Suite 820, Miami Beach, FL 33140, 888-536-7360 or 305-534-2214, fax: 305-538-0914, e-mail: info@imagina tionunlimited.com, website: www.imaginationunlimited.com. Georg Jensen and other Danish silver.

Jane Rosenow, 1210 NW 3rd Ave., Galva, IL 61434, 309-932-3953, fax: 309-932-3068, e-mail: jarose@inw.net. Sterling silver, silver plate, and stainless. Appraisals.

Joan Cookson, PO Box 34, Arnold, CA 95223, 209-795-3034. Silver plate matching.

Joanne Cone Matching Service, 34 Silverwood, Irvine, CA 92604, 949-551-3173, e-mail: jochina@aol.com, website: www.iadm.com. Appraisals.

Just China, PO Box 1401, Merrit Island, FL 32954, 800-5china1 (800-524-4621), e-mail: justchina@msn.com. Discontinued silver flatware patterns.

Kinzie's Matching Service, PO Box 522, Turlock, CA 95381, 209-634-4880, fax: 209-634-1134, e-mail: kinzies@mymailstation.com. Sterling silver and silver plate flatware.

Liberty Silver, 109 Carriage Ln., Contoocook, NH 03229, 603-746-4923, fax: 603-746-5632, e-mail: fredymaj@cscom. Specializes in sterling silver flatware. Appraisals.

Littman's, 51 Granby St., Norfolk, VA 23510, 757-622-6989 or 800-368-6348, e-mail: littmansinc@cavtel.net, website: www.littmans.com. American sterling silver flatware.

M&M Silver, PO Box 460636, San Francisco, CA 94146-0636, 415-821-4221, e-mail: pljohn761@aol.com. Sterling silver matching; some silver plate. Appraisals.

Margaret Lane Antiques, 2 E. Main St., New Concord, OH 43762, 740-826-7414. Specializes in silver-plated flatware. Appraisals.

Martin M. Fleisher, Silversmith, PO Box 305, Copiague, NY 11726-0305, 631-842-2927, e-mail: mfleishe@suffolk.lib.ny.us. Sterling silver flatware: active, inactive, obsolete, and antique. Restoration service.

Matchmaker of Iowa, 109 Discovery Bay St., Sequim, WA 98382, 360-683-7517, e-mail: gakup@olypen.com. Stainless steel, pewter, and some gold flatware.

Maxine Klaput Antiques, PO Box 5628, Carmel, CA 93921, 877-624-8823 or 831-624-8823, fax: 831-624-0956. Sterling silver flatware.

Melange Sterling Silver Shop, 5421 Magazine St., New Orleans, LA 70115, 800-513-3991 or 504-899-4796, fax: 504-899-6265, e-mail: melangesterling@msn.com, website: www.melangesterling.com. Active and inactive patterns of silver flatware.

MidweSterling Flatware, 4311 NE Vivion Rd., Kansas City, MO 64119-2890, 816-454-1990, fax: 816-454-9341, e-mail: info@silverwarehouse.com, website: silverwarehouse.com. Sterling silver, silver plate, and stainless matching service and repair. Garbage-disposal damage fixed, knife blades replaced, professional polishing. Appraisals.

Olympus Cove Antiques, 179 E. 300 South, Salt Lake City, UT 84111, 800-284-8046, e-mail: olympus@uswest.net, website: www.OlympusCove.com. Silver flatware.

Overtons Sterling Matching, 200 Avenida Santa Margarita, San Clemente, CA 92672, 949-498-5330, fax: 949-498-5330, e-mail: edwhiffen @aol.com. Sterling silver flatware. Appraisals.

Past & Present, 14851 Avenue 360, Visalia, CA 93292, 559-798-0029, fax: 559-798-1415, e-mail: P-P@ix.netcom.com, website: www.past present.net. Discontinued silver. Appraisals and restoration.

Pattern Finders Ltd., PO Box 206, Port Jefferson Station, NY 11776, 800-216-2446, fax: 631-928-5170, e-mail: apattern@aol.com, website: www.patternfinders.com. If not sure of your pattern name, mail, fax, or e-mail a photocopy of a knife for silver pattern identification.

Pillsbury-Michel, Inc., 2311 Westheimer Rd., Houston, TX 77098, 877-522-

4797 (toll free), fax: 713-522-4797 (phone/fax), e-mail: info@pillsbury-michel.com, website: www.pillsbury-michel.com. Pattern matching and search services. Appraisals.

R.S. Goldberg, 67 Beverly Rd., Hawthorne, NJ 07506, 800-252-6655 or 973-427-6555, e-mail: rssilver@aol.com, website: rsgoldberg.com. Active, inactive, and obsolete patterns of sterling silver flatware.

Replacements, Ltd., PO Box 26029, 1089 Knox Rd., Greensboro, NC 27420-6029, 800-REPLACE (800-737-5223), fax: 336-697-3100, e-mail: inquire@replacements.com, website: www.replacements.com. Old and new silver by most manufacturers. Silver repair, restoration, cleaning, and polishing. Call the toll-free number, 8:00 A.M.–midnight, seven days a week, for free lists of pieces available in your pattern

Robert D. Biggs, 1155 E. 58th St., Chicago, IL 60637, 773-702-9540, fax: 773-702-9853, e-mail: r-biggs@uchicago.edu. Silver-plated flatware.

Roslyn Berlin, 1500 Palisade Ave., Fort Lee, NJ 07024, 201-461-1633, fax: 201-461-1632. Specializes in Tiffany flatware. Winter address: 3420 S. Ocean Blvd. (15-R), Highland Beach, FL 33487, 561-243-8192, fax: 561-243-4030.

Roundhill's, 6542 46th Ave. NE, Seattle, WA 98115, fax: 206-524-1252, e-mail: jwr8123@msn.com. Silver flatware patterns. Appraisals.

Shirley Stamen Matching Service, 9601 Arby Dr., Beverly Hills, CA 90210, 310-278-4040, e-mail: stajaf1@earthlink.net.

The Silver Girls Silverplated Matching, 168 Riverview Rd. SW, Eatonton, GA 31024, 478-968-5225, fax: 478-968-5225, e-mail: silvergirls@ncommuni comm.com. Discontinued patterns of silver-plated flatware.

Silver Joy Inc., PO Box 1675, Morristown, NJ 07962-1675, 877-745-8759, e-mail: joy@silvercom.com, website: www.silverjoy.com. American sterling silver flatware.

Silver Queen, Inc., 730 N. Indian Rocks Rd., Belleair Bluffs, FL 33770, 800-262-3134 or 727-581-6827, fax: 727-581-0822, e-mail: sales@silver queen.com, website: www.silverqueen.com. Matching active and discontinued sterling silver, plated, and stainless patterns. Call for free catalog and list of pieces available in your pattern.

The Silver Shop, 5630 Dunbar St., Vancouver, BC V6N 1W7, Canada, 604-263-3113, fax: 604-266-4515, e-mail: tarnish@portal.ca. Canadian sterling silver patterns, specializes in Birks, Ellis, Northumbria, Roden.

Silver Smiths, PO Box 5118, Fresno, CA 93755, 559-431-1611, fax: 559-431-1611. Sterling silver flatware, specializes in discontinued patterns.

Sterling Buffet, PO Box 1665, Mansfield, OH 44901, 800-537-5783 or 419-529-0505, fax: 419-529-0506, e-mail: info@sterlingbuffet.com, website: www.sterlingbuffet.com. Sterling silver flatware. Flatware chests, custom drawer liners, tarnish-resistant wraps, and silver polish.

Sterling Shop, PO Box 595, Silverton, OR 97381, 503-873-6315, fax: 503-873-3066, e-mail: juanita@sterlingshop.com, website: www.sterling

shop.com. Discontinued sterling silver and silver-plated flatware and hollowware.

Tabletops Etc, 375 W. Cummings Park, Woburn, MA 01801, 888-242-0994 from U.S. or Canada, 781-932-9882 from other countries, e-mail: service@tabletopsetc.com, website: www.tabletopsetc.com. Online listing of flatware patterns available from a group of independent dealers. Many patterns are pictured.

Vi Walker Silver, 5209 N. College Ave., Indianapolis, IN 46220-3139, 317-283-3753, fax: 317-283-0053, e-mail: vwalker@netdirect.net, website: www.viwalkersilver.com. Silver matching. Appraisals.

Vintage Silver, 33 LeMay Ct., Williamsville, NY 14221, 716-631-0419, fax: 716-433-2850, e-mail: mikekuch@localnet.com. Silver-plated flatware. Appraisals.

Vroman's Silver Shop, 442A Fleetwood Pl., Glendora, CA 91740, 800-824-5174, fax: 626-963-1402, e-mail: vrosilver@aol.com. Specializes in old patterns of sterling silver, silver plate, gold plate, stainless steel, and pewter. Repair and restoration; knives rebladed, tea sets replated, water pitchers dedented, Victorian silver plate restored, etc.

Woodland Antiques, PO Box 3793, Mansfield, OH 44907-3793, 419-756-7171, fax: 419-756-6883. Sterling silver, silver plate, and stainless flatware.

WTC Associates, Inc., 2532 Regency Rd., Lexington, KY 40503, 859-278-4171, fax: 859-277-5720. Silver matching service, specializes in sterling silver. Sterling silver repairs, including replacement of missing parts. Silver plating; silver plate and sterling repairs.

USEFUL INTERNET ADDRESSES

ONLINE AUCTIONS

Amazon, auctions.amazon.com
Bidville, www.bidville.com
Carnaby, www.carnaby.com
eBay, www.ebay.com
ePier, www.epier.com
Internet Auction List, www.internetauctionlist.com (directory of online auctions)
Sotheby's Online, www.sothebys.com
Yahoo! Auctions, auctions.yahoo.com

ONLINE MALLS

Antique Arts, www.antiquearts.com
Antiques World, www.antiquesworld.com (classified ads)
Antique Networking, www.antiqnet.com and www.buycollectibles.com

Collector Online, www.collectoronline.com
Collect.com, www.collect.com (classified ads)
CyberAttic, www.cyberattic.com
Ruby Lane, www.rubylane.com
Shop Mega Now, www.shopmeganow.com
TIAS, www.tias.com
Trocadero, www.trocadero.com

SEARCH ENGINES
Alta Vista, www.altavista.com
DogPile, www.dogpile.com (meta search—looks in a variety of places)
Google, www.google.com
HotBot, hotbot.lycos.com
Lycos, www.lycos.com
MetaCrawler, www.metacrawler.com (meta search—looks in a variety of places)

DIRECTORIES
Google News, news.google.com
InfoSpace, www.infospace.com (has reverse look-up for phone numbers)
LookSmart, www.looksmart.com
Yahoo!, www.yahoo.com (directory-style search—lists by category)

INFORMATION
A to Zee, atozee.com (website guide and collectors' directory)
Antique Resources, www.antiqueresources.com
Curioscape, www.curioscape.com (devoted to antiques & collectibles)
The Great Abbreviations Hunt, www.atomiser.demon.co.uk/abbrev/index.html
Information Please, www.infoplease.com (online dictionary, almanac, atlas, encyclopedia)
Maloney's Online, www.maloneysonline.com
Ms. Information, www.coastside.net/msinfobooks/index.html (out-of-print and hard-to-find books, including trade catalogs and catalog reprints)

Index

A. Walter, 162
Abbreviations, 26; auctioneers, 486; book ads, 56; bottle ads, 64; dolls, 110; numismatic, 263
Abby Aldrich Rockefeller Folk Art Center, 408
Actors, autographs, 48
Adams, Ansel, 303
Addams Family, The, 83
Adrian, designer fashions, 121
Advertising collectibles, 27–39, 53, 65, 73, 96, 232
Advertising, to sell or buy, 14, 17–22, 28, 40
Afors glass, 165
Aguilar, Hector, 201
Airplane-related collectibles, 7, 28
Alcoholic beverages, 7, 14
Aluminum, hammered, 237
Amber jewelry, 204
Amberina glass, 160
Ambrotypes, 302
American Film Institute, 304
American Flyer, 417
American Indians, 7, 28, 48, 453, 457; baskets, 453; beadwork, 453; dolls, 453; jewelry, 211; relics, 14
American Political Items Collectors, 311–312
Americana, 50–51
Amethyst jewelry, 204
AMI jukeboxes, 99
Amish quilts, 406
Amos 'n' Andy, 53
Amusement park collectibles, 76, 78
Andirons, 126
Animal fur, restrictions on selling, 453
Animal license tags, 463, 467
ANRI, 464
Antiquarian book dealers, 55
Apple peelers, 213–214
Applied color labels (ACLs), 64
Appraisal groups, 25, 483–484
Arbus, Diane, 303
Arcade brand toys, 417
Architectural antiques, 39–47
Area codes, 26
Argy-Rousseau, 162
Armstrong, Jack, 419

Armstrong, Rolf, 231
Army discharge papers, 48
Arrowheads, 453
Art Deco Societies, International Coalition of, 467
Art pottery, 323, 344–345
Arts and Crafts jewelry, 204–205
Ashtrays, 379, 464
Asparagus servers, 371
"Association" items, 81
Astronauts, autographs, 48; memorabilia, 81
Atmos clocks, 91
Audubon, John James, 357
Aunt Jemima, 53
Authors, autographs, 48
Autographs, 48–51, 57, 81
Automata, 92
Automobile-related collectibles, 28, 63
Automobiles, toy, 417; vintage, 440–441
Autumn Leaf dishes, 322
Azalea dishes, 322
Badges, 463
Bakelite, 206, 237
Band organs, 78, 80
Banko dishes, 320
Banks, still & mechanical, 417–418
Banners, 129
Bar codes, on books, 57
Bar ware, 466
Barbed wire, 454
Barber collectibles, 51–52; 71
Barbini glass, 165
Bardot, Brigitte, 232
Barometers, 91, 366
Barye bronzes, 238
Baseball, cards, 288, 383; memorabilia, 385
Baskets, 453, 457–460; American Indian, 457; Nantucket, 457; Shaker, 457
Batchelder tiles, 47
Bates, Kenneth, 237
Bathtubs, 47; claw-foot, 42–43, 47
Battery-operated toys, 417
Bauer pottery, 325
Beat Brothers, 293
Bedding, 14
Beekeeping collectibles, 469

Beer, cans, 20, 28, 73; labels, 28–29
Bell Telephone logo, 401
Bells, 463; railroad, 442
Belts, 122; buckles, 29
Benches, garden, 39, 47
Bennett and Co., 201
Bergdorf Goodman, 121
Berlin work, 404
Beswick pottery, 344
Betty Bonnet paper dolls, 231
Betty Boop, 103
Bibles, 56, 62, 286, 463
Bicycles and motorcycles, 441
Bill Blass, designer fashions, 121
Billiards, 385
Bing & Grondahl, 325
Bing toys, 418
Birdcages, 128
Birdhouses, 129
Bitters bottles, 64
Black collectibles, 7, 53–54, 315, 323, 419
Black light, 202
Blenko glass, 165
Bliss, 106, 419
Blown glass, 161
Blueprints, 42
Bobbie Brooks, 121
Boda glass, 165
Bonnie Cashin, designer fashions, 121
Bonwit Teller, 121
Bookbinders, 57, 61
Bookbinding, leather, 54, 57
Bookends, 464
Book-of-the-Month Club, 55–56
Bookplates, 54, 57, 279
Books, 50, 54–62; antiquarian, 60; "association," 57; autographed, 48; children's, 59; decorating, 56; disaster, 56; first editions, 55, 57; girls' series, 59; history, 56; horticulture, 56; instruction, 25; mystery, 55; out of print, xiii; pop-up, 57; science, 56; storage boxes, 61
Bookworms, damage to books, 58
Boots, 453–454
Bottle corks, 65
Bottle openers, 65, 213

Bottles, 27–28, 51, 63–73; Avon, 63; barber, 71; Ezra Brooks, 63; figural, 63–64; go-withs, 63, 65; illegal sales, 68; ink, 64, 460; Jim Beam, 27, 63; machine-made, 63; modern, 63; perfume, 63; poison, 64; "sick," 65; snuff, 72; soda, 64; value hints, 66

Bourke-White, Margaret, 231, 303

Bowling collectibles, 385

Boxes, as advertising collectibles, 28

Boxes, original, 7, 65

Bradley & Hubbard, 219

Brass, 4; showerheads, 46

Bread wrappers, 385

Breweriana, 71, 73–75

Breyer horses, 464

Bricks, collectible, 39

Britains toy soldiers, 417

British royal commemoratives, 464

Bronze, 4, 237–238

Broom labels, 28–29

Brownie cameras, 301

Brundage, Frances, 315

Bubble bath containers, 464

Buckles, 29, 121, 463

Buddy L toys, 417

Butter pats, 466

Buttons, 404, 463

Buy Books Where – Sell Books Where, 55

Buyer's premium, 16

Cabinet cards, 302

Calendar art, 28, 356

California studio pottery, 319; figurines, 321

Cambridge glass, 164

Cameo glass, 162

Cameos, 204

Cameras, 300–302

Candy containers, 192

Canes, 121–122, 124

Canning jar rubber rings, 65

Cans, beer, 20, 28, 73

Cap guns, 464

Capital Changes Daily, The, 397

Carlisle and Finch toy trains, 417

Carnegie, Hattie, 205

Carnival glass, 20, 163–164

Carousels, 75–80; figures, 128

Carr, Gene, 315

Carriages, horse-drawn, 442

Carrier-Belleuse bronzes, 238

Cars, see Automobiles

Cartes de visite, 302, 304

Cartier watches, 86

Caruso, Enrico, 293

Carvings, architectural, 39

Cash registers, 28–29, 39

Castellani jewelry, 201

Castleton dishes, 326

Catalina pottery, 325

Catalogs, collectible, 56

Celebrity memorabilia, 80–84

Celluloid, 310

Cels, animation, 101, 103, 288

Cemetery art, 470

Chains, pocketwatch, 88

Chanel, designer fashions, 121

Chaplin, Charlie, 419

Charitable contributions, 11–12

Chase metalware, 237

Checklist of American Coverlet Weavers, 406

Checks, personal, 20–21

Chein toys, 418

Chelsea figurines, 322

Chihuly, Dale, 165

China matching services, 537–543

Chinese Export porcelain, 320, 324

Chiparus bronzes, 238

Christmas collectibles, 192–195; cards, 192; postcards, 315; ornaments, 5, 192, 193; seals, 393

Christy, Howard Chandler, 231, 315

Chronometers, 85

Church pews, 39

Cigar box labels, 28–29

Cigar clippers, 379

Cigar store figures, 28, 39, 128

Cigarette advertising, 28

Cigarette cases, 379

Ciner jewelry, 200

Circus Historical Society, 466

Civil War writings, 48

Claire McCardell, designer fashions, 121

Clapsaddle, Ellen, 315

Clarice Cliff, 322

Clark & Sowdon, 419

Claycraft tiles, 47

Clocks, 28, 84–93, 213; animated alarm, 85; Atmos, 91; carriage, 85; dial, 85; figural, 85; grandfather, 85; keys for, 90; "marriage" of parts, 85; novelty, 85; Waterbury, 89

Clodion bronzes, 238

Cloisonné, 237

Clothing, vintage, 3, 14–15, 120–126

Coasters, 73

Cobb, Ty, 231

Coca-Cola, 7, 27, 28, 98, 232

Coffee grinders, 28

Coffin markers, 463

Coin-operated machines, 37, 93–99

Coins, 262–270

Collector's Encyclopedia of Dolls, The, 109

Columns, architectural, 42, 44, 46; reproductions, 42

Combs, 121–122

Comics memorabilia, 80, 102; art, 99–105; books, 61, 99–101; characters, 37; strips, 232

Commission, auction gallery's, 11, 16

Compacts, 121–122, 205

Composers, autographs 48; memorabilia, 81

Cone-top beer cans, 73

Conservation supplies, 25, 514–520

Conservators & restorers, 520–531

Consignment shops, 16, 320

Consolidated Glass and Lamp Company, xi

Contracts, with seller, 13, 17

Cookbooks, 56, 213

Cookie cutters, 213

Cookie jars, 213, 321

Coon Chicken Inns, 53

Corbett, Bertha, 315

Corgi toy cars, 417

Cork flooring, 45

Corkscrews, 65

Corn collectibles, 466

Coro jewelry, 205

Counter, store, 28

Courvoisier Art Galleries, 101

Coverlets, 404, 406–407

Cox, Palmer, 231

Cox-Roosevelt political button, 311

Cracker Jack, 28

Crawford, Joan, 253

Cream of Wheat, 232

Credit cards, 18, 20, 21, 265

Credit, risk of extending, 12

Criminals, memorabilia, 81

Crosby, Bing, 293

Crystal matching services, 544–547

Crystal sets, 361

Cupids, 466

Currier & Ives prints, 281–282, 356

Currier & Ives Prints: An Illustrated Check List, 356

Cut glass, 161–162

Czechoslovakian pottery, 320

Daguerreotypes, 301–302, 304; cases, 301

Daum Nancy, 162

De Lamerie, Paul, 370

De Vez glass, 162

Deacidification, 62

Dealers, 9–13, 15, 19, 27

Dean, James, 49, 253

Decals, 29

Declaration of Independence, signers, 48

Decorating books, 56

Decoys, 128–130; fish, 129

DeFoe, Daniel, cigar box label, 29

Delatte glass, 162

Delineator, The, 231

Delivery services, tracking, 26

Dental chairs, 366

Depression glass, xii, 9, 20, 164

Dickens, Charles, 57

Dictionaries, 56, 463

Dining-room sets, 21

Dinky toys, 417
Dionne Quintuplets, 82
Dior, designer fashions, 121
Directory of Obsolete
    Securities, The, 397
Dirk Van Erp, 219, 237
Dishes, filling in sets, 326–327
Disneyana, 81, 103–104, 419
Dispenser, perfume, 93
Displaying collectibles, 25,
    531–533
Dixie cup lids, 383
Doll hospitals, 112
Dollhouses, 106–107
Dolls, 108–120, 453; accessories,
    109; Barbie, xii, 108, 111,
    293, 417; Barbie clothes,
    xii, 109; Ken, xii; Kewpie,
    109; Lenci, 109; Madame
    Alexander, 5, 109; Mattel,
    109; paper, 114–115, 230–231;
    rag, 53; Raggedy Ann, 109;
    Ravca, 109; Schoenhut,
    109; Shirley Temple, 108–
    109; Steiff, 109; Storybook,
    109; Vogue, 109
Dolly Dingle paper dolls, 231
Doorbells, 42
Doorknobs, 42, 185
Doors, 39, 42–47
Doorstops, 236
Dorfan toy trains, 417
Doulton, 344; Royal, 20, 320,
    323, 327
Dover kitchen ware, 214
Drerup, Karl, 237
Drug-related collectibles, 7, 28,
    37
Duffner & Kimberly, 219
Duncan and Miller, 164
Durand glass, 161
Dust jackets, 55, 57
Eagle feathers, restrictions on
    selling, 453
Easter, 193; seals, 393
eBay, 63
Eckhardt, Edris, 165
Egg cups, 466
Egg timers, 178, 213
Eggbeaters, 213, 463
Eglomisé, 276
Eisenberg jewelry, 205
Electrical appliances, 212
Elegant glass, 164–165
Elephant collectibles, 466
Elevator doors, 39
Embroidery, Arts and Crafts,
    408
Emeralite, 219
Emerson radios, 360–361
Enamels, 237, 239
Encyclopedias, 56, 463
Endangered species, 14, 20
Enterprise kitchen ware, 214
Entertainment-related
    memorabilia, 51
Ephemera, 51, 279–289
Epiphone musical instruments,
    256
Erickson glass, 165

Erotica, 28, 231, 462
Erté illustrations, 231
Escrow accounts, 17
Escutcheons, 43
Estate sales, 13–16
Evans, Dale, 83
Explorers, memorabilia, 81
Fabergé, 201
Fada radios, 361
Fairings, 323
Fans, electric, 463
Fans, fashion accessories, 125
Farberware, 237
Farm machinery, 442
Farm toys, 417
Fashion, 120–126; accessories,
    121
Fast food memorabilia, 27
Faucets, 43
FedEx, 26, 49
Fences, 40; iron, 39
Fender musical instruments,
    256
Fenton glass, 164
Fiberboard, pressed, 46
Fiesta, 321–322, 345
Film, nitrate, 254
Finch, Kay, 325
Finials, 43
Fire marks, 466
Fireplaces, 40; equipment,
    126–127; surrounds, 45–46
Fireworks, 463
Fish servers, 371
Fisher, Harrison, 231, 315
Fisher-Price, 418
Fishing, 385, 442
Five Sharps, 293
Flagg, James Montgomery, 231
Flags, 28, 463
Flashlights, 218, 464–465, 467
Flasks, 64, 66
Flea Market Finds with the
    Kovels, xii
Flea markets, 19–20
Flintstones, 102
Flooring, 39, 45–46
Florence pottery, 325
Florenza jewelry, 205
Flower frogs, 465
Flue covers, 465
Folk art, 28, 53, 75–77, 127–131,
    421
Fonda, Jane, 232
Football collectibles, 385
Fore-edge painting, on books,
    57
Forgeries, 49
Fortuny, designer fashions, 121
Fostoria glass, 164
Fountains, water, 39, 47
Fouquet jewelry, 201
Fourth of July, 315
Fox, R. Atkinson, 356
Frames, 131–136
Franciscan dishes, 325–326
Fraternal-order carvings, 129
Frescoes, 45–46
Fretwork, 39
Frog collectibles, 467

Fruit jars, 64–65; closures, 72
Funeral invitations, 462
Furniture, 20, 46, 136–160; beds,
    142; chairs, 140; painted,
    140; pricing of repaired,
    141–143; styles, 138–139;
    wicker, 140
Gallé, 162, 218–219
Galoob toys, 421
Gambling devices, 7, 14
Games, 419–420; video, 96
Garage sales, 13–16
Garden ornaments, 129
Garland, Judy, 253
Garnets, 204
Gas pump globes, 28, 441
Gas pumps, 39, 441
Gehrig, Lou, 231
Gibson Girl, 280, 325
Gibson musical instruments,
    256
Gibson, Charles Dana, 231
Givenchy designer fashions, 121
Glass, 160–184; beveled, 44–46;
    curved, 39; etched, 44;
    liners, for silver salts and
    mustard pots, 72; mid-
    century, 165; modern, 165;
    reference books, 163;
    stained, 42–47, 177–178, 181,
    184
Glass-polishing machines, 72
Glassware, 73, 165–166
Glidden pottery, 325
Gnomes, 467
Godey's Ladies Book, 231
Gold Rush, 48
Gold, identifying, 86
Goldscheider figurines, 322
Golf collectibles, 385
Gone with the Wind, 253
Goss souvenirs, 323
Gouda pottery, 320
Gould, John, 357
Graniteware, 463
Grape shears, 371
Greenaway, Kate, 231
Grey toy cars, 417
Grey, Zane, 59
Grills, architectural, 39, 42
Griswold kitchen ware, 213
Gruen watches, 86
Gum wrappers, 279
Gumball machines, 93
Guns, 14, 20, 248–249, 454;
    laws regarding sales, 248
Gutmann, Bessie Pease, 356
Gutters, 43
Gwinett, Button, 48
Hall pottery, 319–320
Halloween, 192–193, 315
Halls of Fame, 81
Hamilton watches, 86, 91
Hammond instruments, 256
Handel lamps, 219–220, 226
Handkerchiefs, 407
Handles, architectural, 39
Hardware, 39, 42–46, 184–192
Harper's Weekly, 231
Hats, 73